The Reagan Revolution IV
From Victory to the New World Order

Richard C. Thornton

Copyright © 2013, Richard C. Thornton DJT Analytics LLC
All rights reserved.

No part of this book may be reproduced, stored in a retrieval system, or transmitted by any means, electronic, mechanical, photocopying, recording, or otherwise, without written permission from the author.

ISBN 978-1-625-17224-2

Dedication

This book is dedicated to my wife and editor, Joanne, and my sons Douglas and James, who grew up with this project.

Aphorism

Government is the first historian, and its rendering of events is always self serving, however close to the truth. As the only past that exists is that which we, as a nation, choose to remember, the citizen historian's role is to insure that truth prevails over political expediency.

Table of Contents

Introduction ix

Part One
Chapter 1 Strategy and its Discontents 1
Chapter 2 Origins of the Iran Initiative 39
Chapter 3 Crucible of Decision 77
Chapter 4 Shultz and McFarlane Seize Control 117
Chapter 5 The Attempt to Shut Down the Initiative 155
Chapter 6 Israel Entangles the CIA 199

Part Two
Chapter 7 Reagan's Iran Initiative 235
Chapter 8 Moscow Enters the Game 269
Chapter 9 The President Stands Tough 307
Chapter 10 On the Verge of Victory 349
Chapter 11 Collapse of Reagan's Strategy 391
Chapter 12 The Struggle for Power 431
Chapter 13 Defeat and Survival of Ronald Reagan 467
Conclusion 511

Introduction

This fourth volume of the Reagan Revolution series is about victory and defeat; President Reagan's victory over the Soviet Union in the Cold War and his defeat at the hands of his domestic political opponents, who sought accommodation with Moscow over victory. I trace the denouement of a two-decade-long struggle within the American leadership over global strategy. The focal point of the struggle was how to deal with the Soviet Union, a determined adversary armed with intercontinental ballistics missiles (ICBM) and bent on altering the global order to advantage.

The ICBM problem, of course, had arisen in the mid-'50s when both the United States and the Soviet Union had acquired an initial capability. The danger of a nuclear missile conflict had been demonstrated graphically in the Cuban missile crisis. But it was only a decade later in the mid-1960s that the Soviet Union began to deploy ICBMs on a large-scale, presenting the American leadership with the issue of what was to be done. The problem was unprecedented in American history. From the late '60s and for the first time American leaders faced an adversary that could theoretically destroy the nation without warning and against any then-known defense.

As argued in this and my previous works on the Nixon and Carter presidencies, the American leadership split between those who were determined to maintain the containment strategy, which since the beginning of the Cold War had posed the Soviet Union as an adversary, and those who advocated switching strategy from containment to détente and embracing the USSR as a partner.[1] The problem for those advocating détente, whom I have termed "the new world order faction," but who constituted the political establishment, was that the Soviets themselves were unwilling to make the same strategy switch, although they were profuse in their avowals of peace and cooperation. The majority of the American public consistently viewed the Soviet Union with deep suspicion. The new world order faction therefore could not proclaim publicly their preference for a change of strategy and were forced to do so surreptitiously from within, through a complicit media and academic elite.

Moreover, the Cold War codification of containment, which resulted in a global structure of alliances, buttressed by military and economic arrangements that established a forward American position of power and leverage around the periphery of the Sino-Soviet bloc, could not simply be abandoned, but could only be dismantled piecemeal as responses to crises. The containment structure maintained global stability until the late '60s when the impact of two long-developing crises, one geopolitical and one technological, raised questions about its continued viability.

The geopolitical change was the deep involvement of the United States in war in Southeast Asia that stressed the very fiber of the nation. The technological advance was the emergence of the intercontinental ballistic missile, which permanently altered the nature of international politics. The rapid growth of Soviet military power based upon a large deployment of intercontinental ballistic missiles directly threatened the national security of the United States for the first time in its history.

By the time President Richard Nixon had been elected to office, these two changes had produced a veiled but intense debate within the American leadership over the question of strategy. Nixon supported the continuation of the containment strategy against the view of his national

---

[1] Richard C. Thornton, *The Nixon –Kissinger Years: The Reshaping of American Foreign Policy* (St. Paul: Paragon House, 2001, 2nd Ed.) and *The Carter Years: Toward A New Global Order* (New York: Paragon House, 1991).

security adviser, Henry Kissinger, of the new world order faction, who argued that continued adherence to containment would only lead to war. Nixon sought to reach a compromise, agreeing to normalize relations with the Soviet Union, but within the context of the containment strategy, entering into arms control and economic agreements.

President Nixon parleyed rapprochement with China into an honorable withdrawal from Vietnam, which promised not only to lead to a stable settlement in Southeast Asia similar to the one in Korea, but also that it would reinforce the global containment structure against the Soviet Union. By the end of his first term, Nixon's strategy appeared to be succeeding.

With no hope of contending against the president in a second term, during which he would be free to conduct policy with no need for further compromise with what was then the Rockefeller-led establishment, the new world order faction contrived to gain policy leverage by entrapping Nixon in what would become the Watergate scandal.[2] Entangled in a cover-up, Nixon relinquished control over American foreign policy to Henry Kissinger, who from early in 1973 promptly reversed Nixon's strategy from containment to détente and commenced the first steps in the deconstruction of the containment structure with withdrawal from Vietnam. Under President Gerald Ford, Kissinger pressed forward with the strategy of détente, to no avail. The opening to China lay fallow and détente failed to materialize as Moscow mounted the largest military buildup in history.

Jimmy Carter, however, made détente the centerpiece of his presidential campaign. The Carter presidency was clearly the worst in post-war history, but his failures were partly mitigated by the challenges he faced. Foremost among these was fact that the Soviet Union, having moved to the brink of a first-strike capability against U.S. land-based missiles and nuclear superiority over the Eurasian landmass, took to the geopolitical offensive.

---

[2] See Thornton, *Nixon-Kissinger Years*, chapters 4 and 5.

Carter's supine reaction, encouraged by his Secretary of State, Cyrus Vance, of the new world order faction, did nothing to temper Moscow's ambitions. Worse, the collapse of the U.S. relationship with Iran, a further dismantling of containment, and the alienation of Saudi Arabia, opened the door for Moscow to strive for control over Persian Gulf oil, influence over world oil prices, and the prospect for global domination. By the end of his term of office the American economy was in a free fall and U.S. foreign policy in a state of collapse.

Ronald Reagan took office rejecting détente and determined to reestablish American hegemony by reviving the economy, rebuilding military power and reconstructing the Western alliance. At the same time he undercut the Soviet economy. His Strategic Defense Initiative shifted the arms control paradigm from offense to defense and he forced the Soviets into an arms race they could not win. By the end of his first term, Reagan had neutralized the Soviet Union's strategic weapons advantage and thus the basis of its geopolitical offensive.

Having succeeded in his aims and defeating Soviet strategy in the first term, Reagan was intent upon bringing the Soviets to their knees in the second, reestablishing and making permanent American dominance, and completing the reconstruction of the containment structure by strengthening relations with China and restoring relations with Iran. From that position of strength he would be willing to negotiate victory in the Cold War.

The new world order faction, now led by Secretary of State George Shultz, found themselves in the same position vis-à-vis Ronald Reagan that Henry Kissinger and his cohorts had found themselves in vis-à-vis Richard Nixon– and adopted the same approach. Stunningly, Ronald Reagan would suffer the same political defeat that Nixon had, by the same scheme, and for the same reason, as will be detailed in this volume. The only difference between the two was that whereas Nixon chose to fight against the political establishment, and was driven from office, Reagan would compromise with it and serve out his term.

The new world order faction proceeded to entangle President Reagan in what we have come to know as the Iran-Contra scandal. The result was that Reagan turned over control of American foreign policy to Secretary Shultz, who promptly reversed his strategy and strove to reach détente with Moscow. Shultz reversed the entire panoply of Reagan's policies including arms control, relations with allies, economic policy, and support for anti-Soviet resistance movements. Ironically, détente the second time around would not be enough to save the Soviet Union.

******

President Ronald Reagan, entering his second term, was poised to press his strategy against the Soviet Union, as set forth in NSDD-75 of January 17, 1983, the first codification of American strategy since NSC-68 in 1950. This strategy, whose fundamental purpose was to reestablish American dominance over the Soviet Union, posited several broad tasks. Foremost was to continue to strengthen American power and weaken the Soviet Union, particularly its economic base. Another was to maintain the cohesion of the Western alliance, while undermining the Soviet alliance system. The "primary focus" was to "contain and over time reverse Soviet expansionism," which meant raising the costs to Moscow of its support for the conflicts being waged on four continents against Western interests and for its involvement in Afghanistan. Finally, the president sought to parley growing American power into a global structure of peace, in which the Soviet Union could participate, but could no longer disrupt.

The two years following the introduction of NSDD-75 had witnessed Reagan's success in defeating three key Soviet strategic objectives. Reagan had transformed the strategic weapons environment with the introduction of the Strategic Defense Initiative (SDI); he had denied Moscow strategic weapons superiority over the United States by increasing the mobility of strategic forces, and Western Europe and Japan by preempting the Soviet missile deployment to Grenada and completing the deployment of the Pershing II/cruise missile package to Western Europe; and he had defeated Soviet strategy toward Iran.

These Soviet defeats were not irreversible, however, and in the second term President Reagan would attempt to turn Soviet setbacks in these areas into permanent American successes. The president would seek to make permanent the change in the arms balance with a new arms control regime based on defense (SDI) rather than offense (Mutual Assured Destruction, or MAD). He would seek to stabilize Europe through a total elimination of intermediate-range weapons, the zero option, and he would attempt to complete the reconstruction of the containment structure through the re-establishment of a strategic relationship with Tehran.

Determining that the Soviets no longer possessed a strategic weapons advantage, were economically depleted and geopolitically overextended, the president commenced a vigorous support program for resistance movements in Afghanistan, Poland, Angola, Mozambique, Cambodia, and Nicaragua. While the initial strategic purpose was essentially to harass and raise the cost to Moscow and its clients for their involvement, during the second term the president would seek to gain the initiative for these movements, defeating Soviet clients and the Soviets themselves. In short, in the second term, the president sought to shift to the geopolitical offensive and achieve victory for the United States and its allies.

There were growing grounds for optimism that American strategy was succeeding. By mid-1984, not only had the president defeated Soviet strategy, the Russians appeared to be tottering on the brink of general political and economic crisis. Economic sanctions imposed pursuant to the imposition of martial law in Poland, the strengthening of COCOM technology transfer rules, and the tightening of credit restrictions on loans, had significantly impacted Soviet economic performance. Furthermore, the Yamal Siberia-to-Western Europe gas pipeline, now restricted to one strand instead of two, had yet to be completed.

The Soviet economy had ground virtually to a standstill, with growth hovering between 1 percent and zero.[3] Agricultural production was dwindling. The 1984 grain harvest of 170 million tons was the sixth successive year in which production fell substantially short of the

---

[3] Henry Rowen and Charles Wolfe, *The Impoverished Superpower: Perestroika and the Soviet Military Burden* (San Francisco: ICS Press, 1990).

projected target of 250 million tons. Even with record imports of 55.5 million tons of grain, which drained hard-currency earnings, there remained a persistent shortfall.[4] (The 1985 harvest would come in only marginally better at 180 million tons.) The United States appeared to be the only producer with sufficient and consistent long-term excess capacity to meet Soviet needs, although Moscow attempted to diversify imports.

Soviet hard currency earnings from the sale of oil and gas had fallen sharply, as the president's long-term objective of reducing oil prices began to bite. New sources of petroleum and gas were coming on line, from the North Sea, Nigeria, Mexico, Alaska and Canada, increasing overall supply. Oil prices were softening even in the face of cutbacks by OPEC and moderating global demand. The global energy market, on which Moscow depended for nearly three quarters of its hard-currency earnings, was clearly unstable and trending downward. The president was determined to keep the pressure on the Soviet economy by effecting the continued reduction of energy prices.

Indeed, the energy price drop was having a double-barreled effect. Not only were the Soviets earning less, but also the increase in global supply of oil and gas prompted West European countries to renegotiate high-priced contracts for future delivery from the not-yet-completed Yamal gas pipeline. The hard currency needed to finance imports from agricultural commodities to high technology was drying up, forcing increased reliance upon Western credit markets. In 1984, Moscow and its East European clients had nearly tripled their formal borrowing from Western Europe and Japan to just under $3 billion, raising total bloc indebtedness to the West to close to $35 billion.[5]

By 1985, the Soviet Union managed to run down its annual hard-currency trade surplus from over $4 billion to $534 million. This shrinkage had occurred despite a determined effort to increase energy

---

[4] *USSR; Situation and Outlook Report*, (U.S. Department of Agriculture: Washington, D.C., May 1986), 3, 15, 40.
[5] Roger Robinson, "Financing the Soviet Union," *Wall Street Journal*, March 10, 1986, 36.

exports and reduce imports. Moscow also attempted to compensate for its earnings shortfall by increased gold sales, which doubled to 200 tons in 1984.[6] But, there was a clear limit to this approach.

In short, the costs to the Soviet Union of financing its empire, supporting client military operations across the globe, maintaining pace with the American buildup in high technology weapons, and providing for its own people, were exceeding earnings. Long-term trends indicated that conditions would grow worse, rather than improve, raising the fundamental question of: what is to be done?

What was clearly apparent to both the American and Soviet leaderships was that their countries were moving in opposite directions—American power was waxing and Soviet power was waning. Plotted on a graph their respective trends would be viewed as a giant strategic scissors. The problem for the American leadership was how to manage the transition to American supremacy and for the Soviet, how to reverse, or at least, to arrest, the trend?

It was precisely that prospect that prompted the Soviet leadership under Mikhail Gorbachev to change strategy from nuclear coercion to détente in hopes of arresting the negative trend and still achieve fundamental Soviet objectives. These remained the maintenance of strategic weapons dominance over the United States, military superiority over its Eurasian neighbors, and the establishment of decisive leverage over Persian Gulf oil by drawing Iran into the Soviet orbit. Soviet support for so-called anti-imperialist movements was a growing drain on resources, as well as a contradiction in terms of the détente strategy and would have to be written off, but not immediately. An effort would be made to leave Soviet clients with the best possible political prospects, but highly visible Soviet support for what they termed "wars of national liberation" would end.

Soviet objectives were not apparent at the outset, however. Gorbachev's rise was accompanied by a major increase in military spending, an intensification of support for revolutionary conflict, and a

---

[6] Clyde Farnsworth, "Soviet Borrows Heavily as Oil and Dollar Fall," *New York Times*, December 3, 1987, A15.

quantum leap in the level of international terrorism — all directed against the West in general and the United States in particular. Although this prompted some in the Reagan administration to interpret early Soviet policy under Gorbachev as "politics as usual," in retrospect the military emphasis was but prelude to a major shift consistent with the adoption of the strategy of détente.[7] What initially appeared to be politics as usual was an effort to develop an improved bargaining position with the United States on those issues the Soviets were determined to change or liquidate.

Soviet support for international terrorism was in a different category, however. Since the establishment of the Soviet Union in 1917, the Russians had championed state support for international terrorism as an instrument of foreign policy. During the Gorbachev era Moscow would expand and develop an international support base, even while disguising its hand, somewhat in the manner in which Stalin had transformed the Comintern during the era of cooperation with the West in World War II. International terrorism, from Moscow's point of view, was a cheap and effective means of keeping the West in general and the United States in particular off balance and would become one of Moscow's most important, if unacknowledged, successes.

The issue of Soviet support for international terrorism provoked a never-ending debate within the Reagan administration—a debate that intensified following the attack on the Marine Barracks at Beirut. Reagan and his supporters, especially CIA Director William Casey, wanted to publicly identify Moscow's role. Shultz and his supporters, while recognizing the need to combat global terrorism, were eager to identify and take action against Moscow's allies as state supporters of terrorism, advocating the use of military force against them; but they strongly opposed labeling Moscow as a state supporter of international terrorism.

---

[7] See Robert Gates, *From the Shadows: The Ultimate Insider's Story of Five Presidents and How They Won the Cold War* (New York: Simon & Schuster, 1996), 559-66, for a defense of CIA analyses of Gorbachev.

Secretary of Defense Caspar Weinberger vehemently opposed any use of U.S. military power against terrorists, preferring more discreet means. The division within the administration over whether to name Moscow as a state supporter of international terrorism as well as the issue of the use of U.S. military power against terrorists represented a major fault line in the administration. The high-leadership standoff resulted in a decision not to identify the Soviet Union as a state supporter of international terrorism and ipso facto precluded the adoption of a successful strategy to deal with it to the present day.

President Reagan saw Soviet economic deterioration and leadership quandary as an opportunity to bring about a fundamental change in the global order. Therefore, he sought to engage the Soviets in hopes of parleying growing American power into a peaceful transition from Soviet strategic weapons superiority to a new global order based on mutual assured defense, rather than mutual assured destruction. A limited détente, success of the Strategic Defense Initiative, and the negotiated reduction of nuclear weapons were central to his goal of a powerful and secure America and a much weaker and compliant Soviet Union.

Secretary of State Shultz agreed with the idea of engaging the Soviets, but sought a much more equitable outcome for the Russians, the establishment of a mutually beneficial détente relationship. For him and the new world order faction the ultimate objective—to be pursued above all others—was to end the Cold War stand-off and develop the Russians as partners, rather than as subdued adversaries. For him, the failure of Soviet strategy and economic weakness combined with the emergence of a new leadership offered an opportunity to move toward this objective.

Thus, in the short term and on the issue of the growing American strategic advantage, the president's and the secretary's objectives paralleled. However, their long-term objectives were fundamentally opposed. For Shultz, a negotiated strategic weapons reduction, and the maintenance of mutual assured destruction, remained the centerpiece of accommodation and he hoped to leverage SDI as a bargaining chip to get it. The new world order faction sought the further, if not final, deconstruction of the containment structure and the negotiation of what was the unacknowledged fact of a spheres of influence agreement with Moscow.

On the Soviet side, new leader Mikhail Gorbachev recognized that strategic trends were adverse and sought through détente with the United States to buy the time he needed to bring about a recovery of his country's political and economic fortunes. Toward this end he was willing to reach arms control agreements with Washington, but only on condition that the United States forgo, or at least marginalize, SDI, which would reinforce existing Soviet military strength, especially superiority over Western Europe.

The faction associated with the late General Secretary Konstantin Chernenko, led by General Nicolai Ogarkov, opposed the strategy of détente and arms control with the United States as the means to buy time to reinvigorate the Soviet economy. They preferred to continue the pursuit of current objectives, seemingly, even at the cost of further domestic privation. They clung to the outside chance that pursuit of a nationwide missile defense would be successful. Overruled, they appeared to attempt to disrupt the move toward détente through promotion of terrorist attacks against American assets in Europe.

Through 1985 and most of 1986, President Reagan moved systematically toward his objectives, in the face of Shultz's and the new world order faction's attempts to undermine his policies and promote their preferred alternatives. Gorbachev, too, made sufficient concessions both to the United States and his internal opponents, while attempting to promote economic recovery and preparing to cut losses in foreign policy.

The fall of 1986 witnessed the climax of what was a six-year-long struggle between the president and the new world order faction, which the president lost. Similar to the manner in which the political establishment had entrapped President Nixon in scandal in 1972, President Reagan would be entangled in 1986. That scandal, known as the Iran-Contra Affair, resulted in the transfer of control over foreign policy from President Reagan to George Shultz, who, from late in 1986, fundamentally altered American strategy from victory to the new world order.

The point of departure for this volume, then, is the overwhelming electoral victory for President Reagan, which triggered his second-term plans to seek victory in the Cold War over the Soviet Union. At the same time, Secretary Shultz also began to marshal the forces of the new world order in their effort to turn the president's policies in the direction of détente with Moscow. The outcome of their struggle would set the course of American strategy from then until now and is thus worthy of the most intense scrutiny.

Chapter 1
Strategy and its Discontents

In many ways, President Reagan's reelection was a pyrrhic victory. Despite the public euphoria, the president's electoral landslide was not duplicated in the Congress. In the Senate, Republicans lost two seats, which narrowed their margin of advantage to 53-47 and, even though picking up 16 seats in the House, Republicans still trailed the Democrats by a large 71-seat margin 253-182. The continued legislative stalemate was only the tip of the political iceberg, as the division within the administration between the president and his secretary of state grew more pronounced.

Wholesale change within the White House itself also weakened the president's position. Immediately after the election all three members of what had been Reagan's management team, called the troika, began making plans to depart. The first to go was Chief of Staff James Baker, who, seeking a cabinet post, persuaded Treasury Secretary Donald Regan to switch jobs, a change that the president announced in February 1985.[1] At the same time, Counselor Edwin Meese left the White House to become Attorney General and, later in May, Deputy Chief of Staff Mike Deaver left government entirely to set up a public relations firm in Washington, D.C.

The departure of Baker, Meese, and Deaver from the White House did not, however, mean that they had lost influence. According to

---

[1] Michael K. Deaver, *Behind the Scenes*, (New York: William Morrow, 1987), 130, notes "the Treasury swap originated with Baker, but he found a willing buyer in Don Regan." Don Regan, *For the Record* (New York: Harcourt, Brace, Jovanovich, 1988), 220, claims that he proposed the swap.

Regan, Baker requested that both he and Meese be retained as members of the National Security Planning Group (NSPG), giving them a formal voice in policy decisions, and the president agreed.[2] Thus, the Baker-Meese-Deaver troika was not so much broken up, as shuffled into new positions, except for Deaver, who attempted to tutor new Chief of Staff Don Regan until he departed. In consequence, as Cannon observes, "the president was left to fend for himself while Regan underwent on-the-job training in 1985."[3]

Although Regan attempted to keep a tight rein on White House affairs, multiple lines of private access to the president materialized. National Security Adviser Robert McFarlane, in addition to briefing the president daily, had virtually unimpeded access. Secretary of State Shultz had private access to him twice a week arranged by McFarlane, and CIA Director Bill Casey, as before, also had walk-in access as well as a private office in the Executive Office Building adjacent to the West Wing of the White House.[4] Even though Regan was present during most meetings held with the president, the chief of staff was not well versed in matters of foreign policy and strategy, and therefore much escaped him. When he asked McFarlane to explain issues, for example, the national security adviser would invariably demur on the grounds that the chief of staff had "no need to know."[5]

The battle lines were clearly drawn between the president and Shultz in the NSPG, which on paper seemed to favor the president. On one side were Reagan, Casey, Meese, Regan, and Defense Secretary Caspar Weinberger; on the other side were Shultz, McFarlane, and Baker. Vice-president George H. W. Bush, as president-in-waiting, played what by all accounts was an enigmatic role, especially in meetings where he was reticent in voicing opin)ons that could be recorded. Reportedly, in private, he supported the president.

---

[2] Regan, *For the Record*, 235.
[3] Lou Cannon, *President Reagan: Role of a Lifetime* (New York: Simon & Shuster, 1991), 565.
[4] Robert C. McFarlane, *Special Trust* (New York: Cadell & Davies, 1994), 287.
[5] Regan, *For the Record*, 324.

Secretary of State Shultz was the big winner in the musical chairs game, moving to a position of great influence over the policymaking apparatus.[6] In addition to gaining weekly access to the president, he had reestablished State Department preeminence over the policy formulating process through the senior interagency groups (SIGs), and had a strong White House ally in McFarlane. He also reshuffled personnel to advantage, either firing Reagan's supporters, or moving them to less influential positions.[7] For example, Jeane Kirkpatrick, cabinet member and UN representative, sought a more important assignment in the second term; she was denied, and resigned at the end of January.[8] Replaced by Vernon Walters, the UN position was downgraded, removed from the cabinet, and subordinated to the secretary of state.

In the key area of arms control, Reagan had wanted to keep control of the negotiations with the Soviets in the White House, as he had with former National Security Adviser William Clark earlier, proposing to appoint an arms control "czar"; but Shultz strongly opposed it. He insisted that "he personally wanted to lead the American effort to improve Soviet-American relations and get arms talks back on track," and Reagan relented.[9] Shultz promptly reorganized the entire team establishing his and the state department's dominance. Thus, he forced out Reagan's man Ed Rowny, relegating him to advisor status, and replaced him with John Tower. At the same time, he appointed Paul Nitze as his

---

[6] Don Oberdorfer, "Shultz Firmly in Command," *Washington Post*, February 8, 1985, 1 and James McCartney, "Shultz, With Minimal Fanfare, Moves to Strengthen His Role," *Philadelphia Inquirer*, January 27, 1985, 1.
[7] Bill Outlaw, "Conservatives and Shultz Reach Accord in Debate Over Diplomats," *Washington Times*, January 16, 1985, 1 and John McLaughlin, "Shultz's Purge," *National Review*, February 8, 1985.
[8] Bernard Weinraub, "Reagan Is Told By Kirkpatrick She Will Leave," *New York Times*, January 31, 1985, 1.
[9] Hedrick Smith, "For Shultz, Arms Control Talks Offer Fresh Prominence and New Purpose," *New York Times*, January 7, 1985, 8. See also George Shultz, *Turmoil and Triumph* (New York: Macmillan, 1993) 491.

personal arms control adviser, marginalizing Secretary Weinberger and Assistant Secretary of Defense Richard Perle.[10]

Shultz tried but failed to force Weinberger out of government entirely. Shortly after the election, both Shultz and McFarlane spoke disparagingly of him. Shultz insisted to the president that he could no longer "work congenially" with the defense secretary, and suggested that one or the other would have to go, offering his own resignation. Reagan refused the suggestion as well as the secretary's resignation offer.

Then, just before the inauguration, McFarlane repeated Shultz' argument, but the president once again refused, insisting, "We can work with both George and Cap." McFarlane said that left only two choices: "either you delegate to someone within the White House," by whom he meant himself, or, "you've got to expect to become far more involved…in decision-making." Reagan replied presciently: "fine… If that's what it takes, then that's what I'll do."[11] In fact, as we shall see, McFarlane, too, became "more involved…in decision-making."

When McFarlane replaced Judge Clark as national security adviser in the fall of 1983, that change removed control over the NSC from the president and shifted it to the new world order faction, although initially McFarlane played the role of honest broker. By the beginning of the second term, however, he would support Shultz in all important issues and attempt to persuade the president to do the same.[12]

Mayer and McManus thought that McFarlane was acting independently. As they saw it, as the second term began, "McFarlane

---

[10] Don Oberdorfer, "Rowny's Replacement Picked in Stealth," *Washington Post*, January 20, 1985, 29. Edward L. Rowny, *It Takes One To Tango*, (Washington: Brassey's, 1992), 159-60, says the decision was a "stunning blow," which he could not comprehend.

[11] Jane Mayer and Doyle McManus, *Landslide*, (Boston: Houghton Mifflin, 1988), 55-56. McFarlane, *Special Trust*, 286, also discusses these conversations, but reverses their order of occurrence, placing his before Shultz's, and omits the last remark by the president.

[12] See Norman Bailey and Stefan Halper, "National Security for Whom?" *Washington Quarterly* (Winter 1986): 186-88, for an incisive discussion of McFarlane and Shultz's domination of the decision-making process.

decided to make the decisions himself. In effect, he guessed what the president wanted, and acted on that," including signing White House orders FOR THE PRESIDENT in his own name.[13] Reality was more complicated. That McFarlane was making decisions in Reagan's name was true, but that he was acting independently was not. His actions were part of the new world order faction's plans to gain control of the foreign policy decision-making apparatus. As McFarlane put it:

> I decided that the Soviet Union ought to be the leading priority, and Shultz agreed.... We devoted most of our efforts in 1985 to getting the two of us back to the table and developing an agenda that the American people might understand and support.[14]

With Shultz and McFarlane in position to affect the formal policy machinery, not only would the president find it difficult to have his policies enacted through normal channels, his authority over covert operations was also circumscribed. Shortly before the inauguration Shultz made a move to limit the president's authority over covert operations. According to Executive Order 12333 the president and Casey controlled covert operations, but, on January 18, shortly before the inauguration, the president was prevailed upon to sign NSDD 159. On paper, NSDD 159 significantly weakened the president's authority by requiring that a specially configured NSPG "provide a recommendation to the president on each proposed covert action, or proposed modification to an ongoing covert operation."

Where formerly the president and the CIA director decided on covert operations, now a ten-man committee would decide. The membership of the committee was: Reagan, Bush, Shultz, Weinberger, Casey, Regan, McFarlane, Chairman of the Joint Chiefs of Staff General John Vessey, Fielding, and Dawson. (Fred Fielding was counselor to the president, and Tom Dawson was Regan's deputy.)

---

[13] Mayer and McManus, *Landslide*, 65, 61.
[14] Ibid, 65.

Even more important was the stipulation that "the president shall approve of all covert action findings in writing."[15]

Thus, although the president would attempt to implement the "Reagan Doctrine" of building pressure on the Soviet Union to reach agreements to bring the cold war to an end on his terms, his actual ability to execute his plans was limited by George Shultz and Robert McFarlane, who were determined to cajole, pressure, and turn the president's plans toward the main objective of the new world order faction—a more favorable accommodation with the Soviet Union furthered by "negotiated" outcomes of issues in conflict. The fundamental difference in strategy would have ramifications for virtually every proposed policy.

NSDD-159 had a major impact on the means the president chose to implement his two crucial covert policy objectives—aid to the Nicaraguan Contras and the opening to Iran. When Congress cut off funding for the Contras, insiders wondered why the president did not issue a covert action finding to authorize continued funding. After all, the initial program in 1981 was authorized with just such a finding and later actions in 1986 would be authorized the same way. The answer was that with Shultz and McFarlane both on the committee deciding on covert actions, they were in position to block any "proposed covert action or proposed modification to an ongoing covert action," which left Reagan's only recourse a private, off-the-books operation that skirted the edge of legality.

The same was true for the opening to Iran, but with a twist. There was no support from Shultz, or Weinberger either, for an opening to Iran in 1985, although McFarlane surprisingly supported it. Therefore, the president appeared to proceed toward Iran in the same unofficial manner he had with the Contras, running both operations out of the NSC. But appearances were deceiving and the initial approach collapsed.

---

[15]"Covert Action Policy Approval and Coordination Procedures," January 18, 1985. Christopher Simpson, *National Security Directives of the Reagan and Bush Administrations*, (Boulder: Westview, 1995), 493-97.

As we shall see later in this narrative, McFarlane cut Casey out of the action, brought the initiative to the brink of failure, and resigned. After he resigned, however, the president took control of the initiative, signed a covert action finding—three of them, in fact—authorizing arms sales to Iran; but he and his new national security adviser, John Poindexter, kept the findings secret from the secretary of state, or at least they thought they had.

The Reagan Victory Program[16]

As the program unfolded in 1985, President Reagan sought to consolidate the gains of the first term and parley them into a new global order based on American hegemony. What came to known as the "Reagan Doctrine" was the public articulation of NSDD-75, which the president had signed on January 17, 1983. The main objective was to negotiate a new arms control regime with the Soviet Union based on the Strategic Defense Initiative (SDI). The president sought to gain Soviet agreement to make a transition to the strategic defensive, abandon the long-held doctrine of mutual assured destruction (MAD), and sharply reduce inventories of strategic and intermediate-range missiles.[17] Such an agreement would strip Moscow of its military advantage.

At the same time, Reagan wanted to keep the pressure on the Soviet Union, both economically and geopolitically, without which he knew there would be no incentive for Moscow to reach agreement. Economically, the president sought to spur the growth of the United States and the Western allies, while undercutting further the Soviet Union's hard-currency earning capacity, raising the cost of maintaining the Soviet empire. Saudi Arabia would be a secret lynchpin in this endeavor, as success would involve a sharp plunge in the price of oil. Low oil prices would spur Western economic growth

---

[16] Charles Krauthammer, "The Reagan Doctrine," *Time*, April 1, 1985.
[17] For a succinct contemporaneous analysis of the doctrine, see Cord Meyer, "Reagan's Role on World Stage," *Washington Times*, January 11, 1985, 1C.

and at the same time deprive the Soviet Union of needed hard currency earnings.

Geopolitically, the president sought to increase support for those opposing Soviet regimes, especially in Afghanistan, Nicaragua, Poland, Angola, Mozambique, and Cambodia. With the supporting infrastructure put in place during the first term, Reagan now sought to turn up the heat and assist them to victory. Here, too, Saudi Arabia secretly played a major role in providing funding when the U.S. Congress was slow to act, or refused to act, or where secrecy was vital.

The president also strove to complete the global containment structure by reestablishing relations with Iran, the largest single part of that structure. Having blunted Soviet strategy toward Iran in the first term, he now sought to respond to persistent signals from the Tehran leadership of an interest in improving relations. Here, too, Saudi money would play a "bridging" role. Finally, the president was determined to take steps against the growing wave of terror against the United States and its Western allies. Libya, one of Moscow's surrogates, would be a key target.

The secretary of state and the new world order faction had a different agenda. Seeking accommodation with the Soviet Union rather than victory, Shultz opposed to varying degrees every one of the president's policies, while portraying his policy positions as fully in accordance with the president's. The secretary's approach was transparent and necessary. He could not survive politically in open defiance of his president. Alexander Haig's experience was a clear demonstration of that. Thus, whatever his actual position, he would assert unanimity with the president.[18] Besides, he believed that he could persuade the president to his point of view and, if he could not persuade him he would outmaneuver him with and through the bureaucracy.

The secretary's most obvious opposition to the president was over the Iran initiative, where he publicly opposed Reagan, but on all other issues — including the nature of an arms control settlement with the

---

[18] Shultz's memoir, *Turmoil and Triumph*, is a graphic demonstration of this tactic.

Russians, the economic struggle with them, support for anti-Soviet resistance movements around the world, and the issue of international terrorism—Shultz's positions diverged from the president's in more subtle ways.

Indeed, except for Iran, their differences were over the extent of pressure to be applied before coming to the bargaining table, and in all cases Reagan took a tougher stand than his secretary. There was essential agreement between Reagan and Shultz on means; i.e., the need to apply pressure on the Soviet Union and its clients around the globe. Where they differed was over ends, with Reagan seeking victory over the Soviet Union and its clients in the Cold War, while Shultz searched for opportunities to strike a negotiated accommodation at the earliest opportunity.

In practice, it meant that where the president sought to apply sustained and decisive pressure on the Soviet Union, whether over the role of SDI, or support for anti-Soviet resistance groups around the globe, Shultz sought to continue the policies of *bleeding* the Russians and their clients sufficiently to bring them to the bargaining table where a solution could be negotiated to demonstrate the benefits of détente. The policy battle over support for the Afghan resistance was a clear manifestation of this divergence.

Shultz's approach predetermined the result of any ensuing *negotiation,* which was the legitimization and reinforcement of the Soviet-supported side. During the second term, and especially the last two years, when Shultz was in complete control, not a single communist regime would be displaced by means of negotiation. The political outcomes in Nicaragua, Angola, Ethiopia, Mozambique, Poland, and Cambodia reinforced pro-Soviet, communist regimes. Not even in Afghanistan, where the Soviets were driven out, was a pro-Western regime established.

Iran was a special case. Shultz's vociferous opposition to an opening to Iran was based on a fundamental difference in strategy. Restoring relations with Iran would reestablish the essential containment structure around the Soviet Union and involve American support for a pro-Western state on the Soviet border. The new world order faction was committed to dismantling the U.S. forward global position and thus eliminating a presumed obstacle to détente, regardless of how that might impact on the question of the availability and price of petroleum supply and the security of the Persian Gulf.

Contemporaneous observers, the press, and participants in the policy process understood the conflict within the administration, but consistently portrayed it as either personal (Shultz versus Weinberger, or Casey), or institutional (State versus Defense or CIA), rather than fundamental and strategic, involving the struggle between the president and the new world order faction.

Ultimately, the president could always say no, as at Reykjavik where, against all odds, he maintained his stance to preserve SDI against the arguments of both Gorbachev and his secretary of state. He would often be advised by his supporters simply to dismiss Shultz, but Reagan knew that was not possible without major cause, such as with Haig, precisely because of the "compact" between the president and the political establishment. The administration, as discussed in Volume I of this study, was a coalition government made up of Reagan and his supporters and the new world order political establishment and theirs.[19] Besides, Shultz was usefully engaged in what the president wanted, even if he did not want to go as far as the president did.

The Shift to the Strategic Defensive

There was no more important and no more contentious an issue within the administration than arms control, because it would define the relationship with the Soviet Union, and tensions heightened when the Soviets shifted strategy and sought to resume negotiations. The Soviet decision galvanized Shultz into action. As he viewed it, "we were smack in the middle of what was ever more clearly shaping up to be the endgame of the cold war."[20] The president and his aides, especially Weinberger, wanted to tread cautiously, seeing no value in a

---

[19] See Richard C. Thornton, *The Reagan Revolution, I: The Politics of U.S. Foreign Policy*, (Victoria: Trafford, 2003), 56-61.
[20] Shultz, *Turmoil and Triumph*, 501.

precipitous agreement. The strategic tide was running with the United States and the president and his allies wanted to let it run until U.S. power and position improved further, but not Shultz. As the secretary described it, referring to Weinberger:

> They feared agreements. They thought the Soviets would outnegotiate us and then cheat. I disagreed. We could outnegotiate them and catch them if they cheated. But it meant we would have to compromise and have to realize that nothing is perfect or airtight.[21]

Reagan, of course, clearly understood that having defeated the Soviet challenge in the first term, he would need to engage the Russians in the second, if he were to be able to forge a new global order based on SDI. Moreover, it would be vital to do so before the Soviets had become locked into a new strategy. And so, to the consternation of his supporters, who worried about a presidential change of heart, he sided with Shultz. But Reagan, too, understood that they were approaching the "endgame of the cold war," and wanted to end it on his terms.

Secretary Shultz and Soviet Foreign Minister Andrei Gromyko were scheduled to meet in Geneva, January 7-8, to decide on the structure, agenda, and time for resumption of arms control negotiations. In the weeks leading up to the meeting the maneuvering on both sides was intense. Although Weinberger objected to the meeting, the president agreed to it. His objective was first and foremost to bring the Russians back to the bargaining table. Without negotiations there would be no means to gain Soviet agreement for a transition to strategic defense based on SDI and for a sharp reduction in nuclear missiles, both strategic and intermediate, his overarching objectives.

The president knew full well that Shultz saw arms control negotiations as an opportunity to use SDI as a bargaining chip and

---

[21] Ibid, 503.

parley a severely restricted system as the basis for an accommodation. According to Talbott, "Shultz said privately on a number of occasions that he was prepared to 'signal' that SDI was 'open for discussion' as long as Gromyko acknowledged that the Soviet superiority in ICBMs was also negotiable."[22]

To insure that his secretary hewed to his objectives and would *not* attempt to indicate that SDI was negotiable, Reagan issued an unusually detailed and specific set of negotiating instructions for him to follow when he met Gromyko. NSDD-153, which Reagan signed on January 1, 1985, was the product of the combined inputs of Shultz, Weinberger, Casey, the Joint Chiefs of Staff, and the Arms Control and Disarmament Agency (ACDA).[23] McFarlane's accompanying memo to the president highlighted the president's objectives, namely, to "open formal talks within a month or so," and to "begin a process of education and persuasion with regard to your view of how together we can agree on a road which will lead us toward less reliance on offensive systems and more on defensive systems. This latter goal represents a truly historic initiative."[24]

More than a simple set of instructions, the sixteen-page document presented a succinct analysis of the historical evolution of strategic weapons, how the balance had skewed toward Moscow, and how the U.S. strategic modernization program was making it possible to "restore the nuclear balance…by the end of the decade." It explained why Reagan believed that it was important to make a transition to a new arms control regime based on strategic defense, instead of continuing to rely on mutual assured destruction. "If the promise of SDI is achieved, the Soviet advantage accumulated over the past twenty years at great cost will be largely neutralized."[25]

---

[22] Strobe Talbott, *The Master of the Game*, (New York: Knopf, 1988), 213.
[23] Simpson, *National Security Directives, 439,* 469-84.
[24] McFarlane, *Special Trust*, 302.
[25] Simpson, *National Security Directives*, 472.

Nitze had drafted what was termed the "strategic concept," which Shultz was instructed to present to Gromyko when they met. A concise four sentences in length, it stated:

> During the next ten years, the U.S. objective is a radical reduction in the power of existing and planned offensive nuclear arms, as well as the stabilization of the relationship between offensive and defense nuclear arms, whether on earth or in space. We are even now looking forward to a period of transition to a more stable world, with greatly reduced levels of nuclear arms and an enhanced ability to deter war based upon the increasing contribution of non-nuclear defenses against offensive nuclear arms. This period of transition could lead to the eventual elimination of all nuclear arms, both offensive and defensive. A world free of nuclear arms is an ultimate objective to which we, the Soviet Union, and all other nations can agree.[26]

However, the specific negotiating instructions to Shultz, beyond the presentation of the "strategic concept" were muddled and contradictory. Although the secretary was instructed to keep the START and INF negotiating fora substantively and procedurally "*separate*," and offer "corresponding negotiations on nuclear defensive forces," which referred to the Soviet missile defense system, not SDI, which was non-nuclear, he would not be bound by these instructions.

The president authorized him to agree to virtually any formulation that Gromyko proposed, including "a *merger* of talks on reducing medium-range and intercontinental-range nuclear weapons," to get the talks going.[27] However, anticipating that the Soviets would seek to

---

[26] Simpson, *National Security Directives*, 473. For Nitze's original draft, see Paul Nitze et al., *From Hiroshima to Glasnost*, (New York: G. Weidenfeld, 1989) 404-5.
[27] Leslie Gelb, "Unused U.S. Option in Geneva Related," *New York Times*, February 1, 1985, 4. (emphasis supplied)

gain agreement to "prevent the militarization of space," Shultz was instructed at all costs to avoid any pejorative reference to SDI as a "space" weapon. Indeed, he was specifically enjoined to insure that "the word 'space' should not appear in the description of any negotiations...in a manner prejudicial to the U.S."[28]

To insure that the president's views would not be easily circumvented and especially that SDI would not be viewed as a "bargaining chip," before Shultz left for Geneva, the White House issued a report on *The President's Strategic Defense Initiative* explaining the centrality of SDI in Reagan's defense concept and also telegraphed the gist of Shultz's instructions in a series of press articles based on conversations with "unnamed" administration spokesmen. One article outlined the intent to separate the offensive and defensive negotiations.[29] Another revealed that the United States would negotiate arms reductions, but "offer only to hold discussions on future defensive arms."[30] A third said that Shultz would confront the Russians about the ABM treaty violation at Krasnoyarsk.[31] A fourth emphasized, "Reagan has closed the door...on any deals that would limit his 'Star Wars' missile defense program."[32]

The public campaign to keep pressure on Shultz had little effect on the secretary, however, and the negotiating instructions, as is usually the case, were of only marginal relevance to the actual course of the discussions. The same was true for the composition of the delegation that went to Geneva. Although he had been constrained to take a large, 21-man arms control contingent with him to Geneva, representing all

---

[28] Simpson, *National Security Directives*, 478-9.
[29] Lou Cannon, "U.S. Sees Dual Talks Covering Offensive, Defensive Weapons," *Washington Post*, January 1, 1985, 1.
[30] Bernard Gwertzman, "Shultz Instructed to Spurn Russians on Space Weapons," *New York Times*, January 3, 1985, 1.
[31] Walter Pincus, "U.S. to Confront Soviets With Charge of Treaty Violation," *Washington Post*, January 3, 19895, 1.
[32] David Hoffman, "U.S. Firm in Pursuing 'Star Wars,'" *Washington Post*, January 4, 1985, 1.

relevant institutional interests, the secretary excluded all but a select handful to "sit at the table" with him.

On January 5, the day of departure for Europe, Shultz held a meeting of the entire contingent and informed them that only himself, McFarlane, Nitze, Ambassador to the Soviet Union Arthur Hartman, and Russian-speaking State Department note-taker Jack Matlock, would sit at the negotiating table with the Russians. All of the others, representatives from the Defense Department, ACDA, CIA, and the Joint Chiefs, would be relegated to an adjacent room and would not be privy to what would occur.

Shultz further stunned the delegation by imposing a strict no press contact rule, declaring that only Press Secretary Bernard Kalb would be permitted to talk to the press.[33] Thus, while the contingent that accompanied the secretary to Geneva appeared to present a formidable, unified front, the delegates literally had no duties to perform except to sit in an adjacent room while the secretary and his aides negotiated with the Russians. Shultz briefed them after each session, called on them for their particular expertise, when needed, but excluded them from the negotiations. Indeed, the members of the delegation were even kept in the dark about the meeting agenda. Ostensibly to preserve secrecy, they were handed copies of Shultz's talking points only when they boarded the aircraft for Geneva.[34]

The negotiations themselves were conducted in a complete news blackout. Although Shultz claimed that the Soviets accepted "our concept" of linking strategic, intermediate, and space negotiations in an independent, but interrelated fashion, it appears that this was Gromyko's idea, which Shultz accepted.[35] So much for Shultz's boast of being able to "outnegotiate" the Russians. Their agreement bore no relationship to the "strategic concept," of a transition to the defensive, or to the secretary's negotiating instructions.

---

[33] Jay Winik, *On the Brink*, (New York: Simon & Schuster, 1996), 323.
[34] Shultz, *Turmoil and Triumph*, 512.
[35] Ibid, 515-16.

Indeed, Matlock characterized Gromyko's approach as one of "double linkage." As he described it, "there could be no agreement on INF... without one on START. Additionally, there could be no agreement on either of these weapons types without an agreement regarding 'space weapons.'"[36] Shultz weakly complained that to "hold up progress in one area until all three were resolved," was a formula for stalemate, but acquiesced.[37] Of course, as far as Shultz was concerned, as SDI was not sacrosanct, linkage was preferred.

As expected, it was the "space" issue on which Shultz and Gromyko differed most. Gromyko wanted to define SDI as a "space strike weapon," which Shultz rejected, while Shultz wanted to describe SDI as "space defense," which Gromyko thought a contradiction in terms. The talks appeared headed to failure over the Soviet insistence that the focus of the talks was to prevent an "arms race in space." Stalemated, Shultz consulted Richard Perle waiting in the anteroom. The Defense Department's arms control specialist suggested adding on to the phrase "preventing an arms race in space" the words "and terminating one on earth," a solution which both Shultz and Gromyko accepted.

Nevertheless, the Soviets managed to insert into the final communiqué the suggestion that SDI was an offensive weapon by claiming that the negotiations would be about "nuclear and space arms." A following clarification ameliorated the point, declaring that the objective of the talks was to

> work out effective agreements aimed at preventing an arms race in space and terminating it on earth, at limiting and reducing nuclear arms and at strengthening strategic stability.

The negotiations, it was agreed, would be conducted by a delegation from each side, divided into three groups. The subject of the negotiations was to be a "complex of questions" concerning

---

[36] Jack Matlock, *Reagan and Gorbachev*, (New York: Random House, 2004) 104.
[37] Winik, *On the Brink*, 331.

nuclear and space arms, strategic and intermediate range missiles, "with all the questions considered and resolved in their interrelationship."[38]

Shultz could hardly have been serious in reporting to the president that "we got what we wanted," in the structure of the talks. Except for agreeing to recommence talks, which, in truth, both sides did want, the Russians had gotten their way almost entirely. For his part, the president declared that there was a glimmer of "hope" in the forthcoming dialogue with the Russians. But, he warned, "It takes two sides to have constructive negotiations.... For our part, we will be flexible, patient and determined. We now look to the Soviet Union to help give new life and positive results to that process of dialogue."[39]

To set a high bar for the upcoming negotiations, and, perhaps to satisfy critics on the right, on February 1, the president released a report on Soviet arms control violations. It was the third such report issued in the past thirteen months, the first having been issued on January 13, 1984, citing seven violations; the second on October 10, citing seventeen violations; and the current report, citing eleven violations out of thirteen findings.[40] Four violations involved the ABM Treaty, the most serious being the Krasnoyarsk radar, which suggested, "the U.S.S.R. may be preparing an ABM defense of its national territory."[41]

In his letter of transmittal, the president said that for arms control agreements "to have meaning," there must be full compliance and "this administration will not accept anything less." His goal in the coming negotiations was to "reverse the erosion of the ABM Treaty and to seek equitable, effectively verifiable arms control agreements

---

[38] "Text of the Communique," *New York Times*, January 9, 1985, 11.
[39] Bernard Gwertzman, "Reagan Sees Hope of 'New Dialogue' With the Russians," *New York Times*, January 10, 1985, 1.
[40] "The President's Unclassified Report To The Congress On Soviet Noncompliance With Arms Control Agreements," February 1, 1985, Simpson, *National Security Directives*, 502-12.
[41] Bernard Gwertzman, "U.S. Says Soviet Violates ABM Treaty," *New York Times*, February 2, 1985, 3.

which will result in real reductions and enhanced stability." The Soviet Union, he noted, has "thus far not provided satisfactory explanations nor undertaken corrective actions sufficient to alleviate our concerns."[42]

Tass, the Soviet news agency, immediately replied by charging the Reagan administration with plans for a "crash militarization of outer space." Military analyst Vladimir Bogachev said that it was Washington, not Moscow that was preparing to "violate the ABM treaty by developing a space-based antimissile system."[43] Not to be outdone, Defense Secretary Weinberger retorted that the United States was, indeed, considering the "partial deployment of a "Star Wars" anti-missile defense system without waiting for it to be fully completed." This would, he maintained, "strengthen our existing deterrent....[and] could make a major contribution to the prevention of nuclear war before a fully effective system is deployed."[44] The exchange guaranteed that the coming talks would receive wide attention.

Arms control negotiations would resume on March 12, but would be immediately overshadowed by the death of Party Chairman Konstantin Chernenko and the ascendance of Mikhail Gorbachev, who became personally involved in the negotiations thereafter. By that time, the president had already set in motion the other major elements of the Reagan Doctrine.

Signaling Opposition to Moscow

King Fahd of Saudi Arabia was scheduled to visit the White House in the second week of February. As Reagan was counting on the King's support for much of what he planned to do it was important to signal publicly the administration's second-term direction to him, as

---

[42] "Arms Control Violations—The 1985 Report," *National Security Record*, No. 77 (March 1985), 1-3.
[43] "Cheating on Arms Denied by Moscow," *Washington Post*, February 3, 1985, 18.
[44] James McCartney, "Weinberger: Early 'Star Wars' Deployment is Weighed," *Philadelphia Inquirer*, February 4, 1985, 7.

well as to the American people, and other interested parties. First to sketch out what would soon be described as the *Reagan Doctrine* was Bill Casey. In a speech to the Union League Club of New York, on January 9, Casey announced, "the tide has changed."

> Whereas in the 1960s and 1970s anti-Western causes attracted recruits throughout the Third World, the 1980s have emerged as the decade of freedom fighters resisting communist regimes. In many places, freedom has become as exciting and revolutionary as it was here in America over 200 years ago.[45]

Although the Soviets had acquired "surrogates in Cuba, Vietnam, Ethiopia, Angola, South Yemen, Mozambique, Nicaragua, and Afghanistan," he said, they were overextended. It was costing Moscow $8 billion annually to support these regimes and they were running out of money. The good news was that "hundreds of thousands of ordinary people are volunteers in irregular wars against the Soviet army or Soviet-supported regimes." Oppressed people, he said, "want freedom and are fighting for it. They need only modest support and strength of purpose from nations that want to see freedom prevail..."[46]

On February 6, during his State of the Union address, the president picked up Casey's theme:

> We cannot play innocents abroad in a world that is not innocent; nor can we be passive when freedom is under siege. Without resources, diplomacy cannot succeed. Our security assistance programs help friendly governments defend themselves and give them confidence to work for peace.
>
> We must stand by all our democratic allies. And we must not break faith with those who are risking their lives-on every continent, from Afghanistan to Nicaragua-to defy Soviet-

---

[45] Herb Meyer, ed., *Scouting the Future: The Public Speeches of William J. Casey*, (Washington, D.C.: Regnery, 1989), 171.
[46] Ibid, 172.

supported aggression and secure rights, which have been ours from birth.

> The Sandinista dictatorship of Nicaragua, with full Cuban-Soviet bloc support, not only persecutes its people, the church, and denies a free press, but arms and provides bases for Communist terrorists attacking neighboring states. Support for freedom fighters is self-defense and totally consistent with the OAS and U.N. Charters. It is essential that the Congress continue all facets of our assistance to Central America. I want to work with you to support the democratic forces whose struggle is tied to our own security.[47]

King Fahd's visit to Washington a few days later, February 11-15, marked the high point of a carefully nurtured, unwritten, and, as it turned out, short-lived alliance between the United States and Saudi Arabia. Its impetus had been the Soviet invasion of Afghanistan, and heavy military involvement in Ethiopia and South Yemen, which had belatedly convinced the Saudi leadership of earlier U.S. claims that the Soviet Union was attempting to encircle the kingdom with a ring of pro-Soviet client states.

Earlier U.S. efforts at policy suasion during the Carter years had been disastrous, alienating the Saudis who believed that Carter had not only abandoned the shah of Iran, but also had repudiated his own Camp David pledge to provide for Palestinian self-rule. In addition, during the South Yemen invasion of North Yemen, the administration's clumsy efforts to depict the Soviet threat as being greater than the Zionist threat had only deepened suspicion of American intentions. The result was that by mid-1979 the Saudis had

---

[47] "State of the Union," February 6, 1985, *Public Papers of Ronald Reagan.* See also Lou Cannon, "Reagan Hails 'New Freedom,'" *Washington Post*, February 7, 1985, 1 and Don Oberdorfer, "Reagan Declares U.S. Again a Leader of the Free World," *ibid.*, 18.

turned away from Washington with a vengeance, sending oil prices sky high.[48]

The Soviet invasion of Afghanistan changed everything. Throughout 1980 as the United States sought to counter the Soviet thrust by constructing, or refurbishing a string of bases and access points to the region from Turkey to Diego Garcia, and sought to demonstrate its readiness to come to the aid of the kingdom, a genuine coincidence of interests began to evolve. Carter's support of Iraq against Iran involved the Saudis as financier for Saddam Hussein's war. There was no little irony in the fact that it now took little to persuade them that the Shiite threat was genuine and that the Soviet threat was at least as great as the Zionist threat.

The Carter administration parleyed Saudi concern of the Shiite threat into greater cooperation as the Saudis granted to United States the use of Saudi territory and facilities in case of emergency. More importantly, they agreed to construct a massive $80 billion defense network according to U.S. design and specifications. During the decade of the '80s the Saudis greatly expanded their defense infrastructure, building six major new air bases, nine new ports, dozens of airfields, and new pipelines linking Iraqi oilfields to export terminals on the Red Sea.

The purpose of the new defense infrastructure was to upgrade the kingdom's own defense capability and also to facilitate a seamless transition for American forces in the utilization of the bases, if and when it ever became necessary for the United States to come to the direct defense of Saudi Arabia. Few could have foreseen that when the emergency did arise in 1990 the threat would come not from Iran, but from Iraq.

Ronald Reagan sought to build on the relationship as soon as he came into office, consummating with some difficulty the *AWACs* sale in 1981. Washington had deployed a number of the aircraft to Saudi Arabia upon the outbreak of the Iran-Iraq war the previous September.

---

[48] See Richard C. Thornton, *The Carter Years: Toward a New Global Order (New York: Paragon House, 1991)*, chapter 7.

The Saudis were so impressed with the technical capabilities of the planes that they insisted on acquiring them for their own defense. As the crisis over Lebanon erupted and Israel invaded in mid-1982, Reagan supported a greater peace-keeping role for the Saudis in the region, but with no success, as they were averse to assuming a public role in the peace process, which involved negotiation with the Israelis.

By mid-1984, the beginning of a quid pro quo was nevertheless apparent. In return for additional substantial support for Saudi national defense, the king broadened his support for anti-Soviet resistance movements. The administration arranged to deploy an additional aerial refueling tanker to extend the range of the kingdom's fleet of *F-15* aircraft, as well as to provide additional wing-tanks for them. To assist in the Saudi air defense, Reagan authorized the unprecedented sale of 400 *Stingers*, the first time the highly advanced, man-portable missile launcher had been transferred to another country, and over two years before they were introduced into Afghanistan.

The Saudis were already supporting the Afghan resistance against the Soviets at a rate of one dollar for every dollar put up by the United States. At this point, their joint contribution was running over $1 billion annually. In the fall, the Congress had cut off funding for the Contras and the king had agreed to provide funding at the rate of $1 million per month for eight months, until the next congressional vote in early 1985.[49] Thus, by the time the king arrived in Washington for his state visit on February 11, the U.S.-Saudi relationship was well on the way to an unofficial alliance. Reagan and the king would take it a giant step forward.

The President, the King, and the Reagan Doctrine: Lynchpin of Victory

King Fahd arrived in Washington as the crisis within the American leadership over the strategy toward the Middle East-Southwest Asia

---

[49] Robert Kagan, *Twilight Struggle*: American Power and Nicaragua, 1977-1990 (New York: Free Press, 1992), 340-41.

region consumed the administration. Secretary of State Haig had sought to support Iraq as Carter had done and as the new world order strategy of dismantling the containment structure dictated, while Reagan was determined to hold open the possibility of a rapprochement with Iran, as called for by the strategy of rebuilding containment. Shultz's replacement of Haig had only intensified the differences between them, as Shultz' power grew and as the president moved forward toward his Iran initiative at the beginning of the second term.

In retrospect, President Reagan and King Fahd appear to have reached four major agreements in support of the president's strategy against the Soviet Union. The first was a $3 billion arms package, which initially included 42 *F-15s* to go with the 60 already in the Saudi fighter inventory. This part of the arms package would be canceled in May because of intense Israeli opposition expressed through the U.S. Congress, but arrangements were made to provide a comparable aircraft through Great Britain.

The second agreement was for the Saudis to expand and broaden their support for anti-Soviet resistance movements. The kingdom would increase its support for the Afghan Mujahideen as congressional funding increased and triple its support for the Nicaraguan Contras, from $8 million to $24 million. In addition to increasing support for the Mujahideen and the Contras, the Saudis also agreed to provide funds for arms deliveries to Jonas Savimbi's UNITA forces struggling against the Soviet-backed MPLA regime in Angola and to support the Mozambique resistance movement, RENAMO, against the Soviet-backed Maputo regime.[50]

There also appears to have been an agreement for the king to support Reagan's intended opening to Iran. What would make possible the opening to Iran would be Saudi financing of arms transfers, which may have reflected the assumption presumably made by the president

---

[50] Peter Schweitzer, *Victory: The Reagan Administration's Secret Strategy That Hastened the Collapse of the Soviet Union* (New York: Atlantic Monthly Press, 1994) 217-19.

and his aides that the best way to resolve the Shiite threat to the kingdom was by co-opting it, rather than contending against it. At the same time, the Saudis continued to funnel some American weapons to Iraq to insure that no Iranian offensive would succeed.[51] The objective remained to perpetuate a stalemate in the war.

In any case, regarding Iran, Saudi involvement appeared in the person of Adnan Khashoggi, who would not only establish contact with Iranian middlemen and Israelis, but also provide bridge financing for arms sales. His role would be similar to that played by Prince Bandar, who became the conduit for funds to the Contras. In both cases, there can be little doubt that action required the prior approval of the king.

The issue that would have the most decisive impact on Moscow would be the issue of oil. The price trend of oil had been on a gradually downward sloping trajectory since 1981. OPEC had attempted to maintain prices by cutting output as non-OPEC production—North Sea, Mexico, Canada, the Soviet Union—increased. Saudi Arabia, as the swing producer, had cut production from 10 million bpd to 3.4 million bpd, in an unsuccessful attempt to prop up prices.[52] For Riyadh the result was a sharp drop in oil revenue from a 1981 high of $119 billion to a 1985 low of $26 billion. Foreign exchange reserves dwindled and the country began to run a budget deficit, forcing the kingdom to cut back ambitious development programs initiated when income was at its height.[53]

Loss of revenue and market share began to marginalize Saudi Arabia's regional and global role. The Saudis were underwriting the policies of OPEC members who were circumventing agreed quotas for their own gain. For example, Iran and Iraq, attempting to pay huge war costs, were openly flouting OPEC quotas by heavily engaging in countertrade, bartering oil for arms. In effect, Saudi Arabia was losing

---

[51] "The Arming of Saudi Arabia," *Frontline*, February 16, 1993, (transcript of show number 1112).
[52] "Saudi Arabia Crude Oil Production by Year," *Index Mundi* http://www.indexmundi.com/energy.aspx?country=sa&product=oil&graph=production
[53] "Oil Price History and Analysis," *WTRG Economics* http://www.wtrg.com/prices.htm

money by propping up oil prices for the benefit of those who were cheating, including its enemy Iran.[54]

It is safe to assume that when the king arrived in Washington he was ready to listen to any plan that would help alleviate his no-win situation. President Reagan and his aides offered the king just such a plan. In secret meetings behind all the pomp and circumstance that attend state visits, Reagan and his aides proposed what was in a nutshell a plan, as Ambassador Richard Murphy pithily phrased it, to "let the free market dictate prices."[55]

As it was obviously proving impossible to maintain high price levels and the Saudis were losing revenue by cutting production in an attempt to keep prices high, Reagan and his aides proposed to abandon the strategy. They proposed that instead of maximizing income by price to maximize income by volume of output. This approach would allow market forces of supply and demand to determine prices, which meant that the growing abundance of supply would depress prices further. Lower prices were what the president wanted to generate Western economic growth and curtail Soviet hard-currency earnings, but they would also enable the Saudis to recover market share and increase income, regaining the kingdom's rightful place as the preeminent power in the gulf.

As oil prices fell, the president's aides argued, the United States, Western Europe, and Japan would consume more and increase economic growth, while those countries like the Soviet Union, Libya, Iraq, Iran and others dependent upon oil for hard-currency earnings, would suffer sharply reduced earnings. Simply put, their friends would gain and their enemies would lose.

Acceding to this proposition, the next steps were to dismantle the oil pricing arrangements that were in place to keep prices high. The Saudis brought the refiners on board by arranging netback deals guaranteeing per-barrel profits regardless of price. Refiners were given an incentive to maximize profits through volume of production, rather

---

[54] Daniel Yergin, *The Prize*, (New York: Free Press, 1992) 728.
[55] "The Arming of Saudi Arabia," *Frontline*, February 16, 1993.

than by restricting production. It would not matter what the barrel price was. Their profit margin would be the same whether the price was $30 dollars a barrel, or $10 dollars a barrel. The netback deals meant that the Saudis would no longer cut production to support an official price. Once the Saudis decided upon a market share strategy, everybody else would be forced to do the same.

The agreement, it is said, was entirely based on "unwritten understandings," but these understandings would be reinforced by each party's public actions.[56] Reagan took the first step. Less than two weeks after King Fahd left Washington, Prime Minister Margaret Thatcher arrived, February 19-21. During that visit, Reagan convinced Thatcher that it was in Britain's interest, too, to go along with the plan to change oil strategy.

The issue was the role that the British National Oil Company, BNOC, played in setting prices. BNOC bought 51 percent of North Sea output at a specified price and resold it to refiners. In a market where demand was greater than supply this was a profitable enterprise, but a losing one when the reverse was true. Thus, as the market softened in the early '80s, BNOC found itself buying high and selling low, losing money for the British treasury.[57]

Thatcher was therefore willing to consider proposals that would end market losses and here Reagan's proposal was simply that BNOC discontinue its price-setting role and let the free market determine prices. As Thatcher was outspoken in her support for free market solutions, this was a proposal that appealed to her. Therefore, the prime minister later in May removed BNOC from the business of attempting to set prices.

But, of course, as everyone associated with the petroleum business understood, in a glutted oil market the removal of price restrictions meant that prices would go in only one direction—down—and fast. How fast depended on when Saudi Arabia began to increase production. But first the ducks had to be lined up. No doubt, the U.S.-

---

[56] Ibid.
[57] Yergin, *The Prize*, 727.

Saudi Joint Commission on Economic Cooperation, which met April 22-23, in Washington, played a role in working out details and timing.

CIA Director Casey's trip to Riyadh in late spring may have been to signal that the time had come to move. The CIA director also conveyed information that would enable the Saudis to earn additional revenue when he divulged that the United States would commence a gradual dollar devaluation in the fall, which meant that non-dollar Saudi assets would rise in value.[58]

Whether or not Casey's visit was the trigger, the king clearly signaled his intentions at the June OPEC meeting a few weeks later when he said: "If member countries feel they have a free hand to act...then all should enjoy that situation and Saudi Arabia would certainly secure its own interests."[59] At that point, even though OPEC output had fallen to a twenty-year low of 13.7 million bpd, prices continued to soften. In early September word began to get around that the price fall was coming.[60] Then, on September 13, oil minister Sheikh Ahmed Zaki Yamani announced that Saudi Arabia would no longer protect oil prices at all. The ducks were lined up.

Resigned to the inevitable, at the end of November OPEC convened and announced that its members had decided to compete as a group with non-OPEC producers to regain market share without regard to price. Over the next five months the price of oil plummeted. West Texas Intermediate dropped from its peak of $31.75 to under $10, with some cargoes selling for as low as $6 per barrel. A price correction would not come until May 1986 when prices would level and fluctuate in a new, much lower, $17-$19 per barrel price range, which remained more or less steady until the end of the century, except for a price spike in 1991 precipitated by the Gulf War and a price dip in 1999.

Needless to say, the sharp fall of oil prices devastated the Soviet Union's hard-currency-earning capability. In 1986 alone the

---

[58] Schweitzer, *Victory*, 232-33.
[59] Yergin, *The Prize*, 729.
[60] John Berry, "Saudi Oil Price Cut Rumored," *Washington Post*, September 5, 1985, E2.

Soviets lost over $20 billion in expected revenue, even though increasing production. Clearly, the change in the oil regime was one of the major factors that drove the Soviet Union into bankruptcy and contributed to its collapse in 1991.

By all accounts, however, this was not a foregone conclusion in early 1985 when the president initiated the Reagan Doctrine. Indeed, it was not evident that the "doctrine" would live up to its promise, as new Soviet leader Mikhail Gorbachev ascended to the Chairmanship of the Soviet Union.

Shultz's Struggle with the President

On February 16, during his weekly radio address on the subject of Central America, Reagan, echoing Casey's views, declared that

> "...the move against communism and toward freedom...is sweeping the world. In the Soviet Union and Eastern Europe, we see the dissidents; in Poland, the Solidarity movement. We see freedom fighters in Afghanistan, Ethiopia, Cambodia, and Angola. These brave men and women are fighting to undo the infamous Brezhnev doctrine, which says that once a nation falls into the darkness of Communist tyranny, it can never again see the light of freedom.[61]

The president went on to plead for support for the Nicaraguan Contras, those "freedom fighters" who were seeking to restore democracy to their country in much the same way Americans themselves had done two centuries earlier. They were "our brothers. How can we ignore them? How can we refuse them assistance when we know that, ultimately, their fight is our fight?"

Secretary Shultz moved quickly but carefully to blunt the main thrust of the president's strategy. While Reagan had clearly articulated the anti-Communist, anti-Soviet emphasis of his policy during these

---

[61] Ronald Reagan, "Radio Address to the Nation on Central America," February 16, 1985.

early weeks of his second term, Shultz sought to deemphasize its anti-Soviet focus and, instead, emphasize "independence, freedom, and human rights." In a speech to the Commonwealth Club of San Francisco, six days later, on February 22, Shultz seemed to play off the president's speech, declaring that "a revolution is sweeping the world today—a democratic revolution." It was "fashionable in some quarters," he said, to claim that democracy was passé, yet, in fact, the great American experiment has "today captured the imagination and the passions of people on every continent."

> The Solidarity movement in Poland; resistance forces in Afghanistan, in Cambodia, in Nicaragua, in Ethiopia and Angola; dissidents in the Soviet Union and Eastern Europe; advocates of peaceful democratic change in South Africa, Chile, the Republic of Korea, and the Philippines...[62]

Coming months would see these different emphases play out in the policy struggle between them. Shultz would drag his feet on support for anti-Soviet resistance forces, except in the special case of the Contras, while focusing his efforts on actively supporting "peaceful democratic change" for America's allies in South Africa, Chile, the Republic of Korea, and the Philippines. "Peaceful democratic change" was simply a codeword for weakening Washington's relations with these countries. New Zealand, too, would receive special treatment, as part of the long-range plan to dismantle the containment structure in the South Pacific.

Nicaragua was a special case. Shultz had risked the president's ire by meeting directly with Daniel Ortega in mid-1984 and setting up direct U.S.-Nicaraguan talks paralleling the Contadora process, which only involved indirect contact. The discussions at Manzanillo, a small resort town in Mexico, showed some initial promise, but were broken off in December.

---

[62] George Shultz, "America and the Struggle for Freedom," US Department of State, *Bulletin*, April 1985.

(The U.S. invasion of Grenada had alarmed the Sandinistas and, it seems, they had agreed to talks in hopes of forestalling a possible attack on themselves. In any case, the outcome of the Nicaraguan elections, which the Sandinistas unsurprisingly won handily, and the U.S. elections, with Democrats gaining in both houses, persuaded the Sandinistas that they had little to fear from invasion and proceeded to stiff the U.S. In short, as Kagan notes, Shultz had been "burned.")[63]

When the president took a strong public position of support for the Contras, and demanded that the Sandinista regime be "removed," Shultz decided to cut his losses for the time being. Reagan had made his demand at a nationally televised news conference the night before Shultz spoke to the Commonwealth Club. Asked if he wanted the Sandinistas removed from power, Reagan replied: "removed in the sense of its present structure, in which it is a communist totalitarian state, and it is not a government chosen by the people."[64] In other words, yes.

For Shultz, the prospects for engaging a new Soviet leadership far outweighed possible gains from talks with the Sandinistas, to whom, moreover, Reagan was viscerally opposed. Thus, on Nicaragua, he became, in Kagan's words, "a devoted and outspoken hawk, following the lead of his president." Some astutely attributed his shift as an attempt to "mollify conservative critics...so that he might have a freer hand in dealing with the Soviet Union." [65] Shultz had not been "converted." He would continue efforts to reach a diplomatic settlement with Managua, but do so in more subtle ways and over a longer timeframe. Most important, he did not want to be seen as being in open opposition to the president on this highly visible issue.

Shultz's more long-range approach toward the Sandinista problem was to chip away at the foundations of the Contra program. Here, he was only partly successful. As we shall see, the president's promotion

---

[63] Kagan, *Twilight Struggle*, 351.
[64] Lou Cannon, "Reagan Sees Change Due Nicaragua," *Washington Post*, February 22, 1985, 1. See also "President's News Conference on Foreign and Domestic Issues," *New York Times*, February 22, 1985, 14.
[65] Kagan, *Twilight Struggle*, 351.

of an informal support program for the Contras, augmented by third country financial support from the Saudis and Israelis, translated into better military performance on the battlefield by late 1984.[66] But, it backfired. The timely Soviet supply of *Mi-24 Hind* attack helicopters, flying tanks they were called, to Managua emboldened the Sandinistas to take the fight to the Contras, driving them back across the border to their Honduran base camps in early 1985. The Soviets were willing and able to supply more advanced weapons to the Sandinistas than the Contras were receiving.

The strengthened presence of Sandinista forces on the border created great tension within the Honduran leadership, who demanded a "written guarantee" from the United States against Nicaragua in return for continued support for the Contras.[67] The turmoil in Tegucigalpa opened an opportunity for Shultz and McFarlane to undercut support for the Contra presence in the border areas, even as the secretary publicized his support for the president's policy.

In late January, for example, McFarlane went to Tegucigalpa ostensibly to reassure the Honduran leadership. Instead, he provoked a disagreement over the issue of a guarantee, which further roiled political waters. Relations were only patched over two months later when Vice-President Bush traveled to Honduras and publicly declared U.S. support.[68] Increased aid, $88 million in military assistance and $142 million in economic aid ameliorated, but failed to dispel,

---

[66] The Saudi contribution was only one factor accounting for improved Contra performance. Another was a sharp influx of weapons donated by the Israelis valued at well over $10 million. In a project initiated by Casey known as Operations Tipped Kettle I and II, and Project Elephant Herd, Israel donated to the DOD weapons they had captured from the PLO during the 1982 invasion of Lebanon. DOD turned the weapons over to the CIA for distribution to the Contras "as appropriated funds ran out." Maj. Gen. Richard Secord negotiated the initial Israeli contribution and after he retired was later tapped to run the Contra supply program in 1984. See the "Stipulation of Fact" in *The United States of America v. Oliver L. North*, no.88-0080 02, U.S. District Court, Washington, D.C.
[67] Roy Gutman, "U.S. Policy Squeezes Honduras," *Long Island Newsday*, February 8, 1985, 3.
[68] Kagan, *Twilight Struggle*, 349.

Honduran concerns. Tension and rumors of a military coup persisted, along with questions about the U.S. presence. A State Department official openly questioned the value of a U.S. presence: "It would be silly to go down for exercises if this turmoil continues....If a coup takes place while we are there, we'd look bad."[69]

Shultz's main success was to engineer the "surprise" removal of General Paul Gorman, head of Southern Command and a major figure in provision of support for the entire program in Central America. Reportedly, "Shultz had actually lobbied the White House and the Pentagon to force the 57-year old general out of the critically important job." President Reagan, Secretary Weinberger, and General Vessey "all tried to persuade General Gorman to remain at his post or take another government job," but the general said he was "disgusted with State Department opposition to his hard-line policies on communist guerrillas."[70] For Shultz, the retirement of Gorman, who was the administration's "major strategist" for Central America, was a major plus, especially as he was being considered for promotion to either the Command of U.S. forces in Europe, or to Chairman of the Joint Chiefs of Staff when Vessey stepped down.[71]

Shultz's objective was to remove or make very tenuous Honduras as a base for the Contras. Weakening the Contras by undermining their support base presumably would make them more amenable to compromise with the Sandinistas. The problem with this line of reasoning was that the Sandinistas were the more powerful party. Weakening the Contras would not hasten a negotiated settlement; it would simply insure a military victory by the Sandinistas. Indeed, in early 1985 the Sandinista army was just reaching the point where it could go on the sustained offensive. The balance, thanks in great part to the congressional funds cut-off, was tipping against the Contras.

---

[69] Roy Gutman, "Turmoil Tests Key U.S. Ally," *Long Island Newsday*, March 31, 1985, 5.
[70] Walter Andrews, "Tough U.S. General Retires Early From Command in Latin America," *Washington Times, January 11, 1985*, 1.
[71] Bill Keller, "General to Leave Top Latin Position," *New York Times*, January 11, 1985, 4.

This was, perhaps, the key reason that Shultz took a firm stand in support of the Contras early in the second term, for there would be no disguising the State Department's responsibility in a defeat.

Shultz and the Resistance Movements-Afghanistan

In addition to the Nicaraguan Contras, President Reagan had repeatedly declared American support for the "freedom fighters" of Afghanistan, Angola, Mozambique, Ethiopia, and Cambodia. In all of these cases, Shultz and the State Department dragged their feet, or actually opposed support for the anti-Soviet movements.

In Afghanistan, Congressman Charles Wilson (D- Texas) leveraged his position on the House Appropriations Committee, to become a major force in gaining increased funding for the Mujahideen. Obsessed with defeating the Soviets, Wilson moved out front in a personal campaign to provide better weapons for the resistance fighters.[72] It was a common complaint, however, that increased congressional appropriations for the Afghan resistance fighters had been accomplished with "no help from the State Department," which continued its policy of "dragging its heels on providing aid."[73]

The State Department was only partly at fault for not responding promptly to the president's call. Support for the resistance had originated with former President Jimmy Carter, who had authorized a modest program designed to harass the Soviets in Afghanistan, but not to defeat them. Defeat was thought to be impossible and in truth undesirable because Carter naively harbored the hope that cooperation, even détente, with Moscow was still obtainable. President Zia ul-haq of Pakistan, through whom the program functioned, was of a similarly

---

[72] See George Crile, *Charlie Wilson's War*, (New York: Grove Press, 2003) for an entertaining, informative, but critically flawed narrative of Wilson's efforts. The flaw in Crile's argument is the failure to acknowledge the president's and the CIA director's command role, attributing fundamental decisions to Wilson alone.

[73] Benjamin Hart, "Rhetoric vs Reality: How the State Department Betrays the Reagan Vision," January 31, 1986, *Heritage Foundation*, Backgrounder #484.

cautious belief. Zia insisted that the U.S. profile be minimized and that the program be run by the Pakistani intelligence service, ISI.

Reagan had inherited and tried to build on this program, but State and CIA officials assigned under Carter were still in place essentially to oversee and manage the program. The arrangement with Pakistan kept the U.S. role masked and indirect. Washington supplied weapons to Pakistan and the ISI distributed them to the Mujahideen in Afghanistan at its discretion. While this enabled the United States to keep a low profile, and a pseudo plausible deniability, it fooled no one and gave ISI great latitude to distribute weapons favors to preferred recipients, not to mention siphon off a considerable percentage for themselves.

The downside to this arrangement was obvious. Even though the quantity and quality of weapons supplies increased by several times over the Carter levels during the first term, not only was there not a proportional increase in the distribution of supplies to the Mujahideen, but also the ISI funneled the bulk of what they did deem fit to distribute to only one of the seven resistance organizations, led by their favorite, Gulbadin Hekmatyar.

Hekmatyar may have been an appropriate recipient from the ISI's point of view, but he was by far not the ideal choice from the point of view of strengthening the resistance to the Soviet Union. Hekmatyar's men spent as much time fighting against the six other resistance organizations as they did fighting against the Soviets. One source claimed that he "cooperated with Soviet troops in persecution and subsequent defeat of other resistance factions."[74] Although "loyalty" was a fragile concept, at best, among the resistance groups in Afghanistan, Hekmatyar, having been trained in the Soviet apparatus from his youth, was not someone in whom to place an inordinate amount of trust to fight the Soviets.

Several factors combined to produce the president's second-term call for increased support for anti-Soviet resistance fighters. By early

---

[74] Imran Akbar, "Gulbuddin Hekmatyar had Links with KGB," *The News International (Paris)*, October 8, 1992.

1985, Congressman Wilson had seen first-hand that the "system" put in place by State and the CIA to support the resistance was not doing the job. The personnel sent to manage it were firmly of the belief that bleeding the Russians was all that should be done, lest they get angry and retaliate against Pakistan.

Nor was the increased supply of weapons getting into the hands of the most effective resistance organizations. Finally, the stepped-up Soviet offensive early in the year, just as in Nicaragua, was succeeding. The Soviet winter attack took the Mujahideen by surprise. A combined-arms concept of aerial bombing, helicopter gunship assaults, armor attacks and Spetznaz (special forces) strikes threatened to whittle down the resistance into ineffectiveness.[75]

Early in the year, however, Reagan was presented with crucial intelligence from a source on the Soviet General Staff. The report detailed Soviet plans for a general offensive of all of its client forces around the world and for the Soviets themselves in Afghanistan. In Afghanistan, with great fanfare, the Soviets assigned a new commander, General Mikhail Zaitsev, who was given two years to achieve victory.[76] Behind the scenes, however, Valentin Varrennikov, the general in overall command of Soviet third-world clients took charge.[77] One wonders whether the knowledge that the Soviets were going onto the general offensive in early 1985 played a part in Reagan's decision to publicize the Reagan anti-Soviet resistance Doctrine.

In late January, at an NSPG meeting, when the discussion turned to Afghanistan, the president forcefully directed his aides to "do whatever you have to do to help the Mujahideen not only survive, but win." The result was the formulation of a new directive, NSDD-166, which the president signed in mid-March, incidentally, just a few days after Mikhail Gorbachev had been named the successor to Chernenko. The directive fundamentally changed the objective in Afghanistan

---

[75] Mohammad Yousaf and Mark Adkin, *The Bear Trap* (London: Leo Cooper, 1992), 134.
[76] Schweitzer, *Victory*, 212-13.
[77] Crile, *Charlie Wilson's War*, 344-45.

from Carter's goal of "harassing" the Soviets, to Reagan's goal of "victory."[78]

Yet, even though NSDD-166 formally changed U.S. policy in Afghanistan and even though support for the "freedom fighters" was immensely popular in Congress, it would take months before the supply and distribution system was changed, personnel changed, training improved, and a more integrated weapons mix developed. And it would be over a year before the decisive weapon of the war, the anti-aircraft *Stinger* missile was introduced. Simply put, key officials in the CIA, State Department, and in Pakistan's ISI deliberately dragged their feet.

John McMahon, number two behind Casey at CIA, Shultz, Pakistan station chief Howard Hart, and ISI's Mohammad Yousaf, were particularly obstructive, for varying reasons. McMahon and Hart supported Shultz's strategy of merely bleeding the Russians, and used "every bureaucratic trick in the book" to delay shipment of the Stinger, while Yousaf determinedly resisted all efforts by the CIA to gain greater control over the distribution of weapons.[79]

To some degree, their obstructionist efforts could be attributed to General Zia himself, who subtly resisted the introduction of *Stingers* until early in 1986. It was only when Reagan issued an executive order on provision of *Stingers* to Savimbi of UNITA that the dam broke and Zia finally accepted introduction of *Stingers* into Afghanistan. McMahon resigned at the end of February 1986, clearing away the major obstacle within CIA. George Shultz, seeing the policy shift coming, jumped on board the resistance "bandwagon." Casey removed

---

[78] Schweitzer, 213. Simpson, *National Security Directives*, 446-47, describes the thrust of the directive as supporting a "significant escalation," but does not use the term "victory."

[79] On McMahon's role, See Jack Wheeler, "Charlie Wilson and Ronald Reagan's War," *To the Point News*, December 27, 2007, http://www.tothepointnews.com/content/view/3019/2/. For Hart's and Yousaf's roles, see Crile, *Charlie Wilson's War*, 351-53; see 417-18 for the author's attempt to downplay McMahon's obstructionism and opposition to supply of the Stinger.

Hart as station chief and replaced him with Milt Bearden, and Yousaf, who also saw the handwriting on the wall, suddenly became more accommodating.[80] The *Stingers* would deny Moscow control of the air and the Mujahideen would defeat them on the ground.

The president would attempt to follow a similar policy pattern of support for all of the resistance movements, but his main areas of focus would be on rebuilding a strategic relationship with Iran and on gaining Soviet agreement to shift to the strategic defensive. It is to the president's early efforts to seek an opening to Iran that we now turn.

---

[80] Ibid.

Chapter 2
The Origins of the Iran Initiative

President Reagan's defeat of Soviet strategy toward Iran would have profound consequences for both the president and the nation. Moscow shifted from a strategy of attrition in the Iran-Iraq war to support of Iraqi victory. As Iran sought to reach out to the United States, the Soviets activated their Middle East terror network to prevent it. The president saw an opportunity to reestablish relations with Iran, but his internal opponents, the new world order faction, did everything possible to sabotage it. These key developments unfolded in a highly complex milieu, involving parallel and competing Israeli interests, international arms sales to Iran and Iraq, and a highly developed terrorist contract network involving Iran, Libya, Syria, and the Soviet Union.

Moscow's strategy change regarding Iraq was wrapped in the larger strategy shift to détente. The shift was a change in means but not in ends and initially involved an increase in the use of conventional force not a decrease, virtually across the board. The Soviet Union continued to pursue its three main objectives: strategic weapons preeminence over the United States, regional military superiority over its Eurasian neighbors, and leverage over Middle East oil, specifically, by drawing Iran into its orbit. The fundamental purpose in the strategy shift was to disarm the United States politically, turning away from direct military confrontation, while moving stealthily toward the same objectives.

Thus, as Mikhail Gorbachev came to power proclaiming *perestroika* at home and détente abroad, Moscow's actual policies seemed to change little as the Soviet Union increased defense spending, continued to upgrade its weapons systems, continued work on elements of a nationwide missile defense, and intensified support for its client states around the world, including its occupation and suppression in Afghanistan.[1]

The big change was toward Iraq, where Moscow's strategy had failed. Whereas from 1980 to 1983 Soviet policy was to arm Saddam Hussein's forces sufficiently to prevent defeat in a war of attrition, from mid-1984, the Soviets began to provide Iraq with a major infusion of offensive weaponry that offered the prospect of victory. Compared to Saddam's armament levels when the war began in 1980, by mid-1984 the Soviets had dramatically increased his inventory. Moscow sent over two thousand main battle tanks, increasing Iraq's total from 2,750 to 4,820. The Soviets more than tripled artillery from 1,040 to 3,200; and increased Iraq's aircraft from 332 to 580. To utilize this infusion of new weaponry, Saddam increased overall troop levels from 535,000 to 675,000.[2]

Iran still retained the battlefield initiative as it pressed human-wave attacks across the Iraqi border in repeated but largely fruitless attempts either to seize Basra, or Baghdad, or cut the road connecting them. Thus, in the ground war, for many more months to come, Iraqi forces would remain on the defensive. But, from the summer of 1984, with deliveries of *Mirage* and *Mig-23* strike aircraft, tanks, and *Scud* missiles, Iraq intensified military pressure on Iran from the air and at sea, striking cities and petroleum facilities and ships in the Gulf, while buttressing its ground defenses.

The large additions to Iraq's weapons' inventory, especially in tanks and aircraft, presaged inevitably an eventual turn to the offensive and sent Iranian arms purchasers on a frantic worldwide search for weapons to counter Iraqi firepower. It was this unheralded but ominous turn in the military balance that persuaded Iranian leaders to

---

[1] Robert Gates, *From the Shadows* (New York: Simon & Shuster, 1996), 331-37.
[2] Anthony Cordesman and Abraham Wagner, *The Lessons of Modern War*, Vol. II. (Boulder: Westview, 1990), 192.

seek out and make contact with Western governments and American representatives in the fall of 1984.

These same battlefield developments had registered on U.S. analysts, who, perceiving an opening to Iran, began to propose a change in American policy toward the war. The failure of Soviet strategy toward Iran and the Iranian extension of feelers to the United States, as described in volume three of this series, generated high-level interest in the possibility of a rapprochement with Tehran. The president saw the prospects unfolding of not only restoring relations with the Iranian regime, but also of completing his strategic goal of replacing what was perhaps the most important single part of the containment structure in his drive for victory in the Cold War.

Unfortunately, neither the president nor his advisers anticipated the means and the lengths to which Moscow would go to prevent a U.S.-Iranian rapprochement. The new world order faction, led by Secretary of State Shultz, in strongly opposing the president's initiative toward Iran, wittingly or unwittingly supported Soviet strategic objectives.

The Strategic Issues in Dispute

President Reagan and the new world order faction had been engaged in a struggle over U.S. strategy since taking office. As demonstrated in the first three volumes of this study the president sought to pursue a strategy of victory in the Cold War by expanding American and undercutting Soviet economic power, reestablishing hegemony through a shift to the strategic defensive combined with a sharp reduction in nuclear weapons, restoring alliance relationships in a new containment structure that also included China, and fracturing the Soviet alliance system by raising the cost of its maintenance. These were very large structural objectives that required the implementation of a myriad of policies, which, by the end of the first term, had been largely successful, or were on the verge of being successful.

Policy-making is an inherently messy process and there were continuous policy disputes in the administration over the implementation of the president's strategy. This was, however, the essentially healthy argument of how best to pursue the president's objectives. There were also principled disagreements, such as the Secretary of Defense's strenuous objections to the actual application of U.S. military power. But the fundamental conflict within the administration was strategic; between the president's strategic vision and the new world order faction's.

The new world order faction, led first by Secretary of State Haig and then by Secretary Shultz, pursued a diametrically opposite strategy, whose central objective was détente and accommodation with the Soviet Union, not victory over it. They sought a world order in which the United States and the Soviet Union would be equal partners who would cooperate to maintain a new, peaceful, world order. They, therefore, sought to counter, undermine, and otherwise oppose any policy that contradicted their strategic conception.

In truth, the mere articulation of the strategy of détente exposed its incongruity. A new world order based on a cooperative global condominium was without historical precedent and in reality suggested more surrender than cooperation. Worst of all, it rested on the very fragile assumption that the Communist rulers of the Soviet Union sought the same objective. Yet, this was the strategic conception that Shultz sought to press on the president at every policy opportunity.

The three public issues in dispute between the president and his secretary which carried over into the second term were: the nature of the relationship sought with the Soviet Union, a dispute which played out in the arms control negotiations; the structure of the global balance of power, which centered on the issue of relations with Iran; and the Soviet system of alliances and client states, which involved the Reagan Doctrine of support for those peoples opposed to them. The strategic differences between Reagan and Shultz were fundamental. Over the long-term there could be no compromise, although there could be short-term, tactical cooperation until decisive policy points were reached.

With regard to the Soviet Union, for example, the president sought a new balance of power based on defense rather than offense. He sought a transition from a system based on mutual assured destruction to one based on strategic defense, with a sharp reduction in offensive weapons. The Strategic Defense Initiative was the centerpiece of this strategic conception.

Shultz and the new world order faction sought to perpetuate the balance of power based on mutual assured destruction, or MAD; some offensive missile reductions were acceptable, even desirable, to assure a balance, but there could be no missile defense, which they viewed as destabilizing. Shultz saw value in SDI solely as a bargaining chip to gain agreement, but not as the basis for a new strategic paradigm, as the president did. In his view, SDI was simply an instrument to be dispensed with as part of an arms control bargain.

There were similar differences over the structure of the global order. Reagan was intent upon rebuilding the global containment structure, adding China to it, and reestablishing close relations with a post-Khomeini Iran. Iran had been the largest single state in the containment structure whose loss had not only fractured the structure, but also weakened the security of the Persian Gulf and its oil supplies. Reagan sought to rebuild the structure and reestablish security over the gulf. He had reestablished close relations with King Fahd, as we have seen, and Moscow's policy change toward Iraq had opened up the slimmest possibility of engaging Iran.

Shultz was totally opposed to restoring relations with Iran. Dismantling the containment structure was in the new world order faction's view the necessary pre-condition to entering into a détente relationship with Moscow. Reestablishing relations with Iran would reverse that strategy. They did not perceive a Soviet threat either to Iran or to gulf security. Here, too, Reagan and Shultz could cooperate on the short-term goal of promoting a stalemate in the war, but their long-term goals were totally opposed, as Shultz saw American interests best served by an alliance with Saddam Hussein's Iraq.

On the Reagan Doctrine, too, the president and Shultz were opposed, but differences varied by case. Shultz initially opposed, but came around to support military assistance to the Contras as the president made such support a litmus test within his administration. On Afghanistan, Shultz supported a policy of bleeding the Russians against the president's goal of defeating them and driving them from the country. On Angola, Shultz and the president differed over the goals and means of forcing the Cubans to withdraw. In all cases, as opportunities presented themselves, Shultz sought to achieve negotiated settlements with the Russians, rather than their defeat.

Early Maneuvering Over Iran

Anticipating the time when it would become feasible to attempt to reestablish relations with Iran as part of his general strategy of rebuilding containment, the president had twice during the first term explored the legal ramifications of providing arms to Iran, while Shultz sought to foreclose any opening. The first time was in 1981 when Attorney General William French Smith had asked the Department of State counsel for a ruling on the sale of arms to Iran, as Tehran was not then eligible for arms sales under the Foreign Assistance Act, or the Arms Export Control Act.[3]

The State Department's legal adviser, Davis R. Robinson, informed Smith that "the United States could sell weapons to foreign countries outside the Foreign Assistance Act and Arms Export Control Act....The president could instead use the Economy Act and the National Security Act..."[4] Both the FAA and the AECA contained provisions for prior public notification of Congress and set a low threshold of sales over $14 million requiring congressional approval. But, under the Economy Act and National Security Act, if weapons were first transferred between agencies, such as from DOD to CIA, the reporting requirements did not apply. In this way the president could legally skirt the restrictions of the FAA and AECA.

Then, in early 1983, after passing on information from Soviet KGB defector Vladimir Kuzichkin regarding Soviet plans to subvert the Iranian government and in anticipation of the Iranian government's crackdown on the pro-Soviet Tudeh party and its potentially disruptive consequences, the president sought again to ascertain whether there

---

[3] *Report of the Congressional Committees Investigating the Iran-Contra Affair* (Washington, D.C.: GPO, 1987), 176, 189n42. [Cited hereafter as *"Iran-Contra Affair."*]
[4] Theodore Draper, *A Very Thin Line* (New York: Hill and Wang, 1991), 247-48.

were any legal impediments that would prohibit the provision of arms to Iran in case the situation deteriorated and action had to be taken quickly.[5]

Responding to the president's inquiry regarding the use of the Economy Act or the Foreign Assistance Act, W. George Jamison, Assistant General Counsel of the Central Intelligence Agency, issued a memorandum on January 7, 1983, ruling "there were no general legal restrictions that would preclude the CIA from providing equipment to Iran as proposed. Rather, the relevant constraints involve policy considerations that may have to be weighed before undertaking the activity proposed."[6] The proposed activity implicit in Jamison's reply was the clandestine provision of arms. Indeed, arms sales as a means of gaining access to the Iranian leadership was the crux of it. (It should be noted that all this preceded the taking of a single hostage and makes clear the president's intent to reestablish relations with Iran.)

Later in the spring, using his discretionary authority, however, Secretary Shultz sought to close off any government sales by instituting *Operation Staunch*, which he justified as a means of drying up weapons sales to both sides. When implemented later in the year, however, the State Department's efforts were heavily biased in favor of Iraq and against Iran.[7] Indeed, the secretary would go to great lengths to build support for Iraq *against* Iran.[8]

Over the next two years Special Ambassador Richard Fairbanks and his staff cajoled, jawboned, and threatened Washington's allies and friends against continued involvement in the estimated "$3 billion to $4 billion" per year Iranian arms market.[9] As 39 countries were

---

[5] Vladimir Kuzichkin, *Inside the KGB*, (New York: Ballantine, 1990), 369, and Gary Sick, "Iran's Quest for Superpower Status," *Foreign Affairs* (Spring 1986), 709.

[6] W. George Jamison, "Restrictions on Exports to Iran," January 7, 1983, *National Security Archive—Iran-Contra Collection*, George Washington University.

[7] George Shultz, *Turmoil and Triumph* (New York: Macmillan, 1993), 236-37.

[8] For discussion of Shultz's efforts, see Richard C. Thornton, The Reagan Revolution, III: Defeating the Soviet Challenge (Victoria: Trafford, 2009), 447-56.

[9] John Fialka, "How Iranian Dealers Buy Arms of All Sorts Through British Office," *Wall Street Journal*, January 30, 1987, 1.

involved in arms sales to Iran, theirs was a Herculean task and obviously not completely successful. U.S. laws, the Munitions Control List and technology transfer licenses, and the threat of a cut-off from the U.S. market were effective levers in persuading allied governments, in particular, to curtail direct sales.[10]

The evidence suggests, however, that while governments did curtail direct sales, they deftly shifted operations to less identifiable *grey* market operations, clandestine sales to illegal destinations using fake documentation, and/or to private arms dealers operating on the black market.[11] Iran had in the meantime set up purchasing offices in key cities throughout Western Europe. Some of the largest were in London, Madrid, Paris, Hamburg, Rome, Malmo, Brussels, Lisbon, and Zurich.

London, in particular, was a major center for Iranian purchasing agents. Their Logistics Support Center, with a staff of 320, was "the largest military mission in London after that of the United States."[12] It was located in the same building as the National Iranian Oil Company, which was "next to Britain's Department of Trade and Industry." Reportedly, as much as 70 percent of Iran's arms purchases were managed by the London office through private, off-shore dealers and shipping brokers. However, "many of the so-called private arms dealers… [were] really agents for governments."[13]

Israel was a special case with a long history of arms sales to Iran dating back to the time of the shah. Following a brief hiatus after the shah fell Israel resumed arms sales to Iran. President Carter attempted unsuccessfully to put a stop to them, which impacted negatively on his efforts to gain the freedom of the hostages. When Reagan took office,

---

[10] Kenneth Timmerman, *Fanning the Flames: Guns, Greed & Geopolitics in the Gulf War,* chap.7. http://www.kentimmerman.com/krt/fanning_index.htm#Contents
[11] Ibid.
[12] Amir Taheri, *Nest of Spies: America's Journey to Disaster in Iran* (New York: Pantheon, 1988), 159.
[13] Fialka, "How Iranian Dealers Buy Arms…"

Secretary of State Haig had given his quiet approval for sales, as part of his strong support for Israel.[14]

In 1983, after Shultz had replaced Haig and Yitzhak Shamir had replaced Menachem Begin, *Operation Staunch* appears to have succeeded in curtailing Israeli arms sales, at least direct sales.[15] Ambassador Fairbanks acknowledged that he and his staff "leaned pretty heavily on Israel....We told them they just didn't want to be selling arms to Iran."[16] But Israel, like practically all of the others, continued to sell arms *in*directly.[17] Before being pressured to curtail sales, according to the *Observer*, Israeli arms sales to Iran were "valued at between $500 million and $800 million a year."[18]

Crucial developments in 1984, especially the change in Soviet strategy toward Iran, produced a new calculation in Washington. The initial Soviet strategy toward Iran, the use of Iraq as defensive bulwark, as anvil, so to speak, against Iran's hammer, in a war of attrition against Iran, had failed and produced a fundamental change. By early 1984, it was clear to attentive observers throughout the region that the new Russian strategy was to turn Iraq into an offensive force capable of defeating Iran.

From late 1983 the Soviets had replaced "every piece of ground equipment Iraq had lost during the first two years of the war." Then, they began to provide Iraq with a major infusion of new weaponry. In March 1984, the Soviets offered Saddam a $4.5 billion package, "the biggest arms package the Soviets had ever proposed." Moscow

---

[14] Seymour Hersh, "The Iran Pipeline: A Hidden Chapter/A special report; U.S. Said to have Allowed Iran to Sell Arms to Iran," *New York Times, December 8, 1991,* 1.
[15] Trita Parsi, *Treacherous Alliance: The Secret Dealings of Israel, Iran, and the U.S.* (New Haven: Yale, 2007), 113.
[16] Kenneth Timmerman, *The Death Lobby: How the West Armed Iraq* (New York: Houghton-Mifflin, 1991), 141.
[17] Ari Ben-Menashe, *Profits of War: Inside the Secret U.S.-Israeli Arms Network*, (New York: Sheridan Square Press, 1992), claims that clandestine sales continued throughout.
[18] *The Observer*, September 29, 1985, cited by Bishara Bahbah, "Arms Sale: Israel's Link to the Khomeini Regime," *Washington Report on Middle East Affairs* (January 1987), 10.

prepared to "rush deliveries of additional MiG-21 and MiG-23 fighters, Mi-25 *Hind* helicopter gunships, and 350 *SCUD-B* missiles." By the summer of 1984 Soviet cargo vessels were arriving at the Jordanian port of Aqaba, and "endless truck convoys traveled across the desert to Baghdad."[19]

It was this unheralded but ominous turn in the military balance that persuaded Iranian leaders to seek out and make contact with American representatives in the fall of 1984 and prompted President Reagan to prepare the grounds for a response.

The Iranians attempted to make contact in a variety of ways, some not entirely positive on the face of it. Their agents in Beirut, the *Hezbollah*, in the context of a proclaimed campaign to drive the Americans from Lebanon, began attacking and kidnapping Americans and other foreign nationals. First, was the murder of Malcolm Kerr, president of the American University of Beirut on January 18, 1984. On February 11, an American, Frank Regier, and a Frenchman, Christian Joubert, were abducted. On March 7, CNN bureau chief Jeremy Levin was kidnapped. Regier was freed on April 15 when a rival group of Amal militiamen raided the Beirut hideout where he was being held. Levin escaped, or was allowed to escape, nearly a year later on February 14.

Identification of those responsible for these early incidents was muddied by the fact that Hezbollah was not the only terrorist organization operating in Lebanon. If the Iranians were employing terrorists to force contact with the U. S., the Soviets, through their minions, were attempting to use the same tactics to prevent it. Muamar Qadaffi, in particular, seems to have funded terrorists to take actions designed to block any Iranian-American contacts. Thus ensued a period of competitive hostage-taking among rival terrorist organizations.

Qadaffi apparently backed the Lebanese terrorist, Imad Mugniyeh in the execution of several terrorist acts. Mugniyeh, operating a small cell within Hezbollah called Islamic Jihad, carried out several hostage

---

[19] Timmerman, *Death Lobby*, 185.

seizures and airline hijackings in hopes of gaining release of prisoners held in Kuwait, called the Dawa 17, one of whom was his brother-in-law, Mustafa Badredienne.[20] Tripoli, Damascus, and Tehran all supported terrorist groups, especially in Lebanon, where they competed with each other as often as they cooperated and contended with the Israelis. It was difficult to place terrorists with organizations and differentiate between the isolated acts of terrorists and state-supported activities. Radio intercepts were a crucial means of tracking and sorting out the many groupings.

But, the abduction of William Buckley on March 16 was a different matter. On-scene intelligence reports claimed that Buckley had been quickly transferred to Tehran.[21] These reports appeared, in retrospect, to have been incomplete. Buckley may have been transferred to Tehran, but he was soon returned to Lebanon. Later hostage accounts revealed that Buckley had been held in Beirut for most of his time of captivity, until his death in mid-1985.

Nevertheless, the linkage to Iran served the purpose intended in Washington, especially in the CIA, and in Iran. Buckley was the CIA's Beirut station-chief, and one of the agency's top operatives in the Middle East. Iranian leaders correctly assumed that Washington's clandestine service would do everything in its power to gain the release of its valuable intelligence agent. Two other Americans were taken hostage in 1984, Benjamin Weir, on May 8 and Peter Kilburn on December 3.[22]

Iran also employed more "traditional" means of making contact. In early June 1984, parliamentary leader Hashemi Rafsanjani declared that Iran wanted "talks and meetings" to avoid intervention by both the Soviet Union and the United States. As the United States posed no

---

[20] David Martin and John Walcott, *Best Laid Plans: The Inside Story of America's War Against Terrorism* (New York: Touchstone, 1988), 204-5.
[21] "Subject: Meeting with [excised] Re: Beirut Kidnapping," March 17, 1984 and "Subject: Update on Contact with Iranian Terrorist Source," March 17, 1984, *Iran-Contra Collection*, National Security Archive, The George Washington University.
[22] It is frequently incorrectly asserted that Weir was kidnapped two months earlier on March 8.

threat to intervene, this was, of course, but a thinly veiled expression of concern regarding the Soviet threat and an invitation to Washington.

Rafsanjani went on to indicate Iran's interest in contact by saying that "as far as is possible we will prevent such a disaster for humanity from happening by diplomacy and by appropriate talks and meetings."[23] At a press conference in early July, Rafsanjani made a direct reference to the United States, albeit to praise the quality of American arms. He would not rule out the possibility of purchasing American arms "directly or indirectly," he said, because they were better than Soviet or French weapons.[24]

In late July, West German Foreign Minister Hans-Dietrich Genscher traveled to Tehran for a state visit. He was the first Western foreign minister to visit Iran since 1979. In addition to signing a long-term oil agreement, Rafsanjani made a point of urging "other countries" to help bring the war to an end.[25] After Genscher departed, a Kuwaiti newspaper reported that the West German foreign minister had passed on a U.S. proposal for an "amelioration" of relations with Washington.[26] This report was probably planted by the Iranians to elicit a response from Washington. If it had been true, there would have been no reason for the convoluted sequence of events that followed.

There was also an unsuccessful attempt to establish contact through Canada. Ayatollah Mohammad Reza Mahdavi Kani, a member of the ruling circle, sought, during a trip to Ottawa and Toronto in November, to persuade the Canadian government to act as an intermediary with the United States.[27] No doubt the Canadian government passed on this message to the State Department, but no response was made, understandably, because Shultz opposed any opening.

---

[23] Jonathan Randal, "Iraq Moves Tanks to Southern Front," *Washington Post*, June 3, 1984, 15.
[24] Samuel Segev, *The Iranian Triangle* (New York: Free Press, 1988), 130-31.
[25] "Iran Said To Seek New Ties To West," *New York Times*, July 23, 1984, 1.
[26] Foreign Broadcast Information Service-South Asia, *FBIS-SA*, July 27, 1984.
[27] Taheri, *Nest of Spies*, 164.

At the same time that Iranian leaders were extending feelers to make contact with Washington, they were intensifying their efforts to acquire additional weaponry. Their purchasing agents scoured the international arms markets seeking weapons with which to counter the stepped-up Iraqi attacks. As their weapons systems were U.S.-based, as Rafsanjani stated, they were particularly interested in acquiring U.S. anti-tank and anti-aircraft weapons to contend with the growing Iraqi advantage in tanks and strike aircraft.

Reagan Prepares a Response

The failure of Soviet strategy toward Iran and the Iranian extension of feelers to the United States, Reagan recognized, opened the possibility of a rapprochement with Tehran. The president saw the prospects unfolding of not only restoring relations with the Iranian regime, but of completing the containment structure around the Soviet Union and strengthening his drive for victory in the Cold War.

Secretary Shultz, anticipating the president's moves toward Iran, sought to preempt him. On January 20, 1984, he designated Iran a state sponsor of international terrorism, adding another argument to those used in advocating the cessation of arms sales to Iran under *Operation Staunch* initiated a month earlier, on December 15, 1983. At the same time he insured that the State Department would turn away all Iranian attempts to make contact.

The president's response came in the immediate aftermath of the abduction of William Buckley. The numerous Iranian signals of a desire to make contact obviously did not go unnoticed, and the president set the wheels in motion to bring about an opening. He sought to do this in several ways: legislatively, by strengthening anti-terrorism law; administratively, by attempting to change current policy toward Iran; operationally, by assigning to CIA chief Bill Casey the task of attempting to rescue Buckley, a process that would *inter alia* involve making high-level contacts with Iranian leaders; and through extension of subtle policy signals.

Sometime in early April 1984 (the exact date and the actual decision-document are still classified), the president signed

NSDD 138, defining the government's anti-terrorism policy. The directive authorized the conduct of "guerrilla warfare against guerrillas," and action against states supporting terrorism, singling out Iran, Libya, Syria, Cuba, Nicaragua, North Korea, and the USSR.[28]

On April 26, the White House sent four separate legislative bills to the Congress designed to strengthen the government's efforts to combat international terrorism. The first was to establish federal jurisdiction over any kidnapping whose purpose was to "compel third parties to do or to abstain from doing something." Second was the Aircraft Sabotage Act, designed to bring American law into conformity with international law. Third, was an act to authorize the government to pay rewards for information on terrorists. And fourth was a proposed act to prohibit the support or training of terrorists.[29]

There matters stood until the summer of 1984 when the change in Soviet policy toward Iraq had become apparent. As the first step, the president sought through the formal interagency policy process to reevaluate policy toward Iran. On August 31, McFarlane requested that the Department of State lead an interagency study of U.S. relations with Iran after Khomeini. The study preempted and incorporated data from a Special National Intelligence Estimate (SNIE) the CIA was preparing. As Shultz controlled the interagency process, the result was fully predictable.

On October 19, State circulated its study, concluding that any changes in American policy would have to await the death of Khomeini. The United States had "no influential contacts" in the Iranian government or with influential political groups and there was "little that the United States could do to establish such contacts."

---

[28] "NSDD 138, "Preemptive Strikes Against Suspected Terrorists," Christopher Simpson, *National Security Directives of the Reagan and Bush Administrations* (Boulder: Westview, 1995), 365.
[29] "President's Anti-Terrorist Legislation," April 26, 1984, in ibid, 407.

Charles Hill, Shultz's aid, wrote the cover letter stating the secretary's belief that American "powerlessness... would continue indefinitely."[30]

Later in December, John McMahon, CIA Director of Operations, number two in the agency after Casey, but Shultz's ally, sent a letter to Admiral Poindexter, deputy director of the NSC, echoing the same view as the State Department of American "powerlessness." Regarding the utility of covert operations in Iran, McMahon thought that the Mujahideen were "well organized, influenced by the Soviets, and likely to succeed Khomeini."[31] In short, there was nothing that the United States could do.

The State Department then "distilled these views into a draft National Security Decision Directive (NSDD) at the end of 1984." When approved by the president, an NSDD formalizes policy. This decision document would have directed the U.S. government to be ready to "exploit opportunities that might arise in Iran," but reaffirmed existing policies. In its essence, the draft would have reinforced *Operation Staunch*, the policy of discouraging arms transfers to Iran.[32] In the rules-based policy maneuvering that characterized American politics, Shultz seemed to have gotten the better of the president, but Reagan simply declined to approve the NSDD, leaving the policy issue open.

On the other hand, the president had approved subtle measures to send signals of his own to Tehran. Early in 1984 he had authorized Commerce Secretary Malcolm Baldridge to allow some sales of dual use equipment to Iran. Through the first half of the year Commerce had authorized the sale of one hundred jeeps and the release of two Boeing 707 jets the shah had purchased, but which were still in the U.S. for refurbishing at the time of the hostage crisis. Both Weinberger

---

[30] John G. Tower et al., *Report of the President's Special Review Board: February 26, 1987* (Washington, D.C.: GPO, 1987). [Hereafter referred to as the *Tower Report*], III-3, B-2.
[31] Ibid.
[32] *Tower Report*, B-2-3.

and Shultz had opposed the actions, but Baldridge supported them as part of the president's aggressive export policy.[33]

Sales of military equipment went through intermediaries. International arms dealers routinely employed fake end user's certificates to disguise the destination of weapons shipments. In July, for example, the *Christian Science Monitor* disclosed that 25 *F-5* jets were being shipped to Iran, although their purported destination was Turkey. In this instance, Lloyds of London had been asked to insure delivery. Both Britain and Turkey were heavily involved in sales and services to both sides.[34] Indeed, the Turkish air corridor was the most direct way into Iran. Nothing came of these probes.

But, what seemed to be the most promising avenue of contact was Casey's efforts to obtain the release of William Buckley based on the assumption that he was being held by Iran, or by Iran's surrogates. Casey had ordered "a major drive to recruit former members of SAVAK who had fled into exile in Western Europe and the United States."[35] He assumed that some of these men would have remained in touch with former colleagues in Tehran. At the same time, he asked retired, former CIA deputy director of operations, Theodore (Ted) Shackley to quietly explore these contacts.[36]

From the group of SAVAK exiles, the CIA approached the shah's former head of counterespionage, General Manuchur Hashemi, and arranged for him to meet Shackley. The result of their meeting was a plan for Hashemi to introduce Shackley to his Iranian contacts in Hamburg, West Germany, an enclave of Iranian exiles. In the latter part of November, Shackley traveled to Hamburg where he was

---

[33] Scott Armstrong et al., *The Chronology: The Documented Day-by-Day Account of the Secret Military Assistance to Iran and the Contras*, (New York: Warner Books, 1987), 59-60. [Hereafter referred to as *The Chronology*.]

[34] ibid, 61, and "Britain Says It Is Training Troops From Both Sides," *Manchester Guardian*, April 2, 1984, 1.

[35] Taheri, *Nest of Spies*, 166.

[36] "Theodore (Ted) Shackley," *Spartacus Educational* (online at http://www.spartacus.schoolnet.co.uk/JFKshackley.htm). Shackley was a renowned clandestine agent, who had retired from the agency under a cloud.

introduced to Ayatollah Mehdi Karoubi, a close confidant of Khomeini's, and Manuchur Gorbanifar, an Iranian exile and self-styled dealmaker and entrepreneur. It would eventually turn out that Gorbanifar would become Iran's designated interlocutor, but his role and status were unclear at the beginning and controversial thereafter. Nevertheless, in wide-ranging talks, November 19-21, the prospects seemed bright not only for ransoming Buckley, but also for establishing contact with high-level Iranian leaders.[37]

The Iranians wanted an answer from Washington by December 7 about Buckley, but Ghorbanifar, whose own path to the meeting with Shackley had been circuitous, warned him not to deal with the CIA, because, he said, the agents he had dealt with in the past had treated him deceitfully. Shackley accepted this position and immediately upon returning to Washington sent his report to his former colleague, Vernon Walters, instead of to Casey. Walters had been a deputy director of CIA, but was now serving as an Ambassador at-large in the State Department.

Walters passed Shackley's report to Shultz's aides, Richard Murphy, head of Near Eastern Affairs, and Robert Oakley, head of counterterrorism. Both men regarded Gorbanifar's proposals, particularly his plan to ransom Buckley, as a "scam," and deep-sixed the effort.[38] Their reply to Shackley was: "thank you but we will work this problem out via other channels."[39] In short, Shackley's effort was dismissed. Once again, Shultz had headed-off an attempt to make contact with Iranian leaders.

Except for his close aides, Casey's views did not dominate the agency. Supporters of the new world order establishment dominated the upper ranks of the CIA, especially in the directorate of operations under John McMahon. That explains why Shackley agreed with Gorbanifar not to go through the CIA, but it does not explain why he failed to report directly back to Casey. Sending his report to the State

---

[37] *Iran-Contra Affair*, 164.
[38] ibid.
[39] *Tower Report*, B-3.

Department, even though it was through former CIA colleague Walters, guaranteed that the approach would fail.

Manuchur Gorbanifar's meeting with Shackley was his fifth attempt in 1984 to make contact with American leaders from his base in Western Europe. In January, he had sent a letter to Reagan that was never received. Later that month he sought to make contact through U.S. Army intelligence that went nowhere. In March and June he had contacted the CIA in Frankfurt, offering access to high Iranian leaders and a scheme to ransom Buckley. In attempting to determine his credibility, the CIA administered lie-detector tests on both occasions, which Gorbanifar failed ignominiously. Deciding that he was a "nuisance," on June 25 the Frankfurt office declared him a "fabricator," and issued a "burn notice," which meant that agency officers could have nothing to do with him.[40]

Although the Frankfurt office issued the burn notice, McMahon had made the decision at Langley. On its surface, the decision to discredit Gorbanifar appeared to have been an error. Expendable, deniable, private intermediaries were the common and principal means of brokering initial contacts between adversaries. As we shall see, Gorbanifar was to Iran what Adnan Khashoggi was to Saudi Arabia, what Michael Ledeen was to the United States, and what Yakov Nimrodi and Adolf Schwimmer were to Israel.[41] It is true that in the Iranian case there were several exiles who claimed influence in Tehran and it was not easy to determine their bona fides. What seemed to be an error, however, was completely consistent with McMahon's and Shultz's efforts to close off any contact with Iranian interlocutors. Later, when the opportunity arose, Casey would choose to work with Gorbanifar.

---

[40] *Iran-Contra Affair*, 164.
[41] See Michael Ledeen, *Perilous Statecraft* (New York: Scribner, 1988), 100, 106, for a discussion of a nation's needs for "deniable intermediaries."

The Israeli Connection

American leaders were not the only ones to note the change in Soviet strategy and its implications for themselves. Israeli leaders, too, recognized the change and quickly realized both the negative implications for Israel in an Iraqi victory and the positive implications for a resumption of arms sales to Iran. For a variety of reasons, both domestic and foreign, Israel's leaders recognized that a change of its own leadership had become necessary. The Israeli economy was staggering badly under the burden of the Lebanon invasion and relations with Washington were still cool at best under Yitzhak Shamir, whose antipathy toward the United States was well known.

Consequently, in April 1984, the 10th Knesset was dissolved a year early, requiring a new election. Although a Labor Alignment victory was expected, the election of July 23 produced a surprising result; neither of the two main parties, Likud or the Labor Alignment, received a clear majority out of 120 seats. In fact, while remaining the dominant two parties, both lost seats compared to the previous election, Labor dropping from 47 to 44 and Likud dropping from 48 to 41.

The Labor-Alignment's Shimon Peres, the vote leader, was tasked with putting together a majority government, but after over a month of negotiations, failed to obtain the needed sixty-one-seat plurality. Realizing that only Labor/Likud cooperation stood a chance a putting together a stable majority, it was decided to form a National Unity Government. However, as former Ambassador Samuel Lewis observed: "they joined forces in a coalition cabinet, but with great reluctance and only for lack of any alternative."[42]

They agreed that Peres would be prime minister for the first two years and Shamir foreign minister; then they would switch posts for the last two years. Yitzhak Rabin would be Minister of Defense and David Kimche remain as Director of the Foreign Ministry. Peres' position appeared to be strong, but appearances were deceiving.

---

[42] Samuel Lewis, "Israel: The Peres Era and Its Legacy," *Foreign Affairs*, America and the World, 1986.

Although he had appointed Amiram Nir as his counterintelligence adviser, replacing Likud's Rafi Eitan, Shamir and his allies held control of Mossad and the Finance Ministry. Rabin, a fellow Labor Party leader, was a rival of Peres. Kimche, whose patron was Ariel Sharon, was also from Likud, but his relations with Mossad, his former place of employment, were not good. Although Peres, Shamir, and Rabin were known as the "prime minister's club," the reference was ironic, for their interests obviously did not coincide in all matters.

Seven years of Likud rule had resulted in Likud men being sprinkled in important positions throughout the government bureaucracy, especially in the intelligence community. Under the terms of the unity government Peres was unable to replace Likud personnel with Labor personnel. With Shamir in control of the intelligence apparatus, Peres decided to construct his own parallel, but much smaller, organization, a job he entrusted to Nir. Strikingly, the *Mossad* played no apparent role in the events that followed.

A key decision was to restart the arms sales to Iran, an important strategic issue, which would also represent not only a strong source of revenue, but also a way of resuming the repatriation of Iranian Jews. Most importantly, however, the decision reflected the realization that the military balance was tipping against Iran. As Israel's main enemy in the region was Iraq, long-term strategy was to ally with Iran against Iraq, a strategy that had become more complicated but not invalidated with the ascent of Khomeini. Weapons sales represented an important entrée to the Iranian leadership, despite public hostility.

Shamir, however, would not agree to turn control of the operations of the Joint Committee on Israel-Iran relations, which was in charge of arms sales, over to Peres, or permit Mossad to cooperate. The impasse prompted the prime minister to establish his own arms sales conduit to Iran, which involved two steps.[43] First, it was necessary to establish independent contact with Iranian leaders and, second, to get permission from Washington to resume sales.

---

[43] Ben-Menashe, *Profits of War*, 167-68.

Peres assigned David Kimche the task of overseeing the Iran project and charged two of his wealthy friends the task of exploring the possibilities.[44] The two men were: Al Schwimmer, an arms dealer and father of Israel's aircraft industry, and Yakov Nimrodi, who had been Israeli military attaché to Iran in the '60s, and had opened the first arms channel under the shah. Both were experienced dealmakers with extensive international contacts, and deep knowledge of Iran, especially Nimrodi.

The major obstacle to resumption of arms sales was the United States. *Operation Staunch* had largely shut down overt sales of American and Israeli weapons and spare parts, although the Joint Committee had continued to broker covert sales through Poland and North Korea.[45] At a minimum, Peres sought to gain Washington's permission to resume sales of Israeli weapons. In discussions with President Reagan during his state visit on October 9, there can be no question that among the topics discussed, the issue of resumption of arms sales was one of them. Indeed, it appears that despite public denials, Reagan had agreed to permit the resumption of limited sales of Israeli arms to Iran. Later in October, Iraqi, Saudi, and no doubt American intelligence identified and began to track flights, presumably arms shipments, between Israel and Iran.[46]

On the second task of making contact with Iranian leaders, according to Kimche, some time in mid-1984 he and his small group had made contact and begun discussions with disaffected Iranians in Hamburg, who were "both willing and able over time and with support to change the government."[47] Their principal interlocutor was none

---

[44] Ledeen, *Perilous Statecraft*, 117, erroneously claims, "Kimche knew nothing of the [Iran] initiative until [July 1985]."
[45] Ben-Menashe, *Profits of War*, 143-44.
[46] Bishara Bahbah, "Arms Sale: Israel's Link to the Khomeini Regime," *Washington Report on Middle East Affairs*, January 1987, 10.
[47] Robert C. McFarlane, *Special Trust* (New York: Cadell & Davies, 1994), 19. David Kimche, *The Last Option: After Nasser, Arafat & Saddam Hussein* (London: Weidenfeld and Nicolson, 1991), 211, leaves the impression that his first involvement in the Iran initiative was his meeting with McFarlane on July 3, 1985.

other than Manuchur Gorbanifar. And the person who had introduced them was Adnan Khashoggi.

Casey and the Saudi-Iranian Connection

Khashoggi's appearance was a function of King Fahd's and Bill Casey's mutual interest. During Casey's visit to Riyadh in February 1984, the king had "suggested" that the United States approach the Iranians.[48] It seems that the Saudis, too, realized that the battlefield balance was on the verge of swinging to Iraq. Although the Saudis were financing Iraq, it was not unusual for them to play both sides in a conflict. Whoever won, they would be on the winning side. They were more than willing to pay insurance for their oil tankers moving through the gulf. And they wanted to insure against inflammation of Shiite minorities in the region, especially in their own state.[49]

Casey's response at the time was "muted," as the administration was only just in the early stages of internal deliberations over a change in Iranian policy. Within a month, however, with Buckley's abduction, Casey became intensely interested in seeking an approach to the Iranians, who, he believed, were holding Buckley. Thus, King Fahd's personal middleman, Adnan Khashoggi, became active "beginning in the summer of 1984," renewing acquaintances with old business partners Schwimmer and Nimrodi, making contact with Iranian exiles, and, as word got around, eventually encountering Ghorbanifar.[50]

Through mutual Iranian acquaintances Khashoggi met Gorbanifar in the fall in Hamburg at a private sale of the former shah's Persian rugs. Their discussions ranged far and wide focusing on a change in Tehran's policy and also its need for U.S. arms. Gorbanifar, who, recall, was at this moment also engaging with Ted Schackley, offered information that

---

[48] Peter Schweizer, *Victory: The Reagan Administration's Secret Strategy That Hastened the Collapse of the Soviet Union* (New York: Atlantic Monthly Press, 1994), 181.
[49] Wolf Blitzer, "A Saudi Finger in Every Pie," *Jerusalem Post*, November 28, 1986, 5.
[50] *The Chronology*, 58.

Tehran would not seek to disrupt pilgrimages to the Grand Mosque the way Shiites had in 1979. This was enough for Khashoggi to invite him to Riyadh to meet with Saudi officials. While there, Gorbanifar arranged for the Saudi foreign minister, Saud Al-Faisal, to visit Tehran and, as a sign of good faith, the Saudis financed a small arms deal to Iran through Khashoggi and Gorbanifar.[51] Thus, by the end of 1984, a Saudi-Iranian connection had been established.

In early 1985 after the election, as noted in chapter one, the president determined to implement the "Reagan Doctrine," intensify the offensive against the Soviets, and move forward with his Iran initiative. In this context, Shultz and the new world order faction stepped up their efforts to block the president's policies and implement their own. The first step, January 18, as noted above, was to constrict the president's power to authorize covert operations, which was accomplished with the signing of NSDD-159.

NSDD-159 diluted the president's authority by requiring all covert operations be ratified by a ten-man committee, instead of the previous arrangement whereby the president and CIA director Casey possessed sole authority. Moreover, all "findings" were henceforth to be "in writing."[52] Now Shultz could theoretically block any attempt to change policy toward Iran formally, through the interagency process, as before, and now through the new authorization process for covert operations. The master bureaucrat had thwarted the president once again, or so it seemed.

---

[51] Segev, *Iranian Triangle*, 14. Later, Khashoggi was very careful to say that he was not acting on the explicit instructions of the king. He asked Fahd: "do you give me the freedom to discuss it with the Americans? With the Egyptians? With others? He said, 'I give you nothing. I know nothing. You are a free man.' So I went to Egypt..." Later, he also went to see Peres. Deborah Hart Strober and Gerald S. Strober, *Reagan: The Man and His Presidency* (New York: Houghton-Mifflin, 1998), 400. See Ledeen, *Perilous Statecraft*, 110-11, who offers a quite different chronology.

[52] "Covert Action Policy Approval and Coordination Procedures," Simpson, *National Security Directives*, 493-97.

Casey was also active in supporting the president and moving his agenda forward. Following the Shackley dead-end, in January 1985, the CIA director had a meeting in London with his old friend and fellow entrepreneur, Roy Furmark. Casey told Furmark that the United States "was secretly permitting arms sales to Iran."[53] Casey's intent was to encourage his old friend to set up a private arms operation to Iran, perhaps along the lines of what he had already succeeded in doing in Central America. (Casey's revelation strengthens the view that the president had authorized the resumption of Israeli sales during the Peres visit, although Casey did not identify Israel by name.)

With information of this potential financial opportunity in hand Furmark approached Samuel Evans, former chief counsel for Adnan Khashoggi, and asked him to arrange an introduction. (One must assume that Casey had directed Furmark to contact Khashoggi, who had already established contact with the Iranians.) When they met, a few weeks later, Furmark brought along an associate of his, Cyrus Hashemi, a naturalized American citizen of Iranian extraction, who was a banker and arms trader, operating out of London.[54] Hashemi also had a relationship with Casey, having been involved in the release of the American hostages from Iran in 1980-81. More importantly, the previous May, he had been caught in an FBI sting of a group attempting to sell arms to Iran. In seeking to obtain a dismissal of charges against him, Hashemi agreed to act as an informant.[55]

Saudis, Iranians, and Israelis

On March 5, at a meeting in London, Khashoggi introduced Hashemi to Gorbanifar, but also brought in Nimrodi and Schwimmer, assuring them that "King Fahd and Prince Sultan know about this meeting and gave me their blessing." Agreeing to cooperate, with

---

[53] James Traub, "Katzenjammer Falcon," *New York Magazine*, February 9, 1987, 38. See also, William Rempel, "Casey Reportedly Knew of Iran Arms Deals in Early '85," *Los Angeles Times*, January 6, 1987, 1.
[54] Traub, "Katzenjammer Falcon," 39.
[55] Draper, Very *Thin Line, 134.*

Furmark's help, Khashoggi and Hashemi set up the World Trade Group as a shell company to sell arms to Iran, while Nimrodi and Schwimmer returned to Tel Aviv to report to Peres.[56]

Nimrodi and Schwimmer told Peres that Gorbanifar proposed to broker the purchase of $2 billion in Israeli weapons, presumably through the World Trade Group. Peres was undoubtedly interested in such a major arms deal, but cautiously responded with a counteroffer to sell food, but no arms. Understanding that this was just the beginning of a negotiation, the prime minister appointed Schlomo Gazit, former head of military intelligence, to coordinate future contacts. The two Israelis flew to Geneva to pass on Peres' reply. Gorbanifar was "disappointed." He had expected a positive response, especially as "King Fahd had given Khashoggi the go-ahead for the deal." Still hoping to go forward, explaining that the situation at the front was desperate and arms were vitally needed, he compiled a smaller list of weapons amounting to $33 million.[57]

At Schwimmer's suggestion, Peres agreed to bring Gorbanifar and Hashemi to Israel to check them out. They arrived on April 9, staying for three days at Nimrodi's house in the suburbs of Tel Aviv. While they were there, Peres received a lengthy background report on the two men from the Mossad. The report recommended against any dealings with Hashemi on the grounds that he was unreliable, perhaps suspecting that he was an FBI informant, but, suggested that if Gorbanifar, an equally shady character, could provide proof of his contacts in Iran, they could work with him.[58] The Israelis quietly dropped Hashemi from their plans, as did Khashoggi; the World Trade Group would remain an unused and empty shell.

To prove his veracity, Gorbanifar telephoned Mohsen Kangarlu, Iran's deputy prime minister, from Nimrodi's home with the Israelis

---

[56] "Roy Furmark deposition," *Iran-Contra Affair,* Appendix B, volume 11, 164 and Segev, *Iranian Triangle,* 14-15, 18. From a comparison of their accounts, it is evident that both the congressional committees and Segev had access to, and cite, the Israeli government's *Historical Chronology,* which, however, is unavailable.
[57] Segev, *Iranian Triangle,* 18-19.
[58] Ibid, 20.

listening in on the conversation. The call left no doubt that Gorbanifar had contacts at the highest level in Tehran. Peres concluded that although Gorbanifar was untrustworthy, he was Tehran's interlocutor. The top Israeli leadership—Peres, Shamir, and Rabin— debated the merits of doing business with Gorbanifar over the next two weeks, bringing him back for another visit, without Hashemi.

The clincher came when Nimrodi went to Geneva to check out Gorbanifar's finances. He found an account belonging to the Iranian National Oil Company, to which $100 million had recently been deposited and "Gorbanifar's access to the account... authorized by Iran's Prime Minister and oil minister." Peres thereupon approved the plan to work with him, but to keep ties unofficial and to restrict the circle of those knowledgeable, he substituted Nimrodi for Gazit. Nimrodi now had the job of managing the relationship with Gorbanifar.[59] In effect, Peres had cut Israeli intelligence out of the action, assigning the operation to trusted, private operators.

With funds available, Peres agreed to go forward with the small $33 million arms deal Gorbanifar had proposed the previous month. Code-named *Operation Cosmos*, Nimrodi used his own funds to guarantee shipment and preserve deniability for the Israeli government. A freighter was loaded and ready to sail from Eilat on April 23 and, as agreed, an Iranian officer had flown to Israel to inspect the cargo and escort the ship to Bandar Abbas. Just before the ship set sail, however, Gorbanifar called from Geneva and asked for a delay, due to "internal difficulties" in Tehran.[60]

A few days later, at the end of April, Gorbanifar flew to Tel Aviv, his third trip, to apologize for the mishap and plead for a delay of a month or two in the Israeli weapons shipment. What Iran needed immediately, he said, was to purchase American-made anti-tank TOW missiles to counter the growing Iraqi superiority in tanks. Amid great consternation and name-calling, at what was now a costly venture for Nimrodi, Gorbanifar swore that he was acting on the authority of the

---

[59] Ibid, 21-23.
[60] Ibid, 24.

Iranian prime minister, that he would make up any losses suffered in the postponement, and that he would try to obtain the support of the Americans by offering to gain the release of Buckley.[61]

In retrospect it is clear that the Iranians cancelled the arms deal because there was no American involvement. However, having drawn the Israelis in, they now used them to gain access to the Americans. On the other hand, the Israelis, realizing that there would be no arms sales without American involvement, now had every incentive to approach Washington.

Gorbanifar's request for American weapons created a new situation. If the issue were solely the sale of Israeli weapons, Peres would face no difficulty. But he was not prepared to accede to an Iranian request to purchase American equipment from Israel without the president's approval, as required by United States law, and without amending the understanding he had reached with Reagan during his visit to Washington the past October.

When Khashoggi was informed of the new request, he sent a note to NSC head, Robert McFarlane on May 2 "to ready Washington for Iran's request through the Israeli channel." He urged the administration to be receptive to Tehran because "the succession struggle could begin in earnest even before Khomeini's death and that it was in America's interest to try to influence the choice of successor."[62]

---

[61] Ibid, 24-25.
[62] Ibid, 134-35. Draper, *Very Thin Line*, 626n.45, basing his view on Dan Raviv and Yossi Melman, *Every Spy A Prince* (Boston: Houghton Mifflin, 1990), 334-35, claims that Segev confused Khashoggi's message with an analysis done by Gorbanifar on the same date. But the authors and the content of their messages are completely different. Gorbanifar analyzed the internal situation in Iran, while Khashoggi addressed Iran's request to Washington. Moreover, Segev, x, claims that he interviewed "most of the Israeli participants and...had access to government papers not yet declassified." Mention of "government papers" implies a reference to the classified Historical and Financial chronologies the Israeli government provided to the U.S. House and Senate conferees who prepared the *Iran-Contra Affair* study. A comparison of the references to the chronologies in their report with relevant passages in Segev's book makes it clear that he made use of them.

Richard C. Thornton

Crisis and Opportunity in Washington

Khashoggi's memo reopened the issue of Iran policy in a new way, bringing to a head the worst fears of Shultz and the new world order faction. As Howard Teicher, the NSC officer charged with managing the interagency policy process for southwest Asia noted: by "the end of April...the interagency process on southwest Asia was deadlocked over the question of policy toward Iran."[63] In other words, up to this point, Shultz had successfully fended off all attempts to bring about a change in policy. The memo, the tortuous, long-range result of Casey's initiative of over a year earlier, had turned the Iran issue on its head by raising the question of what the United States should do *if the initiative came from Iran?*

Shultz, McFarlane and the new world order faction knew what the president's response would be. The cooperation of the Saudis, Israelis, and Iranians had produced the opening the president sought. Other recent events, they also knew, would only increase the pressure on him to act. From early in the year, Hezbollah had gone on a hostage-taking spree in Lebanon. Between January and mid-June militants had taken a dozen men hostage. Five were Americans: Father Lawrence Jenco, on January 8, Terry Anderson, on March 16, David Jacobson, on May 28, and George Sutherland, on June 9. As noted above Regier and Levin had been seized but escaped and three others, a Swiss and two Englishmen, had been taken and released after a short time. There were seven Americans in captivity and five Frenchmen.

The combination of circumstances left no doubt that Reagan would seize upon an Iranian request to effect an opening. Shultz and the new world order faction therefore decided that their only course of action was to seize control of the initiative and sink it. Fortunately, they had a man ideally placed to undertake this mission in Robert McFarlane, who, in policy discussions espoused a pro-Iran stance. For the next six months, he would almost single-handedly and with considerable skill

---

[63] Howard Teicher and Gayle Radley Teicher, *Twin Pillars to Desert Storm* (New York: William Morrow, 1993), 330-31.

manage and orchestrate the Iran initiative from its inception to its apparent demise, and then promptly retire from government, mistakenly believing that he had accomplished his mission of sinking the initiative.

(This was not the scheme of a former Kissinger aide attempting to duplicate the feats of his mentor. McFarlane was acting on behalf of the new world order faction desperate to prevent an opening to Iran, which would compromise their strategy of accommodation with the Soviet Union. Throughout, and afterward, McFarlane would claim that he was acting on the president's instructions, but could never produce a scintilla of evidence to support his claim.

In fact, he was acting on the instructions of Shultz, although their collusion was carefully masked. McFarlane was in an extremely delicate situation torn between his loyalty to the president and the demands of the new world order faction. The evidence indicates that the weight of this plan of deception created enormous psychological stress on the NSC chief. Ultimately, the pressure of this contradiction would lead McFarlane to attempt suicide.)

Naturally following the unfolding events, McFarlane's first move was to confirm the Iranian request. To maintain secrecy, he, like Peres, would operate completely outside formal government channels and use a private emissary. His choice for this mission was Michael Ledeen, a journalist-scholar, who, whether unwittingly or not, was deeply entwined with the new world order faction. Haig had brought him in as a political adviser to the State Department in 1981 where McFarlane met him. In November 1984, McFarlane hired him on as a consultant to the NSC to work on terrorism issues and Iran.[64]

McFarlane would utilize Ledeen as his private interlocutor throughout the opening to Iran, despite strong objections from NSC colleagues. As Walsh observed, by using Ledeen as his private messenger, McFarlane "pretended not to have official NSC involvement in these overtures." Ledeen testified that he "had an

---

[64] Ledeen, *Perilous Statecraft*, 100.

understanding with Mr. McFarlane that neither of us would keep anything in writing regarding this initiative." [65]

Ledeen's main value was the personal relationships he had with several world leaders, including Italian Prime Minister Bettino Craxi and Israeli Prime Minister Shimon Peres. Craxi was an old friend of twenty years and Ledeen had met Peres when he was consultant in the state department in the early eighties and the prime minister was leader of the Labor opposition to Likud. These relationships would prove to be very useful when it was necessary to convey private messages by trusted emissaries. That was the case here.

In fact, McFarlane had planned to send Ledeen on a "mission of inquiry" to Western Europe in January and had instructed his deputy Admiral John Poindexter to write a letter of introduction for him. For one reason or another, that trip never came off. But Ledeen did travel to Western Europe in March where he reportedly was advised by an intelligence colleague to consult the Israelis for information about Iran. Accordingly, McFarlane agreed to send Ledeen to Israel in April, but objections arose from several senior members of the NSC staff.

Director of political-military affairs of the NSC, Don Fortier expressed these reservations in a note to McFarlane on April 9. Although he had no objection to him carrying messages, he "disapproved of using Ledeen as the government's 'primary channel for working the Iran issue with foreign governments.'"[66] Responding to Fortier the same day, McFarlane sought to allay his concerns. "I want to talk to Shultz so that he is not blindsided when Sam Lewis reports—as he will surely find out—about Mike's wanderings. So for the moment let's hold on the Ledeen aspect. I will get back to you."[67]

---

[65] Ledeen, *Grand Jury Testimony*, September 18, 1987, 34, as cited in Lawrence E. Walsh, *Final Report of the Independent Counsel for Iran-Contra Matters*, (Washington, D.C.: United States Court of Appeals for the District of Columbia Circuit, August 4, 1993), 88. [Hereafter referred to as *Final Report*.]
[66] *Tower Report*, B-4 and Draper, *Very Thin Line*, 138.
[67] *Tower Report*, B-5.

Ledeen's Trip and its Aftermath

That was where matters stood for the next three weeks until McFarlane received word of Iran's imminent weapons' request from Khashoggi, whereupon he hurriedly sent Ledeen to meet with Peres to confirm it. In his haste, McFarlane did not confer with Shultz beforehand, or notify Ambassador Lewis that Ledeen was making the trip, even though he knew that Ledeen's presence could not be kept secret. On the other hand, he instructed Ledeen on precisely what to say to Peres.

According to Ledeen's recollection, McFarlane "told me specifically what to say and what tone of voice I was to use when I said it to Peres." Ledeen was to say that the U.S. was interested in an information exchange on Iran as a "research project" undertaken for the NSC and that Ledeen would report directly to McFarlane.[68] In other words, no one else in the U.S. government would know.

Meeting Peres on May 4, the Israeli prime minister was cautious about sharing information. He allowed as how "it was possible that Israeli information about Iran was better than the American's, but it was still insufficient." After more information was developed, he said, then "there could be another discussion to examine to what extent it was possible to frame a new Iran policy." Ledeen claimed that Peres was "happy to work together to try to develop better information about Iran,"[69] and sent him to have a talk with Schlomo Gazit to arrange an information-sharing program. In fact, the "information program" was a code word for the incipient Iran initiative and Gazit would become its coordinator. The entire arrangement would be informal and outside government, as Gazit was then president of Ben Gurion University.[70]

Toward the end of their discussion, Peres broached the subject that McFarlane had actually sent Ledeen to confirm. He said that "Iran wanted to purchase artillery shells and other weapons and military

---

[68] Draper, *Very Thin Line*, 138.
[69] *Tower Report*, B-5.
[70] Ledeen, *Perilous Statecraft*, 102.

equipment from Israel, but that Israel was not prepared to do so without American consent." Peres wanted Ledeen to "sound out McFarlane about the Iranian request."[71]

Peres' statement to Ledeen was curious, to say the least. Whatever his personal relationship with him, the Israeli prime minister was not prepared to divulge highly classified information to an unofficial envoy. Indeed, Ledeen notes that he himself "was not eager" to get involved and told Peres that he "preferred not to be the channel for this request." After some further discussion, however, he "agreed to pass the message."[72]

As noted above, if the question was merely one of selling Israeli weapons and equipment, not only could Peres decide that question himself, he had already done so. Israel was already selling its own weapons to Iran, with American assent, which he knew that McFarlane knew. Therefore, one must deduce that Peres' mention of "artillery shells and *other* weapons and military equipment from Israel," was a veiled reference to an Iranian request to purchase American weapons from Israel's inventory.

That McFarlane understood Peres' meaning was reflected in his next move. After Ledeen returned to Washington to report on May 13, the NSC adviser authorized him to tell Peres "it's okay, but just that and nothing else."[73] In other words, McFarlane, on his own authority and without reference to Reagan, or American law, authorized Peres to make a one-time shipment of Israeli-owned, American weapons to Iran, establishing the precedent for future sales.

Then, McFarlane ordered an update of the previous year's SNIE on Iran, which would reflect the gist of the message from Peres, that friendly states sell arms to Iran. This was a new notion, which, moreover, flew directly in the face of *Operation Staunch*. Graham Fuller, the CIA's National Intelligence Officer for Near East and South Asia, and Howard

---

[71] Segev, *Iranian Triangle*, 137.
[72] Ledeen, *Perilous Statecraft*, 103.
[73] *Tower Report*, B-6. Mayer and McManus, *Landslide*, 125, also note that "McFarlane told Ledeen to authorize a single small Israeli arms sale to Iran," but assume that it was "the mortar shells that Gorbanifar had wanted."

Teicher, of the NSC, worked together on the update, but the idea of friendly states selling arms appeared first in a memo Fuller sent to Casey four days later, on May 17.

Fuller argued that the Khomeini regime was "faltering," and a succession struggle would soon break out. Moscow held the advantage and the United States needed to develop a "broad spectrum of policy moves designed to give us some leverage." Without naming Secretary Shultz, Fuller attacked his policy of attempting to deny arms to Iran and being ready to use force against Iran, if Tehran was involved in a terrorist attack. This, he thought, was "no longer sensible," and "may now serve to facilitate *Soviet* interests more than our own." After discussing a variety of possible options, Fuller concluded: "the best course...was to have friendly states sell arms that would not affect the strategic balance as a means of showing Tehran that it had alternatives to the Soviet Union."[74]

Meanwhile, Fuller and Teicher were hard at work revising the previous fall's SNIE. Circulated for discussion on May 20, the revised estimate, *Iran: The Post-Khomeini Era*, included the carefully worded recommendation that the extent to which "European states and other friendly states—including Turkey, Pakistan, China, Japan, and even Israel—can fill a military gap for Iran will be a critical measure of the West's ability to blunt Soviet influence." Even though this formulation also called for the reversal of *Operation Staunch*, it was sufficiently subdued that it passed through the interagency process without arousing controversy.[75]

The SNIE then became the basis for a new draft NSDD on Iran. On May 28, Don Fortier sent a memo to McFarlane to say that he and his colleagues, including Graham Fuller, with whom they "worked closely," would need a few more days before completing a final draft. He said: "the Israeli option is the one we have to pursue, even though

---

[74] Fuller to DCI/DDCI, "Toward A Policy on Iran," May 17, 1985, *Tower Report*, B-6-7.
[75] "Iran: The Post-Khomeini Era," SNIE, May 20, 1985, *Tower Report*, B-7-8.

we may have to pay a certain price for the help." Finally, Fortier continued to object to Ledeen as the "right interlocutor."[76]

McFarlane's answer to Fortier was to approve another trip by Ledeen to Israel, but he quickly postponed it when he received a cable from Shultz protesting Ledeen's earlier trip.[77] It seems that on May 30 Ambassador Lewis got wind of Ledeen's earlier trip, described as "a secret mission from the White House," and inquired at both Minister of Defense Rabin's and Prime Minister Peres' offices about its purpose. Peres' office declined to respond, but a spokesman at the Defense Ministry told Lewis that the subject was "too hot" to discuss with him and that Rabin would discuss it with the secretary upon his arrival in Washington. However, when Rabin met with Shultz on June 1 the subject did not come up; hence, Shultz's protest to McFarlane.[78]

Shultz's protest was made by cable from Lisbon on June 5, four days after his meeting with Rabin. If the issue was of importance to the secretary he most certainly would have raised it immediately with McFarlane while in Washington, instead of waiting four days to send him a cable from Lisbon. Not only the delay, but also the form of the protest suggested that something else was going on here besides Shultz's objection to Ledeen's trip to Tel Aviv.

That something was Fuller's memo on the need for a new Iran policy, a copy of which Casey had sent to Shultz on June 4.[79] Shultz's protest to McFarlane was in reality a response to Fuller's proposal. It allowed him to go on record in opposition to collaboration with Israel and at the same time distance himself from the actions of the national security adviser to avoid what was already a spreading sense of their

---

[76] Fortier, "PROF note to McFarlane," May 28, 1985, *Tower Report*, B-8.
[77] *Iran-Contra Affair*, 165.
[78] Segev, *Iranian Triangle*, 139, says Rabin met with Shultz on June 1, but Shultz, *Turmoil and Triumph*, 793, claims that he met with Rabin on June 3 and was in Lisbon the next day. If true, it would mean he probably had no time to discuss the issue with McFarlane personally, but neither meeting date affects the reason for sending the cable, as a response to Fuller's memo.
[79] *Tower Report*, B-7. Martin and Walcott, *Best Laid Plans,* 223, claim that Casey "hand-delivered" Fuller's memo to Schultz.

collusion. That might actually have been an equally important reason for the cable, as McFarlane himself noted, fears were running "rampant," especially in the Pentagon, that there was a "McFarlane-Shultz cabal," influencing the views of the president.[80] Thus, Shultz declared:

> Israel's agenda is not the same as ours. I consequently doubt whether an intelligence relationship such as what Ledeen apparently has in mind would be one which we could fully rely upon and it could seriously skew our own perception and analysis of the Iranian scene. We of course are interested to know what Israel thinks about Iran but we should treat it as having a bias built in.

Next, Shultz considered it "deleterious to encourage or even merely acquiesce in someone like Mr. Ledeen undertaking a mission such as this without our Ambassador in Israel being informed." It suggested that the White House had no confidence in its own representative. Finally, Shultz said that he only learned of Ledeen's mission from Lewis, but not the defense minister himself when they met, which made him all the more "unhappy." "I would appreciate," the secretary concluded, "hearing from you what you know about it."[81]

McFarlane had no inkling of Shultz's motives, and was taken aback by the reprimand. Replying two days later, he expressed his "disappointment" at the secretary's "prejudgment." Clearly rattled, he told Shultz a string of falsehoods to exculpate his actions. He denied that he had sent Ledeen, who, he claimed, had gone "on his own hook." (McFarlane himself authorized his trip.) He excused his failure to notify the secretary because he had only heard from Ledeen "last week" and hadn't had time to speak with him. (Ledeen had reported to McFarlane on May 13, three weeks earlier.) He claimed that it was

---

[80] McFarlane, *Special Trust*, 316.
[81] Shultz to McFarlane, June 5, 1985, in Shultz testimony, *Iran-Contra Affair*, 100-9, 494-5.

Israel that had posed the question of cooperation to Ledeen, (when it had been the reverse).

Then, McFarlane declared that he would send "unequivocal instructions" that the United States had "no interest at all." Although he thought that that might not be "wise," he said that he was "turning it off entirely (and, of course, would never have turned it on without talking to you)." In fact, however, McFarlane did not turn off the initiative; quite the reverse. But, his final remark about not doing anything without first talking to the secretary, simply reinforced suspicions of a "McFarlane-Shultz cabal."[82]

A New Draft NSDD and International Complications

On June 11, Fortier and Teicher submitted their draft NSDD to McFarlane, recommending that he provide copies only to Secretaries Shultz and Weinberger for their comments. Six days later, however, McFarlane sent copies not only to Shultz and Weinberger, but also to Casey, noting in his cover memo that the CIA's updated SNIE, which had also just been distributed, made plain that instability was accelerating in Iran and that it seemed "sensible to ask whether our current policy toward Iran is adequate to achieve our interests." If they agreed a policy change was warranted, then, McFarlane said, "I would refer the paper to the SIG(FP) in preparation for an NSPG meeting with the president."[83]

The draft described an Iranian regime facing increasingly adverse political, military and economic circumstances—growing indecision in the face of Khomeini's fragility, disillusionment over a seemingly endless war, and declining revenue from oil production. The authors saw Iran on the verge of a succession struggle whose course was "impossible to predict." Within the government there was division but no clear opposition leader. Opposition groups, however, were

---

[82] McFarlane to Shultz, June 7, 1985, Ibid, 100-9, 498.

[83] SIG(FP) stood for Senior Interagency Group (Foreign Policy). Peter Kornbluh and Malcolm Byrne, *The Iran-Contra Scandal: The Declassified History* (New York: New Press, 1993), 220.

proliferating and were clearly demarcated into conservative, radical, and military factions, with the Revolutionary Guard portrayed as an additional instrument of state power. Although deeply fractured, "in any scenario," the guard would be at the center in any power struggle.

The authors believed that conservative groups within the government and leaders in the regular army were inclined to be more pro-Western, but radicals and the revolutionary guard would undoubtedly seek to move Iran in the opposite direction and reject cooperation with Washington. The analysis' shortcoming, however, was its lack of specificity. The conservative-radical-military breakdown identified no one in particular. Indeed, the only name mentioned was Khomeini's.

The analysis of Iran's position between east and west was more straightforward. The Soviet Union was far better positioned to take advantage of a succession struggle than was the United States and would exert a maximum effort to prevent the restoration of a pro-western government. "Without a major change in U.S. policy," Washington's position would not improve. Toward that end, the United States must undertake a range of short and long-term initiatives "to enhance our leverage in Tehran," minimize that of Moscow's, and ultimately bring about the normalization of relations with Iran.

First and foremost, the United States must "encourage Western allies and friends" to help Iran to meet its import requirements to diminish the attractiveness of Soviet trade and assistance. This included the "provision of selected military equipment" to Iran on a case-by-case basis. The authors also recommended that Washington establish contact with allies and "be ready to communicate through them to Iran." We should be ready to establish links with receptive Iranian leaders, but continue to oppose the regime itself and be ready to take action against the Iranian-supported terrorist infrastructure. Nothing in the draft NSDD, nor the SNIE which underlay it, mentioned the issue of hostages.[84]

---

[84] Ibid, "U.S. Policy Toward Iran," NSDD (draft) June 17, 1985, 221-26.

The draft, its authors noted, was "provocative," in that it called for a dramatic reversal of policy toward Iran, without stating that it would mean the repudiation of the policy championed by Secretary of State Shultz. Reaction from the secretaries, however, was delayed by the intrusion of a major event on June 14, which, as Cannon notes, "plunged" the president into "one of the gravest crises of his presidency."[85] This was the seizure of an American airliner flying from Athens to Rome with 153 passengers and crew, including 135 U.S. citizens. The event—due to extensive worldwide television coverage—would capture the attention of the Western world for 17 days and bring to a head the Reagan administration's policy deliberations on a range of issues.

---

[85] *Lou Cannon, President Reagan: Role of a Lifetime (New York: Simon & Shuster, 1991), 605.*

Chapter 3
Crucible of Decision

The hijacking of TWA-847 created a crisis of the first order in the Reagan administration whose outcome moved the president to make three crucial decisions, two secret and one public. The secret decisions were to strike powerfully at Muamar Qadaffi, whose role as a Soviet surrogate in instigating the crisis was the proverbial last straw for the president, and to move forward with an opening to Iran, whose assistance in resolving the crisis indicated Tehran's interest in improving relations, despite the involvement of its sometimes uncontrollable agents in terrorist acts against Americans in Lebanon. The increasingly evident divisions within the Iranian leadership appeared to make an opening feasible. The public decision, announced as the crisis was being resolved, was the president's agreement to meet with Soviet leader Mikhail Gorbachev in November.

The president's decisions were not supported unanimously within the leadership. Secretary Shultz and the new world order faction, while supporting the president's decision to move forward with the Soviet Union, was lukewarm regarding the decision to strike at Qadaffi, and continued vehemently to oppose opening relations with Iran.

The Strategy of Terror

The hijacking of TWA-847 was the first attack against an American airline since the early seventies, but one of several airline hijacks in the Middle East within the past year.[1] The hijacks coincided with a general upsurge of terrorism in the region carried out by several armed, terrorist groups. These groups, all connected to national sponsors, at times acted in the name of their organizations and at times in the name of organizations with which they falsely claimed a connection. Falsely claimed or attributed attacks were a common way of providing self-protection.

Lebanon was the chaotic scene of intense civil strife between Palestinians and Lebanese factions as they fought for control over Beirut. Arafat's PLO was holed up in the refugee camps, Sabra, Shatila, and Bourj el Barajneh, encircled by Syria's Amal, Iran's Hezbollah, Israel's Maronites and the Druze. These were but the most visible of the armed, terrorist groups, whose relationships were constantly fluctuating according to the issue of the moment.

All but the Maronites and the Druze opposed Israel, which had withdrawn from Beirut, but maintained a position in southern Lebanon; and the United States for supporting Israel. The Israelis had added insult to injury by imprisoning several thousand men, mostly Shiites, as they withdrew, releasing them sporadically afterward, in return for captured Israelis. Washington had strongly objected to what in effect was Israeli hostage-taking and demanded they be released.

Terrorist actions also occurred in an international context. To the extent that terrorist attacks weakened U.S. and Israeli positions in the region, as well as forestalled any contacts between the U.S. and Tehran, they served the strategic interests of the Soviet Union in its determination to drive the United States from the region and Iran into its orbit.

The Soviets, from the beginning in 1917, had constructed a global clandestine apparatus to serve their needs in the struggle against the

---

[1] In July 1984, terrorists diverted an Air France jet to Tehran's Mehrabad airport. In December, four or five Arabs of Hezbollah commandeered a Kuwait Airways flight and diverted it to Mehrabad. Two days before the hijacking of TWA-847, a Royal Jordanian plane had been seized, flown to Beirut and blown up. See Barry Hillenbrand and Johanna McGeary, "The Gulf: Horror Aboard Flight 221," *Time*, December 17, 1984.

West. As terrorism increased in value as a low-cost instrument of state policy, the Soviets devoted more resources to it. The Soviet role in support of international terrorism was well understood by American leaders, who chose, however, not to publicize it.[2]

By the '80s, Moscow had established a mature, worldwide system of training camps located on its own territory and throughout the territories of its client states where operations could be staffed, planned, and practiced.[3] They managed a complex apparatus that could recruit personnel, socialize them into terrorist "causes," and train them in required skills, like bomb making. Moscow's logistics network managed the travel and special needs of its operatives, including the provision of false documents, laundered money, safe houses, weapons, explosives, and secure communications. Finally, the Soviets advised and consulted their client states on how to develop their own systems.[4]

Indeed, in January 1985, the foreign ministers of Libya, Syria, and Iran met ostensibly to map out a new anti-American strategy, agreeing to "escalate terrorism against U.S. interests and personnel on a worldwide scale." Reality seemed to be less grandiose than the headlines. Sources "close to the Syrian government" said that Damascus and Tripoli "spearheaded the drive" to develop coordination among the

---

[2] See Richard C. Thornton *The Reagan Revolution, III: Defeating the Soviet Challenge* (Victoria: Trafford, 2009), 452-53, for a discussion of the Long Commission Report and the decision not to identify the Soviet Union as a state supporter of international terrorism.

[3] *Soviet Support for International Terrorism and Revolutionary Violence*, SNIE 11, May 27, 1981, Central Intelligence Agency (Washington, D.C., 1981). See also, *The Soviet Bloc Role and International Terrorism and Revolutionary Violence*, NIE 11-2, August 1986, Central Intelligence Agency (Washington, D.C., 1986) and Drew Middleton, "Soviets Seen Adopting 'Low-Intensity Warfare,'" *Air Force Times*, August 5, 1985, 69.

[4] As the authors of *The 9/11 Commission Report: Final Report of the National Commission on Terrorist Attacks Upon the United States* (New York: Norton & Company, 2004), 365, put it: "A complex international terrorist operation aimed at launching a catastrophic attack cannot be mounted by just anyone in any place." See also, William Jasper, "No State Sponsors, No Terror," *New American*, August 18, 2009.

three countries. However, "at Iran's urging," the group avoided creation of a formal alliance that would appear to put the group on the side of the Soviet Union; "Iran doesn't want to appear to be on either side of the superpower struggle."[5]

The Syrian-Libyan effort was consistent with Moscow's interest in preventing Iran from shifting toward the United States and Tehran's refusal to be pigeonholed was consistent with Iran's interest in developing relations with the United States, while not burning bridges to Moscow. On the other hand, Assad was especially sensitive to Qadaffi's repeated attempts to make inroads into Lebanon, which he considered to be a Syrian preserve. Thus, the "cooperation" of the three countries was more apparent than real and, in essence, represented yet another of Qadaffi's many attempts to gain influence through organizational schemes.

TWA-847

On June 14, 1985, at 10:00 in the morning and an hour behind schedule, TWA-847 lifted off the runway at Eleftherios Venizelos airport in Athens, Greece, on its daily scheduled flight to Rome. On board the Boeing 727 were 145 passengers, mostly Americans, and eight crew members. Minutes after reaching cruising altitude, just after Captain John Testrake had turned off the fasten-seatbelt sign, two young Palestinian males, who had been seated in the last row, leapt from their seats brandishing guns and hand grenades and rushed to the cockpit.

Before the two hijackers could force their way into the cockpit, Captain Testrake pressed the 7500 number on the plane's transponder, signaling to monitoring air traffic controllers that there was a "hijack-

---

[5] "Libya, Syria and Iran Coordinate Schemes To Strike U.S. Targets, Arab Sources Say," *Wall Street Journal*, June 19, 1985, 34. The *Journal* article said their meeting was held in Tehran, but Yossef Bodansky, *Target America: Terrorism in the U.S. Today*, (New York: S.P.I. Books, 1993), 44, claims the meeting took place in Hermel, in the Bekaa Valley, Lebanon, and was attended by senior intelligence officials, not foreign ministers, and accorded a much greater initiative to Iran.

in-progress." The seven-hour time difference between Athens and Washington, made it a few minutes before four o'clock in the morning when word reached Washington that the hijack of an American airliner was under way.[6]

The hijackers demanded that Captain Testrake fly them to Algiers. Testrake, co-pilot Phil Maresca, and flight engineer Christian Zimmerman, responded as best they could to make the two men understand—they spoke no English—that there was insufficient fuel to reach Algiers. It was common airline practice to fuel an aircraft for the scheduled distance to be flown. For the 655-mile flight to Rome the plane's tanks were just over a third full, 2,600 gallons (17,000 pounds), which was not nearly enough to fly the 1,120 miles to Algiers. (In retrospect, this indicated poor planning on the part of the hijackers.)

Fortunately, the language barrier was broken when chief flight attendant Uli Derickson explained that she was German, not American, and found that one of the hijackers spoke German—a completely chance occurrence. With Derickson interpreting, Testrake said they could reach Cairo, just less than seven hundred miles away; but the hijackers told him to fly to Beirut, 734 miles away, for "fuel only."[7]

There were originally three hijackers, but one had been bumped from the overbooked flight, another organizational glitch. Well after the fact the two on board would be identified as Mohamad al Hamadi and Hasan Izz al Din. The bumped third member, Ali Atwa, although failing to get a seat on the flight, would subsequently participate in the hijack. All had flown to Athens from Beirut the previous day.

On the flight to Beirut the hijackers terrorized and cowed the passengers by running up and down the cabin aisle brandishing their weapons and randomly beating them with seat armrests used as clubs.

---

[6] David Martin and John Walcott, *Best Laid Plans: The Inside Story of America's War Against Terrorism* (New York: Touchstone, 1988), 163.
[7] John Testrake, *Triumph Over Terror, On Flight 847* (Eastbourne: Kingsway Publications, 1988), 70-71.

They moved the men to the window seats, and forced all to keep their heads down to prevent them from seeing anything, or communicating with one another. With the help of the flight attendants the hijackers identified and dispersed among the passengers seven navy divers. They also sought unsuccessfully to find out if there were any Jews on the plane.

On approach to Beirut International airport, just before noon local time, tower control initially refused permission to land, but grudgingly relented when the hijackers threatened to crash-land and blow up the plane. Two days before, a Royal Jordanian Airways plane had been hijacked and blown up on the runway and its wreckage was still smoldering as TWA-847 taxied by.[8]

Over the radio the hijackers demanded fuel, threatening to "kill an American" unless their demands were met. To hasten a response they began loudly beating one of the navy divers, Robert Stethem. As the plane was being refueled, they also demanded to speak with an official of Amal, the group that controlled southern Beirut and the airport. No Amal official was willing to talk to them, indicating serious differences and obviously no prior coordination between the hijackers, who were apparently part of Hezbollah, and Amal.[9]

At the same time, the hijackers spewed out a series of demands over the radio in Arabic that no one aboard the plane understood. They demanded that governments across Europe and the Middle East release jailed Shiites everywhere. Specifically, they demanded the release of the Kuwait 17, seven hundred prisoners held by Israel, two held by Spain, and two held by Cyprus. They also demanded "world" condemnation of Israel and of the United States for its support for Israel.

With tanks full, passengers and cargo combined put the aircraft 15,000 pounds overweight, a condition that enabled Captain Testrake and Uli Derickson to persuade the hijackers to release 17 women and

---

[8] "Logbook of Terror," *New York Times*, June 17, 1985, 6.
[9] "Remembering the 1985 Hijacking of TWA Flight 847," *Securitas Magazine* (May-June 2005).

two children to lighten the load. At that point, 1:30 in the afternoon, an hour-and-a-half after arriving, the plane took off for Algiers 1,800 miles away.

The initial early morning response from Washington was understandably disjointed based on fragmentary information. When the plane landed in Beirut, President Reagan sent the first of several cables to Syrian president Hafez al-Assad asking for assistance.[10] When the plane took off and it was determined that it was headed for Algiers, the focus shifted there. U.S. ambassador, Michael Newlin, was directed to request of the president of Algeria, Chadli Benjadid, that the plane be permitted to land and then be detained. President Reagan also sent a personal message imploring him to attempt to convince the hijackers to surrender.

Meanwhile, at 3:30 in the afternoon, exclaiming that they were running out of fuel, Captain Testrake was given permission to land at Houari Boumediene International airport. Airport security surrounded the plane and officials arrived to talk, a process that dragged on for the better part of four hours. The hijackers' basic public demand was for the release of the 766 prisoners held by Israel in Atlit prison. For "humanitarian reasons" they released 21 more passengers, but threatened to kill others, if an attempt was made to assault the plane.[11]

As they talked the hijackers demanded that the plane be refueled, but Algerian authorities stalled. To convince them to cooperate they began severely beating Stethem, but, as he was barely conscious and could not cry out, took another American, army reservist Kurt Carlson, and began beating him and directing his shouts into the cockpit radio.[12] After several tense moments and the passage of three deadlines, a fuel truck arrived, but the driver demanded prepayment for the fuel. Once again, flight attendant Derikson saved the day, producing a Shell gas card for payment, whereupon the plane's fuel tanks were topped off at

---

[10] Lou Cannon and John Goshko, "U.S. Stands Firm Against Demands Of Jet's Hijackers," *Washington Post*, June 20, 1985, 1.
[11] Testrake, *Triumph Over Terror*, 81.
[12] Martin and Walcott, *Best Laid Plans*, 172.

just over nine thousand gallons. Derikson was charged six thousand dollars, but the larger point was that the Algerians refused to cooperate with the hijackers, except minimally.[13]

Original Plan Gone Awry

At 8:15 in the evening, TWA-847 took off from Algiers, destination unknown. Once airborne, the hijackers told Captain Testrake to head back to Beirut. To him this meant, "the hijackers didn't really have a game plan. They'd known what to do to get this far—but not what to do afterward."[14] Indeed, getting to Algiers was their objective, but, having failed to accomplish their unspecified purpose once they got there, they were now on the way back to Beirut to determine their next course of action.

Approaching a blacked-out Beirut International a few minutes past two in the morning, tower control again refused permission to land informing Captain Testrake that barricades had been placed on the runway. Declaring his aircraft to be in distress and nearly out of fuel, the captain related the hijackers' threat to crash-land the plane. Relenting, the tower controller advised Testrake to circle the airport while he arranged to have the barriers removed. After circling the airport several times, runway lights switched on, and Testrake was given permission to land.

Wary of a trap, the hijackers had Testrake brake the plane in the middle of the runway while they began to converse with the control tower. In addition to demanding food and fuel, they evidently demanded that Amal join in the hijacking, which was refused. They also threatened to kill the eight Greek passengers on board, if the Greek government failed to release their accomplice, who had been apprehended at the airport.[15] As their argument intensified, one of the

---

[13] Testrake, *Triumph Over Terror*, 80-81.
[14] Ibid, 81.
[15] Shortly after the hijack was reported, Israel's intelligence representative in Athens went to the airport, discovered that one of the three hijackers' tickets had not been used, and concluded that the third hijacker, Ali Atwa, was still probably in the

hijackers suddenly dragged the barely conscious seaman Stethem to the doorway, shot him in the head and dumped his body onto the tarmac, screaming that they meant business and that unless their demands were met in five minutes they would kill another.

At this, the tower gave permission for Testrake to taxi over to the refueling area. When they got there and as the plane was being refueled a group of gunmen, variously estimated to number between five and a dozen, charged onto the plane. Although the hijackers had attempted to draw Amal into their action, those who boarded the plane were Hezbollah gunmen. Indeed, one of them was the leader of the group, Imad Mugniyeh, who identified himself simply as Jihad.

A radical cell within the Iran-sponsored Hezbollah group, the Islamic Jihad, apparently carried out the TWA-847 hijack. To reporters searching for information, some "people identifying themselves as spokesmen" for the group claimed that Islamic Jihad bore responsibility for the hijacking. Others, however, *denied* the group's responsibility, vowing "retaliation against media that say Jihad was responsible."[16] The implication was that Imad Mugniyeh was a member of this cell, but had acted independently of it, undertaking this particular operation supported by a different sponsor.

For the past two years Mugniyeh's Islamic Jihad had concentrated attacks mostly against American and French targets in Lebanon. Islamic Jihad's objectives, like every other group's, were proclaimed to be the removal of American and Israeli presence in the Middle East in general and Lebanon in particular. But Mugniyeh had additional motives that made him one of the most vicious and feared terrorists.

Mugniyeh pioneered the use of suicide bombers and was behind the terrorist bombings of the American embassy in Beirut in April 1983, the Marine barracks and the French legation in October, and the U.S. and French embassies in Kuwait in December. When Kuwaiti

---

airport. With the support of the airport police, they paged Atwa, saying he had an important call, and when he appeared he was arrested. See, Ronen Bergman, *The Secret War With Iran* (New York: Free Press, 2007), 101.

[16] Christopher Dickey, "Hijackings: Tool of Terrorism," *Washington Post*, June 16, 1985, 18.

authorities captured, tried and sentenced a group of those behind the attacks, Mugniyeh obtained an additional rationale. One of the seventeen terrorists convicted and sentenced to death was reportedly his cousin and brother-in-law, Mustafa Badredienne. Thus, all subsequent attacks, including hostage seizures from the first months of 1984 in Lebanon, had included the demand for the release of the Kuwait 17.

But there was more. According to Woodward, Casey, with the support of the Saudis, had arranged to take out Sheikh Fadlallah, the spiritual leader of Hezbollah who had been deeply involved in the bombings of American and French facilities.[17] On March 8, 1985, a huge car bomb exploded outside his headquarters killing 80 people and wounding over two hundred. Fadlallah escaped unscathed, but among those who perished was Mugniyeh's brother, Jihad.

President Reagan denied responsibility, declaring that "never would I sign anything that would authorize an assassination....I never have, and I never will, and I didn't."[18] McFarlane later agreed that Reagan had no involvement. He suggested that CIA-trained "rogue operatives" from Lebanese intelligence carried out the attack without CIA approval. The CIA, however, was widely believed to have been responsible.[19]

Mugniyeh, who spoke English, assumed control of the hijack operation from the moment he boarded the aircraft, making two decisions. The first was to go back to Algiers, to attempt to fulfill the original plan, and the second was to take out hostage insurance against any rescue attempt. (Word had already gotten out that the United States had dispatched a Delta Force team to the Middle East.)

For insurance, the hijackers selected out two groups of seven and five men from among the passengers, took them off the plane, and sequestered them in the slums of West Beirut. One group included five

---

[17] Bob Woodward, *Veil: The Secret Wars of the CIA, 1981-1987* (New York: Simon & Shuster, 1987), 397.
[18] "Did A Dead Man Tell No Tales?" *Time*, October 12, 1987.
[19] "Target America: Terrorist Attacks on Americans, 1979-1988," *Frontline* video archive.

military men and two Greeks and the other included two Americans with Jewish-sounding names and three others selected at random. Mugniyeh would control one of these two groups until the very last minutes of the crisis.

Algiers Redux

A little over three hours after landing at Beirut, with the plane refueled and passengers fortified with sandwiches and soft drinks, TWA-847 took off at daybreak headed again for Algiers. While en route the hijackers radioed a demand for the release of their accomplice Ali Atwa, in return for which they would release the Greek passengers. If he were not released they would begin to kill them. The Greek government immediately complied, flying Atwa to Algiers that afternoon where he was permitted to join the gunmen on the plane.

Upon learning that the plane was headed back to Algiers, Secretary Shultz instructed Ambassador Newlin to request that the Algerian government permit the plane to land and allow the United States to send in a rescue force. Newlin forcefully objected to the instruction about trying a rescue. He did not believe that the Algerians would "ever consent to have a foreign military force operate on their territory." Any attempt to try would provoke "armed opposition from the Algerians, and the terrorists would probably blow up the plane with everybody in it."[20]

The plane landed in Algiers at 7:45 A.M. Shultz thought the best option was to keep the plane in Algiers, where "the Algerians could try to bring the crisis to an end," although he still clung to the hope that, failing that, they would agree "at some point to let our shooters...take over the plane."[21]

But the Algerian government would have none of it. As Newlin had said, they flatly opposed any U.S. military presence, let alone

---

[20] David Wills, *The First War on Terrorism: Counter Terrorism Policy During the Reagan Administration* (New York: Rowman & Littlefield, 2003), 94.
[21] Shultz, *Turmoil and Triumph*, 654-55.

operations, on their soil. At the same time, Algerian foreign ministry officials persuaded the hijackers to release not only several Greek passengers, but also all of the women, children, and flight attendants, in exchange for Atwa. Left aboard the aircraft were 44 male passengers, the three-man flight crew, and about a dozen hijackers.[22]

Based on their discussions, the Algerians believed that "they could probably persuade the hijackers to release the passengers, if the United States could guarantee that Israel would release the Atlit prisoners" they held.[23] The release of the Atlit prisoners in exchange for the passengers seemed to offer the prospect of a prompt settlement. Although the president supported this idea, Shultz strongly opposed a "swap," insisting that American policy was not to make deals with terrorists and not encourage others to do so.[24]

Although President Reagan repeatedly in internal discussions proposed this idea, Shultz refused to agree to it. In the end, a swap is what would actually transpire, but two weeks would be spent attempting to work out staggered releases by Israel and the hijackers to avoid the appearance of a swap and maintain the façade of adhering to principle. This fooled no one. Shultz's opposition and the president's disinclination to override him meant the loss of an early opportunity to resolve the question in Algiers.

By early morning on Sunday, June 16, however, the hijackers had already been in one place too long and had become concerned about an attack on the plane. (They would spend over 24 hours on the ground in Algiers.) Waking early, Mugniyeh demanded the plane be refueled. To overcome reticence by the tower to send the fuel truck, Mugniyeh said to the captain "we want to play a little game here." He opened the microphone and told the crew to yell loudly to pretend that they were being beaten. At the same time, he fired a few shots from his pistol through the open cockpit window. The fuel truck arrived in minutes.[25]

---

[22] Stephen Labaton, "Aid Obstacles to Passenger List, Fate of 15 Unclear," *Washington Post*, June 17, 1985, 16.
[23] Wills, *First War on Terrorism*, 97.
[24] George Shultz, *Turmoil and Triumph* (New York: Macmillan, 1993), 656.
[25] Testrake, *Triumph Over Terror*, 90-1,

Discussing their destination as the plane was being refueled, Mugniyeh said, "we want to go to Aden." When the captain pointed out that South Yemen was well beyond the range of the aircraft and would require a refueling stop in Cairo, Mugniyeh replied: "Okay, we will fly back to Beirut for fuel. Then we will go somewhere else." As the hijackers talked among themselves, Testrake could make out the word "Tehran," a "somewhere else" he did not want to go. As he noted later: "It was obvious to all of us that the hijackers were fresh out of ideas and were just fumbling about without a real plan of attack."[26] Whatever their objective had been in returning to Algiers a second time, they had failed to achieve it.

At eight o'clock in the morning, Sunday, June 16, over the objections of Ambassador Newlin, TWA-847 took off from Algiers heading back to Beirut. When Newlin asked why, his Algerian interlocutors said that they had heard that Delta Force was on its way and assumed the hijackers probably heard about it, too, because they were threatening to blow up the plane.[27] It seems that the Algerian authorities, too, had been concerned about an American attack on the plane, and permitted it to depart before anything could happen.

An Intelligence Discovery

While the plane was en route to Beirut, American intelligence produced surprising information that would have a bearing on the developing crisis. Reports based on "hard intelligence" concluded, "two senior officials of the Greek government of Andreas Papandreou [were] implicated, though perhaps indirectly, in the hijacking…" The two officials were Costas Naliotes, an aide to the prime minister, and Agamemnon Kostosgeorges, Minister of Interior. Both were known "supporters and protectors of international terrorism in Greece," who had been the "focus of administration criticism…for quite some time."[28]

---

[26] Ibid, 92.
[27] Martin and Walcott, *Best Laid Plans*, 182.
[28] Ted Agres, "Two Greek Officials Implicated in Hijack," *Washington Times*, June 20, 1985, 1.

When Israel drove the Palestinians from Lebanon during the 1982 war, over two hundred were evacuated to Greece and Cyprus. The Greek government had helped some of these refugees obtain work permits and employment "on the grounds crews at Athens International Airport." Indeed, the Director of Public Order, Athanassios Trouras, acknowledged that weapons "might have been hidden aboard the aircraft as it stood on the tarmac after arriving from Cairo."

American intelligence thus concluded that "the weapons used by the Moslem Shi'ite terrorists—9mm Mauser handguns and grenades—were positioned aboard the TWA Boeing 727 while it was being serviced during its stopover in Athens, allowing the hijackers to bypass the airport's metal detectors and other security equipment."[29] A member of the service crew, probably one of the cleaning crew, secreted the weapons' package in one of the lavatories on the aircraft.

One of the passengers, Peter Hill, a tour operator from Chicago, offered corroboration. Hill was sitting in the back row of the plane next to the two hijackers. Before takeoff one of the Arabs pushed his way into the lavatory, refusing to keep seated as requested by the cabin attendant. Hill "next heard 'a tremendous crash, a smashing of glass....' Shortly afterwards, the Arab returned to his seat...and began whispering to his companion."[30]

The reports also pointed to the instigator of the hijacking, although were mute on his purpose. It turned out that Muamar Qadaffi had contributed "large sums of money" to Papandreou's 1981 election and that "Libya and other Arab extremist groups therefore had a certain ability to collect favors from the Greek government." One of those "favors" was to look the other way on "terrorist operations occurring within Greece, but not directed against that country."[31]

Thus far, the evidence strongly suggested that Qadaffi had arranged to provide for the placement of weapons on board TWA-847

---

[29] Ibid.
[30] Martin and Walcott, *Best Laid Plans*, 161-62.
[31] Agres, "Two Greek Officials..."

for an Imad Mugniyeh-led terrorist mission to hijack the plane, but said nothing about its purpose, except that their mission was to fly to Algiers. The purpose surely could not have been primarily to bargain for the release of prisoners held by Israel who were already in the process of being released. To accelerate the process may have been in the interests of Mugniyeh, but Qadaffi? Why had he instigated the hijacking?[32]

It was too soon to work through the larger reasons for Qadaffi's motives, but, for the moment, at least, the president could proceed with reasonable confidence that Hafez Assad was not a co-conspirator. This came through in the persistent refusal of his Lebanese surrogate, Amal, to become involved in the hijacking. Iran's role, too, was as yet unclear, but it seemed unlikely that the Iranians would sponsor an action that would undercut their concurrent attempt to establish an arms relationship with the United States, although it was possible that a faction opposed to such an attempt was involved.

Based on this information, it is reasonable to speculate on the contents of the president's letter to Assad of June 16, while TWA-847 was en route to Beirut for the third time. Shultz says that, in the letter, "we asked him to work on Berri to try to end the crisis." The reference was to Nabih Berri, the leader of Amal, who, up to this point had determinedly stayed out of it, twice attempting to prevent the plane from landing in Beirut, and refusing to talk to the hijackers.[33] But obviously there was more to the letter than that.

To encourage Assad's cooperation through Amal, the president most assuredly told him that he knew that Qadaffi was the perpetrator and that Assad had nothing to gain from supporting the Libyan dictator, who he knew was attempting to encroach on his turf in Beirut.

---

[32] It was in this immediate context that, on June 17, Secretary Weinberger initially responded to the draft NSDD on Iran with the comment that opening up to Iran would be similar to "asking Qadaffi over for a cozy lunch." He would send a fuller, more restrained, but still opposed response a month later. Caspar W. Weinberger, *Fighting for Peace: Seven Critical Years in the Pentagon* (New York: Warner Books, 1990), 363.

[33] Shultz, *Turmoil and Triumph*, 656.

(In the Shiite-PLO battle for control of Beirut, Qadaffi supported the Palestinians.) But it was most immediately important to safeguard the remaining passengers to prevent the hijack from exploding into a crisis that would engulf Syria itself. Thus, having Berri and Amal take control of the passengers from Hezbollah when the plane arrived was the most prudent course.

Shultz, however, persisted in an attempt to use force to take control of the plane, seeking to persuade Captain Testrake to fake engine failure and land at Larnaca, Cyprus, where a rescue could be attempted. Weinberger and the Joint Chiefs disagreed. JCS Chairman John Vessey noted "the prospect for a successful rescue mission was virtually nonexistent." In his view, the "only safe way is to talk them out."[34]

Captain Testrake had a larger concern, fearing that the hijackers wanted to go to Tehran.[35] When the hijackers were not in the cabin he began to ask over the radio: would the passengers be safe in Tehran? Once there would they be permitted to leave? But the only answer that came back, from the tower at Athens, was the suggestion to divert to Larnaca. Testrake and his crewmembers wanted no part of a rescue attempt, which they recognized would only mean the probable deaths of many passengers, crew, and terrorists. He agreed with the idea of faking engine failure, but disregarded the suggestion of landing at Larnaca, and instead proceeded to Beirut.[36]

At just after 2:30 Sunday afternoon, June 16, Captain Testrake made his final approach as airport personnel removed fire trucks from the runway. Walid Jumblatt, leader of the Druze and also Transport Minister in the Lebanese government had first given the order to

---

[34] Wills, *First War on Terrorism*, 102 and Martin and Walcott, *Best Laid Plans*, 185.
[35] Samuel Segev, *The Iranian Triangle: The Untold Story of Israel's Role in the Iran-Contra Affair*, (New York: Free Press, 1988), 142, says that "the Iranian government announced that it would not allow the plane to land on its territory," indicating that the hijackers had contacted Tehran while en route.
[36] Testrake, *Triumph Over Terror*, 93.

refuse permission to land, but controllers relented when Testrake told them he was running out of fuel.[37]

The captain and crew had decided to shut down the engines so the plane could not fly anywhere else. Thus, by the time the aircraft was rolling to a stop on the runway, the crew had faked engine failures on two of the three engines. Claiming that the engines were "way overdue for an overhaul" and that replacement engines would have to come from the United States, which would take "at least two to three weeks," Testrake had neatly put an end to any schemes Mugniyeh might have had that the plane could fly on from Beirut. The hijack problem, in short, would be resolved one way or another in Beirut.[38]

Assad and Berri Take Charge

As TWA-847 came rolling to a stop on the runway, American intelligence noted, "contingents from the Amal militia were arriving at the airport."[39] This, it would shortly become clear, was the first step in Assad's decision to take control of the hijacking away from Mugniyeh and Hezbollah, but it would not be clean-cut, or easy. Amal's leader, Nabih Berri, would be his agent in the effort. His objective was to surround the Hezbollah hijackers with his men, but also position them for a defense against a possible rescue attempt.

According to observers "several jeeps loaded with Amal militiamen pulled up to the plane." After some discussion the hijackers agreed to send a representative from the group "to meet with Mr. Berri, the Amal leader, at his home." The hijackers promised no harm would come to the passengers while the talks with Mr. Berri proceeded, but reiterated their threat to blow up the plane if their demand for the release of the Lebanese detainees was not met.[40]

---

[37] Joseph Berger, "Gunmen Negotiate As Hostages Plead For Reagan To Act," *New York Times*, June 17, 1985, 1.
[38] Testrake, *Triumph Over Terror*, 97-98.
[39] Wills, *First War on Terrorism*, 98.
[40] Berger, "Gunmen Negotiate…"

While the negotiations were occurring in Beirut, back in Washington, the NSPG was meeting. They would meet sometimes several times a day throughout the crisis. Reagan attended most of the meetings, and was in contact when he was elsewhere.[41] The NSPG membership consisted of Reagan, Bush, Shultz, Weinberger, McFarlane, Regan, Poindexter, and Vessey. Baker and Meese, also members, attended occasionally. Others would be invited as needed. In the absence of hard information about the situation among the Beirut factions, or on the plane itself, Shultz repeatedly proposed ways to assault the plane, whether in Beirut, or in Jordan, even as he acknowledged the reservations of Weinberger and Vessey about the inevitability of "lots of casualties."

At the 1:00 P.M. meeting (eight in the evening in Beirut), Shultz informed the group that Assad had replied to the president's letter and confirmed that he had "stimulated" Berri to take control of the situation.[42] This was very important information, confirming that Assad was not one of the sponsors, which promised the way to a resolution.

The immediate problem, however, was how to respond to the Israelis, who seemed to want no part of the crisis. Against the backdrop of large-scale demonstrations in Tel Aviv in opposition to the recent decision by the government to swap 1,100 Lebanese for three Israeli soldiers, protestors demanded that the government hold on to the Atlit prisoners.

A government spokesman said that Israel would not agree to any "exchange" of prisoners for passengers. Defense Minister Rabin told reporters that while the government would meet with Red Cross representatives, "the Americans will have to crawl on all fours before we even discuss" releasing the Lebanese detainees. Another

---

[41] Wills, *First War on Terrorism*, 214. While an invaluable account, Wills contradicts himself in the view that "there is little evidence of Reagan's involvement" in the crisis. He compounds his error by the observation, 218, that "most documents from that crisis remain classified," making his conclusion both wrong and a non sequitur.
[42] Ibid, 101.

spokesman said that Israel "would consider a formal U.S. request to swap the prisoners for the passengers."[43]

Parsing these statements went to the heart of the coalition government then in power, the "marriage of inconvenience," as one commentator described it.[44] The author of the no exchange line was obviously deputy Prime Minister Yitzhak Shamir, whose visceral hatred for the United States was well known. Defense Minister Rabin, who was only slightly less antagonistic, was willing to discuss a swap, if the Americans crawled on all fours for it. And Prime Minister Peres was the obvious author of what became the initial official position; that the government would consider an exchange, if Washington requested it.

Secretary Shultz, assuming Peres' position to be the official one, interpreted, or perhaps, *mis*interpreted, his point. He considered the call for a "request" to be an invitation for "us to ask them to release all or nearly all of the many Lebanese Shiite prisoners they held in exchange for the release of TWA-847 and its remaining passengers. ...putting the responsibility on us." In his view, this meant "if people were killed, we couldn't say it was because of Israel's refusal to swap prisoners for hostages."[45] In reality, the split in Israel's coalition and domestic opposition dictated a passive approach. The important point was that Peres had invited Washington to discuss it.

Finally, the secretary read a statement signed by 32 passengers aboard the plane, imploring the president "not to take any direct military action" and "negotiate quickly our immediate release by convincing the Israelis to release the 800 prisoners as requested. Now."[46] Perhaps reassured, the president and his advisers decided not to force Israel's hand and to go slow and not precipitate any unwanted action by those holding the passengers.

---

[43] Ibid, 98.
[44] Joseph Kraft, "Marriage of Inconvenience," *Washington Post*, June 25, 1985, 15.
[45] Shultz, *Turmoil and Triumph*, 655-56.
[46] Berger, "Gunmen Negotiate As Hostages Plead..."

Meanwhile, Mugniyeh and his gunmen on the aircraft were surrounded by Amal gunmen on the tarmac, as they argued all Sunday afternoon and into the evening over the radio with Nabih Berri and his representatives in the control tower. Finally, late in the afternoon, Berri announced the outcome of their "negotiations." He would place the passengers under his "protection" and mediate for the hijackers. In fact, they divided control of passengers, plane and crew. After midnight his men removed all of the passengers from the plane, and dispersed them in small groups throughout the squalid neighborhoods of West Beirut, while the flight crew remained on board the aircraft.[47]

The situation as of Monday morning, June 17, now was: Berri had 43 passengers under guard in West Beirut (he sent one of the passengers, who was ill, to the local hospital), while Mugniyeh had the plane and its three-man crew. CIA informants had located and discovered that the two leaders also divided control of the two groups removed from the plane during the second stopover.[48] Finally, heavily armed Amal militiamen and Hezbollah gunmen surrounded the airport, which now made a rescue attempt out of the question.

Berri put a humane face in place of the murderous visage of the terrorists, turning the hijack into a quasi-diplomatic hostage negotiation. Berri's presence was somewhat comforting to the American people, who were treated to full television coverage of the event, because he had lived in America and frequently visited. His six children were educated there, his ex-wife lived there (in Detroit), and he still held a green card.[49]

Staking Out Negotiating Positions

That morning around nine o'clock (2:00 A.M. Washington time), Robert McFarlane, who had met Berri in 1983 when he was the

---

[47] Andrew Borowiec, "Shi'ites Said Holding Hostages in West Beirut," *Washington Times*, June 18, 1985, 1.
[48] Wills, *First War On Terrorism*, 99.
[49] Jonathan Randal, "Crisis Go-Between: Berri, With Ties on Both Sides, Could Find Leadership Tested," *Washington Post*, June 18, 1985, 9.

president's envoy to the Middle East, spoke with him over the phone to reinforce Reagan's view that he held the key to resolution of the crisis. As McFarlane put it, it was now his game to win or lose. White House spokesman, Larry Speakes, emphasized that message, declaring that Berri "was the key to it, he has control over the situation."[50]

Berri wasn't buying that characterization, turning the tables. At a press conference later in the morning, he acknowledged that he was now "responsible" for the passengers, but it was still an "American problem." If Washington failed to press Israel to release the detainees he would "wash his hands" of the passengers and return them to the Hezbollah "to do with them as they pleased."

Washington's response to that and to the Israeli government was a White House Statement read by Larry Speakes: "We do not make concessions and we don't encourage others to make concessions." The hijack situation, he said, had "effectively blocked Israel from proceeding with plans to release its Shiite prisoners." If it were cleared up, "it might be possible the Israelis would proceed on the schedule they'd previously announced."[51] To provide some incentive to Assad, it was announced that the aircraft carrier *Nimitz* and six other ships were proceeding to the Eastern Mediterranean.

Berri met with the British and Italian ambassadors, who warned him against underestimating Reagan. They pointed out that the United States and Jordan were just then beginning military exercises, which could be a cover for a rescue attempt. There were also reports of Israeli aircraft over flights. On Tuesday, June 18, to forestall hasty action, Berri announced that he was releasing the remaining six Greek passengers as a friendly gesture for the earlier Greek release of Ali Atwa. And he announced that his men were assuring the safety of the rest.[52]

The important news was Assad's reply to Reagan's letter requesting his assistance. Assad wanted to know whether the president

---

[50] Bernard Weinraub, "Passengers Taken From Hijacked Jet, Lebanese Reports," *New York Times*, June 18, 1985, 1. U.S. leaders understood that Assad controlled Beirut and that Berri was his agent. Thus, putting pressure on Berri made little sense.
[51] Ibid.
[52] Wills, *First War On Terrorism*, 107-8.

would "exert efforts" to gain the release of the Israeli detainees and "make public" the administration's view that holding them was a violation of the Geneva Convention? Reagan was receptive. White House spokesman Larry Speakes responded during the morning briefing that the United States "would like Israel" to "go ahead and make the release" of the detainees.

Shultz was apoplectic. While not saying so, he knew that Speakes had not spoken out on his own authority. It was Reagan who had authorized his remark, which was consistent with the position the president had been taking in the NSPG from the beginning. Furious, Shultz went to the president and demanded that he control the "action." All questions, he insisted, "were to be referred to the State Department."

The president relented, issuing a statement containing the "no concessions" line. Reagan also sent a message to Assad reiterating the no deals line and insisting that the hostage takers were the ones "blocking the release of the prisoners held by Israel."[53] On the other hand, the president decided to tell the Israelis "privately" that they could make the "exchange" of detainees for passengers.

The president's message seems to have been part of a plan to use the Red Cross as an intermediary. After visiting both groups, the "administration could cobble together an unspoken agreement in which each party's objectives were met, and the U.S. and Israel could not be accused of conceding to the terrorists' demands." The Israelis rejected the ploy. The Red Cross "are not a party to it. We deal with the U.S.," insisting on an American "request."[54]

Tuesday evening, the president held a news conference to reaffirm the policy. America, he said, will make no concessions, nor ask others to do so. He demanded the passengers be freed forthwith. In responding to a question, he made public, as Assad had requested, the U.S. opposition to Israel's detention of prisoners "in violation of the

---

[53] Shultz, *Turmoil and Triumph*, 658.
[54] Edward Walsh, "Israel Agrees to Red Cross Meeting," *Washington Post*, June 19, 1985, 1 and Wills, *First War on Terrorism*, 109.

Geneva accords," but he said, the United States would not "interfere" with Israel's decision on whether or not to release the prisoners. There was no "linkage" with the passengers.

Finally, when asked about his policy of "swift retribution," the president said that was so when it involved the actions of a government. In this case, there was "a problem identifying the perpetrators and their accomplices." Therefore, "I have to wait it out as long as...we have a possibility—I'll say a probability—of bringing them home."[55]

With the press conference statements, the president had reestablished the U.S. "no concessions" negotiating position and declared that the ball was now in Berri's court. Whatever the hijackers' objectives had been, they had not achieved them. The "swap" of the Atlit detainees for the passengers was now the only issue on the table. The next several days witnessed a sustained attempt by those behind the hijackers to effect a change in public opinion, while negotiations continued by third parties.

On Wednesday June 19, Assad made an unannounced trip to Moscow to meet with Gorbachev, who reportedly told him to make sure none of the passengers were harmed. It may be surmised that he also agreed that it was time to wrap up the crisis. On the same day, Iran sent a message "to the effect that Tehran wanted to do as much as it could to end the TWA crisis." The State Department sent a stiff reply, saying: "It is the view of the United States that the government of Iran cannot escape its responsibilities...to help secure the release of the hostages."[56] Finally, the Algerian government reported that Berri was willing to release the passengers if the United States could provide a "silent but firm guarantee" that the Israelis would release their prisoners by a "date certain."[57]

---

[55] Bernard Weinraub, "President Bars 'Concessions'; Orders Antihijacking Steps; 3 More T.W.A. Hostages Freed," *New York Times*, June 19, 1985, 1. See page 18 for transcript.
[56] John G. Tower et al., *Report of the President's Special Review Board: February 26, 1987* (Washington, D.C.: GPO, 1987), B-13.
[57] Wills, *First War on Terrorism*, 110.

Reagan thought this was a promising step and wanted to call Berri and encourage him to release the hostages and then "work on the Israelis, but not as a quid pro quo." Shultz and McFarlane were concerned about an "unstructured call," and suggested a cable be sent first followed by a call. As for dealing with the Israelis, Shultz wanted nothing "in writing" that could be interpreted as collusion in brokering a deal.[58]

Meanwhile, this promising movement was obscured by what one of the passengers, Peter Hill, called a "bloody circus." First, on Wednesday, Hezbollah brought several reporters and TV cameramen to the plane for a "news conference" with the captain and crew. Responding to questions, they all assured the press that they were being treated fairly and warned against any rescue attempt.[59] The following evening there was a press conference with five of the passengers brought in from town, which, was terminated early when a scuffle broke out between some two hundred reporters and the gunmen. They also pleaded that no rescue attempt be made.[60]

On Thursday, the administration settled on its nothing- in-writing approach. *New York Times* reporter, Bernard Gwertzman, quoting unidentified sources, said that Israel had agreed to release all Shiite prisoners to the Red Cross "within a few hours" of the release of the forty passengers, but Berri was reportedly insisting that there be a "simultaneous" transfer.[61] Shultz was concerned that the Israelis would misread this report, which, he said, was untrue. Pleading innocence, he admitted they may have believed that "we had deliberately leaked this news...to send a signal to, or pressure, them."[62]

Whether it had been a deliberate leak, or not, the press report had the desired effect. The day before Shultz had put a question to Peres, asking what precisely Israel would do with the Atlit prisoners, if "there

---

[58] Ibid, 114.
[59] Testrake, *Triumph Over Terror*, 131-33.
[60] "Hostages, at Beirut News Session Beseech U.S. Not to Try a Rescue," *New York Times*, June 21, 1985, 1.
[61] Bernard Gwertzman, "U.S. Warns Shiites About Becoming Global 'Outcasts,'" *New York Times*, June 20, 1985, 1.
[62] Shultz, *Turmoil and Triumph*, 660.

were no TWA-847 hostages being held?" This, of course, was merely a clumsy way of asking the Israelis what they would do *after* the TWA passengers had been released. Still in disarray, with Shamir objecting to any cooperation, the Israelis stalled.

After the Gwertzman article appeared, Shultz repeated the question. Peres answered early on June 21, his reply now endorsed by Shamir and Rabin. In the absence of the hijacking, he said, Israel would have proceeded with the release of the detainees depending on developments. In view of the hijacking, "we are not inclined to do this in a way that would appear to give in to the terrorists." In any case, detainees could appeal to a board headed by a district judge. One appeal already resulted in a decision to release 31 detainees the following week.[63]

Although Shultz interpreted this as a "complex and indefinite response," he had achieved the purpose of unifying the fractious Israeli government behind the position of releasing detainees piecemeal once the passengers had been released. Moreover, the question of who the detainees were came into focus. The Israeli defense ministry announced that "of the 766 detainees still in Atlit, 570 are Shiite Moslems, 147 are Palestinians and 49 others are Druze, Christians, and Sunni Moslems."[64] Algerian negotiators "could not imagine that the Shiites would knowingly seek to secure the release of Palestinians."[65]

Word came from Ambassador Reggie Bartholomew in Beirut that Berri was having some success in persuading the hijackers to give up, except for an "inner group of terrorists...not under anyone's control, not Iran's and not Hezbollah's." Shultz correctly surmised that they were "related by family to the Dawa prisoners held by Kuwait," but did not know by whom they were led. Later, when the FBI examined the plane, Mugniyeh's fingerprint was found in the toilet, enabling analysts to establish that it had been Mugniyeh and his small band that

---

[63] Shultz, *Turmoil and Triumph*, 661.
[64] Thomas Friedman, "Israel To Release 31 Prisoners Seized In Lebanon," *New York Times*, June 24, 1985, 1.
[65] Shultz, *Turmoil and Triumph*, 663.

was "not under anyone's control."[66] At least, not Iran's nor Hezbollah's.[67] The question would become: who had leverage over the group. That very morning Mugniyeh, in a mask, had mobilized several hundred Hezbollah demonstrators at the airport shouting "death to America" and "death to Reagan," to demonstrate his defiance.[68]

Tension Increases—Worldwide

Two days after he had said he would "wait it out," the president reversed position, declaring, "our limits have been reached." The evening before, in San Salvador, two gunmen dressed in Salvadoran army uniforms had opened fire on a crowd at an outdoor cafe, killing thirteen people, including six U.S. Marines, whom they apparently had "sought out." The gunmen were believed to be from the Farabundo Marti National Liberation Front that has been battling the government for the past five years. The president's shift seemed to be directed at "diminishing political fallout" from the Beirut hostage crisis as well as from the Salvadoran killings.[69]

Additional terrorist attacks occurring over the next couple of days suggested a global pattern. In Chile, terrorist bomb attacks on three electrical towers knocked out power in the grid feeding electricity to the capital, Santiago, a city of four million people. At Frankfurt International Airport, West Europe's busiest, unidentified terrorists set

---

[66] Bergman, *Secret War With Iran*, 101.
[67] Shultz, *Turmoil and Triumph*, 662. Actually, three days earlier a U.S. Navy source in the Middle East said, "there is also...some evidence that the identities of the original pair of Lebanese Shiite hijackers...is now known to U.S. authorities." Michael Getler, "Smaller Group Said to Include Military Persons," *Washington Post*, June 21, 1985, 1.
[68] Wills, *First War on Terrorism*, 116.
[69] Robert Merry, "Reagan Vows Determination on Terrorism," *Wall Street Journal*, June 21, 1985, 31 and Robert McCartney, "Gunmen Seen Singling Out U.S. Marines," *Washington Post*, June 21, 1985, 1.

off a bomb near the ticket counters of Iranian, Spanish, and Greek air carriers. Three people were killed and over 40 injured.[70]

Worst of all, on Sunday June 23, two terrorist bombings of aircraft pushed the Reagan administration to its limit. An Air India flight from Toronto to New Delhi, after refueling in London blew up over the Atlantic near Ireland scattering debris over a five-mile radius of ocean. Three hundred and twenty-nine persons perished, with no survivors. At the same time a Canadian Pacific flight from Vancouver to Tokyo made a successful flight, but a bomb exploded in baggage from the plane after it landed at Tokyo International airport. Two baggage-handlers were killed and four injured. Had the bomb detonated in flight the carnage would have resembled the Air India attack.

Baggage on the flights came from Toronto and Vancouver, cities with sizable Indian communities and "baggage originating in both those cities had been on both planes." The Canadian Pacific flight had left Vancouver after taking on connecting passengers from Toronto and passengers boarding the Air-India flight in Toronto included twenty-nine connecting passengers from Vancouver.[71]

To those in the administration following these events it was difficult not to recall CIA deputy director Herb Meyer's warning months earlier that the "current outbreak of violence is more than coincidence....I believe it signals the beginning of a new stage in the global struggle between the Free World and the Soviet Union....What we are seeing now is a Soviet-led effort to fight back, in the same sense that the Mafia fights back when law enforcement agencies launch an effective crime-busting program."[72]

---

[70] "Chile: Bombings Leave Capital in the Dark," *USA Today*, June 21, 1985, 4 and "Frankfurt Terminal Bomb Kills 3, Leaves Dozens Hurt," *Washington Times*, June 20, 1985, 10.

[71] "Air-India Crash Kills 329," *Baltimore Sun*, June 24, 1985, 1.

[72] Herbert Meyer, "Why Is the World So Dangerous?" memorandum to the Director of Central Intelligence, November 30, 1983 (Washington, D.C. 1983). http://www.foia.cia.gov/sites/default/files/document_conversions/89801/DOC_0000028820.pdf

The Key Players Convene

Meanwhile, as the Israelis were releasing thirty-one of the Arab prisoners from Atlit, generating objections from Berri that that was not enough, American intelligence was tracking the movements of the relevant players in the TWA-847 crisis.[73] Rafsanjani had traveled to Tripoli on June 21 for a three-day stay with Qadaffi and Hafez Assad had returned from his visit to Gorbachev in Moscow in time to receive Rafsanjani in Damascus on June 24. There was a strong presumption that the conversations in Tripoli, Damascus, and Moscow would be decisive. Indeed, gathering in Damascus were not only Rafsanjani and Assad, but also Sheik Fadlallah and Nabih Berri.

While Rafsanjani was still in Tripoli, on June 22, Shultz sent a message to Assad. The U.S. government, he said, understood the domestic constraints under which Berri operated and the limits of his influence with Hezbollah, but urged that Assad support him "in moving to release the passengers and crew." It was "the continued detention of passengers, crew and aircraft [that] constitutes a specific impediment to Israel's publicly-expressed policy to release the Atlit prisoners." Then, he said, disclosing his knowledge that Rafsanjani "may soon visit Damascus,"

> We believe that it would be useful... [to] urge your Iranian visitors to use their influence with those groups in Lebanon and which Iran is in contact to urge not only the release of the passengers and crew of TWA-847, but also the release of the American, British, and French kidnap victims—some of whom have now been in captivity for more than a year.[74]

Assuming that Iran's influence with Hezbollah would be decisive in gaining the release of the passengers, the secretary also sought to enlist Assad's support in pressuring Iran to gain the release of the

---

[73] Edward Walsh, "31 Arabs Are Freed By Israel," *Washington Post*, June 25, 1985, 1.
[74] As cited in Wills, *First War on Terrorism*, 118.

seven hostages it was holding in Lebanon. He only achieved part of his objective, because Hezbollah did not control the seven hostages; Mugniyeh's Islamic Jihad did.

When Rafsanjani ended his visit with Assad, he publicly denied Iran's responsibility for the hijacking in unmistakable terms, but was silent on the seven hostages. Referring to the hijacking, Rafsanjani said: "had [Iran] known in advance about this kind of action, it would have acted to prevent it." The Iranian leader then met with Sheik Fadlallah, who was also in Damascus to take part in this meeting. It was, of course, Fadlallah who had influence with Mugniyeh, who not only controlled the seven hostages, but also four of the passengers. Berri controlled the rest. Sensing that the meeting of the main figures involved in this matter would be decisive, the Reagan administration imposed a news blackout in Washington, "a sure sign," according to Martin and Walcott, "that the posturing had ended and the dealing had begun."[75]

Assad had hosted this meeting, no doubt on advice received from Gorbachev, with whom he had spent the previous few days. Assad had control over Beirut and northern Lebanon, by virtue of the extension of Syrian political/military presence and through his agent Nabih Berri, but under his umbrella operated other terrorist groups, such as Hezbollah and Islamic Jihad, that were not under his control. That was where Sheik Fadlallah and Rafsanjani came in. Rafsanjani held sway over Hezbollah, but not Islamic Jihad. If anyone held any influence over Islamic Jihad and its leader, Imad Mugniyeh, it was Sheik Fadlallah, which gave significance to Rafsanjani's meeting with the cleric.

Curiously, there was a major absence in the gathering. If American intelligence was correct in identifying Muamar Qadaffi as the facilitator, if not instigator, of the hijacking, his absence from the gathering in Damascus suggested that the others were not cooperating with him and were prepared to settle. The willingness of the hijackers to release the Greek passengers aboard the plane suggested the Qadaffi-Papandreou tie and added another point to the thesis that the Libyan dictator was the perpetrator.

---

[75] Martin and Walcott, *Best Laid Plans*, 196 and Wills, *First War on Terrorism*, 120.

Qadaffi himself appeared to throw a monkey wrench into the gathering in Damascus. After Rafsanjani left Tripoli, Libyan state radio declared that Libya and Iran had announced plans to "promote 'Islamic revolution' on a worldwide scale and to form an army to 'liberate Palestine.'" Qadaffi's number two, Abdel Salam Jalloud, appeared to level a direct challenge to Syria's dominance in Lebanon, saying "Libya and Iran have decided to work together in order to reunite the Moslem and Palestinian forces in Lebanon."[76]

This was clearly an attempt by Qadaffi to create bad blood between Rafsanjani and Assad. He knew, as did everyone else, that at this moment, in Lebanon, Syrian-supported Shiites were attempting to destroy Arafat's PLO in the battle for control of Beirut. Their reconciliation was hardly imminent, or likely. Moreover, Assad had "given ample evidence" that he would not "tolerate intervention in Lebanon by any foreign state, be it Arab, or non-Arab."[77] Furthermore, Rafsanjani's public remark that Iran would have "prevented" the hijacking had Tehran known about it in advance made plain that neither he, nor Assad was working with Libya. Qadaffi's ploy had failed.

End Games

The unfolding of events is much more clear-cut in retrospect than at the time. Still, the question was: did the Reagan leadership realize that Assad and Rafsanjani had combined to resolve the crisis and put on a display of resolve of its own to demonstrate to the public that it had determined the outcome? Or, were they still uncertain that the crisis was coming to an end and resolved to give it a push?

Whatever the truth of the matter, and the timing is unclear, after the NSPG meeting of June 25, the president divulged that he had decided on a series of ever-escalating steps that he hoped would force

---

[76] "Libya and Iran Pledge to 'Liberate Palestine,'" *Wall Street Journal*, June 25, 1985, 34.
[77] Ibid.

a resolution of the crisis.[78] White House Spokesman Larry Speakes announced that if diplomatic efforts were not successful in freeing the passengers "within the next few days," the president was considering using military and economic means to shut down Beirut airport and blockade Lebanon.

The president, it was said, was hopeful the crisis would be resolved soon, but becoming concerned that the hijacking stalemate was beginning to resemble the Iranian hostage crisis. Although public opinion was still strongly behind the president, there was also growing sentiment that he should "do something." Thus, his decision seemed to be saying to Assad, in particular, "now is the time to act or be tagged with some of the blame and some of the consequences if you fail to do so."[79]

Raising the ante succeeded. The Israelis responded first through a back channel Shultz had set up with Benjamin Netanyahu, Israel's ambassador to the United Nations. Peres sent word to Reagan that a public request was no longer necessary. Israel would do "whatever the United States wanted." Peres' shift opened the door for an exchange of letters formalizing what came to be known as the "no deal deal," the agreement for Israel to release the Atlit detainees as soon as the TWA passengers were released.[80]

Berri responded the next day, June 26. After freeing one of the passengers for medical reasons, he offered to transfer the remaining thirty-nine to either the French or Swiss embassies in Beirut, or to Damascus, to be held "in escrow" until the Atlit detainees were released. But he also demanded that the United States remove all of its ships from the vicinity of Lebanon and pledge not to attack Lebanon once the passengers were released.[81] The president dismissed the escrow idea, as did the Swiss and French, who wanted no part of it. He

---

[78] Don Oberdorfer, "Reagan's Shift Risks Forcing His Hand If Deadline Passes," *Washington Post*, June 26, 1985, 17.
[79] Ibid. See also Lou Cannon and John Goshko, "U.S. Weighs Blockading Lebanon, Airport Boycott," *Washington Post*, June 26, 1985, 1.
[80] Martin and Walcott, *Best Laid Plans*, 197-98.
[81] Bernard Gwertzman, "U.S. Weighing Shiite Offer on Moving Hostages," *New York Times*, June 27, 1985, 1.

also rejected the demand to remove U.S. ships, which were in international waters, but felt that the state department should be prepared to respond positively to the no-retaliation demand, which would not be inconsistent with declared policy toward Lebanon. Shultz, however, procrastinated in issuing a statement.

Assad also responded, sending a message to Reagan affirming that progress was being made. Attempting to insinuate himself into Israeli politics, positing an explicit quid-pro-quo, he asked: "what if the hijackers were informed that Syria would guarantee the release of the Lebanese prisoners after the TWA passengers were freed?" Shultz, in his response to Assad, insisted that there was no connection between the two: "Syria may be confident in expecting the release of the Lebanese prisoners after the freeing of the passengers of TWA-847, without any linkage between the two subjects."[82]

The secretary believed that this was the "moment" when a resolution of the crisis became "imminent." Indeed, he, the president, and vice-president, all sought to parley the imminent resolution of the TWA crisis into the release of the seven hostages held by Mugniyeh and Islamic Jihad, demanding publicly that they be included with the passengers. It was a long shot, but it played well with the families of the hostages who throughout had pressed the president in public appearances and newspaper ads to take action on behalf of their loved ones.

It was also a long shot because American leaders were still uncertain "whether Islamic Jihad exist[ed] as a coherent organization, or is merely a shadowy coalition of extremist Shiites loosely affiliated with Iran....[whose] radicalism contrasts with the more moderate policies of Mr. Berri's Amal faction." They "assume that the captors of the seven, or of some of them, are at least tolerated by Syria, which also is loosely allied with Iran."[83] Nevertheless, the president was not willing to press this demand to the point of fouling resolution of the TWA crisis.

---

[82] Shultz, *Turmoil and Triumph*, 664.
[83] Henry Trewhitt, "U.S. Says 7 Seized Earlier Must be Released as Well," *Baltimore Sun*, June 28, 1985, 1.

At this delicate moment, Muamar Qadaffi deftly tossed yet another political hand grenade into the mix, which held the potential at the very most to blow apart a solution to the crisis at the last moment and at the very least to undercut and embarrass Hafez Assad. But the grenade was lobbed from an unexpected quarter—from Malta by Qadaffi's new ally, the Prime Minister of Malta, Carmelo Bonnici. Qadaffi and Bonnici had signed a treaty of "friendship and cooperation" the previous November, effectively incorporating Malta into the Soviet-Libyan scheme.[84]

Thus, on June 28 an "unsolicited offer of assistance" came from a senior Maltese official to Ambassador James Rentschler. The Maltese official offered to contact and persuade Berri to send the passengers to Israel. Then, they could appeal to the Israelis for their release and the release of the detainees, an appeal which Israel could hardly refuse coming from Americans who had suffered seventeen days of captivity.[85]

Rentschler had "no cause to question" the official's motive and thought the offer "well meaning, but greatly muddled." Unfortunately, it was more than that. If adopted, this "Maltese option" would have cut Assad out completely, required the unlikely cooperation between Amal and Israel, turned Berri against Assad, disrupted U.S. cooperation with Syria, and Syrian cooperation with Iran. Coming at the very moment that Assad and Rafsanjani were putting the final touches on a settlement, switching to the Maltese option would have been a very bad mistake, and the U.S. government wisely avoided this trap.[86]

By June 29, after Reagan had telephoned Assad to reiterate his previous assurance than Israel would release the Lebanon detainees once all of the hostages were released, everything seemed to be in order. Passengers were assembled for transport from Beirut to

---

[84] "The Libyan-Maltese Alliance," Joseph Churba, ed., *Focus On Libya: February 1984 to June 1989* (Washington, D.C.: Pemcon publishers, 1989), 89-92.
[85] Wills, *First War on Terrorism*, 130.
[86] Shultz, *Turmoil and Triumph*, 665, refers implicitly to this episode in noting that many "diplomatic volunteers," had suddenly "emerged from all over the landscape, offering to get involved in 'the release.'"

Damascus, while the Pentagon dispatched a C-141 transport plane to Damascus. At the last minute, however, it was discovered that the four hostages being held (we now know) by Mugniyeh as insurance, were not among the passengers.

Mugniyeh insisted that the United States issue to Syria a public guarantee that there would be no retaliation. Without it, the crisis would drag on indefinitely. McFarlane thought that this was more an attempt to make Berri look bad than a genuine fear of an American attack. In any case, it was agreed, "a restatement of the administration's formal policy concerning the sovereignty of Lebanon would be accepted by Hezbollah as a non-retaliation pledge."[87] A statement was promptly issued.

Assad, however, also sought to squeeze the lemon. He wanted Israel to transfer the Atlit detainees to Syria and not simply release them into Lebanon. But Shultz maintained that the passengers and detainees were separate issues and that the detainee matter would have to be discussed after the passengers were released. Assad's ploy may have been intended to disguise the fact that he could not produce the four still being held by Mugniyeh and Shultz's response implied an absence of leverage over Israel.

At this point, McFarlane claimed he instructed Ollie North to contact Rafsanjani—reportedly through Manuchur Gorbanifar—to obtain his assistance in gaining the release of the last four passengers. Although Ledeen relates the story of Ghorbanifar's participation, the timing of North's involvement in the opening to Iran seems premature.[88] In any case, it is not clear that Rafsanjani was able to exert leverage on Mugniyeh, but Assad was.

Humiliated by the failure to finalize the arrangements to which he had agreed, Assad took action. After meeting with representatives from Iran and Hezbollah, he contacted the Iranian Revolutionary Guards Headquarters in Baalbeck. To them he issued an ultimatum: "release the hostages or get out of Lebanon" and sent his chief

---

[87] Wills, *First War on Terrorism*, 132.
[88] Michael Ledeen, *Perilous Statecraft: An Insider's Account of the Iran Contra Affair* (New York: Scribner, 1988), 114.

intelligence officer for Lebanese affairs, Brig. Gen. Ghazi Caanan, to ensure compliance.[89]

The four remaining passengers were released at just after noon on June 30 and the entire group set out in a Red Cross convoy for Damascus an hour later. Their ordeal was over. Reagan sent a cordial note of thanks to Rafsanjani, but what was to have been a similarly cordial telephone call to Assad turned out badly. The president harangued the Syrian leader mercilessly, repeatedly condemning Syrian policies and demanding that Assad bring the hijackers to justice and produce the seven hostages. Vice-President Bush, appalled at Reagan's outburst, sent his own note of thanks to Assad in an attempt to repair the damage of the president's intemperate remarks.[90]

Aftermath

That evening, President Reagan addressed the American people on national television to announce that the 39 passengers were at last free. The president demanded justice and declared that the United States would not rest "until the world community meets its responsibility." And trying one last time to pry the seven hostages from Hezbollah's grip, he called upon "those who helped secure the release of these TWA passengers to show even greater energy and commitment to secure the release of all others held capture in Lebanon." Finally, he put the terrorists on notice, declaring "we will fight back against you in Lebanon and elsewhere."[91]

In remarks to reporters, White House officials then loudly, and brazenly, denied there had been any "deal" with the Israelis. "They had made no deals with Israel to free the Lebanese prisoners it holds." An administration official, evidently Secretary Shultz, declared "at no

---

[89] Wills, *First War on Terrorism*, 132, and 249-50, n.155. Martin and Walcott, *Best Laid Plans*, 200, say the threat was to "get out of the Bekaa Valley."
[90] Ibid., 202, and Lou Cannon, *President Reagan: The Role of a Lifetime* (New York: Simon & Shuster, 1991), 607.
[91] David Hoffman, "39 U.S. Hostages Freed After 17-Day Ordeal; Reagan Vows to 'Fight Back' at Terrorism," *Washington Post*, July 1, 1985, 1.

time, from the first day to the last, did we ever urge, cajole, suggest directly or indirectly by any U.S. official to my knowledge, absolutely never any hint of it from the president, that [the Israelis] alter their policy about no concessions, or, in this case, no releases, at any point..."[92]

There could be only one reason administration officials adopted this patently false position. They must have obtained secure knowledge that Israel was not going to carry through on its commitment to release promptly the 766 detainees held in Atlit prison. Denying the existence of any deals meant that the United States could not be held responsible for, or forced to exert pressure on, Israel's subsequent actions.

On July 3, Israel released only three hundred detainees from Atlit. As for the remaining four hundred and sixty-six, Defense Minister Rabin said they would be "released in accordance with developments in South Lebanon." No date was mentioned. In fact, it would not be until September 10, ten more weeks, that the remaining four hundred and sixty-six would all, finally be released.[93]

If Israel reneged on the promise to release all 766 detainees upon the release of the TWA passengers, the United States, too, reneged on its pledge not to retaliate against Lebanon. On July 2, President Reagan issued orders for the government to "put Beirut International Airport out of action." Washington terminated the once-a-week flight between Beirut and Washington by Lebanon's Middle East Airlines as well as flights by U.S. and Lebanese cargo carriers to Beirut, and was attempting to influence other countries to do the same.[94]

There was an immediate outcry from Lebanon against the U.S. government's actions. Lebanon's Prime Minister, Rashid Karami lodged a formal protest. Finance Minister Camille Chamoun called upon Washington to "reconsider the measure and not carry it out."

---

[92] Ibid.
[93] Shultz, *Turmoil and Triumph*, 667 and "Release of Captives by Israel Set for Today in Border Zone," *New York Times*, July 3, 1985, 14. Some accounts put the number of detainees at 735.
[94] Nora Boustany, "Lebanese Criticize America," *Washington Post*, July 3, 1985, 14.

Amal leader Nabih Berri bemoaned the fact that the Americans had broken their promise that there would be no reprisals. Islamic Jihad issued a statement proclaiming a great victory over the United States, but also its intent to create a "nightmare" for America, striking at its interests "in the region and throughout the world."[95]

Behind the scenes at this time, the president made three key decisions. First, culminating four months of negotiations, was the press release issued on June 29 announcing that President Reagan and Mikhail Gorbachev had decided to meet in the fall.[96] A few days later it was disclosed that they would meet in Geneva, Switzerland, November 19-21. Their meeting would not be the "well-prepared summit" that Reagan had insisted upon all during the first term, but the two leaders would "do more than just get acquainted and shake hands."[97] The timing of the announcement seemed to indicate some connection to the just concluded TWA crisis.

Officials declined to discuss an agenda, though likely topics were arms control and trade relations. Reagan was understood to be interested in "sitting down with the Soviet leader without prenegotiated agreements to sign," although expectations for direct results were "quite low." The view from the state department, however, was decidedly more upbeat. A spokesman said, "we believe we can and should solve all outstanding problems in the agenda before us."[98]

Despite his decision to meet with Gorbachev, however, the president took the opportunity of the TWA settlement to point once again to the "close relationship" the Soviets had to terrorist states. In a speech at the Annual Convention of the American Bar Association on July 8, he urged his audience to "look beyond" the spate of recent terrorist acts and "not allow them—as terrible as they are—to obscure

---

[95] Richard Beeston, "Shi'ites Warn More Anti-U.S. Blows Coming," *Washington Times*, July 3, 1985, 1.
[96] John Wallach, "Gorbachev and Reagan Agree on Fall Talks," *Baltimore Sun*, June 29, 1985, 1.
[97] Gary Lee, "Reagan-Gorbachev Meeting Set for Nov. 19-21 in Geneva," *Washington Post*, July 3, 1985, 1.
[98] Ibid.

an even larger and darker terrorist menace." We must avoid the temptation "to see the terrorist act as simply the erratic work of a small group of fanatics." The terrorist attacks of the past few years, he said, "form a pattern of terrorism that has strategic implications and political goals. And only by moving our focus from the tactical to the strategic perspective, only by identifying the pattern of terror and those behind it, can we hope to put into force a strategy to deal with it."

The president noted the alarming increasing trend of terrorist acts against the United States and its allies. From some five hundred in 1983, "to over 600" in 1984, and "at the current rate, as many as 1,000 acts of terrorism will occur in 1985." The Middle East has been one principal point of focus for these attacks; Western Europe and NATO another.

The president singled out Iran and Libya as supporting "state-approved assassination and terrorism," then added three more states—North Korea, Cuba, and Nicaragua—that were also "actively supporting a campaign of international terrorism against the United States, her allies, and moderate Third World states." These states were not the only ones that support international terrorism, "they are simply the ones that can be most directly implicated." This terrorism, he averred, was "part of a pattern, the work of a confederation of terrorist states." Those involved were being "trained, financed, and directly or indirectly controlled by a core group of radical and totalitarian governments—a new, international version of Murder, Incorporated."

"We can be clear on one point," Reagan stated. "These terrorist states are now engaged in acts of war against the Government and people of the United States. And under international law, any state which is the victim of acts of war has the right to defend itself."

Then, toward the end of his speech, the president focused on the Soviet Union. "The question of the Soviet Union's close relationship with almost all of the terrorist states that I have mentioned and the implications of these Soviet ties on bilateral relations with the United States and other democratic nations must be recognized." During the recent hostage crisis, the Soviet government "suggested that the United States was not sincerely concerned about this crisis, but that we were, instead, in the grip of—and I use the Soviets' word here—'hysteria.'"

The Soviets also charged that the United States was simply looking for a "pretext" to invade Lebanon. There was, he concluded, a non-Soviet word for "that kind of talk...an extremely useful, time-tested original American word, one with deep roots in our rich agricultural and farming tradition." [Laughter][99]

Press coverage of the president's speech noted the conspicuous absence of Syria from the president's list of state-supporters of terrorism, suggesting "Mr. Reagan seemed to be noting the role of Syrian President Hafez Assad in helping to free the TWA hostages." But two accounts, in particular, in the *Wall Street Journal* and the *New York Times*, also curiously omitted one of the president's most important points: the relationship of the Soviet Union to these terrorist states.[100]

Reconstruction of Events

At the outset of the crisis the administration had assumed that Syria and Iran sponsored the hijack and Hezbollah carried it out. But as evidence accumulated, it became clear that a quite different interpretation fitted the facts, one more consistent with the prevailing strategic context. It had been Moscow and Qadaffi, not Syria and Iran that were the sponsors of the hijacking, and Imad Mugniyeh, not Hezbollah, who was the perpetrator. In fact, Hafez al-Assad of Syria and Ayatollah Rafsanjani of Iran had played critical roles in resolving the crisis both directly and through their surrogates in Lebanon, Amal and Hezbollah.

The Soviets hoped to use the hijack to erect a barrier to U.S.-Iran rapprochement. They enlisted Qadaffi in this scheme because it would also serve his interests. In NSDD-168, April 30, 1985, the Reagan administration had decided to contain Qadaffi by strengthening

---

[99] Ronald Reagan, "Remarks at the Annual Convention of the American Bar Association," July 8, 1985.

[100] See David Ignatius, "Reagan Warns 5 Nations of U.S. Right To Defend Itself Against Acts of Terror," *Wall Street Journal*, July 9, 1985, 3 and Bernard Weinraub, "President Accuses 5 'Outlaw States' Of World Terror," *New York Times*, July 9, 1985, 1.

relations with Libya's neighbors. Improving relations with Algeria was the centerpiece of this strategy.[101] In flying the hijacked plane to Algiers, Qadaffi hoped to disrupt U.S. efforts to improve relations with that country.

To execute the hijacking, Qadaffi enlisted arch terrorist, Imad Mugniyeh, who also had an interest. Not only had Mugniyeh been on a terrorist rampage, his brother-in-law, Mustafa Badredienne, was one of the Dawa 17 imprisoned by Kuwait for terrorist acts against American and French embassies in November 1983. Indeed, his younger brother had been killed in a U.S.-sponsored, Lebanese government attempt to kill Sheik Fadlallah in March of 1985. So, for reasons of revenge and the possibility of gaining the freedom of his brother-in-law, Mugniyeh accepted this contract.[102]

Ironically, the hijacking had the opposite effect from that desired by the Russians and Qadaffi. Reagan had decided to strike at Qadaffi and proceed with an opening to Iran. The ongoing political struggle between the president and the new world order faction would greatly affect the way both of these decisions would be executed in the months ahead, but the president's general course had now been set. It is first to the question of the opening to Iran that we now turn.

---

[101] "U.S. Policy Toward North Africa", *NSDD 168,* April 30, 1985, in Christopher Simpson, *National Security Directives of the Reagan & Bush Administrations* (Boulder: Westview, 1995), 528-32.
[102] See Bergman, *Secret War With Iran,* 72-74, for a full account of Mugniyeh's activities.

Chapter 4
Shultz and McFarlane Seize Control

The TWA crisis in June 1985 offered a positive way forward toward an opening to Iran for the president. Reagan had made contact with and thanked Rafsanjani for his assistance in resolving the crisis, opening a direct channel of communication to Tehran. At the same time, during the crisis, CIA Director Casey had developed what appeared to be two direct channels of access to the Iranians. It was also increasingly clear that the Iranian leadership sought contact, as it was in desperate need to acquire American weapons to counter the growing strike power of Soviet-supplied Iraq.

The prospect of an imminent opening of direct contact with Iran caused alarm within the new world order faction, whose leaders, Secretary Shultz and NSC adviser McFarlane, moved quickly to take control. This same prospect greatly concerned Israeli Prime Minister Peres, who feared that Israel would be cut out of the action and denied the opportunity of lucrative arms sales. The result was the evolution of a surprising, but temporary coincidence of interests between the new world order faction and Peres.

Shultz and McFarlane realized they could use Israel to preempt Reagan, based on the Israelis' desire for arms sales to Iran, cut out Casey in the process, seize control of the gambit themselves, and derail it. For the new world order faction, however, the coincidence with Peres would be a temporary expedient, lasting only until the objective of derailing the opening to Iran was accomplished.

The Israeli leadership understood fully that American and Israeli interests did not coincide in all respects and that their role in American policy was limited. The Israelis sensed the discord within the Reagan leadership and sought repeatedly to ascertain whether the decision to approve Israeli arms sales was an agreed position within the administration. As a matter of insurance, they sought to draw the United States government more deeply into the arms sales venture, which only added to the complexity and consequences for all concerned.

Cutting Casey Out

Shultz's and McFarlane's first tasks were to close off the initiatives Casey had developed, which had reached a promising point by the middle of June coincident with the outbreak of the TWA crisis.[1] Casey's efforts had produced two avenues of direct contacts to Tehran. The first was through Cyrus Hashemi to deputy Prime Minister Mohsen Kangarlu, and the second was through Adnan Khashoggi to Ayatollah Hassan Karoubi. Both contacts, ironically, involved the

---

[1] George Shultz, *Turmoil and Triumph* (New York: Macmillan, 1993), 793, claims that his knowledge of the Iran affair "amounted to a series of isolated fleeting moments," information that was "fragmentary at best and perhaps was not even representative of what had in fact happened." However, Lawrence Walsh, the independent counsel came to a much different conclusion. According to Walsh, *Final Report of the Independent Counsel for Iran-Contra Matters*, (Washington, D.C.: United States Court of Appeals for the District of Columbia Circuit, August 4, 1993), 325-26, contrary to their public testimonies, Shultz and McFarlane were in close contact throughout 1985 and 1986. Inside the State Department, Shultz and eight of his top aides had "significant contemporaneous knowledge" of the Iran initiative. Shultz, Deputy Secretary John Whitehead and Under Secretary Michael Armacost "met daily to keep each other informed." Executive Secretary Nicholas Platt and Shultz's assistant Charles Hill kept a "detailed handwritten record" of the secretary's activities. Assistant Secretary Richard Murphy, Deputy Assistant Secretary Arnold Raphel, and Ambassador Robert Oakley were referred to as the "floating directorate," that kept track of "U.S. and Israeli contacts with Iranians and arms shipments to Iran during 1985 and 1986." Shultz misrepresented his "contemporaneous knowledge" of events to the Tower Board, the Senate-House investigators, and in his memoirs. It was only five years later that Walsh and his team unearthed the data of Shultz's and McFarlane's close monitoring of events.

essential participation of Gorbanifar; indeed, it was the case that all avenues to Tehran passed through him.

Shultz and his CIA allies quietly sank the Hashemi opening in a bureaucratic haze. After Khashoggi and the Israelis had dropped Hashemi in early April (see chapter 2), he sought to join up with Gorbanifar and approach Casey on his own. Thus, in mid-June, acting through John Shaheen, a friend of Casey's, Hashemi offered to set up a meeting with "a high-ranking Iranian official" in Western Europe.

After bringing American and Iranian officials together, Hashemi hoped to arrange the purchase of *TOW* missiles for Iran, facilitate the release of the Dawa prisoners in Kuwait, the hostages in Lebanon, and, in return for all this, obtain a nullification of the charges against him as a result of his entrapment in an FBI sting the previous year. Although Shaheen whittled down the proposal he sent to Casey to simply arranging a meeting with a high-ranking Iranian official, he obviously had informed the director of Hashemi's larger agenda because Casey's report of June 17 to the CIA's Near East Division Chief carried the subject heading: "release of the hostages."[2]

The Near East Chief passed on Casey's memo to Under Secretary Richard Murphy at the State Department on June 22 with the notation that Casey was "very anxious to move ahead" on a meeting with the Iranian official, with no mention of hostages, or arms sales. Murphy's memo to Under Secretary Michael Armacost carried the subject heading: "Possible Iranian Contact." Armacost approved a plan for a meeting two days later.[3]

In "early July," however, when Hashemi identified the participants in the proposed meeting as Deputy Prime Minister Mohsen Kangarlu, referred to as the "second Iranian," and Manuchur Gorbanifar, the CIA balked. Willing to meet with Kangarlu, the agency refused to "do

---

[2] "Casey memo 6/17/85 to CIA Chief of the Near East Division, Subj: Release of the Hostages, C-8965-66," *Report of the Congressional Committees Investigating the Iran-Contra Affair* (Washington, D.C.: GPO, 1987), 171 [Cited hereafter as *Iran-Contra Affair*.]
[3] Ibid, "Richard Murphy memo, 6/22/85, to Armacost. Subj: Possible Iranian Contact, S-3812-13."

business" with Gorbanifar, the deemed "fabricator." Although some effort was made to arrange a meeting with Kangarlu, it led nowhere.[4] It is apparent that, despite Casey's expressed desire to "move ahead" on this contact, highly placed leaders at the CIA and the State Department blocked a meeting with the deputy prime minister of Iran on the grounds that his interlocutor was an undesirable character.[5]

Meanwhile, at about the same time that the new world order faction was sinking the Hashemi approach, Shultz took on the task of torpedoing the draft NSDD on Iran. On June 29, just as the TWA crisis was being resolved with Rafsanjani's crucial and timely assistance, the secretary sent in his "comments" on the draft NSDD. Couched in a pseudo-academic, almost professorial tone, Shultz thought the draft constructive and perceptive, but disagreed "with one point in the analysis and one specific recommendation." The secretary then proceeded to attack the proposed new policy in its entirety. He objected to the central policy recommendation that "Western friends and allies" provide arms to Iran and insisted that the arms ban remain in force. Even if the draft were revised to reflect this concern, he wanted "to see the draft again before it is put in final form."[6]

He also disputed the interpretation that the Soviets were "better positioned" than the United States to take advantage of a succession struggle. He thought that the "limits" on the Iranian-Soviet relationship were "underplayed," although "hints of possible improvements in Iranian-Soviet relations [were] worrisome." In his view, the "Soviets, while conscious of the strategic prize Iran constitutes, have other important regional relations and interests." His formulation was vague,

---

[4] CIA memos dated July 9, 15, and 23, on Shaheen, Hashemi, and a possible meeting with the "Second Iranian," indicate that the effort to arrange a meeting fizzled out by the end of July. *Iran-Contra Affair*, 171-72.

[5] William Rempel, "Iran Arms Dealers May Use Secret CIA Links as Defense," *Los Angeles Times*, August 4, 1988, 1.

[6] Shultz to McFarlane, "U.S. Policy Toward Iran: Comments on Draft NSDD," June 29, 1985, (declassified and released, July 21, 1987), John G. Tower et al., *Report of the President's Special Review Board: February 26, 1987* (Washington, D.C.: GPO, 1987), B-9.

but the implication was that the Soviets had other interests that took priority over Iran.

> The draft NSDD appears to exaggerate current anti-regime sentiment and Soviet advantages over us in gaining influence. Most importantly, its proposal that we permit or encourage a flow of Western arms to Iran is contrary to our interest both in containing Khomeinism and in ending the excesses of this regime. We should not alter this aspect of our policy when groups with ties to Iran are holding US hostages in Lebanon. I therefore disagree with the suggestion that our efforts to reduce arms flows to Iran should be ended.[7]

In these "comments" Shultz, for the first time in all of the discussions regarding an opening to Iran, raised the issue of "groups with ties to Iran...holding US hostages in Lebanon." This was an obvious reference to the last-minute glitch in the TWA hijack which Rafsanjani had assisted in resolving, but which had had no impact on gaining the release of the other seven American hostages still in captivity. In other words, Shultz sought by this reference to dismiss prospects of an opening to Iran.

His view of "our fundamental policy goal," however, was crystal clear. While claiming that the goal was to "wind down" the Iran-Iraq war, which meant stalemate, all understood that the Soviets were rapidly arming Iraq and that there was "a steady decline in Iran's military capability." The inevitable outcome of these trends was obvious—an Iraqi victory, a policy result Shultz had been supporting for over two years.

Shultz also ignored the obvious consequence of blocking arms shipments to Iran—that a successful embargo would force the Iranians into Moscow's arms, if only for self-protection. In short, the essence of Shultz's "comments" was to insist on a policy course that would only result in Iran's defeat and slide into the Soviet sphere—the very

---

[7] Ibid.

outcome that the NSDD warned against. Once again the issue was starkly strategic. Should the United States attempt to bring Iran back into the western camp, as the president desired, or back Iraq against Iran, as the new world order establishment demanded?

Shultz's opposition stymied the formal attempt to enact a change of policy toward Iran. From the hindsight of a quarter of a century, the judgment of history clearly is that this was a monumental strategic blunder; a blunder, moreover, based upon a terrible error in judgment that withdrawal from Iran (and other concessions) was a necessary condition for détente with the Soviet Union. Finally, it overlooked the fact that the Soviet Union was unable to match the qualitative surge in American military power then under way and was straining mightily to keep its very system intact.

Preempting Direct Contact By Cutting In the Israelis

By the end of June the Iranian regime was becoming increasingly desperate to acquire weapons from the United States to counter the growing Soviet-supplied Iraqi armed forces. The one-time, McFarlane authorized, Israeli shipment of American weapons in mid-May had led to nothing. Therefore, some time in the third week of June Ayatollah Khomeini agreed to a change in policy toward the United States, appointing a five-man committee to manage a new approach.[8]

Appointed to the committee were Rafsanjani, as chairman; members were Mir Hossein Moussavi, the prime minister; Rafiq Doust, minister in charge of the revolutionary guards; Mohsen Rezai, commander of the revolutionary guards; and Ahmed Khomeini, the Ayatollah's son. Mohsen Kangarlu, deputy prime minister and chief of intelligence, would be added soon afterward.

The Iranian decision was to authorize Gorbanifar to reach out to the Americans through their Israeli contacts, Kimche, Nimrodi and

---

[8] Samuel Segev, *The Iranian Triangle: The Untold Story of Israel's Role in the Iran-Contra Affair* (New York: Free Press, 1988), 147. See also, "The Ayatollah's Big Sting," U.S. News and World Report, March 30, 1987, 18-28, which places this meeting in January 1985.

Schwimmer, and Saudi middleman Khashoggi. Within days, on June 19, Gorbanifar met with them in Hamburg to propose the sale of one hundred *TOW*s, claiming that the sale would be followed by release of the American hostages.[9] His timing, however, could not have been worse, as Shultz and President Reagan repeatedly declared during the TWA hijacking– under way at that moment– that the United States would make no deals with terrorists.

For Iran, the hostages had served the purpose of drawing U.S. attention, but were now an obvious impediment. (They would become useful leverage again once negotiations/discussions began.) Hostage-taking was not all done by pro-Iranian terrorists as Shultz incessantly maintained. As we have seen, some, if not most, were taken by Imad Mugniyeh, who did contract work for a number of state sponsors, including Qadaffi and the Russians. It is not at all clear that the American leadership, or analysts in the intelligence agencies, understood the distinction between Hezbollah and Islamic Jihad at this point, or that Imad Mugniyeh was the terrorist responsible for the recent hijackings.[10] The plain fact was that Iran did not "control" Mugniyeh and therefore could not deliver the hostages.

In any case, the Iranians shifted their approach to get around the hostage impediment. As we have seen, Rafsanjani was instrumental in obtaining the release of the TWA passengers. Now, using the Gorbanifar-Israeli-Saudi channel, they proposed direct contact with the American leadership. The Iranian *démarche* came on July 1 in the form of a 47-page analysis of the internal Iranian political situation passed by Adnan Khashoggi to key interested leaders, including King Fahd of Saudi Arabia, King Hussein of Jordan, President Mubarak of Egypt, Prime Minister Peres of Israel, and McFarlane. In his cover letter to McFarlane, Khashoggi said the analysis had been written in

---

[9] *Iran-Contra Affair*, 166.
[10] According to Ronen Bergman, *The Secret War With Iran* (New York: Free Press, 2007), 96, Mugniyeh was an unfathomable mystery to Israeli intelligence, which could not determine where he "fit in," in the terrorist infrastructure of the Middle East.

part by "a single senior individual…in charge of Iranian intelligence in Western Europe."[11]

The detailed analysis described a leadership in turmoil, with three broad but fluid factions maneuvering to succeed Khomeini. None questioned the legitimacy of the regime, or sought to reverse the Islamic revolution. But so-called "moderates" led by Hassan Karoubi and "pragmatists" led by Ayatollah Rafsanjani were willing to cooperate with the West against the Soviet Union, as opposed to "extremists" led by President Ali Khamenei and Prime Minister Mir Hussein Moussavi, who insisted on uncompromising domestic policies, the exportation of the Islamic revolution, and, presumably, cooperation with the Soviets.[12]

Khashoggi's cover letter was an invitation to the United States, through pursuit of a "wise and flexible" policy, to attempt to influence the outcome of the struggle. Sensing an opportunity to affect how that could be done was the question and Prime Minister Peres moved quickly. Apparently alone among the four heads of state who received Khashoggi's packet, Peres immediately charged Kimche, who was traveling to Washington on foreign ministry business, to meet with McFarlane to offer a way forward.

Kimche met with McFarlane on July 3 and although McFarlane had the communication from Khashoggi in hand when they met there is no suggestion in the record that it was discussed. But, of course, it must have been discussed, as Iran was the purpose of Kimche's visit. Kimche said that "Israel had contacts with Iranians who had direct access to leading figures in Iran's political establishment and who had expressed a desire eventually to meet official American representatives on an unofficial basis." He claimed that McFarlane "enthusiastically

---

[11] Theodore Draper, *A Very Thin Line: The Iran-Contra Affairs* (New York: Hill and Wang, 1991), 152, believes this "senior individual" to have been Ghorbanifar, but it is not clear who he was. Gorbanifar was not, of course, "in charge of Iranian intelligence in Western Europe." Moreover, Draper's source, Khashoggi, in a cover letter to McFarlane, *Iran-Contra Affair*, Appendix B, volume 11, 190, does not identify the senior individual and says he is in contact with several Iranian officials.
[12] Segev, *Iranian Triangle*, 154-55.

encouraged us to continue these contacts," but warned that "in all probability," there would come a point where "we would be faced with a request for some American arms."[13]

McFarlane, as is the case on almost every issue, has provided contradictory accounts. To the Tower Board he reinforced Kimche's view, but added a point that Kimche omitted, namely that the Iranians believed that "they could influence the Hizballah in Lebanon to release the hostages" and wanted to know where to deliver them.[14] In his memoir, published last among all of the publications of those involved in the events, he went further. He claimed that Kimche intimated that if the U.S. agreed, the Israelis were willing to assassinate Khomeini and "accelerate matters" in the region. McFarlane claims to have rejected the suggestion out of hand. "We cannot engage with you in an enterprise in which anyone's purpose is to assassinate the Ayatollah."[15]

McFarlane recounts that he informed Reagan of his meeting with Kimche "a day or so" later and that the president was especially keen on the possibilities of opening up a dialogue with the Iranians. "Gosh, that's great news," he reportedly said. McFarlane claimed, however, there was "a precondition." In getting back to Kimche, McFarlane said that before "opening any dialogue...we would need evidence of their genuine power in the form of the release of all our hostages."[16] McFarlane's account thus connected an opening to Iran with release of the hostages, but not arms for hostages, and assumed that Iran could deliver the hostages.

---

[13] David Kimche, *The Last Option: After Nasser, Arafat & Saddam Hussein* (London: Weidenfeld and Nicolson, 1991), 211.
[14] John G. Tower et al., *Report of the President's Special Review Board: February 26, 1987* (Washington, D.C.: GPO, 1987), B-14.
[15] Robert C. McFarlane, *Special Trust* (New York: Cadell & Davies, 1994), 20-21. Kimche denied that he discussed a plot to kill Khomeini. See Walter Pincus, "Reagan Ex-Aide Details Start of Iran-Contra in Book," *Washington Post*, September 11, 1994, A11.
[16] McFarlane, *Special Trust*, 23-24.

There are reasons to doubt McFarlane's account of a conversation with Reagan "a day or so" after his meeting with Kimche, or at any time before he spoke to the president in the hospital on July 18 recovering from an operation on his colon. First, on July 8, in an address before the American Bar Association, the president pointedly singled out Iran and Libya as supporting "state-approved assassination and terrorism," which he considered to be "acts of war against the Government and people of the United States."[17] Surely, the possibility of a dialogue with Iran would have caused him to temper his statement, if McFarlane had just informed him of Iran's inquiry.

Second, Reagan, in his largely ghostwritten memoir, even though clearly designed to comport with the new world order rendition of this history, completely ignored the episode. Instead, he says "during Bud McFarlane's visit to Bethesda Naval Hospital [on July 18] and in following meetings, he informed me that representatives of Israel had contacted him secretly to pass on information from a group of moderate, politically influential Iranians."[18] Reagan thus dated his introduction to the Iran story nearly two weeks after McFarlane says he did.

Third, Don Regan, chief of staff, also disputed McFarlane's claim to have told Reagan of his conversation with Kimche before he entered the hospital. Regan was present during McFarlane's daily briefings of the president and would have been privy to such a conversation, if it had taken place. After Reagan had entered the hospital, McFarlane demanded that he be permitted to see him immediately after his operation. According to Regan "…if he had [told the president earlier] I don't know why he would have felt such a sense of urgency ("I've just got to see the president") to tell him the same thing a second time."[19]

---

[17] David Ignatius, "Reagan Warns 5 Nations of U.S. Right To Defend Itself Against Acts of Terror," *Wall Street Journal*, July 9, 1985, 3.
[18] Ronald Reagan, *An American Life* (New York: Simon & Shuster, 1990), 504. *Iran-Contra Affair*, 167, supports the president's view.
[19] Don Regan, *For the Record* (New York: Harcourt, Brace, Jovanovich, 1988), 20.

Greed, Politics, and the New World Order Faction

The chronology of events is particularly important here, as the period between Kimche's meeting with McFarlane and McFarlane's meeting with the president brackets the moment when the new world order faction saw an opportunity to seize control of the Iran initiative, divert it away from direct contact with the Iranians, and sink it with an arms for hostages deal. According to Segev, "Kimche left Washington empty-handed," but while in Paris on a stopover en route to Jerusalem "received a telegram from Peres instructing him to proceed to Geneva."[20]

In Geneva, July 7, Kimche met with Schwimmer, Nimrodi, Gorbanifar, and Khashoggi and was informed that Ayatollah Hassan Karoubi would be in Hamburg the next day to dedicate a Moslem study house. They all proceeded to Hamburg the next day for a meeting with Karoubi at the *Vier Jahreszeiten* (Four Seasons) Hotel. The import of the Iranian cleric's view was that his people wanted "a free and independent Iran with good relations with all, but especially with the United States." Kimche averred that Israel "would like to serve as a bridge...between you and the west." Karoubi declared, "we must set a common goal and frame appropriate methods of action" and promised to "submit a detailed proposal in writing that can serve as a basis for discussion between us."[21]

After reporting the results of their meeting to Peres, the prime minister, acting in accordance with the channel set up by McFarlane, sent Schwimmer to Washington on July 11 to meet with Ledeen.[22] Schwimmer carried with him a transcript of the meeting with Karoubi

---

[20] Segev, *Iranian Triangle*, 155.
[21] Ibid, 157, 159.
[22] Michael Ledeen, *Perilous Statecraft: An Insider's Account of the Iran Contra Affair* (New York: Scribner, 1988), 119, notes that during Kimche's meeting with McFarlane on July 3, the Israeli "asked him whether the American government was truly interested in pursuing the matter [of an opening to Iran] and, if so, whether I was the proper channel. McFarlane had said yes to both questions, and Schwimmer had accordingly flown to the United States to brief me."

and urged Ledeen to meet with Karoubi himself through Gorbanifar, their interlocutor.

Ledeen left a message for McFarlane regarding his meeting with Schwimmer, saying:

> It is indeed a message from [the] Prime Minister of Israel; it is a follow-on to the private conversation he had last week when David Kimche was here. It is extremely urgent and extremely sensitive and it regards the matter he told David he was going to raise with the President. The situation has fundamentally changed for the better....This is the real thing and it is just wonderful news.[23]

McFarlane's desk calendar confirmed that he met with Ledeen two days later during which the latter undoubtedly passed on the transcript of the meeting with Karoubi.[24] As shown in the transcript, Karoubi asked for nothing but a high-level dialogue with the United States. He made no request to purchase arms, or reference to the hostages.[25]

But the Israelis, Gorbanifar, and Khashoggi were not satisfied with merely establishing a high-level dialogue for the United States. Their interest was in making money, in the short run by selling arms, and, beyond that, to becoming major commercial brokers to benefit from the financial bonanza that would flow when Iran's contacts with the west had been reestablished. Thus, according to Ledeen, it was Gorbanifar who put together the package that included not only the establishment of high-level contacts and development of a "dialogue," but also permission for "Israel to sell several hundred *TOW* antitank missiles to the Iranians," which would gain the release of the hostages.[26]

McFarlane, on the other hand, says that it was "the Israelis" who pressed for some "tangible show" of the Iranians' ability to deliver and the Iranians who said they could obtain the release of the seven

---

[23] *Tower Report*, B-16, n.10.
[24] Ibid.
[25] For the transcript, see Segev, *Iranian Triangle*, 157-59.
[26] Ledeen, *Perilous Statecraft*, 118.

hostages held in Lebanon, but would need to show "some gain," in the form "specifically" of "delivery from Israel of 100 *TOW* missiles."[27]

There is little doubt that McFarlane understood the distinction between opening a "dialogue" and trading arms for hostages and absolutely no doubt about who wanted what. He immediately sent a message to Shultz, who was traveling in Australia, combining all three elements—dialogue, arms sales, and hostage release—into one package the way Gorbanifar had, although stating that "the larger purpose would be the opening of the private dialogue with a high level American official and a sustained discussion of U.S. Iranian relations."[28] The NSC adviser favored "going ahead," but would "abide fully by your [Shultz's] decisions."

Shultz replied immediately, instructing him "we should make a tentative show of interest without commitment." The secretary's immediate priorities, however, were the hostages, not a strategic opening. He did not "think we could justify turning our backs on the prospects of gaining the release of the other seven hostages and perhaps developing an ability to renew ties with Iran under a more sensible regime..." Finally, wanting to keep knowledge of this proposal secret from other members of the administration, especially Casey, the secretary told McFarlane to "manage this probe personally." "The two of us should discuss its sensitivity and the likelihood of disclosure after my return." He said to tell Schwimmer that "you and I are in close contact and full agreement every step of the way."[29]

Shultz closed his message to McFarlane with the startling observation that conveying their "full agreement" was "all the more important in view of the present lack of unity and full coordination on the Israeli side." Was this reference to the obvious discord among Peres, Rabin, and Shamir? If so, it was quite ironic considering the deep split between the president and the new world order faction.

---

[27] *Tower Report*, B-16-17.
[28] Ibid, B-17.
[29] Ibid.

Discussing this message in his memoir, Shultz observed, "McFarlane could be deceived into unwise actions, I feared."[30] Shultz, in other words, would decide.

Shultz's reply to McFarlane was extraordinary, to say the least. Just two weeks before, in his comments on the draft NSDD on Iran, he had railed against changing policy to permit "Western friends and allies," which emphatically meant Israel, to sell arms to Iran as "contrary to our interests." Yet, here he was expressing his "full agreement" to this very proposal! Shultz's concern about McFarlane being deceived was misplaced. In fact, McFarlane was more the deceiver, than the deceived. Immediately upon receiving Shultz's reply, he began pressing Regan to arrange a meeting for him with the president.

The problem was that the president had entered Bethesda Naval Hospital on Friday, July 12, to have a small polyp removed from his colon. During the procedure doctors discovered a much larger, cancerous polyp, and the president decided to have it removed immediately. Therefore, the next day, Saturday July 13, the president underwent a second operation. This time because it was a more invasive procedure it was decided to invoke the 25th amendment designating George Bush acting president during the hours Reagan was incapacitated.

Following successful surgery, and after reclaiming his presidential powers, Nancy Reagan decided to prohibit all visitors, except for herself and chief of staff Don Regan, while the president recuperated. Thus, the president was incommunicado during the next four days, much to McFarlane's chagrin as he importuned Regan daily with pleas that he had "just got to see the president."[31] His urgency increased with the arrival on July 16 of the memorandum promised earlier by Karoubi. The memo was quickly passed to Ledeen, who immediately

---

[30] Shultz, *Turmoil and Triumph*, 795.
[31] It was during these days, too, that both Secretary of Defense Weinberger and CIA Director Casey sent in their responses to McFarlane regarding the NSDD Draft on Iran, Weinberger, on July 16, opposing and Casey, on July 18, supporting it.

turned it over to McFarlane.[32] Ledeen left for a trip to Israel the evening of July 16, which was partly a family vacation, but also partly another mission for McFarlane to meet with Gorbanifar.[33]

Karoubi said that Iran faced two possible futures if current trends continued. Iran would either descend into a Lebanon-like chaos, or become a Soviet "puppet state." To avert either of these outcomes, "we must immediately begin to bring together the moderate and patriotic forces of pro-Western sympathies who oppose the extremists and the anti-Western Left." Within a month he promised to "send you the final plans…and details of the things we need…." For the moment, in anticipation of the coming presidential and Majlis elections, Karoubi sought "some financial aid," for distribution among the clergy in Qom, merchants in the bazaar, and in south Tehran. Finally, to demonstrate his credibility, he appended a list of "people who support our line."[34]

What was striking about the memo was the focus on political cooperation to the complete exclusion of any other matter, let alone request for arms, or any discussion of hostages. At this point, Karoubi only wanted American financial support for pro-Western candidates in the coming elections. Successful election of pro-Western candidates held the potential for a peaceful turn in Iran and McFarlane and Shultz knew that Reagan would respond to this plea with alacrity. Thus, it was vital for them to head this proposal off at all costs and as soon as possible.

Karoubi's memo gave McFarlane added incentive to pester Regan for an appointment to see the president. Finally, on the morning of July 18, Nancy Reagan relented, agreed that the president was sufficiently recovered to begin receiving visitors, and McFarlane was admitted. Only the president, McFarlane, and Regan were present. What was

---

[32] *Iran-Contra Affair*, 167.
[33] Segev, *Iranian Triangle*, 161-63. Ledeen, *Perilous Statecraft*, 119, obscures the memo transferral, not to mention its content, by claiming that McFarlane saw the president on July 16, a falsehood. As we will see below, it is clear that McFarlane lied to him.
[34] Segev, *Iranian Triangle*, 162-63.

discussed is in dispute and for good reason, for the hospital meeting marked the beginning of the long road to scandal surrounding arms for hostages.

McFarlane's Bait and Switch on Reagan

According to Don Regan's notes and recollection, during a conversation lasting no more than "ten or twelve minutes," McFarlane "asked the President if he was interested in talking to the Iranians." He reasoned "this was a good idea because the United States ought to be talking to the Iranians about the future so as to have established contacts if and when a new government came into being in Tehran." The hostages were "discussed in a general way," in the sense that "the Iranians, who had already been helpful in connection with the TWA hijacking might be disposed to be helpful in other situations if we were more friendly to them."[35]

But, noted Regan, "there is nothing in my notes or in my memory to suggest that the idea of swapping arms for hostages was mentioned by either man on this occasion." Any mention of such a scheme, he continued, "would have made me prick up my ears."

> It hardly seems likely that an entirely new policy, involving a brusque departure from past practices and established principle—and bringing in a third country, Israel, as a middleman in a secret arms sale—could have been decided on in such a brief encounter.[36]

Thus, according to Regan, McFarlane asked the president if he was interested in a dialogue with the Iranians, not to authorize an Israeli arms sale, or a swap of arms for hostages. The president was, indeed, interested in "talking to the Iranians," and instructed McFarlane to "go ahead. Open it up."[37]

---

[35] Regan, *For the Record*, 20-21.
[36] Ibid, 21.
[37] *Tower Report*, citing Regan's testimony, B-16.

But that is not what McFarlane did. Here was the bait and switch. Although asking and receiving permission from the president to open up a "dialogue" with the Iranians, McFarlane immediately informed Kimche that, "in principle," the president had approved "the sale of *TOW*s by Israel."[38] In short, McFarlane authorized Israeli arms sales when the president authorized only talks, and he did so as part of the new world order scheme to prevent an opening to Iran.[39] Furthermore, he made no record of the decision because it would document his perfidy.

What is even more remarkable about this sequence is that McFarlane already had authorized Ledeen to convey this message to the Israelis *two days* before he met with the president in the hospital. The point centers on the confusion regarding when McFarlane actually saw the president. Although the fact is clearly established that McFarlane saw the president on the morning of July 18, several sources say that the meeting took place two days earlier, on the 16th, which is manifestly not the case, but essential to make the claim that McFarlane's instructions to Ledeen were based on authorization from the president. Ledeen recounts that he and his family

> Were scheduled to leave for Israel on the evening of July 16th.... The president was facing surgery at Bethesda Naval Hospital that very morning. McFarlane undertook to discuss this sensitive issue with Reagan prior to my departure, and did so on the morning of the 16th, after the president's surgery. *As McFarlane described it to me early that afternoon,* it was the first matter raised with Reagan after he emerged from

---

[38] *Iran-Contra Affair*, 167. Caspar W. Weinberger, *Fighting for Peace: Seven Critical Years in the Pentagon* (New York: Warner Books, 1990), 369, comes to the same conclusion, observing that McFarlane "took it upon himself to advise the Israelis it was all right for them to sell the weapons we had furnished them..."
[39] Ibid. Weeks after the scandal erupted, on November 21, 1986, McFarlane claimed that the president was "all for letting the Israelis do anything they wanted at the very first briefing in the hospital," but he was never able to produce a shred of evidence to substantiate this claim. Nor does the extant record support it.

anesthesia, and I suspect that this is one reason why the president's memory about the discussion has always been rather fuzzy.[40]

The dating conflict is best explained by yet another of McFarlane's unilateral actions, all part of the bait and switch. He informed Ledeen that he had seen the president when he obviously hadn't, in order to allow him to travel with the "authority" of the president to Israel. Ledeen had no means of verifying, and no reason to doubt, the word of his chief. McFarlane's need to "cover" this action with an actual conferral of presidential authority, however, was what undoubtedly lay behind his insistent demands to see the president.[41]

McFarlane's go-ahead message to Kimche for arms sales, along with Ledeen's arrival, no later than July 18, precipitated a flurry of activity over the next twelve days, and while the sequence of events is not completely clear, the substance is crystal clear. Ledeen reinforced McFarlane's authorization for arms sales and Kimche immediately alerted Peres' team, Khashoggi, and Gorbanifar.

Toward the end of the month, Khashoggi set up a meeting in Hamburg, reportedly attended by "Gorbanifar, Kimche, other Iranians and Israelis, and two Americans, possibly from the National Security Council." The Israelis were most likely Kimche and Nimrodi (Schwimmer was on a business trip in China), but the identities of the "other Iranians...and two Americans" is unknown.[42] Ledeen also mentions a Hamburg meeting, affirms that Kimche attended, but says that it occurred before he arrived in Israel.[43] One must question how he

---

[40] Ledeen, *Perilous Statecraft*, 119. (Italics supplied)
[41] Ledeen was not the only one to claim that McFarlane's meeting with the president occurred on the 16th. Draper, *Very Thin Line*, 156, also made this claim because it was the only way to connect the presumed chain of authority—from Reagan to McFarlane to Ledeen.
[42] Scott Armstrong et al., *The Chronology: The Documented Day-by-Day Account of the Secret Military Assistance to Iran and the Contras* (New York: Warner Books, 1987), 137.
[43] Ledeen, *Perilous Statecraft*, 121.

knew. Did the Israelis tell him, or was he himself one of the Americans at the meeting? More to the point, there was no reason to hold a meeting until "authorization" had been given by the president, and that did not happen until July 18.

The Israeli Historical Chronology says that unidentified "Israelis," presumably Kimche and Nimrodi, but not Ledeen, met with Gorbanifar in Israel on July 25 where the essential quid pro quo of arms for hostages was worked out. They then briefed Ledeen separately on the 28th.[44] Ledeen claims that he met with them all, including Schwimmer, on July 29.[45] Although Ledeen denies that he was sent to negotiate in any way and says that his "role was always…to attend meetings, listen, ask questions, find out as much as I could, and then report back," it is clear that he participated in what was clearly a negotiation.[46]

According to Segev, during their meeting "Gorbanifar made the link between supplying weapons and freeing the hostages explicit," describing it as "a necessary test to prove the sincerity of both sides." Kimche said "Israel would be ready to supply the missiles only if secrecy could be guaranteed and the hostages freed." Gorbanifar said realistically that while some hostages would be released within "two or three weeks," the Iranians would keep some others as a "bargaining card."[47]

Having reached the fundamental decision that weapons would come before a dialogue, there was a tacit agreement to drop Ayatollah Hassan Karoubi, who wanted no arms, and deal with Mohsen Kangarlu, who did. Thus, Gorbanifar called Kangarlu to brief him on the proposed arrangement. The Iranian leader thought the release of Buckley would be a fair exchange for the weapons, but the Israeli side made it plain that the weapons would have to be paid for in advance.[48]

When Kimche reported back to Peres, Shamir, and Rabin on the proposed deal, Rabin objected to dealing with Ledeen, a messenger.

---

[44] *Iran-Contra Affair*, 167.
[45] Ledeen deposition, *Iran-Contra Affair*, Appendix B, volume 15, 978.
[46] Ibid, 974.
[47] Segev, *Iranian Triangle*, 164-65.
[48] Ibid., 165. Buckley, it was later learned, had died on June 3.

He observed that from his experience as ambassador to the United States, "he knew that it was best to negotiate with the decision-makers and not with their occasional messengers." In short, Rabin insisted on a "more unequivocal U.S. authorization."[49] When informed of Rabin's reaction, Ledeen replied, "the Israelis had already received sufficient authorization from the response that the president had given in the hospital." Nevertheless, "the Israelis were insistent on confirmation."[50]

According to Ledeen, afterward on July 30, he and the Israelis met and decided to report immediately to McFarlane. But, he claims, not wishing to cut short his vacation and as Kimche was going to Washington anyway, it was agreed that Kimche would "report on these conversations to McFarlane."[51] Much of what Ledeen claims may be true, but its essence was not. As it was the Israeli leadership that insisted on direct confirmation from McFarlane, Kimche would have been assigned the task of obtaining it regardless of what Ledeen did. Thus, on August 2, Kimche flew to Washington "to meet with McFarlane and to obtain the specific U.S. position on Israel's sale of the *TOW*s."[52]

Meanwhile, Gorbanifar was also active. Following the meetings, he proceeded to Marbella, Spain, to meet with Khashoggi. Roy Furmark, New York oil consultant and Casey's "go-between" with Khashoggi, was present on Khashoggi's yacht moored off Marbella when Gorbanifar arrived. No one else was there. The Iranian was excited about the prospect of an Israeli arms deal with Iran, but, given the mistrust of the two parties for each other, it would be necessary to provide outside "bridge financing" for the transaction. Khashoggi readily agreed to provide the money, offering to make a million dollar prepayment.[53]

After their meeting, Furmark and Gorbanifar flew to Tel Aviv to inform the Israelis of Khashoggi's willingness to provide the million-

---

[49] Segev, *Iranian Triangle*, 166.
[50] *Iran-Contra Affair*, 167.
[51] "Ledeen Deposition," *Iran-Contra Affair*, Appendix B, volume 15, 986.
[52] *Iran-Contra Affair*, 167.
[53] "Roy Furmark Deposition," *Iran-Contra Affair*, Appendix B, Volume 11, 73-76.

dollar bridge money. Attending this meeting were Nimrodi, Schwimmer, and, for the first time, Prime Minister Peres' counterterrorism adviser, Amiram Nir, but not Kimche, who was on his way to Washington to put the final piece of the proposal into place—approval of President Reagan.[54]

Kimche had traveled to Washington expressly to obtain approval for the proposal worked out over the previous few weeks, the proposal that McFarlane himself—through Ledeen—had initiated. Before they agreed to engage in the proposed arms sale, however, the Israeli leadership wanted several assurances. They wanted Washington's confirmation that the proposed plan was indeed strategic, that is, aimed at an opening with Iran, and not merely a tactical maneuver to gain the release of Buckley and the other hostages; that the plan had the "agreement of the president and his cabinet"; and that the president agreed to timely replenishment of the weapons the Israelis sold with "new and modern" models.[55]

Kimche put these questions to McFarlane during two days of meetings, August 2-3. Once again, attempting to avoid a paper trail, McFarlane violated standard procedure and "made no memorandum of the meetings," thus his view is based on his recollection, which changed over time. Based on McFarlane's testimony before the congressional committees, the initiative came from the Israelis. It was the Israelis, he claimed, who "asked for permission to sell 100 *TOW*s," and that he, McFarlane, had merely "agreed to present the issue to the President."[56] This, however, was the very opposite of the truth.

Based on Israeli classified data, the Kimche-McFarlane meetings explored the parameters of the arms sales proposal and Israeli concerns. On the strategic question of establishing ties to Tehran, Kimche gave McFarlane Karoubi's memo (which he already had), with its attached name list of Iranian supporters. He claimed that this "moderate" faction needed to acquire the weapons to demonstrate its

---

[54] *Tower Report*, B-18,
[55] Segev, *Iranian Triangle, 166*.
[56] *Iran-Contra Affair*, 167.

superior contacts to the United States and ability to "deliver" over rival factions. In addition, the weapons would help "broaden its base of support in the army and the Revolutionary Guard."[57]

Then, Kimche put forward the proposed deal worked out with Gorbanifar, Khashoggi, and Ledeen. In exchange for the delivery of 100 *TOW* missiles, Iran would arrange for the release of four hostages. Israel would be prepared to deliver four hundred additional missiles, depending on the outcome of the first deal. Kimche wanted to know whether the United States would replenish the weapons within thirty days of delivery.

On the matter of the president's consent, McFarlane agreed to put the question before the president to establish whether arms shipments were "consistent with American policy and goals," but affirmed that on the question of replenishment, Israel "has bought weapons from the United States for years and always will, and so you don't need to ask whether you can buy more weapons."[58] McFarlane thus left the "general impression...that the U.S. would reply favorably."[59]

Reagan Says No; McFarlane Says Yes

As the Tower Board put it, "what followed is quite murky," in large part because McFarlane continued his practice of making no record of any of the discussions between the president and his top aides. The Board concluded that there had been several meetings in early August with "one or more of the principals in attendance" at each one. At the same time "White House records...show no meetings of the NSC principals in August scheduled for the purpose of discussing [Iran], although there were meetings at which "this issue could have been discussed." Worse, in another McFarlane "lapse," defying standard procedure, "no analytical paper was prepared for the August discussions and no formal minutes of any of the discussions were made."[60]

---

[57] Segev, *Iranian Triangle*, 167-68, n.3.
[58] *Tower Report*, B-19.
[59] Segev, *Iranian Triangle*, 169.
[60] *Tower Report*, III-6.

Most of the NSC principals recalled a meeting on August 6, during which the Israeli proposal was discussed. They agree that both Shultz and Weinberger expressed strong objections and that the president made no decision. But that is where agreement ends. Weinberger says that Shultz, McFarlane, Regan, and either Casey or his deputy John McMahon met with the president in the sitting room in his White House quarters. Weinberger omitted Vice-President Bush and was unsure whether Casey attended or not.[61]

Secretary Shultz testified to the congressional committee that Reagan, Bush, Shultz, Weinberger, Regan, and McFarlane, but neither Casey nor McMahon, was present on August 6.[62] Yet, to the Tower Board and in his memoir, he recalled the meeting on that date as "one of my regular meetings with the president," during which "Bud McFarlane brought up the idea of talks with Iran." Thus, for Shultz, there were two meetings on August 6 where the Israeli proposal was discussed.[63]

In his memoir, McFarlane presents yet a third story, claiming that in attendance were the president, Bush, Weinberger, Regan, and General John Vessey. Moreover, he says that the Israeli proposal was piggybacked onto another matter, a briefing by Weinberger and Vessey to discuss "proposed changes to our nuclear targeting doctrine."[64] This would appear to explain why there was no White House record of a meeting to discuss Iran.

For this information, however, McFarlane relied upon the White House attendance log, which betrayed him. Vessey had been scheduled to brief the president, but the briefing had been canceled at the last minute. As described by Walsh, "Weinberger had first offered Vessey a ride to the White House meeting and then, after checking, had to tell Vessey that he was not invited. The next day, Weinberger

---

[61] Weinberger, *Fighting For Peace*, 368.
[62] *Iran-Contra Affair*, 167.
[63] Shultz, *Turmoil and Triumph*, 796 and *Tower Report*, III-7.
[64] McFarlane, *Special Trust*, 32.

told Vessey that he 'wouldn't believe what was being proposed,' namely negotiation with the Iranians."[65]

McFarlane says neither Shultz, nor Casey, attended the meeting, although he avers that he had spoken to Shultz "earlier, on the phone," when the secretary expressed his opposition to any arms deal. As McFarlane described it Bush and Regan were "mildly supportive of the plan, Shultz and Weinberger were opposed, while he, McFarlane, supported it. The president's response was to say, "I'll think about it."[66] (Tellingly he omits any reaction by Vessey. He also omit's Shultz's message to him of July 14 expressing his "full agreement" to proceed. See p.129 above.)

Despite differences in recollection of who attended the crucial meeting of August 6, all agreed that the president made no decision to authorize an Israeli arms sale. According to Chief of Staff Regan, "the President told McFarlane to 'go slow' at the August meeting," so as to "make sure we know who we are dealing with before we get too far into this."[67] However, in his testimony, McFarlane said that he informed Kimche of the president's affirmative decision on that day, August 6.[68]

In an interview with Mayer and McManus, McFarlane claimed that the president's decision came "a day or so" after the August 6 meeting. The president called him at home from Camp David to say that he wanted to "go ahead with the Iranian matter we discussed." Thus, according to his second account, the president authorized the Israeli arms deal "a day or so" after the August 6 meeting.[69]

However, once again McFarlane's claim was exposed as a falsehood and he subsequently changed his story. If the president had

---

[65] Lawrence E. Walsh, *Final Report of the Independent Counsel for Iran-Contra Matters* (Washington, D.C.: United States Court of Appeals for the District of Columbia Circuit, August 4, 1993), 406 n.10.
[66] McFarlane, *Special Trust*, 32-34.
[67] *Iran-Contra Affair*, 167.
[68] "McFarlane Testimony," *Iran-Contra Affair*, Hearings, 100-2, at 48-50.
[69] Jane Mayer and Doyle McManus, *Landslide: The Unmaking of the President* (Boston: Houghton Mifflin, 1988), 128.

authorized the Israeli sale, it would have been one of the major decisions of his presidency, requiring a formal record. Yet, as reporters Mayer and McManus discovered, not only was no directive issued, there was no White House record of the telephone call, nor did McFarlane make any note of a call from the president.

Worse, between Tuesday, August 6, and Saturday, August 10, the president had not traveled to Camp David. He remained at the White House where McFarlane saw him each of those days. On August 11, the president flew to his ranch in California and McFarlane accompanied him on *Air Force One*. As Mayer and McManus put it, "there was no obvious reason for Reagan to call his aide at home, something he rarely did in any case."[70] There was ample opportunity to convey his decision to McFarlane in person, if in fact he had done so.

The Tower Board and the congressional committees accepted McFarlane's account, despite its many and obvious contradictions, concluding that the president "most likely approved the Israeli sales before they occurred." It was their view that "McFarlane had no motive to approve a sale of missiles to Iran if the President had not authorized it."[71] But, as this account maintains, he had both motive and opportunity. In any case, after his story was exposed as false, he changed it once again in his memoir.

In his memoir, McFarlane placed the call from Camp David *before* his meeting with Kimche and said that it had come to his White House office on Saturday July 27, where he happened to be, not to his home. In the call, the president was said to want to "find a way" to do the "Israeli thing." Then, *after* the meetings of August 6, McFarlane said that "a little after noon" the president called him into the Oval Office to tell him that he wanted to go ahead with the Israeli arms sale because "it's the right thing to do."[72] Again, no record was made of the decision, or of the telephone call, or of his visit to the Oval Office.

---

[70] Ibid, 129.
[71] *Iran-Contra Affair*, 168 and *Tower Report*, III-8.
[72] McFarlane, *Special Trust*, 31, 34.

Compounding McFarlane's problems is Segev's assertion that McFarlane notified Kimche that the president had authorized the sale on August 6, the day of the meeting.[73] This assertion invalidates McFarlane's initial testimony that the president authorized the sale "a day or so" after August 6, but, at least, makes physically possible his revised story. Plainly, contrary to the Tower Board and congressional committees which accepted McFarlane's claim, not only does the evidence strongly indicate that the president gave no authorization for an Israeli arms shipment to Iran before it occurred, but also that McFarlane had a clear motive to undertake this action on his own.

McFarlane and The First Arms Shipment

As soon as McFarlane notified them the Israelis prepared the first shipment of *TOW* missiles for delivery to Iran, code-named "Operation Cappuccino." The way McFarlane had arranged the deal must have given the Israeli leadership some qualms, as it was apparent to those closely following the action that the American leadership remained sharply divided, and the Israelis politically at risk. "Rabin refused to allow Israel to ship the weapons without written authorization from the U.S." Reportedly, McFarlane provided authorization "after consulting with Reagan."[74] However, once again, there was no record of a prior presidential authorization.

Khashoggi wired the promised $1 million to Nimrodi's Credit Suisse bank account in Geneva on August 7, (which incidentally reinforces the view that McFarlane had notified the Israelis on the 6th.) With funds in hand, Schwimmer took care of the logistics. McFarlane had arranged for a CIA proprietary in Miami, Florida, to ship the weapons, so Schwimmer flew to Miami where he chartered a DC-8 cargo jet from an American company, re-registered it in Belgium, and

---

[73] Segev, *Iranian Triangle*, 169.

[74] Scott Armstrong et al., The Chronology: The Documented Day-by-Day Account of the Secret Military Assistance to Iran and the Contras (New York: Warner Books, 1987), 148.

hired a three-man American crew. Plane and crew arrived in Tel Aviv on August 18, followed by the arrival of Gorbanifar the next day.[75]

In the meantime, McFarlane arranged a secure communications scheme with Kimche through Ledeen. Ledeen had returned to Washington from his vacation in Israel in the second week of August. In his report to McFarlane he said he had become "extremely suspicious" of Gorbanifar because he was simply "too good to be true." McFarlane was noncommittal, but, "a couple of days later," having heard from Kimche that the operation was set to go, the national security adviser had another meeting with Ledeen and told him that "the president had approved this test." Ledeen was "to meet with Kimche as quickly as possible to assure [him] that the President had in fact made this decision and to arrange a way [to]…communicate with the Israelis securely without going through the normal communication systems in the Israeli embassy or the American Embassy in Tel Aviv."[76]

Ledeen flew to London on August 20. Meeting in a hotel room at Heathrow airport, Ledeen passed on an elementary code scheme that would enable them to establish secure telephone communications and Kimche handed Ledeen typed notes of their July conversations with Gorbanifar.[77] Kimche cautioned him that the Iranians would not deliver everything they promised, but, even if they "delivered significantly less than what they had promised," it was still worth a try.[78]

---

[75] Segev, *Iranian Triangle*, 172-73. The company was International Airline Support Group, Inc, owned by Richard R. Wellman. The CIA's airline proprietary project officer later testified that this August flight "was not an Agency flight." Furthermore, the agency only "found out after the fact" that the proprietary had chartered the plane. "Airline Proprietary Project Officer deposition," *Iran-Contra Affair*, Appendix B, volume 1, 18. Furthermore, the authorization for the flight came from McFarlane, not the CIA. According to the CIA Air Branch chief, when asked about the cargo regarding the August flight, he replied: "you don't ask unnecessary questions when it comes out of the White House." "CIA Branch Chief deposition," Ibid, volume 4, 818.

[76] "Michael Ledeen deposition," *Iran-Contra Affair*, Appendix B, volume 15, 988-89.

[77] Ibid, 993.

[78] *Tower Report*, B-25.

Around midnight on that same evening of August 20, the DC-8 took off from Tel Aviv for Iran loaded with 96 *TOW* missiles, four short of the agreed 100. The missiles were packed in pallets of twelve missiles per pallet; thus eight pallets were shipped.[79] In addition, according to Ledeen, the Israelis were determined to avoid a repeat of the April fiasco, and insisted that Gorbanifar accompany the cargo or the mission would be canceled.[80]

Taking off from Ben Gurion airport, the unmarked cargo plane flew west for a time before turning 180 degrees to enter Cyprus airspace where the pilot requested and was given over flight clearance across Turkey to Tehran. Nearing Tehran, however, the plane encountered two Iraqi fighter aircraft, which forced the pilot to take evasive action and divert to Tabriz. Mohsen Kangarlu and several aides met the plane. From Tabriz the plane flew on to Tehran where Ali Shamkhani, deputy commander of the Revolutionary Guards met the plane and took control of the missiles, after receiving the concurrence of Prime Minister Moussavi.[81]

When the first arms delivery occurred, McFarlane was in California with the president. The president had left Washington on August 11 and would remain at his ranch until September 2 as part of his recovery from cancer surgery. While at the ranch his only contact with White House business was through Regan and McFarlane, and Nancy Reagan limited that to "written communications and phone calls."[82] In other words, during the period of the first Israeli arms delivery, the president was at the ranch, out of the White House, and, it seems clear, out of touch.

Meanwhile, after his meeting with Kimche, Ledeen flew to Los Angeles. After delivering a scheduled speech, he traveled up the coast to the Biltmore Hotel Resort in Santa Barbara where the presidential

---

[79] *Israeli Historical Chronology*, as cited in *Iran-Contra Affair*, 172, n.93.
[80] Ledeen, *Perilous Statecraft*, 131.
[81] Segev, *Iranian Triangle*, 174.
[82] Mayer and McManus, *Landslide*, 132, observe that in addition the two aides were "locked in a debilitating rivalry and by the summer of 1985 their fighting had descended to...a mean and petty level."

party stayed. There he briefed McFarlane on his meeting with Kimche and turned over the typed report of the July meetings.[83]

When informed of the Israeli delivery McFarlane realized that the scheme to sink the opening to Iran had reached a critical point. Up to now, all of the action had involved McFarlane maneuvering the Israelis and Iranians into an arms-for-hostages transaction. The U.S. government was completely uninvolved, save for his own assurances to the Israelis and Gorbanifar that the president was committed to the operation. But, McFarlane knew that the Israelis would immediately place before Weinberger a request for prompt replenishment of the weapons and he had to get to the secretary before they did.

So, on August 22, McFarlane flew back to Washington. Aboard Air Force One, he called Weinberger to arrange a meeting, and, as soon as he landed that evening went directly to the Pentagon for a forty-minute conclave with the defense secretary, his aide Colin Powell, and General Charles Gabriel, Acting Chief of the General Staff.[84] McFarlane informed the secretary that the president had approved the Israeli missile transfer and also the decision to replenish Israeli stockpiles.[85] According to Powell's recollection:

> McFarlane described to the Secretary the so-called Iran Initiative and he gave to the Secretary a sort of a history of how we got where we were that particular day and some of the thinking that gave rise to the possibility of going forward with such an initiative and what the purposes of such an initiative would be...[86]

---

[83] "Ledeen Deposition," *Iran-Contra Affair*, Appendix B, volume 15, 993.
[84] "Weinberger Diary," August 22, 1985, as cited in Walsh, *Final Report*, 407 n.15, 16.
[85] Robert Parry, "Colin Powell: Failed Opportunist," *Consortiumnews*, November 26, 2004. http://www.consortiumnews.com/2004/112604.html
[86] "Colin Powell Deposition," *Iran-Contra Affair*, Appendix B, Volume 21, 228 passim. Powell remembered the conversation with McFarlane, but was vague as to the date.

Powell recalled that the secretary's response was "negative," repeating his oft-stated opposition to the so-called "initiative." But, despite his suspicions that this was another instance of McFarlane acting in the president's name without authorization, Weinberger complied, failing to confirm with the president. In retrospect, he certainly should have. There was no record, no directive; nothing but McFarlane's say-so. Had Weinberger checked and called the president to confirm, the Iran-Contra debacle might never have occurred. But, he didn't, although he did procrastinate on replenishing the *TOW*s.

Entangling Reagan in an Arms For Hostages Scheme

Arranging for replenishment was the necessary step in McFarlane's and the new world order faction's derailment plan. From this point onward, McFarlane's efforts focused on drawing the president, the CIA, Defense Department, and the NSC, into the arms for hostages scheme, while keeping Shultz and the State Department out, and extricating himself and Ledeen from it, as well. Indeed, he began to speak of retiring from government service.

The day after his meeting with Weinberger, August 23, McFarlane called the president at the ranch on what Reagan referred to as his "secret phone" to alert him to the possibility of a hostage release. His message was cryptic, saying only "a man high-up in the Iranian govt believes he can deliver all or part of the 7 kidnap victims."[87] McFarlane mentioned nothing else, making no reference to the Israeli arms shipment, or replenishment of arms, or that it was the result of the president's policy.

According to Regan, during a daily briefing after the president had returned from the ranch in early September, McFarlane informed him that the Israelis had shipped arms to Iran. Reagan had become "quite upset" at the news because he had not known anything about it. McFarlane

---

[87] Ronald Reagan, "Diary," August 23, 1985, as cited in Walsh, *Final Report*, 407 n.12.

brazenly disclaimed any knowledge or connection to the Israelis, declaring that they "simply had taken it upon themselves to do this."[88]

However, it soon became apparent that something was wrong. Although the Israelis had delivered the *TOW*s, the Iranians failed to obtain the release of a single hostage. Extremely agitated, Nimrodi called Gorbanifar, who was in Tehran, and arranged to meet him in Nice. In a rancorous discussion on August 27, at first Gorbanifar claimed that as the Revolutionary Guards had seized the missiles, the "moderates" felt no obligation to free hostages.[89] Of course, this argument effectively demolished the idea of a separate "faction," moderate or otherwise, that could be armed against the government because it was the government that was receiving the weapons.

Then, Gorbanifar argued that the 100 missiles were really the first part of the "test" they had discussed and that the entire deal included the 400 remaining missiles, which would result in the release of at least one hostage. To indicate Iran's commitment, Gorbanifar showed the Israelis that the Iranian government had transferred $1,217, 410 to his account to repay Khashoggi, plus expenses. He also disclosed the Saudi financier's agreement to provide additional bridge money, $4 million, for the rest of the shipment of four hundred *TOW*s.[90]

When informed of this meeting, McFarlane immediately sent Ledeen back to Europe to confirm it. During a "hard" meeting at the King George V Hotel in Paris, on September 4, Ledeen and the Israelis- Kimche, Schwimmer, and Nimrodi- emphasized to Gorbanifar Iran's need to honor its side of the bargain. Gorbanifar, in order to demonstrate Tehran's commitment, called Kangarlu in Tehran, who reaffirmed the arrangement. To verify Gorbanifar's claims, both the Israelis and the NSA listened in on the call.[91]

---

[88] *Tower Report*, B-24 and Walsh, *Final Report*, 518-19 n.89.
[89] Segev, *Iranian Triangle*, 175. Ledeen, *Perilous Statecraft*, 132, thought that rather than a scam, "the Iranians themselves were surprised at what had happened."
[90] *Iran-Contra Affair*, 168.
[91] "Ledeen Deposition," *Iran-Contra Affair*, Appendix B, Volume 15, 995-96 and Segev, *Iranian Triangle, 176.*

It was agreed that Israel would ship four hundred *TOW*s and the Iranians would release a hostage. According to McFarlane, he was given the choice of which hostage to be released and asked for Buckley, but, when told that he was too ill to travel, he picked Benjamin Weir, the longest-held hostage. (Although unknown to the U.S. side at that time, Buckley had already succumbed in early June from harsh treatment and medical malpractice.)[92]

In his testimony to the Tower Board, however, McFarlane told a different story, that Kimche had called him in the second week of September just prior to the second delivery of the 400 *TOW*s to say that "a hostage would be released and that he expected all the hostages to be released soon." There was no reference to Buckley, or of offering the national security adviser a choice of whom to release.[93]

In fact, McFarlane acted weeks before Kimche's call, in late August, to begin the process of entangling the U.S. government in his scheme. Assuming that a hostage would be released following the second Israeli arms shipment, McFarlane instructed NSC staff member Lt. Col. Oliver North to prepare "contingency plans for extracting hostages…from Lebanon."[94] North had not been involved in McFarlane's "Iran initiative" up to this point and now was tasked specifically with "extracting hostages…from Lebanon," not an opening to Iran.[95] McFarlane picked North because, in addition to his assignment to support the Contras, North was then the NSC coordinator of the Counterterrorism Task Force, a recently formed offshoot of the Terrorist Incident Working Group (TIWG) that had been set up the previous year.[96]

---

[92] McFarlane, *Special Trust*, 38, acknowledges that he selected Weir after learning that the Iranians would not release Buckley.
[93] *Tower Report*, B-26.
[94] *Tower Report*, B-25.
[95] Oliver L. North and William Novak, *Under Fire: An American Story*, (New York: Harper Collins, 1991), 26, claims his "operational involvement" in the Iran initiative began on November 17 when Israeli Defense Minister Rabin telephoned him.
[96] Ibid, 198-99.

The Task Force had been created during the TWA-847 crisis and was primarily responsible for making the arrangements to bring the passengers home. Reagan had ordered the establishment of the Task Force in the White House because the TIWG, run by Secretary Shultz in the State Department, had proven to be bureaucratically cumbersome with over two dozen members and operationally ineffective during the crisis. The Task Force had fewer than a dozen members drawn CIA, DOD, FBI, State, and JCS.[97]

As soon as he was directed to prepare contingency plans to extract hostages, on August 30 North obtained a passport from the State Department under the name of William P. Goode, for use in "a sensitive operation in Europe in connection with our hostages in Lebanon." The next day, Deputy NSC chief John Poindexter set up a "private method of interoffice computer communication" with him called "private blank check," which enabled North to bypass the normal screening of computer messages by the Executive Secretary of the NSC.[98]

A few days later, on September 12, North tasked Charles Allen, who was CIA National Intelligence Officer for Counterterrorism (and a member of the Counterterrorism Task Force that North coordinated) to "increase intelligence efforts against Iran and Lebanon." He assumed that the Iranian-sponsored Hezbollah had seized Buckley and "might" release him "in the next few hours or days."

Allen wanted to know who should receive the intelligence and, at McFarlane's instruction, North told him to send reports to Vice-Admiral Moreau, of JCS; Casey, or McMahon, in CIA; McFarlane, and North. McFarlane said that he would brief Shultz directly, so nothing should be sent to State. The congressional committee report exonerated Shultz and the State Department completely, concluding

---

[97] Ibid. Noel Koch and Richard Armitage from Defense, Dewey Clarridge and Charles Allen from CIA, Buck Revell and Wayne Gilbert from FBI, Robert Oakley from State, and Arthur Moreau and Jack Moellering from JCS, would all in one way or another be involved in the Iran-Contra affair.
[98] *Tower Report*, B-25.

denied access to the intelligence, the State Department was not told of the Israeli *TOW* shipment, was not advised of the linkage of Weir's release to arms shipments, and was not informed of the President's decision or the U.S. Government's involvement.[99]

As is now known, this was erroneous. Shultz and his close aides were kept completely informed of events, following them closely and daily, but McFarlane's instruction had provided political cover of deniability.[100] Originally, McFarlane had also omitted Weinberger from the list, which meant that he was unaware of the first two *TOW* shipments in advance. Later, however, when the secretary learned from his Assistant Colin Powell that he was being cut out of the intelligence, he demanded and was included in the dissemination list.[101]

The Second Israeli Arms Delivery

Authorized by Peres and Rabin on September 9, the second Israeli arms delivery proceeded along the lines of the first, but more smoothly and with a better result. Schwimmer chartered the same DC-8 transport and hired the same three-man crew that he did for the first trip. Nimrodi accompanied Khashoggi to Geneva to deposit bridge funds as he had in August, only this time the Saudi financier deposited $4 million to pay for the 408 *TOW* missiles to be shipped. On September 11, Kimche telephoned McFarlane to tell him that the arms would be shipped within the next few days and that the Iranians would release one hostage, but it would not be Buckley. When asked if he had a preference for the release of any particular hostage, "McFarlane answered in the negative."[102]

---

[99] *Iran-Contra Affair*, 169
[100] Walsh, *Final Report*, vol. 1, 332-341 and footnote no. 1, above.
[101] *Iran-Contra Affair*, 169 and *Tower Report*, B-25.
[102] Segev, *Iranian Triangle*, 177, thus offers yet a third explanation for the first hostage release. McFarlane, above fn 91 and 92, first claimed that he selected Weir when Buckley was unavailable, then said Kimche simply told him a hostage would

Late on the night of September 14, the DC-8 charter left Tel Aviv, arriving five hours later at Tabriz. A few hours after the delivery, the Rev. Benjamin Weir was released in Beirut near the U.S. embassy. McFarlane ordered Ambassador Reggie Bartholomew to withhold any announcement of his release for a few days, expecting that the "other hostages would be released in three batches without publicity." But no others were released, prompting Shultz to conclude, "Weir had been freed by terrorists who wanted to publicize their demand for their Dawa cohorts to be released from Kuwait."[103]

Weir himself was a decidedly unpleasant surprise. North, who was sent to debrief him found him "openly hostile to the United States and to Israel" and, despite being in captivity for 495 days, was openly sympathetic with his captors. Rejecting a letter from the president requesting his cooperation, he "emphatically refused to provide us with any information that might result in the use of military force to rescue his fellow hostages."[104]

Despite his uncooperative attitude, Weir inadvertently revealed some very important information. He said "he had reached an understanding with his captors about what he would and would not disclose publicly. To protect the other hostages he would not identify his captors, say where he was held or provide details on his repatriation." He also disclosed that on the day of his release he had spoken with Rev. Lawrence Jenco, Terry Anderson, David Jacobson, and Thomas Sutherland, but had not seen either Peter Kilburn, or William Buckley.[105]

In a public speech he warned, as Shultz suspected, "unless the Reagan administration pressures Kuwait to release 17 terrorists convicted of seven bombings in December 1983, the remaining

---

be released without identifying anyone. Kimche himself, *Last Option*, 212, says "it was Gorbanifar who informed us of the imminent release of the Reverend Benjamin Weir after we had delivered 500 *TOW* anti-tank shells."

[103] Shultz, *Turmoil and Triumph*, 797.
[104] North, *Under Fire*, 28.
[105] "Benjamin Weir's Secret Passage," *Time*, September 30, 1985.

Americans may be executed and more U.S. citizens kidnapped."[106] Demanding the release of the Dawa 17 was a clue to who had taken Weir and at least four of the other hostages. During the TWA crisis discussed in the previous chapter, intelligence analysts had determined that the sticking point to a resolution of the crisis had been an unidentified "inner group of terrorists...not under anyone's control, not Iran's and not Hezbollah's."[107]

By the time of Weir's release the FBI, in examining the hijacked TWA aircraft, had found Imad Mugniyeh's fingerprints in the toilet.[108] They were therefore able to conclude that he had been the leader of this "inner group." The fact that Weir had been prompted to make the same demand for the release of the Dawa 17 as the TWA hijackers had meant that Mugniyeh was also the one holding the hostages. If intelligence analysts had examined the personal backgrounds of the Dawa prisoners they would undoubtedly have confirmed this deduction when they discovered that one of the prisoners was Mugniyeh's brother-in-law, Mustafa Badreddine. Shultz himself had concluded that members of this inner group "were related by family to the Dawa prisoners held by Kuwait."[109]

But there was an even more disturbing deduction for the Shultz-McFarlane scheme to entangle the president. If Mugniyeh was not under the control of either Iran or Hezbollah, then neither could deliver the hostages and the new world order scheme for entangling the president in an arms for hostages scandal would not work. McFarlane and Shultz must have realized that the Israelis knew this and that they and the Iranians were entangling them in a pure and simple arms deal.[110]

---

[106] Ibid.
[107] Shultz, *Turmoil and Triumph*, 662.
[108] Bergman, *Secret War With Iran*, 101.
[109] Ibid.
[110] Bergman, *Secret War With Iran*, 96, says, however, that "for years, the Israelis could not fathom the hierarchical arrangements between Hizballah's various components and Syria and Iran …. Where, for example, did Mugniyeh himself fit in? There was a prolonged debate in the intelligence community over whether he was a member of Hizballah, or directly subordinate to Iranian intelligence." A third

Despite his own conclusions that the "inner group" of terrorists was holding the hostages and was not under the control of Iran or Hezbollah, Shultz continued to maintain that "Iran, not Syria, was in the position, if any country was, to call the shots when it came to the remaining American hostages."[111] This view, it is obvious, was contradicted by what Shultz already knew, but was consistent with his ideological predisposition to oppose any dealings with Iran.

The new world order derailment scheme had run into unexpected complexity with the discovery that Mugniyeh was the principal hostage-taker. Worse, if he was not under either Iran's or Hezbollah's control, then his connection to Qadaffi and ultimately to Moscow would inevitably come to light, no matter how well disguised his command links were. The prospect that Moscow could be found to be the deep sponsor of terrorist acts against Americans would be the very opposite of what the new world order faction sought.

It is impossible to know how far the new world order faction intended to take the derailment scheme, but there can be little doubt that the discovery Mugniyeh was the operational mastermind meant that the possibility hostages could be freed was slimmer than thought. For McFarlane it was now more important than ever to move to the end game, extricate himself from his scheme, and implicate the president deeper.

---

possibility, of course, was that he was an "independent contractor," loosely affiliated with several terrorist organizations.
[111] Shultz, *Turmoil and Triumph*, 662 and 667.

Chapter 5
The Attempt to Shut Down the Iran Initiative

In the fall of 1985, the new world order faction moved to close off any possibility of an opening to Iran. Having cooperated with the Peres leadership to set the hook in the form of Israeli arms deliveries and the release of a hostage, McFarlane and Kimche now prepared for the next step, of entangling the United States government illicitly in the scheme. On this narrow objective the two men cooperated, but with full understanding that their interests were not entirely congruent.

The point of divergence lay in the expected outcomes of their scheme. For the new world order faction entangling the United States directly in the arms-for-hostages scheme was designed to close off any possible rapprochement with Iran, but the Israelis calculated it would insure their continued access to the lucrative Iranian arms market. In 1985 alone independent Israeli arms sales to Iran were reportedly valued conservatively at between $500 million and $1 billion.[1] (By way of comparison, in their entirety, U.S.-Israeli arms sales to Iran in 1985 and 1986 that were part of the Iran initiative did not exceed $50 million.)

At the same time, all parties, including the United States, Syria, Iran, and Israel, were sending agents to scour the Lebanese countryside in a search for the hostages, who had become highly valuable commodities. In short, whoever could find the hostages would hold

---

[1] Martin Sieff, "Former NSC Aide Says Iran Arms Worth Much More Than Reported," *Washington Times,* December 5, 1986, 8.

great leverage over Washington, unless, of course, U.S. agents found them first.

Not only was a race going on to find the hostages. Perhaps most important were apparent changes at the global level. Here, two developments were paramount. First, preparations for a Reagan-Gorbachev summit held ominous implications for Iran. As the Iranian leadership saw it, a move to U.S.-Soviet détente implicit in the summit would, as it had in the seventies, consign Iran to the Soviet sphere and leave Tehran to the machinations of Moscow.

Second, was the imminent collapse of oil prices, which would have not only a dramatic impact on Moscow's revenues, but on Iran's, as well. From early September rumors abounded about a coming price drop, which actually began in November.[2] A sharp reduction in oil income would impact heavily upon Iran's ability to finance its war with Iraq. These developments, combined with the growing Soviet supply of Saddam Hussein's forces with missiles, tanks, and aircraft, galvanized the Iranian leadership into a determined attempt to reach an accommodation with Washington.

The Iranian leadership was desperate. Not only were strategic trends increasingly adverse, the situation on the ground in the war with Iraq and with regard to the hostages was of great concern. Moscow's rearming of Saddam's forces portended serious losses, if not defeat, if compensating weaponry were not acquired. Worse, the Iranians knew and suspected that Washington also knew, or would soon realize, that they could not deliver all of the hostages on demand. Hence, the Iranian approach was to pretend that they could deliver the hostages and attempt to strike a large deal, to get as much as they could before the Americans realized the truth.

Each side had tricks to play to maneuver their counterparts into desired positions. The result was a period full of surprises. Deceit reigned, as all sides operated on the false assumptions that the United States genuinely sought rapprochement through arms-for-hostages and

---

[2] See chapter 1.

that Iran actually controlled the fate of the hostages.³ The result was a series of unpredictable and explosive developments that reached a climax at the end of the year in what appeared to be the end of the initiative.

McFarlane's Hand-Off

Having started the arms-for-hostages initiative on his own without presidential authority, McFarlane now sought to implicate the president and draw others in the U.S. government into the scheme, especially CIA and Defense, but not State. McFarlane also handed off the management of this initiative to his untutored deputy in the NSC, Oliver North, while he moved to a less prominent, but still controlling, position. The procedure was remarkably similar to the scheme his mentor Henry Kissinger had employed with regard to Angola in 1974, unilaterally and clandestinely initiating involvement, then later passing the project of supplying the FNLA and Holden Roberto off to the CIA.⁴

When McFarlane directed North to prepare to recover the hostages he thought would be released following Israel's September arms shipment, North went to Charles Allen, the CIA's NIO for counterterrorism to activate intelligence coverage of Iranian leaders and their contacts in the Beirut area.⁵ Thus, the circle of those with knowledge of McFarlane's scheme immediately widened, as intelligence reports began to circulate within the upper echelons of government.

---

³ As John G. Tower et al., *Report of the President's Special Review Board: February 26, 1987* (Washington, D.C.: GPO, 1987), IV-2, concluded: "if the U.S. objective was a broader, strategic relationship, then the sale of arms should have been contingent upon first putting into place the elements of that relationship. An arms-for-hostages deal in this context could become counter-productive to achieving this broader strategic objective."
⁴ See Richard C. Thornton, *The Nixon-Kissinger Years* (St. Paul: Paragon, 2001, 2ⁿᵈ Edition), 360-69.
⁵ Lawrence E. Walsh, *Final Report of the Independent Counsel for Iran-Contra Matters*, (Washington, D.C.: United States Court of Appeals for the District of Columbia Circuit, August 4, 1993), 206.

Immediately after the September 14 release of Rev. Benjamin Weir, and knowing that Casey was receiving the intelligence reports, McFarlane informed him for the first time of his "contacts with Iran."[6] Weinberger, too, hearing of "strange" reports about an arms-for-hostages swap, called Casey to compare notes. Casey was as "surprised" as Weinberger and suspected that "Bud [McFarlane] is not telling us all he knows or has promised."[7] Clearly, the exchange proves that neither Casey nor Weinberger, both of whom were the president's allies, was part of McFarlane's scheme.

The role of Shultz and the State Department in the Iran initiative has been almost completely overlooked because, when the scandal erupted, Shultz denied knowledge of conspiracy and congressional investigators were loath to probe his veracity. The Independent Counsel investigation, however, subsequently uncovered voluminous evidence of the State Department's involvement in the factional struggle. As Walsh notes,

> regarding the November Hawk shipment...Shultz and other senior department officials were informed contemporaneously of many of its details, including...the flight plan, the need for overflight clearances, the delay in the shipment and the reasons the Iranians eventually returned the missiles.[8]

In other words, Shultz and his cadre of aides were also independently closely following the events. Nick Platt saw the downside of Weir's release at once. Three days later Platt observed that the release of only one hostage meant that McFarlane's scheme "appears not going anywhere." He noted cryptically that the hostage-release process had turned into a "race between Syria [and Iran] to round up hostages so [country name redacted, but clearly the United States] can pay or the Israelis can pay Iranians with weapons sales."[9]

---

[6] Ibid.
[7] "Weinberger note," September 20, 1985, in Ibid, 207.
[8] Ibid, 337.
[9] "Platt note," September 17, 1985, in Ibid, 335n73.

A few days later, Shultz and two of his aides, Michael Armacost and John Whitehead, discussed their concerns about the deal. Shultz was "not comfortable" with what he saw as "strange bargaining going on," but did not know what to do about it. McFarlane had "taken control" of the operation and was playing his cards close to the vest. When Armacost asked McFarlane's deputy, John Poindexter, about it, he replied that things were "very confused." (Armacost thought that Poindexter was "being cute" with him, but in fact McFarlane had not yet brought Poindexter into his scheme, either.)[10] Whitehead wondered whether they had told the president. Shultz thought they had, but was concerned that Reagan didn't "appreciate the problems with arms sales to Iran."[11]

A week after Weir's release, McFarlane instructed North to assume the responsibilities held by Ledeen, but to do so in a circumspect manner. Deniability was the criterion. Accordingly, North informed Ledeen "McFarlane has told me I'm supposed to now handle all the operational aspects of this, and McFarlane has no knowledge... that Ledeen is doing anything, much less that North has taken over what he is doing."[12]

To assure a smooth transition from Ledeen to North with the Israelis, Schwimmer flew to Washington toward the end of September where, according to North's calendar, he met with him and Ledeen, on September 26.[13] Schwimmer returned two weeks later with Nimrodi and Ghorbanifar for further introductions, although the issue of hostage William Buckley's fate gave added urgency and dimension to their trip.

---

[10] "Poindexter deposition," *Report of the Congressional Committees Investigating the Iran-Contra Affair, Appendix B, volume 20, (Washington, D.C.:GPO, 1987), 1094.* [Cited hereafter as *Iran-Contra Affair*.] In describing this period, Poindexter said, "In November of 1985 I was very confused as to what had been approved and what hadn't been approved and frankly thought it had been run in a very slipshod manner."

[11] "Hill note," September 21, 1985, in Walsh, *Final Report*, 335n.74.

[12] *Tower Report*, B-28n.19.

[13] Ibid, B-29.

On October 1, the Israelis had carried out a major air raid on PLO headquarters in Tunis in retaliation for the PLO "Force 17" murder of three Israelis aboard a yacht off Cyprus.[14] Two days later Islamic Jihad, Mugniyeh's group, declared that it had executed William Buckley "because of U.S. involvement in Tuesday's Israeli air raid on Yasser Arafat's PLO headquarters in Tunis."[15] There was a presumption, though no confirmation, that Buckley was dead, so North asked Ledeen to arrange for Gorbanifar to come to Washington as soon as possible to discuss Buckley and the other hostages.[16]

Some, like North held out a slim hope that Buckley was still alive, but others, like Charles Allen, thought that he was already dead.[17] (It would be at least another month before it would be confirmed that he died in June of harsh treatment and had not been executed by Mugniyeh.) The prospect of hostages being systematically executed, however, raised the question of whether the United States could have any further dealings with Iran.

Schwimmer, Nimrodi, and Gorbanifar met North briefly in his office in the Old Executive Office Building on October 8, but the seizure of the Italian cruise ship *Achille Lauro* the day before claimed all of North's attention and he left Ledeen in charge of their meeting.[18] Thus, although McFarlane had attempted to move Ledeen out of the picture, circumstances kept him directly involved for several more weeks. He would report directly to McFarlane on the results of their conversations.

The four men engaged in a wide-ranging discussion regarding the continuation of arms for hostages. Gorbanifar assured them of the

---

[14] "Israeli Jets' Raid Target Was Elite Arafat Unit," *Washington Times*, October 4, 1985, 6.
[15] "Terrorists Say They Executed U.S. Hostage," *Washington Times*, October 4, 1985, 1.
[16] *Iran-Contra Affair*, 169.
[17] "Charles Allen deposition," *Iran-Contra Affair*, Appendix B, volume 1, 351.
[18] Samuel Segev, *The Iranian Triangle: The Untold Story of Israel's Role in the Iran-Contra Affair* (New York: Free Press, 1988), *182-3*. Gorbanifar traveled to Washington under the alias of Nicholas Kralis.

hostages' safety and that Tehran could deliver. He also put forth Tehran's desire to acquire a broader category of weapons, beyond the anti-tank *TOW* missile. They were especially interested in acquiring the latest versions of air-to-air weapons, *Phoenix* and *Sidewinder*, as well as the anti-ship and anti-air, *Harpoon* and *Hawk*.[19] "For each bundle of advanced weapons, they were offering one or more hostages," Ledeen observed.[20]

Gorbanifar's request did not include a specific proposal; he was most interested in learning what the American reaction would be to a large arms-for-hostages deal. To pique Washington's interest, he also confided to Ledeen that "it had become possible for us to talk directly to spokesmen for the 'conservative line'…and we were promised meetings within the next month."[21]

During the course of their discussions Ledeen voiced his objections to continuing on the arms-for-hostages track and argued for a straight political dialogue. Schwimmer and Nimrodi immediately objected, ostensibly on the grounds that there were also Israeli Jews in Iran whom they hoped eventually to repatriate, but actually because of their concern to keep open the arms sales connection. A straight political dialogue would cut them, and Israel, out. When Ledeen asked Gorbanifar for his view, the Iranian surprisingly agreed with Ledeen declaring that developing a political relationship "should be the focus of their energies." If we continue on the arms for hostages track "we shall become hostages to the hostages."[22]

In reporting on their discussion to McFarlane, Ledeen strongly expressed the view that not only should the United States get out of the hostage business, based on Gorbanifar's promise of direct contacts

---

[19] The *Phoenix* was a long-range air-to-air missile carried exclusively by the *F-14*; the *Sidewinder* was a short-range air-to-air missile; *Harpoon* was an over-the-horizon anti-ship missile; and the *Hawk* was a medium-range surface-to-air missile.

[20] Michael Ledeen, *Perilous Statecraft: An Insider's Account of the Iran Contra Affair* (New York: Scribner, 1988), 137.

[21] Ibid.

[22] *Tower Report*, B-29 and "Ledeen Deposition," *Iran-Contra Affair,* Appendix B, volume 15, 1015.

with Iranian leaders, he wanted out of it, too. McFarlane agreed, declaring, "I have a bad feeling about this whole operation, and said his intention was to shut the whole thing down." This was not Ledeen's view. "I asked him not to shut the whole thing down, but to let the political thing go ahead." McFarlane said he would think about it. When Ledeen told him that Gorbanifar had arranged a meeting with a senior Iranian official in Europe at the end of the month, McFarlane "approved the trip for me to go and meet with this person."[23]

Islamic Jihad's announcement that it had executed William Buckley had dramatically affected all concerned. Assuming Iran controlled the hostages, it raised the fundamental question of whether any relationship with Iran was possible. This was certainly the case for North, who apparently did not yet realize that the Iranians had precious little leverage or control over Mugniyeh's Islamic Jihad. As noted above, however, Shultz and McFarlane, if not Casey, were fully apprised that Mugniyeh was the wild-card terrorist not under anyone's control, yet acted as if Iran could control the hostages.

Tehran did not control Mugniyeh and therefore could not deliver the hostages on demand, but only insofar as they could persuade or bribe him to part with them. The Iranians, desperate for weapons and realizing that the Americans were dubious about continuing, therefore, through Gorbanifar, were at great pains to insist that they *could* deliver the hostages. Given the American interest in them, to claim otherwise would end their chances of acquiring weapons.

At the same time, they would repeatedly hint at the need to get beyond the hostage issue, as Gorbanifar had just demonstrated in his talks with Ledeen. In any case, sensing that the Americans would realize at any moment that they could not deliver on the hostages the Iranians sought as large a deal as possible, as soon as possible, promising to release all of them in a grand bargain.

The Israelis were, perhaps, affected most by the claim of Buckley's execution. The arms-for-hostages deal was Peres' entrée into the Iranian arms market and if it collapsed the market would disappear.

---

[23] Ibid, 1019-20.

The Israeli answer to this conundrum was to inveigle the U.S. government deeper into the game of supplying arms to Iran. Up to this point, the United States was effectively uninvolved, except for McFarlane's as yet unrealized promise to replenish the weapons the Israelis had sold to Iran. Israeli threats to stop further arms supply unless the United States promptly replenished weapons already delivered was in essence a bluff.

The Israeli need to involve the U.S. government more directly dovetailed perfectly with the new world order faction's objective and was the basis for the collusion between McFarlane and David Kimche which would produce what became known as the *Hawk* deal.

The Hawk deal in International Context

Over two months passed between the September Israeli shipment and the November *Hawk* deal. McFarlane explained the lag in terms of the press of events and his preoccupation with the president's "crowded" schedule. First, was the *Achille Lauro* hijack in the second week of October, which resulted in tense standoffs with Egypt and Italy over the hijackers.[24] Then, in rapid succession came the president's visit to the United Nations in late October with its attendant speeches and meetings, including a meeting with Soviet foreign minister Eduard Shevardnadze, followed by preparations for the Reagan-Gorbachev summit, November 19-21. McFarlane continued, "I spent nearly all my time chairing meetings on our arms control positions and on four major addresses we wanted the president to deliver in support of our goals at the summit." Thus, he says, "I sent the Iran file to the back of my mind."[25]

Indeed, McFarlane was busy. The October-November time frame saw the national security adviser at the center of a major controversy over arms control, which was part of the Washington-Moscow

---

[24] See Michael Bohn, *The Achille Lauro Hijacking: Lessons in the Politics and Prejudice of Terrorism* (Dulles: Potomac Books, 2004). Bohn was director of the White House Situation Room during the events.
[25] Robert C. McFarlane, *Special Trust* (New York: Cadell & Davies, 1994), 40-41.

maneuvering before the summit. In brief, although Gorbachev was a new face and had adopted a more open style compared to previous Soviet leaders, he sought to accomplish the same objectives as had Andropov and Brezhnev—strategic weapons dominance over the United States, intermediate-range nuclear missile domination over Western Europe and Japan, and control over Iran.

After six months of fruitless negotiations at Geneva, in September Gorbachev produced an arms control proposal that promised a fifty percent reduction in offensive forces, but only if the United States cancelled SDI, which, of course, would insure Moscow's strategic weapons dominance. Also, having failed to prevent the U.S. deployment of the Pershing II/Cruise Missile package to Western Europe, Gorbachev sought to define these weapons out of existence.

The Soviets sought to accomplish this by resurrecting their old definition of what constituted a strategic weapon, which was any weapon, including an aircraft that could strike the Soviet Union. The SALT II treaty defined a strategic weapon as any ballistic missile with a range exceeding 3,200 miles. If the Soviet definition were accepted, it would mean that forward-based aircraft and the just-deployed Pershing II/Cruise Missile package to Western Europe would be counted as strategic weapons and be part of the fifty-percent reduction. No Russian intermediate-range weapons would be affected, thus insuring Moscow's nuclear domination of Western Europe and Japan.

As the Soviet Union had more missiles than the United States, a 50 percent reduction on both sides would still leave the Soviets with their existing advantage. There were other hedges in their proposal, but its gist would leave the Soviet Union with strategic and intermediate-range weapons' advantages vis-a-vis the United States, Western Europe, and Japan. In truth, the Soviet proposal's one-sidedness was transparent and patently unacceptable, except as a propaganda and negotiating tactic.[26]

---

[26] Robert Toth, "U.S. Criticizes Soviet Arms Plan, Warns of Allied Split," *Los Angeles Times*, October 9, 1985, 1 and Elizabeth Pond, "US Arms Expert Sees

Conferring with his aides, President Reagan decided to "undermine their propaganda plan by offering a counter proposal which stresses our acceptance of some of their figures, such as a 50 percent cut in weapons and a total of 6000 warheads, etc. Those are pretty much like what we've already proposed."[27] However, he did more than offer a counterproposal. Over the next months the president took steps to clear the way for SDI testing and development to proceed beyond basic research and he raised fundamental geopolitical issues that would have to be discussed at the summit.

Reagan understood that the Soviets were engaging in a bidding game to see if there was a price at which he would give up SDI. It was an open secret that the administration was split between those, like Shultz, who wanted to use SDI as a "bargaining chip" to get an arms control agreement and those like the president and Weinberger, who saw strategic defense as essential to American strategy. But the president was firm: "we would *not* trade away our program of research–SDI—for a promise of Soviet reduction in nuclear arms."[28]

The first step, in which McFarlane was centrally involved, was to strengthen the SDI program by reinterpreting the terms of the 1972 ABM treaty to permit work to proceed beyond mere research to testing and development. Appearing on the television news program *Meet the Press* on Sunday, October 6, and in the course of criticizing the Soviet arms control proposal, McFarlane reaffirmed the president's determination to pursue a vigorous SDI program, which was clearly consistent with the ABM Treaty. Then, he said, "research, testing and development of new defensive weapons 'involving new physical concepts…are approved and authorized by the treaty. Only deployment is foreclosed…'"[29]

Pluses and Minuses in Soviet Proposal," *Christian Science Monitor*, October 11, 1985, 9.
[27] Ronald Reagan, *An American Life* (New York: Simon and Schuster, 1990), 629.
[28] Ibid, 628.
[29] Lou Cannon, "Reagan Aide Faults Soviet Arms Plan," *Washington Post*, October 7, 1985, 1. For the private bureaucratic discussions that preceded McFarlane's public statement, see Don Oberdorfer, *The Turn: From the Cold War to a New Era: The*

His assertion immediately created a storm of controversy. Up to this point, the United States had defined the treaty as permitting only a limited ground-base deployment and prohibiting anything beyond laboratory research on new missile defense components. The new "broad" interpretation would permit the United States to go beyond laboratory research to testing and development of systems based on new physical principles.

Critics howled, demanding that the United States adhere to the treaty as originally understood, but the new interpretation was straightforward.[30] "Agreed Statement D" of the treaty stipulated that "in the event ABM systems based on other physical principles and including components capable of substituting for ABM interceptor missiles, ABM launchers or ABM radars are created in the future, specific limitations on such systems and their components would be subject to discussion..."[31]

The statement "in the event ABM systems based on other physical principles...are created in the future" implied clearly that for a "system" to have been created there would ipso facto have to have been research, testing, and development. As SDI was based on "other physical principles," it followed logically and legally that the program had to go beyond research to testing and development before it could be termed a "system" subject to discussion.

Nevertheless, of all the critics Secretary Shultz howled the loudest. In an "emotionally charged meeting," which one administration source described as a "knock-down, drag-out meeting," Shultz pulled out all the stops in an effort to force the president to back away from the broad interpretation, including another threat to resign. Citing

---

United States and the Soviet Union, 1983-1990 (New York: Poseidon Press, 1991), 123-26.

[30] For one critique, see Alan Sherr, "Sound Legal Reasoning or Policy Expedient? The 'New Interpretation' of the ABM Treaty," *International Security*, vol. II, no. 3 (Winter 1986-87) 71-93. See appendix A for State Department legal adviser Abraham Sofaer's statement before the House Foreign Affairs Committee.

[31] For the treaty and appendices, see Gerard Smith, *Doubletalk: The Story of SALT I* (New York: Doubleday, 1980), 487-502.

"messages of concern" from London and Bonn and support of arms control negotiator, Paul Nitze, Shultz said that a change of such magnitude would cause a storm among U.S. allies as well as in the congress.[32]

The president countered Shultz by citing the State Department's own legal counsel Abraham Sofaer, whose analysis supported the broad interpretation. Sofaer pointed out that the negotiating record showed Moscow's refusal to accept a total prohibition of ABM systems based on other physical principles.[33] He also showed that the illegal Krasnoyarsk radar was part of a very robust Russian missile defense system that flaunted the treaty's restrictions.[34] Nevertheless, the argument that carried the day was that, as it would be some time before the U.S. program would be ready to go beyond the research stage, the broad interpretation was premature.

Thus, the outcome of the argument was Shultz's formulation that the United States would continue to conduct the SDI program "in accordance with a restrictive interpretation" of the ABM treaty, even though "a broader interpretation of our authority was fully justified."[35] Although it seemed that Shultz had forced the president to back down, a White House spokesman later declared that the president's position remained that "research stops short of deployment [but] it encompasses research, testing and development."[36]

---

[32] Don Oberdorfer, "Shultz Was Key in ABM Policy Switch," *Washington Post*, October 17, 1985, 4. Nitze had actually changed his view to support of the broad interpretation.

[33] "Written Statement of Abraham D. Sofaer," October 22, 1985, Appendix A, in Sherr, "Sound Legal Reasoning or Policy Expedient?" 90.

[34] David Yost, "Soviet Ballistic Missile Defense And NATO," *Orbis*, (Summer 1985), 281-93.

[35] Don Oberdorfer and David Ottaway, "U.S. Clarifies ABM Pact View," *Washington Post*, October 15, 1985, 1 and William Beecher, "White House Moved to Save Face on Interpretation of ABM Treaty," *Boston Globe*, October 16, 1985, 18. See also George Shultz, *Turmoil and Triumph* (New York: Macmillan, 1993), 578-82.

[36] Charles Mohr, "U.S. Keeps Options For 'Star Wars,'" *New York Times*, October 20, 1985, 7.

Although the president's position was clear, even if the administration's position was ambiguous, the fact was a major evolution of U.S. strategy had taken place. The public argument had the effect of making it seem—especially to the Soviets–that the SDI program was further along than the administration admitted and ready to enter the "testing" stage.[37]

A few days later the president raised other matters for resolution before an improvement in relations with Moscow could occur. In a major address celebrating the 40th anniversary of the United Nations, the president laid out his agenda for the forthcoming summit. Calling for a "fresh start," the president offered to discuss America's "deep and abiding differences" with the Soviet Union on the basis of complete candor. He began by declaring that the United States, as a free society, "cannot accommodate ourselves to the use of force and subversion to consolidate and expand the reach of totalitarianism." [38]

He pointed to three areas of conflict: Soviet treaty violations, the strategic weapons balance, and regional conflicts. Focusing on the 1972 ban on biological and toxin weapons, the 1975 Helsinki Accords, and U.S.-Soviet strategic weapons agreements, the president said that we feel it will be necessary to discuss "what we believe are violations of a number of the provisions in all of these agreements."

He went on to refer to the recent Soviet arms control proposal, which he said contained several "seeds" we could "nurture," but in discussing the "vital relationship between offensive and defensive systems," he wished to focus on "the possibility of moving toward a more stable and secure world in which defenses play a growing role." "If," he declared, we are "destined by history to compete, militarily, to keep the peace, then let us compete in systems that defend our societies rather than in weapons which can destroy us..."

---

[37] John Fialka, "Reagan Team Justifies Star Wars Plan By Claiming Loophole in ABM Treaty," *Wall Street Journal*, October 22, 1985, 64.

[38] Ronald Reagan, "Address to the 40th Session of the United Nations General Assembly in New York," October 24, 1985, *Ronald Reagan: Public Speeches*.

Finally, he pointed to Soviet involvement in five regional conflicts: Afghanistan, Cambodia, Ethiopia, Angola, and Nicaragua, pledging that American support for "struggling democratic resistance forces must not and shall not cease." At the same time, he proposed a three-part negotiating framework for resolving them, involving discussions between the parties to end each conflict, negotiations between the United States and the Soviet Union on how best to assist in conflict termination, and American developmental assistance once conflicts ended.[39]

Having set the agenda for the coming summit, in early November, the president announced Washington's counterproposal to Moscow's arms control proposal on the eve of Secretary Shultz's trip to meet with Soviet foreign minister Shervardnadze. He characterized the proposal as "deep cuts, no first-strike advantage, defensive research—because defense is safer than offense—and no cheating."[40]

Reagan's proposal in essence took on Gorbachev's bidding game and went one further. Where Gorbachev proposed a reduction to 6,000 total warheads, Reagan proposed more than fifty percent cuts in offensive forces, to a limit of 4,500 total warheads, with 3,000 on heavy missiles. He would set a limit of no more than 350 long-range bombers and 1,500 cruise missiles. Reagan's proposal was unconditional, although it contained no offer on defensive arms, whereas Gorbachev conditioned his offer on the cancellation of SDI.[41] Nevertheless, as the November summit approached, the two sides

---

[39] Raymond Coffey, "Reagan Shows Fist, Open Hand To Soviet," *Chicago Tribune*, October 25, 1985, 1; Lou Cannon, "President Calls for 'Fresh Start' With Soviets," *Washington Post*, October 25, 1985, 1, and "On to the Summit," *Wall Street Journal*, October 25, 1985, 18, and Lou Cannon and David Hoffman, "Arms Control, Regional Peace; Reagan Signaling Gorbachev That 2 Issues Are Linked, Officials Say," *Washington Post*, October 25, 1985, 31.

[40] Lou Cannon, "Reagan Announces Arms Plan; Shultz To Seek 2nd Summit," *Washington Post*, November 1, 1985, 1.

[41] William Chaze, "Back in the Game," *U.S. News & World Report*, November 11, 1985, 28.

appeared to have set the stage for a substantive discussion, if not for an actual agreement.

The "Hawk" Set-up

The September-November period was filled with intense activity and McFarlane was deeply involved in a variety of policy-related moves. Yet, for all of that, he had by no means sent the "Iran file" to the back of his mind. Indeed, the weeks leading up to the Geneva summit were when he and David Kimche put in place the *Hawk* deal, which entangled the U.S. government directly and illegally in the arms-for-hostages scheme.

In late October, on the 27th, McFarlane sent Ledeen to Geneva to meet with Hassan Karoubi, the senior Iranian leader in the meeting arranged by Gorbanifar. Kimche, Schwimmer and Nimrodi also attended. It was Ledeen's first face-to-face meeting with Karoubi, but not the others, who knew him well. Ledeen, of course, was familiar with Karoubi's earlier memo that had been passed to him by the Israelis and prodded McFarlane into action in July.[42]

After professing his group's desire for an improvement in relations with the United States, Karoubi got to his point. He claimed that as a result of the mid-October elections "he and his men were now in key positions and that they could influence their country's policy and bring about the release of the five remaining American hostages." They could also apply pressure on Hezbollah in Lebanon "to refrain from further kidnapping."[43]

In return for getting the hostages out, Karoubi wanted a one-time "blanket order" of 150 *Hawk* missiles, 200 *Sidewinder* missiles, and thirty-to-fifty *Phoenix* missiles. There would be a staggered release of hostages in three groups interspersed with arms deliveries. Although surprised by the large number of weapons being asked for, but

---

[42] See chapter 4, 15-22.
[43] Segev, *Iranian Triangle*, 183.

encouraged by the prospect of the release of the rest of the hostages, Ledeen agreed to present this offer to his superiors in Washington.[44]

Before he left, in a separate conversation, Kimche told Ledeen that Rabin was "very upset about the U.S. failure to "replenish the TOW missiles" and doubted that he would "agree to sending more arms to Iran until arrangements are made for supplying replacements."[45] Although Ledeen had reported previously about Rabin's concern to have the *TOW*s replenished, he promised to bring it up again upon his return.

Ledeen returned to Washington on October 30 to report to both McFarlane and North. Upon hearing what Ledeen had to say, McFarlane expressed skepticism about "the existence of moderate elements in Iran, let alone their ability to come to power." Nevertheless, he did not reject the offer, but instructed North and Ledeen that no weapons would be shipped without the release of "live Americans." Apparently, there was no discussion about the replenishment of the *TOW*s.[46]

The next day, October 31, and unbeknownst to Ledeen, McFarlane received word from Kimche that the Iranians had upped the ante. After the meeting with Ledeen, Gorbanifar had flown to Dubai for a meeting with Kangarlu who was there on a weapons' buying trip. After hearing Gorbanifar's report and checking with Rafsanjani, Kangarlu drafted a formal proposal, which added several inducements, including a written pledge of cooperation, while increasing Iran's demands for sophisticated American weapons worth hundreds of millions of dollars.

> From this moment onwards, Iran pledges not to engage in any hostile acts against the U.S.—neither bombings, nor kidnappings, nor attacks on American interests in the Middle East. Iran likewise pledges to aid the Afghan rebels in their struggle against the Soviet army of occupation and to transfer to them, any equipment made available to them by the

---

[44] *Iran-Contra Affair*, 175.
[45] Segev, *Iranian Triangle*, 184.
[46] *Iran-Contra Affair*, 175.

U.S....As for the hostages, Iran is prepared to guarantee the release of only five of them. Iran has no authority or involvement regarding other hostages.[47]

Kangarlu proposed a five-step plan for weapons deliveries and hostage releases beginning on November 12 and ending on the 25th. Except for the first weapons shipment, when the sequence would be delivery first, hostage release second, Iran would release one hostage at five P.M. on the day of each subsequent delivery, which would arrive at midnight. The Rev. Martin Jenco would be released first, followed by Thomas Sutherland, Peter Kilburn, David Jacobson, and Terry Anderson.

Each delivery would include 35 *Hawk*, 50 *Sidewinder*, and 15 *Phoenix* missiles. These numbers were substantially higher than those specified by Karoubi. By comparison there were to be 175 total *Hawks* compared to 150 in Karoubi's proposal, 250 *Sidewinders* compared to 200, and 75 *Phoenix* compared to 50. Once completed, Iran would host a visit by a senior U.S. representative.[48] On the other hand, Iranian support for the anti-Soviet resistance in Afghanistan was an unanticipated bonus.

Gorbanifar left Dubai for London on October 30 for a meeting with Kimche, Schwimmer, and Nimrodi.[49] When Kimche saw the Iranian offer he knew at once that it boded ill for Israel. If it went forward as proposed, the hostages would be freed, the United States and Iran would reestablish political relations, and Israel would be shut out of the Iranian arms market. Israel would undoubtedly be the main supplier for the five proposed arms deliveries, but after that, when U.S.-Iranian relations were reestablished, Washington would become the main supplier of arms to Iran, and Israel would be relegated to the sidelines. Thus, Kimche could not allow the deal to stand as proposed.

---

[47] Segev, *Iranian Triangle*, 184-85. The reference to "only five" hostages evidently referred to the Americans and excluded the French hostages.
[48] Ibid, 185.
[49] Ibid, 194.

As their discussion progressed, Kimche focused on three points, the number and types of weapons and the release sequence for the hostages. Within minutes, Kangarlu's original proposal lay in shreds. As the discussion continued, "the participants began calling Washington, Jerusalem, and Tehran" for guidance. As Segev notes, "during the following days the Hawk deal would come together in long telephone conversations between American and Israeli officials, and between them and the Israeli and Iranian middlemen." At the very least, this must be taken to mean that Kimche talked with McFarlane and Peres, and Gorbanifar with Kangarlu, if not also Rafsanjani.[50]

Kimche related McFarlane's view that hostages must be released first before any weapons were delivered. Gorbanifar countered with the argument that weapons had to be delivered first, and then hostages would be released. Kimche declared that Israel could not deliver the amount and type of weapons specified "because of the American embargo." Initially, he said, Israel could only deliver the *Hawk* missile. After telephoning Kangarlu and receiving permission to negotiate for "Hawks only," Gorbanifar proposed a way out of the impasse.[51]

Gorbanifar declared that Iran desperately needed *Hawk* missiles to defend against "high flying Iraqi and Soviet planes."[52] He proposed that to break the impasse "Israel supply 80 missiles in a single shipment, with five American hostages and two Lebanese Jews, also captives, being released simultaneously." Afterward, "Kimche briefed McFarlane on his conversation with Gorbanifar."[53] McFarlane must

---

[50] Ibid, 194-95.
[51] Ibid, 194.
[52] Gorbanifar's technical unfamiliarity with weapons specifications—the *Hawk* missile was a low-altitude, not a high-altitude interceptor—would shortly become a major source of friction, although it is true that the Israelis did not correct his misunderstanding.
[53] Ibid, 194. McFarlane, *Iran-Contra Affair*, 175, testified to congressional investigators that he and Kimche had had "a series of meetings...in the fall of 1985." However, the record indicates that there were none between the November 8 meeting and one on December 8.

have agreed, for that is the deal that was supposed to constitute the first shipment. As it evolved, however, the Israelis would not be able to ship all 80 *Hawk* missiles in a single aircraft, which resulted in what was supposed to be three deliveries and a sequential release of the hostages. That, too, would not transpire, as we shall see, for the *Hawk* deal quickly turned into a fiasco. *Operation Espresso*, the Israeli codename for the *Hawk* deal, would leave a bitter taste for all concerned.

The Hawk Entanglement

Both the Israelis and the new world order faction wanted to use the *Hawk* deal to entangle the United States government in arms sales, but for quite different reasons. To reiterate, the Israelis involved were Prime Minister Peres and his men, Kimche, Schwimmer, and Nimrodi; the principal figures for the new world order faction were Schultz and McFarlane, but not their aides, who were unaware of their collusion. Each group used the other to achieve its objectives, which were only partially coincident. And in each group the principals sacrificed their minions in the pursuit of success and to avoid blame.

Schultz and McFarlane wanted to employ the Israelis to entangle President Reagan in an arms-for-hostages deal that would torpedo his plan for rapprochement with Iran. Israel was the vehicle for this objective, but the coincidence of interest was only temporary. Once achieved, as we shall see, the new world order faction would attempt to severely cripple the U.S.-Israeli relationship and close off the Israeli arms conduit.

Peres, on the other hand, understood that Israel's interests were not the same as America's and feared that if the arms-for-hostages deal went through it would mark the end of Israeli arms sales to Iran. McFarlane was threatening to shut the operation down and resign and so to avoid being left hung out to dry Peres sought to go beyond McFarlane and draw the United States government directly into the arms sales business with Iran to insure Israel's own continued access to what was a lucrative arms market.

The two groups colluded over the next two weeks, as McFarlane tried to draw Defense and the CIA into the *Hawk* deal, while the

Israelis tried to involve the State Department. Shultz, who followed events very closely, and McFarlane insured that the state department was not implicated in the arms sales. Weinberger objected strenuously to the *Hawk* deal, and kept Defense out of it, but the CIA illegally became entangled.

The deal with the Iranians agreed in principal, the Israelis wanted face-to-face confirmation of U.S. government participation. In the second week of November Peres sent Kimche, Rabin, and Amiram Nir, his counterterrorism expert, to Washington to talk to McFarlane and North. Kimche arrived on November 8, Nir on the 14th and Rabin on the 15th.

Although Ledeen says he asked Kimche to come to Washington to remonstrate with McFarlane, who was depressed (there were rumors about affairs with a reporter and a White House staffer) and on the verge of resigning his office because of an on-going battle with Chief of Staff Don Regan, Kimche had his own reasons for making the trip.[54] With North now about to become more deeply involved as McFarlane's surrogate, it was important for Kimche to meet him.

More important, however, was the Israelis' need to assess the United States commitment to the deal. Ironically, it appears that Ledeen did not know the true purpose of Kimche's trip and it was only later that he learned of the *Hawk* deal.[55] In any case, Kimche lunched with North and Ledeen on November 9, and the next day lunched with North and McFarlane, without Ledeen.[56] There can be little doubt that McFarlane and Kimche privately worked out the final details of the plan at this time during the "series of meetings" McFarlane testified

---

[54] Theodore Draper, *A Very Thin Line: The Iran-Contra Affairs* (New York: Hill and Wang, 1991), 181, thought it "odd" that a "part-time" consultant should "enlist an Israeli official to come all the way to Washington to strengthen the 'resolve' of an American superior." See also, Ledeen, *Perilous Statecraft*, 149-50.
[55] Ibid, 150-51.
[56] Scott Armstrong et al., The *Chronology: The Documented Day-by-Day Account of the Secret Military Assistance to Iran and the Contras* (New York: Warner Books, 1987), 173.

that he had with Kimche "in the fall of 1985."[57] Moreover, Kimche was now also acquainted with North, who was being groomed to play a larger role.

Following Kimche's visit, that same day McFarlane moved to entangle the defense department. He met with Weinberger and disclosed that the "hostage release efforts were tied to arms sales to Iran." As the defense secretary noted in his diary, McFarlane "wants to start 'negot.' [negotiations] Exploration with the Iranians (+ Israelis) to give Iranians weapons for our hostages." McFarlane presented the issue to Weinberger as if they were at the start of discussions, when, in fact, he had already worked out the deal.

Weinberger, of course, was viscerally opposed to any deals with Iran and their conversation was heated but inconclusive. The next day, however, in a follow-up discussion, Weinberger allowed as how "we might give them—thru Israelis—Hawks but no Phoenix."[58] In this way, Weinberger sought to avoid direct U.S. involvement, while complying with what he thought was the president's policy.

Weinberger's shift of position may have been the result of a change of administration attitude toward "talking to terrorists." On November 8, a packet of letters from four of the hostages was tossed from a car onto the doorstep of the West Beirut Office of *Associated Press*. A cover letter signed by Jenco, Anderson, Jacobson, and Sutherland, urged the president to negotiate with their captors. The result was the administration decided it would "talk directly with terrorists as long as concessions or blackmail are not involved."[59]

White House spokesman Edward Djerejian distinguished between "negotiations" and "talk." We do not negotiate with terrorists, he said, but are prepared to "talk to all parties...even the abductors of American hostages—in an effort to obtain their safe release." The *L.A. Times* reporter, Eleanor Clift, astutely observed that Islamic Jihad was

---

[57] *Iran-Contra Affair*, 175.
[58] Walsh, *Final Report*, 91.
[59] Eleanor Clift, "U.S. Revises Its Stances on Talking to Terrorists," *Los Angeles Times*, November 13, 1985, 1.

thought to be holding the hostages and was demanding the release of the Kuwait-held Dawa 17 in exchange for release of the hostages.[60]

In any case, within days, Secretary Shultz learned of McFarlane's meeting with Weinberger. The secretary's aides, Charles Hill and Nick Platt, each had made a record and in a meeting just before Shultz left for Geneva, the five of them, including Armacost and Whitehead, discussed what they had learned. According to Hill's note: "in last few days Bud asked Cap how to get 600 Hawks and 200 Phoenix to Iran. It's highly illegal. Cap won't do it I'm sure. Purpose not clear. Another sign of funny stuff on Iran issue."[61] Thus, contrary to Shultz's testimony to congressional investigators, he was well informed of the *Hawk* deal days before it occurred.

Amiram Nir arrived for a meeting with North on November 14. The two had worked together during the *Achille Lauro* crisis and North had been impressed and grateful for the help Nir had given in tracking down the terrorists. As it was apparent that Washington was attempting to locate those holding the hostages, Nir offered to cooperate with North in a covert operation to find them. He would remain in Washington for the better part of a week and reach a tentative agreement on two plans, but not on how to fund their operation.[62] His true mission, however, may have been to keep in as close touch with North as possible over the next several days as the *Hawk* deal unraveled.

On the same day that Nir and North began their talks, McFarlane and Poindexter met with Casey and McMahon in the White House for their regular weekly briefing. During the briefing, McFarlane made it a point to tell them that, having heard rumors regarding Weir's release that the U.S. was indirectly involved in shipping arms to Iran, "or at least to wink at some transferred from Israel," he "called David Kimche... on the open line to assure him that that was not the

---

[60] Ibid.
[61] "Hill note," November 14, 1985, as cited in Walsh, *Final Report*, 91 and "Platt note," November 14, 1985, in Ibid, 305.
[62] *Iran–Contra Affair*, 175-76.

case and that no deal had been struck for the release of Weir." Calling on an "open line," rather than a secure line indicated that McFarlane wanted to establish for the record in the intercepts that he had not been involved in an arms-for-hostages arrangement.[63]

When the briefing was over and McMahon had left the room, McFarlane "casually" mentioned in an aside to Casey that the "Israelis plan to move arms to certain elements of the Iranian military who are prepared to overthrow the government."[64] This was an extraordinary remark and its purpose unclear. Israel providing arms for a military coup was never part of any discussion. Was it simply loose talk, or intended to prepare Casey to be supportive of Israel when the CIA was called upon to assist? McFarlane knew that Rabin was arriving the next day, so informing Casey of an imminent aggressive Israeli move would be certain to elicit his approval and support.

Rabin met with Casey the following morning, November 15. When he asked if "the president still approved Israeli arms sales to Iran?" the CIA director reassured him based upon the information McFarlane had just given him the day before.[65] Had McFarlane not informed Casey of the impending action, it is not at all clear that he would have known what Rabin was talking about. McFarlane had only briefed Casey once before on his "contacts with Iran," and that had been almost two months earlier on September 20, in the aftermath of Weir's release.[66] That had been the first inkling Casey had had of McFarlane's Iran initiative. Clearly, the CIA director was not "in the loop."

Following his meeting with Casey, Rabin met with his counterpart, Weinberger. His talking points included discussion of the supply of "American arms to Israel, including construction of new submarines for the Israeli navy." Oddly, he does not seem to have discussed the subject of *TOW* replenishment with the defense secretary, or the

---

[63] "John McMahon deposition," *Iran-Contra Affair*, Appendix B, volume 17, 84-87.
[64] McMahon, "memorandum for the record," November 15, 1985, in Walsh, *Final Report*, 207 and Iran-*Contra Affair*, 176.
[65] Walsh, *Final Report*, 207.
[66] See page 158 above.

impending arms shipment to Iran.[67] He reserved those topics for his discussion with McFarlane.

In his meeting with McFarlane, Rabin informed the national security adviser that Israel would be making another arms shipment within the next few days. He wanted reassurance that the president was behind the arms sales, that it was a "joint project" between the two countries, and that the United States would replenish the weapons Israel delivered. The answers he got, however, were anything but reassuring.

Rabin "wanted to reconfirm that the President of the United States still endorsed this concept of Israel negotiating these arms sales." Instead of a simple "yes," McFarlane replied in his typically vague and circuitous manner: "the president's authorization for Israel to sell arms to Iran subject to replenishment by the United States was still in effect." Then, he said, even more vaguely, that this authorization was based on "recent questions and reaffirmation by the president that I had received."[68]

If Rabin was unsettled by McFarlane's tangential reply as to whether Reagan "still endorsed this concept," he was further disturbed by McFarlane's answer to his next question. Rabin wanted "reassurance that the matter was indeed a joint project between the United States and Israel." McFarlane replied: "while the United States supported Israel's activities, it was going along with Israel on this matter." "Going along with Israel on this matter" was hardly the answer Rabin expected. The only reading of this reply was that it was not a "joint project."[69]

Finally, as to the matter of replenishment, McFarlane assured him that he would be assigning the task to North within the next two weeks "to find a technical means of achieving the replacement." Whatever McFarlane meant by "technical means," replacement of weapons

---

[67] Segev, *Iranian Triangle*, 195.
[68] *Iran-Contra Affair*, 176.
[69] Ibid.

Israel would deliver would not occur for months, if it would be two weeks before McFarlane assigned North the task to do it.[70]

McFarlane's vague and troubling answers to Rabin's very specific questions undoubtedly confirmed in his mind that Israel was about to get itself into a very dangerous position, unless the United States was brought directly into the "project." Thus, whatever his differences with the prime minister, he was prepared to cooperate in the Peres' plan to do just that. The means of bringing the United States in would center on the flight logistics of the first *Hawk* missile shipment to Iran.

The plan was for Israel to botch the shipment and request American assistance in transporting the arms and for McFarlane to respond by facilitating the government's entanglement. Moreover, the president's national security adviser would orchestrate this maneuver from Geneva, Switzerland, where President Reagan and Mikhail Gorbachev were to meet.

The Geneva Summit

When Reagan and Gorbachev met November 19-21, the strategic situation had almost completely reversed since the Carter-Brezhnev meeting of 1979. Then, Moscow was on the offensive with a SALT II-codified strategic supremacy over the United States, dominance over Western Europe and Japan, and support for a worldwide network of revolutionary client regimes, which augured a transformation of the global order to the disadvantage of the United States.

President Reagan not only had defeated this Soviet strategy, but he had also reestablished American strategic and intermediate-range weapons advantage, rebuilt the western alliance, and was providing support for anti-Soviet resistance movements worldwide. He had codified his approach in a new strategic doctrine set forth in NSDD-75, based on strategic defense. The meeting in Geneva was thus the

---

[70] Ibid.

first act for him in a projected long play to create a new, re-designed global order.[71]

Reagan and Gorbachev had come to Geneva committed to a successful meeting, and by all accounts they got along amicably, but with their opposing positions well publicized in advance. In its essence, Reagan wanted to engage Gorbachev, and through him the Soviet leadership, to persuade them that agreeing with his strategy of shifting to the strategic defensive and arms reductions would not leave the Soviets worse off. Gorbachev, on the other hand, knew that he could count on the support of Shultz and most of the political establishment and hoped that the summit would be where he could convince the president to abandon SDI in return for substantial weapons reductions.

Reagan, therefore, needed to establish a negotiating baseline beyond which he would not go. That baseline was the annual report on Soviet treaty violations. On June 10, in NSDD 173, the president had instructed Weinberger to deliver the report by November 15 and to include recommendations of "appropriate and proportionate responses to these violations."[72] The defense secretary delivered his report on November 13.

In a letter accompanying the report, Weinberger addressed the president's Geneva meeting, cautioning him not to compromise on three issues: on continued observance of SALT II, restrictions on SDI research, and on a proposed *communiqué*.[73] Weinberger argued that continued adherence to SALT II would "sharply restrict the range of responses to past and current Soviet violations." Limiting the SDI program to research only "would diminish the prospects significantly that we will succeed in bringing our search for a strategic defense to fruition." Finally, agreement to a *communiqué* that allows "the Soviets

---

[71] See Arnold Horelick, "U.S.-Soviet Relations: The Return of Arms Control," *Foreign Affairs*, Vol. 63, no. 3, 511-537.

[72] Christopher Simpson, National Security Directives of the Reagan and Bush Administrations (Boulder: Westview, 1995), 549-55.

[73] "Weinberger Letter to Reagan on Arms Control," *New York Times*, November 16, 1985, 7.

to appear equally committed to full compliance...will make the difficult task of responding to...violations even more problematic."[74]

In the executive summary of the report, which, as in the previous report, found twenty-three Soviet treaty violations, Weinberger argued, "our original assumptions that the Soviets would not violate agreements ...have been proved false." Consequently, the only path to improved U.S.-Soviet relations was paradoxically through "a vigorous U.S. defense program and forceful responses to all perceived Soviet violations." Otherwise, he said, "current and future Soviet violations pose real risks to our security and to the process of arms control itself."[75]

The report, summary, and cover letter were strictly in conformity with past practice and analysis of Soviet treaty violations. The problem arose when they were leaked to the press just before the summit. The resultant furor seemed to point to Weinberger as the culprit. McFarlane, when asked whether the release was intended to "sabotage the summit talks," responded, "sure it was."[76] Whoever leaked the material, and it was probably not Weinberger, it served the president's purpose of publicly setting the baseline for his discussions with Gorbachev.

Indeed, when asked bluntly whether he would fire Weinberger for "pressing his views too vigorously," the president barked to newsmen "hell no!"[77] Weinberger did not accompany the president to Geneva, but his chief aides, Fred Ikle and Richard Perle did. Perle took with him a secure communication device so that he could be in touch with the defense secretary should the need arise for his advice.[78]

---

[74] Ibid.
[75] Walter Pincus, "Weinberger Urges Buildup Over Soviet 'Violations,'" *Washington Post*, November 18, 1985, 1.
[76] Bernard Weinraub, "Reagan Aides Upset by Disclosure Of Weinberger's Letter on Arms," *New York Times*, November 17, 1985, 1.
[77] Barbara Rehm and Bruce Drake, "'Hell, no,' Cap Won't Go," *New York News*, November 18, 1985, 3.
[78] Jay Winik, *On the Brink* (New York: Simon & Schuster, 1996), 387-88.

In fact, the president hewed to Weinberger's advice, refusing to bend on SDI and insisted on the need to go beyond research to some testing to determine the validity of concepts. The president also refused to agree to Shultz's proposal for a communiqué, but late in the afternoon of the second day agreed to issue a joint statement. *Communiqués* are negotiated in advance and Reagan wanted to insure that any summit statement accurately reflected what he and Gorbachev actually discussed, not what state department officials cooked up beforehand. The issue of continued adherence to SALT II did not arise.[79]

During the course of their talks the president hammered Gorbachev on the human rights issue, which the Soviet leader considered none of the outside world's business, but agreed to evaluate persons on a case-by-case basis.[80] The essence of the meeting from the president's point of view were three proposals he made to Gorbachev: for a transition to strategic defense, treaties on strategic and intermediate-range missiles, and a formula for the resolution of regional conflicts.

Reagan reiterated his concept of a transition from security based on offense to one based on defense, a sharp reduction of strategic missiles and the complete liquidation of intermediate-range weapons. He also offered a formula for the resolution of regional conflicts, calling for termination of military support, sponsorship of negotiations between the parties, and provision of developmental assistance afterward.

Gorbachev avoided any commitments, but did reaffirm that the Soviet Union had altered its strategic conception from "equal security" to "reasonable sufficiency," a major change in their national security requirements. He also responded to Reagan's regional conflicts formula with a hint about withdrawing from Afghanistan, which Reagan ignored.[81]

In response to Gorbachev's demands to end SDI, Reagan declined, but surprised the Soviet leader by offering to "share the benefits" of

---

[79] Jack Matlock, *Reagan and Gorbachev* (New York: Random House, 2004), 149-55.
[80] Shultz, *Turmoil and Triumph*, 603 and Matlock, *Reagan and Gorbachev*, 161.
[81] Shultz, *Turmoil and Triumph*, 601 and "Soviet May Seek Afghan Pullout Plan, U.S. Says," *New York Times*, November 25, 1985, 8. See also Oberdorfer, *The Turn*, 141-42.

any promising missile defense technology that might emerge from research *and* testing. After heated exchange, Gorbachev declared his disagreement, but acknowledged the president's belief in what he said. Reagan went further than his aides expected by also offering to invite Soviet scientists into U.S. laboratories where SDI research was being conducted.[82]

The joint statement, hammered out during an all-night session, was a sober recapitulation of what the two leaders had discussed, and emphasized Reagan's oft-stated view that nuclear war cannot be won and must not be fought.[83] Also, as Reagan wanted, there was no "statement of principles," "guidelines," or "road map." Nor were SALT II, the ABM treaty, and SDI mentioned in the statement, although the two leaders hoped for "early progress" on two issues on which they found common ground: the possibility of a fifty-percent reduction in strategic arms and an "interim agreement" on short-range weapons based in Europe.[84]

After it was over, the president reported to congress that while the two sides remained "far apart," "we met, as we had to meet. I had called for a fresh start—and we made that start.... We understand each other better. That's the key to peace." The president reported that Gorbachev had agreed to an exchange of meetings over the next two years. The summit, he said, was a good start, but for now "our byword must be, steady as we go."[85]

The Arms-for-Hostages Trap

While Reagan was in Geneva, the Israelis carefully orchestrated the *Hawk* deal to entangle the United States government in arms sales to Iran.

---

[82] Matlock, *Reagan and Gorbachev,* 167.
[83] Ibid, 165 and Rowland Evans And Robert Novak, "Reagan's New Realism," *Washington Post,* November 22, 1985, 23.
[84] Walter Pincus, "Little Gained on Arms Reduction," *Washington Post*, November 22, 1985, 11.
[85] David Hoffman, "President Pushed For Missile Defense," *Washington Post*, November 22, 1985, 1.

The August and September *TOW* shipments had been logistically straightforward. The Israelis shipped the missiles by DC-8 charter jets directly from Tel Aviv to Tabriz and Tehran, via the airspace of Cyprus and Turkey, a four-hour trip of roughly 1,500 miles.

The *Hawk* arrangement was quite different, more complex, longer, and open to mishap. Despite the presumed urgency in getting the weapons to Iran, Kimche and Schwimmer chose to ship the weapons first from Tel Aviv to Lisbon, Portugal, and then from Lisbon to Tehran. The Lisbon route would add 5,000 miles to the trip and at least an additional day, counting turnaround time, if all went as planned.

Why not use the same route as before? According to the congressional report, the Israeli "planners chose this circuitous routing because direct flights from Israel to Iran would draw attention given [their] poor relations..."[86] When Poindexter asked North about it, he claimed that a direct flight would "compromise origins and risk eventual uncovering of many operational details."[87] Yet, none of this had concerned the Israelis just two months earlier, least of all their so-called "poor relations" with Iran.

Rabin, too, gave an inherently implausible explanation. He said to North that because of an incident over Turkish airspace "a few months earlier, the Israelis had concluded that direct flights were too dangerous. Instead, they had arranged to move the shipment through several other intermediate points, disguised...as oil-drilling equipment."[88] The implausibility of this explanation was that despite moving the shipment "through several other intermediate points," it was still routed over the same Turkish airspace as the August and September flights.[89]

It was common practice for Israel to move weapons through third countries and use neutral carriers to disguise origins, but why pick Lisbon, the furthest location in Western Europe from Iran? Was it

---

[86] *Iran-Contra Affair*, 179.
[87] *Ibid*, 190n.56.
[88] North, *Under Fire*, 29.
[89] The alternate route into Iran was down the Red Sea, around the Arabian Peninsula and into Bandar Abbas on the Persian Gulf.

because Portugal itself was a major arms shipper to Iran? By 1985, "43.8% of all Portuguese arms exports," $28 million, were going to Iran.[90] Or, was it because Lisbon International Airport was also a major transshipping point for arms exporters of all types? The Israelis themselves were using Lisbon as one of their intermediate points for arms exports. Soprofina was an Israeli front company used for this purpose and Israel Airline Industries had a major warehouse complex located at the airport where arms could be stored, laundered and sanitized, manifests created, and end-user certificates obtained.[91]

Or, did Kimche and Schwimmer pick Lisbon because Richard Secord, North's agent in the contra supply effort, also operated out of the same airport? Secord, the Israelis knew, was arranging weapons shipments for the Contras through DefEx, a Portuguese arms shipper that had a warehouse at the airport.[92] What would be more convenient when the Israelis professed to encounter complications in their shipment than to call on Secord for assistance?

For the moment, all seemed in order. On the morning the president departed for Geneva, November 16, in a brief conversation McFarlane had told him enigmatically "there was something up between Israel and Iran," which "might lead to our getting some of our hostages out, and we were hopeful...." According to McFarlane, the president simply said, "cross your fingers or hope for the best, and keep me informed."[93] The national security adviser did not mention that it was an arms-for-hostages deal and simply left it to the president's imagination to decipher what he meant by "something up."

---

[90] Kenneth R. Timmerman, *Fanning the Flames: Guns, Greed and Geopolitics in the Gulf War*, chapter 7 (1988 online at http://www.kentimmerman.com/krt/fanning_index.htm).
[91] Segev, *Iranian Triangle*, 199 and Ronen Bergman, *The Secret War With Iran* (New York: Free Press, 2007), 118.
[92] Segev, *Iranian Triangle*, 198, claims to the contrary that "only afterward did the Israelis discover that Lisbon was an important logistic base for Secord..."
[93] *Iran-Contra Affair*, 176, misdates this conversation, placing it on November 17, but accurately notes that it occurred before the president left for Geneva, which was the morning of the 16th. See "Scheduled Events at the U.S.-Soviet Summit," *Washington Post*, November 19, 1985, 20.

The very next day, however, the Israelis began to encounter "problems." In retrospect, it seems more than a coincidence that the Israelis chose to commence the *Hawk* mission when President Reagan (and McFarlane) were in Geneva. The day after they had arrived, Rabin called McFarlane to tell him "Israel was unwilling to commence the shipment without satisfactory arrangements for replenishment by the United States."[94] In other words, Rabin said that he was unwilling to wait for McFarlane to task North to make the arrangements in two weeks, after the delivery had occurred. He wanted action now, or Israel would not "commence the shipment."

McFarlane immediately called North as did Rabin. Rabin informed North that Israel planned to move 80 *Hawk* missiles by November 20, but he refused to act "without satisfactory arrangements for replenishment by the United States." After speaking to Rabin, North checked back with McFarlane, who confirmed, "the Israelis are trying to ship some Hawk missiles to Iran. The whole operation is being handled by a couple of private Israeli citizens. They've run into some logistical problems. Get back to Rabin and take care of it. Just fix it. Go up to New York and see Rabin."[95]

Rabin's phone calls to McFarlane and North were the first step in the process of entangling the U.S. government in the arms-for-hostages scheme. McFarlane's assignment of North to "just fix it" was the second. Up to this moment, North had had no involvement in the scheme, except for intelligence monitoring of activity concerning the hostages. Nor had the United States government. As North put it: the

---

[94] *Iran-Contra Affair*, 177.
[95] Oliver North and William Novak, *Under Fire: An American Story* (New York: Harper Collins, 1991), 26-27 and McFarlane, *Special Trust, 42-43*. Both accounts telescope events, but in different ways. Later, when Walsh attempted to subpoena Kimche and Schwimmer, the Israeli government quashed the subpoena in U.S. District Court on the grounds that "Kimche and Schwimmer were acting on behalf of the Israeli Government, not as private citizens, and that any cooperation Mr. Walsh desires from them should be handled on a Government-to-Government basis." See Thomas Friedman, "Iran-Contra Hearings; Israel Gives U.S. Iran Role Report," *New York Times*, August 1, 1987, 1.

calls "marked a major change in the U.S. government's role in the arms sales to Iran." McFarlane "gave me the go ahead for direct U.S. involvement, and assured me that the President had approved it."[96]

Thus was North "thrown into this on the night of November 17." [97] It is difficult to avoid the impression that McFarlane had carefully set North up to play the role he now assigned to him. North would eventually become a major player in the Iran initiative, as he already was in the Contra operation, but in the fall of 1985 when McFarlane assigned him the task of "fixing" Schwimmer's problem, he was an over exuberant, gung-ho, Marine who believed he could solve any problem, but who knew nothing about the history of the Iran initiative, or his boss's machinations.

North flew up to New York City the next day, the 18th, to meet with Rabin and Israel's Defense Procurement Mission Chief, Avram Ben-Yosef. While there, North called Schwimmer in Tel Aviv, who told him that the plan was for Israel to ship 600 *Hawks* to Iran in groups of 100 over the next three or four days. Israel would ship the first 100 from its own stocks, after which all five hostages would be released. Other shipments would follow.

North agreed to authorize the Israeli purchase of 600 replenishment weapons, recording in his notebook: "Schwimmer to P/U [pick up] HAWKS in U.S."[98] He also passed on McFarlane's instruction that Ben-Yosef keep the purchases under $14 million per order. Any number higher than that would have to be reported to congress. (In fact, Ben-Yosef would write up the first purchase for $18 million, which immediately drew congressional scrutiny.)

---

[96] North, *Under Fire*, 27. Kimche called McFarlane and Schwimmer called North on the same day conveying the same message: no replenishment, no deal. See Segev, *Iranian Triangle*, 195-96.
[97] *Iran-Contra Affair*, 177. North testified "I didn't know the details of who [McFarlane] worked it out with, except the persons that he sent to me, first of all, in the case of Mr. Ledeen and second of all, in the case of those who came from overseas to meet with us." Draper, *Very Thin Line*, 186. The reference to Ledeen was to his October 30 meeting with him and McFarlane.
[98] *Iran-Contra Affair*, 177.

Rabin then explained his predicament, saying, "at the last minute they had run into problems with landing rights and other clearances." He wanted North to "find us an acceptable airline that can move this stuff." North replied, "we don't have these kinds of assets sitting around." Rabin reassured him, "don't worry....Our people will take care of the logistics. We just need an airline."[99]

From Schwimmer, North learned that he had arranged for an El Al 747 cargo jet to take 80 *Hawk*s from Tel Aviv to Lisbon, but had "neglected" to apply for landing clearance at Lisbon until the last minute. When he did, "he found that the Portuguese authorities were reluctant to grant them."[100] In retrospect, the landing clearances omission appeared to be a red herring, but North, unfamiliar with transport procedure and under the pressure of the moment, took Schwimmer's explanation at face value. In fact, landing clearances are routinely granted two-to-three days in advance, but in emergencies are granted within hours. It was true, however, that diplomatic authorization was required for flights carrying dangerous goods, but, equally true that there were many firms that provided the service of arranging for necessary clearances.

Schwimmer had employed Israel's national airline, El Al, to ship the cargo. The airline ordinarily would have applied for landing clearance in Lisbon as routine procedure at the same time it filed a flight plan for the trip, arranged for flying time through appropriate air corridors, and set out alternative airports in case of emergencies, bad weather, etc. Schwimmer himself was perhaps the most experienced airman in Israel, which made it extremely unlikely that either he or the airline would have "neglected" a matter of critical importance that was moreover part of standard operating procedure.

To North, however, the solution seemed straightforward: if they could arrange for a landing clearance for the El Al jet there would be no need to find another airline. Checking with McFarlane, North decided to enlist Secord, whom he knew had extensive experience

---

[99] North, *Under Fire*, 30.
[100] Draper, *Very Thin Line*, 185.

shipping arms out of Europe; indeed, out of Lisbon, and from the very airport in question.[101] With the decision to send Secord to arrange for landing clearance in Lisbon, Schwimmer "instantly" agreed to transfer $1 million to Secord's Lake Resources account in Geneva, to give him sufficient monies to charter another aircraft, or bribe officials.[102] The money would, of course, implicate Secord in the scheme.

North arranged to meet with Secord the next day, the 19th, to brief him on the task and to hand him a letter of introduction to establish his bona fides if and when it became necessary. It described his mission as arranging for "the transfer of sensitive material being shipped from Israel," and enjoined him to exercise "great caution" and discretion to insure that the activity not be disclosed. North signed the letter for McFarlane (who, later denied having authorized North to write it).[103] Secord quickly contacted his business agent in Lisbon, Thomas Clines, who happened to be in Washington, and the two of them flew to Lisbon that night.

Meanwhile, McFarlane was attending to two other tasks, which were to entangle the president and also Weinberger in the arms-for-hostages scheme, with mixed success. Late on the morning of the 19th, after the first Reagan-Gorbachev session, and before lunch, McFarlane briefed the president and Don Regan on the arms-for-hostages plan in Regan's small bedroom.[104] In a twenty-minute "difficult to follow"

---

[101] *Iran-Contra Affair*, 178. North, *Under Fire*, 30, says he picked Secord, while Secord, *Honored and Betrayed*, 219, says North told him McFarlane had recommended him.

[102] Draper, *Very Thin Line*, 184, thought that this "crossover" of funds "intermingled" the Iran and Contra operations for the first time, but it did not. There were separate accounts for each funding source. Richard Secord and Jay Wurts, *Honored and Betrayed: Irangate, Covert Affairs, and the Secret War in Laos* (New York: Wiley, 1992), 220, notes, "when Schwimmer was informed, he had the money instantly deposited to Lake Resources." The Lake Resources ledger, however, shows the deposit occurred on November 20. *Iran-Contra Affair*, 179.

[103] *Iran-Contra Affair*, 179.

[104] McFarlane, *Special Trust*, 43, says he briefed the president *before* the first session.

talk, including the cover story about shipping oil-drilling equipment, McFarlane laid out the entire scheme—

> Intermediaries, timing, secret messages, transshipment and verification of weapons, guarantees that the hostages would in fact be released by their captors on the word of people in Tehran and Tabriz who ostensibly had no direct control over their action, only 'influence' and good offices.[105]

According to Regan's vivid recollection, "this was certainly the first time the president had heard the whole scenario," but McFarlane's timing "could not have been worse." The president had "just left Gorbachev; he had had no lunch; and many other items dealing with the summit, which was uppermost in his mind, remained to be discussed."[106] McFarlane did not seek the president's approval, "he simply told the president that the Israelis were about to act."[107]

The oddity about the briefing was that McFarlane knew that the Israelis were *not* about to act. They had been denied landing clearance in Lisbon and without it nothing would move. Why would McFarlane lay out in intimate detail an operation that had yet to be confirmed, let alone begun? A few hours later, he called Shultz at his suite and gave him the same briefing, except to say, "four hostages would be released on November 21." This was even more baffling than his briefing to the president because the number of hostages was five not four, and McFarlane had no way of knowing the exact date of release for an operation that had not yet begun, unless he were privy to Israeli planning.[108]

Shultz's reaction was "stony anger. I told McFarlane that I had been informed so late in the operation that I had no conceivable way to

---

[105] Regan, *For the Record*, 320, claims Shultz was present when he was not. See Shultz, *Turmoil and Triumph*, 798 n.8. McFarlane clearly understood that the Iranians had "no direct control" over Mugniyeh.
[106] Don Regan, *For the Record*, (New York: Harcourt, Brace, Jovanovich, 1988), 321.
[107] *Iran-Contra Affair*, 178.
[108] Schultz, *Turmoil and Triumph*, 797.

stop it."[109] But Shultz lied. His aides had been following events very closely, keeping him informed at every step. Early in the morning of the 18th, Charles Hill had told Shultz that McFarlane had tried to see him the night before about the hostages. "He thinks something's coming down in the next week or so." Shultz responded: "it's a bad deal."[110] Ambassador Oakley also sent a memo to Shultz on the 18th, possibly based on telephone intercepts, noting the "expectation of a possible breakthrough on the hostages on November 20 or 21."[111] Thus, not only was Shultz being kept abreast of events as they occurred, but also, as we shall see, there was an opportunity for him to attempt to "stop" the operation.

McFarlane was also busy attempting to draw Weinberger into the scheme and retroactively cover North's previous "authorization" for Israel to purchase the missiles. The first day of the Geneva Summit, the 19th, he cabled the secretary and "asked him to sell 500 Hawks to Israel, which would transfer them to Iran in exchange for the release of five hostages on November 21."[112] But Weinberger was too crafty for McFarlane and gave him the bureaucratic runaround. He tasked Henry Gaffney, acting director of Defense Security Assistance Agency, to determine the availability of the *Hawks* and the legality of the sale. His report was negative. The *Hawks* could not be sold for re-transfer without congressional notification and intentionally packaging them under $14 million was "a clear violation."[113]

Weinberger promptly passed this message on to McFarlane. The next day, the second day of the summit, McFarlane told Weinberger that, "notwithstanding the legal problems, President Reagan has decided to send Hawk missiles to Iran through Israel." Israel, he said, would sell only 120 not 600 and these would be "older models." He also informed the secretary that the hostages would be released on November 22, which indicated that he was keeping in touch with the

---

[109] Ibid, 798.
[110] "Hill note," November 18, 1985, in Walsh, *Final Report*, 336.
[111] Ibid, "Oakley memorandum," November 18, 1985.
[112] Ibid, "Weinberger Diary," November 19, 1985, 408, 92.
[113] Ibid.

Israelis and North about the clearance problem.[114] McFarlane had worked around Weinberger's block for the moment, but replenishment of Israeli weapons still needed to be addressed. Weinberger, on the other hand, managed to keep the defense department out of McFarlane's Iran scheme, but the CIA would not be as lucky.

The CIA is Caught!

On Tuesday evening, the 19th, relieved at having arranged what he thought was the solution to the problem of obtaining a landing clearance, North stopped off on the way home for a drink and a chance to catch up with two of his former comrades, Dewey Clarridge and Vince Cannistraro. They had met and worked with each other the previous year when North had crafted the Contra support network, but had since been reassigned elsewhere. [115] Clarridge was now the CIA's European Division Chief and Cannistraro was working counterterrorism at the NSC.

They met at a favorite CIA watering hole in Mclean, Va., not far from agency headquarters, a restaurant and bar called *Charley's Place*. Their meeting was significant because, when the crisis broke a year later, Clarridge would be charged with denying he learned at this meeting that the U.S. was involved in shipping weapons to Iran. Walsh would claim that he and the CIA had from that point illegally participated in a covert activity without presidential authorization. As a result, he would be forced into retirement in 1987 and given a formal reprimand for his brief, but critical role.

It is vital to understand the legal framework that established the basis for CIA activity because a concern to have acted within the boundaries of the legal framework drove the behavior of the participants from this point onward. Two edicts, the Hughes-Ryan Amendment of 1974 and NSDD 159, were the main elements in the framework. The Hughes-Ryan

---

[114] Ibid, "Weinberger Diary," November 20, 1985, 409 and 428.
[115] Clarridge had been Latin America Division Chief and Cannistraro Central American Task Force chief.

Amendment required the president to issue a written Finding to authorize CIA or Defense Department involvement in any covert activity. The requirement that a Finding had to be in writing was re-emphasized in NSDD-159, which the president had just signed in January 1985. Moreover, a president's finding could only anticipate future activity and not be retroactive. NSDD-159, in particular, had to be fresh in the minds of those for whom it mattered.

At *Charley's Place*, North undoubtedly recounted the story of the elementary Israeli screw-up in failing to obtain a landing clearance and how he had called on their mutual acquaintance, Richard Secord, to solve it. Clarridge claims that the subject of "Iran did not come up," and that he did not know Secord, but notes that they did discuss Lisbon's "clogged" pipeline, although only in the context of shipping arms to Central America.[116] North may or may not have given Clarridge a "heads-up" call to be ready to help out in case Secord was unsuccessful, but he had no reason to ask for help at this point.

Walsh's charge was based on the recollection of the third party at the meeting, Vince Cannistraro, who recalled that North said "he needed Clarridge's help getting clearance to fly a shipment of military equipment to Iran." Unfortunately for Walsh, Cannistraro could not remember the date of their meeting, which undermined his case.[117]

However, Walsh's charge was dubious for several other reasons. The meeting at *Charley's Place* occurred while Secord and Clines were on the way to Lisbon where they would arrive the next morning. If, as Walsh also notes, Secord was "confident" that he could obtain landing clearance through his contacts, then there was no reason to ask Clarridge for assistance on a problem that had not yet arisen. Moreover, *if* North requested "help" on the 19th, why did Clarridge wait over two days until early in the morning of the 22st to send his first cable to Lisbon? Furthermore, his first cable was simply to

---

[116] Duane R. Clarridge, *A Spy For All Seasons: My Life in the CIA* (New York: Scribner, 1997), 309.

[117] Walsh, *Final Report*, 254, established the date of their meeting as November 19 based on North's calendar; Clarridge claims they met on November 20.

instruct the CIA chief of mission in Lisbon to provide assistance to Secord, who actually declined his help, at first.[118]

Finally, the next day, the 20th, North sent Poindexter a detailed PROF message, which laid out the entire scheme, to commence on November 22, including the provision of "appropriate arrangements" with Lisbon air control, delivery of weapons to Tabriz, and the release of all five hostages in Beirut. He specifically noted, "all transfer arrangements have been made by Dick Secord, who deserves a medal for extraordinary short notice efforts."[119] As all of the parties to this mission were in virtually constant contact by secure communication means, North's message to Poindexter reflected Secord's expectations at that moment.

At that moment, Secord's business colleague, Jose Garnel, one of the owners of DefEx, who had a brother-in-law in the foreign ministry, had contacted Portuguese authorities earlier that day, asking for landing clearance for two aircraft in transit to Iran. He had made his request on Secord's behalf, although Garnel simply identified Secord as a retired U.S. general. (Secord was traveling under the name of "Copp.") Secord himself had spoken with the minister of defense, who assured him that approval was forthcoming, and Secord had called Schwimmer to tell him things were in order.[120]

However, within the Portuguese foreign ministry things were decidedly not in order. When the clearance request was made, Portuguese Ministry officials, fully conversant with declared U.S. policy toward Iran, asked for an explanation from the U.S. embassy. As the ambassador Frank Shakespeare was away, on the 21st, the charge d'affairs, James Creagan, sent the political counselor to the ministry to explain. He told ministry officials that "the shipment was not authorized by the United States and was contrary to U.S.

---

[118] Clarridge, *Spy For All Seasons,* 312. Walsh, *Final Report,* 249, says he sent his first cable late on November 21, but acknowledges in note 16 that the cable is dated November 22.

[119] *Iran-Contra Affair,* 180. The PROF system was a secure email program that Poindexter designed for the NSC.

[120] Segev, *Iranian Triangle,* 198, 200.

Government policy strongly opposing arms sales to Iran."[121] Furthermore, he said, "he knew nothing that would justify the mission, because he had nothing in his channels."[122]

With a red flag from the U.S. embassy, the Portuguese foreign ministry became increasingly reluctant to be a party to the affair and this attitude became more pronounced as the hours passed. What explains the Portuguese foreign ministry's attitude? It would seem that here is where Shultz found the opportunity to throw a monkey wrench into the operation and force the CIA into greater involvement. U.S. embassy officials would not take it upon themselves to respond to the ministry's inquiry without first checking with Washington.[123] It is my conjecture that Shultz's aide, Ambassador Robert Oakley replied to the charge` in the secretary's name with the instruction to restate U.S. policy opposing arms sales to Iran.

Actually, it is more than conjecture because, when the charge` told the CIA's chief of mission what happened, he immediately sent a cable to Clarridge at CIA headquarters "to find out if the Secretary of State, Secretary of State Shultz, was aware of the mission and if he approved [U.S.] involvement."[124] In other words, the CIA chief of mission had been told that Shultz opposed it.

Clarridge passed this message over to Poindexter at the NSC. His response, on the 22nd, which Clarridge forwarded to Lisbon, contradicted the instruction from State. Poindexter said, "the Secretary of State and Ambassador Oakley were the only two State officials who were aware of the mission, that they concurred..." (!) However, because of the operation's "sensitivity," only CIA communications channels were to be used, not the state department's.[125] Poindexter's

---

[121] *Iran-Contra Affair*, 180.
[122] *"CIA Chief deposition,"* Iran-Contra Affair, Appendix B, volume 4, 1159 and "Deputy Chief of Mission deposition," Ibid, volume 8, 271-72.
[123] Ibid. See the embassy's reporting "Cable from American Embassy [Lisbon] to Department of State Headquarters," November 22, 1985, 180 and 190 n.82. Unfortunately, the content of the cable is unavailable.
[124] Ibid, "CIA Chief of Mission deposition," volume 4, 1162.
[125] Ibid, and "Deputy Chief of Mission deposition," volume 8, 272-74

attempt to get around Shultz' opposition would not work. By the time his cable reached Lisbon, events were already careening out of control, entangling the CIA in arms-for-hostages.

Chapter 6
Israel Entangles the CIA

Meanwhile, on the evening of November 21, in Tel Aviv, Kimche, Schwimmer and Nimrodi's assistant, Yehuda Alboher, met to discuss their next steps. After calls to North in Washington, Ben-Yosef in New York, Secord in Lisbon, and Nimrodi in Geneva with Gorbanifar, they assessed the situation.[1] There had still been no resolution of the weapons' replenishment problem, only North's promise, but no decision by the Pentagon, which deeply concerned the Israelis. Worse, the U.S. government still remained on the sidelines of the mission, as only Secord, a private citizen, had become directly involved. North had turned Rabin's initial ploy to have the U.S. provide Israel with an airline into an effort to obtain landing clearance for Israel's own plane, which was promised but not confirmed.

There was another stunning, recent development that preoccupied them. It was the arrest of an American intelligence specialist spying for Israel that threatened to disrupt the entire U.S.-Israeli relationship. On November 18, naval intelligence had detained Jonathan Jay Pollard for questioning. Pollard was an American Jew working as an intelligence analyst for the Naval Investigative Service. Offended that the United States was not sharing all of the intelligence that it should

---

[1] Samuel Segev, *The Iranian Triangle: The Untold Story of Israel's Role in the Iran-Contra Affair* (New York: Free Press, 1988), 198.

with its ally, Israel, Pollard had volunteered his services to Tel Aviv as a "walk-in" spy.[2]

The Pollard Affair

For over a year Pollard had accessed "almost every document in the American intelligence network." He provided Israel with mountains of intelligence, including satellite reconnaissance photos, message traffic, targeting data on the Soviet Union, information on the Middle East, the identity of American agents, ultra-secret technology, and much more. He gave Israel an inside look at America's innermost secrets. Eventually, his actions aroused suspicion among his co-workers, who alerted naval authorities.[3]

Extensive surveillance of his activities led to a decision to call him in for questioning on November 18. Released after questioning, Pollard immediately contacted his handler at the Israeli embassy and demanded assistance to flee the country to Israel. He and his wife, Anne Henderson Pollard, attempted to seek sanctuary in the Israeli embassy three days later, but though gaining entry, were turned over to the FBI who arrested them.[4]

As soon as Pollard called the embassy for help on the evening of the 18th it was clear that his cover had been blown and Pollard's handlers all quickly fled to Israel. Thus, even before he had been arrested on November 21, in Israel "intelligence officials and politicians there already knew" that Pollard's exposure "was bound to harm Israel's relations with the United States."[5]

---

[2] Dan Raviv and Yossi Melman, *Every Spy a Prince*, (New York: Houghton Mifflin, 1990) 306. See also, recently declassified CIA documents on *The Jonathan Pollard Affair*, National Security Archive, The George Washington University, 2013.
[3] Gordon Thomas, *Gideon's Spies: The Secret History of the Mossad*, (New York: Thomas Dunn, 2009), 85-86.
[4] Joe Picharallo, "Navy Employee Is Charged With Passing Defense Secrets," *Washington Post*, November 22, 1985, 1 and "Navy Employee Is Accused of Passing Secrets to Israel," *Wall Street Journal*, November 22, 1985, 6.
[5] Raviv and Melman, *Every Spy a Prince*, 317.

Theories about the Pollard case range from poor spy craft on his part, to a general spy roundup by the FBI; from an extension of internal Israeli politics to Washington, to an extension of internal American politics to Israel. There is a high probability that all of these theories are partially correct. Pollard had become careless in his work. His supervisor "noticed 'huge stacks' of top secret material on Pollard's desk that were not related to his assigned tasks."[6] In this version, suspicion led to surveillance; surveillance to apprehension.

There was a heightened sense of insecurity within the American intelligence community as a result of a string of arrests during 1985 of several spies. Among these were the navy spy ring operated by John Walker, Arthur Walker, Michael Walker, and Jerry Whitworth; Samuel Morrison, a civilian intelligence analyst with Naval Intelligence Command; Ronald Pelton, an NSA communications specialist; Edward Howard, former CIA employee; Larry Wu-tai Chin, CIA analyst; Sharon Scranage, CIA clerk; and Richard Miller, an FBI veteran. The result was a massive government-wide campaign to tighten security throughout the intelligence community.[7]

There was also the view that Pollard had been a deliberate casualty of the ongoing conflict between Israel's Likud and Labor parties. Pollard was connected to a spy network in the United States run by Rafi Eitan called LAKAM, and his exposure severely damaged Yitzhak Shamir's Likud Party. The sensational charge associated with this theory was McFarlane's relationship with Eitan and his role in facilitating Pollard's work, which, it is claimed, was the real reason for the national security adviser's resignation.[8]

The theory in the current work, however, argues that Pollard's arrest was the result of the ongoing conflict between the Reagan and new world order factions. The new world order faction orchestrated the arrest of Pollard to cripple the U.S.-Israeli relationship and shut

---

[6] Ibid, 315.
[7] "Pentagon Orders Security Crackdown on Code Experts," *Philadelphia Inquirer*, November 27, 1985, 12.
[8] Ari Ben-Menashe, *Profits of War* (New York: Sheridan Square Press, 1992), 174-76.

down the Iran initiative. McFarlane, though a member of this faction, was a necessary casualty. Moreover, it was Peres, rather than Shamir, who had to bear the brunt of the ensuing spy scandal.[9] If McFarlane's resignation had any impact in Israel, it was on Peres' strategy to retain and enlarge access to the Iranian arms market.

Over the next several weeks Shultz led a "spy probe" in Israel to determine the scope and propriety of "activities," which "were inconsistent with official Israeli policy."[10] At the same time, what can only be called a witch-hunt took place, as nameless "sources" began to label Jewish-American officials in the U.S. government as Israeli informants.[11] Pollard was tried and sentenced to life imprisonment, "having been found guilty of being the greatest traitor in the history of the United States."[12] But, if the purpose behind the anti-Israel campaign was to frighten Peres off from cooperating with Reagan, it backfired.

The Israelis Prod Washington

Kimche, Schwimmer, and Alboher, meeting that evening of November 21, were undoubtedly alarmed by the news about Pollard. Coming on top of the persistent American reticence to replenish the weapons or failure to obtain landing clearances, they could not but assume that their worst fear of being hung out to dry by the Americans was about to come true. They were therefore more determined than ever to press forward with their plan to bring the United States government directly into the arms-for-hostages scheme.

---

[9] "Peres Reported to Admit that Navy Man was Spy," *Philadelphia Inquirer*, November 26, 1985, 4.
[10] "U.S. Widens Spy Probe in Israel," *Washington Times*, December 10, 1985, 2 and Joseph Harsch, "Spy Case Brings Sea Change in US-Israel Ties," *Christian Science Monitor*, December 20, 1985, 7.
[11] Howard Teicher and Gayle Radley Teicher, *Twin Pillars to Desert Storm* (New York: William Morrow, 1993), 380-84.
[12] Thomas, *Gideon's Spies*, 408.

Beginning that evening, they bombarded McFarlane, North, and Secord with phone calls demanding action. Rabin called McFarlane threatening to call off the mission. "If the Iranian project were not viewed as a joint U.S.-Israel operation, Israel would not undertake it alone."[13] Rabin and Kimche made calls to North demanding that he "put White House pressure on the Pentagon to expedite the replenishment."[14] Ben-Yosef also called North to demand that the United States promptly sell the latest model *Hawk* missiles as replenishments. Privately, however, the Israelis had decided to send older ones to Iran.[15]

Their decisive act, however, was to send the El Al 747 cargo jet to Lisbon even though they knew that landing clearance had not been obtained, thus forcing American involvement. There is confusion in the record surrounding this crucial decision, however. Segev says that Schwimmer called North and Secord on the evening of November 21 and they agreed that the plane would take off twenty-four hours later, on Friday evening, the 22nd.[16]

The joint congressional study contradicts this noting "although the clearance for landing in [Lisbon] had not been authorized on the morning of November 22, the El Al 747 carrying the 80 *Hawk* missiles was ordered to take off..."[17] Draper, also remarks on this decision, describing it as "one of the most peculiar episodes in this melodrama." He says "Schwimmer decided to send an El AL plane loaded with 80 *Hawk* missiles out of Tel Aviv toward Lisbon—without a clearance, "

---

[13] *Report of the Congressoinal Committees Investigating the Iran-Contra Affair* (Washington, D.C.: GPO, 1987), 189 n.16. [hereinafter cited as *Iran-Contra Affair*].
[14] Segev, *Iranian Triangle*, 198.
[15] Ibid, 198-99.
[16] Ibid, 199, 201. Segev is at pains to pass the blame for the failure of this mission on the Americans, who he saw as "incompetent," and to protect Schwimmer, who he says was shocked by their actions.
[17] *Iran-Contra Affair*, 181.

but doesn't say when.[18] The behavior of American officials, however, establishes the plane's departure time as the morning of the 22nd.

Segev notes "on Friday morning Secord called Schwimmer and asked for takeoff to be delayed by a few hours, since he had not yet been able to arrange the landing rights in Lisbon."[19] Asking to delay the takeoff indicates that the plane was about to depart. If the plane was not supposed to depart until evening, there does not seem to be any reason to ask for a delay in the morning. Nevertheless, against Secord's plea, but in accord with their own plan to prod the Americans into commitment, Schwimmer sent the plane out. The result predictably sent North and Secord into a frenzy.

When the Israelis began bombarding North with demands the previous evening of November 21, he became concerned that the United States was verging on the prospect of becoming directly involved and asked McFarlane if there were a covert action finding that would permit it. The answer he received, copying it down in his notebook, was "RR said he would support 'mental finding.'"[20]

Under the pressure of the moment, McFarlane had given North the only answer he could think of. He, of course, knew that findings were highly secret, compartmented documents, not subject to verification by anyone without the "need to know." However, the entire notion of a "mental finding" was preposterous and absurd, requiring the skills of a mind reader. Moreover, it flew in the face of NSDD 159, which McFarlane also knew specifically required that all covert action findings be in written form. But, in the exigency of the moment, McFarlane's answer satisfied North and was the critical act that pushed the CIA into direct and illegal involvement. (Fortunately, North had the presence of mind to jot down McFarlane's authorization).[21]

---

[18] Theodore Draper, *A Very Thin Line: The Iran-Contra Affairs* (New York: Hill and Wang, 1991), 189
[19] Segev, 199.
[20] As quoted in Draper, *Very Thin Line*, 212.
[21] The Foreign Assistance Act, as amended, section 654, says of Presidential Findings: "In any case in which the President is required to make a report to the

North had no reason to question his boss, who, he assumed, was transmitting the view of the president.[22] With authorization in hand in the form of the "mental finding," North called Clarridge for help. Arranging to meet him at his office in Langley at just after four A.M. (which was nine A.M. in Lisbon and eleven A.M. in Tel Aviv), North said that he faced an emergency and needed to obtain landing clearances in Lisbon for an El Al 747 that was "already airborne."

Explaining with the cover story that he needed to assist an Israeli shipment of oil drilling equipment to Iran, Clarridge replied "sending *anything* to Iran was a violation of the U.S. embargo on Iran and in contravention of U.S. policy of not negotiating with terrorists." North reassured him, based on McFarlane's "mental finding" remark, that "the president had approved both lifting the embargo and negotiating for the hostages."[23]

A skeptical Clarridge only became convinced "after hearing North on the phone with McFarlane in Switzerland and Poindexter at the White House." Aside from the fact that McFarlane was then in Rome, not Geneva, it was clear that North was following the orders of his superiors. It was, of course, axiomatic that the mission of the CIA is to support the policies of the executive branch. In any case, Clarridge also checked with Casey who approved. As far as Clarridge was concerned, "the decision had been made by the president."[24]

Clarridge sent "flash" cables to his Lisbon mission chief instructing him to "contact Secord…and offer him assistance" in the

---

Congress…concerning any finding or determination under any provision of this Act…that finding or determination shall be reduced to writing and signed by the President."

[22] Oliver North in North and William Novak, *Under Fire: An American Story* (New York: Harper Collins, 1991), 34, says, "I don't know exactly what McFarlane told the President. I do know that he told me that the President had approved our involvement. "Fix it," McFarlane had said, and that's all I needed to hear. It was the kind of challenge I thrived on, and I jumped right in. I can do it, I thought. I'm a Marine. This whole deal is screwed up, but I can take care of it."

[23] Duane R. Clarridge, *A Spy For All Seasons: My Life in the CIA* (New York: Scribner, 1997), 310-11.

[24] Ibid.

fulfillment of his mission. As noted above, however, at this point Secord felt he had the clearance matter well in hand and declined assistance. But, a few hours later, around 1:00 P.M. Secord was hit with a double whammy that changed his mind. To his astonishment, he learned that not only had Schwimmer sent the plane against his instructions, but also that the Portuguese government had refused to issue the landing clearance. Worst of all, intensifying the pressure, the plane was nearing the turn around point, where, if there were no clearance, it would have to turn around to have enough fuel to get back to Tel Aviv.[25]

Secord in a panic called the CIA mission chief back and made an "urgent request for assistance."[26] He suggested that they bring in the embassy chargé to make a formal request and cabled Clarridge requesting approval. Clarridge obtained approval from Poindexter and replied to his mission chief in Lisbon to say that the "NSC wanted the CIA senior field officer to bring the chargé into the operation and to 'pull out all the stops' because the El Al plane was only one hour from aborting."[27]

Complementing this action, North contacted Oakley in the State Department to obtain his agreement to authorize the Lisbon chargé to support the clearance request. (Here, one wonders whether North was unaware that the State Department was on the other side, or thought that he could personally persuade Oakley, with whom he worked on the counterterrorism task force.) Oakley told North that he would help, but did not. Instead, he called Clarridge and told him "the State Department was aware of the operation," but that "Clarridge should contact the foreign minister...for assistance."[28] In other words, Oakley

---

[25] *Iran-Contra Affair*, 181.
[26] "CIA Cable," November 23, 1985, in Lawrence E. Walsh, *Final Report of the Independent Counsel for Iran-Contra Matters*, (Washington, D.C.: United States Court of Appeals for the District of Columbia Circuit, August 4, 1993), 249.
[27] "Director 625908," November 22, 1985, Ibid, 250. See also "Deputy Chief of Mission deposition," *Iran-Contra Affair*, Appendix B, volume 8, 272-74.
[28] Walsh, *Final Report*, 255. The *Iran-Contra Affair*, 181, errs in stating that Oakley told North that the *Embassy* "could request clearances."

was intent on keeping the State Department out of the action, but willing to push the CIA in deeper.

Secord, meanwhile, applied a second time for a landing clearance and frantically, if clumsily, attempted to gain personal access to both the prime minister and the foreign minister to plead his case. As they were returning from a trip, Secord sought to contact them at the airport, talking his way into the VIP lounge. But when he realized he had gone to the wrong terminal he made a scene and aroused the antipathies of Portuguese authorities, who became more than ever averse to granting a clearance.[29]

Next, the CIA mission chief sought to see the foreign minister, who was in a meeting, but was told that Portugal would need "a formal statement from the U.S. Embassy."[30] The time spent waiting for the foreign minister, who showed no inclination to meet with U.S. representatives, and in deliberating over whether or not to put their request in writing, took the El Al plane to the turnaround point and it was forced to abort and return to Tel Aviv. It would no longer be available.

That afternoon, hoping to reschedule the mission for the next day, North finally convinced McFarlane to call the Portuguese foreign minister to request approval for a landing clearance. At the same time he formulated three options for continuing the mission. They could charter a new airline and pick up the material in Tel Aviv, fly to Lisbon and transfer the cargo to the three DC-8 aircraft Schwimmer had chartered, and proceed to Iran; they could fly the three chartered aircraft to Tel Aviv, pick up cargo and fly back to Lisbon and thence to Iran; or they could fly the three aircraft to Tel Aviv, abandon the Lisbon route, and fly directly to Iran. North observed, "everybody involved '(including Kimche)' believed the first option to be the best."[31] In other words, the situation had now reverted to the very first

---

[29] Draper, *Very Thin Line*, 191.
[30] "CIA Cable," November 22, 1985, in Walsh, *Final Report*, 250.
[31] John G. Tower et al., *Report of the President's Special Review Board: February 26, 1987* (Washington D.C.: GPO, 1987), B-33.

proposal Rabin made to North, which was to "find us an acceptable airline that can move this stuff."[32]

McFarlane, contacted in Rome, promptly called the Portuguese foreign minister that afternoon at five-thirty and claimed to have received approval for a landing clearance to be granted the next morning. McFarlane also claimed that he had "persuaded [the foreign minister] to approve the flights without a diplomatic note." However, when the chargé contacted the ministry the next morning, neither the secretary-general, nor the chief de cabinet knew anything about any agreement and continued to insist on a diplomatic note. Indeed, the foreign minister himself went further, publicly insisting, not only on a diplomatic note, but also on one that said, "the purpose of the mission was to secure the release of the U.S. hostages."[33]

The truth is that while McFarlane did place a call to the foreign minister, he had not persuaded him to grant a landing clearance, but told North that he had.[34] But why? There were three reasons McFarlane lied to North. He did not want to involve the State Department, which sending a note would do (indeed, McFarlane decided not to send one); he wanted to buy some time for Clarridge to arrange for an alternate aircraft, which would bring the CIA into the operation illegally and irreversibly; and he wanted to insure that all other options had been foreclosed.

McFarlane didn't want North to know there was no clearance yet because if he did the solution would simply be to use the three DC-8s Schwimmer had already deployed to Lisbon, fly them to Tel Aviv, pick up the missiles, and fly them to Iran. But that would not involve the CIA, or the U.S. government. So, it was important to buy just enough time for Schwimmer to cancel his charter with the DC-8s, which would leave the operation with no aircraft and force the CIA to provide them.

---

[32] North, *Under Fire*, 30.
[33] Walsh, *Final Report*, 250-52.
[34] Draper, *Very Thin Line*, 188.

Thus, North and Clarridge, operating on the assumption that a clearance would be granted the next morning, the 23rd, and assuming that all they needed was a replacement for the El Al 747, worked out a solution. Reporting to Poindexter at six in the evening, North said two CIA proprietary 707s from St. Lucia airways would be made available to Secord to pick up the *Hawks* in Tel Aviv, deliver them to Lisbon where they would be transferred to Schwimmer's three chartered DC-8s, and flown to Tabriz.[35]

This solution lasted less than an hour. At seven P.M. North reported to Poindexter that Schwimmer had "released their DC-8s in spite of my call to DK [David Kimche] instructing that they be put on hold until we could iron out the clearance problem in [Lisbon]." North thought Schwimmer "released them to save $ and now does not think they can be re-chartered before Monday."[36] Secord suggested using one of the Lake Resources aircraft scheduled to transport ammunition to the Contras. This would delay delivery to the Contras by a few days, but would "at least get this [Iran] thing moving." North concluded: "so help me I have never seen anything so screwed up in my life."[37]

Saturday morning, the 23rd, North learned that the Portuguese government would not issue landing clearances without a note and Secord's idea also fell through, so he began to explore alternate routes, the most obvious being the original route the Israelis had used in August and September, flying directly from Israel to Iran.

These developments had a different impact on Clarridge. As it became evident by afternoon that Lisbon was out and that the CIA was the only remaining transport option, Clarridge, "understood that we as an agency might be on the brink of getting into this endeavor. We'd no longer be simply providing communications, we could be perceived as participating in NSC activities. When I realized that this might bring the CIA into North's operation, I called Ed Juchniewicz for

---

[35] *Tower Report*, B-33.
[36] *Iran-Contra Affair*, 182.
[37] Ibid.

approval."[38] As Casey, McMahon, and Clair George were out of Washington that weekend, Juchniewicz was acting director of operations.

The question was: could the CIA legally provide a proprietary aircraft for this NSC mission? If the mission were construed as a covert activity, then the president would need to issue a finding to authorize it. On the other hand, if it were simply a commercial venture, a finding would not be necessary. Hearing that North was requesting the use of the CIA's proprietary aircraft, Juchniewicz asked: Is this a straight commercial deal? Clarridge replied that it was. North would lease and pay for the use of the aircraft and pilots. On the grounds that it was a commercial arrangement, the acting chief of operations gave his ok.

This entire exchange exposed McFarlane's claim of Reagan's "mental finding" as false. Even though North had used it to gain Clarridge's assistance, Clarridge did not use it to justify the CIA's involvement. He sought approval from Juchniewicz on other, safer, grounds. The "mental finding" would never be brought forward as a justification for anyone else's actions (until McFarlane tried to talk Attorney General Edwin Meese into employing it after the crisis broke, but it was immediately discarded).[39]

But, for Clarridge, it was "important to the Agency that North pay for the use of the aircraft and pilots. That would confirm the commercial nature of the operation. If the arrangement had not been a commercial one and no money changed hands, then it would have become a CIA covert operation in support of the National Security Council," and "require a presidential finding."[40]

---

[38] Clarridge, *Spy For All Seasons*, 313.
[39] Edwin Meese, *With Reagan: The Inside Story*, (Washington, D.C.; Regnery, 1992), 266-68, did argue that Reagan had made an "oral" finding, which was also dubious, but which put the president in a better legal position. See chapter 13.
[40] Clarridge, *Spy For All Seasons*, 313.

Hook, Line, and Sinker

Authorized to support North in a "straight commercial deal," Clarridge sprang into action, assembling the required expertise, as North, Charles Allen, the Air Branch Chief, and intelligence officers congregated in his office "command post" to provide support for the mission.[41] They all assumed, as Allen did, that, although "it was not the norm," it was "a White House request" and they "did not question it." They all further assumed, like the airline proprietary project officer, that they were operating under a finding, which, as was standard, "would be staffed all the way up to the DDO."[42]

(Nobody believed the Israeli cover story about oil drilling equipment, yet all would later deny any certain knowledge that missiles were the cargo, even if they suspected otherwise, because of the legal exigencies under which they operated. When the crisis broke a year later, and it was learned that they had been tricked, that there had been no finding to authorize their actions, the participants sought to cover their activities by claiming they did *not* know missiles were the cargo, until later in January. In January, when the president did sign a finding, their actions became "legal.")[43]

Clarridge contacted his field agents to arrange over flight clearances over Turkey and landing and over flight clearances for Cyprus, as well. Once they decided to dispense with Lisbon and fly direct from Tel Aviv, to disguise the origins of the flight they decided to stop in Larnaca, Cyprus, before proceeding on through Turkey to Iran. All of this required coordination, not only with his agents in the field, but also with Schwimmer and Kimche in Tel Aviv.

Air Branch could not obtain the use of a proprietary 747 on short notice, so two St. Lucia Airways 707s were advanced and by the evening of the 23rd, one had flown in to Tel Aviv. It had been a

---

[41] *Iran-Contra Affair*, 182.
[42] "Charles Allen deposition," Ibid, Appendix B, volume 1, 410 and "Airline Proprietary Project Officer deposition," 139-40.
[43] See Walsh, *Final Report*, for the charges against Clarridge, 260-62, and especially note 170.

remarkably quick response, but problems immediately surfaced. When loading the missiles onto the plane, the size of the missile containers restricted the number the plane could accommodate to eighteen, instead of eighty. This meant that five flights would have to be made to deliver the first tranche of eighty; and, after consultations with Gorbanifar in Geneva, one hostage would now be released after each partial delivery, instead of all five at once.[44] The Iranians, *inter alia*, had re-established the principle of releasing one hostage for one shipment of arms.

Worse, as they were loading the missiles it was discovered that the plane bore a U.S. registry, while the other standing by did not. So, in the interests of maintaining some degree of plausible deniability, the non-U.S. registered aircraft was substituted for the U.S. registered plane—at a cost of some additional delay of unloading and re-loading the aircraft.[45] Schwimmer tried to talk the captain into using the U.S.-registered plane, but disguising it by painting over the registry numbers, which seemed "crazy" to the airline proprietary officer, and he refused.[46]

There were also money problems. As it was absolutely essential that the Israelis pay for the aircraft to maintain the commercial nature of the flight, the proprietary's manager demanded a $30,000 down payment, which didn't sit well with Schwimmer, who claimed he had to scramble for funds.[47] The oddity here was that the Iranians had just deposited over twenty-four million dollars in Nimrodi's account to cover the purchase and transport of 80 *Hawk* missiles.

The Israelis had additional tricks to play. When the plane finally took off for Iran via Cyprus, Schwimmer inexplicably neglected to include a manifest with the flight documents. When they landed in Larnaca, customs officials became suspicious and wanted to inspect

---

[44] Segev, *Iranian Triangle*, 202. See also Draper, *Very Thin Line*, 192-94.
[45] "CIA Air Branch Chief deposition," *Iran-Contra Affair*, Appendix B, volume 4, 847-48.
[46] "Airline Proprietary Officer deposition," Ibid, Appendix B, volume 1, 38-39.
[47] For discussion of these travails, and more, see Segev, *Iranian Triangle*, 202-04 and Draper, *Very Thin Line*, 193-94.

the cargo. The pilot and crew managed to write out a manifest on the spot and talk themselves into the air without disclosing the cargo.[48] Had Cypriot customs inspected the cargo and discovered the missiles the subsequent brouhaha would have led to the probable confiscation of the cargo, if not the exposure of the American role. All of which raised the question of what the Israelis were up to? Would exposure be the next best thing to involvement?

In any case, once the plane was in the air over Turkey, Clarridge received a cable from his man in Ankara, who said that the Turkish foreign ministry wanted to know whether the plane was carrying weapons. Clarridge doubted the story he was told that Turkish air traffic controllers had learned about the cargo from querying the pilot and so reaffirmed the cover story that the plane was hauling oil-drilling equipment. He believed that "someone in the Turkish Foreign Ministry decided to go on a fishing expedition and just threw out the question…to see what the response would be."[49] But, the real question was: who suggested to the Turkish foreign ministry that there might be weapons on board? Could it have been someone in the U.S. embassy?

Yet another change in the flight plan caused in-flight problems. At the last minute, the destination was changed from Tabriz to Tehran requiring a new flight plan. The new route was inconsistent with the over flight clearance request, prompting additional probing questions. As the congressional study observes, "ironically, the pilot told the flight controllers the true nature of the cargo even while Clarridge was spreading the cover story to high level officials…"[50]

The plane arrived in Tehran's Mehrabad airport on the morning of November 25 to the surprise of the airport personnel. Having been diverted from Tabriz, word had not been forwarded to Tehran. Nevertheless, after some slight confusion the unloading of the missiles was uneventful and the plane departed later the same day. Fortunately

---

[48] "Airline Proprietary Officer deposition," *Iran-Contra Affair*, Appendix B, volume 1, 41-42.
[49] Clarridge, *Spy For All Seasons*, 314-15.
[50] *Iran-Contra Affair*, 185.

for the crew, they had left before the missile crates were opened and inspected.

When Iranian technicians took one look at the contents they were outraged, thinking initially that they had been the victims of yet another hoax. As Secord observed, during 1985 and 1986, "every con artist on the planet seemed out to make a buck at Iranian expense."[51] The 18 *Hawk* missiles were not what they had bargained for. Believing that they were ordering high-altitude anti-aircraft missiles to contend with Soviet and Iraqi reconnaissance aircraft penetrating their airspace, what they got were low-altitude anti-aircraft missiles, which could not serve that function. Prime Minister Moussavi was beside himself with rage, railing at Kangarlu in Geneva, "You idiot! They tricked you again. We can't depend on you!" Perhaps as bad, several of the missiles had Stars of David stamped on them.[52]

The Iranians refused to accept the missiles, which were eventually returned (in February 1986), and demanded their money back. Iran had deposited $44 million in Gorbanifar's account on November 22 for 80 *Hawks* and future arms purchases. No bridge money from third parties was involved here, indicating the seriousness of the Iranian side. Gorbanifar transferred $24 million to Nimrodi, who, in turn, paid $11.8 million to the Israeli Ministry of Defense for the planned first shipment of 80 *Hawks*. With the failure of the *Hawk* deal, the Iranians wanted the $24 million back.[53] Some of it, however, had already been spent and arguments swirled around every stage of the money's return.

The Israeli Defense Ministry refunded $8.1 million to Nimrodi, keeping back $3 million plus for the 18 *Hawks* not yet returned. Nimrodi refunded $18.6 million to Gorbanifar for the 62 missiles not shipped. The remainder, minus "expenses," that is money skimmed at each stage, kickbacks, and bribes, would be refunded to Gorbanifar in

---

[51] Richard Secord and Jay Wurts, *Honored and Betrayed: Irangate, Covert Affairs, and the Secret War in Laos* (New York: Wiley, 1992), 222.
[52] Segev, *Iranian Triangle*, 205.
[53] Segev, 206-7 and Draper, *Very Thin Line*, 196-97 offer similar accounts of these money movements.

February 1986, after 17 of the 18 *Hawk* missiles were returned (the Iranians had test-fired one missile).

Despite Clarridge's precautions, the CIA had become directly involved in the *Hawk* mission, not just sending cables, but providing communications support, using its influence in arranging over flight and landing clearances, and supplying planes and pilots. When the crisis broke a year later, the charge against Clarridge would be that he had known all along—from his first meeting with North on November 19—that North was arranging for the shipment of missiles to Tehran and thus not only he but the CIA was engaged in illegal covert activity without the authority of a presidential finding. What was conveniently overlooked, however, was that the CIA's involvement was the direct result of McFarlane's transmission of the president's purported "mental finding" to North, who used it as the basis of his request to Clarridge.

Reagan Turns the Tables

The failure of the *Hawk* deal intensified the struggle between those who wanted to continue with the arms-for-hostages scheme and those who wanted to shut the operation down. The president, now fully apprised of the issues, decided, as he had time and again, to take what had been done and employ it for his own purpose—to attempt to establish a political relationship with Iran—but he did so without informing the leaders of the new world order faction, or congress, of his decision.

The *Hawk* failure was the climax of McFarlane's scheme. He now moved to use it as the rationale for shutting down the initiative entirely, according to the new world order faction's plan, and pirouetted to side with Shultz and Weinberger in opposition to the program. The Israelis also pirouetted to keep the program going and Kimche began to cooperate with North and Secord in developing a new plan.

The president chose a third course, which was for the United States to take control of the arms-for-hostages scheme, subordinate the Israelis to it, and seek to parley it into a diplomatic relationship with Iran. In a very real sense, the president turned the tables on the new world order faction, who had sought to use the arms-for-hostages scheme as their way of *preventing* the establishment of relations with Iran.

The Israelis, too, became victims of their own success. Their plan to draw the United States deeper into the scheme succeeded too well, as Reagan took control of the policy, relegating the Israeli role to logistical support. Of course, Reagan's action did not occur in a vacuum. His was but one successful move in a contest with moving parts; others—the Israelis, the new world order faction, even those who thought they were acting on behalf of the president—would make moves of their own.

As soon as John McMahon learned of Clarridge's actions on the morning of November 25, he recognized the CIA's need for legal authorization to justify "implementation of this mission." After angrily placing a hold on any further CIA involvement, he called the agency's general counsel, Stanley Sporkin, and told him that "I wanted a Finding and I wanted it retroactive to cover that flight." [54] Informed that a finding was being prepared, North called Schwimmer to tell him that there would be no more flights "until we tell you."[55]

McMahon should have been familiar with the law on presidential findings, which stipulated that a finding dealt with "anticipated future intelligence activity," not with what had already been done. Sporkin, however, did know the law, or quickly became informed of it, and told McMahon that there was no need for a finding to cover the proprietary flight. Upon reflection, however, he agreed that it "wouldn't hurt" to cover the CIA's effort in attempting to influence foreign governments to obtain landing clearances,[56] even though he knew it was, at the very least, unprecedented. Sporkin sought to lend some quasi-legal heft to the retroactive feature of the finding by describing it with the Latin phrase *nunc pro tunc* (literally "now for then").[57]

---

[54] *Iran-Contra Affair*, 185.
[55] Draper, *Very Thin Line*, 207.
[56] "John McMahon: Memorandum for the Record," December 5, 1985, *Iran-Contra Affair*, Appendix B, volume 12, 166-67.
[57] "Edward Makowka deposition," Ibid, volume 17, 598-99.

What Sporkin did, however, was to stretch the finding well beyond providing mere cover for the CIA into legal authorization to "facilitate the release of the American hostages." The finding authorized

> assistance by the Central Intelligence Agency to private parties in their attempt to obtain the release of Americans held hostage in the Middle East. Such assistance is to include the provision of transportation, communications, and other necessary support. As part of these efforts certain foreign materiel and munitions may be shipped to the Government of Iran, which is taking steps to facilitate the release of the American hostages.
>
> All prior actions taken by U.S. Government officials in furtherance of this effort are hereby ratified.[58]

This finding represented a serendipitous capstone of the new world order faction's plan to entangle the president in an arms-for-hostages scheme, their way of derailing an opening to Iran. It authorized future (and legalized past) CIA involvement in the scheme, but failed to imbed it in the larger strategic context of a diplomatic opening to Iran. Thus, while the finding's immediate effect was to sanction the CIA's involvement, the longer-term danger was that the unvarnished arms-for-hostages formula would pose a major political liability for the president—if it ever became public.

Sporkin had prepared this finding in less than twenty-four hours and the question is: from whom had he learned that the proprietary flight had been part of an exchange of arms for hostages? Sporkin told McMahon that he intended to speak to the White House counsel, Fred Fielding, and to the Attorney General, Edwin Meese.[59] There is no record of a discussion with Fielding; Findings were routinely sent to the Justice Department to insure "legal sufficiency." However, Meese denied that Sporkin had contacted him or the department.[60]

---

[58] McMahon, "Memorandum for the Record," 186.
[59] "John McMahon deposition," *Iran-Contra Affair*, Appendix B, volume 17, 296.
[60] "Edwin Meese deposition," Ibid, volume 18, 33-34.

The evening of November 25, McMahon sent two of the CIA technicians involved in the proprietary flight to brief Sporkin, the Air Branch deputy chief and the CIA group chief, (but, oddly, neither Clarridge nor Allen, who knew the purpose of the flight).[61] Sporkin claimed that these "two guys from operations...told him the operation was, in essence, an arms-for-hostages trade."[62] However, both men contradicted Sporkin, and testified, "nothing was said to indicate that the proprietary's flight was related to an effort to free hostages." [63] If neither of these men told him of the flight's purpose, who did?

There are three possibilities. Sporkin must have spoken to McFarlane, Poindexter, or North. McFarlane was the obvious candidate because this had been his scheme from the beginning and the finding served his purpose. But he was not in Washington (although location meant little, as these men were, or could be, in contact from anywhere). Poindexter was in Washington holding down the fort at the NSC, had not been privy to McFarlane's scheme, and was only just beginning to get a feel for what was going on.[64] North, on the other hand, was directly and continuously involved; thus, the probability is that Sporkin spoke to North, if not also to McFarlane. It seems that in the matter of the November finding, North became the unwitting agent for McFarlane and the new world order faction,

---

[61] Allen had shown Clarridge "reports indicating that the flight was part of an operation aimed at the liberation of hostages, but the CIA was permitted to reveal only that the flight had a humanitarian purpose." Scott Armstrong et al., *The Chronology: The Documented Day-by-Day Account of the Secret Military Assistance to Iran and the Contras* (New York: Warner Books, 1987), 185.

[62] Walsh, *Final Report*, 540. See also "Sporkin testimony," *Iran-Contra Affair, 100-6, 121, 130.*

[63] *Iran-Contra Affair*, 185-86. The congressional report contradicts the technicians and follows Sporkin's line.

[64] "John Poindexter deposition," Ibid, volume 20, 1094. "In November 1985, I was very confused as to what had been approved and what hadn't been approved and frankly thought [the Iran initiative] had been run in a very slipshod manner."

although his immediate purpose was to provide legal cover for his own actions.[65]

When North heard that McMahon was demanding a finding he realized that McFarlane had lied to him about the "mental finding." If the "mental finding" were valid there would have been no need for another one. North got in touch with Sporkin that evening to insure that the finding he was preparing not only covered the CIA's role in the *Hawk* shipment, but also would legalize the mission itself (and his role in it). If Sporkin spoke to McFarlane he received the same advice. However, from this point onward, McFarlane and North moved along opposing policy paths, although North's realization of McFarlane's opposition was slow in coming.

North had had "nothing to do" with the first draft and by the time he got in touch with Sporkin, one of the chief counsel's aides, Edward Makowka, had already typed up a first draft of the finding in response to Sporkin's directive.[66] It retroactively sanctioned the CIA's support for Israel's shipment of missiles to Iran, including a provision for notification of congressional intelligence committees, but said nothing about facilitating the release of the American hostages.

By the next morning, however, reflecting his conversation with North and possibly McFarlane, Sporkin changed the draft finding entirely. He removed the provision for congressional notification, scratched out Israel and substituted "private parties," erased missiles and substituted "foreign material and munitions," and inserted the phrase "release of the American hostages," three times, to make its purpose unmistakable.[67]

After instructing Makowka to "keep no copies," Sporkin turned in the finding to Casey on Tuesday morning, November 26.[68] The

---

[65] North's prominent role with Sporkin in formulating both the January 6 and 17 findings reinforces the argument that he was also involved with him on this one.
[66] "Sporkin testimony," *Iran-Contra Affair*, 100-6, 212.
[67] "Makowka deposition," Ibid, Appendix B, volume 17, 597-98. "Sporkin testimony," 100-6, 127, denied that he had been "asked to alter the finding."
[68] "Makowka deposition," Ibid, 604. Back-up copies were found later after a search of hard drives.

director immediately called McFarlane and Don Regan to get their approval.[69] In a cover memo to Poindexter, Casey instructed, "it should go to the President for his signature and should not be passed around in any hands below our level."[70] Poindexter, however, kept the finding to himself because Reagan had already left for California that morning. Although the president returned to Washington on the 2nd, Poindexter did not present it to him for signature until three days later, on December 5.[71]

The Policy Scramble

Within a matter of twenty-four hours, indeed, the same twenty-four-hour period surrounding the formulation of the finding, the *Hawk* mission had collapsed in failure. The morning of November 25, in McFarlane's absence, "Poindexter told the president at his regular 9:30 briefing that a shipment of arms to Iran had just taken place."[72] All eagerly awaited the announcement that hostages had been released. They waited in vain; no hostages were freed.

Instead, a few hours later, Gorbanifar called Ledeen on the verge of hysteria to describe the *Hawk* fiasco. Claiming that the Israelis and the Americans, indeed, Reagan himself, had "cheated" Iran, he conveyed a message from Prime Minister Moussavi that he wanted Ledeen to deliver to the White House. The message stated:

---

[69] "McMahon: Memorandum for the Record," December 5, 1985, *Iran-Contra Affair*, Appendix B, volume 12, 166.
[70] "Memorandum from Casey to Poindexter," November 26, 1985, in Walsh, *Final Report*, 208 n.52.
[71] "Donald Regan deposition," *Iran-Contra Affair*, Appendix B, volume 22, 612. Regan claimed that he never saw the November finding. "I don't recall ever seeing nor hearing about the Sporkin finding in November of 1985."
[72] *Iran-Contra Affair*, 185. The president's daily brief (PDB) was a CIA-compiled account of the events of the previous twenty-four hours. In the Reagan administration, however, the CIA did not directly brief the president, but gave the briefing book to the NSC adviser, who did. See John Helgerson, *CIA Briefings of Presidential Candidates* (Washington, D.C.: CIA, 1996), chapter 6 passim.

We have fulfilled our every promise, and now you have cheated us. You must immediately remedy this terrible situation or else dire consequences will follow.[73]

Ledeen drove down to the West Wing "early in the evening," hoping to see McFarlane, but he was in California and "unavailable." Instead, he delivered the message to Poindexter, who, receiving it told Ledeen that he was being "taken off the project," because, he said, "we need people with more technical expertise." Ledeen was stunned, thinking that Poindexter "knew nothing about the political contacts with Iran. Only McFarlane and North…were privy to this information."[74]

In fact, it was McFarlane, who wanted to take Ledeen out of the line of fire to cover his own tracks. His intent, like Kissinger's maneuver over the Angolan affair, was to "bring this operation into the NSC," where he could hide his own responsibility and pin it on someone else, like Poindexter.[75]

Thus, by the evening of November 25, Poindexter learned of the *Hawk* disaster. Did he tell McFarlane, or the president? Although McFarlane was out of town and although there were rumors of his imminent resignation, he was still the national security adviser and Poindexter most certainly spoke with him. In fact, McFarlane was deeply involved in and in frequent contact with the president regarding another airline hijacking that had begun two days before and had just ended very badly.

On November 23rd, Egyptair flight 648 took off from Athens headed for Cairo. Within minutes of being airborne, three Palestinian members of Abu Nidal, led by Omar Rezaq, commandeered the

---

[73] Michael Ledeen, *Perilous Statecraft: An Insider's Account of the Iran Contra Affair* (New York: Scribner, 1988), 161-62.
[74] Ibid, 162.
[75] The next day, November 26, McFarlane wrote North that he was "inclined to think that we should bring this operation into the NSC and take Mike [Ledeen] out of it but will await John's [Poindexter] thoughts. No further communication with Mike on this until I have thought it through." *The Chronology*, 187.

aircraft. In what was another Qadaffi-sponsored terrorist plot,[76] they ordered the pilot to take the plane to Tripoli, but, as the hijackers began to check passengers' passports, an Egyptian Security Service agent pulled out his gun and killed one of the terrorists instantly. In the ensuing gunfight, the Egyptian agent was wounded along with two flight attendants, and the aircraft's fuselage was punctured causing depressurization of the passenger cabin.[77]

As the pilot took the aircraft into an emergency descent to 14,000 feet to allow passengers to breathe without oxygen masks, the hijackers commanded him to land at Luqa airport in Malta. After an emergency landing, which airport controllers initially attempted to prevent, the hijackers demanded fuel for the aircraft, intending to fly on to Tripoli. As Maltese authorities refused to comply unless all passengers were released, the hijackers began shooting them, first two Israeli, then three Americans, to show they meant business. (Fortunately, three of the five survived.)

Maltese Prime Minister Mifsud Bonici, an ally of Qadaffi's, personally assumed control of the negotiations with the hijackers. Indeed, NSA intercepts convinced American leaders that Qadaffi was sending instructions to the hijackers and perhaps to Bonici, who may have expected an outcome similar to the TWA 847 hijacking that ended without excessive violence.[78] But Mubarak had a more forceful response in mind, perhaps to make up for his gaffe in allowing the terrorists to escape in the Achille Lauro affair the previous month.

Bonici was caught between the demands of the hijackers for fuel and free passage and the demands of the Egyptian and American governments to permit Egyptian Special Forces to storm the plane. Shultz declared publicly "terrorists deserve no quarter. Terrorists

---

[76] It was later learned that Libyan embassy personnel had smuggled the weapons into the boarding area in diplomatic pouches, which were not subject to security screening.

[77] J.A. Mizzi, *Massacre in Malta: The Hijack of Egyptair MS 648* (Valletta: Techonografia, 1989).

[78] David C. Wills, The *First War on Terrorism: Counter-Terrorism Policy During the Reagan Administration* (Lanham, MD: Rowman & Littlefield, 2003), 176.

should have no place to hide. We must stamp out this terrorist activity."[79] On *Meet the Press*, he said, "the way to get after these people is with both barrels," endorsing a military raid.[80] A state department spokesman said, "we were prepared to offer all appropriate assistance."[81]

Unlike the TWA instance, this time Shultz would get his wish. Under great pressure, Bonici dragged out the negotiations with the hijackers for almost an entire day before finally agreeing to permit Egyptian Task Force 777 to attack the plane on the evening of November 25. U.S. Delta Force had trained the Egyptian unit and, although the state department offered to send a special operations team to assist them, Bonici rejected the offer.[82]

The plan was to attack the plane after nightfall under cover of delivering food to the passengers. Inexplicably, an hour and a half before the planned time of the raid, the Egyptian commandos stormed onto the plane after detonating explosives attached to the cabin doors and luggage compartment. The explosions ignited a fire that spread rapidly in the cabin, causing a suffocating, toxic smoke.

Realizing they were under attack the two hijackers tossed grenades into the cabin area, killing and wounding many. Casualties mounted as the commandos fired indiscriminately throughout the smoke-filled cabin. In all, 60 of the 91 passengers were killed, and many were wounded. The leader of the hijackers, Omar Rezaq, initially escaped by disguising himself as a wounded passenger, but was later caught. In short, the "rescue" resulted in one of the worst airline hijack tragedies

---

[79] Bernard Gwertzman, "U.S. Lauds Raid, Regrets Deaths," *New York Times*, November 25, 1985, 1.
[80] Terry Atlas, "U.S. Stands Behind Jet Raid," *Chicago Tribune*, November 26, 1985, 1.
[81] "U.S. Says It Was Prepared to Employ Force," *Philadelphia Inquirer*, November 25, 1985, 13.
[82] David C. Martin and John Walcott, *Best Laid Plans: The Inside Story of America's War Against Terrorism* (New York: Touchstone, 1988), 266.

in history, discrediting the feasibility of assaulting a passenger aircraft.[83]

President Reagan, Secretary Shultz, and McFarlane were heavily involved throughout the hijack as Egyptian President Hosni Mubarak asked for and received U.S. assistance. McFarlane called the president early in the morning of November 24 to obtain permission to authorize U.S. planes stationed at nearby Sigonella air base in Sicily to provide protective air cover against a possible interception by Qadaffi's planes as the Egyptians deployed forces to Malta. The next day, the 25th, there was extended discussion of the horrific outcome. Finally, on November 29, McFarlane passed on Mubarak's request for fighter escorts as he extracted his forces from Malta.[84]

The Egyptair crisis thus bracketed the failure of the *Hawk* mission and may well have affected the president's response to it. It also shows McFarlane fully engaged with the president, who had left Washington at 0900 Tuesday November 26 for Los Angeles. McFarlane was already in San Francisco where he joined Shultz for his 65th birthday celebration at the Bohemian Grove, afterward going to Santa Barbara.[85] It is probable that McFarlane delivered the president his daily briefings on the November 27t and 29, the days before and after Thanksgiving.

Detailing the movements of the key players is essential to establish the context for an apparent presidential decision on the morning of November 26. The congressional report asserts that Reagan "authorized continuing the arms-for-hostages transaction" on the morning of the 26th when Casey "sent the Finding to the White House." The report further claims "North's notes indicate that he was so informed by Poindexter at an hour-long meeting." The note read:

---

[83] "Hijack Rescue Leaves Dozens Dead," *Washington Times*, November 25, 1985, 1.
[84] Douglas Brinkley, ed., *The Reagan Diaries* (New York: Harper Collins, 2007), 372.
[85] Robert C. McFarlane, *Special Trust* (New York: Cadell & Davies, 1994), 330, makes no mention of the hijack.

0940-1050. Mtg w/JMP. RR directed op to proceed. If Israelis want to provide diff model, then we will replenish. We will exercise mgt over movment if yr side cannot do. Must have one of our people in on all activities. [86]

The report supports this note by a citation from the *Israeli Historical Chronology* that "later that day, North related to an Israeli official that the Americans wanted to carry on even if the supply of additional arms was needed and even if the weapons had to come from the United States."[87] Draper says North had a second meeting with Poindexter on November 26, citing another North note, where North was instructed to have either Secord or Kimche tell the Iranians that the U.S. was not at fault in the *Hawk* fiasco and was willing to commit to shipping 120 more *Hawks*, if the Iranians would effect the release of all of the hostages "on 1st delivery" and "reiterate" their commitment to no more terror against the U.S. Finally, Washington would arrange a "change of team" to insure success.[88]

However, there are multiple problems with the assertion that Reagan directed the operation to proceed at this moment, beginning with the question of who told Poindexter that the president had authorized the operation to proceed? The best estimate is that, as the president was on his way to California and not informed of the need for a decision on the morning of November 26, it was McFarlane who told Poindexter to proceed, and he promptly relayed that information to North.

These multiple problems further entail the reliability of North's notebook entries, the substance of policy, and its timing. North frequently misdated entries in his notebooks. Indeed, both Draper and the congressional report identify some of North's misdated entries, casting suspicion on their reliability.[89] The widely quoted

---

[86] *Iran-Contra Affair*, 186-87.
[87] Ibid, 187.
[88] Draper, *Very Thin Line*, 200.
[89] Ibid, 632n.101. Draper says North misdated his entry regarding the second meeting of November 26, as October 26, while the congressional report dated it on

Israeli Historical Chronology was and remains a classified document, and thus also unverifiable.

Policy substance is another issue. As it evolved, the president's policy would look only vaguely like that described in North's purported notes of November 26 and it would take over a month of internal wrangling before a decision to proceed with arms sales would be made. Clearly, the decision to assume control of the arms-for-hostages program, whatever its larger rationale was not a matter to be decided lightly, especially as the entire approach of trading arms-for-hostages had not been Reagan's policy in the first place.

The shipment of 120 *Hawks* would never be a part of any plan. The "change of team" formulation was obviously incorrect because at that very moment Kimche, Schwimmer, and Nimrodi were conferring with North and Secord about a new plan. The Israeli team would not be removed from the action until a month later. The replenishment question was yet another matter that would not be resolved for several months and McMahon had stopped CIA support for the proprietary flights, pending the signing of a finding. Thus, literally nothing in the North notes of November 26 was true, or actual policy, at that moment.

Finally, there is the timing issue. Poindexter had not learned of the *Hawk* fiasco until the evening of November 25 and the president left for Los Angeles the next morning at 0900 hours. The finding was sent over to the White House the morning of November 26, but not until after the president had gone. It seems unlikely, therefore, that the president would have made a decision to proceed based upon a document he had not yet seen. In fact, the operation did not proceed because in the absence of a signed finding the CIA continued planning, but stood down.

More importantly, there was not much time to make a decision on the morning of the 26th and while it is possible that Poindexter, the president, if not also Casey, had conferred the evening before, it is

---

November 27. *Iran-Contra Affair*, 210 n.1, says the November 27 entry was misdated October 27. At the very least, there is confusion as to whether the second meeting occurred on November 26, or 27.

unlikely that a decision was made then. The congressional report removes even this narrow decision window by stating that it was not until "after midnight on November 26," that is, early morning of the 27th, that "Allen learned [from radio intercepts] that officials in Iran were upset that the wrong model *Hawks* had been delivered" and, therefore, only sometime after that a decision to proceed was made.[90] Thus, it seems, advancing the decision date obscures the argument that then ensued over whether or not to proceed.

The Issue is Joined

Two policy arguments collided at this time. While McFarlane and Shultz were attempting to use the failed *Hawk* delivery as the reason to shut down the Iran initiative entirely, North, Secord, and Poindexter were actively working out a new arms-for-hostages plan with Kimche, Ghorbanifar et al, to keep it alive. There is nothing in this record to suggest a foregone conclusion that the president had made the decision to take control of the initiative at this point.

There can be little doubt that when McFarlane joined Secretary Shultz for his birthday celebration at the Bohemian Grove outside of San Francisco the two men discussed McFarlane's plan to resign as well as the best way to utilize the act in furthering their larger objective. McFarlane decided to "inform" the president of his "thinking" during his daily briefing on the 29th. Determined to "turn off the Iran arms deals," he told Reagan "this is not working."

> Our hopes at the beginning of this were to be talking to Iranian politicians and to have a political agenda. It has ended up that we are talking to Iranian arms merchants, with no apparent prospect of establishing a political agenda.[91]

According to McFarlane, the president agreed, saying: "OK…Get the guys together," by which he meant to convene an NSPG meeting

---

[90] *Iran-Contra Affair*, 187.
[91] McFarlane, *Special Trust*, 46.

when he returned to Washington. McFarlane immediately called Poindexter, but told him to set up two meetings, not one. The first, as instructed, was of the NSPG for December 7; the second was with Gorbanifar in London the next day.[92] McFarlane's plan was straightforward. At the NSPG meeting he would side with Shultz and Weinberger to shut down the initiative. Then, he would fly to London to inform Gorbanifar that the deal was off.

McFarlane's next step was to hand in his resignation, of which there are two versions. Mayer and McManus say that on Saturday November 30, McFarlane drove up to the ranch and handed the president's military aide his letter of resignation, prompted by word from his secretary that *Newsweek* was about to publish a rumor about it.[93] McFarlane, however, claims that four days later, "on December 4, I wrote my resignation letter and slipped it into the binder I gave the president every morning during the daily briefing…"[94] The president's diary entry, however, settles it, stating that on Saturday, the 30th, the president received an "eyes only" resignation letter from McFarlane.[95]

The next day, Sunday December 1, according to the president's diary, Reagan saw McFarlane in Los Angeles at his Century Plaza hotel headquarters "for a few minutes" to make sure that he truly wanted to leave government.[96] McFarlane confirms that it was during his meeting with the president at the Century Plaza that he discussed his resignation with him.[97] However, as the president had left Los Angeles for Washington, via Seattle, on the 2nd, it was patently impossible for McFarlane to have slipped his resignation letter into the briefing book on December 4 and then discussed his resignation with the president the next day at the Century Plaza hotel in Los Angeles.

---

[92] *Tower Report*, B-44.
[93] Jane Mayer and Doyle McManus, *Landslide: The Unmaking of the President* (Boston: Houghton Mifflin, 1988), 169-70.
[94] McFarlane, *Special Trust*, 330-31.
[95] Brinkley, *Reagan Diaries*, 373.
[96] Ibid.
[97] McFarlane, *Special Trust*, 331-32.

There was more to McFarlane's resignation than is evident. He may not have intended to resign, but to use a threat to resign as part of his and Shultz's plan to shut down the Iran initiative. Both he and Shultz had used the threat to resign as a tactic before.[98] But, if this was the tactic, he was in for a surprise. By this time Reagan was fully apprised of the *Hawk* fiasco as well as McFarlane's role in it. As Mayer and McManus observe, "unlike a year earlier when Reagan had refused to accept McFarlane's resignation, this time he accepted it on the spot—to what others said was McFarlane's great disappointment." Indeed, McFarlane "regretted his resignation almost instantly," but it was too late. He had gambled and lost.[99]

By accepting McFarlane's resignation the president regained control of the NSC with the appointment of Poindexter, which would also strengthen the president's voting position in the NSPG. Once again, the president had turned the tables on the new world order faction, but not completely. In a move reminiscent of the ouster of Alexander Haig, McFarlane retained computer access to the NSC from his home and was allowed to keep his White House pass, but was no longer a regular member of the decision-making process.[100]

In the meantime, North had sent Secord to Tel Aviv as soon as he learned of the botched *Hawk* shipment to find out what had happened. As Secord told it, North had sent him "to Tel Aviv ASAP to get the full story from David Kimche," so he "flew to Israel via chartered Lear jet," arriving by November 28, at the latest.[101] Secord, a retired American general, operating under an assumed name (of Copp), cut an impressive figure, with a Lear jet at his disposal to "shuffle people" around the capitals of Europe.[102]

---

[98] See Draper, *Very Thin Line*, 260, for a list of Shultz's resignation threats.
[99] Mayer and McManus, *Landslide*, 170.
[100] See Richard C. Thornton *Reagan Revolution, III: Defeating the Soviet Challenge* (Victoria: Trafford, 2009), 140-41, for Haig's unusual resignation.
[101] Segev, *Iranian Triangle*, 209, claims Secord went to Paris first, on November 29.
[102] Secord, *Honored and Betrayed*, 221-22, said he was using "the Lear jet...to shuffle people between Tel Aviv, Lisbon [sic] and Paris." He undoubtedly meant London, not Lisbon, as Portugal was not on his itinerary this trip, but London was.

In Tel Aviv, Secord discussed the *Hawk* mission with Kimche, assuring him that "I was not in town on a fault-finding mission, but to prevent any problems from recurring."[103] Kimche simply professed to be "puzzled" by the Iranian rejection of the missiles, but eager to work out a new plan. The perennial issue of replenishment for the first 504 *TOWs* Israel had delivered came up in discussion with Mendy Meron, Director General of the Israeli Ministry of Defense. Secord observed laconically that the U.S. could not "just ship weapons" without congressional approval, indicating that some other means would have to be devised to compensate Israel for these missiles.[104]

Secord's meeting with Schwimmer was quite different. The Israeli was "very defensive" about his handling of the affair claiming that he was simply following the orders of his friend Shimon Peres. He claimed that they had "assumed the "I" in *I-HAWK* meant that the "improved" *Hawk* missile had high-altitude capability, " which it did not. Schwimmer was plainly "embarrassed" by what he had been asked to do. The bill for the two proprietary 707s Clarridge had arranged and the Lear jet Secord was using came to $200,000, which had been paid for out of the $1 million Schwimmer had advanced earlier. He told Secord to keep the remaining $800,000 for future needs.[105]

Secord and Kimche decided to set up a meeting in London for all of the principals to meet and "sort through the issues." At North's direction, however, Secord's next stop was Paris and the Georges V Hotel, where, on November 29, he and Kimche met Gorbanifar and Nimrodi. After a lengthy negotiation, in which Gorbanifar initially sought to place a large order of advanced weapons, including the *Maverick, Dragon*, and the *Phoenix* missile, as well as more *Hawks*, and 4,000 *TOWs*, he eventually agreed to a smaller weapons purchase in return for which all five American hostages and one French hostage

---

[103] Ibid, 220-21.
[104] Ibid, 223.
[105] Ibid, 221. Segev, *Iranian Triangle*, 210, attempting to protect Schwimmer, accused Secord of "exploiting the failure of Operation Espresso to get himself involved in the Iranian dealings, in place of Schwimmer and Nimrodi."

would be released. Fifty *Hawks* and 3,200 *TOWs* were divided into five packages that would be delivered in the course of a single day, December 12, at phased intervals, with each plane delivery followed by release of a hostage. To Secord this was "a ransom deal if I ever heard one," but that was what was agreed.[106]

Secord, Kimche and Gorbanifar agreed to consult their principals, after which they would meet North in London on December 8 to finalize arrangements for the December 12 delivery. Throughout, Secord was in contact with North using a special "brevity code" that enabled them to communicate over commercial phone lines. Kimche, receiving approval from Peres, proceeded to Geneva with Gorbanifar on December 4 to meet with Karoubi. The Iranian leader attempted unsuccessfully to raise the number back to 4,000 *TOWs*, but agreed to 3,300.[107]

Secord's negotiation trip and McFarlane's resignation ploy set the stage for what was expected to be the decisive NSPG meeting of December 7. To prepare for it, North put together a long memorandum for Poindexter based on Secord's meetings with Kimche and Gorbanifar and their colleagues. The memo was equal parts policy review, strategic assessment, operational plan, and emotional plea.

North reviewed the *Hawk* mission, noting that it had "created an atmosphere of extraordinary mistrust on the part of the Iranians," as Gorbanifar charged the Israelis with playing a "cheating game." Nevertheless, Secord and Kimche had managed to renew the dialogue promising hope for "achieving our three objectives." North saw these as providing support for a "pragmatic" army faction, return of the hostages, and the end of terrorism.[108]

Reflecting Kimche's input, North saw Israel's objectives as wanting to perpetuate a stalemate in the Iran-Iraq war, promoting the emergence of a more moderate government, and effecting through arms sales and/or barter arrangements the recovery of Iranian Jews. In view of this, North thought

---

[106] Secord, *Honored and Betrayed*, 227 and Segev, *Iranian Triangle*, 210.
[107] Segev, *Iranian Triangle*, 210-11.
[108] *Tower Report*, B-34.

> We should probably be seeing the return of the AMCIT hostages as a subsidiary benefit—not the primary objective, though it may be a part of the necessary first steps in achieving the broader objectives.[109]

Injecting a note of urgency and alarm, North noted that all agreed that time was running out and to stop now would incur the risk of "never being able to establish a foothold for longer-term goals" and raise the greater likelihood of reprisals in the form of seizures of more hostages and even executions of those still being held.

However, North's description of the hostage situation was oddly uninformed, saying curiously that "the hostages...may be killed or captured/released [sic] by the Syrians, Druze, Phalange or Amal in the near future."[110] If anything, these groups were attempting to locate and free the hostages. Worse, there was no discussion of Hezbollah, or the group that actually was holding the hostages, Imad Mugniyeh's *Islamic Jihad.*

North put forth the details of the deal negotiated by Secord and Kimche with Gorbanifar. The 3,300 *TOWs* and 50 *Hawks* would be broken down into five packages and delivered on December 12 with release of one hostage per delivery. He noted that the Iranians had demonstrated their sincerity by depositing $41 million for purchase of the weapons and had prepared the 17 *Hawks* (minus the one test-fired) delivered in November for return shipment.

Although the hostages were not to be released until after deliveries had begun, to guard against a possible double-cross, North said that if the first two deliveries of 300 *TOWs* each "do not produce the desired outcomes, all else stops." Besides, he said, we had their money: "all $ are now under our control." Then, he said contradictorily, the hostages must be released "before the A/C actually crosses into Iranian airspace." It was not clear whether a hostage was to be released after the first delivery, or while the plane was still in the air.

---

[109] Ibid, B-35.
[110] Ibid, 34-35.

Again, reflecting Kimche's input, North folded into the plan's "opsec," or operational security concerns, replenishment for the missiles and other weapons Israel would deliver, including the 504 *TOWs* sent in August and September. As a sweetener, it would be a cash deal. The Israelis would pay cash for replenishment weapons and not use Foreign Military Sales credits, as was normally the case, which would not draw congressional scrutiny.

As to procedure, North said that Secord, Kimche, Schwimmer and he were to meet on Saturday morning, December 7 in London to go over the deal and if everything was in order, then Kimche and Schwimmer would meet Gorbanifar and his Iranian superior "at another hotel…to formalize the plan." If all agreed, North would transmit the deal to Poindexter and, if the president approved, Kimche and Schwimmer would meet again with Gorbanifar and his Iranian chief on Sunday morning to finalize the agreement.[111]

In his closing paragraphs, North claimed that he and Clarridge had "been through the whole concept twice looking for holes and can find little that can be done to improve it," but, though Clarridge knew a great deal, "the only parties fully aware of all dimensions of what we are about are you and RCM [McFarlane]." Finally, he pleaded, "if we do not at least make one more try…we stand a good chance of condemning some or all [of the hostages] to death and a renewed wave of Islamic Jihad terrorism."[112]

---

[111] Ibid, B-36-37.

[112] Ibid, 37. Clarridge, *Iran-Contra Affair*, 195, denied discussing this plan with North saying that he had a "tendency to use my name with McFarlane and Poindexter because if I said it was a good idea, then they tended to think it was a good idea."

Chapter 7
Reagan's Iran Initiative

From early December of 1985, the Reagan and new world order factions contended over the Iran initiative, which the president would resurrect from the depths to which McFarlane and the new world order faction believed they had consigned it. Signing a covert action finding on January 17, 1986, the president authorized a new and legal approach involving the CIA, the NSC, and third U.S. parties, relegating the Israelis to a supporting role. The president's objective was to bring about a political rapprochement with Iran, which *inter alia* would result in the release of the five American hostages being held in Beirut.

The plan was for a limited delivery of munitions to Iran to result in the release of the hostages, after which a high-level meeting would inaugurate a full-blown rapprochement. Unfortunately, while accepting American weapons, the Iranians stalled on completing their end of the bargain, for two reasons. First, they exercised only limited influence over Imad Mugniyeh, who held the hostages and second, their overall strategic calculation changed.

The Two Factions Collide

North's memo to Poindexter came just as the latter and McFarlane were engaged in "several lengthy meetings," on December 3 and 4, following the outgoing national security adviser's return to

Washington.[1] There can be little doubt that McFarlane told Poindexter of his intent to shut the initiative down. Shultz, speaking to him the next day, gave him the same opinion.[2] Poindexter, of course, was firmly committed to the opposite course, having authorized the formulation of a new plan, which Secord, Kimche, North, and Gorbanifar had just worked out.

When Poindexter realized that McFarlane and Shultz were intent on shutting the initiative down, he decided not to bring up the existence of the unsigned finding he had received from Casey a week earlier authorizing CIA involvement.[3] He also realized that he would have to remove McFarlane from an operational role, so he instructed North to rewrite the new plan, taking McFarlane out of it and shifting his participation into the future.

The next day, December 5, North dutifully rewrote his memo, retitling it "Special Project Re Iran," summarizing its main points, but tweaking it in three areas. He inserted a flat "guarantee" that Iran would release the hostages, added a brief description of Hezbollah in Lebanon, and removed McFarlane from direct participation in the deal.

Their Iranian interlocutors, North said, will "guarantee" the release of the five American and one French hostages in return for delivery of 3,300 *TOWs* and 50 *Hawks* and also that "no further acts [of] Shia fundamentalist terrorism" will occur.[4] They "are cognizant of the pressure being placed on the Hizballah [sic] surrogates in Lebanon and that the leverage they now exercise "may no longer be available in the near future." What he meant by "Hizballah surrogates" was left to the reader's imagination.

---

[1] *Report of the Congressional Committees Investigating the Iran-Contra Affair* (Washington, D.C.: GPO, 1987), 195. [hereinafter cited as *Iran-Contra Affair*]
[2] John G. Tower et al., Report of the President's Special Review Board: February 26, 1987 (Washington, D.C.: GPO, 1987), B-40
[3] *Iran-Contra Affair*, 195. 197. McFarlane "does not recall any discussion of the status of the covert action finding..." and "Poindexter did not even mention the finding" in his call to Shultz.
[4] *Tower Report*, B-41.

With regard to McFarlane's role, North neatly took him out of the current operation and shifted his participation to the future. Thus, where in the December 4 memo North had suggested a McFarlane "meeting with the Iranians to obtain release of the hostages" *before* delivery, in the December 5 memo he said that "McFarlane would step in to supervise achieving the longer-range goals" *after* the hostages were released.[5]

On Thursday morning, December 5, Poindexter delivered the president's daily brief, at which he claimed to have "presented" Sporkin's November 26 finding to the president, who, he says, "signed it." But had he? The evidence for his assertion is flimsy in the extreme. Reagan himself later said flatly "I do not recall signing a Finding relating to Iranian arms transactions in November or December 1985. I am aware that an unsigned version of such a Finding exists...although I am told that a signed version has not been found."[6]

Don Regan, who attended the briefing, said that neither he, nor any members of his staff "can remember seeing that document." McFarlane, too, did "not recall any discussion of the status of the covert action finding." Poindexter says that he gave the finding to legal counsel Paul Thompson for deposit in his safe at the NSC.[7] That was the only copy, which was contrary to procedure. Copies should have been passed to the CIA and other involved department heads.

While Poindexter insists that the president signed the finding, he could not recall the "precise date" he signed it.[8] The December 5 date seems to have stemmed from McMahon's "memorandum for the

---

[5] Ibid, B-37, 42. See also Theodore Draper, *A Very Thin Line: The Iran-Contra Affairs* (New York: Hill and Wang, 1991), 224.
[6] Reagan, "response to Grand Jury Interrogatories," cited in Lawrence E. Walsh, *Final Report of the Independent Counsel for Iran-Contra Matters* (Washington, D.C.: United States Court of Appeals for the District of Columbia Circuit, August 4, 1993), 470. Arthur Liman, lead congressional investigator, in "Hostile Witness," *Washington Post*, August 16, 1998, said that he did not believe Poindexter.
[7] *Iran-Contra Affair*, 195-97. See also, "The Iran-Contra Hearings: Excerpts; Hold Body and Soul Together," *Los Angeles Times*, May 12, 1987, 1.
[8] "John Poindexter deposition," *Iran-Contra Affair*, Appendix B, volume 20, 1101.

record," in which he noted "someone told him on December 5 that the president had signed [it]." No one, it seems, except Poindexter, admits even to seeing the finding. Thompson, who was supposed to have put it in his safe, never saw it, only the folder in which it had been placed.[9] North claimed that the finding had been signed, but admitted that he "never saw" the draft, either.[10] There is additional circumstantial evidence that the finding was not signed on December 5, or earlier. That day, Poindexter called Shultz to brief him about the planned operation and the meeting for the 7th, but made no mention of the finding.[11]

Why did Poindexter maintain that Reagan signed a finding on December 5? Given the preparation for the delivery/swap of the 12th, Poindexter may have wanted to insure that the CIA continued planning to carry out its presumed role. Hence, Poindexter let McMahon know that the president had signed the finding, even though he was "never happy with it" and "wanted to get a broader finding."[12] Nor did he let anyone else know it existed, which, in fact, defeated its purpose. Finally, the main reason that Reagan would not have signed the finding was that to do so would have acknowledged his attempt to cover up an illegal action he had never authorized.

North left for London via New York on December 6, to meet with his Israeli and Iranian colleagues, as planned. In New York City, he met with Israeli procurement chief Ben-Yosef about the replenishment of the 504 *TOWs* Israel had shipped in August and September. Based on what actually transpired later, North's advice was simply to add the 504 replacement missiles onto a future weapons sale to Iran.

However, the sole source for North's discussion with Ben-Yosef, the *Israeli Historical Chronology*, presents an entirely different, and incredible picture. Three Israeli officials were privy to the discussions. One, unidentified, "made handwritten notes of their meeting on

---

[9] "Paul Thompson deposition," *Ibid*, Appendix B, volume 26, 998-99.
[10] *Tower Report*, B-40.
[11] *Iran-Contra Affair*, 197.
[12] "John Poindexter deposition," *Ibid*, Appendix B, volume 20, 1025, 1104.

December 12, 1985." The other two "did not recall the remarks of North." They should have, for North allegedly told Ben-Yosef that the "U.S. did not have the money to pay for the 504 missiles already supplied to Iran." If Israel wanted to be repaid, " he said, it should get the money from the two Israeli arms dealers," Nimrodi and Schwimmer.[13] The problem with this account, however, is that their discussion was not about repayment, but replenishment.

The unidentified Israeli also claimed that North told them "he intended to divert part of the profits [from arms sales] to the Contras." Both Segev and the congressional report repeat this claim, which also lacks credibility, particularly as the notes of the meeting were reportedly written six days after the event and two of the three persons present could not substantiate the conversation.[14]

The explanation lies, perhaps, in what transpired between North's visit and the cancellation of the December 12 delivery. The Israelis simply concocted the notes when it became clear that there would be no deal in order to plant the seeds of later controversy and divert blame from themselves. Certainly, North, properly sensitive to security, had no reason whatsoever to discuss with the Israelis what he planned to do with "profits" from Iran arms sales and every reason not to. They had no need to know.

In any case, North flew from New York City to London, arriving on December 7 to meet with Kimche, Gorbanifar, Nimrodi, Schwimmer, and Secord, to iron out the final details of the deal for 3,300 *TOWs* and 50 *Hawks*.[15] Gorbanifar, seeking to stress the urgency of the moment confided that "nine Hizbollah leaders had been summoned to Tehran on Friday [December 6] and that, given the pressure inside Lebanon, all it would take for the hostages to be killed

---

[13] Samuel Segev, *The Iranian Triangle: The Untold Story of Israel's Role in the Iran-Contra Affair* (New York: Free Press, 1988), 213.

[14] Ibid, and *Iran-Contra Affair*, 197.

[15] Segev, *Iranian Triangle*, 214-15, claims that North met first with Kimche and then with the others.

would be for Tehran to 'stop saying no.'"[16] This was not an entirely empty threat, but, as the hostages had been taken to obtain policy leverage, to have killed them would have been self-defeating.

On the same day, however, Iran made a move that greatly heartened these men. Iran's foreign minister, Ali Akbar Velyati began a three-day visit to Saudi Arabia, the first such visit by an Iranian since the 1979 revolution. The meeting with King Fahd was read as a signal "Iran really was abandoning its ambition of exporting its Islamic revolution."[17] It was in this "atmosphere of expectation," then, that the Americans, Israelis, and Iranians awaited the arrival of Robert McFarlane.

The New World Order Faction Blocks Action

Just as North was arriving in London on Saturday morning, the president was meeting with his top aides in the White House family residence. Present for this informal NSPG meeting, the first full discussion by the American leadership of a specific plan for the Iran initiative, were Shultz, Weinberger, Regan, McFarlane, Poindexter, and McMahon, standing in for Casey, who was traveling abroad. Vice-President Bush, to avoid taking sides, decided to attend the Army-Navy football game.

Discussion swirled around the Secord-Kimche-Gorbanifar plan to sell 3,300/50 missiles for the hostages. Shultz repeated his now all-too-familiar refrain objecting to any deals with Iran or terrorists. Weinberger supported him, adding that any arms shipments would violate the Arms Export Control Act. McMahon declared that there were no moderates in Iran to support. McFarlane, who was the initiator of the deals, swung to support Shultz and Weinberger in

---

[16] Scott Armstrong et al., *The Chronology: The Documented Day-by-Day Account of the Secret Military Assistance to Iran and the Contras* (New York: Warner Books, 1987), 207
[17] Segev, *Iranian Triangle*, 215.

"recommending an end to them."[18] Regan's position surprised the president most when he said that the best solution to a losing proposition was to "cut your losses."[19]

The president, "fully engaged," wanted to proceed, claiming "the American people will never forgive me if I fail to get these hostages out," because of legal technicalities. Interestingly, the Sporkin finding, supposedly signed just two days before, which the president could have produced as a *fait accompli* to legalize the deal, did not come up. Furthermore, even though Poindexter had Casey's proxy vote in favor,[20] the balance of voting opinion at the meeting was at best four against four, or five to three against the president, depending on where Regan stood. Bush's vote would have been crucial, but he was not there to cast it.

In the face of the deadlock, (Weinberger thought the deal was "finished"; Shultz wasn't so sure), the president cancelled the 3300/50 plan. Instead, he decided that McFarlane should go to London and propose to Gorbanifar an alternative. If the Iranians released the hostages, then the United States would be prepared to provide weapons in the context of a political dialogue. Otherwise, the United States would not sell weapons to Iran, or permit others, which meant Israel, to do so.[21] Shultz "did not object" to this approach, although he thought, "the prospects for success were minimal."[22]

McFarlane left Washington that evening of the 7th, arriving in London the next morning. After breakfast with North and Secord at the Hilton Intercontinental, McFarlane met privately with Kimche to give him advance notice of the policy change. Kimche was understandably "upset," believing that the United States was "missing a big

---

[18] *The Chronology*, 207-08. *Iran-Contra Affair*, 198, incorrectly claims that McFarlane "spoke in favor of continuing the initiative."
[19] "Donald Regan deposition," *Iran-Contra Affair*, Appendix B, volume 22, 583. In his testimony to the Tower Board, B-45, however, Regan claimed that that he "favored keeping the channel open, if necessary selling a modest amount of arms."
[20] Walsh, *Final Report*, 206.
[21] *Ibid*, 199 and *Tower Report*, B-44-45.
[22] George Shultz, *Turmoil and Triumph* (New York: Macmillan, 1993), 799.

opportunity." There was a need for "patience," he argued. But McFarlane responded, "well, we just don't see that; and further, we think it is being skewed off in the wrong direction."[23] With that, they went off separately to the meeting with Gorbanifar.

McFarlane, North, and Secord arrived at Nimrodi's duplex off Hyde Park around one in the afternoon. There to meet them were Kimche, Schwimmer, Nimrodi, and an Israeli general representing Rabin. Gorbanifar was alone. The Iranian started the conversation by immediately doubling the price of the agreed package of 3,300 *TOWs* and 50 *Hawks* for the five American and one French hostage to 6,000 *TOWs*, plus *Hawks* and *Phoenix* missiles. He declared that the new price was "one box for one thousand TOWs," referring to the hostages as "boxes." And, he went on, "if you ship another thousand immediately, I can guarantee two boxes." He could also deliver "one box for some Phoenix missiles, if you deliver them immediately."[24]

McFarlane's response, however, stunned the Iranian. Without haggling about price, as Gorbanifar undoubtedly expected, McFarlane simply informed him "under instructions" that the arms sale deal was off. Instead, McFarlane put forward the proposal that the Iranians free the hostages first, after which the United States would enter into a political relationship that would include the subsequent provision of weapons.[25]

Gorbanifar, thunderstruck, thought McFarlane was "crazy." He claimed that the Iranians were "desperate," and "too weak for political talk." A political relationship must wait, he said, until his clients "get strong and take power." That meant weapons sales had to come first. He shrieked "if I take this news back to my colleagues, they will go mad! They might say, to hell with the hostages! Let the Hezbollah kill them!"[26]

Gorbanifar was not the only one who had been stunned by McFarlane's performance. Both North and Secord, who flew back to

---

[23] *Tower Report*, B-45.
[24] Richard Secord and Jay Wurts, *Honored and Betrayed: Irangate, Covert Affairs, and the Secret War in Laos* (New York: Wiley, 1992), 231.
[25] Robert C. McFarlane, *Special Trust* (New York: Cadell & Davies, 1994), 48.
[26] Ibid, 49.

Washington with McFarlane aboard the Gulfstream III jet, were also dumbfounded. Instead of coming to *sanction* the deal they had painstakingly put together with the Israelis and Iranians, McFarlane had shut the entire project down. However, although the new world order faction appeared to have won the battle, the war continued. Before the three men had landed at Andrews Air Force Base outside Washington, the next battle was already underway.

Iran: The End and the Beginning

On the plane back from London, December 8, while McFarlane was preparing his report for the president about shutting down the initiative, North, on the same plane, was preparing a memorandum entitled "Next Steps." Addressed to McFarlane and Poindexter, North presented an entirely different interpretation of what had happened in the meeting with Gorbanifar. Where McFarlane described Gorbanifar as the most "despicable" man he had ever met, with whom the United States could not do business, North and the Israelis saw him as "genuine," and "the deepest penetration we have yet achieved into the current Iranian government."[27]

While acknowledging, "information is incomplete," motivation "uncertain," and "our operational control tenuous," North argued, "much of our ability to influence the course of events...depends on the validity of what Gorbanifar has told us." However, "while it is possible that Gorbanifar is doubling us or simply lining his own pockets, we have relatively little to lose in meeting his proposal." The worst case would be if the Israelis delivered a small number of *TOWs* and no hostages were released. On the other hand, "a supply operation now could very well trigger the results he claims."

"Our greatest liability throughout has been lack of operational control over transactions with Gorbanifar." North pinned the blame for the *Hawk* fiasco on Schwimmer, who arranged for weapons "not

---

[27] "Next Steps," North to McFarlane/Poindexter, December 9, 1985, *Tower Report*, B-48-49.

requested by Gorbanifar" and negotiated terms "disadvantageous to the IDF," making it difficult for us to replenish the Israelis. His latest proposal would have swapped 3,300 *TOWs* for three hostages, but "at a price which would not allow the IDF to recoup expenses, thus complicating our ability to replenish IDF stores."

"The question which now must be asked is should we take a relatively small risk by allowing …a small Israeli-originated delivery of TOWs and hope for the best, or should we do nothing?" Raising the specter of hostage executions, North said there appeared to be four options available: go forward with the Gorbanifar/Schwimmer 3,300 plan; carry out a rescue raid with its attendant risks; allow the Israelis to deliver only 400-500 *TOWs*, maybe get a hostage out, and pick up the *Hawks* still in Iran as a "show of good faith"; or "do nothing."

Then, he added, as if in afterthought, "there is a fifth option which has not yet been discussed." "We could, with an appropriate covert action Finding commence deliveries ourselves, using Secord as our conduit to control Gorbanifar and delivery operations." North thought this option had "considerable merit," in that it would make it easier to replenish Israeli stocks, and provide weapons that the Iranians want and Israelis do not have, like the advanced *Hawk (PIP II)*.

On December 10, McFarlane reported to the president on his trip. Present also were Weinberger, Casey, Regan, Poindexter, and possibly Bush and North.[28] Shultz was *en route* to a NATO ministerial meeting in Brussels. McFarlane "recommended that we not pursue the proposed relationship with [Gorbanifar]." But, in discussion of the options in North's memo, the president, concerned about reprisals against the hostages, asked if we couldn't continue to "let Israel manage this program" without any commitments from us.[29]

The president "felt that any ongoing contact would be justified and any charges that might be made later [about trading arms for hostages]

---

[28] Ibid, B-49. *Iran-Contra Affair, 199-200,* says that North was there and Weinberger was not. McFarlane gave two versions. In one he thought Bush was there and Casey was not, and in the other he recalled that Casey and Weinberger were there, and Shultz was not. See *Tower Report,* B-50.
[29] Ibid. and *Iran-Contra Affair,* 200.

could be met and justified as an effort to influence future events in Iran." The president made no decision at this briefing, although Weinberger thought the initiative had been "strangled" and Armacost reported to Shultz that it had been agreed to drop it. Casey, however, "had the idea that the president had not entirely given up on encouraging the Israelis to carry on with the Iranians."[30] Regan and Poindexter thought the same. They were right.

After the briefing, Poindexter instructed North to "keep the Iran initiative moving forward," but contrary to the congressional report, the president's immediate decision was not to authorize either a resumption of Israeli arms shipments, or a raid.[31] Instead, he decided to pursue a diplomatic approach and sent Ambassador Dick Walters to Damascus with a message asking President Assad for his assistance. As Weinberger noted in his diary "President still wants to try to get hostages released—but forcible storming would mean many deaths—decided to send Dick Walters to Damascus."[32] Unfortunately, the approach to Assad yielded nothing because the Syrian leader had even less influence over Mugniyeh than the Iranians, at least at this point in time.

Draper says that North went to see Sporkin about a new finding on December 9, the day *before* the briefing. This could only have been a heads-up call based on his 5th option in the *Next Steps* memo, because it obviously was not a result of decisions yet to be taken at the December 10 meeting. Draper does acknowledge, however, that

---

[30] "Casey to DDCI," December 10, 1985, in *Tower Report*, B-50-52 and *Iran-Contra Affair*, 200.
[31] *Iran-Contra Affair*, 200, says "following the briefing" Poindexter told North to prepare a new finding, change the Israeli team, and find a legal way to sell arms to Iran. In fact, these steps would not be taken until early January.
[32] "Weinberger Diary," December 10, 1985, in Walsh, *Final Report*, 410 n.64. In *Fighting for Peace*, 373, Weinberger says of McFarlane's trip and subsequent report "to the best of my knowledge, McFarlane had no instructions, nor do we know what he actually had told the Iranians. He 'debriefed' some of the December 7 attendees on December 10, but I always felt that McFarlane's 'debriefings' were imaginary reports on what he wanted his auditors to hear."

"actual work" on the new finding "did not start until January 2, 1986," twenty-four days later.[33]

The decision to resume discussions with the Israelis came after a series of emotional meetings the president had with the families of the hostages a few days later, in mid-December, to "tell them that attempts to free the hostages by Christmas [had] failed." After these very emotional meetings, the president ordered Poindexter and Regan to "redouble efforts to gain their release." Poindexter immediately directed North to contact Amiram Nir.[34]

After communicating with North, Nir persuaded Prime Minister Peres to add him to the Kimche, Schwimmer, Nimrodi team, and Peres agreed. In a meeting with Schwimmer on December 25 the prime minister explained "given McFarlane's resignation and Nir's close ties to Poindexter and North, it was worth bringing Nir onto the Israeli team." Schwimmer "had no objections."[35] At this point, it was not yet a case of changing the team, just adding to it. Besides, Nir had some new ideas about recovering the hostages and obtaining American weapons.

Drawing on past Israeli experience, Nir's idea involved Israel selling 4,000 *TOWs* to Iran from its own stocks, and the United States pre-positioning a like amount of U.S. *TOWs* in Israel. "In case of an emergency" with Syria, Israel would purchase these weapons from proceeds obtained in the sale to Iran. Then, as in the TWA-847 crisis, he proposed the swap of twenty or thirty Israeli-held Shiite prisoners in Al Haim prison in Southern Lebanon for the five American hostages held in Beirut. In this concept, Israel would bear all the responsibility and the United States could deny any involvement.[36]

Before Nir's ideas could be formulated into a concrete proposal to Washington, however, two terrorist attacks at airports in Rome and Vienna, in which over a hundred people were either killed or

---

[33] Draper, *Very Thin Line*, 240.
[34] *The Chronology*, 225.
[35] Segev, *Iranian Triangle*, 222-23.
[36] Ibid.

wounded, coalesced administration attitude on the problem of terrorism and Qadaffi, who was implicated. Indeed, the problems of Qadaffi, international terrorism, and the Iran Initiative intertwined within Reagan's inner circle over the next several weeks.

Qadaffi and State-Supported Terrorism

The administration had been singularly unsuccessful in its efforts at combating terrorism in general and at confronting Qadaffi in particular since taking office. Although Reagan had signed NSDD 138 in April 1984 authorizing a "proactive" approach to terrorism, its main effect had been to precipitate a public debate between Shultz and Weinberger over the best way to combat terrorism. Shultz pressed for the proactive use of American military power against terrorists, while Weinberger sought to narrow the circumstances under which it could be used. The result was, as Noel Koch, Assistant Secretary of Defense for International Security Affairs observed: "no part of it was ever implemented."[37] It was all talk and no action, but the administration began to focus on Qadaffi in 1985.

In March, the CIA released a Special National Intelligence Estimate that concluded that Qadaffi was sponsoring a worldwide campaign against American interests and supporting a phalanx of terrorists groups of all stripes, including the PLO, Abu Nidal, and Imad Mugniyeh.[38] On April 30, the president signed NSDD 168, "U.S. Policy Toward North Africa," which was designed to contain and isolate Qadaffi by improving relations with his neighbors. An interagency group was authorized to review U.S. policy toward Libya and "prepare policy options to contain Qadaffi's subversive activities."[39]

---

[37] Joseph Stanik, *El Dorado Canyon: Reagan's Undeclared War with Qadaffi*, (Annapolis: Naval Institute Press, 2003), 95-97.
[38] *Libya's Qadaffi: The Challenge to U.S. and Western Interests* (Washington: Central Intelligence Agency, 1985).
[39] Stanik, *El Dorado Canyon*, 100 and Simpson, *National Security Directives*, 448, 528-32.

What emerged from the review was a two-pronged policy proposal, code-named *Flower,* whose components were *Tulip* and *Rose. Tulip* was a covert operation to support anti-Qadaffi groups that sought to overthrow the dictator. *Rose* was a U.S.-supported attack by Egypt against Libya. However, neither policy proposal fared well in inner councils. Both Shultz and Weinberger opposed *Rose,* as did Mubarak of Egypt, and the Senate Intelligence Committee vetoed *Tulip*.[40]

After the TWA crisis, with pressure mounting on the president to take action, on July 20, he signed NSDD-179, creating a government-wide task force on combating terrorism and placing Vice-President Bush in charge. Bush was tasked with devising plans for "preemptive or retaliatory actions to combat terrorism" and accorded the authority to call on virtually all sectors of the U.S. government for assistance in his task.[41]

The administration did not initially connect Qadaffi to the spate of American hostage seizures in the first half of the year. But he was identified as a supporter of Imad Mugniyeh, whose men had hijacked TWA-847 in June and Mugniyeh was determined to have masterminded the seizure of the hostages. Qadaffi was also identified as the supporter of Abu Nidal, whose men had seized the *Achille Lauro* in October and hijacked Egyptair 648 in November. Although Qadaffi denied involvement in all of these events the evidence was more than circumstantial. However, most of it was classified and publicly unusable, leaving the president frustrated and hamstrung.

The massacres at the Rome and Vienna airports changed that. Two days after Christmas, at just after nine in the morning, four young men, high on amphetamines, mingled in with the crowd in front of the ticket counters at the Leonardo da Vinci airport outside Rome. In their bags they carried thirteen grenades and four AK-47 automatic rifles. Without warning they began rolling grenades across the floor and raking the terminal with bullets, hitting people in line at the El Al,

---

[40] Stanik, *El Dorado Canyon,* 102-3.

[41] Ibid, 101 and Christopher Simpson, *National Security Directives of the Reagan and Bush Administrations* (Boulder: Westview, 1995), 454, 576-77.

TWA, and Pan Am ticket counters. The shooting rampage went on for five minutes. Eventually, airport police killed three of the four terrorists, but the cost was high–a dozen dead and seventy-four wounded, including several Americans.[42]

At about the same time three young men rushed into the second-floor departure area at Vienna's Schwechat airport, opening fire with AK-47 rifles and rolling grenades at passengers waiting to check in for an El Al flight to Tel Aviv. After two minutes, the gunmen fled the terminal, commandeered a car and tried to escape. In a running gun battle with the police the assailants were captured two miles from the airport. The toll was three dead, including one of the terrorists, and forty-seven wounded.[43]

Qadaffi publicly hailed the terrorists as "heroic," and acknowledged that he had provided Abu Nidal shelter in Tripoli. Indeed, his fingerprints were soon found figuratively all over these massacres, although the terrorists attempted to implicate Assad of Syria, as, for their own reasons, did the Israelis.[44] The grenades used by the assailants were traced to Libyan munitions stocks, the forged travel documents traced to passports confiscated from Tunisian guest workers, and communications intercepts linked Qadaffi to Abu Nidal.[45]

President Reagan was stunned and, while he declared the evidence against Qadaffi "irrefutable," the United States' public response was muted.[46] Behind the scenes, however, within hours of the massacres, planners had begun work on contingency measures, identifying

---

[42] Ed Magnuson, "Terrorism: Ten Minutes of Horror," *Time*, June 21, 2005.
[43] Ibid.
[44] The Soviets were redeploying SAM missiles, including mobile missiles, to the Bekaa along the Syrian-Lebanon border to replace those that the Israelis had knocked out during the 1982 war. Thus, Peres was seeking reasons to strike at Syria. See William Smith, "Middle East: An Eye for an Eye," *Time*, June 21, 2005.
[45] Daniel Bolger, *Americans At War, 1975-1986*, (San Francisco: Presidio, 1988), 386, Stanik, *El Dorado Canyon*, 106, and David C. Wills, *The First War on Terrorism: Counter-Terrorism Policy During the Reagan Administration* (Lanham: Rowman & Littlefield, 2003), 177.
[46] George Wilson, "Reagan Denounces Warning by Qadaffi on Retaliation," *Washington Post*, January 3, 1986, 1.

political, military, and economic options against Libya. After almost ten days of discussions at upper levels of the bureaucracy key meetings were held on January 6 and 7 to decide on the course of action to take.[47] Coincidentally, these would be the same two days when key decisions were made regarding the Iran initiative.

A Decision on Israel and Iran

Both Peres and Rabin had approved Nir's ideas and authorized him to go first to London to meet with Nimrodi and Gorbanifar to obtain the approval of the Iranians and then to Washington to present the proposal to the Americans. In London, on December 30, Nimrodi introduced Nir to Gorbanifar and briefed him on the previous deals. Nir was supposed to meet Schwimmer in New York before going to Washington, but instead went directly to Washington to meet with North and Poindexter, on January 2. This marked the beginning of a serious rift among the Israelis, as Schwimmer believed that he had been "tricked" and complained to Peres that Nir was attempting to cut him and the others out.[48]

In Washington, Nir's proposal to North and Poindexter was for Israel to undertake unilaterally the sale of 4,000 *TOW* missiles to Iran and with the proceeds purchase replacement missiles from Washington. At the same time, Israel would release twenty or thirty Shiite prisoners from the Al Haim prison in southern Lebanon and Iran would release the five American hostages. To "test Iran's intentions," Israel would make an initial delivery of 500 *TOWs*. If the hostages were freed, Israel would deliver the remaining 3,500; if not, Israel would bear the cost of the 500 and the operation would be terminated.[49]

Poindexter said the United States would not preposition missiles in Israel, but would either sell them, or in an emergency, fly them in. To

---

[47] Wills, *First War on Terrorism*, 177-81.
[48] Segev, *Iranian Triangle*, 223-24.
[49] Ibid, 224-25. Cf. *Iran-Contra Affair*, 201.

Nir's stand that replenishment of missiles was "a precondition for any further Israeli sales to Iran," North responded that Israel just couldn't buy missiles from the Pentagon. "There was a legal process, including congressional approval." But, he reassured Nir that "the price tag would be within Israel's means." North agreed that Israel would sell weapons to Iran at an "inflated price" and use the proceeds "to buy replacements for Israel and to fund joint, covert activities, mostly in the area of counterterrorism."[50]

The congressional report claims that during these discussions with Nir in early January, North's mention of "joint covert operations" also referred to the "finance [of] U.S. activities in Nicaragua," or what would later become known as the "diversion." This seems unlikely. Later in the same account, the report quotes North himself saying that "other operations" did *not* refer to the contras. "I do not believe [Nir] mentioned contras at that meeting, but my recollection is we began to talk in early January about other joint U.S.-Israeli, and in some cases unilateral Israeli operations of a certain kind."[51] By "operations of a certain kind," North meant the possibility of an Israeli rescue of the hostages.

After contacting Casey, who liked Nir's plan, Poindexter instructed North to go see Judge Sporkin to draft a new finding. Over the next few days, and after several re-writes, North and Sporkin produced a finding. The objective was threefold: to bring about the establishment of a moderate government in Iran; to acquire intelligence from Iran unavailable elsewhere; and to further the release of the five American hostages held in Lebanon.

The third point, release of the hostages, was not inserted until the final draft. North had wanted to keep it out, but Sporkin, with Casey's assent, reinserted it. To achieve these ends the United States was prepared to provide various forms of assistance, including arms, to friendly selected liaison services and third countries. Because of the

---

[50] Segev, *Iranian Triangle*, 224-25.
[51] *Iran-Contra Affair*, 201-202.

project's "sensitivity," the president elected to "limit prior notice" to Congress until otherwise directed.[52]

During the president's daily briefing on the morning of January 6, attended by the vice-president, Deputy NSC Adviser, Don Fortier, and Regan, Poindexter raised the subject of the Israeli proposal. According to Regan, "the president decided that we should pursue this line, that we should be prepared to sell arms, and that we should make a Finding that would authorize and justify [it]..." Poindexter then handed the draft finding to the president, saying that this was the proposal to be discussed the following day, and the president mistakenly signed it.[53]

Later that day, Sporkin realized that the wording of the finding was inconsistent and confusing regarding whom the United States was to assist. In one place it said the United States was prepared to assist "selected friendly liaison services and third countries" and in another place said "third parties and third countries." So, to be consistent, Sporkin inserted the following language "selected friendly liaison services, third countries, and third parties...." The change was prescient. Sporkin thought at the time that the term "third parties" referred to Gorbanifar and the Iranians, but it would come to refer crucially to Secord, instead.[54] Sporkin's emendation meant that the draft would have to be retyped and, of course, signed again.[55]

However, between the time that the finding was retyped and signed by the president on January 17, the entire initiative would be restructured in almost every aspect, requiring yet a new finding. On January 7, after a full NSPG meeting that dealt with Qadaffi, which will be discussed below, the president gathered his top aides for a principals only meeting in the Oval Office.[56] In attendance were the president, vice-president, Shultz, Weinberger, Casey, Meese, Regan, and Poindexter.

---

[52] *Tower Report*, B-58-60.
[53] Ibid, B-60-61.
[54] *Iran-Contra Affair*, 208.
[55] *Tower Report*, B-61.
[56] "Recollection of Attorney General Edwin Meese," in *Tower Report*, B-61.

In contrast to the meeting a month earlier, on December 7, where McFarlane, McMahon, Shultz, Weinberger, and Regan had all voiced opposition to the initiative, at this meeting the president had almost unanimous support. Casey was there instead of McMahon, Poindexter was there instead of McFarlane, Meese was there for the first time, Bush was also there, and Regan had changed his mind.

Although Weinberger claimed that the discussion of Nir's proposal was "very much a re-run" of the December 7 meeting, the very opposite was true.[57] Nir's plan was substantially different from the Schwimmer/Gorbanifar plan discussed in December; there was no American role. After a vigorous discussion in which everyone had his say, the president had overwhelming support for going forward with Nir's plan. As Shultz noted "it was clear to me by the time we went out that the President, the Vice-President, the Director of Central Intelligence, the Attorney General, the Chief of Staff, the National Security Adviser all had one opinion and I had a different one, and Cap shared it."[58] The voting margin was six to two, but even that understated the president's support and Shultz's isolation.

It was true that Weinberger shared Shultz's opinion, but unlike Shultz accepted the president's decision, even though reluctantly. Aside from his visceral objections to dealing with the Iranians, the defense secretary's main substantive objections had been to their legality. Israeli sales of U.S. weapons to Iran would violate the Arms Export Control Act, as would U.S. sales to replace those arms Israel sold to Iran. Moreover, such sales would have to be reported to Congress.

But Reagan had brought Attorney General Meese to the meeting specifically to provide a ruling on this matter. Meese produced the 1981 opinion by his predecessor, William French Smith, which ruled that the CIA, obtaining weapons from the Defense Department under the Economy Act, could legally sell them to third countries. The

---

[57] *Iran-Contra Affair*, 203.
[58] *Tower Report*, B-63-64.

Economy Act permitted intra-governmental transfers, which meant weapons could be sold at or below cost.

Furthermore, reporting requirements under the Economy Act were less stringent. Meese's ruling meant that the finding would have to be rewritten to include reference to the authority contained in the Economy Act, which was not in the January 6 draft.[59] Weinberger reluctantly accepted the ruling.[60] "We would carry out the Commander-in-Chief's orders to do this, and obviously hold it as closely as possible because that was not only the direction [directive] but the obvious thing to do."[61]

North immediately sent Nir a message in rudimentary code (whose meaning, unfortunately, even a beginner code-breaker could decipher, not to mention the Soviets, who undoubtedly intercepted it). The message read:

> Joshua has approved proceeding as we had hoped. Joshua and Samuel have also agreed on method one. Following additional conditions apply to Albert. (A) Resupply should be as routine as possible to prevent disclosure on our side. May take longer than two months. However, Albert says if crisis arises Joshua promises that we will deliver all required by Galaxie in less than eighteen hours. (B) Joshua also wants both your govt and ours to stay with no comment if operation is disclosed. If these conditions are acceptable to the Banana then Oranges are ready to proceed.[62]

Aside from confusing Joshua with Albert in the sixth sentence, it was self-evident that Joshua was the president and Samuel, connected to resupply, was the secretary of defense. The only indecipherable term was "method one," which referred to direct sale of weapons to

---

[59] For Poindexter's memo accompanying the January 6 finding, see *Tower Report*, B-58-60.
[60] *Iran-Contra Affair*, 203.
[61] *Tower Report*, B-65.
[62] *Iran-Contra Affair*, 204.

Israel, instead of Nir's idea of prepositioning. The rest of the message was straightforward, except for the silly but transparent references to Banana and Oranges.

North obviously wanted to respond positively to the Israeli proposal, but his message was premature. The U.S. government was not "ready to proceed." The reason Reagan had not produced the finding he had signed the day before was because when Meese ruled that the Economy Act could be the legal authority for selling weapons the president realized that the finding would need to be revised to include it. In addition, he had not decided how weapons would be sold, or at what cost. Although Poindexter later noted the finding had not been fully staffed, in fact it had not included the legal authority justifying the president's decision.

And One On Libya

Meanwhile, these same two days saw the president preoccupied with the issue of what to do about Qadaffi. These meetings were the culmination of arguments that had swirled throughout the bureaucracy and the leadership for the previous ten days. On January 6, after his daily brief the president went into an NSPG meeting where Shultz argued for an immediate air strike against Libya. He buttressed his proposal with a legal opinion from Abe Sofaer, State Department legal counsel, that Qadaffi's support for terrorist acts against the United States justified armed retaliation.[63]

Weinberger objected that all diplomatic and economic options had not been exhausted. Furthermore, air attacks would strike civilians and many of the one thousand-plus Americans working in Libya could become hostages. This argument, in particular, persuaded the president against hasty action, and he postponed a decision. Instead, he instructed Casey to move forward on *Tulip*, the covert operation to

---

[63] Wills, *First War on Terrorism*, 181.

support anti-Qadaffi dissidents, and Weinberger to intensify efforts on *Rose*, the plan to support an Egyptian invasion of Libya.[64]

By the next day, January 7, at a follow-on NSPG meeting, the president had decided on a strategy. Rather than act precipitously, as Shultz demanded, or avoid military action altogether, as Weinberger cautioned, the president decided upon a several months-long, diplomatic, economic, and military plan that would clear the decks for action. The gradual build-up of pressure on Qadaffi would either cause him to discontinue support for terrorist acts, or, if he continued, the United States would carry out attacks against him.[65]

The strategy of pressure would involve a public information campaign, economic sanctions, diplomatic suasion of allies, and increasing naval pressure in the Gulf of Sidra. President Reagan established the basis for the new strategy with the issuance of Executive Order 12543, which declared Libya to constitute "an unusual and extraordinary threat to the national security and foreign policy of the United States." The order banned the import or export of "any" Libyan goods or services, denied entry into the United States of any ships or aircraft, and generally prohibited provision of any credit, services, travel, or trade with Libya.

That evening, in a nationally televised press conference, the president announced the terms of the executive order. Declaring a "national emergency," he said that there was "irrefutable evidence" of Qadaffi's involvement in the Rome and Vienna massacres and denounced him as a "pariah" for his "longstanding involvement in terrorism," and castigated Libya as an "outlaw regime."[66]

---

[64] Stanik, *El Dorado Canyon*, 109 and Wills, *First War on Terrorism*, 177-81
[65] Douglas Brinkley, ed., *The Reagan Diaries* (New York: Harper Collins, 2007), 381. As Reagan put it in his diary entry for this day: "If Mr. Q decides not to push another terrorist act—O.K. we've been successful with our implied threat. If on the other hand he takes this for weakness & does loose another one, we will have targets in mind & instantly respond with a h—l of a punch."
[66] Bernard Weinraub, "President Breaks All Economic Ties With The Libyans," *New York Times*, January 8, 1985, 1.

Acknowledging that earlier steps taken against Qadaffi had "not been sufficient," the president promised that if the steps he was now introducing "do not end Qadaffi's terrorism, I promise you that further steps will be taken." Concerned for the safety of the 1,000 to 1,500 Americans working in Libya, he warned them "to leave immediately." Those who refused, "will be subject to appropriate penalties upon their return" to the United States.

One commentator viewed Reagan's action as "anticlimactical" because he had already banned oil imports from Libya in 1982 and total trade had already dropped from its high of $7.6 billion in 1980 to $300 million. Furthermore, Libya's assets in the United States were left undisturbed. The small print made it even worse because the sanctions did not apply to subsidiaries of American companies, which further muted their effect. That provision was said to have been insisted upon by Secretary Shultz, who was concerned that the Europeans would refuse to cooperate.[67]

The next day, January 8, Reagan issued NSDD-205, which set in motion the strategy against Qadaffi.[68] Although all future decisions would be shrouded in secrecy, the early stages were featured in the press. The press campaign focused on the many and varied means by which the United States could deal with Libya. Economic sanctions were activated, now including the freezing of all Libyan assets in the United States.[69] Shultz sent his aides, Whitehead and Oakley to Europe to gain allied support. And Weinberger ordered the fleet in the Mediterranean to begin freedom of navigation exercises in the Gulf of Sidra.

From the outset the president's policy encountered bumps in the road. Whitehead's and Oakley's European trip was singularly unsuccessful. Leaders in West Germany, Britain, France, Italy, Holland, Spain, and Belgium all expressed skepticism about the "effectiveness" of economic sanctions. French Prime Minister Laurent

---

[67] Bernard Gwertzman, "Why Reagan Shuns Force," *New York Times*, January 8, 1985, 1.
[68] Simpson, *National Security Directives*, 654-55.
[69] Robert Greenberger, "Libya's U.S. Assets Frozen by Reagan In Retaliatory Step," *Wall Street Journal*, January 9, 1985, 25.

Fabius captured the sentiment of the European leaders when he said "there is no point beating the air with a sword. If sanctions are going to be ineffective, they have no interest."[70]

Qadaffi immediately reinforced the European attitude, calling in envoys from France, Italy, Belgium, the Netherlands, Spain, and Greece to assert their "common interests." He noted that there were 45,000 Europeans working in Libya in 230 companies. This represented, he said, $13 billion in contracts, with $36 billion more planned for those who cooperate. But, raising the specter of war, Qadaffi declared that if the United States attacked Libya from European bases, then "we will close our eyes and ears and hit indiscriminately." We will react with suicide squads to hit ports, towns and more. "If it comes to war, we will drag Europe into it."[71]

In short, the Qadaffi problem essentially would be Reagan's. But, even within the administration, there was criticism. Vice-President Bush's secret report on terrorism, leaked to the press, recommended that the president "stop making warlike threats of retaliation unless he intends to take military action."[72] Then, an unnamed State Department official claimed that the United States had "only circumstantial evidence linking Libya to the Abu Nidal terrorist group." The official said, "there isn't any smoking gun."[73] Shultz himself disagreed, declaring that Qadaffi was not only "harboring terrorists.... he is a terrorist" and the United States "could use military force" against him.[74]

Over the next several weeks, both the Soviets and the Americans moved pieces around the Mediterranean. The Russians moved their Mediterranean flagship, a submarine tender, to Tripoli and deployed a new *SAM-5* ground to air missile battery to Sirte to provide anti-

---

[70] "Allies Spurn U.S. Call For Libya Sanctions," *Washington Post*, January 9, 1985, 18.
[71] Christopher Dickey, "Libya Seeks To Divide U.S., Allies," *Washington Post*, January 10, 1985, 1.
[72] James McCartney, "Reagan Draws Fire on Terror Threats," *Philadelphia Inquirer*, January 8, 1985, 1.
[73] Greenberger, "Libya's U.S. Assets Frozen..."
[74] James Morrison, "Shultz Warns Force Remains an Option to Stop Terrorism," *Washington Times*, January 10, 1985, 1.

aircraft coverage over the Gulf of Sidra. The Russians realized, however, that there was little they could do to protect Qadaffi and would not go to war with the United States over Libya. At the same time, Qadaffi crowed "Reagan has backtracked from war," but, "if it comes, I believe it will be in the sea hundreds of miles away from land."[75]

At the same time, the United States initially sent a second carrier, the *Saratoga*, to the Mediterranean to join the *Coral Sea* already on station. In March, Weinberger ordered a third carrier, *America*, to join the other two. By mid-March, the United States would have deployed three carrier task groups comprising 26 combatants, with 250 aircraft.[76] Qadaffi had drawn a line across the northern Gulf of Sidra, which he called the "line of death." By mid-March, the U.S. Navy was preparing to cross it.

Taking Control of the Iran Initiative

Pursuant to President Reagan's decision to proceed with Nir's plan, between January 9 and 13, Assistant Secretary of Defense Noel Koch and head of the Israeli Procurement Mission, Ben-Yosef, were designated to work out the details of the "replenishment sales." At this point, the plan was still for Israel to sell 4,000 *TOW* missiles to Iran and use the proceeds to purchase replacement missiles from the United States. After a few days of intense haggling, however, in which Nir and North also played major roles, the negotiations collapsed.

At the outset, Nir informed North that the proceeds Israel derived from the August-September 1985 sales "had been used for other purposes" and were "not available" now. Koch informed Ben-Yosef that the lowest price the basic *TOW* had ever been sold for was $6,800. Nir responded by insisting that Israel "could pay only $5,000-$5,500 per missile." The two sides were at an impasse.

---

[75] "Qaddafi Says Reagan 'Has Backtracked,'" *Washington Post*, January 15, 1986, 5.
[76] Stanik, *El Dorado Canyon*, 130.

To narrow the difference, North postulated that if Israel charged Iran $10,000 per missile, then, they would receive ten million for the first one thousand missiles and forty million for four thousand. After deducting administrative costs, commissions to Gorbanifar and Schwimmer, and a contribution to their covert operations fund, Israel would be able to purchase 4,000 replacement *TOWs* at $6,000 each, or 4,500 *TOWs* at $5,333 each, the latter number including the 500 *TOWs* from August-September 1985.[77]

When North explained this formula to Koch, the latter said that the sale of 4,000 *TOWs* would immediately signal to interested observers, like the Russians, that they exceeded Israel's needs and therefore were for a third party, which would raise questions. Secondly, the dollar amount would greatly exceed the $14 million level requiring congressional notification. The solution was to "go black," have the president issue a finding and conduct the sales covertly under the Economy Act, which would allow them to set a lower price.[78] (Ironically, without knowing it, Koch and his aides at DOD had come to the same approach that Meese had proposed at the January 7 NSPG meeting.)

When Koch talked to Weinberger about the negotiations the secretary was greatly agitated, exclaiming that the president's initiative "was a very foolish undertaking." Referring implicitly to their common background experience of Watergate, Koch asked: "was there a legal problem with this? Is somebody going to go to jail?" Weinberger replied: "yes," but Koch did not think the secretary "intended it seriously," and he therefore "did not take that seriously." He had "assumed if there was any prospect of its being illegal, that [Weinberger] would have stopped it. Since he didn't…I assumed it was legal.[79] Weinberger, although reluctantly following orders, nonetheless remained adamantly against involvement.

---

[77] *Iran-Contra Affair*, 204.
[78] Ibid.
[79] Walsh, *Final Report*, 411n.68 and *Iran-Contra Affair*, 205.

At the same time, however, CIA lawyers raised more fundamental concerns. An internal memorandum for Sporkin outlined the difficulty. Arms previously obtained by Israel under the Arms Export Control Act, or the Foreign Assistance Act, "could not be sold to Iran" without U.S. consent, notice to Congress, and the eligibility of the third country recipient. As there was to be no prior notice and Iran had been designated a "terrorist state," the proposed approach of Israeli sales, not to mention replenishment of weapons already sold, "was not feasible." However, hitting upon the same solution as DOD and Meese, the lawyers also suggested that it would be legal under a presidential covert action finding to use the Economy Act, whereby the DOD could sell to the CIA, which, in turn, could sell to either Israel or Iran.[80]

Another issue was the role of Gorbanifar, whom the Israelis still viewed as a necessary interlocutor with Iran. So did the new world order faction. When word got around in early December that Reagan was going to press forward with the initiative, McFarlane had contacted Ledeen and told him to put Gorbanifar in touch with Casey.[81] Astoundingly, after only a few days before calling Gorbanifar the most "despicable" person he had ever met and refusing to deal with him, McFarlane was putting him back into the game.

The new world order faction's vacillating attitude toward Gorbanifar made it abundantly clear that he was simply an instrument in their scheme. At the earliest stage of the opening to Iran, the new world order faction turned off Casey's initiative on the grounds that Gorbanifar was a "fabricator." McFarlane, however, deliberately included Gorbanifar in his arms-for-hostages scheme with the Israelis. Then, in December, McFarlane turned off the scheme on the grounds that Gorbanifar was a "despicable" character. Now, here was McFarlane bringing Gorbanifar back into the game. Clearly, the on-again, off-again use of Gorbanifar had nothing to do with his character, but with his utility at any particular moment. In this case, it

---

[80] Ibid, 205.
[81] *Tower Report*, B-52.

seems, McFarlane hoped Gorbanifar would do what he could not—bring down the initiative.

Ledeen met with Charles Allen and Clarridge, telling them that he "had McFarlane's approval" and mentioned that Kimche was also still involved.[82] The ostensible reason for bringing Gorbanifar back in was his "important intelligence about Iranian-backed terrorism in Western Europe." Casey met Ledeen on December 19 and arranged for the head of the CIA's Iranian desk to meet with Gorbanifar. After meeting with him, however, they still didn't like him, describing Gorbanifar as "a guy who lies with zest."[83]

Despite the reservations of his people, Casey sent a memorandum to the president on December 23, saying that while we had "to be careful talking to Gorbanifar," he agreed to take another polygraph test, which Casey felt was "worth doing for what we might learn." Gorbanifar took the test on January 11 and "showed deception on almost all questions." Tellingly, the test revealed that Gorbanifar "knew ahead of time that the hostages would not be released [in November] and deliberately tried to deceive us..."[84] The recommendation was that "the Agency have no dealing whatsoever with Gorbanifar."[85]

Unwilling to accept the polygraph results, Casey sent Allen to meet with Gorbanifar and provide a personal assessment. After a five-hour session, on January 14, Allen told the director that the Iranian was "hard to pin down" and was "very clever." Allen called him "a con man," to which Casey replied jokingly that he himself was "a con man's con man." In short, Casey decided that Gorbanifar would continue to play a role in the initiative.[86]

Casey, and perhaps others, had begun to realize that the United States should structure the initiative the same way that the Israelis and

---

[82] *Tower Report*, B-52. Ledeen, *Perilous Statecraft*, 201, says that it was his idea to approach Casey, which North approved.
[83] *Tower Report*, B-53.
[84] Ibid, B-54-55.
[85] *Iran-Contra Affair*, 205.
[86] Ibid, 206.

Iranians had by using private cut outs. Peres had used private individuals, Kimche, Schwimmer, Nimrodi, and now Nir to deal with both Iran and the United States and Iran was using Gorbanifar in the same role. Moreover, it became increasingly clear that Gorbanifar was eager to bypass Israel and deal directly with the United States. Thus, was conceived the idea of using Secord as an "agent" for the United States to deal directly with Iran.

On January 14, the issue of Secord's role crystallized. At first, North proposed that the DOD sell directly to Secord, bypassing the CIA. In this scheme, Secord would deliver the *TOWs* to the Israelis, who would transfer them to Iran under arrangements made by Gorbanifar. When apprised of this idea, Koch declared that Weinberger, who objected to Secord's involvement, "will blanch," forcing a change. Casey had wanted to avoid agency involvement, too, but, with Weinberger's objection, agreed that Secord could be an "agent for the CIA," with the agency otherwise uninvolved. Under this scheme, DOD would sell to Secord as the CIA's agent; he would then sell and ship to the Israelis, who would transfer to Iran through Gorbanifar.[87]

However, the CIA's lawyers objected to the use of an agent, who would have "no connection with CIA other than to act as a 'middle man.'" George Clarke, one of Sporkin's staff lawyers, insisted that he "would feel more comfortable if the CIA were directly involved in the activity and that it would be essential that we act in furtherance of a traditional covert action objective." There was, in short, "no way" to structure the deal "without the CIA's getting involved."[88] The CIA had become involved, marginally, to be sure, but now legally for the first time in the Iran initiative.

The persistent problem was how to replace the *TOWs* Israel had sold to Iran in August-September 1985. Israel had acquired these weapons under the AECA and therefore retransfers, or sales, would require "U.S. consent, notice to Congress, and [consideration of] the

---

[87] *Iran-Contra Affair*, 206.
[88] Ibid, 207.

eligibility of the third country recipient for U.S. aid."[89] As Poindexter had not been privy to any of McFarlane's dealings with the Israelis, he directed North to contact him and "find out what the understanding had been on replenishment of the first 504 TOWs."

McFarlane, of course, had no choice but to continue the lie and falsely said that the "United States had undertaken to sell, over time, 'requisite TOWs to replace the TOWs'" that Israel had sold to Iran for Weir.[90] The truth was the president had undertaken no such commitment, which was why, some six months later, nothing had yet been done. There had been no consent, no notice to Congress, and Iran was ineligible for aid. Finally, as was the case in *all* of McFarlane's machinations on this issue, there was no paper trail. The best he could ever come up with was a "mental" finding.

On the morning of January 16, North devised a solution to the problem of replenishment of the 1985 sales. He proposed that for the first 1,000 *TOWs,* they cut out the commissions for Schwimmer and the Iranians, which would mean that Secord would receive a larger share. With that larger sum, he "could purchase 504 TOWs from the United States and ship them to Israel as replenishment for the 1985 transactions."[91] North's proposal was under consideration that afternoon as Poindexter convened key participants to resolve outstanding issues.

Meeting in Poindexter's office were Weinberger, Casey, Meese, Sporkin, and possibly North. Shultz was not present, nor, unusually, it seems, was Regan. After mulling over the legal impediments, Attorney General Meese made a momentous decision. "Israel should not ship weapons out of its stocks." Instead, he recommended "the United States...sell directly to the Iranians." Direct sales, under the authority of the Economy Act, he said, "would avoid the restrictions of the Arms Export Control Act, including Congressional reporting

---

[89] *Iran-Contra Affair*, 205.
[90] Ibid, 207. Cf. *Tower Report*, B-68, which cites North's PROF note to Poindexter of January 15, 1986, reporting his conversation with McFarlane.
[91] *Iran-Contra Affair* says, 207, their commissions should be cut by 25% and 15%, respectively, and 208, "cut out" completely. Cf. Draper, *Very Thin Line*, 254.

requirements." Weinberger was stunned, declaring that he wanted to have his lawyers "look at it and see that the analysis is correct."

By the next morning, Friday, January 17, Weinberger sent word that his lawyers "agree with the analysis and...have signed off on the project."[92] After the president had returned from a "brief talk" to the American Legislative Exchange Council, he met with the vice-president and Regan. They were joined by Poindexter and Don Fortier, who went over the details of the hastily rewritten memorandum. After discussing it for a few minutes, the president "gave the go-ahead" and signed the finding.[93]

There is confusion in the record over the January 17 finding. The *Tower Report* and the *Congressional Report* both state, respectively, that the January 17 finding was "identical to the January 6 document with Sporkin's revision..." and that the two documents were "almost identical." Draper follows this interpretation, describing the two findings as "almost identical" and "virtually the same."[94] The implication is that the policy authorized by the two findings was also the same, which it decidedly was not.

All findings come in two parts, a memorandum describing the policy and the finding authorizing it. While the authorizations in the January 6 and 17 findings were "almost identical," the policies being authorized were completely different. The January 6 finding authorized an Israeli plan to "unilaterally commence selling military material to western-oriented Iranian factions." Israel would also release Shiite prisoners from jail and Iran would effect the release of the five American hostages. In this plan the "only requirement the Israelis have is an assurance that they will be allowed to purchase U.S. replenishments for the stocks that they sell to Iran."

The January 17 finding specifically rejected the Israeli plan, but supported the objective of promoting a "more moderate Iranian

---

[92] *Iran-Contra Affair*, 208.
[93] *Tower Report*, B-65-67 and Brinkley, *Reagan Diaries*, 384. The oft-repeated phrase, "I agreed to sell TOWS to Iran," does not appear in the president's diary entry for January 17.
[94] *Tower Report*, B-65, *Iran-Contra Affair*, 208, and Draper, *Very Thin Line*, 256-57.

government." The memorandum stated "the objectives of the Israeli plan could be met if the CIA, using an authorized agent as necessary, purchased arms from the Department of Defense under the Economy Act and then transferred them to Iran directly after receiving appropriate payment from Iran."

Israel's role under the new plan, as Segev notes, was changed from being an arms seller to serving solely as a "liaison with Gorbanifar and his contacts in Tehran."[95] The Israelis would "make the necessary arrangements for the sale of 4,000 TOW weapons to Iran" and insure that "sufficient funds to cover the sale would be transferred to an agent of the CIA." Left unstated in the memo was the identity of the CIA's "agent," who was Richard Secord, and the transshipping point to Iran, which would be Israel.[96] Secord would take delivery of weapons in the United States; ship them to Israel, and from there forward them to Iran.

The memorandum closed with a test for success and a loophole. "If all of the hostages were not released after the first shipment of 1,000 weapons, further transfers would cease." This test suggested that the main purpose was to gain the release of the hostages, but the next sentence altered that perception entirely. It stated "on the other hand, since hostage release is in some respects a byproduct of a larger effort to develop ties to potentially moderate forces in Iran, you may wish to redirect such transfers to other groups within the government at a later time."[97]

Also included in the memorandum, but not in the finding itself, was the recommendation that the president exercise his "statutory prerogative to withhold notification of the finding to the Congressional oversight committees until such time that you deem it to be appropriate." This was not an attempt to circumvent the Congress, as was later claimed, because the assumption was the hostages would be released after the first delivery of *TOW* missiles. Thus, the time frame envisaged by the recommendation was, at most, a few days. Unfortunately, this was not how it turned out.

---

[95] Segev, *Iranian Triangle*, 231.
[96] *Tower Report*, B-66.
[97] Ibid.

To avoid the charge that the administration was dealing with the Khomeini regime, the justification given for direct arms sales was to support "moderates," who could change Iranian policy. The fact was that the concept of Iranian moderates was that of the Iranians themselves, who passed it on to Washington. American analysts perceived no "moderates" in the Iranian leadership. American leaders, however, adopted it for its obvious political utility, or "cover."

There was another potentially explosive issue, which was that Reagan had decided to cut the Israelis out. Meese had justified direct U.S. sales, instead of indirect sales through Israel, on the grounds that it would avoid violating the Arms Export and Control Act. However, the United States did not employ that law; it legalized arms sales under the Economy Act, which just as easily could have justified sales through Israel. Thus, it seems, the January 17 finding was the first step in a series designed to cut Israel out of the initiative. It would be easier said than done.

After two weeks of discussions and intense legal scrutiny the president's advisers had formulated a covert action finding that would allow the United States to sell arms directly and legally to Iran. The objective was to reestablish political relations severed seven years earlier and in the process gain the release of the five American hostages being held in Lebanon. "Operation Recovery" was under way. The assumption was that the Iranians, too, wished to reestablish political relations. It was an assumption that would be put to the test in coming days.

Chapter 8
Moscow Enters the Game

President Reagan's decision to proceed in secret with a now fully legal Iran initiative did not occur in a vacuum. It was part of a larger set of decisions to implement NSDD-75, the strategy toward the Soviet Union adopted in early 1983.[1] Having defeated Soviet strategy in 1983-84, Reagan sought to deal from a position of "greater relative strength" to begin the process of putting his own strategic construct in place.[2]

Thus, in early 1986, to increase pressure on the Soviets, the president decided to include provision of *Stinger* anti-aircraft missiles and other military assistance to resistance forces in Angola and Afghanistan and communications equipment for the Contras in Nicaragua. More would be sent once Congress appropriated requested funds for the Contras. Similarly, increased financial support was funneled into Eastern Europe to support dissidents in Poland and Czechoslovakia, into Africa for anti-Soviet forces in Mozambique, and into Southeast Asia for anti-Vietnamese forces in Cambodia.

---

[1] See Richard C. Thornton, *The Reagan Revolution, III: Defeating the Soviet Challenge* (Victoria: Trafford, 2009). For NSDD-75, see Christopher Simpson, *National Security Directives of the Reagan and Bush Administrations* (Boulder: Westview, 1995*)*, 255-63.

[2] In his *Annual Report to the Congress,* Fiscal Year 1987, 3-4, Secretary Weinberger openly declared the change. "Rather than dealing from weakness...the United States is now beginning to deal from strength and the promise of greater relative strength....Nothing could so enhance the prospects for long-term peace as Soviet acceptance of the proposition that they can achieve no significant exploitable military advantage over us."

The president's strategy was designed to vanquish the Soviet Union in the Cold War and bring about a new global balance based on American hegemony. The president and his close aides fully understood that the policies enacted in early 1986 would very likely, if successfully implemented, take a major step toward achieving this general objective because they calculated that the Soviets were overextended geopolitically and the Soviet economy was visibly faltering and moving toward a crisis of the regime. The Russians, in short, were going broke and could no longer compete with the United States in the global arena.

In the course of the year the president guided the nation onto an active course against the Soviet Union and its allies. In addition to funneling increased military support to anti-Soviet forces, he authorized a major strike against Moscow's Libyan ally, Qadaffi, in an attempt to dissuade the Libyan dictator from further support for international terrorist activities. He supported clandestine sabotage by Afghan rebels against targets inside the Soviet Union itself. Then, he countered Gorbachev's arms control gambit at Reykjavik designed to maintain the status quo with a new strategy of his own.

Gorbachev, though promoting détente and arms control, responded to the president's challenge with a significant change in Soviet strategy. The core objectives of the Soviet Union under Brezhnev, Andropov, and Chernenko had been to perpetuate strategic weapons superiority over the United States, maintain military dominance across the Eurasian landmass, and draw Iran into Moscow's political orbit. Gorbachev had recognized that this core strategy had failed and so revised each element of it in an attempt to retain some advantage.

An outgrowth of his "new thinking," Gorbachev abandoned the long-term Soviet strategy of seeking change and advantage through nuclear coercion and shifted to one of seeking détente with the United States and mutual cooperation with other states and clients. As I have argued elsewhere, only a dramatic reduction in security costs would enable

Gorbachev to modernize his failing economy.[3] The shift from a zero-sum to mini-max approach would be codified at the 27th Party Congress at the end of February 1986, but several of its policy parts would be put into practice beforehand.

The centerpiece of Gorbachev's strategy was détente with the United States and he made politically extravagant proposals to dissuade American leaders, especially the new world order faction, from pursuing Reagan's strategy. After digesting the results of the Geneva Summit, Gorbachev offered détente to the United States and in a January 1986 letter to Reagan proposed the complete abolition of "all nuclear weapons" by the end of the century.[4] The proposal, like all Soviet proposals, had a catch, which was the demand that Reagan agree to cancel the Strategic Defense Initiative, which dimmed some of the luster from this transformational idea, which was best understood as pie in the sky instead of SDI.

On the Eurasian balance, Gorbachev renounced the aim of nuclear superiority, while offering détente with both European and Asian states. During a visit to Paris in October 1985, he offered Soviet inclusion in a common European "home," another remarkable idea, and said that Moscow now sought "reasonable sufficiency,"[5] rather than nuclear superiority. He offered dramatic improvements in relations with both Japan and China, as well. In fact, Gorbachev's proposals would have considerable appeal among the political left in all of these countries, but would have uneven results.

Gorbachev also sought to take up Reagan's earlier proposal of a zero option for Europe in an attempt to reverse the failure to prevent the deployment of the *Pershing II*/Cruise missile package to Western Europe. In this proposal the United States would remove the *Pershing II* and Cruise missiles and the Soviet Union would scrap its *SS-20* force. If accepted, this quite transparent plan would eliminate

---

[3] See Richard C. Thornton, "Mikhail Gorbachev: A Preliminary Strategic Assessment," *World and I* (January 1993), 583-93.
[4] Don Oberdorfer, *The Turn: From the Cold War to a New Era: The United States and the Soviet Union, 1983-1990* (New York: Poseidon Press, 1991), 156-58.
[5] Ibid, 141.

American missiles from Western Europe and reestablish Soviet ballistic missile advantages over Eurasia once again, because the Russians would simply replace the SS-20 with other missiles, particularly the SS-25. At the stroke of a pen, the situation would revert to that which had existed prior to the deployment of the Pershing II/Cruise missile.

Gorbachev's proposals, however, contrasted sharply with Soviet policy behavior. Although professing a desire for regional political solutions, Gorbachev continued to supply heavy weapons for Afghanistan, Angola, and Nicaragua, and supported police crackdowns against dissidents in Eastern Europe.[6] In this context, Gorbachev's most skillful gambit came in southwest Asia, where it went virtually unrecognized by American leaders and was designed to keep alive Moscow's Iranian strategy by frustrating Reagan's attempt to reestablish relations with Tehran.

Moscow's Shift on Iran

The essence of Moscow's Iranian strategy since 1979 had been twofold. First, it was to create a geopolitical pincer against Iran, with Iraq on the western flank and the Soviet Union—from its position in Afghanistan—on the eastern flank. Second, it was to weaken Iran in a war of attrition against Iraq, leaving it vulnerable to an internal takeover. Saddam's role, after the first weeks of the conflict, had been to play anvil to Iran's hammer.

When Reagan foiled Moscow's Iran strategy in early 1984, the Soviets abandoned it and began to rearm Saddam's forces for a war of conquest. The Iranian response had been to intensify ongoing worldwide efforts to obtain weapons to counter the Iraqi buildup. In that context, they extended feelers for reestablishment of relations with the United States, their hated enemy, as the only means of counterbalancing Soviet support for Iraq.

---

[6] See Peter Rodman, *More Precious Than Peace: The Cold War and the Struggle for the Third World* (New York: Scribner's, 1994).

Those were the circumstances, which had offered President Reagan the opportunity to develop a political relationship with Iran and fulfill the objective of reconstituting the containment structure around the Soviet Union. As demonstrated in previous chapters, the president sought to respond positively to the Iran opening, but by the end of 1985 his internal foes, the new world order faction, had thwarted this opportunity with the arms-for-hostages deal, turned fiasco.

Nevertheless, for Moscow, the fiasco raised alarm at the prospect of an American-Iranian rapprochement, which had to be prevented at all costs, or it would completely defeat Soviet strategy. This prospect prompted Gorbachev to make another policy shift, in hopes of avoiding that dreaded outcome. The overriding problem was how to avert the worst case of U.S.-Iran rapprochement and keep Iran isolated. Moscow's pincer strategy had failed and arming Saddam for a war of conquest had backfired, driving the Iranians into Washington's arms.

Gorbachev decided to reverse course, which was to dismantle the pincer put in place in 1979-80, relax Iraqi military pressure against Iran, and withdraw from Afghanistan. Gorbachev adopted as a plan of strategic deception an even-handed approach toward Iran in the conflict, offered to improve relations, and provide additional weapons from Soviet clients.[7] The objective was to dissuade the Iranian leadership from taking the fateful step of reestablishing relations with the United States and assuming an anti-Soviet posture in the U.S. containment structure.

The Soviets hoped that by beginning the process of withdrawing from Afghanistan, holding back the Iraqis, relaxing military pressure on Iran, and offering improved relations, the Iranians would believe that they were in no danger of defeat and would refrain from taking an irrevocable step toward the United States. The Soviets hoped that with less concern about military defeat, the Iranians' basic antagonism toward the United States would resurface and they would decline the

---

[7] "Moscow Shift: Animosity to U.S. Doesn't Make Mideast Pro-Soviet," *Economist*, February 12, 1986.

reestablishment of diplomatic relations—Moscow's worst case–and maintain an independent stance. Only this would keep open the possibility of drawing Iran into Moscow's orbit later on.

The first step was to gain Saddam Hussein's agreement, which would be no easy task. The Soviets had built up Saddam's forces and were putting Iraq in position to achieve victory in the long war. He would have to be dissuaded from such a course and apprised of its dangers at the present moment. Therefore the Soviets invited Saddam for a state visit on December 16-17, his first visit in seven years. It was also Saddam's first trip outside Iraq since the war began. Upon arrival, he and Iraqi Foreign Minister Tariq Azziz met with Gorbachev and Soviet Foreign Minister Sheverdnadze for a two-hour discussion, reportedly on "the Iran-Iraq war and bilateral relations."[8]

It was clear from the press accounts of both countries that the discussion had been difficult. *Al Thawra* said that the two men agreed on "most" of the issues discussed, while *Pravda* described the meeting as "businesslike, frank, and friendly."[9] The code words "most," "businesslike," and "frank," all implied that the atmosphere was "cool" and that there had been disagreements. Furthermore, in an unprecedented omission, no communiqué was issued after the visit.

Andrei Gromyko, in his new role as president of the USSR, also met with Saddam, Azziz, and his key generals. In a statement after their talks, in addition to announcing the provision of "new types of weapons" at current levels, he complained about the Iraqi attitude in a way that indicated what the Russians had asked of Saddam:

> Those who contrary to any reason are calling for the war to be continued 'to a victorious end,' considering it as a means to settle accounts with the adversary and impose their will upon him, are behaving irrationally.[10]

---

[8] Haim Shemesh, *Soviet-Iraqi Relations, 1968-1988: In the Shadow of the Iraq-Iran Conflict* (Boulder: Lynne Rienner, 1992), 198.
[9] Ibid.
[10] Ibid.

In his own speech after their meeting, Saddam hinted his agreement as he called upon "friendly states, among them the Soviet Union, to increase urgent efforts either in the Security Council or at other levels to establish a just and comprehensive peace."

Pravda's report on the talks after his departure noted that both sides "vigorously opposed any attempts to impose from outside...regimes which are alien to them."[11] Parsing these hints, it seems that the Russians were asking Saddam, at least for the time being, to postpone a continuation of the war "to a victorious end" and he had, no doubt reluctantly, agreed. What else he agreed to would shortly become clear on the battlefield.

On Afghanistan, according to Gorbachev, the decision to withdraw was "adopted in October 1985." He maintained "a clear goal ha[d] been set—to speed up the process in order to have a friendly country and leave."[12] Recall, at the Geneva Summit, he had hinted to Reagan a willingness to withdraw with appropriate guarantees and afterward Washington had "expressed its willingness in principle to guarantee an Afghan accord."[13]

While Saddam was still in Moscow, and no doubt with his agreement, the Soviets sent a message to Tehran promising to pursue a "neutral policy" in the war.[14] At the same time, they reinforced the change in Afghan policy by having their Afghan client Najibullah reiterate to Pakistani authorities that the Soviets had decided on a withdrawal timetable.[15] Afghan negotiators passed this information to U.N. mediator Diego Cordovez, during the sixth round of the U.N.-

---

[11] Ibid, 198-99.
[12] "Notes From Politburo Meeting, 13 November 1986," *Bulletin, Cold War International History Project*, 14/15, (Winter/Spring, 2003-2004), 144.
[13] John W. Parker, *Kremlin in Transition/ Vol. II, Gorbachev, 1985 to 1989* (Boston: Unwin Hyman, 1991), 85.
[14] Shemesh, *Soviet-Iraqi Relations*, 201.
[15] According to Rodman, *More Precious Than Peace*, 326, the Soviets had begun informing UN interlocutors of their intent to withdraw according to a timetable from mid-1985.

sponsored proximity talks with Pakistan, December 16-19, again, while Saddam was still in Moscow.[16]

(Gorbachev's position would become unmistakable a few weeks later when in his speech to the 27th Party Congress in late February he described Afghanistan as a "running sore," and declared that a "step by step withdrawal [plan] has been worked out with the Afghan side.")[17]

Thus, by the end of the year, Gorbachev had put in place the new policy structure toward the region. To insure that Iranian leaders fully understood the new shift, in early February, on the 2nd, he sent first deputy foreign minister Georgi Kornienko to Tehran– the highest official to visit Tehran since the establishment of the Islamic Republic. In talks with the top Iranian leadership Kornienko discussed and evidently resolved to Iran's satisfaction the entire gamut of issues outstanding between the two countries.

Two public irritants resolved were the continuing fallout from the Kuzichkin case, the Soviet resident KGB chief who had defected to the West in 1982, and the wholesale expulsions of Soviet personnel from Iran the following year.[18] Indicating improved relations, Iran's foreign minister Ali Akbar Velyati accepted an invitation to visit Moscow and the two sides agreed to resume airline service between their countries.

Although there is no record of other topics discussed, Majlis leader Rafsanjani's remarks at a news conference suggested that matters relating to the ongoing war with Iraq were discussed. Kornienko's visit, he said:

> Will have a great effect on our relations with the Soviet Union and the Eastern World. One can be optimistic in fields such as technical military, economic, and possibly political relations.[19]

---

[16] Parker, *Kremlin in Transition, II*, 85.
[17] Ibid.
[18] John W. Parker, *Persian Dreams: Moscow and Tehran Since the Fall of the Shah* (Washington: Potomac Books, 2009), 21.
[19] Itamar Rabinovitch and Haim Shaked, eds, *Middle East Contemporary Survey, 1986*, vol. 10 (Syracuse: Syracuse University Press, 1986), 45-46.

Kornienko's visit was followed a week later by the beginning of an Iranian offensive against Iraq, which resulted in a victory at the Al Faw peninsula. By all accounts it was a "stunning victory that....sent a psychological shock throughout the region."[20] The near-unanimous view also claimed that the occupation of Al Faw put Iran into position to attack Basra from the south, cut off access to Kuwait and strongly affect Iraq's naval access to the gulf. A closer look, however, belied these claims on every count but one–that it had been a psychological victory.

Throughout the previous fall both Iraq and Iran had strengthened their respective positions in anticipation of renewed fighting. Iran had deployed some two hundred thousand men to the southern sector of the front from north of Basra to the mouth of the Shatt al-Arab on the gulf and an assault on Basra was widely anticipated. To strengthen defensive positions, Iraqi forces struck first on January 6, recapturing most of the Majnoon oil complex north of Basra, but the Iranians managed to hold on to a small position on the island.[21]

On February 9, Iran commenced a series of attacks in two broad thrusts, north of Basra and against Al Faw. The first was a two-pronged amphibious attack under cover of heavy rains and darkness across the three hundred yard wide Shatt al Arab toward Al Faw. One Iranian division of 10,000 men took the island group of Umm al-Rasas and another the town of Siba. Iraqi forces quickly engaged and retook Umm al-Rasas, but on the 11th the force at Siba pressed southward to take Al Faw, an abandoned oil depot at the very tip of Iraq, and held it.[22]

At the same time, Iranian forces struck north of Basra at Qurna and Amara in the area of the Howiza Marshes, the scene of several small-

---

[20] Mohiaddin Mesbahi, "The USSR and the Iran-Iraq War: From Brezhnev to Gorbachev," in Farhang Rajaee, ed., *The Iran-Iraq War: The Politics of Aggression* (Gainesville: University of Florida Press, 1993) 82.

[21] Edgar O'Ballance, *The Gulf War* (London; Washington: Brassey's Defence Publishers, 1988), 173.

[22] Anthony H. Cordesman and Abraham R. Wagner, *The Lessons of Modern War*, Vol. II (Boulder: Westview, 1990*)*, 219-20.

scale skirmishes the previous year.[23] After three days of heavy fighting, Iraqi firepower drove back the invaders with heavy losses. Iraqi commanding general, Abdul Maher al-Rashid, told journalists visiting the front that he had requested permission from Saddam Hussein "to launch a counterattack into Iranian territory," which would have encircled and cut off Iranian forces from support, but Saddam had "refused" his request.[24]

By the middle of February, Iranian forces had consolidated a position of some one hundred and fifty square miles on the southern half of the Al Faw peninsula. As Pelletier notes, Iraqi forces had quickly "set up blocking lines to the west and north of the occupied area." In fact, Al Faw occupied a "dead space in the Gulf and up to this point in the war had been of no military significance." The peninsula was honeycombed with defense works, which enabled the Iranians to fend off Iraqi attacks, but they could not utilize the peninsula as a springboard for an attack north toward Basra, or to cut off access to Kuwait. "Penned up there, their military effectiveness would be nil. Indeed, they could be left there for the duration of the conflict."[25]

The victory at Al Faw had a much greater impact politically than militarily. While the Iranians were never able to exploit their position to break out of the peninsula, the political significance of their success had an immediate impact on Iran's response to the United States. Indeed, it would seem that the victory at Al Faw related to what Gorbachev and Saddam Hussein had agreed to in their meetings in December.

The Iraqis had been slow to respond to the Iranian move to Al Faw, which they considered to be a diversionary attack. The dilatory response gave Iran the chance to secure a bridgehead on the peninsula. The heavy rains explain the failure to provide timely air support.

---

[23] Anthony H. Cordesman, *The Iran-Iraq War and Western Security, 1984-1987* (London: Jane's, 1987), 92.
[24] O'Ballance, *Gulf War*, 179.
[25] Stephen Pelletiere, Douglas Jonson, and Leif Rosenberger, *Iraqi Power and U.S. Security in the Middle East* (Carlisle: U.S. Army War College, 1990), 9.

Moreover, Iraq had positioned only a small, one thousand-man force of reservists to guard the port town, which had been rapidly overrun.

Cordesman thought, "Iraqi planners [did] not seem to have fully considered the possibility of an Iranian amphibious assault in this area" and criticized the area commander, who "[did] not seem to have realized the need to destroy an enemy landing force before it can secure a bridgehead."[26] Yet, he also noted that Iraqi intelligence for months had observed the Iranian stockpiling of small craft and pontoon bridging equipment south of Abadan, the training of amphibious commando units, and their infiltration to the southern front in the latter half of 1985.[27]

Given the many months during which Iraqi intelligence observed Iranian preparations for amphibious operations, it is highly unlikely that Iraqi commanders failed to "realize" what the Iranians were planning and take contingency measures. Iraqi counter deployments along the southern front confirm their understanding of Iranian options. Moreover, Iraq held an overwhelming five-to-one advantage in firepower over Iran.

Rather, as argued here, the delayed Iraqi response was deliberate. The delay could be explained on the grounds that Basra was Iran's actual objective, not the relatively insignificant target of Al Faw, or because bad weather hindered a rapid response. I believe Saddam decided to allow the Iranians a small victory to encourage them in the belief they could still succeed without making an irrevocable political commitment to the United States.

The Iranian Response to Washington

President Reagan had informed Secretaries Shultz and Weinberger of his decision to proceed with the Iran initiative at a family group meeting in the White House after he had signed the finding on the

---

[26] Cordesman, *Iran-Iraq War and Western Security*, 93.
[27] Ibid, 89.

morning of January 17.[28] However, he apparently had not shown either man the actual finding. Shultz would later testify that he had not known of the president's decision until after the crisis broke in November.[29] Weinberger would also claim that "neither Secretary Shultz, nor I, nor even Don Regan, saw the final, January 17 finding (until it was revealed publicly)."[30] Weinberger was wrong about Regan, whom Poindexter had briefed along with the president and Bush, on January 17, but it was true that Regan was uninvolved in the project thereafter.

Both Weinberger and Shultz had been disingenuous about their knowledge of the initiative. Not only had Weinberger learned of the president's decision on the day it was made, the next day Poindexter informed him that he should prepare 4,000 *TOWs* for sale to Iran. Although briefly considering resignation, the secretary decided to stay on, follow orders, and hope to be able to reverse the policy later on.[31] Indeed, no weapons could have been sold without the secretary's authorization. Thus, he knew about the initiative, even if he had not seen the finding.

Shultz was an altogether different matter. Claiming minimal knowledge throughout, in fact, as Walsh reveals, "the notes of Hill, Platt, and others…reflect Shultz's awareness of ongoing arms-for-hostages negotiations during nearly this entire period [between December 1985 and May 1986]."[32] He had also placed an ally, Peter Rodman, into the NSC, who kept him informed. Indeed, Poindexter, North, and Fortier

---

[28] Lawrence E. Walsh, *Firewall: The Iran-Contra Conspiracy and Cover-Up* (New York: Norton & Co., 1997), 328.
[29] *Report of the Congressional Committees Investigating the Iran-Contra Affair* (Washington, D.C.: GPO, 1987), 209 [hereafter cited as *Iran-Contra Affair*]; and George Shultz, *Turmoil and Triumph* (New York: Macmillan, 1993), 812.
[30] Caspar W. Weinberger, *Fighting for Peace: Seven Critical Years in the Pentagon* (New York: Warner Books, 1990), 376.
[31] Ibid. 83-84.
[32] Lawrence E. Walsh, *Final Report of the Independent Counsel for Iran-Contra Matters*, (Washington, D.C.: United States Court of Appeals for the District of Columbia Circuit, August 4, 1993), 337-38. In *Firewall*, 328-30, Walsh also details Shultz's knowledge throughout.

briefed Rodman on the January 17 finding in February, and he thought the policy was "crazy."[33] As will be noted below, Shultz on at least two occasions would attempt to place bureaucratic roadblocks into the path of the initiative in an attempt to stop it.

Meanwhile, North immediately contacted selected CIA and DOD personnel to arrange for the agency's acquisition of the *TOWs* to be shipped. The decision to keep the process secret even within those organizations led, according to the congressional report, to a "significant pricing error" for the *TOWs*, which "North exploited to the advantage of the Enterprise."[34] The price the DOD charged the CIA was $3,469, instead of $8,435, which resulted in a significantly larger profit for the CIA "agent" Secord. However, there was no pricing error. Under the Economy Act, as an intra-governmental transfer, the DOD "sold" weapons at cost, not at the price it would charge to an outside buyer, or at replacement cost, both of which would have been much higher.

Within a few days the pricing and transportation arrangements were settled and North and Secord flew to London to meet Nir. At the same time, Nir had arranged to cut out Kimche, Schwimmer and Nimrodi in what was a messy, unpleasant series of exchanges filled with recriminations. Nir had argued that those involved in the initiative had changed on the American side. With North now the lead player, and, as he knew North well, Kimche, Schwimmer and Nimrodi should stand aside. Objecting, the trio appealed to Peres, who upheld Nir.[35]

In London, January 22, North and Secord met with Nir to work out the details of the Israeli role. The next day the three of them met with Gorbanifar to reach agreement with the Iranian side. As North laid it out in a fifty-step, "notional timeline" for Poindexter after his return,

---

[33] Rodman, *More Precious Than Peace*, 421. On May 22, Rodman wrote a critical memo to Poindexter "warning that the policy seemed to be degenerating into an arms-for-hostages deal. He did not include me in important deliberations after that point." The memo is reprinted in *Tower Report*, B-100.
[34] *Iran-Contra Affair*, 215.
[35] Samuel Segev, The *Iranian Triangle: The Untold Story of Israel's Role in the Iran-Contra Affair* (New York: Free Press, 1988), 236-38.

the United States would sell and ship 4,000 *TOW* missiles to Iran in four tranches, pick up and return the rejected *Hawks* to Israel, and also furnish an "intelligence sample" to Iran. Israel would repay Iran $5.4 million for the returned *Hawks* and release 100 Shiite prisoners held by the Southern Lebanon Army (part of Nir's original proposal). Iran would pay for the weapons and arrange for the release of the five hostages.[36]

North had tape-recorded the session with Gorbanifar, establishing for the record that they had discussed using the profits from the arms sales, or "residuals," for other purposes. Gorbanifar waxed ecstatic, claiming that the profits would enable the United States to resolve the hostage problem, the terrorist problem, and support for the Contras, all "free of charge. ...Everything free." North later acknowledged, "using the Ayatollah's money to support the Nicaraguan resistance was the right idea."[37]

The entire series of shipments and exchanges were to take place between January 24 and February 25 and set the stage for a meeting soon after between high American and Iranian officials to begin the process of reestablishing relations between the two countries. The crucial phase, however, was the first. According to North's notes, the Iranian Government was to deposit $40 million in Gorbanifar's Swiss account. He would deposit $10 million to Secord's account for the first 1,000 *TOWs*. Secord would transfer $3.5 million to the CIA, which would confirm to DOD that funds had been transferred. Defense would then make the weapons available for pickup by Secord. The CIA would furnish an intelligence package, Secord would ship the missiles, Israel would release Shiite prisoners, and Iran would arrange for the release of the hostages. All this would be accomplished by February 9, an ambitious schedule to say the least.[38]

---

[36] John G. Tower et al., Report of the President's Special Review Board: February 26, 1987 (Washington D.C., 1987), B-71-73.
[37] *Iran-Contra Affair*, 216.
[38] *Iran-Contra Affair*, 215-16 and *Tower Report*, B-71-73.

North's notional timeline was an impressive feat of logistical planning, which, however, immediately became obsolete, except as a baseline schedule to be repeatedly adjusted. It also included the fantastic prediction, which Gorbanifar proclaimed would come true, that on February 11, the Ayatollah Khomeini would step down as supreme leader of Iran.[39] When North returned to Washington, he informed Poindexter that he had "found a way that we can provide some funds to the democratic resistance through funds that will accrue from the sale of arms to the Iranians." After thinking it over for a few minutes, Poindexter agreed.[40]

According to North's timeline, Gorbanifar was to transfer $10 million to Secord's account on January 29 to pay for the first 1,000 *TOWs*, which would be delivered on February 8. The Defense Department, on Weinberger's orders, would do nothing until it had money in hand. Once Secord transferred funds, the department would move weapons from the storage depot in Anniston, Alabama, to Kelly Air Force Base, Texas, where Secord would pick them up and fly them to Israel.

When Gorbanifar failed to deposit the $10 million on January 29, a concerned North called him and was reassured that the money would be deposited on February 4. North then got together with Secord and the CIA's Near East Division Chief, Thomas Twetten, to "develop another schedule based on an anticipated bank transfer to the CIA account on February 4."[41] Yet, that schedule slipped, too, as North jotted in his notes "Gorba going to bank to make transaction tomorrow." However, there was no deposit on February 5, either.

During the January 22 meeting, the four men had agreed to meet again in London, on February 6, to authorize the final go ahead. Gorbanifar's failure to transfer funds on January 29, February 4, or 5, lent great urgency to the scheduled meeting of February 6. When

---

[39] Ibid, B-73.
[40] *Iran-Contra Affair*, 216.
[41] *Iran-Contra Affair*, 217; and Theodore Draper, *A Very Thin Line: The Iran-Contra Affairs* (New York: Hill and Wang, 1991), 282, who identifies DC/NE and C/NE as Twetten.

North, Secord, and Nir arrived in London for the meeting, however, Gorbanifar failed to appear. As Secord recounted it "We tried to track him down on the phone using a dozen numbers Nir carried for that purpose—Gorba's contacts and relatives in Nice, Paris, Frankfurt, and Bonn—but with 'no joy,' as military pilots say when their target is not sighted."[42] Needless to say, without Gorbanifar the entire scheme was dead in the water.

What had happened? Although many on the American side impugned Gorbanifar for his failure to perform according to agreement, it seems obvious that Gorbanifar, as interlocutor, was responding to the decisions of those higher up. It was the leaders in Tehran that had decided to hold off on the transaction with Washington. The Russians had gotten to the Iranians just before they accepted the American offer. Kornienko had arrived on February 2, as noted above, and persuaded the Iranians to hold off taking any irrevocable steps until they could evaluate the result of the imminent battle, which began on February 9. The Soviet leader's extraordinarily well-timed visit raises the question of Moscow's knowledge of American policy.[43]

The Iranian decision to stall created a major crisis for Gorbanifar. As interlocutor he bore the brunt of the American ire and if the "stall" became a permanent decision against establishing a relationship he faced irrelevance. The fact is the Iranian government, having decided to hold off regarding the U.S., had not transferred $40 million into Gorbanifar's account and therefore there were no funds for him to transfer to Secord. Unless and until he could find a way to find the funds to keep the project alive, the deal would be off, so he stayed away.

Scrambling for funds, Gorbanifar appealed to Adnan Khashoggi. As Gorbanifar told it, Khashoggi lent him $10 million on February 7,

---

[42] Richard Secord and Jay Wurts, *Honored and Betrayed: Irangate, Covert Affairs, and the Secret War in Laos* (New York: Wiley, 1992), 245.

[43] Of course, we know now that Aldrich Ames, the mole in the CIA, was providing Moscow with a great deal of information. Were White House policy decisions among them? Were knowledgeable Iranian, or even Israeli opposition leaders passing information to Moscow?

depositing it "directly" into Secord's Lake Resources account at the Swiss bank Compagnie de Services Fiduciaire (CSF).[44] It would take a few days for the funds to clear and not be until February 10 and 11 that funds were transferred from the Lake Resources account to the CIA accounts, which were in the same bank, two deposits of $1.85 million each, totaling $3.7 million.[45]

This sequence also implies that Gorbanifar must also have appealed successfully to Tehran to let him keep the Americans in play. Tehran, of course, still wanted weapons, but now no political commitment. So they agreed to Gorbanifar's weapons' purchase scheme on condition that he arrange for outside financing. As this was now, strictly speaking, Gorbanifar's deal and not Tehran's, there could have been no commitment regarding the hostages simply because Gorbanifar had no influence over Mugniyeh.

Indeed, as Gorbanifar recounted the Khashoggi loan: "there was no talk of release of hostage. There was no hostage. So it is proof to you that there is no deal on hostage. There is no deal for hostage, tit for tat—give me, take this."[46] Moreover, the Iranian government now saw the hostages as insurance *against* any political commitment in the same way that hostages had been used before in 1979 and 1980.

Gorbanifar had "resurfaced" with funds in hand on February 7, as Secord noted, giving "some improbable explanation for his disappearance." Did the president realize what had happened? As I will recount in the next chapter, it appears that Reagan began to prepare for a tactical shift in his approach at this time. But, for the moment, he decided to press on. Indeed, he had little choice, but to see how events would play out. Thus, North and Secord rescheduled delivery of the first 500 missiles for February 17 and also set up the meeting with an Iranian leader in Frankfurt for February 19.[47]

---

[44] *Tower Report*, B-74. Willard Zucker, an American tax lawyer, controlled the bank. See Walsh, *Final Report,* chapter 8, "The Enterprise and its Finances," 79-104.
[45] *Iran-Contra Affair*, 217.
[46] *Tower Report*, B-74.
[47] Ibid. and Secord, *Honored and Betrayed*, 252.

Ignoring Tehran's failure to deposit the funds on time and despite numerous adjustments in schedule, it seemed the president had decided to risk the sale of a relative handful of weapons to establish official contact with Iran, the main objective of his policy. It was now a transaction with Gorbanifar, not with Tehran, but did Reagan know that? The evidence is that he did. Although Secord claimed he did not discover that Khashoggi was bankrolling Gorbanifar, not the Iranian government, until August 1986, North knew by early May, but apparently not in February.[48] One must presume others in the government were also fully aware of the change in procedure. Gorbanifar underestimated the capabilities of U.S. intelligence, for, as the Tower Report notes, he "went to…much trouble to keep [this secret] from us."[49]

North's PROF note to Poindexter of February 13 following his return to Washington laid out the new timetable. The first 500 missiles would now be delivered to Bandar Abbas on Monday February 17, instead of February 8, and "the meeting we had wanted to pass the second set of intel has now been slipped to Weds [February 19] by Gorba." The second 500 missiles were to be delivered on Friday, the 21st and 25 Hezbollah prisoners would be released "shortly after." Then, and only then, "if all goes according to plan," the hostages would be released on Sunday, the 23rd, two weeks after the original date of February 9.

This was not simply a new schedule, but a new deal. There would be no release of the hostages after the first 500 *TOWs* had been delivered, but only after the first thousand. And the hostages would be released only after the Hezbollah prisoners were released. In other words, Gorbanifar's insistence that there had been no arms-for-hostages deal was literally true. It was to be a trade of prisoners for hostages, preceded by a separate sale of weapons. In any case, the

---

[48] In a PROF note to Poindexter on May 5, North said "we know that Khashoggi is the principal fund raiser for Gorba and that only after Gorba delivers a cargo does he get paid by the Iranians." *Tower Report*, B 93-94.
[49] Ibid, 283.

president decided to gamble that a demonstration of American good faith with delivery of the weapons, would gain both the release of the hostages and a meeting with the Iranians.

An Opening to Iran?

According to the new timetable, Secord delivered the first five hundred *TOWs* to Bandar Abbas, on February 17. The aircraft then flew to Tehran, picked up the 17 previously rejected *Hawks*, and returned early the next day to Ben Gurion airport in Israel. That morning, Gorbanifar called Secord to arrange for the promised meeting at the Iranian embassy in Frankfurt on February 19. He said that Kangarlu would head a six-man delegation and wanted to exchange names and titles with the American participants.[50]

Reporting on this call, Secord said that Gorbanifar also wanted to confirm the delivery of the second 500 *TOWs* scheduled for Friday morning, February 21. He promised that "they will release all the hostages, if repeat, if intelligence is good," either Friday, or Saturday. He also promised to arrange the long-sought future meeting with Iranian leaders, while the U.S. was delivering the remaining 3,000 *TOWs*. Gorbanifar "repeatedly stressed need for good current intelligence." Secord ended his message, saying that he had rejected the Iranian embassy in Frankfurt as a venue and they had agreed to meet at a hotel, instead.

North immediately asked Casey for another intelligence package and tasked Clarridge with arranging fake identification documents for himself, Secord, and Albert Hakim, Secord's partner in the Enterprise. Gorbanifar knew North and Secord so it made no sense to assume different identities. It would only cast suspicion on U.S. motives when he pointed out that they were not who they said they were. Hakim was another matter. As a prominent former member of the shah's regime, he was considered an enemy of the state, who could not afford to be

---

[50] *Tower Report*, B-75.

recognized. He donned a disguise (a wig and glasses) and participated as a DIA official under the name of Ibrahim Ibrahimian.[51]

The problem was that the Iranian side as transmitted by Gorbanifar had once again changed the nature of the arrangement by interjecting the value of the intelligence as a pre-condition for the release of the hostages. As the value of the intelligence lay in the eye of the beholder, this raised the distinctly unpleasant prospect that the release of the hostages could be delayed indefinitely. Nevertheless, the ever-optimistic North concluded, "we appear to be much closer to a solution than earlier believed. Kangarlu's attendance at the [coming] Frankfurt meeting tends to support our hope that this whole endeavor can succeed this week, if we *appear* to be forthcoming."[52]

When North, Nir, Twetten, and Hakim arrived in Frankfurt on February 19 (Secord was in Tel Aviv supervising the weapons delivery to Iran), it was a case of déjà vu, only this time it was the Iranian delegation that did not show. Placing a call to Tehran, Kangarlu told Gorbanifar "his bosses would not release him and had given him other assignments." Frustrated, North angrily rejected Gorbanifar's pleas to wait and decided to return to Washington until Kangarlu actually came to Frankfurt. He also canceled delivery of the second 500 *TOWs*, scheduled for February 21, which produced a prompt Iranian agreement to meet on the 24th.[53]

The day before the scheduled meeting, Gorbanifar telephoned Allen, a call that the latter recorded. When Casey decided to work with Gorbanifar, he assigned Allen the task of keeping in contact with him, ostensibly for his value with regard to counterintelligence matters, but, in fact, also as a way the CIA could monitor the evolving relationship with the Iranians.

Obviously intending to encourage the American side, Gorbanifar declared that the Iranians had finally "made up their minds." It was, he

---

[51] North traveled as Mr. Goode and Secord as Maj. Gen Adams. Draper, *Very Thin Line*, 282, saw this as "youthful playacting" on North's part.
[52] *Tower Report*, B-76. (emphasis in original)
[53] Secord, *Honored and Betrayed*, 253

said, "a real breakthrough." Exuding more than his usual confidence, he said, "these people...are ready to make a real firm response and [agree to] collective cooperation for the future." Concluding, he observed, "I think this time with all the strings I have pulled now it is going to work out."[54]

Thus, when North, Secord, Nir, Hakim, and Twetten arrived at the Frankfurt Sheraton hotel on the evening of February 24 for the first meeting between American and Iranian officials in over six years, expectations could not have been higher. Gorbanifar introduced them to Mohsen Kangarlu, a deputy prime minister, who was accompanied by three intelligence officials. As they began their discussion, it soon became apparent that each side had come to the meeting with radically different expectations of the other, courtesy of Gorbanifar.

Gorbanifar had enticed Kangarlu to Frankfurt based on his assurance that the Americans were willing to sell the most advanced weapons to the Iranians. He had told the Americans that Iran was going to release the hostages and prepare for a high-level meeting with President Khamenei, Prime Minister Moussavi, and Majlis Speaker Rafsanjani. Thus, Kangarlu wanted to talk about weapons, while North sought to arrange the high-level meeting. Gorbanifar, as interpreter, attempted to reconcile these irreconcilable expectations, "intentionally" mistranslating what was being said, until Hakim, after repeatedly correcting him, was asked to take over the job.[55] The first meeting, in short, was a disaster.

The next day, however, once Kangarlu was disabused of the notion of acquiring the highly sophisticated *Phoenix* air-to-air missile and other advanced weapons, discussion centered on the American agenda: delivery of the second 500 *TOWs*, release of the hostages, and a high level meeting. They agreed that delivery of the second shipment of *TOWs* would result in the release of "a couple of hostages," presumably two. The rest would be released "after a meeting among

---

[54] Draper, *Very Thin Line*, 283.
[55] "C/NE deposition," (Twetten), *Iran-Contra Affair*, Appendix B, volume 5, 936-37 and *Tower Report*, B-77.

high-level officials at Kish Island off the coast of Iran." When all the hostages were released, the United States would deliver the remaining 3,000 *TOWs*.[56]

North departed Frankfurt on February 26, having assured Kangarlu that the second 500 *TOWs* would be shipped the next day. Secord and Hakim stayed overnight, meeting with both Nir and Gorbanifar the next morning, and then with Kangarlu later to confirm delivery of the second shipment. In a message to North on the 27th, Secord reported that Kangarlu emphasized the need for strict secrecy and "a quick meeting at Kish." He intimated that he could "possibly surprise us by getting some hostages released before the meeting."[57]

Immediately upon his return to Washington, North conferred with Casey, Poindexter, Twetten, and George to go over the results of the meeting. They agreed, "we are indeed headed in the right direction."[58] Overlooking the "money problem" and despite all the "adjustments in schedule," after a remarkably brief period of time, just six weeks from signing the finding, the American side seemed to think that the president's initiative was on the verge of success.[59]

A word about the decision-making process. Although the president does not appear in the record as the main decision-maker, and Casey, Poindexter, North, and Secord appear prominently in apparent decision-making roles, it is obvious that the president was in overall command. Poindexter briefed him every morning and there is no doubt whatsoever that the president guided the process from the Oval Office.[60] The idea that Poindexter, North, or even Casey would make crucial decisions affecting the fate of the president's policy without his

---

[56] *Iran-Contra Affair*, 219.
[57] *Tower Report*, B-78.
[58] Ibid.
[59] The congressional report interprets this moment as reflective of just "another promise" by the Iranians, rather than the point of possible breakthrough. See *Iran-Contra Affair*, 221.
[60] In his deposition to Walsh, *Firewall*, 155, Vice-President Bush artfully "acknowledged that the Iranian initiative had been discussed in the president's intelligence briefings more often than once a month but less often than once a week."

input is, frankly, preposterous, their willingness to take responsibility for failure after-the-fact notwithstanding. The axiom of politics is that the president takes credit for successes; his staff takes responsibility for failures.

At this critical moment, when it appeared that an opening to Iran was imminent, the president decided to move forward with a unified leadership and so offered the new world order faction an opportunity to close ranks. Thus, as preparations for the meeting on Kish Island began, the president through Poindexter offered McFarlane the opportunity to lead the U.S. delegation, an offer that he accepted without hesitation. North elaborated on the events leading up to this point in an exchange of PROF messages with him, advising him to "pack your bags and be ready to go in about a week or so."[61]

At the same time, the president instructed Poindexter to brief Secretary Shultz on the upcoming meeting and solicit his support. According to the secretary, Poindexter said to him the hostages would be released, but

> the Iranians wanted a high-level dialogue, covering issues other than hostages. He said the White House had chosen McFarlane for the mission, and that he would go to Frankfurt...to meet with a deputy of Rafsanjani....The Iranians had asked for help on intelligence as to what the Soviets were doing on the Iranian border and in Afghanistan. [Poindexter] saw a path to reemerging relations.[62]

Shultz was shown McFarlane's negotiating instructions and approved them, but thought it "unlikely" he would succeed. Nevertheless, he said, "well, if you've got that arrangement, that's great."[63]

The situation was not clear-cut. No hostages had been released since Weir the past September and the United States had delivered one thousand missiles. Moreover, the atmosphere surrounding the

---

[61] For the exchange, see *Tower Report*, B-78-80.
[62] Ibid, B-79.
[63] Ibid.

meetings had reeked with suspicion, deception, and mistrust. Kangarlu hinted that the U.S. and Iran should have direct talks, which alarmed Nir and Gorbanifar, who, fearing they would be cut out, repeatedly stressed their relevance to the proceedings. North and Hakim also tried to convince Kangarlu that Gorbanifar was no longer necessary as a conduit and Hakim began regular contact with Kangarlu, bypassing Gorbanifar. Word of this reached Peres, who, also concerned about being cut out, immediately sent a letter to Reagan promising continued Israeli assistance.[64]

Backbiting intensified among the Americans, too. The CIA, perhaps sensing a historical moment approaching and wanting to be a part of it, tried to cut out Secord and Hakim on the grounds that they were "outsiders," but North would not have it. He insisted that both remain on the team. Finally, at Claire George's and Tom Twetten's insistence, North agreed to bring George Cave, a retired CIA agent who spoke fluent Farsi, into their operation.[65] Counter intelligence chief Charles Allen, also became increasingly involved.

The situation facing the President Reagan on Iran was directly analogous to the situation Nixon faced with China fifteen years earlier. Although McFarlane would be denigrated for attempting to duplicate the feat of his mentor, Henry Kissinger, by embarking on the secret mission to Iran, the relevant analogy was not McFarlane and Kissinger, but Reagan and Nixon.

Then, Nixon had sought to present a unified leadership in the opening to China and so sent Kissinger, of the new world order faction, to lead the secret trip to Beijing. Now, Reagan sought to do the same and unify the American leadership in the opening to Iran. In both cases, incidentally, the new world order faction would attempt to sabotage these respective openings.[66] So much for bipartisanship in strategic matters, but including the opposition in a great if obviously

---

[64] Segev, *Iranian Triangle*, 247-49 and Draper, *Very Thin Line*, 286.
[65] *Iran-Contra Affair*, 222 and *Tower Report*, B-80.
[66] For Nixon's approach, see Richard C. Thornton, The *Nixon-Kissinger Years: The Reshaping of American Foreign Policy* (St. Paul: Paragon, 2001, 2nd Ed.), chapters 1, 3, and 9.

risky matter of state is an unspoken rule of politics. The intent was to insure that, depending on the outcome, neither side could blame the other for failure, but both could claim credit for success.

In the China instance, Mao was determined to establish relations with the United States and so Kissinger's efforts failed until later when he became secretary of state. After Nixon resigned, the U.S.-China relationship would founder until President Carter resuscitated it in 1978.[67] McFarlane would be more "successful" because the Iranian leadership was not sufficiently convinced that an opening to the Great Satan was then in its interest.

Tehran Plays a Delaying Game

The Iranian leadership had shifted to a delaying game based on their mistaken beliefs that they were achieving success on the battlefield against Iraq and that Moscow would end support for Saddam Hussein. A series of incremental successes, beginning with the taking of the Al Faw peninsula and followed up with battlefield advances along the front, including seizure of a strip of Iraqi territory at Salaimaniyeh in the Kurdish north, fed these beliefs.[68] In fact, none of these "victories" was in any way decisive, although the propaganda campaign accompanying them claimed otherwise.

It was against the backdrop of these battles that the turn in Tehran's position occurred, prompting a reciprocal turn by the president. A few days after North returned to Washington, in early March, he received word, apparently separately from both Hakim and Nir, that the Iranians had changed their mind about both the Kish Island meeting and the weapons they wanted.[69] Hakim reported that

---

[67] For the history on these developments, see Richard C. Thornton, *China: A Political History, 1917-1980* (Boulder: Westview Press, 1982) and *The Carter Years: Toward A New Global Order* (New York: Paragon House, 1991).

[68] Cordesman and Wagner, *Lessons of Modern War*, 217-24.

[69] *Iran-Contra Affair*, 222, says that Kangarlu called Hakim, who told him, but Secord, *Honored and Betrayed*, 254, says Nir called North, to pass on Gorbanifar's message.

Kangarlu had reverted to his earlier position and wanted to buy the *Phoenix* and *Harpoon* missiles before any hostages would be released and Gorbanifar passed word that Iran wanted a preparatory meeting in Paris before setting up the Kish meeting.[70] These "messages" raised doubts among agency officials that Gorbanifar could deliver the hostages, and concern that the Iranians were attempting to use "salami" tactics simply to obtain more weapons.

Gorbanifar was also becoming uneasy as Washington became increasingly suspicious of his ability to deliver. North had told Nir about Kangarlu's conversation with Hakim, intensifying both Nir's and Gorbanifar's fears that they would be cut out. Gorbanifar called Allen in Washington in an attempt to establish his own direct channel through the CIA.[71] Although there was growing dissatisfaction with Gorbanifar's performance and pressure grew to seek another means of access to the Iranian leadership, the fact was that it was Tehran's position that was changing.

Nevertheless, North, Twetten, and Cave went to Paris to meet with Gorbanifar and Nir on March 8. Gorbanifar launched into what had become a common refrain about how essential he was to the initiative and how with the sale of a few more weapons the hostage problem could be cleared up and profits could be used for the Contras. Specifically, he reiterated Kangarlu's demand for *Phoenix* and *Harpoon* missiles, in addition to the pending order of 3,000 *TOWs*. He also said that the Iranian military needed spare parts for its mostly inoperative *Hawk* missile system and submitted a request for 240 items.[72] Finally, he said that the leadership had decided that Kish Island was unacceptable; the high-level meeting would have to take place in Tehran.[73]

---

[70] See North memo to Poindexter, "Terms of Reference U.S.-Iran Dialogue," April 4, 1986, *Tower Report*, B-86-90, the so-called "diversion" memo. *Iran-Contra Affair*, 225, titles this memo as "Release of American Hostages in Beirut."
[71] Segev, *Iranian Triangle*, 254.
[72] *Tower Report*, B-87. The list would not be received until March 28.
[73] Segev, *Iranian Triangle*, 254 and *Iran-Contra Affair*, 223.

Despite Nir's exhortation to the Americans that these sales would result in the release of all of the hostages, North smelled a rat. They had clearly taken a step backward. Changing the site of the meeting meant further delays. Aside from reiterating to Gorbanifar Washington's willingness to meet, he made clear that the United States would not sell anything before all of the hostages were released. During this exchange, however, North disclosed U.S. intelligence regarding the decrepit state of Iran's weapons' capability. Responding to the demand for advanced weapons, he observed that even if the United States sold them, the *Hawk* "launchers for these missiles were in such disrepair that the missiles could not be launched."[74]

The real tipoff to Tehran's stall was the spare parts list itself. Secord, who had "crafted, installed, and verified" Iran's *Hawk* missile system a decade earlier, saw the list as "meaningless." "From the first time I eyed the list, I knew the Iranians were in deep yogurt militarily—through a lack of technical competence and knowledgeable leadership." They asked for "high value" electrical generators, which "could be obtained easily from their own internal market." They also asked for "printed circuit boards, simple cable connectors...and an oscilloscope—Radio Shack stuff that had little or nothing to do with the HAWK's mission peculiar systems."[75]

When North reported to Poindexter upon his return, the national security adviser reacted very negatively, recognizing the stall. No doubt conveying the president's instructions, he said that he was "fed up and wanted to just cut it off entirely." He turned to North and said, "forget it. It wasn't going anywhere."[76] Accordingly, over the next three weeks, until the end of the month, North made no further effort to contact Gorbanifar, or Nir. Nor would he take their calls. At this point, it appeared as if the initiative was dead, but it wasn't. In fact, it was during this time that the president decided to change tack, as will be discussed in the next chapter.

---

[74] *Tower Report*, B-87.
[75] Secord, *Honored and Betrayed, 258.*
[76] *Tower Report*, B-82.

Unable to reach North, Gorbanifar and Nir tried to keep up contact through Allen, calling him every few days. On March 9, Gorbanifar assured him that the Paris meeting had been "successful, although additional effort remained."[77] Gorbanifar went to Tehran on March 13, returning on the 17th to consult on the next steps forward. Upon his return, he immediately called Allen to claim that he had been in discussions with the top Iranian leadership and that they wanted to move forward with another meeting.[78]

Nir also called Allen, passing on news that Gorbanifar was "under pressure in Tehran," and was in "financial difficulty," although the "Israelis were helping him." Later in March, Gorbanifar called Allen again, upset because the FBI was seeking information about him. His "California girlfriend's house had been entered, as had Furmark's office in New York." He blamed the CIA, but ever suspicious, believed he was being cut out.[79]

Point at the mulberry leaf to curse the locust leaf[80]

There were other reasons for Poindexter, and the president, too, to be "fed up" with the Iranians besides their dilatory tactics. Larger issues occurring at this time were consuming most of their attention. The United States was about to enter the third phase of the plan decided upon in early January (see chapter 7) to gradually increase pressure on Qadaffi, isolate him, and reduce his value as a Soviet strategic asset. The means to this end, as in 1981, was the right to navigate freely in the international waters of the Gulf of Sidra.[81]

During the first two phases, January 26-30 and February 12-16, Task Force 60 commanded by Admiral Frank Kelso had sent the carrier

---

[77] C. Allen, "Conversation with Subject," March 11, 1986, *Tower Report*, B-83.
[78] Draper, *Very Thin Line*, 294.
[79] C. Allen, "Memoranda for the Record," *Tower Report*, B- 85 fns 61, 63.
[80] Ancient Chinese stratagem, *zhi sang ma huai*, means to strike at your adversary's smaller ally as a means of sending a signal to your adversary.
[81] Howard Teicher and Gayle Radley Teicher, *Twin Pillars to Desert Storm* (New York: William Morrow, 1993), 340-343.

groups *Coral Sea* and *Saratoga* on freedom of navigation exercises just north of 32 degrees 30 minutes' north latitude. This placed his carrier group outside the Gulf of Sidra, but sent his combat air patrols into the Tripoli FIR, or flight information zone, over the Gulf of Sidra. Qadaffi had claimed the international waters south of thirty-two thirty as Libyan waters and declared the latitude the "line of death," vowing to destroy all intruders.

The day before the first exercise, Qadaffi boarded the missile patrol boat *Waheed* at the port of Misrata and declared that he would sail to Benghazi to demonstrate that the Gulf of Sidra belonged to Libya. Dressed in a yellow silk flightsuit and wearing a navy cap, he declared "I am going out to the parallel 32.5 which is the line of death, where we will stand and fight with our backs against the wall..."[82] Ignominiously, rough seas forced the *Waheed* back to port in Misrata in less than an hour.

During the two exercises, however, there was no fighting. No Libyan ships ventured out to sea, although 150 Libyan aircraft were intercepted without incident, encounters that provided American airmen with a wealth of tactical combat information about Libyan procedures and tendencies.[83] These essentially routine and peaceful interactions would all change in phase three.

On March 14, at an NSPG meeting, President Reagan authorized the execution of phase three, code-named *Prairie Fire*. The third exercise would commence on March 23 and be far different from the first two. A third carrier, *America*, had joined the task force, bringing the American force complement to three carriers, twenty-six ships, and two hundred and fifty planes. Kelso positioned the three carriers one-hundred and fifty miles north of latitude thirty-two thirty, while the Aegis cruiser *Ticonderoga*, and destroyers *Scott* and *Caron* were poised to sail south past the "line of death" into the international

---

[82] Michael Goldsmith, "Qadaffi Sails Near U.S. Exercises," *Washington Post*, January 26, 1986, 21.
[83] Joseph Stanik, *El Dorado Canyon: Reagan's Undeclared War with Qadaffi* (Annapolis: Naval Institute Press, 2003), 123-126. The following account of *Prairie Fire* generally follows Stanik.

waters of the Gulf of Sidra, under the cover of carrier aircraft flying combat air patrols.

At noon on March 24 the *Ticonderoga* and the two destroyers pushed across thirty-two thirty latitude over thirty miles into the gulf, commencing four days of action carried out almost entirely under cover of darkness. Qadaffi's forces fired first, launching a salvo of SAM-5 missiles at U.S. fighters and then attempted to penetrate the battle group with several anti-ship missile boats. It was a futile effort.

U.S. air and naval units, demonstrating the use of the latest weapons systems, like the *Aegis* radar, *Harpoon* anti-ship missile, *HARM* anti-radiation missile, and *Rockeye* cluster bomb, sank two and probably three missile boats, and put the Soviet-manned, *SAM-5* missile battery at Sirte out of action.[84] The Libyan air force, which had flown over a hundred and fifty sorties during phases I and II, stayed in their hangars because the majority lacked night-fighting capability.[85]

Anticipating the humiliation his forces were about to suffer at the hands of the American navy, on the second day of *Prairie Fire*, March 25, Qadaffi sent cables to the People's Bureaus in East Berlin, Paris, Rome, Madrid, Geneva, and Belgrade, ordering terror attacks against American military and civilian targets. The cables, intercepted by American intelligence, which was on special alert, expressly called for execution of the "plan" that would "cause maximum and indiscriminate casualties."[86] Three days later he issued a formal public call for "all Arab people to attack anything American."[87] He had also

---

[84] "Soviet Advisers Reported in Libya," *Washington Post*, January 1, 1986, 26. Reporting on a leak to the Egyptian newspaper, *Al Ahram,* it was revealed that "the Soviet experts who run these missiles receive their orders directly from Moscow....Libyans are banned from entering those bases."

[85] Stanik, *El Dorado Canyon*, 131-139 and Daniel Bolger, *Americans At War, 1975-1986* (San Francisco: Presidio, 1988), 292-400.

[86] Stanik, *El Dorado Canyon*, 142-143. Seymour Hersh, "Target Qadaffi," *New York Times*, February 22, 1987, 25, says that NSA moved a satellite to a new position over the Mediterranean to improve coverage.

[87] Weinberger, *Fighting for Peace*, 182.

apparently contacted his agents Abu Nidal and Yasir Arafat, by personal courier, as it was one of these two whose men struck first.

A week later, on April 2, Flight TWA-840, on its daily run from Rome to Athens, suffered a mid-air explosion as it was descending into Athens, but managed to land safely. Four American passengers, of the 115 on board, were sucked through the hole in the fuselage created by the explosion, falling to their deaths fifteen thousand feet below. The prime suspect was a known Lebanese terrorist, who went by the name of May Elias Mansur and the pressure-timed explosive a signature trademark of Abu Ibrahim, a master bomb-builder of the Palestinian group called May 15.[88]

Under the circumstances, it was easy to indict Qadaffi, who applauded the terrorist act, but there was no direct tie-in. However, there were clearly ties between him and Abu Nidal and Yasir Arafat, both of whom also had connections to the May 15 group. The Arab Revolutionary Cell, an Abu Nidal front group, claimed responsibility, saying it was retribution for U.S. attacks on Libya in the Gulf of Sidra.[89] As one Western diplomat observed "the renegade Palestinians are an obvious source of men and know-how. They don't cost very much to finance, and it is very difficult to trace any links back to Libya."[90]

If the connection between Qadaffi and the terrorist attack on TWA was murky, the next series of events was more clear-cut. Two days later, British intelligence intercepted a message from the Libyan People's Bureau in East Berlin to Tripoli saying "we have something planned that will make you happy." At just before two o'clock in the morning of April 5 a bomb exploded in the restroom of La Belle Discotheque, a popular nightclub in West Berlin. The bomb injured 229 people, including 78

---

[88] Stanik, *El Dorado Canyon*, 143. May 15 commemorates the displacement of Palestinians from Israel after the 1948 war.
[89] David C. Martin and John Walcott, *Best Laid Plans: The Inside Story of America's War Against Terrorism* (New York: Touchstone, 1988), 285, says that "later, intelligence officials concluded the bombing was probably the work of a close associate of Yasser Arafat who called himself Col. Hawari and who had recruited two expert bomb makers trained by Abu Ibrahim."
[90] William Smith, "Terrorism Explosion on Flight 840," *Time*, April 14, 1986.

American servicemen, and killed two. Literally, minutes afterward, a second message to Tripoli was intercepted saying, "an event occurred. You will be pleased with the result."[91]

The shock of the West Berlin attack dominated the headlines, overshadowing the wave of Qadaffi-inspired terror attacks that accompanied it. On the same day the French government expelled two Libyan diplomats for "plotting an attack with hand grenades and machine guns on the American visa office in Paris." The next day, Libyan agents attempted to fire rocket-propelled grenades into the American embassy in Beirut and sought to buy the hostages being held by terrorists in Beirut. They also attempted to kidnap the American ambassador to Rwanda.[92]

Over the next few days intelligence came in reporting that Qadaffi was planning "about three dozen operations against American diplomatic missions, military installations, and commercial interests overseas." The CIA specifically identified "nine Libyan operations either ordered by Qadaffi or already underway," creating a powerful sense of urgency in the White House.[93] But there was an even larger concern.

For over two months, the CIA had been reporting from its agents that the KGB was planning a terror campaign in West Germany against Americans and American interests. The Soviets were looking for "restaurants near U.S. military bases where it could hide 'minibombs.' The KGB planned on exploding these bombs when the restaurants were busy, and then blaming the carnage on German terrorists."[94] Were the Soviets planning on using Qadaffi's terror campaign as the cover for their own? Was this Gorbachev's work, or that of his internal adversaries?

---

[91] Hersh, "Target Qaddafi," 25 and Leslie Gelb, "How Libya Messages Informed U.S.," *New York Times*, April 23, 1986, 6.
[92] Martin and Walcott, *Best Laid Plans*, 289 and Keith Richburg, "U.S. Had Word of More Plots," *Washington Post*, April 15, 1986, 1.
[93] Stanik, *El Dorado Canyon*, 147.
[94] Pete Early, *Confessions of a Spy: The Real Story of Aldrich Ames* (New York: Putnam, 1997), 194.

Reagan's decision was to strike hard at Qadaffi, authorizing a much larger attack than had been planned. Certainly, the larger attack was intended to insure the infliction of maximum damage, but it was also designed to dissuade Qadaffi and Moscow from taking any further terrorist action. If the Soviets were deterred, it would send a clear signal that the correlation of forces had changed in America's favor. If they failed to protect Qadaffi, all of Moscow's clients would be forced to reconsider the value of Moscow as an ally. If they carried out their planned wave of terror, they would have to reckon with a no-longer passive America and the end of their push for détente.

On April 9, with the "smoking gun" of the intelligence intercepts in hand, the president met with his chief advisers to decide on a final target list. Five targets were selected, three in Tripoli and two in Benghazi. UK-based F-111 bombers would strike targets in Tripoli: the military airfield, where Qadaffi's IL-76 transports were located; the Murat Sidi Bilal terrorist training camp; and the Bab al Azizziya barracks, a walled, 200-acre compound housing his East German security forces, residence, and headquarters.

Carrier-based aircraft would attack the two targets in Benghazi, the Benina airfield, where a squadron of Mig-23 *Flogger*, Qadaffi's only night-flying aircraft were based and the Jamahiriya Guard Barracks, his eastern command center. Contrary to some later commentary, there was no attempt to target Qadaffi himself, which was against American law.[95] For security purposes, Qadaffi never slept in the same bed two nights in a row, making it virtually impossible to target him. However, it was the consensus that if he happened to perish in the attacks, no one would shed any tears.

The decision to carry out a large raid, instead of a surgical strike was passed to Air Force planners on April 12. Since January, when contingency planning began at Lakenheath Air Base in England, they "had been planning for a small, surgical raid by no more than six jets. Now, however, with very little time left to adjust, the size of the mission had been tripled." The planners were stunned by what they

---

[95] Hersh, "Target Qadaffi."

believed was a serious tactical error that "major changes to the targets…and especially to the raid's size were all being made within forty-eight hours of the planned takeoff time."[96]

Then came worse news, the most direct route would not be available. The president had sent UN Ambassador Vernon Walters to Western Europe over the weekend of April 11-13, to confirm allied support for the coming strike. Except for Prime Minister Thatcher, the results were disappointing. Thatcher agreed to permit U.S. aircraft to employ British bases for the mission, which she saw as a matter of self-defense. She had her own reasons for striking back at Qadaffi. The Libyan leader had supported the IRA attempt to assassinate her in October 1984 and a Libyan diplomat had shot and killed a British policewoman performing crowd control duties in front of the People's Bureau in London earlier in April of that year.

Aside from Thatcher, no other West European leader supported the U.S. plan. Francois Mitterand and Jacques Chirac stunned Walters by refusing permission for U.S. aircraft to overfly French territory. The recent French election had installed Chirac in a co-leadership role with Mitterand and he rejected the U.S. request "out of hand," taking what was described as a "traditional Gaullist line" of non-intervention.[97] He also claimed incorrectly that the United States had not given France sufficient advance notice. The fact was that since early February, U.S. and French officials had been engaged in "joint military planning" for the raid.[98] Spanish Prime Minister Felipe Gonzalez, following the French lead, also refused over flight permission.

The West Germans and the Italians, as Libya's largest trade partners, also refused to offer support. West German Foreign Minister, Hans-Dietrich Genscher, warning against "hasty action," "rejected economic sanctions as too ineffectual and military force as too reckless

---

[96] Robert Venkus, *Raid on Qadaffi* (New York: St. Martin's, 1993), 86.
[97] Jeremiah O'Leary, "Mitterand Favored Raid to Oust Qadaffi," *Washington Times*, April 21, 1986, 1.
[98] Teicher and Teicher, *Twin Pillars*…, 345. Howard Teicher and Walters had arranged for the cooperation during a visit to Paris in early February. Chirac may not have been briefed about this arrangement.

in dealing with Qaddafi."⁹⁹ According to Shultz, Prime Minister Craxi told associates "he hoped the United States would…take out Libya's military infrastructure, and bring about Qadaffi's downfall." Of course, he admitted, "public opinion in Italy meant that he could not openly support such an effort, indeed, he would have to oppose it."¹⁰⁰

Craxi did more than oppose U.S. action, he tipped-off Qadaffi. According to a report by Abdel-Rahman, then Libya's ambassador to Italy, which was confirmed by Italy's foreign minister Giulio Andreotti, Craxi secretly sent word to Qadaffi that there would be "an American raid against Libya."¹⁰¹ Craxi's message came immediately after his meeting with Walters, giving Qadaffi time to prepare his defenses several days in advance.

Although the Russians adopted a very low profile in Libya, in anticipation of the American attack, it would appear that Moscow got word to Qadaffi just before the planes arrived over Tripoli enabling the Libyan leader to escape harm. American intelligence had pinpointed Qadaffi "at work in his tent" just before midnight Tripoli time, which was "the last fix" obtained on him.¹⁰² That was just over two hours before the bombs began to fall.

When the mission was "well underway," Secretary Shultz called in the Soviet chargé d'affaires and "informed him of the operation."¹⁰³ Perhaps, Shultz did not wait long enough, for Qadaffi was warned and fled to safety minutes before the attack. There can be no doubt that the chargé immediately sent word back to Moscow. The question is: Did Moscow have sufficient time to warn Qadaffi? Certainly his ally

---

⁹⁹ William Drozdiak, "Walters Discusses Terrorism With European Leaders," *Washington Post*, April 14, 1986, 15.
¹⁰⁰ Shultz, *Turmoil and Triumph*, 682 and Bernard Weinraub, "U.S. Says Allies Asked for More In Libya Attack," *New York Times*, April 22, 1986, 1.
¹⁰¹ Nick Squires, "Italy 'tipped off' Libya about 1986 US raid," *The Telegraph*, October 30, 2008, 1.
¹⁰² Hersh, "Target Qadaffi," 22.
¹⁰³ Stanik, *El Dorado Canyon*, 180.

Bonici of Malta did, telling him that the raid was under way, as American planes were sighted streaking over Maltese airspace.[104]

Eighteen F-111 *Aardvarks*, forced to fly 2,800 miles over the Atlantic and around the Iberian peninsula because of the French refusal to grant over flight permission, pummeled targets in Tripoli, while fifteen carrier-based A-6E *Intruders* struck targets in Benghazi. One F-111 bomber was lost. Over fifty additional aircraft, from refueling tankers, to defense suppression FA-18 *Hornets* and A-7 *Corsairs*, electronic countermeasure EF-111 *Ravens*, and SR-71 *Blackbird* reconnaissance planes, supported the mission. It was the "longest fighter combat mission…in the history of military aviation."[105]

The raid on Tripoli not only crippled Libya's terrorist infrastructure, but also more importantly marked a "turning point" in the use of American power against international terrorism.[106] In eleven minutes over target, thirty aircraft dropped over ninety, mostly laser-guided 2,000-pound bombs on the five selected targets in Tripoli and Benghazi. Two bombs went off target, causing some collateral damage, including to the French Embassy. Qadaffi claimed that his adopted fifteen-month old daughter, Hana, was killed in the attack, a claim that lingered for years, but was false. Hana grew up to become a medical professional in Libya.[107]

Qadaffi escaped harm, although he was badly shaken by the near miss and went into seclusion for several months to plot his revenge. Some authors, like Hersh, claimed that the U.S. had sought to assassinate Qadaffi, which was false. The most obvious target for such an attempt was the Libyan leader's tent. As Venkus notes "the tent

---

[104] Kennedy Hickman, "International Terrorism: Bombing of Libya (Operation El Dorado Canyon)," *About.com*.
[105] Venkus, *Raid on Qaddafi*, xi.
[106] Lou Cannon and Bob Woodward, "Reagan's Use of Force Marks Turning Point; More Terror and Retaliation Seen," *Washington Post*, April 16, 1986, 1.
[107] Martin Evans, "Libya: Hana Gaddafi 'alive and well,'" *The Telegraph*, August 26, 2011. See also Colin Freeman and Robert Mendick, "Emails show British Government knew Hana Gaddafi was still alive," *The Telegraph*, September 24, 2011.

should have been targeted if that was the mission's goal."[108] It was not. Most important, the American strike had made Libya's vulnerability and isolation starkly obvious to all.

Moscow had declined to enter into even the standard friendship treaty with Libya, as it had done with South Yemen, for example, and, in the current crisis, had failed to provide anything but lukewarm diplomatic support and replenishment of Libya's weapons.[109] Seeking some minimal protection from the communist camp, at the end of April, Qadaffi secretly applied for membership to the Warsaw Pact. Even here, "the Soviet Union insisted on certain conditions before the application [was] processed."[110] It was not granted.

President Reagan addressed the nation after the raid had ended. "Today, we have done what we had to do. If necessary, we shall do it again." Administration officials hastily declared that future actions would be on a case-by-case basis, not the beginning of a long war. They declared that the bombing was designed "to show the Libyan military that there was little it could do to combat American power and little that the Soviet Union would do to protect Libya."[111]

Privately, Poindexter focused on the raid's impact on Moscow. The attack, he said, had "helped to demonstrate to the Soviet Union and others throughout the world that we were not going to be stepped on, that if provoked we were going to respond with deadly force. I don't think that lesson was lost on the Soviets."[112] It was not lost on the Iranians, either. Even as the United States was preparing to confront Qadaffi in the Gulf of Sidra, the Iranians were backing away from improving relations, but trying to keep open the door to weapons sales from Washington.

---

[108] Venkus, *Raid on Qaddafi*, 154.
[109] See "Gorbachev's Condolence Message to Qaddafi," *New York City Tribune*, April 29, 1986, 11.
[110] "Libya Is Said to Apply to Warsaw Pact," *Baltimore News American*, April 26, 1986, 2.
[111] Leslie Gelb, "U.S. Aides Deny Attack Is Start of an Escalation," *New York Times*, April 16, 1986, 15.
[112] Robert Timberg, *The Nightingale's Song* (New York: Touchstone, 1995), 379.

Chapter 9
The President Stands Tough

By the middle of March 1986, President Reagan had managed to bring Shultz and the new world order faction into agreement on the need to adopt tougher measures against the Soviet Union and its allies. He had also offered McFarlane an opportunity to make a secret trip to Tehran in a renewed effort to reestablish relations with Iran. But the president knew that the new world order faction would attempt to kill an opening to Iran again as they had in the past, so, this time, the president added a twist in an attempt to foil his adversaries.

At the same time, Reagan continued to spar with Gorbachev over the next steps in arms control and a formula for the resolution of third-world conflicts. Over the past year, Gorbachev, while professing interest in better relations with the United States, had continued to resupply Soviet clients in Angola and Nicaragua, as well as Soviet forces in Afghanistan, with sufficient military strength to enable them to maintain the advantage against the resistance fighters.

Gorbachev's blatant hypocrisy enabled the president to convince the Congress and Secretary Shultz of the need for tougher measures against the Soviet Union and its clients. Even so, throughout 1985, there had occurred a bruising bureaucratic struggle over the implementation of the Reagan Doctrine. The indecision over whether or not to apply pressure on Qadaffi, and to adopt a more aggressive policy against international terrorism, discussed above, had been part of that struggle, as had battles over whether or not to increase support for the anti-Soviet resistance movements in Afghanistan, Angola, and Nicaragua.

There is a substantial record detailing each facet of this struggle, which, taken together reflected the conflict over grand strategy.[1] Secretary Shultz and others in the bureaucracy, like John McMahon, Deputy Director of the CIA, had argued persistently that a strategy of "bleeding the Russians" would eventually lead to negotiated solutions. This was, of course, the fundamental thrust of the new world order faction's détente strategy.

The Russians did not cooperate. They reinforced their allies, delivering powerful Mi-24 *Hind* armored helicopters and special operations forces (*Spetznaz*) to their clients (in Nicaragua, Cubans were the functional equivalent), enabling them to dominate their adversaries. Even though the United States allocated more funds and weapons to the resistance forces during the year, it had become increasingly obvious that the strategy of bleeding the Soviets had failed to elicit an interest in negotiating outcomes anywhere.

Soon after the Soviet introduction of armored helicopters the idea of providing *Stingers*, the very effective infra-red-guided, anti-aircraft missile, to counter them was advanced and debated for most of 1985. The new world order faction opposed the provision of *Stingers*, based on the notion of "plausible deniability," and sought to disguise the U.S. role by purchasing communist-bloc weapons for the resistance fighters. This scheme was not only ineffective, but also naive. The Soviets understood full well that the United States was buying weapons from its clients to support the resistance movements and

---

[1] On Afghanistan, George Crile, *Charlie Wilson's War* (New York: Grove, 2003), Steve Coll, *Ghost Wars* (New York: Penguin, 2004), Mohammad Yousaf and Mark Adkin, *The Bear Trap*, (London: Leo Coper, 1992), Kirsten Lundberg, *Politics of a Covert Action: The US, the Mujahideen, and the Stinger Missile* (Boston: Harvard, 1999). On Angola, Chester Crocker, *High Noon in Southern Africa* (New York: Norton, 1992), J.E. Davies, *Constructive Engagement?* (Oxford: James Curry, 2007). On Nicaragua, Roy Gutman, *Banana Diplomacy* (New York: Simon & Shuster, 1988), Peter Rodman, *More Precious Than Peace* (New York: Scribner's, 1994), James M. Scott, *Deciding to Intervene* (Durham: Duke University Press, 1996).

sabotaged as many communist-bloc weapons the U.S. purchased as possible.²

By early in 1986, it was clear that Reagan had won the Stinger battle for Angola and Afghanistan, but not for Nicaragua. Both Savimbi of Unita and President Zia of Pakistan had expressed their wishes for the Stinger, but the Contras had to be satisfied with the *Redeye*, the much less effective precursor of the Stinger, and would not receive it until much later. Nevertheless, it was clear that the notions of "bleeding the Russians" and "plausible deniability" had been repudiated. The CIA's chief proponent of "bleeding the Russians," McMahon, resigned at the end of February and Shultz reluctantly agreed that more pressure was needed, although he "continued to have reservations" about the visibility of American arms.³

Finally, the long-sought meeting with the Iranians was arranged for late May and the president offered McFarlane the opportunity to head the mission. He did this fully aware that the new world order faction opposed an opening to Iran, but offered the opportunity nonetheless. Reagan was less concerned about achieving immediate success with Iran than laying the foundation for future relations, but he did anticipate solving an immediate funding need for the Contras.

Funding the Contras

The problem of how to deal with Nicaragua and its communist government seemed to be intractable. The powerful Democrat majority in the House of Representatives had since 1982 systematically squeezed off the president's ability to support the Nicaraguan resistance forces by refusing to authorize lethal aid and restricting government involvement through annual amendments to the defense appropriations bill, known as the Boland Amendments.

---

[2] John Walcott and Tim Carrington, "Role Reversal: CIA Resisted Proposal to Give Afghan Rebels US Stinger Missiles," *Wall Street Journal*, February 16, 1988.
[3] Peter Samuel, "Decision to Give Stingers to Rebels Is Hailed," *New York City Tribune*, March 31, 1986, 1. See also Lundberg, *Politics of a Covert Action*.

A critical moment occurred in the spring of 1984 when the CIA's involvement in mining Nicaraguan harbors was revealed. The resulting flap prompted the House and the Senate to pass nonbinding resolutions prohibiting the use of U.S. funds to support mining. Worse, the flap placed in jeopardy all funding for the Contras. The president had responded by arranging for temporary funding by third countries and parties and by directing the NSC to establish a logistics support system for the Contras. The plan was to use private funds until the House could be persuaded to restore full government funding and involvement. The Senate, with a Republican majority, supported the president's proposals.[4]

Shultz and McFarlane attempted to prevent the president from soliciting funds from third countries, postulating that it might be an impeachable offense, but the attorney general ascertained that such funding was legal as long as there was no quid pro quo.[5] Cleared to proceed, within months the president had raised over $10 million for the Contras. The private fund-raising effort was entirely legal and public, although donor identities were not announced.

On Casey's recommendation, in mid-1984, North tapped Richard Secord to set up a logistical network to funnel weapons and supplies to the Contras.[6] By September, press reports were quoting administration officials and rebel leaders that the administration had already raised over $10 million.[7] (Indeed, the major donor was King

---

[4] Gutman, *Banana Diplomacy*, 199-203.
[5] Lawrence E. Walsh, *Final Report of the Independent Counsel for Iran-Contra Matters*, (Washington, D.C.: United States Court of Appeals for the District of Columbia Circuit, August 4, 1993), 2 and fn4. See also Peter Kornbluh and Malcom Byrne, *The Iran-Contra Scandal: The Declassified History* (New York: New Press, 1993), 77.
[6] Oliver North and William Novak, *Under Fire: An American Story* (New York: Harper Collins, 1991), 251.
[7] Walsh, *Final Report*, 161-63 and Philip Taubman, "Nicaragua Rebels Reported To Raise Millions In Gifts," *New York Times*, September 9, 1984, 1. Taubman named Israel, Argentina, Venezuela, and Guatemala, in addition to Taiwan, but made no mention of Saudi Arabia.

Fahd of Saudi Arabia, who secretly agreed to provide a million a month through the end of the year. Fahd was also secretly providing matching funds for the Afghan rebels.)

Attempting to thwart the president's effort, the House passed the most restrictive amendment yet, Boland III, on October 12, 1984, mandating that no funds appropriated to the CIA, Defense Department, or "any other agency or entity...involved in intelligence activities" could be spent on or in support of military or paramilitary operations in Nicaragua. The loophole was a ruling by the Intelligence Oversight Board that the NSC fell outside the definition of an entity involved in intelligence activities, as it was part of the president's office.[8] An additional loophole enabled the president to pay involved NSC personnel out of his own office contingency fund.

By the spring of 1985, the arrangement by which donations went to Contra leader Adolfo Calero, who paid Secord and others to acquire arms, was viewed as unsatisfactory. There was concern that Contra leaders were refusing to coordinate their efforts and were skimming funds from the donations. Accordingly, the decision was made to unify the resistance leadership and to centralize the finances.

At a meeting in Miami in June 1985, North brought together the three main Contra leaders, Calero, Arturo Cruz, and Alfonso Robelo and renamed the resistance as the United Nicaraguan Opposition (UNO). At the same time, North removed Calero from control over donated funds. He decreed that all future donations would go to Secord's Enterprise, specifically to the Lake Resources account, although Calero could retain for his use whatever funds still remained from earlier donations.

Referring to the Lake Resources account, North later testified, "when private money was raised for the Contras, this was where it was sent."[9] The decision to shift control of funds from Calero to Secord had an

---

[8] For the Democrat and Republican interpretations of the amendments, see *Report of the Congressional Committees Investigating the Iran-Contra Affair* (Washington, D.C.: GPO, 1987), 395-407 and 489-499 [hereafter cited as *Iran-Contra Affair*]. The Boland amendments would be enacted annually through October 1986.
[9] North, *Under Fire*, 268.

unintended consequence. When Secord later became involved in Iran arms sales, it established the presumptive basis for the explosive charge that he had diverted profits from Iran sales to the Contras.[10]

The charge, however, was difficult to substantiate. In his exhaustive analysis of money transfers, Walsh notes, from mid-1985, "the money originally used to purchase weapons [for the Contras] came from commingled funds in Enterprise accounts—including U.S. funds generated by the sale of arms to Iran and funds donated to the Contras" from the Saudis, Taiwanese, and private sources.[11] By commingled funds, he meant that the money from various sources had become so entangled in Secord's books that it was impossible to determine which funds went to purchase what.

For example, although Walsh claimed that the $1 million the Israelis delivered to Secord in November 1985 derived from Iranian arms sales, he acknowledged (in a footnote) that "because of the commingling of funds in the Lake Resources account it is not possible to directly tie the Israeli deposit to an expenditure of funds on the Contras."[12] Indeed, he also acknowledged that this was true for all of the funds in Secord's possession. "Because of the commingling of Enterprise funds, it was not possible to determine precisely how much money was diverted."[13]

In this judgment, Walsh echoed Secord, who said, "lax financial controls…allowed funds from various sources and intended for certain projects—Contra or Iranian—to become commingled."[14] Nevertheless, Walsh insisted, despite his own lack of evidence, that a diversion had

---

[10] See John Singlaub, *Hazardous Duty* (New York: Summit, 1991), 451ff, for an unflattering treatment of Secord and North. Singlaub competed with Secord for the role of main Contra supplier.

[11] Walsh, *Final Report*, 164. Walsh claimed that profits from Iranian arms sales belonged to the U.S. government, a claim that was disputed and which will be dealt with below.

[12] Walsh, 168n32.

[13] Ibid, 171.

[14] Richard Secord and Jay Wurts, *Honored and Betrayed: Irangate, Covert Affairs, and the Secret War in Laos* (New York: Wiley, 1992), 254-55.

occurred and estimated that a minimum of $3.6 million of surplus Iranian funds had been spent on the Contras.

In any case, from mid-1985 Secord used his newly acquired pool of funds to establish an air supply network. He purchased seven old aircraft of various types, hired crews, set up a full-service repair and refurbishment facility in Miami, an arms warehouse in Lisbon, Portugal, and also purchased a cargo ship.[15] Operating from airbases in Ilopango, El Salvador, Aguacate, Honduras and later Santa Elena, Costa Rica, Secord began supply operations in early 1986. The trials and tribulations of setting up and running this network have been well-documented, but the best that can be said for it is that it sustained the Contra forces at a bare bones level, but was not sufficient to make them a threat to the Nicaraguan regime.[16]

Meanwhile, the Soviets had taken advantage of the opportunity afforded by the cutoff of Contra funds to strengthen the Sandinistas. By November 1984, in addition to other military supplies, they had deployed Mi-24 *Hind* helicopter gunships to Nicaragua, just as they had to Angola and Afghanistan.[17] The results were the same in all three countries, as their clients wreaked havoc among the resistance forces, who had no defense against the "flying tanks." Over the next

---

[15] Ibid, 262, claims that he "never saw" funds from Saudi Arabia or Taiwan, but the probable explanation is that when the funds were transferred from Calero they were not identified as to source. Walsh, *Final Report*, 160, for example, lists the source of $11.3 million transferred to Secord's account simply as coming from the "Contras."

[16] Secord, *Honored and Betrayed;* Robert Kagan, *Twilight Struggle: American Power and Nicaragua, 1977-1990* (New York: Free Press, 1996); Gutman, *Banana Diplomacy;* Rodman, *More Precious Than Peace*.

[17] "Official: Nicaragua has Soviet Helicopters," *Evening Herald* (South Carolina), November 16, 1984, 10. The helicopter deployment was a U.S. intelligence fiasco. Intelligence reports identified a dozen crates aboard a Soviet freighter headed for the port of Corinto; the supposition was that the crates contained MIG-21 jet fighters and the United States duly filed a public protest. However, as Shultz described it, "the Soviets and the Nicaraguans ...lured us into visible protests in opposition to MIG-21s and then supplied the kind of aircraft [MI-24] that, ironically, would do far greater damage to the Contras in the field than would jet fighters." George Shultz, *Turmoil and Triumph* (New York: Macmillan, 1993), 424-25.

year, Moscow had built the Nicaraguan army into a force one hundred thousand strong, the largest armed force in Central America. By comparison, although the Contras had also grown, their forces had not yet reached fifteen thousand.[18]

Given their superior forces, the Sandinistas were disinclined to negotiate with the Contras, most of whom had withdrawn from Nicaragua to Honduras.[19] Even the Democratic Left in the House conceded that the balance had skewed. Secretary Shultz, who had pressed hard for adoption of a political solution in Nicaragua was also forced to concede that the Contadora process was at a dead end. The Reagan leadership had moved into rare agreement on the need to strengthen the Contras. If there were to be any chance of reinvigorating the negotiating process, the Contras would have to be strengthened.

Opinion in the House and Senate also seemed to have reached the tipping point. In December 1985, while reauthorizing the Boland amendment, the Congress also authorized classified amounts to the CIA to assist the Contras in "communications" and to provide "advice" on logistics. However, although Senate Intelligence Committee Chairman David Durenberger (R-MN) believed that the CIA could provide advice on logistical matters, House Intelligence Committee Chairman, Lee Hamilton (D-IN) emphatically declared that such advice was "not appropriate."[20]

Believing that opinion in the Congress and, indeed, in the nation was swinging in favor of aid to the Contras, the president determined to give it a push.[21] In private, Reagan signed a finding on January 9, 1986, positively interpreting the congressional authorization. Thirteen million dollars were designated to provide communications assistance

---

[18] James LeMoyne, "Most Contras Reported To Pull Out of Nicaragua," *New York Times*, January 30, 1986, 10.
[19] Ibid.
[20] John G. Tower et al., Report of the President's Special Review Board: February 26, 1987 (Washington: GPO, 1987), C-6n5.
[21] Robert Merry, "Congress Shifts Toward Reagan On Aid for Contras in Nicaragua," *Wall Street Journal*, January 13, 1986, 30.

and logistical advice, although Hamilton continued to rule that CIA "participation in planning or execution of military activities, or acting as military advisors, is prohibited."[22]

Publicly, the president requested that the Congress authorize $100 million in support for the Contras. In this "first major test of the 'Reagan Doctrine,'" the president's advisers calculated that "if the president can present the request as part of a strategy for forcing the Nicaraguan government to negotiate seriously with the opposition, Congress might support him."[23] A major public relations campaign accompanied the request.

Secretary Shultz also lent his support for aid. In congressional hearings in February, the secretary declared that the "Sandinista game plan was…to persuade people not to help the Contras for long enough so that, with this big Soviet buildup of advanced weapons, they will wipe them out before we wake up." For any negotiations to occur, let alone succeed, he said, Congress had to approve Contra aid first. Only if the Sandinistas realize that they cannot win will they agree to negotiate. In short, "if you do not have any cards to play," he argued, "you cannot get into the card game."[24]

Believing that the ground was prepared, the president, on February 25, formally requested that Congress authorize $100 million in aid for the Contras. The bulk of it, $70 million would be for military assistance, the rest for humanitarian aid. No new money would be involved. The request was to permit the president to reprogram, that is, to transfer, funds from one account to another in the existing defense budget. The $27 million in humanitarian aid the Congress authorized the previous year would run out at the end of March and the Contras were sorely in need of weapons.

---

[22] Bob Woodward, "CIA Provided Contras $13 Million in Assistance Under Reagan 'Finding,'" *Washington Post*, January 14, 1987, 1.
[23] Robert Parry, "Swing Votes Could Deliver Contra Aid," *Washington Post*, January 27, 1986, 4.
[24] Kagan, *Twilight Struggle*, 423.

"You cannot fight Soviet helicopter gunships flown by Cubans with food and boots and bandages," Shultz said.[25]

In an unexpected response, however, the House balked. Four House committees quickly voted to bar any aid to the Contras. Voting mainly along party lines, the Committee on Intelligence, the Sub-Committee on Western Hemispheric Affairs, the Appropriations Committee, and the Foreign Affairs Committee all voted against. Only the Armed Services Committee recommended approval. Even some Senate Republicans supported the Democrats. Sen. Nancy Kassebaum (R-KS) complained that the administration's approach was based on "simplistic reasoning," was filled with gross "distortions," and was "highly offensive."[26]

The sharp congressional rebuke prompted efforts to work out a compromise, but, after a few days, the president himself ruled it out. "In the last few days here in Washington there has been talk of compromise on this issue: smaller amounts of aid, delay in providing it, restrictions on the uses to which it could be put, all the usual temporizing and quibbles," Reagan said. The reason for hardening against compromise was the belief that it was undermining the effort to gain passage of the president's request.[27]

Reagan decided to make a direct appeal to the American people to bring pressure to bear on the Congress. In a television address on March 16, the president condemned Nicaragua as a "cancer" that "poses a direct threat to the United States." Posing a challenge to the House Democrats, he said, "stopping Communism and international terrorism there would serve as a historic test of his presidency." He

---

[25] David Shipler, "Reagan Asks $100 Million for Contras," *New York Times*, February 26, 1986, 3.
[26] Milton Coleman and Edward Walsh, "2 More House Panels Bar Contra Aid," *Washington Post*, March 7, 1986, 4 and Steven Roberts, "House Panels Bar Help For Contras," *New York Times*, March 6, 1986, 9.
[27] Edward Walsh and Milton Coleman, "Idea of Compromise On Contra Aid Fades," *Washington Post*, March 12, 1986, 7 and Bernard Gwertzman, "Reagan Aides Open Compromise Talks on Aiding Contras," *New York Times*, March 9, 1986, 1.

appealed to the American people to "demand that Congress endorse the Administration's $100 million aid package."[28]

Three days later, the Democrat-controlled House voted to reject the president's aid package for the Contras. Sixteen Republicans joined 206 Democrats to defeat the proposal 222 to 210. In a statement issued after the vote, Reagan predicted ultimate victory, vowing, "to come back again and again until this battle is won, until freedom is given the chance it deserves in Nicaragua."[29] There was general sentiment on both sides of the aisle that the president would eventually win passage for aid, as it would require only six Republicans to change their votes, but it would be at least a month, or more, before another vote would be taken. The problem was what to do in the meantime.

Reagan Rips Off the Ayatollah

The president was clearly stung by the congressional rebuff and hurt by his failure to generate popular pressure on the House. Sixteen Republicans had deserted him and his aides had failed to do their homework. They had encouraged the president to climb out onto a limb, which the Democrats gleefully sawed off. Allowing the president to suffer such an embarrassing defeat was unprecedented. One author, Gutman, characterized the Contra aid plan as an amateurish "caricature of a legislative strategy."[30]

If there was a moment when what would later be termed the "diversion" of funds to the Contras began to be considered seriously, it was when the House rejected President Reagan's proposal for a $100 million support package for the Contras on March 20, 1986. However, the term "diversion" is a misnomer, and both the term and the concept need definition. The term to divert is defined as to cause something to change course, as to divert water from a channel. As such the concept

---

[28] Bernard Weinraub, "Reagan Condemns Nicaragua In Plea For Aid To Rebels," *New York Times*, March 17, 1986, 1.
[29] Edward Walsh, "House Defeats Reagan Request For Contra Aid," *Washington Post*, March 21, 1986, 1.
[30] Gutman, *Banana Diplomacy*, 322-23.

is of a flow, which is changed from one direction to another. Neither the term nor the concept correctly describes what occurred, for there was no flow and no change of direction.

There was no flow of funds. In fact, there were only three instances when profits from arms sales to Iran were recorded in Lake Resources books and could have been "diverted": February, May, and October 1986. Secord acknowledged a $5 million surplus from the February sale, but showed that $2 million was set aside for aircraft insurance, $1.7 million to purchase and retrofit the cargo ship, *Erria*, and $300,000 for miscellaneous expenses. This left approximately $1 million for the Enterprise. It is unknown how much, if any, of the $1 million was expended on direct purchase of weapons or supplies for the Contras, but it was obviously not much.[31] More to the point, at this time there was no pressing need to fill a gap in funding as the president was at that moment in late February just making his request for funds to the Congress, and he expected prompt passage.

If the February shipment was too early for the diversion, the October shipment was too late. Congress had authorized the $100 million for the Contras in late June and funds had begun to flow in mid-October. This leaves the May sale, which occurred during the period when the Congress had rejected the president's request and bridging funds were most needed. In fact, the May arms shipment of *Hawk* missile spare parts recorded the largest sale, of $15 million.

According to Secord, after all payments were made to the CIA for the cost of the parts, shipping, and insurance, there was an estimated surplus of somewhere around $3 million. This was not far off from Walsh's estimate of $3.6 million and appears to be the likely point when funds were "diverted" to support for the Contras.[32] At the time, however, North mistakenly thought there would be a surplus of $12 million, enough to sustain the Contras in the field for five or six months and bridge the gap until Congress would vote to resume funding.

---

[31] Secord, *Honored and Betrayed*, 254.
[32] Ibid, 260.

As to a change of direction, there could only be a diversion if there was a specific purpose from which funds could have been diverted. The profits from arms sales were expressly dedicated to build up Secord's private company, the Enterprise, and support its activities, central to which was support for the Contras. The use of money for any activity which strengthened the Enterprise was wholly appropriate and therefore not a diversion.

Surplus funds from the May Iran arms sale were indeed used to support the Contras in their time of dire need, but it was not a diversion and was entirely legal. Secord, in effect a private donor, was free to use his funds in any way he wished. Secord had no contractual relationship with the U.S. government, was not even named in the January 17 finding, and operated on a handshake agreement. But this would not be the view of congressional Democrats who rushed to the attack when the initiative was exposed and insisted that all surplus funds from arms sales belonged to the government. No court ever validated that claim.

In March of 1986, determined to sustain the Contras, Reagan hit on the idea of using surplus monies from Iran arms sales. The idea of using surplus funds for other purposes had been floating around the NSC for a couple of months. So it was no surprise that it came up for consideration as Congress voted down the president's request, and conveniently just at the moment that the Iranian government proposed a new arms deal for Iran.

As recounted in the previous chapter, Poindexter had told North to break off contact with the Iranians and so from March 9 he had refused to accept any calls from either Gorbanifar or Kangarlu. In the interim, Gorbanifar had traveled to Tehran and returned with another idea, which he asked Nir to pass on to North.[33] Before North could respond, Kangarlu also communicated with him via the "phone-drop in Maryland which we had established for this purpose." He asked, "why we had not been in contact" and urged that we proceed expeditiously because conditions in Beirut were "deteriorating rapidly." A

---

[33] "North PROF note to McFarlane," March 20, 1986, *Tower Report*, B-85.

subsequent call led to the president's decision to resume negotiations on the *Hawk* spare parts package worked out earlier.[34] North then contacted Gorbanifar and arranged for him to come to Washington to negotiate a deal.

After meeting with Nir in London on April 2, Gorbanifar took the three and a half-hour supersonic *Concord* flight to Washington, arriving the next day. Upon arrival Gorbanifar joined North, Cave, Twetten, and Allen for an all-night session at a hotel in Herndon, Va., not far from CIA headquarters.[35] The U.S. team was composed of three CIA officers (although Cave was retired) and North. During their deliberations Gorbanifar called Kangarlu in Tehran several times to clarify various points.[36] The result was an agreement that would involve the sale of 240 *Hawk* spare parts, a high-level meeting of U.S. and Iranian leaders, and release of *all* of the remaining hostages "as soon as the U.S. delegation arrived in Tehran."[37]

Immediately afterward, North sent a memo to Poindexter "to forward to the President," detailing the terms of the agreement and how the profits from the sale would be distributed.[38] On April 7, the Iranian government was to deposit $17 million in the Israeli account in Geneva. The Israelis would retain $2 million for themselves and transfer $15 million to Lake Resources. Secord would transfer $3.65 million of it to the CIA account for the *Hawk* spare parts. Once paid for, the Defense Department would assemble the parts for transport.[39]

Kangarlu confirmed that when McFarlane and his team arrived in Tehran on April 20 Rafsanjani and his delegation would meet them. In a matter of hours the hostages would be released in Beirut and an Israeli cargo jet would deliver the *Hawk* spare parts to Bandar Abbas.

---

[34] Ibid, B-87.
[35] The *Iran-Contra Affair*, 224, omits Allen, while *Tower Report*, B-86, includes him as part of the negotiating team.
[36] Samuel Segev, The Iranian Triangle: The Untold Story of Israel's Role in the Iran-Contra Affair (New York: Free Press, 1988), 256.
[37] *Iran-Contra Affair*, 224.
[38] *Tower Report*, B-86.
[39] *Iran-Contra Affair*, 225.

With the hostage obstacle out of the way, the two teams would begin the process of reestablishing relations.

As for the surplus from the arms sale, North's memo continued, the $2 million withheld by the Israelis would be used to replace the 508 *TOWs* Israel sold to Iran in the fall of 1985. Twelve million dollars would be used

> to purchase critically needed supplies for the Nicaraguan Democratic Resistance Forces. This materiel is essential to cover shortages in resistance inventories resulting from their current offensives and Sandinista counter-attacks and to "bridge" the period between now and when Congressionally approved lethal assistance...can be delivered.[40]

(When the scandal erupted and investigators showed North this memo he "remembered that Poindexter requested drafting of the April memorandum about diversion." What Poindexter clearly meant by diversion was how much of a surplus there would be from the arms sale that could be used to support the Contras. Poindexter, however, denied directing North to prepare such a memorandum, insisting that he "directed North to put nothing in writing about the diversion." North, in turn, denied receiving this direction.

In a further twist, Poindexter went on to say that while he "admitted leading North to believe that the President had approved the plan...he [Poindexter] denied ever discussing it with the President." Parsing this dispute, it is North's account that rings true. Poindexter did in fact instruct North to draft a memorandum specifically "for Poindexter to forward to the president." Furthermore, the PROF computer system was the primary means by which these men communicated with each other between meetings, which meant that almost everything was in writing. North's voluminous memo output was proof enough to reject Poindexter's denial, which amounts to a

---

[40] *Tower Report*, B-88.

classical instance of a subordinate falling on his sword for his superior.)[41]

Curiously, North's arithmetic was slightly off, $3.65 million from $15 million was not $12 million, but $11.35 million. Immediately, however, there was a larger problem. The Iranian government failed to deposit funds on April 7, as agreed, but Gorbanifar called Allen the next day, the 8th, to tell him that he had "good news...an agreement had been reached in accordance with Washington's wishes."[42] The implication was that Kangarlu had sold the deal to the Iranian leadership after some difficulty and that the money would be forthcoming momentarily. Yet, another week passed with no deposit, a week in which momentous events occurred.

If the Iranian leadership was balking at handing over $17 million before the middle of the month, the American air strike on Libya, on April 14-15, positively spooked them. The Iranians immediately sought to put some distance between themselves and the United States by raising new demands. Within hours of the attack, Gorbanifar called Allen to pass on new terms from Kangarlu. He now wanted a meeting in Frankfurt before a meeting in Tehran, insisted on a sequential release of the hostages instead of their release all at once, and then said Iran would only begin the release process after all the spare parts had been delivered.[43] "If the U.S. did not deliver all the HAWK spares with the arrival of the U.S. delegation, only one hostage would be released." This was, Gorbanifar said, a "take it or leave it" proposition.[44]

After a series of frantic phone calls involving North, Nir, Gorbanifar, Kangarlu, and Allen, North proposed to Poindexter that he make a quick trip to Frankfurt to meet with the Iranian interlocutors. Poindexter, clearly angered by the delays, replied:

---

[41] *Iran-Contra Affair*, 226.
[42] C. Allen, "Conversation with [Gorbanifar]," April 8, 1986, *Tower Report*, B-90.
[43] C. Allen, "Conversation with Subject [Gorbanifar]," April 16, 1986, *Iran-Contra Affair*, 227 n.125.
[44] "North PROF note to Poindexter," April 16, 1986, *Tower Report*, B-91 n.65.

You may go ahead and go, but I want several points made clear to them. There are not to be any parts delivered until all the hostages are free in accordance with the plan that you laid out for me before. None of this half shipment before all are released crap. It is either all or nothing. Also, you may tell them that the President is getting very annoyed at their continual stalling. He will not agree to any more changes in the plan. Either they agree finally on the arrangements that have been discussed or we are going to permanently cut off all contact.[45]

Impact of the Libya Air Strike

Reagan and his aides apparently had not anticipated the impact the air strike on Libya would have on Iranian sensibilities, although Cave would come close to it later. In the immediate aftermath of the strike Gorbanifar put off the proposed meeting with Kangarlu in Frankfurt. As Allen and Nir attempted to get into contact with him to reschedule the meeting, other disturbing news arrived.

On April 18, the dead bodies of American hostage Peter Kilburn and British hostages, Leigh Douglas and Philip Padfield were found outside Beirut. Qadaffi had "bought" them from their captors and had them killed as a reprisal for the raid. A different group from the one that held the other American hostages had held Peter Kilburn. Nevertheless, reports about Qadaffi trying to buy the other hostages were unsettling.[46] Kilburn's case was especially galling, as North had attempted to cooperate with the CIA in freeing him in a ransom deal that had gone wrong just before the raid.[47] Had the Iranians been involved? If the Iranians controlled Hezbollah and could influence the hostage-takers, had they been involved in, or responsible for, the killing? These were unsettling questions that could jeopardize everything.

---

[45] "Poindexter PROF note to North," April 16, 1986, *Tower Report*, B-91.
[46] David C. Wills, The First War on Terrorism: Counter-Terrorism Policy During the Reagan Administration (Lanham: Rowman & Littlefield, 2003), 212.
[47] David C. Martin and John Walcott, *Best Laid Plans: The Inside Story of America's War Against Terrorism* (New York: Touchstone, 1988), 345-46.

After several days of intermittent contact and cancellation of another Frankfurt meeting because Kangarlu would not appear, Cave attempted to reconstruct what was happening. He believed that Kangarlu

> had probably received some kind of authority to cause the release of the hostages prior to our Libyan action and that the current delays and efforts to force new concessions are a consequence of internal disputes over what the Iranians should do about this matter in the wake of the U.S. action in Libya.[48]

Cave's interpretation was insightful and plausible, but crucially incorrect. His assumption that Tehran possessed some sort of "authority" that could bring about the release of the hostages had little or no foundation.[49] It was increasingly understood that Imad Mugniyeh held the hostages, but the flawed assumption was that Hezbollah controlled and directed his actions, which was not the case, as we have seen. This assumption was the big disconnect in the American leadership's understanding of the dynamic interconnectivity of the terrorist network.

Cave's surmise that the Libyan strike had triggered "internal disputes" about how to deal with the hostages was closer to the mark, but confused the issue. The question of how Tehran could position itself between the United States and the Soviet Union was an ongoing issue within the Iranian leadership since the beginning of the year and not the result of the Libyan strike. It had become increasingly apparent that Iranian strategy had shifted from seeking to reestablish relations with the United States to taking an equidistant position between the two superpowers.

In fact, the Tehran stall pre-dated the Libyan strike by two months, although the attack had clearly strengthened the Iranian leadership's

---

[48] "North PROF note to McFarlane," April 21, 1986, *Tower Report*, B-91.
[49] "George Cave Deposition," *Iran-Contra Affair*, B, vol.3, 844. In fact, he would shortly change his view to say that Tehran had influence but no control over the hostages.

resolve. The reason for the stall was the Iranian government's decision to maintain a middle position and also began before Cave himself became involved. This was why Iranian officials would not meet with the Americans and the government would not advance its own funds for weapons. Instead, Tehran forced Gorbanifar to scramble to find the money to pay for the weapons.

Indeed, during April two of his deals blew up in his face. The first was a U.S. Customs sting involving Cyrus Hashemi. Hashemi, working as an informant, cooperated in the arrest of six Israelis, including an Israeli general, and several others ostensibly attempting to purchase arms for Iran. Gorbanifar, implicated as a financial backer for the arms dealers, had been arrested briefly by the Swiss police, but released.[50]

Gorbanifar's second operation involved an attempt to involve British business magnate Roland 'Tiny' Rowland in a large sale of arms and other goods to Iran. Gorbanifar, Khashoggi, and Nir approached the British entrepreneur in early April with a proposal to use his company, Lonrho, as an umbrella organization for the transaction. The trio claimed that the White House had secretly approved the sales, had cut out the State Department, and that the point man was Poindexter.[51]

Dubious, Rowland checked out the story with the embassy and Ambassador Charles Price passed word back to the department. Shultz, as might be expected, "expressed strong opposition on legal and moral grounds as well as concern for the President." Rowland was advised, "to stay out of the plan" to sell arms to Iran. But Shultz, feigning ignorance of the president's arms sale plan, confronted Poindexter, who acknowledged there was "a shred of truth" to the assertion of White House involvement with Gorbanifar and the others, but denied that the approach to Rowland was "our deal."[52]

---

[50] *Iran-Contra Affair*, 226. See also, Michael Fredericks, *The Octopus Eagle* (Tallahassee: Loiry Publishing, 1987) and Ari Ben-Menashe, *Profits of War*, (New York: Sheridan Square, 1992), 177-84.
[51] *Iran-Contra Affair*, 229.
[52] Ibid.

Shultz was in Tokyo with the president for an economic summit in early May. When informed of the approach to Rowland and although claiming that he sought out the president, Shultz never spoke to him about it. But he did express his anger and frustration to Don Regan, demanding "he should go to the president and get him to end this matter once and for all."[53] Regan, blindsided, "expressed alarm and promised to raise the matter with the President."[54] In truth, as Walsh noted, Shultz and his aides were monitoring every move made by North and Poindexter in the Iran arms plan, looking for opportunities to derail it.[55]

By the time the Rowland episode broke, North had finally arranged to meet Gorbanifar in London, even though Kangarlu still refused to leave Tehran. (Poindexter told North to travel *incognito* to London and stay away from the embassy so as not to inflame Shultz.)[56] North noted to Poindexter that he and Cave "intend to tell [Gorbanifar] that unless a deposit is made by the end of the week, the whole operation is off."[57]

When they met the next day, May 6, at the Churchill Hotel, Gorbanifar confidently assured them that "financing had been arranged," but, he said, he would deposit the funds in an account controlled by Nir, not Secord.[58] Again, this seemed to be a way for Iran to keep distance from direct contact with the Americans and disguise the fact that the money was coming from Khashoggi not the Iranian government. Their discussion of the arms package was now expanded to include two radars, to sweeten the pot, which pushed the CIA's cost up to $12.6 million. Secord's markup raised the price to

---

[53] *Tower Report*, B-93.
[54] *Iran-Contra Affair*, 229.
[55] Walsh, *Final Report*, 340-41.
[56] "Poindexter PROF note to North," May 5, 1986, *Tower Report*, B-94. It was, of course, not true as the *Iran-Contra Affair, 229,* claims, "Shultz would remain in the dark." Walsh, *Final Report*, 340-43, shows definitively that Shultz was kept continuously informed of the initiative's progress, or lack thereof.
[57] "North PROF note to Poindexter," May 5, 1986, in *Tower Report*, B-94.
[58] Ibid.

$15 million and Gorbanifar's much higher to $23.6 million, $8.6 million over Secord's.[59]

North emphasized that the procedure must follow Poindexter's sequencing: a high-level meeting, release of hostages, and then delivery of the 240 spare parts. He also expected the Iranians to have sent a delegation to Beirut by the time the Americans arrived in Tehran. Thus, the Iranians would arrange for the release of the hostages in Beirut at the same time that the Americans were negotiating with them in Tehran. If all went as planned, the parts would be delivered.

Gorbanifar confirmed Kangarlu's earlier offer that top Iranian officials would meet with the Americans, but now he also sweetened the pot. Not only would Rafsanjani lead the Iranian delegation, he said, but it would also include Prime Minister Moussavi, President Khamenei, and possibly also Khomeini's son, Ahmed, and conservative leader, Ayatollah Farsi.[60] These arrangements were even better than those negotiated during the February meetings and should have raised eyebrows. Even heads of state would not be afforded as high-level a meeting as was being promised.

When Cave got on the phone with Kangarlu to confirm the terms of the deal, however, a "major snag" immediately arose. Kangarlu demanded delivery of spare parts first, followed by a meeting, and then release of the hostages—the exact reverse of the American position. Indeed, Kangarlu wanted the Americans to bring the entire parts package with them. When that was rejected, after much haggling, they agreed the delegation would bring as many parts as the plane could hold. Only then would the Iranians send a delegation to Beirut "to barter for the release of the hostages," which clearly implied that there was no guarantee that all would be released and probably none while the Americans were in Tehran.[61]

---

[59] *Iran-Contra Affair*, 230.
[60] "George Cave Deposition," *Iran-Contra Affair*, Appendix B, volume 3, 627-28. Cave was quite "skeptical" that they would actually meet with Iran's highest leaders.
[61] *Iran-Contra Affair*, 230.

Given this impasse, North's PROF note to Poindexter when he had returned to Washington was either a blatant breach of discipline, or something else, which will be discussed below. He wrote, "we have succeeded. Deposit being made tomorrow....Release of hostages set...in sequence you have specified....Thank God—he answers prayers."[62] North had claimed success where there had been no success. The Iranians had not agreed to Poindexter's sequence, yet North's erroneous report asserting otherwise would be the basis for McFarlane's negotiating instructions in Iran.[63]

North expected Gorbanifar to deposit $17 million on May 8, but no money arrived for nearly a week, and when it did there was only $15 million, and that was deposited on May 14 by Khashoggi, not the Iranian government. One of the checks for $5 million bounced, delaying confirmed receipt of the funds until May 16. The Israelis deposited $1.6 million for the replacement *TOWs* on the 15th.[64]

The "rubber check" precipitated a blunt exchange between Secord and Gorbanifar, with the general declaring that he could no longer "tolerate" Gorbanifar's deceitful tactics and would recommend that he be "terminated." Gorbanifar misunderstood the remark to mean that Secord wanted him killed, which amused the general, who later explained that he only wanted to end all dealings with the Iranian.[65]

Secord's angry response had been based on the assumption that the Iranian government was providing the funds and Gorbanifar was skimming off the top. It was only later, *after* McFarlane's failed mission to Tehran that he discovered Adnan Khashoggi had provided the funding for Gorbanifar, not the Iranian government—"a bit of

---

[62] "North PROF note to Poindexter," May 8, 1986, *Tower* Report, B-94 and *Iran-Contra Affair*, 231.
[63] Jane Mayer and Doyle McManus, *Landslide: The Unmaking of the President* (Boston: Houghton Mifflin, 1988), 226, come to the same conclusion, observing, "as North knew, the Iranians had not committed themselves specifically to release all the hostages. But North told Poindexter they had, and Poindexter so briefed McFarlane—which would lead to one of the major misunderstandings of the Tehran visit."
[64] Walsh, *Final Report*, 169.
[65] Secord, *Honored and Betrayed*, 261.

information that, all by itself, would've caused me to slam on the brakes and stop the transaction for security reasons, making the debate over McFarlane's trip academic."[66]

North, however, did know beforehand that Khashoggi was financing the arms transaction, but did not disclose this information to Secord. As he reported to Poindexter in early May before the meeting with Gorbanifar in London: "We know that Khashoggi is the principal fund raiser for Gorba and that only after Gorba delivers a cargo does he get paid by the Iranians."[67] Of course, the only way for North to "know" how the funding worked was from information provided by U.S. government agencies, particularly the CIA and U. S. Treasury, which were tracking the money flows.

In any case, unaware of the origin of Gorbanifar's funds, Secord deposited $6.5 million into the CIA's Geneva account on May 16, an amount that covered the cost of the spare parts ($4.3 million) and the 508 *TOWs*, but not the radar purchase, which was set aside for the time being.[68] That left roughly $10 million available in Lake Resources accounts. Secord, in later attempting to account for the funds, explained that the cost of transportation, crews, and miscellaneous came to $1.2 million, and $900,000 was set aside to repay Israel for the original $1 million given the previous November, which, according to Secord, left between $8.1 million and $7.9 million. Then, after setting aside $4 million for self-insurance for the planes, the remaining $3.9 million was "surplus."[69]

In attempting to explain away this surplus, Secord attempted to do some financial juggling. He double-counted the transportation, crew, and miscellaneous expenses, which were actually built into the CIA price and his claim of a $900,000 repayment to the Israelis was made up out of whole cloth. Schwimmer had told him months earlier that the funds were his to use as he saw fit and need not be repaid. As we shall

---

[66] Ibid, 283.
[67] "North PROF note to Poindexter," May 5, 1986, *Tower Report*, B-93-94.
[68] *Iran-Contra Affair*, 231 and *Tower Report*, B-94 n.66.
[69] Secord, *Honored and Betrayed*, 260.

see, at this moment there was actually over $6 million in surplus funds available for the Contras.

There was yet another aspect to this shell game, the radars. The CIA price of $12.6 million included the cost of the radars, as well as the spare parts and the *TOWs,* but the explanation for setting aside the radar purchase was because "Iranian funds were never sent for the radars."[70] It was literally true that *Iranian* funds were not sent, but $15 million had been deposited in Lake Resources accounts, sufficient to cover the cost of the radars, but, as noted, Secord only deposited $6.5 million in the CIA account. A second explanation was that the Department of Defense refused to sell the radars because the request "came only from the CIA," not from the White House.[71] Both "explanations" were clearly specious and suggest an effort to explain away missing "surplus" funds spent on the Contras.

On May 16, just as Secord was depositing the funds in the CIA Swiss account activating the arms sale to Iran, the president was calling an NSPG meeting to address the issue of soliciting funds for the Contras. The meeting included not only principals, but also note takers. Thus, North, Alan Fiers, Raymond Burghardt, Edward Djerejian, Craig Fuller and several other aides were sitting along the wall behind the principals.[72] When Shultz said he thought the Congress would procrastinate on authorizing the $100 million, he was asked to "prepare a list" of countries to approach for assistance. The secretary suggested that the Saudis should be asked to help, unaware of the fact that the president already had solicited $32 million from King Fahd.[73] Shultz's suggestion was quietly shelved. (McFarlane would tell him later).

As the discussion progressed, Walsh reveals, the president "startled the group in the situation room by asking, 'can't Ollie find funds until

---

[70] *Iran-Contra Affair*, 231 and 235 n.157.
[71] Ibid, 236 n.185.
[72] Scott Armstrong et al., The Chronology: The Documented Day-by-Day Account of the Secret Military Assistance to Iran and the Contras (New York: Warner Books, 1987), 368.
[73] *Iran-Contra Affair*, 231.

we get the hundred million dollars?'"[74] The president's outburst stunned those in attendance, especially the note takers. Although Don Regan immediately changed the subject and insured that the president's question did not appear in the minutes of the meeting, it was clear especially to the note takers in attendance that the president had let slip the fact that he was deeply involved in the search for funds. Furthermore, he clearly not only knew who North was, but also that he was fully aware of his efforts to obtain funds for the Contras.

North, having just received word from Secord of the deposit of funds into Lake Resources before the meeting, was about to respond to the president's question when Poindexter hushed him up.[75] Afterward, North sent Poindexter a PROF note stating that the Nicaraguan resistance "now has more than $6M available for immediate disbursement [which] reduces the need to go to third countries for help."[76] In his reply, the national security adviser explained that he had hushed him up because "I just didn't want you to bring it up at NSPG. I guessed at what you were going to say."[77]

Incredibly, in yet another instance of protecting the president, Poindexter later claimed, "he did not tell the president of the sudden availability of 'bridge funds.'"[78] Since the House rebuff of the president's $100 million request in late March, Reagan had been desperately searching the world for funds. Indeed, the very purpose of the May 16 meeting was to brainstorm fundraising possibilities, in part, because as far as the president then knew Iranian funds had yet to come in. It strains credulity to believe that Poindexter, having just learned of the answer to the president's predicament, would not have informed him of it.

---

[74] Lawrence Walsh, *Firewall: The Iran-Contra Conspiracy and Cover-Up*, (New York: Norton, 1997), 286.
[75] Mayer and McManus, *Landslide*, 227.
[76] "North PROF note to Poindexter," May 16, 1986, *Tower Report*, B-96. The *Iran-Contra Affair*, 231, puts it slightly differently, having North say: "there is now 6M available for the resistance forces."
[77] "Poindexter PROF note to North," May 17, 1986, *Tower Report*, B-96.
[78] *Iran-Contra Affair*, 231.

The Tehran Set-up

The secret mission to Tehran, May 25-28, was originally designed to bring about the immediate release of the remaining hostages and establish the beginning of a new relationship with Iran, but, by the time it occurred the president had dramatically altered its purpose. It had been clear to the president since the end of January that the Iranians were stalling, trying to shift to an equidistant position between Washington and Moscow, while still seeking weapons from the United States.[79] He also understood that Tehran had little or no control over Imad Mugniyeh and therefore could not obtain the release of the hostages, except as a result of a negotiation with him. Thus, he knew that the stated objectives of the January 17 finding were beyond realization at this time. Only a change in Iranian policy would reopen the possibility of success.

Therefore, sometime during this period the president decided to change tack. Reagan had faced similar problems on three occasions in the first term when Helmut Schmidt, Zenko Suzuki, and Deng Xiaoping had all sought to maintain a middle position between the United States and the Soviet Union. In each case, Reagan had shifted tactics after initial policy had failed and brought those nations into closer alignment with the United States.[80] Admittedly, the broken Iranian-American relationship represented an added level of difficulty, but the structural problem was the same.

Also the same was the vehement opposition of the new world order faction to any improvement in relations with Iran. To deal with his internal opposition, Reagan drew the same play from the playbook he used against Haig, when he sent the former secretary of state to Beijing in 1981.[81] After the secretary quashed the proposed plan to develop a strategic partnership with Beijing, the president then

---

[79] See chapter 8 *passim*.
[80] See Richard C. Thornton, *The Reagan Revolution, II: Rebuilding the Western Alliance* (Victoria: Trafford, 2005), chapters 3 through 8.
[81] See Ibid, and the author's *The Reagan Revolution, I: The Politics of U.S. Foreign Policy* (Victoria: Trafford, 2003), chapter 2.

excluded him from the action, taking control of the China issue to negotiate the August 17 communiqué that established the basis for future U.S.-China relations.

The president used the same play now by naming McFarlane to head the mission to Tehran. In doing so, the president understood that it put him into position to insure its failure, which, however, would then justify exclusion of the new world order faction from any future involvement. Indeed, McFarlane's 'all or nothing' negotiating instructions, and what he was told to expect from his counterparts, guaranteed a deadlock in Tehran.

The president's decision explains the curiously erroneous note North sent to Poindexter after the May 6 meeting with Gorbanifar in London, when the impasse with Tehran had become glaringly evident. North's false PROF note to Poindexter that the Iranians had agreed with the president's terms, when they had not, was part of the plan to set up the new world order faction into believing that a deal was possible. The mission would, however, also serve to demonstrate American *bona fides*, if and when Tehran decided to seek better relations at a later date, and also *inter alia* provide the necessary bridge funds for the Contras.

North's note to Poindexter had not been sent immediately following the London meeting, but only after he had returned to Washington on May 8. North thus had ample time to discuss with Poindexter what the content of his note should be before he sent it. It was vital to show that the meeting had been a success because his note would be part of the negotiating record Poindexter would show to McFarlane when he briefed him before he left for Tehran. The president also met with him prior to his trip.[82] It is obvious that only the prospect of success would persuade McFarlane to agree to undertake what was a very risky mission.

The irony was that both Reagan and McFarlane thought the odds were small that the meeting could succeed, but diverged on the reason for having it. Reagan saw it as earnest money for the future, while

---

[82] Armstrong et al., *The Chronology*, 375.

McFarlane thought that there was an eighty percent chance that this was "just another elaborate con" by the Iranians and hoped that by going he could convince the president to terminate the initiative, this time "once and for all."[83] In other words, McFarlane's intent was to kill the initiative.

Reagan agreed to permit newly appointed head of NSC Political-Military Affairs, Howard Teicher, to be a part of the group, because of his "past relationship with McFarlane...," but excluded him from any role in preparation for the trip, because, as North told him, he "did not have a need to know." [84] Both McFarlane and Teicher opposed the participation of Amiram Nir, but acquiesced in deference to Prime Minister Peres, who pointed out that the Israelis were after all providing planes, warehouse space, and a forward base for the operation.[85] The group that flew to Tehran from Tel Aviv was McFarlane, North, Cave, Teicher, Nir, a CIA communication specialist, and two pilots. A second communications specialist would man a comm-link in Tel Aviv to permit secure, real time contact between Tehran and the White House.

McFarlane was not informed that his plane would also be carrying one palette of spare parts and there is a discrepancy in the record regarding the total spare parts package. The congressional report states that a total of 13 pallets were shipped to Israel. The McFarlane aircraft carried one to Tehran and a second plane was to deliver the remaining twelve, pending release of the hostages.[86] Cave, however, said that there were only four pallets in total, the McFarlane aircraft carrying

---

[83] Robert C. McFarlane, *Special Trust* (New York: Cadell & Davies, 1994), 54.
[84] Howard Teicher and Gayle Radley Teicher, *Twin Pillars to Desert Storm* (New York: William Morrow, 1993), 363-364. Howard Teicher was the newly appointed head of NSC Political-Military Affairs. When the crisis broke in November, a "senior White House official" would describe him as the "mastermind" of the whole affair! (see p. 372).
[85] Ibid, 365.
[86] *Iran-Contra Affair*, 232.

one.[87] Depending on which is correct, McFarlane either brought with him one fourth of the total package, or one thirteenth.

Iran's complex agenda, however, disrupted the proceedings from the start. The Iranians wanted no strategic relationship with Washington, but did want to keep the channels open to procure weapons. The Iranians also knew they could not deliver the hostages as the Americans demanded, but claimed they could because it guaranteed Washington's continued interest. Both sides' objectives were diametrically opposite. The Iranians demanded delivery of weapons before anything else, while McFarlane demanded release of the hostages before delivery of weapons.

Thus, from the first moments after arrival, the American group became the objects of a carefully contrived Iranian negotiating approach. This meant, in the first instance, repudiating any prior agreement and eventually renegotiating another, which they also could not, or would not, honor. The procedure was intentionally intimidating and humiliating to the Americans, who were taken aback by their treatment, but it was designed to browbeat them into submitting to Iranian demands for weapons.

As the Iranians wanted no strategic relationship they denied they had agreed to ministerial meetings and would not permit their leaders to meet with the Americans, sending only bureaucratic functionaries to deal with them. As they could not deliver all of the hostages they denied they had agreed to do so. Finally, as their objective was to obtain the spare parts, they demanded that they be delivered before any steps were taken to gain the release of the hostages.

Gorbanifar had preceded the McFarlane team to Tehran by three days, in more than enough time to be instructed in the role he was to play. He would be the greedy messenger, who deceived both sides in the interests of his own profit, and be blamed by both sides for his deception. Although this characterization fit Gorbanifar perfectly,

---

[87] "George Cave deposition," Ibid, Appendix B, volume 3, 629. Gorbanifar, in a July 8 letter to his Iranian chief, said that the Americans "brought more than one fifth of the requested spare parts...," *Tower Report*, B-133.

Iranian negotiating tactics should not be blamed on him. Gorbanifar was the convenient scapegoat blamed by both sides.

There was no question about the arrival time of the aircraft, or the agreement upon which the trip had been arranged. In the aftermath of the failed mission, on July 8 Gorbanifar wrote a letter to his superiors attempting to repair the damage and reminding them of what had happened in Tehran. He revealed that the Iranian negotiating strategy had, indeed, in McFarlane's words, been "just another elaborate con." Gorbanifar declared that

> prior to the arrival of the US team and myself in Tehran on 25 May 1986, there was full agreement that upon arrival of the high-ranking US delegation in Tehran, bringing some of the requested items, the Iranian authorities would begin immediately mediating for the release of all American hostages in Beirut, all together, and collectively. And that after this, the remaining items requested by Iran would arrive in Tehran.[88]

Into Tehran

The Iranian ploy commenced the moment the unmarked Israeli 707 touched down at Merabad airport outside Tehran. There was no one to receive them and they were forced to languish in the formerly resplendent, but now shabby V.I.P. lounge for over an hour and a half before Gorbanifar arrived with Kangarlu, and a crew of revolutionary guards, claiming that the plane had arrived early. McFarlane, according to one account, had expected to have been met at the airport by Rafsanjani himself and transported to the meeting place in a motorcade.[89]

After taking their passports (all of the group traveled with fake Irish passports), confiscating a cake that North brought for Gorbanifar's mother, and decorative pistols intended as gifts for the

---

[88] *Tower Report*, B-133.
[89] Theodore Draper, *A Very Thin Line: The Iran-Contra Affairs* (New York: Hill and Wang, 1991), 315.

Iranian leadership, the hosts bundled the Americans into cars for a quick ride downtown to the Independence Hotel, the former Tehran Hilton. This took the Americans aback, as the agreement had called for them to be housed in private lodging outside the city.[90]

At the hotel came another unpleasant surprise. Just as the Americans were settling in to the top (15th) floor of the hotel, a scuffle broke out in the parking lot. One group of revolutionary guards got into a shoving match with another and word filtered up to the Americans their guards had foiled an attempt to arrest them.[91] In all likelihood, this was a staged event designed to raise the anxiety level among the Americans, emphasize their isolation, and soften them up for the hard line the Iranians were about to take.

But not immediately. Although Gorbanifar kept reassuring McFarlane that everything was progressing smoothly and release of the hostages was imminent, no Iranian interlocutor appeared at the hotel until 5:00 P.M., nine hours after their arrival. Worse, the Iranian official who arrived was not Rafsanjani, or some other high official; it was a deputy prime minister introduced as Ali Najavi. His name was probably a pseudonym like those of other persons who drifted in and out of the hotel—and the Irish names used by the Americans. The Iranians, however, knew the identities of the Americans and Nir; Gorbanifar had told them.

Although disappointed, McFarlane went through his brief, emphasizing U.S. willingness to assist Iran, warning of Soviet designs on Iran, and the extreme unlikelihood that Moscow would permit Iraq's defeat in the war. He also put forward the U.S. understanding of the sequence to be followed involving release of the hostages before anything else. "We are pleased that informal talks resulted in agreement on release of American hostages. Once that is completed we can begin serious talks."[92]

---

[90] Segev, *Iranian Triangle*, 272.
[91] Draper, *Very Thin Line*, 315.
[92] Howard Teicher, "Memorandum of Conversation," May 25, 1986, *Tower Report*, B-103.

The Iranian official responded by asserting Iran's core position "we don't want to ally with East or West, but that doesn't mean we don't want relations." He then surprised McFarlane by disclosing they had already off-loaded the palette from the plane without authorization and declared, "we expected more than what came on the aircraft." McFarlane's startled reply was that "we could not bring it all on the plane. But the rest can be brought forward."[93]

The Iranian tossed two more surprises. First, regarding the hostages, he said that Iran "will send a delegation to Beirut to solve that problem." This, too, startled McFarlane, who had been led to believe that the Iranians had already sent people to Beirut for that purpose. This meant that gaining their release while he was still in Tehran would be extremely unlikely.

Then, Najavi said the Iranian military were suspicious of the individual remaining aboard the aircraft because the plane was on the military side of the airfield, and suggested that he come to the hotel. McFarlane immediately objected, saying "we can't do that....He performs communications functions."[94] To acquiesce would have meant that they would be completely cut off from contact with the outside world.

McFarlane did not take the exchange well, exploding repeatedly, venting his frustrations. Regarding the hostages, he exclaimed, "I have come. There should be an act of goodwill by Iran." Then again, regarding the single palette "I have come from U.S.A....I did not have to bring anything. We can leave now!" Najavi merely responded that he was not a decision maker. "We just give you a message and take your message."[95] In his reporting memo to Poindexter, McFarlane

---

[93] Ibid, B-104. George Cave, "deposition," *Iran-Contra Affair*, Appendix B, volume 3, 837-38. Cave noted that the pilots had told them that while the Iranians had unloaded the palette they had not opened it, so he was at a loss to explain how Najavi could have determined what was inside the crate, or its condition.
[94] *Tower Report,* B-105.
[95] Ibid.

said, "the incompetence of the Iranian government to do business requires a rethinking on our part..."[96]

The next afternoon, at 3:30 P.M., Najavi arrived again and McFarlane decided to force the issue. He declared that

> There are crucial matters related to the Soviet Union, Afghanistan and Iraq that we should discuss. But we cannot begin to address these matters until preliminary problems are solved. Perhaps your government is not ready to deal with these larger issues. Maybe we should wait for another day. But I must depart tomorrow night. I would like to meet with your Ministers. But I cannot if preliminary problems have not been solved. I have no more to say.

McFarlane closed the meeting by insisting that he wished to meet with ministers. "No other meetings are necessary." To Najavi's reply that an "important authority" would be arriving shortly, McFarlane said, "he would not meet the person. He came to meet with Ministers. The staff can meet this other person."[97]

This "other person" was Ali Najafabadi, Chairman of the Majlis Foreign Affairs Committee and a senior adviser to Ayatollah Rafsanjani. Although scheduled to arrive at four he did not appear until after nine that evening. There can be no doubt McFarlane's adamant refusal to meet with anyone but a "minister" had an impact on his delay.

McFarlane's decision to stay in his room left the floor to North, who, along with Cave, Teicher, and Nir engaged in a lengthy discussion with Najafabadi, a fluent English speaker who exuded confidence and a sense of power. In McFarlane's absence, North laid out the internal U.S. political situation being careful not to be too explicit because Teicher was present taking notes.

---

[96] Ibid, B-101.
[97] Ibid, B-106.

Immediately after exchanging pleasantries, North warned "there are factions in our governments that don't want something like this to succeed." His next words were "that is why McFarlane grew angry when things didn't take place as I suggested they would." If North seemed to be suggesting that he and McFarlane were on opposite sides, Najafabadi certainly understood it that way. After his meeting with McFarlane the next day, he proposed that he and North work out terms of agreement without McFarlane![98]

North followed up his warning about an opposing faction in the U.S. government with an offer to provide a secure communications system to fool the Soviets, who were "trying to find out" what we were doing and "will make a major effort to expose us." Then, North offered to sweeten the spare parts package by including the radars back into the mix. "If your government can cause the release of the Americans held in Beirut, 10 hours after they are released, aircraft will arrive with the HAWK missile parts. Within 10 days of deposit [of funds], two radars will be delivered."[99]

As their discussion continued, Najafabadi said, "we have the same problem that you have. Some here oppose relations with the U.S." Moreover, "we see the Russian danger much more than you....We feel it, touch it, see it. It is not easy to sleep next to an elephant you have wounded."

In his next breath, Najafabadi demolished the twin assumptions on which the trip had been based. Claiming a "misunderstanding," he said when we agreed to the meeting "it did not mean a direct dialogue would occur on the spot. It is too early at this stage." Furthermore, "there was no agreement that when McFarlane led the team it would lead to Ministerial meetings. Let us turn the key in a way that will work." Then, dropping a bombshell, he said "We don't see the release of hostages as the key."[100]

---

[98] Howard Teicher, "Memorandum of Conversation," May 26, 1986, in Ibid, B-107.
[99] Ibid, B-108.
[100] Ibid, B-109.

North said nothing about the hostages, but protested that he "was told" there would be ministerial meetings. When Najafabadi questioned his source, North said that Gorbanifar "had stated that the U.S. team would meet with the senior leadership." But Najafabadi's retort was "the last phone call did not mention Ministerial meetings. We did not agree to such meetings for McFarlane. We keep our word."[101]

Najafabadi's reference to the "last phone call" was undoubtedly reference to the May 6 meeting where the final arrangements for the trip had been confirmed. Recall, that was the meeting that produced North's false memo declaring that both sides had reached full agreement on the terms of the meeting. Here was further confirmation that that was not the case and that the memo was part of the set up of McFarlane.

Najafabadi had an inducement of his own, declaring that Rafsanjani had said officially that Iran was willing to purchase weapons from the United States and that Khomeini had said Iran was "ready to establish relations with all the world except Israel." There was a "$2.5 billion" deal on the table, "but you have to remove the obstacles." North asked whether a "secret meeting" could be arranged with Rafsanjani, but Najafabadi said no, it was too soon. McFarlane "would have to wait or come back" after some period of time, "after the hostages are free and the deliveries are completed." The Iranian ended their conversation, saying "we sent a man to Lebanon" and hope to have "news" by tomorrow.[102]

The next morning, Tuesday May 27, Najafabadi arrived at ten with news from Beirut. It was not good. Mugniyeh (we now know) demanded that before any hostages were released Israel must withdraw from both the Golan Heights and Southern Lebanon; Shiite prisoners taken by Colonel Lahad, commander of Israel's Southern Lebanon Army, must be returned to Beirut; and the Dawa 17 prisoners in

---

[101] Ibid, B-110.
[102] Ibid, B-110-11.

Kuwait must be freed. Finally, all expenses incurred by the hostage taking must be paid.[103]

The Iranian immediately tried to soften these clearly impossible demands, declaring, "we told them these conditions must be reduced. We can't make this work....We are negotiating other conditions [and] we are hopeful..." However, he then attempted to couple the spare parts issue to it by complaining that Washington "should" deliver the rest. The implication was that delivery of the spare parts package would lead to a reduction of terrorist demands. What it really meant, however, was that there was now a third negotiating partner, a negotiating trap that promised indefinite delay.[104]

At this point, McFarlane, who was listening to the exchange, called down to invite Najafabadi to his suite. In a session lasting almost three hours he reiterated his brief about the Soviet threat and the agreement they had, stressing the sequence of hostage release first, followed by delivery of the spare parts. Najafabadi demanded to know "just who had agreed to these terms?" When McFarlane named Gorbanifar and Kangarlu, Najafabadi declared "these were not the terms as he understood them," insisting "all deliveries [were] to occur before any release took place."[105]

When Najafabadi produced a letter from Gorbanifar purporting to support his interpretation, McFarlane brought in Cave, who pointed out that the letter was entirely in Gorbanifar's handwriting and bore no mark of American input. His bluff called, Najafabadi "asked for a break to confer with his colleagues." McFarlane agreed, but "hoping to build a little fire under them," reiterated that they had to leave that night. McFarlane's "judgment [was] that they are in a state of great upset, schizophrenic over their wish to get more from the deal but sobered to the fact that their interlocutors may have misled them." [106]

---

[103] Howard Teicher, "Memorandum of Conversation," May 27, 1986, Ibid, B-112.
[104] Ibid.
[105] Ibid, B-113-14.
[106] Ibid, B-114.

In retrospect, Najafabadi's request for a break to consult with his colleagues marked a turning point in the negotiation. Now faced with a deadline, with their bluff called, from the resumption of the talks that afternoon Najafabadi became much more conciliatory. Before the talks resumed, however, Gorbanifar, who "did not seem concerned that his duplicity had been unmasked," arranged for his mother to prepare a sumptuous lunch for the visitors, "their only good meal of the trip."[107] During the meal, Gorbanifar took Cave aside to ask him to confirm to the Iranians, if they asked, that the $24.5 million price tag for the weapons was correct. Cave asked North about it and the two of them questioned Nir. The Israeli reassured them that the price was correct, involving "other deals" and "enormous expenses."[108]

When Najafabadi returned at 5:00 P.M. to resume their negotiations, at first he tried one last time to obtain agreement on the delivery-first scheme. "If the plane arrives before tomorrow morning, the hostages will be free by noon," he said. But McFarlane wouldn't budge, responding "...release the hostages, advise us, and [we] will deliver the weapons." The Iranian simply said "OK," and then asked for the "staff to work out an agreement." By "staff" he meant North and Cave. He wondered, "perhaps if we can reach agreement on this the staff can stay and complete the work?" McFarlane's response to this request was to say, "I will seek the president's decision, [but] I cannot know what he will say."[109] The meeting ended at 6:00 P.M. (In fact, McFarlane would not seek the president's decision.)

When Najafabadi returned at 9:30 P.M. North presented a 6-point draft proposal for their consideration. It was a restatement of the American position, stipulating that the plane carrying the spare parts will depart Tel Aviv at 0100, May 28, to arrive in Tehran at 0900. The Iranians will "cause the release" of the hostages "not later than 0400." If the hostages are not safely in the hands of U.S. authorities by 0400

---

[107] Mayer and McManus, *Landslide*, 240-41.
[108] Ibid.
[109] Howard Teicher, "Memorandum of Conversation," May 27, 1986, in *Tower Report*, B-115.

the plane "will be turned around." If the hostages are released the U.S. government will deliver two radar sets within ten days of receiving payment for same.[110]

The final two points committed the two governments to continuation of a "secret" political dialogue on the Soviet threat, Afghanistan, Nicaragua and other agreed topics "until such time as both sides agree to make such a dialogue public." To facilitate this dialogue, the U.S. government shall "provide a secure channel of communications between our two governments."[111]

After reading it, the Iranians talked animatedly among themselves, until Najafabadi asked plaintively, "how are we supposed to free the hostages by 0400?" When North reminded them they had offered to gain their release by noon, Najafabadi said, Yes, but "it is now late," and switched topics to ask about the Dawa 17. North said that the U.S. could issue a statement about making every effort to insure "just and fair treatment" for the Shiite prisoners, but could not interfere in the internal affairs of Kuwait.[112]

At around 11:00 P.M., McFarlane took Najafabadi aside for a private discussion. Half an hour later, he emerged looking grim. "Let's pack up and go," he said, "they're just stringing us along."[113] But North replied that they could not depart because the plane had not yet been refueled. Semi-stranded, with a failed negotiation, the Americans fumed as they began to pack up.

At 2:00 A.M., Najafabadi returned again, pleading for a few more hours, until 6:00 A.M. They should be able to "get an answer on the hostages by then." McFarlane said, OK, we'll give you until six-thirty and, if "you give us a time we will launch the aircraft so that it will

---

[110] George Cave, "Record of Meetings," in Ibid, B-118-19.
[111] Ibid.
[112] Howard Teicher, "Memorandum of Conversation," May 27, 1986, Ibid, B-116, claims that North also offered to "achieve the release" of the prisoners, but Cave emphatically disputed it. According to Cave, North did not "say anything about the release of...prisoners." See "George Cave Deposition," *Iran-Contra Affair*, Appendix B, volume 3, 869.
[113] Mayer and McManus, *Landslide*, 242.

land here two hours after the hostages are in U.S. custody."[114] Najafabadi said he would be back in touch before six.

What happened next is filled with controversy. McFarlane accused North of launching the plane from Tel Aviv without his authorization; North claimed he sent a message to launch the plane to Dick Secord "with McFarlane's permission."[115] It is Secord, however, who reconciles these otherwise irreconcilable claims and in the process exposes McFarlane's attempt to blame North and Gorbanifar for the failure of the mission.

Secord says, "shortly after midnight on the 28th I received a message to launch...the second aircraft...but to be ready to turn it around on command."[116] The flight from Tel Aviv to Tehran would take about eight hours along a route that went over the Red Sea, around the Arabian Peninsula, and then north to Tehran.

McFarlane claimed that North sent the message to launch while he was asleep, but the time difference of one-and-a-half hours between Tel Aviv and Tehran makes this highly unlikely.[117] Two o'clock in the morning in Tehran was 12:30 A.M. in Tel Aviv. As noted, Najafabadi had returned at 2:00 A.M. to plead for more time. Thus, McFarlane could not have been asleep when the message to launch was sent at "shortly after midnight" Tel Aviv time, lending support to North's account.

Secord then notes that "four hours into the flight," he received instructions to turn the plane around. Unfortunately, he was unable to contact the plane, which was then at the southern end of the Red Sea. There were anxious moments until they restored contact, but "since the pilot had not received confirmation to continue, he followed his

---

[114] Howard Teicher, "Memorandum of Conversation," May 28, 1986, in *Tower Report*, B-117.
[115] McFarlane, *Special Trust*, 63 and North, *Under Fire*, 58.
[116] Secord, *Honored and Betrayed*, 267.
[117] McFarlane, *Special Trust*, 63. In his "testimony," *Iran-Contra Affair*, 241, McFarlane said that while he was "asleep," North "violated" his orders and "directed Secord to send the plane..."

instructions and returned to Tel Aviv, where he landed without incident."[118]

McFarlane claims that when awakened at six and told that the plane had launched, he "angrily countermanded" North and turned the plane back just before it had reached the mid-point in the flight. The implication is that had he not countermanded North's order, the plane would have flown on to Tehran.

The former national security adviser, however, bases this argument on a surprisingly faulty understanding of flight operations. All air missions have a planned fail-safe point requiring final confirmation to proceed. Failing receipt of confirmation at the fail-safe point the mission is automatically scrubbed and the plane returns to base. That is in fact what occurred in this case when Secord was unable to communicate with the plane.

Secord believed that McFarlane had decided to launch the plane as a "negotiating ploy" to "create a tangible deadline." It failed because he did not realize that the Iranians did not control the hostages. In short, "Bud's demands for an 'instant' hostage release to match the transit schedule of the second plane was simply unrealistic." In other words, McFarlane had set conditions that were highly unlikely, if not impossible, to be met.

But not according to McFarlane. For him, North "had been deceiving Poindexter and the President, and now me." Indeed, "the collapse of the entire mission was due to lies and deceptions on the part of both North and Gorbanifar."[119] But McFarlane's claim of innocence was simply designed to divert attention from his own actions in scuttling the mission. Iranian inability to gain the release of the hostages and disinclination to enter into a strategic relationship with the United States were decisive, but, for McFarlane and the new world order faction, rapprochement with Iran was to be prevented at all costs, even if McFarlane had to create impossible conditions to do it.

---

[118] Secord, *Honored and Betrayed*, 267-68.
[119] McFarlane, *Special Trust*, 57-58.

It was at ten minutes to eight in the morning, several hours *after* the plane had turned back to Tel Aviv, that Najavi arrived to offer a compromise on the hostages. "They think two can get out now but it will require 'joint action' on the other two." Ten minutes later, Najafabadi arrived to reaffirm the offer. McFarlane replied: "It's too late." "You are not keeping the agreement." "We are leaving."[120]

Teicher's notes left out the dispute that then ensued between McFarlane and North. The Iranian offer was to obtain the release of two hostages before delivery of weapons and possibly the remaining two after delivery. North thought this a deal worth taking and wanted McFarlane to call Poindexter and ask for guidance, but McFarlane would not consider it. At the same time, all the way to the airport and literally up to the plane's stairway the Iranians pleaded with McFarlane to reconsider, but he remained obdurate.[121]

The intelligence evidence surrounding the trip was ambiguous. On the one hand, NSA radio surveillance of Beirut indicated "no evidence that 'the hostages were about to be released or that anything unusual was taking place.'"[122] On the other hand, North reported that the CIA had informed them "Rafiq Dust, Iran's deputy foreign minister, had left Tehran for Damascus, as he had in previous cases when Western hostages were actually released."[123] The implication was that Iran had to coordinate with Syria on hostage matters and that the offer to release two might have worked.

In reporting to the president the next day that the mission had failed, McFarlane, according to Mayer and McManus, said "the Iranians had insisted on the delivery of all the HAWK parts before releasing any of the hostages."[124] That, as the above account demonstrates, was not remotely true. McFarlane had declined to tell

---

[120] Howard Teicher, "Memorandum of Conversation," May 28, 1986, *Tower Report*, B-117.
[121] North, *Under Fire*, 59-61.
[122] *Tower Report*, B-118.
[123] North, *Under Fire*, 60.
[124] Mayer and McManus, *Landslide*, 245-46.

the president of the compromise offer at the end and, indeed, urged that he discontinue the initiative.

The mission to Tehran had two very important consequences, one immediate and the other longer ranged. In the immediate sense, it was a success for the new world order faction. The mission had failed to obtain the release of the hostages and reestablish relations with Iran. But, in a longer-term sense, its failure enabled the president to proceed with his plans to develop relations with Tehran without further participation of the new world order faction, although, as we shall see, Shultz and McFarlane continued to play roles from off-stage, as it were, and would ultimately be successful in killing the initiative.

Chapter 10
On the Verge of 'Victory'

By the summer of 1986, President Reagan's general strategy of rebuilding the Western alliance and defeating Soviet strategy seemed to be succeeding, or on the verge of succeeding, on all major fronts. In arms control, the president had reclaimed command of the negotiations from Shultz and set a high bar for Soviet compliance in his quest for a shift to the strategic defensive based on SDI. He had marshaled congressional and cabinet support for greater arms assistance to anti-Soviet resistance forces, especially in Angola, Afghanistan, and Nicaragua. Most important, he had secretly cleared the way for direct interchange with the Iranian leadership.

Secretary Shultz and the new world order faction opposed the president's strategy, favoring détente with the Soviet Union and accommodation to Soviet interests around the world. Shultz sought through arms control to establish détente based on mutual assured destruction, albeit at lower levels of weapons, and was willing to sacrifice SDI to get it. His objective in third world conflicts was to negotiate settlements rather than defeat Soviet client regimes. His agreement to support increased arms to Angola, Afghanistan, and Nicaragua stemmed from the fact that the Soviets were increasing the supply of arms to their clients, who were winning and not interested in negotiations. On the issue of Iran, Shultz was totally opposed to reestablishing relations, insisting that the United States support Iraq, instead. Despite Shultz's objections, by the summer of 1986, President Reagan appeared poised to take decisive steps toward the realization of his policy objectives.

Reagan in Command

The most highly visible aspect of President Reagan's strategy was the Victory Program of supporting anti-Soviet resistance forces, especially in Angola, Afghanistan, and Nicaragua. By mid-year, the decision to supply the *Stinger* missile to counter the Soviet deployment of helicopter gunships to Angola and Afghanistan was being implemented. *Stingers* were already in use with Savimbi's forces in Angola and the CIA was in the process of training Afghans in their use in the United States.[1] The appearance of *Stingers* on the Afghan battlefield would come in September. In both places they would turn the tide of battle.

Another success was the House vote at the end of June to approve the president's $100 million program for the Contras. The vote reversed five years of continuous opposition by the House expressed in the Boland Amendments. Even so, Speaker Tip O'Neill's skillful legislative tactics delayed the beginning of money flows until the coming fiscal year, in October, but the CIA began active planning to resume its role in full support of the Contra forces as soon as the vote was cast.

In retrospect, however, the issues that would decide the struggle between Reagan and Shultz and the new world order faction occurred largely outside the public view. These were the arms control negotiations with the Soviet Union and the Iran initiative, which unfolded in secret over the second half of 1986. Shultz and the new world order faction were determined to achieve détente with Moscow through the arms control negotiations, while Reagan sought to strengthen the containment structure around the Soviet Union through the reestablishment of a strategic relationship with Iran.

Shultz and the new world order faction sought an accommodation with Moscow based on existing strategic doctrine,

---

[1] "Rebels Get First Load of Stinger Missiles," *Washington Times*, April 21, 1986, 5. See also Milt Bearden and James Risen, *Main Enemy: The Inside Story of the CIA's Final Showdown with the KGB* (New York: Random House, 2003*)*, 215; and Mohammad Yousaf and Mark Adkin, *The Bear Trap* (London: Leo Cooper, 1992), 182.

mutual assured destruction, while Reagan sought to dispense with MAD and persuade the Soviets to agree to a transition to strategic defense, based on sharp reduction of nuclear weapons and emphasis on missile defense. Both sides agreed on weapons reductions and SDI, but disagreed on their purpose.

After the Geneva Summit (and McFarlane's resignation and replacement by John Poindexter) the president decided that he would become directly involved in the arms control process and "negotiate the key elements personally" with Gorbachev.[2] Recall, Secretary Shultz had in early 1985 demanded and obtained control of the negotiations. Taking this responsibility away from Shultz, even though he would obviously still have a major input into the process, may have been the reason the secretary made another of his offers to resign.

When he made it, the president's reaction startled him. Reagan said that "he wanted him to stay, but wouldn't try to talk him out of leaving."[3] Shultz' resignation threat was a bluff to regain control of the negotiations. His bluff called, he decided to stay, for the obvious reason that there was no guarantee that his successor would come from the ranks of the new world order faction, which would effectively kill arms control as the path to détente.

From early in the year, paralleling the negotiations under way in Geneva, Stockholm, and Vienna, Reagan and Gorbachev exchanged a series of letters, in which each leader made clear his respective position.[4] The letter format put the president in charge of the process. In its essence, Reagan sought to gain Gorbachev's agreement to reduce nuclear weapons and make a transition to strategic defense based on missile defense, while the Soviet leader offered to reduce strategic and intermediate-range weapons, but only if Reagan would renounce SDI. Reagan's agenda included formulas for the resolution of regional

---

[2] Jack Matlock, *Reagan and Gorbachev*, (New York: Random House, 2004), 175.
[3] Ronald Reagan, *An American Life* (New York: Simon and Schuster, 1990), 642.
[4] In addition to the arms control negotiations taking place in Geneva, Stockholm hosted the Conference on Security and Cooperation in Europe, and in Vienna representatives from NATO and the Warsaw Pact were negotiating reductions in conventional weapons.

disputes, treaty violations, and human rights issues, while Gorbachev focused almost entirely on the U.S.-Soviet weapons balance.

Gorbachev sought to set the agenda with his letter of January 15. The core of his proposal was an offer to eliminate all nuclear weapons by 1999, including all intermediate-range weapons from Europe, but *only* if Reagan were willing to renounce the "development, testing, and deployment" of SDI. In letters of February 6 and 22, just before the opening of the Soviet Union's 27th Party Congress, Reagan replied, agreeing in principle with the ideas of the zero option for intermediate-range missiles in Europe and a fifty-percent reduction in U.S.-Soviet "nuclear arms," but wanting no limits on "strategic defense research."[5] In short, "by late March," as Oberdorfer notes, "almost everything seemed bogged down in the usual suspicions and discord."[6]

Two events in April only served to harden these positions further. The first was the strike against Qadaffi on April 14, a punch that Reagan subtly telegraphed in his letter of February 6. Discussing regional conflicts, the president sent a rather clear signal, which, in combination with other intelligence Moscow was receiving, indicated that the United States was preparing to strike Qadaffi. "What are we to make," he said, "of your sharply increased military support of a local dictator who has declared a war of terrorism against much of the rest of the world and against the United States in particular?" And further, he asked, was the Soviet Union "so recklessly seeking to extend its influence in the world that it will place its prestige...at the mercy of a mentally unbalanced local despot?"[7]

When the attack came, Moscow's unwillingness to protect Libya, or do more than supply another SAM-5 missile unit, was a major demonstration of ineffectualness. The Soviets bitterly criticized the United States, cancelling a scheduled meeting between Soviet Foreign Minister Shevardnadze and Shultz, which suggested that an

---

[5] Reagan, *American Life*, 650-58.
[6] Don Oberdorfer, *The Turn: From the Cold War to a New Era: The United States and the Soviet Union, 1983-1990* (New York: Poseidon Press, 1991), 166.
[7] Reagan, *American Life*, 655.

improvement in relations was not imminent. Then, ten days later came the shocking nuclear incident at Chernobyl. Moscow's, indeed, Gorbachev's, inept handling of the crisis, failing even to acknowledge there had been one until Western European nations began to identify nuclear fallout over their countries, clearly cast a pall on Soviet efforts to indicate that the Soviet Union under Gorbachev was changing for the better.

Gorbachev had at Geneva agreed to an exchange of visits, with the first to come in Washington. U.S. representatives repeatedly pressed their Soviet counterparts to set a date and the president extended an invitation for a late June visit, but the Soviets declined. Reagan's reaction was to continue to raise the issue, but also to increase the price Gorbachev would have to pay for a visit. Reagan wanted no arms control agreement without "substantial progress in other areas," like a Soviet withdrawal from Afghanistan, progress on treaty violations, and human rights, while Gorbachev would not agree to a visit without the certainty of an arms control agreement beforehand.[8]

Content to increase the pressure, on May 27, the president announced that the United States would no longer be bound by the SALT II treaty. After what was a "fierce argument," in which Shultz argued against denouncing the treaty, the president compromised announcing that while the United States would no longer be bound by the unratified treaty, it would remain in compliance with it for the time being by dismantling two twenty-year-old *Poseidon*-class submarines to make way for a new *Trident* sub, the *Nevada*, just beginning sea trials.[9] The immediate outcry from congress, including some on the Republican side, and of course from the Soviets, prompted a clarification. Arms control adviser Paul Nitze, explained that the president was committed "to take another look," if the Soviets "should take the initiative...to satisfy U.S. concern on arms issues."[10]

---

[8] Matlock, *Reagan and Gorbachev, 176.*
[9] Oberdorfer, *The Turn,* 168 and Lou Cannon and Walter Pincus, "Compliance With Salt Continued," *Washington Post,* May 28, 1986, 1.
[10] Don Oberdorfer, "U.S. Is 'No Longer Bound' By SALT II, Weinberger Says," *Washington Post,* May 29, 1986, 1.

The Soviet response came almost immediately, no doubt prepared earlier by knowledge of the argument that was riling the administration. In Geneva, on May 29, Soviet negotiators put forth the defense part of an offense-defense package. Their proposal called for "strengthening" the ABM Treaty with "limits on testing and a ban on deployment of antimissile systems" of all kinds. They wanted U.S. commitment to adhere to the treaty for "fifteen to twenty years" and to stricter definitions of treaty terms. Their proposal, as Nitze observed, "would tighten the ABM treaty even more than the so-called narrow interpretation."[11]

On June 11, the Soviets presented the offense part of the package. Moscow would be willing to negotiate an INF agreement separately from START, with zero missiles for the U.S. and the Soviet Union and leaving undisturbed British and French systems. He also agreed to freeze Soviet missile forces in Asia. U.S. forward-based systems in Europe, including the Pershing II and cruise missile bases, would be removed, as would Soviet SS-20s.

The Soviets proposed to reduce "strategic arms" by thirty percent, instead of their earlier proposal of fifty, but to increase the number of nuclear warheads and bombs by twenty-five percent, from six thousand to eight thousand. They also spoke only of "significant reductions" in throw-weight, a retreat from an earlier willingness to reduce throw-weight by fifty percent.[12] The Russians seemed to be signaling a preference for negotiating an INF agreement over a START accord.

Gorbachev would include these proposals in a letter to Reagan on June 15, but the president began to formulate a response as soon as he received word from Geneva. On June 12, in a principals' only meeting of the president, Shultz, Weinberger, Casey, and Poindexter, a lengthy debate began on what would culminate in the president's July 25 letter to Gorbachev. These discussions would not circulate below the

---

[11] Paul Nitze et al., *From Hiroshima to Glasnost* (New York: G. Weidenfeld, 1989), 416.
[12] Ibid, 417.

principals' level and the information was not circulated to the Joint Chiefs for comment, or to the arms control bureaucracy.[13]

Shultz advocated as he had before that "we propose a trade-off of fifty percent reductions in nuclear arms for a willingness to forgo deployment of a strategic defense for the period during which reductions would take place."[14] Shultz also questioned whether "development and testing of SDI was permissible under the 1972 ABM Treaty." Weinberger argued that both were fully allowed under the "broad" interpretation of the treaty. Reagan "sided with Cap." He was "committed to the search for an alternative to the MAD policy." SDI, he maintained, was "not a bargaining chip."[15]

Weinberger departed completely from his past, persistent opposition to any agreement by offering the surprise proposal to "eliminate all ballistic missiles!" The idea had bubbled around the Defense Department for some time. Its essential thrust was that as the Soviet nuclear arsenal relied almost exclusively on ballistic missiles, while the U.S. was more diverse, including bombers and cruise missiles, the elimination of all ballistic missiles would work to U.S. advantage.[16]

The president's letter, as it finally evolved, built on Gorbachev's proposal for offensive reductions and offered a compromise on SDI, consistent with his goal of a transition to the strategic defensive. The letter remained classified until 2009.[17] Thus, most of the works that discussed it presented only partial accounts. The only contemporaneous information about the letter came from newspaper leaks and later memoir references.[18]

---

[13] Admiral William J. Crowe, *The Line of Fire*, (New York: Simon & Shuster, 1993), 265-66.
[14] George Shultz, *Turmoil and Triumph* (New York: Macmillan, 1993), 722.
[15] Reagan, *American Life*, 666.
[16] Oberdorfer, *The Turn*, 170-74.
[17] Martin Anderson and Annelise Graebner Anderson, *Reagan's Secret War* (New York: Crown, 2009), 282-83, provides a lengthy excerpt.
[18] Walter Pincus and Lou Cannon, "Star Wars Compromise Discussed," *Washington Post*, July 10, 1986, 1, Leslie Gelb, "Reagan Reported To Stay Insistent On 'Star

Without exception, the leaks focused on Reagan's proposals for SDI and said little or nothing about his proposals for offensive force reductions. Of the memoirs, Weinberger says nothing. Reagan hints that he sent Gorbachev a "sweeping new arms reductions proposal."[19] Shultz provides more, but badly distorts Reagan's proposal on missile reductions, saying: "A letter finally emerged that covered much familiar ground, including reductions by 50 percent in strategic weapons."[20] In fact, it was a "sweeping new...proposal." Reagan called for 50 percent reductions in ballistic missiles, which meant the heavy SS-18, not simply strategic weapons, and sought to move toward the "total elimination of nuclear weapons."[21]

Shultz's distortion of the July 25 letter stemmed from the fact that he opposed the proposal as well as the strategy of the transition to the strategic defensive. But the letter itself casts new light on the arms control negotiations, including and especially on the Reykjavik meeting later in October and the events leading up to it.

On the defense side, the president proposed a five-year "program of research, development and testing, which is permitted by the ABM Treaty," to determine whether a system was feasible. If after this period either side decided to deploy missile defense, it would be obligated to "share the benefits of such a system," provided "there is mutual agreement to eliminate the offensive ballistic missiles of both sides."

> Once a plan is offered to this end, the details of the sharing arrangement and the elimination of offensive ballistic missiles

---

War' Test," *New York Times*, July 24, 1986, 1, and Leslie Gelb, "Reagan Seeks Soviet Agreement On the Deployment of 'Star Wars,'" *New York Times*, July 25, 1986, 1, and Don Oberdorfer, "Reagan Called Ready to Make Deal on Defensive Arms," *Washington Post*, August 4, 1986, 1.
[19] Reagan, *American Life*, 665-66.
[20] Shultz, *Turmoil and Triumph*, 723.
[21] "July 25, 1986: Reagan to Gorbachev," 3, in Jason Saltoun-Ebin, *The Reagan Files: Reagan-Soviet Letters* http://jasonebin.com/thereaganfiles/id70.html

would be the subject of negotiations for a period of no more than two years.[22]

If there were no agreement after two years "either side will be free to deploy unilaterally after [giving] six months notice..." The seven-and-a-half year testing/negotiation period was in part a response to Moscow's proposal that both sides adhere to the ABM Treaty for fifteen-to-twenty years. It was also partly a response to Shultz's proposal to "give up those deployment rights that we could not exercise anyway."[23] And it included a modified version of Weinberger's proposal to eliminate all offensive ballistic missiles.

There was also an offense side to the president's proposal that went far beyond that suggested in the memoirs of Reagan and Shultz. The president proposed that the two countries "begin moving toward our common goal of the total elimination of nuclear weapons," by first implementing the principle of a fifty percent reduction of "strategic ballistic missiles warheads." The president said he was also prepared to limit long-range cruise missiles "below our current plan," and to limit the total number of ICBMs, SLBMs, and heavy bombers "to a level in the range suggested by the Soviet side."

Reagan next proposed to take immediate steps to eliminate the "entire class" of intermediate-range missiles worldwide, "which is consistent with the total elimination of all nuclear weapons." He thought an immediate agreement "would be the best outcome," but he wrote, "an interim approach, on a global basis, may prove the most promising way to achieve early reductions." On the question of Gorbachev's proposal for a complete ban on nuclear testing, the president demurred. While a complete ban was a long-term U.S. objective, "we believe a safe, reliable and effective nuclear deterrent requires testing."[24]

---

[22] Ibid.
[23] Shultz, *Turmoil and Triumph*, 718.
[24] "July 25, 1986: Reagan to Gorbachev," 5.

With the July 25 letter Reagan had taken the high ground from Gorbachev by offering a concrete plan to rid the world of all nuclear weapons, but, contrary to Gorbachev's proposals, as part of a shift to the strategic defensive. It was a bold proposal that would heavily impact the Soviet Union's superpower status, which was based almost solely on possession of nuclear weapons. Indeed, Gorbachev's response to Reagan's letter was—silence. It would be almost three months, mid-October, before he would reply and then circumstances would have changed dramatically.

In Washington, meanwhile, a major turn of events on the Iran/hostage front, made clear that the president had not shut down the Iran initiative, but was continuing it. That news, combined with the president's dominance of the arms control process, not to mention his successes in supporting anti-Soviet resistance forces, created a major crisis for the new world order faction.

Secret Contact with Iran

During the Tehran meeting, although no immediate breakthrough had occurred in U.S.-Iranian relations, unbeknownst to McFarlane there had been a major development. When North disclosed to Najafabadi in McFarlane's absence that there existed a government faction opposed to opening relations with Iran, the Iranians understood that a direct approach to the president would be necessary. Thus, they offered to dispense with Gorbanifar as an intermediary and establish direct contact. As Cave reported

> In Tehran, the Iranians talked about the undesirability of the Gorbanifar [Kangarlu] channel. So...they agreed to look for a new channel and we were to consider the new channel.[25]

---

[25] "George Cave Deposition," *Report of the Congressional Committees Investigating the Iran-Contra Affair* (Washington, D.C.: GPO, 1987), Appendix B, volume 3, 690. [Cited hereafter as *Iran-Contra Affair*.]

> When we were in Iran, the Iranians told us that they were not happy with the Gorbanifar [Kangarlu] channel. But, they said, if you guys insist on using it, it's all right with us. We, of course, had the problem with the Israelis on Gorbanifar, even after Tehran. The Israelis were insisting ...that Gorbanifar had to be used. We decided to look for a second channel.[26]

This was, of course, precisely what the president had hoped to accomplish with the mission. He wanted direct contact unfettered by intermediaries and allies and without the knowledge of his factional adversaries. For two reasons, however, the president decided to keep Gorbanifar in play, but held at arms length. One, there was some concern that, if cut off entirely, Gorbanifar would blow the whistle on the operation and ruin the opening. Two, keeping him in play served to divert attention away from the secret effort to establish direct contact through a second channel.

From June, then, Secord and Hakim were tasked with searching for the new channel, while North, Allen, and Cave were charged with fending off Gorbanifar and Nir, although Cave would become involved with the second channel after contact was made. Indeed, it seemed that the Iranian leadership, too, as intimated during the Tehran meeting, was attempting to distance itself from Gorbanifar.

Shortly after the Tehran meeting, Gorbanifar, Kangarlu, and Nir sought to contact North, proposing a new arms deal they insisted would produce the hostages. For Gorbanifar, especially, there was particular urgency. Khashoggi had arranged to provide the $15 million financing for the *TOWs*, spare parts, and radars that were supposed to be a part of the Tehran mission. With only one palette of arms delivered, the Iranians refused to make any payments—and Khashoggi wanted to be paid, with interest. The only way for Gorbanifar to clear his debt to Khashoggi was for the United States to ship the rest of the spare parts order to Iran.[27]

---

[26] Ibid, 849.
[27] *Iran-Contra Affair*, 245.

However, when Gorbanifar tried to get in touch with the American side through Nir, and Kangarlu contacted Cave by telephone, both found that the Americans stood firmly on their demand that the hostages had to be released before the rest of the spare parts shipment would be delivered. As before, Kangarlu demanded shipment before any more hostages would be released.

Gorbanifar found himself locked in the middle and made extravagant promises to each side in an effort to break the logjam. To the Iranians he promised without authorization from the Americans that the United States would deliver additional missiles with the spare parts, if a hostage were released. To the Americans he claimed that the Iranians were preparing to release a hostage as a "gesture" for the fourth of July.

At the same time, the Iranians produced a price list for American weapons showing that they were being overcharged by six hundred percent. In discussions with Cave, Kangarlu attempted to place the blame on the Americans for the overcharge and to protect Gorbanifar, but it was clear that the Iranian leadership blamed Gorbanifar for the price gouge.[28] The arms merchant claimed "he had increased the price of the spare parts by only 41 percent," implying that it was the Americans who were at fault.[29] The effect of Iranian complaints about over-pricing was simply to stiffen American disinclination to resume any dealings with the Gorbanifar-Kangarlu channel.

Indeed, that may have been its actual purpose. Cave thought that the Iranians were not at all surprised that Gorbanifar was overcharging them.[30] As to the "price list," it was a Defense Logistics Agency list, which was not really a price list, but a list designed "to get the serial numbers and descriptions correct for ordering [weapons]." All pricing was based on replacement cost, in any case, which was much higher

---

[28] Theodore Draper, *A Very Thin Line: The Iran-Contra Affairs* (New York: Hill and Wang, 1991), 378.
[29] Ibid, 379.
[30] "George Cave Deposition," 638-39.

than the DLA list.[31] The Iranians knew all this, which, in Cave's view, meant that they were simply using it as a "device."

At the end of June, Gorbanifar heard from Kangarlu that the Iranians would release a hostage as a humanitarian gesture in connection with the fourth of July. Gorbanifar told Nir, who called North. North immediately sent a recovery team to Weisbaden, West Germany, to receive the hostage. But the holiday came and went without the release of a hostage. The fiasco prompted North to refuse to take any more calls from Nir. Thus, by the end of June, North had put distance between himself and both Gorbanifar and the Israelis.

Meanwhile, the search for the new channel had begun and was showing promise. Secord and Hakim were placed in charge of the search, but it was actually Hakim who got in touch with friends and former colleagues, particularly in London, at the Iranian Purchasing Mission, to determine who among them might be informed that a new channel would be coming out of Iran. Recall, that the Iranian Purchasing Mission was Iran's largest weapons' acquisition organization outside of Iran.

By mid-June, Hakim had contacted an old colleague, Sadegh Tabatabai, who had worked for him years earlier and was reputed to be "well connected" to the Iranian leadership, including Rafsanjani. Hakim's enticement was the promise of commissions from the expected lucrative business with Iran. Before long Tabatabai had assembled half a dozen contacts from among the exile group in Frankfurt and Iranians working in the Purchasing Commission in London. North brought Tabatabai to Washington on June 27 for a meeting and, to assess his reliability, arranged for a polygraph.[32] The "vetting" of Tabatabai occurred just as Gorbanifar, Kangarlu, and Nir were promising the fourth of July release of a hostage that failed to occur.

There was considerable interest, then, when a few days later, in early July, Tabatabai "reported to Albert [Hakim] that the Relative had come out and asked for an American contact." It was not clear who

---

[31] Ibid, 670-71.
[32] *Iran-Contra Affair*, 249.

the Relative was, in this instance. Later, the term was used to refer to the second channel, who was then identified as Ali Hashemi Bahramani, Rafsanjani's nephew.[33] As Cave recalled, "we assumed that this was the Iranian effort also to set up a second channel."[34] North brought Tabatabai back to Washington again for more meetings. Hakim and Cave met with him on July 10 and 11 as did North, separately, on the same days.[35] Undoubtedly, North gave Tabatabai instructions on how to proceed when the Relative came out again.[36]

Two days earlier, Gorbanifar, now in a panic over his debt to Khashoggi, had sent a letter to Kangarlu proposing three options to settle the spare parts issue and his own debt problem. Two options were for what was termed a "sequential delivery" whereby the Iranians would release one or two hostages, reimburse Gorbanifar $4 million, and the United States would deliver the spare parts. Then, they would release another one or two hostages and the United States would deliver additional equipment, radars and *TOWs*, after which there would occur a high-level meeting. His third option was for Iran to return the initial palette of weapons, close the case, and "pretend nothing happened."[37] Alternating delivery of weapons with the release of hostages would now become the norm in dealing with the Gorbanifar, Kangarlu, Nir channel.

Jenco's Release and the New World Order Faction

Contrary to Shultz's later testimony that "from May 4, 1986...until...November 3, 1986...I received no information indicating that an arms transfer to Iran had occurred," Walsh demonstrates

---

[33] See Draper, *Very Thin Line*, 400, for a discussion of the Relative, who might have been Rafsanjani's nephew, or his eldest son, Mehdi Bahramani.
[34] "George Cave Deposition," 851.
[35] Ibid, 675-76.
[36] *Iran-Contra Affair*, 249, states that the second channel had not been identified until "late July."
[37] "Gorbanifar, July 8, 1986 letter," John G. Tower et al., *Report of the President's Special Review Board: February 26, 1987* (Washington: GPO, 1987), B-134-35.

conclusively that his testimony was false. Shultz and his top aides closely monitored the president's Iran Initiative throughout.[38] They were fully informed about McFarlane's trip to Tehran, knew that negotiations had resumed with Gorbanifar and Nir afterward, and were apprised of the proposed hostage release timed for the fourth of July. None of that was cause for alarm as far as the new world order faction was concerned, for there appeared to be no prospect for success. But that would change with the events surrounding the release of hostage Father Lawrence Jenco.

Shultz's aides were initially unaware of the president's secret search for a second channel, but by the end of July began to suspect that something was up. They were unable to keep track of Secord and Hakim, who, as private citizens were off the new world order faction's radar, but they were able to monitor Cave's movements. Indeed, it may have been through keeping track of Cave that they stumbled onto the early contacts with the new channel. The discovery occurred in the context of the release of hostage Father Lawrence Jenco.

On July 21, North reported to Poindexter that Nir told him that the Iranians had decided to release a hostage. To "preclude a repeat of July 4," he decided not to alert a recovery team, but did notify assets on the ground in Beirut. Then, on what he termed a "related subject," North informed him that "George Cave will proceed to Frankfurt to meet w/ Tabatabai, the cousin of the man I met with here" to determine his "real access" and whether he could "act as an interlocutor" to the Iranians.[39] (North erred here. As will become clear in a later message on July 25 to Poindexter cited below, Cave was to meet with Tabatabai and Speaker Rafsanjani's brother.)

---

[38] Lawrence E. Walsh, *Final Report of the Independent Counsel for Iran-Contra Matters*, (Washington, D.C.: United States Court of Appeals for the District of Columbia Circuit, August 4, 1993), 341. Walsh's conclusions were based on new data from Shultz's aides that had not been made available to the Tower Commission, or to Congressional investigators. He restates his view in *Firewall: The Iran-Contra Conspiracy and Cover-Up* (New York: Norton & Co., 1997), 320-335.

[39] "North to Poindexter," July 21, 1986, *Tower Report, B-138.*

There had been of late a flurry of activity, as foreign diplomats interacted with Iranian leaders. An unnamed Turkish official had had a discussion with Iran's Deputy Foreign Minister, Ali Larijani, who expressed Iran's interest in an "easing of relations" with Washington. His memorandum of conversation had been passed to Secretary Shultz and to the NSC. Upon receiving it, North proposed sending a positive reply to Tehran through this emissary, pending Shultz's approval. Shultz's reaction, however, revealed that he had learned of Cave's trip to Frankfurt, although not its purpose.

In a note to Poindexter, Shultz agreed to send a message through the emissary, but then asked "about a Cave meeting in the next few days." He explained his interest by saying that "he just wanted to be sure that we did not have any disconnect between what the [emissary] will be telling them and what Cave tells them."[40] Shultz was clearly fishing for information about Cave's trip and its purpose. Poindexter was noncommittal, but told North.

North replied to Poindexter later that same day to say, "Cave is meeting w/ [a relation of a powerful Iranian official] and Tabatabai to determine level of access and current political sentiments toward the present regime."[41] In other words, Cave was to meet with Tabatabai, who would introduce him to "a relation of a powerful Iranian official." According to Taheri, the man Cave met on July 27 was Mahmoud Rafsanjani, the brother of the Iranian Speaker.[42]

In any case, the amount of activity regarding Iran had suddenly intensified and what happened next seems to have alarmed the secretary and the new world order faction. The release of Jenco on July 26 came at the moment that Cave was making the first substantive contact with the relative of top Iranian leader, Rafsanjani. Looked at from Tehran's point of view, the timing of Jenco's release must be

---

[40] "Poindexter PROF note to North," July 25, 1986, Ibid.
[41] "North PROF note to Poindexter," July 25, 1986, Ibid, B-138-39.
[42] Amir Taheri, *Nest of Spies: America's Journey to Disaster in Iran* (New York: Pantheon, 1988), 217.

considered as a diversion to distract attention from the imminent high-level meeting with the president's representatives.

We now know that the notion of three competing Iranian factions was only partly true and that most if not all of the top leaders were involved, or at least informed, of the opening to the United States. It seems likely therefore that the Iranian leadership's decision to release Jenco at this moment was intended to create a diversion from Cave's meeting with Mahmoud Rafsanjani.

The president's men were also bent on diverting attention from Cave's meeting, and pointed to Gorbanifar. Poindexter claimed Gorbanifar "convinced" Kangarlu to release Jenco, but all knew that Kangarlu was a manager not a decision-maker.[43] The decision to release Jenco had been taken at a higher level and Kangarlu ordered to execute it. Similarly, the decision to pay Gorbanifar $4 million suggests that the Iranian leadership sought to put into effect one of Gorbanifar's July 8 options, as a step toward settling with him and prompting delivery of the rest of the spare parts ordered earlier.[44]

Cave, meanwhile, had been very busy. Not only had he met with Rafsanjani's brother, Mahmoud, on July 27, but also later that same day he joined North, who had traveled to Frankfurt, for a meeting with Gorbanifar and Nir. Kangarlu participated in their meeting by telephone. Both Gorbanifar and Kangarlu claimed credit for the release of Jenco and insisted that now the United States must deliver the remainder of the spare parts package.[45] North agreed.

On the day Jenco was released, McFarlane probed Poindexter to find out how it happened. The president's men, Poindexter, North, and Director Casey, as well, all wrote memos claiming that Jenco's release had been "directly related" to McFarlane's trip. Casey insisted that the Gorbanifar-Kangarlu channel had "worked for the second time" and that it should be continued because they and Nir had every incentive to

---

[43] "Poindexter PROF note to McFarlane," July 26, 1986, *Tower Report*, B-139.
[44] "What We Know of the Jenco Release," North to Poindexter, July 26, 1986, Ibid, B-139-40.
[45] *Ibid,* B-142.

work for "further release of our hostages." He also agreed that the United States should deliver the remaining spare parts, if only to avoid the loss of face for those involved, including Peres and Rabin.[46]

Casey's memo, and North's and Poindexter's messages to McFarlane had all been sent the day of Jenco's release, making it highly doubtful that they, or anyone, knew the reasons for it. It seems that this, too, was a pattern of internal disinformation designed to achieve the same objective from the American side that Jenco's release had been designed to do from the Iranian side. It was in the paramount interest of both sides to keep the second channel secret as it was being established. Indeed, once the relationship had been firmly established in the third week of September, less than a month away, the United States would peremptorily shut down the Gorbanifar-Kangarlu channel and Casey would inform Shultz that they had opened a new channel.

But, if the president's men were attempting to deceive the new world order faction about its developing clandestine relationship with Tehran, they failed. The very fact of Jenco's release was a shock to them. On the day he was released, several of Shultz's top aides sent memos arguing that the hostage release "was part of an arms deal," which they expected would continue.[47] Coming the day after the president's July 25 letter to Gorbachev, the situation looked bleak from their point of view.

Then, a few days later, on August 4, their suspicions were confirmed when the United States delivered the remainder of the spare parts package. The events meant to them that the president, having boxed in the Soviets on arms control, was also succeeding in his efforts to establish relations with Iran.

Shultz's immediate reaction was to submit his resignation once again. So the next day, August 5, he went to the president and said he wanted to resign. As the president put it, "although he had never stopped letting me know that he didn't approve of the Iranian policy,

---

[46] "American Hostages," memorandum from Casey, attached to "North PROF note to Poindexter," July 26, 1986, *Tower Report*, B-140-41.
[47] Walsh, *Final Report*, 343.

that wasn't his reason. He thought that Cap Weinberger, Bill Casey, and John Poindexter were ganging up on him and pushing foreign policy issues that he opposed behind his back. He felt that I'd lost faith in him."[48]

According to Shultz, "I didn't want to abandon [the president], but I felt that he must correct the indecisiveness and backbiting involved in the current NSC and White House processes. I also knew that when it came to anti-Communist dictators, he and I were just not on the same wavelength. And I was sick and tired of fighting the same battles on Soviet matters over and over again."[49]

Compared to his willingness to allow the secretary to depart in January, Reagan refused to accept his resignation this time. The reasons were clear. In January, after Geneva, the president's policy had not been formulated and Shultz's departure would not have had an adverse impact. Now, in August, the president's policies toward the Soviet Union and Iran were in place and Shultz's resignation would signal to Americans and non-Americans alike that there was major dissension in the president's ranks. So the president remonstrated with his secretary, telling him to take some time off.

Shultz spent the next few days at his home in Palo Alto, California, and when he got back, he gave Don Regan his demands. He demanded greater control over the foreign policy process. Couched in terms of complaints about "the way the White House operates," Shultz wanted the right to form his own "team to deal with the Soviets," wanted the right to place his own people in important positions, demanded that the leaks from the White House and Defense Department stop, wanted a single channel, his, "going out to foreign governments," and he wanted to put an end to the CIA's "politically motivated distortion of intelligence."[50] This was nothing less than a repeat of Al Haig's demand to be the vicar of American foreign policy. Reagan, of course, wanted Shultz on board, just not in control.

---

[48] Reagan, *American Life*, 523.
[49] Shultz, *Turmoil and Triumph*, 725.
[50] Ibid, 726.

In Shultz's view, the "White House and NSC staffs...were operating on the fringes of loyalty to the president and of common sense." In truth, however, Shultz's complaints about the White House, NSC, defense, and the CIA were indirect attacks on the president himself and were a clear expression of the differences between them.

At the end of the month, the president was in Santa Barbara at the ranch and Shultz had gone to his farm in Massachusetts. The secretary was "mulling over how best to persuade [the president] to change his White House and NSC decision-making process."[51] "Just then," he recalled, a fresh Soviet-American crisis flashed onto my screen," which offered him the opportunity to do exactly that.

Crises and Opportunity for the New World Order

Shultz and his new world order cohorts did more than mull over how best to persuade the president. Marginalized in the administration and desperate to gain a dominant voice and change the president's strategy, they implemented three actions that they hoped would enable them to turn things around.

The first was enactment of an amendment to the AECA on August 27 that augmented the Secretary of State's counter-terrorism authority. The bill included a prohibition on weapons sales to countries designated by the secretary to be supporters of terrorism.[52] The amendment to the AECA would have established a clear impediment to arms sales to Iran, if the president's policy had been based on it, but

---

[51] Ibid, 727.
[52] The Omnibus Diplomatic Security and Anti-terrorism Act of 1986, P.L. 99-399, Title V, Section 509, amended the Arms Export Control Act to preclude the export of items on the U.S. Munitions List to any country determined by the Secretary of State to have repeatedly provided support for acts of international terrorism. The president could waive the prohibition of a particular export if he determined it to be in the national interest, and submitted a report to Congress justifying the determination. The waiver would expire after 90 days unless Congress passed a law to extend it.

unbeknownst to Shultz the president had used the Economy Act instead.

Second was a plan to precipitate an espionage crisis, which would enable the secretary to engage in direct negotiations with his Soviet counterpart. The crisis would be triggered by the arrest of a KGB agent for spying in New York City, with the full understanding that the Russians would retaliate in Moscow. Shultz would parley the espionage crisis into the Reykjavik Summit.

Third was a scheme to utilize American intelligence to leak information to a Lebanese journal exposing the Iran Initiative. The Lebanese leak triggered a crisis of the president's foreign policy. Although the AECA impediment amounted to nothing and the president was able to weather the Reykjavik meeting without giving up his arms control strategy based on SDI, he would be less successful in managing what became the Iran-Contra crisis.

As part of a government-wide crackdown on espionage in the United States, the large Soviet spy presence in New York City was an obvious target. The Soviet UN Mission had 275 "diplomats," and over 800 Soviets worked in the UN Secretariat and other organizations where it was estimated that at least a fourth of them were spies. The diplomats at the Mission held diplomatic immunity and if caught spying could only be expelled from the United States. Employees at other UN organizations, like the Secretariat, however, had no immunity and, if caught, could be tried and sent to jail.

Nevertheless, the Soviets were brazenly using many of their employees in the Secretariat to "run agents" and the FBI had been closely monitoring one such employee, Gennady Zakharov, a physicist by training, for over three years. In August, the bureau had planned a "sting" operation to catch Zakharov in the act of receiving classified information from one of his contacts, a Guyanese employee, who was a double agent.

As was standard practice, on August 21, the bureau sent around to the CIA and Department of State a request to authorize the arrest of Zakharov. When the form arrived at the desk of Jack Matlock, NSC coordinator for Soviet Affairs, he was "surprised...that the State Department made no objection to the arrest since retaliation against an

American was likely to follow." Indeed, he thought "we could expect the KGB to arrest an American without diplomatic immunity in the hope of forcing a trade."[53]

Given Shultz's well-known antipathy to any actions that could impinge negatively on U.S.-Soviet relations, Matlock was at a loss to explain state's approval. Oberdorfer claims that Shultz and the top officials concerned with Soviet affairs "were all on vacation" and that a lower level official signed off on it.[54] Whether Shultz was on vacation when the request arrived, or not, the secretary always traveled with secure communication equipment, and so certainly would have been apprised of anything involving relations with the Soviets. In short, one must conclude that Shultz approved of the FBI sting.

Why approve of an action that would assuredly lead to a crisis as soon as Moscow retaliated? Under any other conceivable circumstance, as Oberdorfer notes, the State Department's response would have been to "tell the Soviets quietly to send Zakharov home to avoid an all-but-certain crisis."[55] That state declined to take this approach goes to the stalemate in U.S.-Soviet relations that had developed over the summer. Even though delegations from the two countries continued to meet on arms control and other matters, there had been no progress at any level. What was needed was a way to move the relationship forward and the proposed arrest of Zakharov offered Shultz that opportunity.

The FBI arrested Zakharov on August 23, an event not highly publicized, and the KGB responded a week later with the arrest of Nicholas Daniloff, an American journalist of Russian descent, who had been working for *U.S. News and World Report* in Moscow for the previous five years. His arrest exploded in the U.S. media. The Russians insured that their sting mirrored the FBI's. Both men were set up by acquaintances, handed some classified material, and arrested. Neither had diplomatic immunity and both were charged with spying.

---

[53] Matlock, *Reagan and Gorbachev*, 198.
[54] Oberdorfer, *The Turn*, 176.
[55] Ibid.

The fundamental difference, of course, was that Zakharov was a spy and Daniloff was not. Nevertheless, as in previous cases, Moscow wanted a trade.

Anticipating the arrest of an American, Shultz hoped to negotiate a resolution of the crisis and open the way to a summit meeting between Reagan and Gorbachev. It would be a classic case of not allowing a crisis to go to waste. Shultz would be creating a problem in order to solve it and parley the outcome into better relations. And he would be in the driver's seat, not the president or the NSC, working out a solution with his opposite number, Eduard Shevardnadze, whom he was scheduled to meet in Washington, on September 19.

The most recent precedent for the Zakharov-Daniloff arrests had occurred eight years earlier. On May 20, 1978 the FBI arrested two Soviets, Rudolph Chernayev and Valdik Enger, on espionage charges. Both were working for the UN Secretariat and thus did not have diplomatic immunity. On June 12, the Soviets arrested an American businessman, Jay Crawford, who also had no diplomatic immunity, on currency violations. Two weeks later all three were remanded to the custody of their respective ambassadors. The Soviets convicted Crawford of black market currency dealings and then deported him. The two Soviet UN employees were tried, convicted, and sentenced, but then traded for five imprisoned Soviet dissidents.[56]

Shultz would attempt to follow this precedent closely, and the outcome would be identical in structure, but he had to struggle against the president who demanded that there be no trade because the two cases were not equivalent. In his view, Zakharov was a spy and Daniloff a hostage. Matlock agreed, advising that the president demand Daniloff's release before proceeding on any other matters and begin "periodic expulsions" of KGB agents until Daniloff was released.[57]

---

[56] The precedent was discussed widely in the press. See Bernard Gwertzman, "Soviet Is Given New U.S. Offer In Daniloff Case," *New York Times*, September 11, 1986, 1. Neither Shultz, nor Oberdorfer, mentions this precedent in their accounts.
[57] Matlock, *Reagan and Gorbachev*, 199.

When Matlock attempted to coordinate policy with the State Department, however, the director of Soviet affairs told him bluntly: "the secretary wants to negotiate this....We mustn't do anything precipitous." He "wants to work it out himself and he wants you guys to stay out of it. He'll talk directly to the president on this."[58]

Before Reagan returned to Washington to meet with Shultz, however, he and Gorbachev engaged in a game of tit for tat. The president first tried to obtain Daniloff's release, sending a letter to Gorbachev informing him that the journalist was not a spy. Moscow responded by charging him with espionage.[59] Reagan then warned Gorbachev that unless Daniloff was freed, "there is no way to prevent this incident from becoming a major obstacle in our relations."[60]

It was in a highly charged atmosphere, then, that Shultz and the president met the morning of September 9, with the president's warning headlined in the press. Shultz presented him with his recommendation, which was designed to bridge the difference between the president, who did not want a trade, and the Soviets, who did. Shultz's solution was based on the 1978 precedent. He proposed that the two men be remanded to their respective ambassadors. Zakharov would be held for trial and Daniloff expelled. If Zakharov were convicted the administration "would seek to trade him for Soviet refuseniks." Reagan authorized him "to make it work" as long as it was not an obvious trade.[61]

For his scheme to work, therefore, Shultz had to show "how to keep a trade from being obvious."[62] If Daniloff could legitimately be considered a spy under Soviet law that would at least superficially make the two cases equivalent. Casting doubt on Daniloff's innocence outraged the president and his men, but in Shultz's view was the path

---

[58] Ibid, 199-200.
[59] Felicity Barringer, "Jailed American Charged in Soviet With Being A Spy," *New York Times*, September 8, 1986, 1.
[60] Gerald Boyd, "Reagan Sees Peril To U.S.-Soviet Ties In Reporter Case," *New York Times*, September 9, 1986, 1.
[61] Shultz, *Turmoil and Triumph*, 735.
[62] Matlock, *Reagan and Gorbachev*, 202.

to a solution acceptable by both sides. Fortunately for Shultz, Soviet law was so ambiguous as to cover almost any eventuality. Article 65 on spying held that any foreigner in possession of information that could be used "to the detriment of the U.S.S.R." could be punished by several years in prison, exile, or even death.[63]

Daniloff had unwittingly become entangled in CIA operations in Moscow as a transmitter of information. A CIA official also identified him during a telephone call the Russians had taped. Thus, even though Daniloff was not spying, he had been unknowingly caught up in a clandestine web. Worse, Shultz strengthened Moscow's hand by passing a message on to Oleg Sokolov, the Soviet charge d'affairs in Washington, "about the way the CIA station in Moscow had implicated Daniloff" without his knowledge.[64] Blaming poor CIA spycraft not only tended to alleviate Daniloff's predicament, it also cast Casey in a poor light, something Shultz seemed always eager to do.

On September 12, it was agreed to remand Zakharov and Daniloff to their respective ambassadors, completing the first step in Shultz's plan. Still, even though the stage was set for a resolution of the crisis along the lines of the 1978 precedent, several days passed without any movement. Soviet foreign minister Shevardnadze would be meeting with Shultz on September 19 and to give the Soviets a nudge, the day before he arrived, the administration announced that the United States was expelling twenty-five Russian "spies" from the Soviet UN Mission.

The administration had informed the Soviets of the decision to reduce their mission by twenty-five in February, to 218, but had not identified by name those who would have to leave by October 1st. Now this moment was chosen to do so, partly based upon information gleaned from Zakharov after his arrest. Reportedly, under interrogation "he sang like a tweetie bird," revealing the names of the KGB and GRU station chiefs, who were placed on the list.[65] Shevardnadze

---

[63] "The Soviet Law on Spying," *New York Times*, September 8, 1986, 14.
[64] Matlock, *Reagan and Gorbachev*, 210. Shultz, *Turmoil and Triumph*, 739, only includes part of this message.
[65] "Admitted Spy Zakharov Named Two High Soviet Agents, U.S. Official Says," *Los Angeles Times*, October 17, 1986, 1.

immediately howled, warning that "years of 'confrontation and dangerous contention' might be ahead," if the issue was not promptly resolved.[66]

Shevardnadze's visit with Shultz and the president marked the beginning of a ten-day process that not only resolved the Zakharov-Daniloff affair, but also reached agreement for the Reagan-Gorbachev summit that followed. It was clear from that first meeting when the Soviet foreign minister handed the president a letter from Gorbachev that the way was being cleared for a summit.

In the letter, after complaining that the Zakharov-Daniloff affair had been "exaggerated out of all proportion" and noting that the arms control negotiations "will not get anywhere if you and I do not involve ourselves personally," Gorbachev proposed

> We meet one on one close by... in Iceland or in London, maybe just for a day, for a completely confidential, closed, frank conversation (possibly only in the presence of our ministers of foreign affairs). The result...would be instructions to our appropriate departments for draft agreements on two or three questions that you and I could sign during my visit to the United States.[67]

Reagan agreed to this proposal, but only on condition that Daniloff be released without trial beforehand. The letter made clear that the Soviet leader was prepared to settle the Zakharov-Daniloff affair on Reagan's terms in order to obtain agreement for a "one on one" meeting. Shultz's reaction, however, was odd. As he saw it, it was only on September 20 that the president and his aides began to realize that the U.S. case on Daniloff was "weak!" Paradoxically, he then said, contradicting himself, "that was the day when I finally felt sure

---

[66] Bernard Gwertzman, "High Soviet Official Warns U.S. on Ties," *New York Times*, September 19, 1986, 8 and Celestine Bohlen, "Parallel Seen In Response on Daniloff, KAL," *Washington Post*, September 22, 1986, A20.
[67] Matlock, *Reagan and Gorbachev*, 208.

that we would resolve the problem on our terms and that we were headed for a summit."[68]

Shultz and Shevardnadze spent the next week meeting in Washington and New York hammering out an agreement whose purpose was to clear the way for a summit meeting. The agreement bore a strong resemblance to the 1978 outcome, but with two added twists. The Soviet Union would permit Daniloff to leave without trial. Zakharov would stand trial, plead no contest, and be expelled. The Soviet Union would permit dissidents Yuri Orlov and his wife to emigrate. So much was quite close to the 1978 precedent.

In this sense, strictly speaking, Daniloff's release was an independent act and Zakharov was traded for the Orlovs. Virtually everyone, however, considered the solution nothing more than a thinly disguised trade. The added twists were that the Soviet Union would accept a reduction in their UN Mission to 218 and the two countries would announce that Reagan and Gorbachev would meet in Reykjavik, Iceland, October 10-12.[69]

Shultz had negotiated through a complicated diplomatic and political thicket in more ways than one. Unnamed administration officials said, "key decisions...had been made by a small group of senior officials, which did not include Secretary of Defense Casper W. Weinberger, a skeptic on arms control." They said that "all this was done in the closet by three men," the president, Shultz, and Poindexter.[70]

But, while the president and his secretary of state were cooperating in the matter of relations with Moscow, which the president was eager to do, the new world order faction and the president were in sharp conflict at this very same time over the president's initiative toward

---

[68] Shultz, *Turmoil and Triumph*, 744.
[69] Ibid, 747. Lou Cannon, "Daniloff Freed by Soviets; U.S. to Release Zakharov," *Washington Post*, September 30, 1986, 1 and Gerald Boyd, "Reagan and Gorbachev Agree to Meet Next Week in Iceland; Zakharov, Freed by U.S. Leaves," *New York Times*, October 1, 1986, 1.
[70] Michael Gordon, "U.S. Hopes To Use Meeting In Iceland To Spur Arms Pact," *New York Times*, October 2, 1986, 1.

Iran. At the critical moment, when a breakthrough with Iran appeared imminent, the new world order faction executed a behind-the-scenes move that exposed the president's secret initiative.

Contact with the Second Channel and its Repercussions

Once again, as in late July, the president's men, Poindexter and North, used a meeting with Gorbanifar and Nir as a cover for meetings with Mahmoud Rafsanjani in early August. North requested travel orders for a trip to Frankfurt on August 6, but got off at Heathrow for meetings in London, instead.[71] There he joined Hakim and Mahmoud Rafsanjani for a meeting on August 7 and met the next day with Cave, Nir and Gorbanifar. Hakim, meanwhile, went on to Madrid for another meeting with Iranian contacts on the 10th.[72]

North's meeting with Gorbanifar and Nir (Kangarlu participated again by telephone) produced another sequential delivery plan to gain the release of hostages with an arms deal. Kangarlu complained that numerous items in the spare parts package were deficient, missing, or inoperable. North advised that they hold onto them pending another shipment. In fact, there would be no additional shipments through the Gorbanifar-Kangarlu channel, as the Second Channel materialized.[73]

Hakim's meetings with representatives of the Second Channel on the other hand brought results. On August 19, Hakim informed North that he had arranged for a meeting with the Second Channel, identified as Ali Bahramani, Rafsanjani's eldest son, or nephew, depending on the source. They were to meet in Brussels on August 25. Bahramani said "he had come with instructions to act as an intermediary, and that he was even willing to come to the United States."[74]

---

[71] *Tower Report*, B-148 n.86.
[72] Samuel Segev, The Iranian Triangle: The Untold Story of Israel's Role in the Iran-Contra Affair (New York: Free Press, 1988), 294, 298.
[73] "Next Steps With Iran," North PROF note to Poindexter, September 2, 1986, *Tower Report*, B-150.
[74] Draper, *Very Thin Line*, 399.

Secord and Hakim met with Bahramani for eight hours of discussions that constituted a *tour d'horizon* of all issues, including the Soviet threat, Iran-Iraq war, weapons needs, and Iran's postwar economic development needs. Secord made it clear that all things were negotiable once the hostage issue was settled and Bahramani expressed himself confident it would be resolved. He also revealed that he knew all about the efforts of Gorbanifar and Kangarlu, the Israeli connection, and the McFarlane mission, characterizing Gorbanifar as a "crook." When it was over, Secord reported, "we have opened up a new...channel into Iran."[75]

While North, Cave, Hakim, and Secord were attempting clandestinely to establish a Second Channel, it seems that the new world order faction was a step ahead in attempting to preempt them. During the meeting with Bahramani, the Iranian divulged that two groups, led by Alexander Haig and Senator Edward Kennedy had attempted to meet with him, but he declined, preferring to deal with the president's representatives, instead.[76] This meant that the new world order faction, too, knew the identity of the man code-named the Relative, were tracking his movements, and were trying to prevent a connection to the president.

Thwarted in their efforts at contacting the Iranian leadership, the new world order faction turned to a plan to expose the initiative. The plan was to utilize the DIA's agent and courier network in the Middle East to leak information about McFarlane's secret mission to Tehran. The information included "details of money transfers and bank accounts, with dates and places, most of it based on incidents and conversations that could only have been known to the Iranian or American negotiators."[77]

In Beirut, DIA's Tony Asmar ran an agent network whose main task was to keep track of the whereabouts of the hostages.

---

[75] "Secord (Copp) to North," August 26, 1986, *Tower Report*, B-149.
[76] Ibid.
[77] Donald Goddard with Lester Coleman, *Trail of the Octopus*, (New York: Signet, 1994), 191.

Lester Coleman was the agent/courier who was tasked with passing him the damning material. To insure security, the data was incorporated into a special electronic chip in a Mattell *Speak'n'Spell* children's toy, which could only be accessed when Coleman and Asmar both typed in special code words.

Coleman, under cover as a TV news cameraman, flew from Washington, Dulles airport on September 4 bound for Heathrow, thence to Larnaca, Cyprus. From Larnaca, he took the ferry to Jounieh, Lebanon, where he met Tony Asmar on Monday, September 8 at his office in Karantina. His instructions were to "sit down with Tony, punch in your code word, he'll punch in his, and you'll retrieve the data we've loaded in. He'll know what to do with it." When they did

> Out poured a detailed account of visits made by Robert McFarlane and Lt. Colonel Oliver North to Iran, traveling on Irish passports, to organize the sale of TOW missiles and launchers to the Iranian government in exchange for the release of American hostages.[78]

One of Asmar's men "delivered the *Speak'n'Spell* material to a relative who worked for *Al Shiraa*, Beirut's pro-Syrian, Arabic-language news magazine." The editor of the magazine, Hassan Sabra, a supporter of Montazeri's, sought confirmation of the story from his sources in Tehran.[79] It would take the better part of a month before the new world order faction's time bomb exploded in Tehran and in Lebanon, but by the first week in September, it was ticking. By then, too, every interested party had taken note of and reacted to the opening of the Second Channel.

In fact, Reagan's attempt at secrecy was more honored in the breach than in the observance. Gorbanifar, Kangarlu, Nir, Prime Minister Peres, and the Russians all responded to the now genuine prospect of Washington's reestablishment of relations with Iran. At the end of the

---

[78] Ibid, 190-91.
[79] Segev, *Iranian Triangle*, 283-86.

month, a few days after Secord's meeting with Bahramani, Kangarlu passed word to Gorbanifar that the Americans had opened up a separate channel and that at least one meeting had already been held.[80]

This was devastating news for Gorbanifar because with no further arms deals he would have no means of paying off his considerable debt to Khashoggi and other creditors. In fact, Reagan had decided to cut him off unless there was no other alternative. Gorbanifar would begin to work out a scheme to blackmail the Americans by threatening to expose the initiative. Over the next several weeks he would demand payment of various large sums, ranging from $4 million to $10 million, but for the moment, his immediate reaction was to inform Nir.

Nir, up to this point working on the assumption that the deal sketched out in London in early August was still in the works, quickly arranged to travel to Washington to plead his case. The implication of the new channel was that Israel, too, would be cut out of the operation. This prospect also prompted Prime Minister Peres and Defense Minister Rabin to include the issue as part of their agenda during visits to Washington, September 10 and 15, respectively. Peres would be making his final visit as Prime Minister before handing off the position to Yitzhak Shamir, as per their arrangement two years earlier.

The Russians, of course, had the most to lose. Reestablishment of U.S.-Iran relations would completely defeat the Soviet strategy of drawing Iran into their orbit. Their choice was to promote the taking of another hostage in hopes of driving a wedge between Washington and Tehran. On September 8, a small group of toughs seized Frank Reed, Director of the Lebanese International School, an American institution. Word was put out that Mugniyeh's Islamic Jihad was responsible, but Bahramani quickly called Hakim to say "Reed was not, repeat not, held by Islamic Jihad, that no Iranian 'influenced' groups were responsible, and that Iran will do whatever they could [sic] to find him

---

[80] *Iran-Contra Affair*, 251.

and either return him or tell us where he is being held."[81] American intelligence shortly confirmed that Reed "was taken by elements other than Hizballah—although they may have him in their hands now."[82]

Ironically, Kangarlu also decided to authorize the taking of a hostage, but for the opposite reason. He thought that it would make the Americans more cooperative. On September 12, three men seized Joseph Cicippio, Controller of the American University of Beirut, as he walked to work. The group that seized him called itself the Revolutionary Justice Organization. North thought that both Reed and Cicippio were "probably in the hands of Libyan controlled group which earlier bought/killed Kilburn."[83]

American intelligence, monitoring Kangarlu's communication channels, learned that he had authorized the seizure of at least one of the hostages. Contrary to Kangarlu's assumption, however, the seizure of new hostages gave the Americans another reason for not dealing with the Gorbanifar-Kangarlu channel. When Gorbanifar and Nir called their American contacts, North let them know that "new kidnappings had forced the United States to cut off any new arms shipments." North also hinted that he had "proof" that Kangarlu had been behind at least one of the hostage takings.[84]

As Peres, Rabin, and Nir would be coming to Washington in the second week of September, the president decided on September 8 on "new guidance." He would pursue the Second Channel and cut out Gorbanifar except as a fallback and provide a full briefing to the Israelis. They remained indispensable as a forward logistical base. Therefore, the president instructed Poindexter and North to express

---

[81] "North PROF note to Poindexter," September 11, 1986, *Tower Report*, B-155. Reed would languish in captivity for three-and-a-half years before being released in May 1990.
[82] Ibid, B-163.
[83] "North PROF note to Poindexter," October 10, 1986, Ibid, B-167. The Revolutionary Justice Organization also seized the American book salesman, Edward Tracy on October 21. They sometimes referred to themselves as Islamic Dawn.
[84] Segev, *Iranian Triangle*, 305-6.

appreciation for their assistance to date, but, given the Iranian antipathy to Israel, the United States would be establishing the relationship directly.[85]

Indeed, while Peres was still in Washington, the president authorized the very bold act of bringing Bahramani to the Capitol on September 19-20. In discussing preparations for the Iranian's trip, the question arose as to when or whether to inform Shultz and the new world order faction. North was still peddling the line to McFarlane that the United States was attempting with difficulty to work out the August 8 deal with the Gorbanifar-Kangarlu channel.[86]

Casey said that he "planned to tell Shultz in general terms that we were talking to another high level Iranian and that we would fill him in after the interview." North protested, saying that "experience showed that Shultz would talk," and eventually word would leak to the press, but Casey was determined. The director may have realized that the secret was already out and failing to inform the new world order faction would only work to their disadvantage.[87]

Washington and Frankfurt

Meanwhile, Secord flew Bahramani and his party from Istanbul to Washington, D.C. for two days of high-level talks designed to demonstrate sincerity of purpose. Their meetings took place in North's office in the Executive Office Building and Secord's office in Tysons Corner. Cave and Allen also participated. After the conclusion of talks on the first evening, North gave the Iranians a tour of the White House, including the Oval Office, Cabinet Room, and Roosevelt Room. The president was out of town, spending the weekend at Camp David.

Bahramani explained that the majority of Iran's top leadership had agreed to improve relations. He mentioned: Rafsanjani, Rafiq-Dust, Jalalai, Moussavi, and Khamenei. Khomeini's son, Ahmed, briefed his

---

[85] For the "talking points" for Nir, Peres, and Rabin, see *Tower Report*, B-154-56.
[86] "North PROF note to McFarlane," September 3, 1986, Ibid, B-151.
[87] "North PROF note to Poindexter," September 17, 1986, Ibid, B-156-57.

father on the progress of the initiative. He did not mention Ayatollah Montazeri, who was known to be viscerally opposed to reopening relations with the United States. Nevertheless, it was significant that the majority of the top Iranian leadership supported this effort.

The talks focused on the establishment of a strategic relationship, but also explored their differences. The two sides disagreed on the Soviet threat. The increase in Soviet aid flowing to Saddam Hussein was the driving force behind Iran's search for a counterweight and the United States sought to parley Iran's search for weapons into an anti-Soviet stance. The Iranians, however, while seeking weapons, also intended to maintain a middle course, seeing the Russians as neither enemies nor friends.

Similarly, on the Iran-Iraq war, the U.S. side sought neither victory nor defeat for either side; the Iranians wanted "some kind of victory" and the downfall of Saddam. The Americans made no commitment about Saddam, but were willing to meet Iran's practical weapons needs, such as ammunition and replacement barrels for artillery.[88] The Iranians, of course, were playing both sides. While the talks were occurring with Washington, Tehran was engaging in similar high-level discussions with the Russians. Nevertheless, the Americans were impressed with Bahramani's political acumen and sincerity.[89]

Both sides downplayed the hostage obstacle. Bahramani believed that it could be resolved quickly, although he admitted that Iran did not have complete control over the hostage takers. North expressed U.S. willingness to expedite the process with additional arms sales. On Gorbanifar, North advised that "Iran should pay him whatever they owe him so he will be quiet," but Bahramani replied "he had received all his money." This surprising reply raised the suspicion, never far from the surface as far as Gorbanifar was concerned, that he might be attempting to blackmail the United States.[90] He also discouraged

---

[88] Richard Secord and Jay Wurts, Honored and Betrayed: Irangate, Covert Affairs, and the Secret War in Laos (New York: Wiley, 1992), 290-91.
[89] Taheri, *Nest of Spies*, 227-28.
[90] Draper, *Very Thin Line*, 410-12. In attempting to reconstruct payments to Gorbanifar, Casey believed that Iran had paid him $4 million at the end of July, $6

further contact with Gorbanifar on the grounds that they had discovered a KGB agent on Kangarlu's staff.[91]

While no specific agreements were reached, Bahramani had presented an eight-point list of weapons needs and proposed the creation of a commission that would meet secretly in Lisbon or Istanbul to address issues of concern.[92] The main accomplishment had been to establish direct contact and the decision to continue meeting to work out a detailed plan for the development of relations. The American side was unanimous in believing that relations were headed in a very positive direction.

On September 26, as a show of good faith and a down payment on future arms purchases, Bahramani deposited $7 million into the Lake Resources account. North instructed Secord to deposit payment for 500 *TOWs* and *Hawk* parts into the CIA's account. No shipment would be made until after another meeting with Bahramani, which would have to include a resolution of the hostage obstacle.[93]

On October 2, Bahramani called Secord requesting that they meet in Frankfurt on the 6th. He claimed there was "now an internal consensus on how to proceed with regard to the hostages 'obstacle.'" Bahramani also indicated that he would be bringing along an official who had been involved in the previous negotiations and a Koran for the president. He asked that North bring a definitive sample of intelligence.[94]

North, Cave, Secord, Dewey Clarridge, and Tom Twetten brainstormed a memo titled, "next steps for Iran," in which they devised their negotiating strategy for the Frankfurt meeting and a scheme to pacify the Israelis, that is, Nir, while still keeping him out of

---

million in early August, and $8 million on August 21st. These payments supposedly squared accounts by mutual agreement. See "Casey memorandum to Poindexter," regarding Roy Furmark's Comments on the Hostage Situation, no date, but probably written on October 23, 1986. *Iran-Contra Affair*, Appendix B, volume 3, 1062-64.
[91] "North PROF note to Poindexter," September 22, 1986, *Tower Report*, B-158-59.
[92] Secord, *Honored and Betrayed*, 290-91.
[93] "North PROF note to Poindexter," September 26, 1986, *Tower Report*, B-160.
[94] *Iran-Contra Affair*, 253.

the action. They decided that the intelligence they would provide would be "a mix of factual and bogus information" in hopes of enticing the Iranians to accept a communications team in Tehran that could provide real-time intelligence.[95]

As Bahramani said he was bringing a Koran, North's team decided to reciprocate by responding with a Bible, inscribed by the president. As for Nir, the objective was to relegate him to a supporting role without affecting Israel's important political and operational role. Toward this end, Secord would go to Tel Aviv on the way to the Frankfurt meeting to brief Nir about the second channel but not include him at this stage. He would carry a letter from the president reaffirming the "joint effort" of the two countries.[96]

North, Cave, Secord, and Hakim met Bahramani in Frankfurt on October 6. The first surprise was the official who accompanied him. It was Ali Samii, the Iranian equivalent of a political commissar, who had actually been present in the background of both the February meetings with Gorbanifar and the Tehran meeting with McFarlane. They had nicknamed him the "Monster," the "Engine," and the "General," because he clearly possessed the authority to make decisions. The two Iranians would adopt the good cop/bad cop approach in negotiations with the Americans.

The second surprise was the admission that despite the so-called "internal consensus" on how to resolve the hostage obstacle, they had no solution. They admitted that they did not in fact control, nor could "100 percent" influence, Mugniyeh, who held Jacobson, Anderson, and Sutherland. They noted that these men were being held in two locations and could gain the release of one, Jacobson, but not the other two. Furthermore, they had no idea where the two most recent hostages, Reed and Ciccipio, were being held, but it was not by any of their men, or Mugniyeh.

North presented a seven-point proposal, which, although laden with promises of weapons, intelligence, and technical support, had as

---

[95] "Next Steps for Iran," October 2, 1986, *Tower Report*, B-160-64.
[96] Ibid.

its initial step the release of all three hostages upon delivery of the first 500 *TOWs*. It fell like a thud as soon as he put it forth. The evaporation of any prospect for gaining the release of all three hostages may have accounted for North's uncharacteristically grandiose, even shrill, representation of himself as the president's personal aide and confidential adviser as he strove to persuade the Iranians to reconsider.[97]

Instead, Samii proposed his own plan of nine points, which offered the release of one hostage after delivery of the *TOWs*, but sought to put the United States in the position of negotiating the release of the remaining two hostages by interceding with the Kuwaiti government for the release of the Dawa 17 prisoners. Three, including Mugniyeh's brother-in-law, Mustafa Badradienne, had been condemned to death. Five had been given four-year sentences, and nine sentenced to longer terms. Cave claimed that the Iranians were told that the U.S. could do nothing about the three condemned to death, could attempt to insure that the five with four-year terms were in fact freed on time (sometime in 1987), and perhaps influence the release of two others.[98]

That was difficult enough, but the deal breaker was Samii's demand that the United States and Iran "work within the framework of the Hague settlement process to provide Iran with military items...that Iran had paid for...but had been embargoed after the Embassy seizure."[99] The "Hague settlement process" was a euphemism for the $12 billion in Iranian assets, including all weapons contracts that the United States had frozen after the embassy seizure in 1979. Implicit in the Iranian proposal was the request that the United States change policy and support Iran against Iraq and reopen the arms spigot full force.

This demand went well beyond North's brief and he pointed out that his seven-point proposal was the president's list. "That's all he authorized....That is everything he authorized me to talk about."[100]

---

[97] See Draper, *Very Thin Line*, 421ff.
[98] "Cave deposition," 951-52.
[99] *Iran-Contra Affair*, 256.
[100] Draper, *Very Thin Line*, 426.

North saw the two countries passing each other "like two ships in the night" and was afraid that he had "failed in my mission."[101]

North faced a quandary. He could not agree to negotiate a commitment on behalf of the United States to interfere in the legal processes of an ally, especially to seek the release of convicted terrorists responsible for the deaths of many Americans. Nor did he have any authority to negotiate about Iran's frozen assets, or discuss a major change in policy. There can be no doubt that he called Poindexter for advice.

The decision was that discussion about frozen assets and a change of policy were simply ruled out. But, in order to prevent the negotiation from falling apart entirely, North, a representative of the U.S. government, would extricate himself and permit Hakim and Secord, private citizens, to attempt to find a solution to the Iranian demand that the United States negotiate with the Kuwaiti government.

North's abrupt decision to take himself out of the negotiation and return to Washington has received various explanations. North himself implies that he left because of the controversy that had arisen over the shoot down of a Contra supply plane on October 5, in which the Sandinistas captured the lone survivor, Eugene Hasenfus.[102] He also claims that Secord also departed "to deal with the firestorm."[103] Draper follows this line of argument.[104] Segev says simply the decision was "hard to explain."[105]

The congressional study states simply "North had to return to Washington," without explanation, but does note that he "suggested to

---

[101] Ibid.
[102] The Hasenfus shoot down is an unresolved mystery. Walsh, *Firewall*, 79, says even after "it was learned from the CIA that the Nicaraguans had anti-aircraft weapons ready for a C-123 flight, William Cooper and Wallace Sawyer were nonetheless ordered to fly the C-123 mission in which they had died and Eugene Hasenfus had been captured." The implication is that they were deliberately sent into harm's way.
[103] Oliver North and William Novak, *Under Fire: An American Story* (New York: Harper Collins, 1991), 296.
[104] Draper, *Very Thin Line*, 427.
[105] Segev, *Iranian Triangle*, 308.

the group, 'why don't you guys hold this discussion after I'm gone, O.K.?'"[106] Another curiosity is that all accounts, save one, claim that North, Cave and Secord all left Hakim to continue the negotiations alone, much to the consternation of the Iranians, who did not know how to interpret what had happened.

Secord is the exception, who repudiates all of these accounts. He says that he learned of the shoot down on the 6th and informed North of it as soon as he arrived in Frankfurt that day. "There was nothing either of us could do about it now, especially with a critical meeting coming up, except to stay informed and pray that our local people could keep the thing contained."[107] Thus, North knew of the Hasenfus shoot down before the meeting with the Iranians began and it was unlikely that that was the reason for his abrupt departure a day later.

Secord also states unequivocally that while he did excuse himself briefly to change plane reservations, he returned to join Hakim in the negotiation. He also addresses the Dawa 17 issue, stating that instead of the U.S. government becoming directly involved, the solution was for the United States to offer a plan for the phased release of the prisoners, which Iran would take as their own and present to Kuwait. The United States would mediate, but not be directly involved. The Iranians "accepted" this plan.[108]

Hakim, Secord, Samii and Bahramani worked out a nine-point plan that was sent to North just as he was arriving in Washington. Known as "Hakim's plan," North obtained approval of it from Poindexter, Casey, and Twetten. The president, too, approved those parts of the plan "that applied to the U.S. government," that is, *excluding* the plan to influence the Kuwaiti government.[109] As reworked by North, the plan provided for the following:

The Iranians would pay $3.6 million for 500 *TOWs*, which the U.S. would deliver nine days after payment. Secord and Hakim would "help

---

[106] *Iran-Contra Affair*, 256.
[107] Secord, *Honored and Betrayed*, 295.
[108] Ibid, 300-01.
[109] *Iran-Contra Affair*, 258 and Draper, *Very Thin Line*, 434-35.

prepare a plan for approaching the Kuwaitis to guarantee no more terrorism against the Amir and by which the Amir will use a religious occasion to release some of the Dawa. They will take this plan to the Hizballah as their idea (face saving gesture with the Hizb)." One and possibly two hostages would be released within four days of *TOW* delivery. If only one "whole process stops and we meet again." If two, then deliveries of additional *TOWs*, technical support, intelligence, etc., would commence.[110]

The plan as reworked left out any mention of the Hague settlement process, identified only *TOWs* for delivery and possibly *Hawk* spare parts, but made no reference to Bahramani's eight-point weapons list, and identified Hakim and Secord, not the United States government, as being responsible for the plan for addressing the Dawa 17 problem with Kuwait.[111] Finally, the plan called for the release of "some" of the Dawa prisoners, not all of them.

The Iranians apparently privately insisted that the United States become involved directly with the Kuwaiti government over the Dawa 17 issue. But the United States made clear its position in "press guidance" issued from the White House on October 14, ostensibly in response to a *Newsweek* magazine article speculating about a trade of Dawa prisoners for American hostages. "We will not negotiate the exchange of innocent Americans for…convicted murderers held in a third country, nor will we pressure other nations to do so."[112]

Although appearing definitive, this formula was quite close to that used to resolve the TWA-847 hostage incident that became known as the "no deal deal," in which the United States in fact looked the other way as Israel released prisoners and Mugniyeh released passengers. Implicit was the prospect of another no deal deal, but that was not to be.

What was also omitted was a response to the Iranian request that the United States change policy. The decision to focus narrowly on arms

---

[110] *Iran-Contra Affair*, 257-58.
[111] When the crisis broke in November, North blamed Hakim for the Dawa arrangement, while Poindexter blamed Secord. See Draper, *Very Thin Line*, 434.
[112] Ibid.

and hostages would have a predictable result. In less than a month the president's Iran initiative would lay in shambles, the result of an exposure of its secret negotiations. In the meantime, the president was off to Reykjavik, Iceland for what was supposed to be a tête-à-tête preparatory meeting with Gorbachev, but what turned out to be potentially the most far-reaching deal in the history of U.S.-Soviet relations.

Chapter 11
The Collapse of Reagan's Strategy

From the first week in October through the end of the month, in the context of a heated mid-term congressional election campaign, the president's strategy began to collapse like a slow-motion train wreck. The downing of the Contra supply plane and the subsequent claim of the lone survivor, Eugene Hasenfus, that the aircraft was part of an illegal, CIA-run operation began a slowly building crisis led by congressional Democrats. The crisis was first muted by the focus on the Reykjavik summit, which seemed to offer promise, but then produced no agreement. Negotiations with the Iranians at the end of the month also seemed at first to show promise, but led nowhere. By the end of the month the administration seemed to be in a state of suspended animation.

The No Summit Summit at Reykjavik, Iceland

There was a deeper significance to the meeting at Reykjavik than met the eye. In remarks before the meeting, the president said that it was to be a "planning session" to prepare for Gorbachev's visit to Washington, either later in 1986, or in 1987, "a base camp before the summit," Reagan said. He played down expectations for an arms control agreement and, instead, said he would "press" Gorbachev on human rights issues and regional conflicts, like Afghanistan.[1] In fact, however, the president planned a major demarche that would focus

---

[1] Lou Cannon, "Reagan Vows to Pursue Human Rights, Regional Issues With Gorbachev," *Washington Post*, October 7, 1986, 1.

almost exclusively on arms control, and involve a proposed fundamental change of strategy. In short, the president sought to bring about the end of the Cold War on his terms.

The meeting at Reykjavik was the culmination of a two-year-long negotiation that resembled a high-stakes card game, in which each leader attempted to outbid and/or bluff the other into submission. But in this game Gorbachev was running out of chips. Reagan's strategy of promoting low energy costs had jump-started the American economy as well as those of Western Europe, Japan, and also China, while continuing to depress earnings for the Soviet Union, which depended heavily upon oil and gas exports for revenue. The costs to Moscow of maintaining its very large military infrastructure, its alliances, and far-flung commitments around the globe were escalating beyond the Soviet Union's ability to pay and impoverishing the nation.

In his July 25 letter, Reagan had offered Gorbachev a fundamental way out of the *cul de sac* into which the Soviet Union was heading—a shift to the strategic defensive. As Gorbachev well understood, the Reagan military modernization program had effectively neutralized Moscow's leverage against the United States and the *Pershing II* deployment eliminated it in Europe. Even though the actual numbers of weapons still favored the Soviet Union, the momentum clearly lay with the United States.

Reagan's proposed abandonment of the doctrine of mutual assured destruction and adoption of a new strategy based on strategic defense, offered Gorbachev the opportunity to eliminate the crippling costs of maintaining its massive, yet increasingly dysfunctional, strategic weapons arsenal designed to exert leverage on the United States and its European and Asian neighbors. Adoption of a defensive strategy would allow Gorbachev to shift scarce resources to needed modernization and developmental ends.

It was, therefore, with a high degree of anticipation that the president awaited Gorbachev's response to his proposal. The key questions were: did the Soviet leader have the wit, courage, and political power to make a truly historic decision to accept Reagan's proposed change of strategy? When his answer came, during their very first session, it was clear that Gorbachev would not accept the president's offer. He strove to maintain the Soviet Union's strategic weapons advantage, regain lost leverage over Europe, retain it in Asia, and prevent the United States from moving onto the path of strategic defense.

Once it was clear that Gorbachev was bent upon maximizing Soviet advantage within the existing strategy of mutual assured destruction, Reagan also shifted his approach to attempting to get what he could in terms of weapons reductions, while keeping open the prospect of moving onto his preferred strategy based on strategic defense, with or without the Soviet Union.

Despite all the hoopla about reducing and even eliminating nuclear weapons as a threat to world peace, Gorbachev came to Reykjavik with the objective of maintaining the Soviet Union's advantages at the strategic and intermediate levels. His scheme was to offer even greater reductions than before in return for Reagan's abandonment, or neutering of SDI. His intentions became obvious at their very first session, where Gorbachev presented a package of proposals, which amounted to a response to Reagan's July 25 letter.[2]

In the July letter Reagan had reiterated the agreement reached at Geneva for a 50 percent reduction in strategic arsenals, but with a new twist, now specifically focusing on reducing "strategic ballistic missile warheads." He also offered to limit air-launched cruise missiles below current plans and reduce the total number of inter-continental ballistics missiles, submarine-launched ballistics missiles, and heavy bombers "to a level on the range suggested by the Soviet side." Gorbachev's response was to agree to a minimum of 50 percent reduction in strategic offensive forces, especially the Soviet Union's heavy missiles and the United States' submarine-launched ballistic missiles (SLBMs).[3]

On Intermediate-range forces, Reagan had proposed to begin immediate reductions with the goal of the total elimination of

---

[2] For a brilliant synthesis of the Reykjavik meeting, see Walter Pincus, "Reagan's 'Dream' Was to Eliminate Ballistic Missiles," *Washington Post*, October 14, 1986, 1.

[3] "July 25, 1986: Reagan to Gorbachev," in Jason Saltoun-Ebin, *The Reagan Files: Reagan-Soviet Letters* http://jasonebin.com/thereaganfiles/id70.html. Gorbachev's response is taken from the Russian "Transcript of Reagan-Gorbachev Summit in Reykjavik," *FBIS-USR,* May 17, 1993, 1-4.

intermediate-range nuclear missiles "worldwide," also referred to as a "global solution," by which he meant Europe and Asia. Gorbachev proposed the "complete elimination" of intermediate-range missiles from Europe, but not in Asia. In what he said was a major concession, he announced that the Soviet Union would disregard the missile forces of Britain and France and in return asked that the United States "withdraw the question of Soviet medium-range missiles in Asia," about which he was prepared to begin negotiations as reductions in Europe commenced.

Reagan had proposed that once the two countries had "achieved a 50% reduction in...strategic nuclear missiles" and "make progress in eliminating long-range INF missiles, we would continue to pursue negotiations for further stabilizing reductions. The overall aim should be the elimination of all nuclear weapons." Gorbachev was silent about future negotiations for "further stabilizing reductions," and the goal of total "elimination of all nuclear weapons," but offered to freeze and begin negotiations on missiles "with a range of less than 1,000km," a category of weapons Reagan had not mentioned in his letter.

Reagan's proposal had not included a time period for the reduction of offensive missiles, but did for missile defense. He had proposed a five-year period in which both sides could carry out research, development, and testing, as permitted by the ABM Treaty, to determine feasibility of concept. If feasible, they would negotiate for an additional two years a treaty to share the developed technology, provided "there is mutual agreement to eliminate the offensive ballistics missiles of both sides." If that failed, then either side could give six-months notice and be free to deploy missile defense.

Gorbachev's counterproposal to Reagan's seven-and-a-half-year program was to "strengthen" the ABM Treaty and make it "timeless." He wanted adherence to the Treaty for ten years, with no right of withdrawal, after which the two sides would commence a negotiation for three to five more years when both sides would "decide what to do," in effect giving the Soviet Union a permanent veto.

Development and testing of SDI components would be confined to laboratories with "prohibition of outside-of-laboratory testing of means intended for space-based destruction of objects in space and on earth." There would, however, be no prohibition on "testing permitted under the ABM Treaty, i.e., testing of stationary ground-based systems and their components." It would also be necessary, Gorbachev said, to "prohibit anti-satellite means" because "if this were not done, then in the course of creating anti-satellite means it would be possible to develop antimissile weapons."

Gorbachev's determination to constrain or neuter SDI was actually a desperate attempt to close two growing loopholes in the ABM Treaty that had emerged since 1972 contained in Article IV and Agreed Statement D. Agreed Statement D stated that "in the event ABM systems based on other physical principles...are created in the future, specific limitations on such systems and their components would be subject for discussion...." Article IV stipulated that the treaty's limitations "shall not apply to ABM systems or their components used for development or testing...within current or additionally agreed test ranges."[4]

The "future" mentioned in Agreed Statement D had arrived. The two loopholes meant that the United States (and also the Soviet Union) could develop and test current or future ABM systems at test ranges. Moreover, there was no requirement to discuss limitations on "systems based on other physical principles" until a "system" had been created. As the United States had not yet developed and tested a "system," as Gorbachev acknowledged, there was nothing yet to discuss and was why Gorbachev wanted to prevent testing "means," i.e., components, in space and confine testing to laboratories. But his determined fixation on SDI was implicit recognition that the Soviets believed that the United States was developing a missile defense in space based on "other physical principles."[5]

Reagan commented briefly on Gorbachev's package of proposals at the end of the morning session, but his full response would come

---

[4] Gerard Smith, *Doubletalk: The Story of SALT I* (New York: Doubleday, 1980), 489, 495.

[5] Many, if not most, U.S. arms control specialists, including Nitze, tended to argue that most SDI technology did come under the category of "other physical principles." See Paul Nitze et al., *From Hiroshima to Glasnost* (New York: G. Weidenfeld, 1989), 472-73.

only after he had consulted with his aides. Immediately after the morning session, when Shultz and the president gathered with their advisers in the secure bubble set up to prevent eavesdropping, the usually taciturn Shultz giddily described Gorbachev's proposals as laying "gifts at our feet." The president, however, was less sanguine, saying that Gorbachev had "brought a whole lot of proposals, but I'm afraid he's going after SDI."[6]

The Second Meeting

Reagan decided to obtain agreement on arms reductions first and then try to persuade Gorbachev that his strategy of a transition to defense was in both countries' interest. When the afternoon session began, Reagan immediately declared, "reductions are the highest priority" and the "heart of the matter is reducing ballistic missile warheads." For its part, he continued, the United States was "prepared for appropriate corresponding reductions in all ballistic missile systems," as well as air-launched cruise missiles (ALCMs) and bombers.[7]

He was, however, disappointed by Gorbachev's INF proposal, which by failing to include zero for Asia, represented a "step backward" from his September letter. Indeed, the president "had thought we had agreed to pursue an interim global agreement" and insisted that the "issue must be dealt with on a global basis." After some discussion, the president said, "so let's agree to have 100 units

---

[6] Jay Winik, *On the Brink*, (New York: Simon & Schuster, 1996), 505. George Shultz, *Turmoil and Triumph* (New York: Macmillan, 1993), 760-61, also describes this scene, but leaves out the president's remark about SDI.

[7] U.S. "Memorandum of Conversation," second Reykjavik meeting, October 11, 1986, *National Security Archive: The Reykjavik File,* Document 11, The George Washington University.

[missiles] each in Europe and Asia, and then we will be making some headway."[8]

Reagan welcomed the fact that Gorbachev raised the issue of shorter-range missiles and the readiness to freeze them. "You and I can agree to instruct our diplomats to coordinate on the matter of limiting lesser-range missiles within the framework of an interim agreement." We can also agree on verification measures, including exchange of data and on-site inspections. Finally, he proposed to instruct our diplomats to formulate a "legally binding" INF treaty, which will limit these systems while negotiators reach agreement on further reductions of them.

Having expressed his interest in reaching agreement on missile reductions, the president turned to SDI. Saying that he had taken Gorbachev's concerns into account in his July 25 letter, Reagan "proposed a mechanism by which we could move toward a regime based on high reliance upon defense." This would not replace the ABM Treaty, although as a result of our negotiations "new provisions…would replace some provisions of the ABM Treaty." His proposal envisaged a stable, verifiable "transition… to a new balance of offensive and defensive weapons, and later on, to elimination of offensive ballistic missiles."[9] In other words, the president was proposing a new relationship in which neither power could attack the other with ballistic missiles.

He forcefully denied the notion that "space-based weapons could be used to destroy targets on the ground," noting "we already have an agreement prohibiting deployment of mass destruction weapons in space." Besides, the ICBM was the most effective and reliable weapon to strike targets on earth. He also denied that the United States could carry out a first strike and use its defense to prevent retaliation. "We do not have the capability for carrying out a first strike," he said.[10]

---

[8] Russian "Transcript of Gorbachev-Reagan Reykjavik Talks," October 11, 1986, *FBIS-USR, July 12, 1993, 1-6.* The U.S. translation is less precise than the Russian here, failing to mention the September letter, or the phrase "step backward."
[9] Ibid, 2.
[10] Ibid.

However, Reagan continued, Gorbachev's concerns had led him to "propose a treaty now which would lead to the elimination of all offensive ballistic missiles. Once we do that, the issue of a combination of offensive and defensive forces giving one side or the other an advantage would not arise."[11] With this formulation the president had subtly reversed the position he had taken in their morning session. Then, he had argued that SDI would make missile reductions possible. Now, he said that the elimination of ballistic missiles would make SDI possible.

Missile defense, the president said, would reinforce stability at lower cost, "protect each of us against cheating," and against the missiles of third countries. We were even prepared to "share the benefits of strategic defense" and were willing to "agree now to a Treaty committing to do so in conjunction with the elimination of ballistic missiles." But, he concluded, Gorbachev's proposal for a test ban was a non-starter. "Neither a test moratorium nor a comprehensive test ban is in the cards for the foreseeable future," although he was prepared to fix the defects in the verification protocols of the Threshold Test Ban Treaty and the Peaceful Nuclear Explosions Treaty signed, but not ratified, a decade earlier.

Then, it was Gorbachev's turn and he attempted to pin the president down to specific commitments. First, he attempted to obtain Reagan's agreement to the transparently unfair 50% cut of nuclear weapons "across the board," acknowledging that "the structure will remain the same but the level would be lower." Reagan at first said, "this should be taken up by the experts," but then observed that although he himself "did not have all the numbers...he did know that the Soviets outnumber us by a lot. If we cut 50%, they would still have more than we do."

Gorbachev tried to bulldoze the president into making a commitment on the spot, saying "this is not a matter for the experts." He handed the president a sheet of weapons data and said, "here is the data, let us cut this in half." Reagan said "the idea was interesting," but

---

[11] U.S. "Memorandum of Conversation," second Reykjavik Meeting, October 11, 1986.

he would have to "give the U.S. side a chance," meaning to give the experts a chance to review it. Shultz chimed in on Gorbachev's side to say, "it was a bold idea, and we need bold ideas." "Gorbachev agreed that this was what we need." By this time, Reagan had recovered and asked Gorbachev again "if he agreed to his proposal for a meeting of experts" and Gorbachev, realizing that he had failed to bulldoze the president into an unwise decision, agreed.[12]

On INF, Gorbachev asked the president three times whether he accepted the zero option for Europe and Reagan replied "yes," each time, but insisted that any solution had to be "global," to include Europe and Asia. Finally, Gorbachev asked: "if we find a solution on Asian missiles, do you accept zero in Europe?" Reagan's affirmative response sent this issue, too, off to the experts for resolution.

It was obvious that Gorbachev's primary objective on INF was the removal of the *Pershing II* missiles from West Germany, but his newfound reticence on zero for Asia was somewhat puzzling. It was equally obvious that the SS-20s were mobile missiles, which could be moved from Asia to threaten Europe in the future after the *Pershings* had been withdrawn, but their presence also complicated Soviet prospects for any improvement of relations with China and Japan.

Gorbachev argued that they should work toward a total ban on nuclear testing, but in stages. "In the first stage," they could consider reducing yields, the number of tests, and the future of the treaties. "It would be clear movement had begun toward a total ban, at some stage." Reagan thought this proposal "interesting" and said that "their people should take it up."

Coming to his main argument, Gorbachev said that if we were going to "reduce strategic missiles and eliminate medium-range missiles," how could we abandon the ABM Treaty? It was "only logical" to strengthen the treaty by agreeing not to withdraw from it while "large-scale reductions would be taking place." "Otherwise, one side could believe that the other was doing something behind its back." Furthermore, his proposal to confine research to the laboratory was

---

[12] Ibid.

really "accommodating to the U.S. side." It would enable the U.S. "to see whether it wanted a full-scope three-echelon strategic defense or something else."

At this point, Reagan tossed a bombshell, saying that "with the progress we are making we do not need 10 years. He could not have said that a few years ago...[but] we do not think it will take that long. Progress is being made." Gorbachev was taken aback. After declaring that the Soviets were "not going to proceed with strategic defense themselves," an astounding remark given the extensive work the U.S. knew the Russians were conducting on defense, including the phased-array radar at Krasnoyarsk, he then said he "took note of the president's statement that less than 10 years would be needed." He quickly moved to end the session. "Let us turn our experts loose to work.... The two of us have said a lot. Let them go to work now."

But Reagan wasn't quite ready to stop. Noting that they had been "so wrapped up" in arms matters that "they had not touched on regional, or bi-lateral, or human-rights issues," he proposed they set up a separate experts' group for these issues. Gorbachev readily agreed. As they were finishing, Reagan noted that Gorbachev had said the Soviets would not develop strategic defense. If the Soviets come up with a better solution than SDI, "maybe they can give us theirs."

Gorbachev replied that their solution "would not be better, but different." Evading an answer to the question about sharing their solution with the United States, Gorbachev declared that he could not take Reagan's proposal about sharing SDI technology "seriously." As the United States was unwilling to share even the simplest technology, including milk factories, with the Soviet Union, he thought it would require "a second American revolution" to share missile defense technology, which "would not happen."[13]

---

[13] Ibid.

The 'Experts' All-Nighter

If the Americans did not realize what Soviet strategy was after the first day–and Shultz's remark about Gorbachev "laying gifts at our feet" and Reagan's about his "going after" SDI suggest that they did not–the all-night session by the "experts" made it abundantly clear. They were now, as Shultz notes, in a full-fledged negotiation.[14] The experts were divided into two groups, one devoted to the arms control issues discussed thus far, and another to discuss regional, bilateral, and human rights issues. Paul Nitze and Sergei Akhromeyev led the former group; Roz Ridgway and Alexander Bessmyrtnekh the latter.[15] The appearance of Akhromeyev, chief of the Soviet general staff, surprised the Americans, who had not expected a military man to be there, let alone be involved in the negotiations. In fact, he was the chief negotiator.[16]

The two groups met at eight P.M. that evening. The arms control group wrestled all night with the main issues Reagan and Gorbachev had discussed, not ending their discussions until six o'clock in the morning. The Ridgway-Bessmyrtnekh group wrapped up their discussions shortly after midnight. As Matlock, a participant in the Ridgway group saw it, they made "little progress" beyond compiling a "list of cooperative projects that might be undertaken."[17] Although

---

[14] Shultz, *Turmoil and Triumph*, 762.

[15] In Nitze's group were Richard Perle, Max Kampelman, Mike Glitman, Ronald Lehman, Henry Cooper, Bob Linhard, Adm. Jonathan Howe, Gen. Ed Rowny, and Ken Adelman. In Akhromeyev's group were: Victor Karpov, Valentin Fallin, Evgeni Velikhov, Georgi Arbatov, and Yuli Dubinin.

[16] Both Rowny and Shultz claim that Akhromeyev told them the identical story about being the "last of the Mohicans," a reference to James Fennimore Cooper's book. Either Akhromeyev told them the same story, or one of the authors is mistaken. As Rowny spoke Russian and Shultz did not, the likelihood is that Akhromeyev told Rowny the story during an off moment, as he claims. See Edward L. Rowny, *It Takes One To Tango* (Washington: Brassey's, 1992), 184, and Shultz, *Turmoil and Triumph*, 763.

[17] Jack Matlock, *Reagan and Gorbachev* (New York: Random House, 2004), 223.

neither group made breakthroughs, the Soviets made plain their determination to continue with the strategy laid out by Gorbachev.

Akhromeyev followed Gorbachev's lead in attempting to gain acceptance of the 50% cut, category by category. In any percentage arms reduction scheme the Soviets, as Reagan observed, would emerge with the advantage because of the larger overall numbers of weapons in its arsenal. The Russians held a 9000 to 7000 advantage in overall weapons. Nitze countered by proposing "equal numerical end levels." Eventually, Akhromeyev accepted the equal end levels formula of 6,000 weapons and 1,600 delivery systems, but he had a fallback plan.[18]

While arms reductions according to an equal numerical end levels formula would benefit the Russians less, they would still benefit because of the throw weight preponderance of their heavy weapons and the sheer reduction in the number of U.S. targets. To counter this, Nitze proposed sub-limits on categories to prevent concentrating a preponderance of weapons in a given category, but Akhromeyev refused to consider sub-limits. It was obvious that the Russians were determined to maintain strategic weapons advantage at whatever level of weapons was decided upon. As with all areas of disagreement, Nitze reserved the right to raise the issue again at the Geneva negotiations.

On INF, Akhromeyev followed Gorbachev's lead here, too, proposing zero for Europe and refusing even to discuss reductions in Asia. As Rowny noted, the Soviet general used an American expression to make clear he was not authorized to discuss Asian limits, saying, "that decision can only be made by someone above my pay grade."[19] It would be up to Gorbachev to make that call. The Soviet

---

[18] "Russian transcript of Negotiations in the Working Group on Military Issues," October 11-12, 1986, Soviet-American Summit, Reykjavik. *National Security Archive: The Reykjavik File*, Document 17, The George Washington University. See also, Paul Nitze et al., *From Hiroshima to Glasnost* (New York: G. Weidenfeld, 1989), 430. Edward Rowny, *It Takes One To Tango*, (Washington, D.C.: Brassey's, 1992), 182, says Akrhomeyev proposed the formula.

[19] Rowny, *It Takes One To Tango*, 185.

objective was to obtain the complete removal of the *Pershing IIs*, while retaining some mobile SS-20s in Asia.

On SDI, Akhromeyev reiterated Gorbachev's pitch that research and testing be confined to the "laboratory." Nitze proposed that they compose a memorandum laying out their areas of disagreement: on the length of the nonwithdrawal period from the ABM Treaty, and what was permitted during and after withdrawal. But Akhromeyev refused even to agree on "how we disagreed."[20]

Nitze raised the subject of nuclear testing and presented a proposal that tied "step by step limitations on nuclear testing" to "reduction and elimination of nuclear weapons." Akhromeyev responded by proposing a "full ban on nuclear testing," without a link to weapons reductions. Soviet skepticism was evident in Georgi Arbatov's reaction to Nitze's expressed interest in the "complete liquidation of nuclear testing," when he said it would happen "in a 100 years."[21] In the matter of a nuclear test ban, it seemed, both sides were bluffing. Everyone knew that to end testing meant the certain atrophication of nuclear weapons.

On INF it was the same. Zero for Europe meant the elimination of *Pershing II* and SS-20s positioned against each other, but the refusal to consider reductions in Asia meant that the Soviet Union would still have SS-20s deployed and the United States would have no countervailing weapon, if the SS-20s were subsequently moved within range of Western Europe.

The Soviet approach to SDI was double-barreled. Not only did Gorbachev demand an indefinite veto over an American decision to deploy missile defense years in the future, he also wanted to prevent any possibility of testing SDI components in space, which the ABM Treaty permitted. Here, on the pretext of "strengthening" the treaty, he was in fact demanding that it be rewritten to Soviet advantage.

---

[20] Nitze, *From Hiroshima to Glasnost*, 432.
[21] "Russian transcript of Negotiations in the Working Group on Military Issues," October 11-12, 1986, Soviet-American Summit, Reykjavik.

Day Two, the Games Begin

When the two leaders reconvened Sunday morning for what was scheduled to be their final meeting it was apparent that Reagan had decided on a subtle shift in his negotiating strategy, perhaps recognizing that Gorbachev was not going to budge. When briefed before the meeting about the all-night negotiations, according to Rowny, the president was "delighted that progress had been made on START and was particularly pleased with the Soviet INF offer."[22]

When he began the meeting with Gorbachev, however, he professed dissatisfaction with the negotiators' efforts. It was part of the act. In fact, Reagan put a positive spin on their work, even though there had been no positive result. He hoped that by agreeing to nearly everything Gorbachev wanted he would persuade him to relent on his demands on SDI. Ironically, Gorbachev had decided to adopt the same strategy, but hoped for the opposite outcome, that Reagan would agree to constraints on SDI.

Reviewing the night's work of the arms control team the president said he was "disappointed with what had been achieved." However, it was his "understanding that the working group had been able to agree on a formulation for the outlines of a 50% reduction of strategic arsenals that should move the negotiations substantially ahead." On INF, after lecturing Gorbachev at length on the long-held U.S. position, which Gorbachev knew well, of the need for a global solution, the president said that "in the right context we could accept 100 in Europe and 100 in Asia" and offered to "settle now" on that formula "and instruct our negotiators to work out details."[23]

On defense and space, Reagan acknowledged that they were at an impasse, but suggested that they relegate the issue to their negotiators and instruct them to focus on three issues "to move our positions closer together." First, to "synchronize" an investigation of strategic

---

[22] Rowny, *It Takes One To Tango*, 186.
[23] U.S. "memorandum of conversation," final Reagan-Gorbachev meeting, October 12, 1986, *National Security Archive: The Reykjavik File,* Document 15, The George Washington University, 1-2.

defense with their "shared goals of eliminating ballistics missiles." Second, to examine the timeframe for a transition to strategic defense. Third, to determine what "common understandings might be reached" for testing of advanced strategic defenses under the ABM Treaty. Reagan's proposal was to instruct their negotiators to do what he and Gorbachev would not—determine how and when and under what conditions the two powers could shift to strategic defense.[24]

On the question of nuclear testing, Reagan made a one hundred and eighty degree reversal of position, although carefully camouflaging the change by criticizing the negotiators "lack of imagination." Where he had earlier declared to Gorbachev that any test ban was "not in the cards," he now agreed to begin "immediate negotiation on testing issues." When an undoubtedly privately alarmed Gorbachev asked, "what you have in mind," Reagan read from the paper Nitze presented the night before."[25]

> The U.S. and Soviet Union will begin negotiations on nuclear testing. The agenda will be…first to resolve remaining verification issues associated with existing treaties. With this resolved, the U.S. and U.S.S.R. will immediately proceed, in parallel with the reduction and elimination of nuclear weapons, to address further step-by-step limitations on testing, leading ultimately to the elimination of nuclear testing.[26]

---

[24] Ibid, 3.
[25] Ibid and Russian "Transcript of Reagan-Gorbachev Reykjavik Talks," morning of October 12, 1986, in *FBIS*, August 30, 1993, 2.
[26] U.S. "memorandum of Conversation," fourth Reagan-Gorbachev meeting, October 12, 1986, 4. The Russian translation is significantly different. "The United States and the USSR begin negotiations on questions of nuclear testing. Their agenda will include all aspects of nuclear testing, including the unresolved questions, existing treaties, monitoring, limits on the power of explosives, and others. These talks could occur together with stage-by-stage elimination of nuclear weapons and would ultimately lead to stopping nuclear testing." In the U.S. version, limiting testing was to proceed "in parallel" with weapons reductions. In the Soviet version, testing limitation "could occur together with stage-by-stage elimination of nuclear weapons."

To say Gorbachev was taken aback would be an understatement. Reagan had not only called his bluff, he raised the ante. By formally proposing to tie the end of nuclear testing to reductions in weapons inventories he was laying out a plan for the early end to their programs. This was anathema to Gorbachev.Therefore, he did not reply directly to the president's new proposal, but, instead, began a lengthy review of where things stood, emphasizing the "major concessions" he had made and demanding that the president reciprocate. It was a "dangerous mistake," he averred, to think that the Soviets needed nuclear disarmament more than the United States does; that "if you put a little pressure on the Soviet Union it will raise its hand and surrender....It is not going to happen."[27]

We took U.S. concerns into consideration, he said, when we agreed that the "principle of 50% reductions should apply to all components of strategic forces, both platforms and warheads."[28] On INF, he probed again for the elimination of the *Pershing II* from Europe, asking," if we could find a concrete solution to the problem of intermediate-range missiles in Asia...you would agree to complete elimination of Soviet and American missiles, to a zero-level solution in Europe?"

Reagan would not agree to remove all of the *Pershing II* in Europe as long as SS-20s remained in Asia and so replied, with zero in Europe "it is not hard for you to move [SS-20s] from one place to another." You would have, he said, "an absolute advantage because we would have no deterrent in Europe." Trying to browbeat Reagan, Gorbachev said, "you appear to have forgotten the existence of English and French nuclear forces....When we talk about a zero level for Europe, we are in fact talking about a zero level for ourselves."

As for moving Asian SS-20s, he said disparagingly, "I actually find it a little awkward to hear that in a conversation on our level." We could include treaty text that says, "the transfer of just one missile from Asia to Europe would be grounds for abrogation of the treaty."

---

[27] Russian "Transcript of Reagan-Gorbachev Reykjavik Talks," Part 3, October 12, 1986, *FBIS-USR*, August 30, 1993.
[28] Ibid.

This was a semantic evasion. He knew that it was not necessary to transfer SS-20s "to Europe" for them to be in range of Europe, but he thought he could shame Reagan into buying his argument.

On the ABM Treaty, Gorbachev wanted to strengthen the treaty to insure that while "unprecedented" reductions in strategic and intermediate missiles are occurring neither side would be "doing anything behind the back" of the other. Thus, he reiterated his insistence that both sides agree to a ten-year non-withdrawal commitment from the treaty and that the United States agree to confine all SDI testing to the "laboratory." Gorbachev wanted to have it both ways. While implying that the United States might do something "behind the back" of the Soviet Union to gain an advantage, he was offended by any suggestion that Moscow might do the same.

Reagan could not understand Gorbachev's objection to missile defense after the two sides had eliminated their missiles. They would obviously not need a defense against each other, but only against third parties, unless, of course the Russians cheated. He explained again that he was committed to the full exploration of missile defense, but was willing to commit to a treaty obligation to share the technology with the Soviet Union, if it proved fruitful. All this could be made part of the ABM Treaty, strengthening it.

After going round and round with no give on either side, Gorbachev finally replied to Reagan's proposal about nuclear testing, but claimed that the president's proposal was one-sided. "You suggest talking about the problem of testing, but not about conducting negotiations on a complete end to testing."(!) In fact, Reagan had proposed "the elimination of nuclear testing," but Gorbachev was intent upon separating the testing question from reduction of weapons. Gorbachev invited the president to comment, employing an American saying that "it takes two to tango."

Recalling the historical record when "the Soviet side used the period of the moratorium to prepare to create new types of nuclear weapons," Reagan insisted that "proper control" was necessary. "Only after finishing the development of controls will we be ready to stop testing." There was a good American saying that reflected this caution, he said, "once burned twice shy." At this, Reagan repeated his proposal tying testing stoppage with weapons reductions, but Gorbachev peremptorily declared, "that wording does not suit us" and proposed to set it aside by "having our experts sit down and work out a formula."

After this exchange, which clearly demonstrated Gorbachev's disinclination to accept the president's formula, their discussion became disorganized, moving seemingly randomly from obscure topic to obscure topic. They discussed their respective country's political systems, philosophies, political parties, movies, trade, and human rights, in a desultory fashion. In response to Gorbachev's claim that "the possibilities of agreement are exhausted," Reagan replied, "it seems to me that we have agreement on nuclear testing." But Shevardnadze immediately spoke up to turn the discussion away from testing. "I would still like to return to the question of the ABM Treaty," he said, and Gorbachev immediately seized on that idea.

Gorbachev declared that his proposals were "a definite package and would ask you to consider it as such." Reagan's plea that there need not be a "link" between offensive reductions and the ABM Treaty fell on deaf ears. Finally, observing that "X-hour is approaching," Gorbachev said "maybe, if the president does not object, we will declare a break for 1-2 hours" and let our ministers try to propose something. Thus ended the morning session.[29]

The Focal Point is SDI

Secretary Shultz and Foreign Minister Shevardnadze and selected aides met to try to "propose something." Shultz attempted to raise the issue of nuclear testing, claiming that he thought it was a "solvable drafting problem,"(!) but Shevardnadze peremptorily cut him off. "Almost taunting" Shultz, he claimed that "the Soviets had made all the concessions....Now, it was our turn." Everything, he said, depended on "how to handle SDI."[30]

---

[29] Ibid.
[30] Shultz, *Turmoil and Triumph*, 768.

Bob Linhard and Richard Perle, sitting at the other end of the table, were prepared, having discussed a possible compromise based on the July 25 letter the previous evening with Poindexter and Shultz.[31] They hurriedly put together a proposal that included the Soviet demand for a ten-year non-withdrawal from the ABM Treaty, a 50 percent reduction of strategic nuclear arsenals during the first five year period, elimination of all offensive ballistic missiles during the second, and the right to do research, development, and testing permitted by the treaty. After ten years, either side would be free to deploy defenses. Shultz handed the proposal to Shevardnadze, who thought it was "worth considering," but he believed Gorbachev would not agree with the right to deploy defenses after ten years.[32]

As soon as they broke up, the two sides briefed their leaders on the new proposal. Reagan liked it, observing, "he gets his precious ABM treaty, and we get all his ballistic missiles. And after that we can deploy SDI in space. Then it's a whole new ballgame."[33] Gorbachev, as Shevardnadze noted, did object to the right to deploy after ten years, but he took the proposal and used it as the basis for a counterproposal, which he offered to the president as soon as they reconvened.

Gorbachev's counterproposal contained two changes and one omission. He insisted that "testing of all space components of ABM defense in space shall be prohibited except for laboratory research and testing." His formulation used the term "strategic offensive weapons" compared to the U.S. use of two terms, "strategic nuclear arsenals" in the first five-year period and "offensive ballistic missiles" in the second. Finally, Gorbachev omitted the sentence about the two sides being free to deploy defenses after the ten years were up.[34]

Their ensuing discussion revolved around the issues of testing and what could be done after ten years. Reagan insisted that testing permitted by the ABM Treaty be allowed and that after ten years each

---

[31] Winik, *On The Brink*, 513 and Nitze, *From Hiroshima to Glasnost*, 433 n.6.
[32] Winik, *On The Brink*, 513.
[33] Ibid, 514.
[34] Russian "Transcript of Reagan-Gorbachev Reykjavik Talks," Part 4, October 12, 1986, *FBIS-USR*, September 20, 1993, 2.

side could have the right to deploy defenses. But Gorbachev insisted that testing be confined to laboratories and stipulated against a unilateral right to deploy defenses after the ten-year period. He claimed that laboratory research would enable the U.S. to determine whether defense was feasible. After the ten years were up, the two sides would continue discussions and "negotiate a mutually acceptable solution concerning their future course of action." In other words, Gorbachev reinserted the Soviet right to veto an American decision to deploy missile defense.[35]

At an impasse, they decided to take another break to "sort out the differences between the two texts." During the break, Reagan asked his aides whether the U.S. "could carry out research under the restraints the Soviets [were] proposing?" Perle responded with an "unequivocal" no, but Shultz and Nitze "counseled him to accept the language proposed by Gorbachev," arguing that "they could worry about whether research could be conducted in the laboratory later."[36]

When they returned for their final session that evening at 5:30 P.M. it was clear that Reagan had sided with Perle. He presented his proposal again, altered slightly to reflect Gorbachev's objections, but it still contained the permission to conduct "research, development, and testing, as permitted in the ABM Treaty." He also included the right to deploy after ten years. Slightly amended, it now read: "At the end of the ten-year period, either side could deploy defenses if it so chose, unless the parties agreed otherwise."

Gorbachev dropped the issue of what would happen after ten years and shifted to two other issues. He wanted to know why Reagan had left the word "laboratory" out of his proposal. Reagan replied that, as the two sides had different views on testing, "their people in Geneva must decide what is permitted." Why had he employed two different terms for the weapons to be eliminated? Reagan's somewhat confused reply was that he thought "the Russians were mainly interested in

---

[35] U.S. "memorandum of conversation," final Reagan-Gorbachev meeting at Reykjavik, October 12, 1986, 4.
[36] Winik, *On The Brink*, 515.

ballistic missiles." Gorbachev repeated that they were interested in reducing "strategic offensive weapons."[37]

At this point the discussion veered wildly as each leader offered more in terms of weapons to be eliminated to convince the other, until Reagan said:

> Do we have in mind—and I think it would be very good—that by the end of the two five-year periods all nuclear explosive devices would be eliminated, including bombs, battlefield systems, cruise missiles, submarine weapons, intermediate-range systems, and so on?[38]

Gorbachev replied: "we could say that, list all those weapons. Shultz chimed in: "then, let's do it." Reagan replied: "If we agree that by the end of the 10-year period all nuclear weapons are to be eliminated, we can turn this agreement over to our delegations in Geneva so that they can prepare a treaty which you can sign during your visit to the U.S." Gorbachev, then said: "Well, all right. Here we have a chance for an agreement."[39]

Then, Gorbachev threw what Reagan would later call a "curve."[40] The term "laboratory" as a restriction on SDI testing had to be included as part of the overall package. Without it, there was no deal. Reagan was dumbfounded and said, "he could not confine work to the laboratory." Each man tried to convince the other "as a personal favor" to give in, to no avail. Gorbachev insisted that it was a matter of "principle." Reagan replied that Gorbachev was "asking him to give up the thing he'd promised not to give up."

After a few minutes, it was over. They had come close to an historic agreement, but in the end could not bridge the strategic

---

[37] U.S. "memorandum of conversation," final Reagan-Gorbachev meeting at Reykjavik, October 12, 1986, 8-9.
[38] Russian "Transcript of Reagan-Gorbachev Reykjavik Talks," Part 4, October 12, 1986, *FBIS-USR*, September 20, 1993, 8.
[39] Ibid.
[40] Ronald Reagan, *An American Life* (New York: Simon and Schuster, 1990), 677.

differences that separated them. Reagan had offered an opportunity to shift away from strategic offense to strategic defense and bring an end to the Cold War, but Gorbachev was not prepared to do away with the weapons that underpinned the very essence of the Soviet global position.

The outcome, however, was actually favorable to the United States. With no restrictions on the strategic defense initiative the way was clear to proceed with testing, development, and deployment. The strategic weapons balance and the European missile balance were both more than acceptable positions. Indeed, the outcome at Reykjavik left the United States and its European allies in the best possible position. It was inevitable, as Reagan understood, that the Russians would come back to the negotiating table to attempt to redress these outcomes.

After Reykjavik

The meeting at Reykjavik had occurred at the climax of the congressional election campaign and the Democrats seized on the president's presumed failure to reach an agreement to further their own cause. Democrats (as well as Shultz and the new world order faction) saw SDI as a bargaining chip to be used to obtain an arms control agreement. But, the president stood his ground. In his national broadcast to the American people after his return from Iceland, Reagan declared that as it was the SDI program that had brought the Soviet Union back to the arms control talks in the first place, he was not going to accept Gorbachev's attempt to "kill SDI" as the price for an agreement. SDI, he maintained, was America's "insurance policy" that the Russians would keep the commitments made at Reykjavik.[41]

As details began to filter out about the negotiations, troubles mounted for the president from within his own administration as well as from allies. The president had neither consulted nor informed the joint chiefs of his proposal to eliminate all nuclear weapons in ten

---

[41] Gerald Boyd, "President Won't Give Up 'Star Wars' but Says Pacts Are Possible," *New York Times*, October 14, 1986, 1.

years and news of this proposal caused great consternation within military circles.[42] Many believed that the forfeiture of nuclear weapons would open up the United States and the western alliance to Soviet blackmail because of Moscow's conventional force advantage.[43]

NATO allies also sought reassurance from Washington that any arms deal with Moscow would not de-couple Western Europe.[44] Before Reykjavik, it was thought that the United States would seek a "phased withdrawal" of intermediate-range missiles. "They were taken by surprise when the superpowers suddenly agreed to go directly to zero."[45] Thatcher was astounded.[46] West German Chancellor Kohl and President Mitterand of France issued a joint statement declaring that any elimination of missiles must also "be accompanied by cuts in superior Soviet conventional forces."[47]

In Washington, Democrats were intent upon demonstrating that the administration was violating the Boland amendment in Central America, hoping to forestall the activation of the $100 million in aid the Congress had passed for Contra assistance earlier in June. Hasenfus had claimed that the CIA was directly involved in running the program, a charge not easily rebutted.[48] Eleven House Democrats sent a letter to the Justice Department demanding that Attorney

---

[42] George Wilson, "Reagan's Offer Baffles Military, Hill Specialists," *Washington Post*, October 14, 1986, 17. See also Admiral William J. Crowe, *The Line of Fire*, (New York: Simon & Shuster, 1993), 268-69.

[43] Mark Thompson, "U.S. Offer At Odd With Pentagon," *Philadelphia Inquirer*, October 15, 1986, 11; Michael Gordon, "Reagan's Missile Offer Sets Off a Shifting Debate," *New York Times*, October 24, 1986, 14.

[44] Gary Verkey, "Nervous NATO Allies Seek US Assurance on Superpower Arms Deal," *Christian Science Monitor*, October 23, 1986, 9.

[45] Don Cook, "Europeans, Buffeted by Missile Foes and Superpower Seesaw, Wait and Worry," *Los Angeles Times*, October 26, 1986, 2.

[46] Richard Beeston, "Thatcher to Warn Reagan on Arms," *Washington Times*, November 12, 1986, 7.

[47] "Soviets' Conventional Forces Worry West Germany, France," *Baltimore Sun*, October 29, 1986, 2; Steven Erlanger, "For British, Germans, Arms Failure May Hurt," *Boston Globe*, October 21, 1986, 16.

[48] Lydia Chavez, "Salvadoran Air Base Is Called Center for C.I.A. Operations," *New York Times*, October 15, 1986, 1.

General Meese assign a special prosecutor to determine the extent to which the government was complying with, or deviating from the Boland restrictions.[49]

At the same time, Senate Foreign Relations Committee "staff members said they would begin taking sworn depositions from persons willing to give testimony on additional allegations that…the Contras have been involved in gunrunning, drug trafficking, and money laundering." However, Senate leaders, in a close 50-47 vote, rejected a demand that the president report to Congress on the aid program.[50]

Exposure of the Contra supply network strained ties with El Salvador and Honduras, whose airfields were being used for the operation.[51] Stories circulated about the "vast" private supply network supplying the Contras.[52] An earthquake in San Salvador offered an opportunity to provide economic assistance and the president moved quickly to sign the necessary orders to start the aid to the Contras flowing from U.S. government coffers.[53]

Relations with Moscow were also strained. On Sunday, October 19, the Soviet Union expelled five American diplomats in retaliation for the expulsion of twenty-five Russian members of the Soviet mission to the UN on September 17. On October 21, the Reagan administration ordered the expulsion of fifty-five Soviets from the

---

[49] Joanne Omang, "Democrats Demand a Contra-Aid Special Prosecutor," *Washington Post*, October 18, 1986, 15.

[50] Christopher Simpson, "Senate Won't Demand Report on Contra Aid," *Washington Times*, October 17, 1986, 4.

[51] Julia Preston, "Clandestine Missions Described," *Washington Post*, October 17, 1986, 1; Stephen Engleberg, "U.S.-Salvadoran Ties Called Strained," *New York Times*, October 21, 1986, 3;

[52] "Private Pipeline To the Contras: A Vast Network," *New York Times*, October 22, 1986, 1; Robert Reinhold, "Ex-General hints at Big Role As U.S. Champion of Contras," *New York Times*, October 14, 1986, 6.

[53] Stephen Engleberg, "Shultz Tours Salvadoran Rubble And Promises More American Aid," *New York Times*, October 17, 1986, 15; James Morrison, "Regan order Could Get Aid for Contras Flowing Today," *Washington Times*, October 22, 1986, 1; Joanne Omang, "Reagan Restarts Contra Aid," *Washington Post*, October 25, 1986, 17.

United States, the largest number of diplomats ever expelled from the country at one time.[54] Moscow responded immediately by barring 260 local Russian employees from working at the U.S. embassy in Moscow and the consulate in Leningrad.[55] The Soviet action placed embassy personnel in "a stressful" situation for several months until the State Department could recruit and train replacements, but it brought an end to the "tit for tat" expulsions.[56] President Reagan managed to weather these relatively minor storms, but his main current focus was on the Iranian initiative, which had reached a critical point.

Forebodings of Failure

Following the October 6 meeting in Frankfurt, Cave and Hakim were in periodic, secure telephone contact with Bahramani and Samii in Tehran, awaiting a response to the 9-point plan. While they waited, however, a threat to the initiative appeared from an entirely different quarter. Adnan Khashoggi, concerned that Gorbanifar had been cut out and that he would not recoup his investment, conjured up a threat to the initiative that he communicated through an associate of his, who was also a friend of Casey's.

To recapitulate, moving to the second channel left Gorbanifar with no means of generating income to repay his and his investors' investment. The Iranians had not produced the hostages, the Americans had not delivered the remaining spare parts and radars, and the Iranians refused to pay Gorbanifar, who, in turn, could not repay Khashoggi.

Hoping to prod the Americans into action, Khashoggi sent his "sometime partner," Roy Furmark, to see CIA Director Casey, an old

---

[54] Bernard Gwertzman, "U.S. Is Expelling 55 In Latest Reprisal On Soviet Envoys," *New York Times*, October 22, 1986, 1.
[55] Celestine Bohlen, "Soviets Retaliate, Limit U.S. Embassy," *Washington Post*, October 23, 1986, 1.
[56] Matlock, *Reagan and Gorbachev*, 242; David Ottaway and John Goshko, "U.S. Seeks to Halt Round of Expulsions, Act on 'Larger Issues'," *Washington Post*, October 24, 1986, 1.

friend.[57] Visiting Casey on October 7, Furmark laid out the finances of the May arms deal, Khashoggi's $15 million investment, and the $10 million shortfall. Furmark disclosed that Khashoggi had involved two Canadian investors in the deal, who, if they did not receive their funds back, would divulge the initiative to Democrat members of the Senate Intelligence Committee.[58] Casey was non-committal, perhaps realizing that such an action would insure that they would lose their investment, but told Furmark to give all the details to one of his "guys."

A few days before, on October 1, Allen, reading the intelligence traffic, had grown concerned that too many people were knowledgeable of the Iran initiative and took his concerns to deputy director Robert Gates. Gates, only recently promoted following McMahon's resignation in February, was only dimly aware of what was going on and was surprised by what he was told.[59] Allen was worried about operational security because North had comingled the Iran and contra operations by using Secord in both. He feared that both operations were "spinning out of control."[60]

Gates agreed and took Allen to see Casey, as it happened, shortly after the director had met with Furmark on October 7. Raising their concerns about North's actions, Casey expressed his admiration for North as "a man who gets things done," but shared their concerns about "opsec" and promised to look into it. In the meantime, Casey instructed Allen to put his views in writing.[61] Two reports in the same

---

[57] Samuel Segev, The Iranian Triangle: The Untold Story of Israel's Role in the Iran-Contra Affair (New York: Free Press, 1988), 308-9.
[58] As Theodore Draper, *A Very Thin Line: The Iran-Contra Affairs* (New York: Hill and Wang, 1991), 450, notes, the Canadians, Donald Fraser and Ernest Miller, "were real enough, but their roles in Khashoggi's scheme had been invented." The actual investors behind Khashoggi were Saudis, but, in order to lend political heft to his threat to disclose the initiative, Khashoggi enlisted his old Canadian acquaintances in the scheme.
[59] "Charles Allen deposition," *Report of the Congressional Committees Investigating the Iran-Contra Affair* (Washington, D.C.: GPO, 1987), Appendix B, volume 1, 824. [cited hereafter as *Iran-Contra Affair*.]
[60] "Robert Gates deposition," Appendix B, volume 11, *Iran Contra- Affair*, 973.
[61] Draper, *Very Thin Line*, 441.

day detailing difficulty with the initiative clearly got Casey's attention. He quickly wrote a memorandum for the record of his conversation with Furmark and called Poindexter to alert him of the gist of his meetings.[62]

Two days later, on October 9, Casey included Gates for lunch in his office with North to get a status report on the Iran operation. After being briefed on the state of play there and the anticipated breakthrough with the second channel, Gates says he asked North about Hasenfus' charge about the Contra supply effort being a CIA operation. North replied bluntly that there was "absolutely" no CIA involvement.[63]

North, however, tells a different story about the meeting. He claimed he said, "sooner or later the real story [about the supply effort] was going to come out." Although Gates says that Casey mildly admonished North to "get this straightened out," North claims that Casey told him that Project Democracy was "over" and that he was to "shut it down and clean it up." Now that Congress had passed the aid legislation, Casey said, the agency "was going back in." North also said "Nicaragua wasn't the only thing on Casey's mind." He was "unhappy to hear that Furmark, an outsider, had detailed knowledge about Lake Resources, the use of the residuals, and my own involvement in all of this."[64]

Contrary to Gates, North says that "Casey's admonition to 'clean it up' meant more than just bringing back the pilots and others who had worked for Secord [in Central America]. Between the Hasenfus problem and Furmark we were facing the strong possibility of the imminent exposure of all our operations, including the hostage recovery effort." It was from this point, North claims, that he "tried to destroy all documents that mentioned the 'diversion,' or the names of people who might conceivably be at risk." This included the "ledger"

---

[62] "Allen deposition," 829-30.
[63] "Gates deposition," 988.
[64] "Gates deposition," 988 and Oliver North and William Novak, *Under Fire: An American Story* (New York: Harper Collins, 1991), *Under Fire*, 297-98.

that Casey had given him to keep track of the money and the names of individuals and organizations "whose public exposure would have been a disaster."[65]

On that same day, October 9, as Allen was preparing to write his memorandum, Nir telephoned him to emphasize that Gorbanifar was at wits end and would somehow "take his revenge" if he were not paid.[66] Nir's alarmist tone reinforced Allen's misgivings. Allen's memo of the 14th thus described the ongoing initiative in alarmist tones as a "disaster of major proportions" that is "likely to be exposed soon unless remedial action is taken."[67]

Allen recommended an "orderly, damage-limiting shutdown" of the Gorbanifar-Kangarlu channel, preparation of "press guidance" in the event of exposure, and the establishment of a high-level "planning cell" in the White House headed by "two or three" outside experts of high stature, like Henry Kissinger(!), or former CIA Director Dick Helms.[68] Allen's recommendations assumed that the White House had no "plan to deal with the potential disclosure" and his recommendation to bring in someone like Kissinger betrayed no indication that he understood the strategic conflict raging within the administration. Nevertheless, he had put down on paper the essence of the president's Iran Initiative and predicted "disaster."

Allen turned his memo in to Gates on the 15th and he immediately gave it to Casey. The two men went that same day to see Poindexter. The National Security Adviser read the memo betraying no sense of

---

[65] North, *Under Fire*, 298-99. Draper, *Very Thin Line*, 443, says "the impression left by Gates' account is that Casey and North were remarkably unperturbed at this meeting" and suggests that Casey told North "privately" to clean things up. But, he concludes that "Casey had been holding out on his deputy, Gates." Jane Mayer and Doyle McManus, *Landslide: The Unmaking of the President* (Boston: Houghton Mifflin, 1988), 287, also say that Casey called North later "that week" to tell him to "clean things up."
[66] Draper, *Very Thin Line*, 443.
[67] Charles Allen, "memorandum for Casey," October 14, 1986, *Iran-Contra Affair*, Appendix B, volume 11, 1049-57.
[68] Ibid, 1055-56.

anxiety.[69] Casey suggested that perhaps it was time to go public and advised Poindexter to consult the White House counsel, Peter Wallison, to insure that they were on firm legal ground. But the national security adviser disagreed and said, "I don't know that I can trust the White House counsel." Casey subsequently decided, on the advice of Gates, to talk to the CIA's own counsel to review the case. The counsel, David Doherty, "did not believe there were any concerns from a legal or proprietary standpoint for CIA."[70]

Casey sent Allen to see Furmark, who turned the screw further, telling him that the "Canadians" were about to talk to Democrat Senators, Patrick Leahy, Daniel Moynihan, and Alan Cranston. They intended to tell them that the government had been engaging in a back channel arms deal with Iran and had swindled them out of their investment. They also intended to sue Khaghoggi, who, in turn, would reveal U.S. government involvement.[71] But, Furmark thought that the way out of the mess was for the administration to make at least a partial shipment of the remaining spare parts, so Tehran could pay off Gorbanifar.[72]

Although their meeting was brief, Furmark having to return to New York, Allen was stunned by his depth of knowledge of the affair. Furmark had been present from the beginning in January 1985 and described its subsequent twists and turns, which meant he knew more about it, especially its origins, than even Poindexter, North, and Secord, who had only become involved themselves months later. It was also evident that he was closely associated with Khashoggi, Gorbanifar, and the Israeli officials involved. Allen's view was that the risk of exposure was "growing daily" and recommended that a "group be formed" that was knowledgeable of the Gorbanifar channel to "consider how to cope with this burgeoning problem."[73]

---

[69] "Gates deposition," 981-82.
[70] Draper, *Very Thin Line*, 442, 446.
[71] "Roy Furmark deposition," *Iran-Contra Affair*, Appendix B, volume 11, 133.
[72] "Allen Memorandum to Casey and Gates," October 16, 1986, Ibid, Appendix B, volume 1 1180-82.
[73] Ibid, 1182.

Casey immediately called Furmark and offered him a ride back to New York in his plane, as he was going there, too, for a public function. On the plane, Furmark gave him the same story he had given Allen, urging that the administration "try to send a small shipment so that Gorbanifar may be able to take another 5 million to take the pressure off Khashoggi." Casey's reaction was that he would look into it and told Furmark to "just sit tight."[74]

Casey next arranged for Allen to go to New York to finish his debrief of Furmark and sent Cave along with him. No doubt, Casey wanted Cave's reaction to Furmark. On the evening of October 22 they met for dinner at the Chrysalis restaurant where they went over the details yet again. Cave revealed his direct involvement in the affair as a "logistician," and observed that it took sixty days for the financing of the previous deal to be concluded. The implication was that the Canadian investors were still within a reasonable time frame for concluding the deal and should not panic.

Furmark argued that the U.S. had simply not completed its contract and completing it would lead to a "perfect result." Otherwise, Khashoggi also stood to lose the collateral he had put up for the loan, an astounding $30 to $35 million, he claimed. Then, turning the screw further, for the first time Furmark revealed, "Gorbanifar believed that… $15 million had gone to Nicaragua."[75] Allen had suspected for some time that profits from the arms sales had been used for the contras and now his suspicions were confirmed. It is curious, to say the least, that the CIA, having labeled Gorbanifar a "fabricator" and a liar throughout this process, was eager to believe him now.

Nevertheless, Cave wrote up a memorandum of conversation combining his and Allen's notes of the meeting with Furmark and the two of them briefed Casey on it the next morning of October 23.[76] Casey was "deeply disturbed" and immediately talked to Poindexter on the secure phone. But, although Casey said he would send the

---

[74] "Roy Furmark deposition," 135.
[75] Ibid, 140-41.
[76] "Allen deposition," 843-45.

memo over to Poindexter, he did not, because, as Allen told it to the Tower Commission afterward, "it fell into the wrong out box." [77]

We may be profoundly skeptical that the Cave-Allen memo got lost in the shuffle. At the same time, we may agree wholeheartedly with Chairman John Tower's observation that "anything that critical...he [Casey] would have discussed with Admiral Poindexter" (and not put it in writing).[78] Time was of the essence. Casey wanted nothing more than to deep six the Allen-Cave memo because it had laid out the covert operations on paper just at the moment of the expected breakthrough with the Iranians.

The Iranian Calculus Changes

When Bahramani presented the 9-point plan to the Iranian leadership, they immediately realized that North had pulled the wool over his eyes. (As they would tell the Americans when they next met: they considered North's 7-point plan the "official position" of the U.S. government and "the 9-point plan as simply a private agreement between Hakim and [Bahramani].")[79] Indeed, Bahramani was chastised and temporarily prevented from continuing as a negotiator.

Worse, what he had brought back was a change in U.S. policy. The Iranians had sought to take the middle position between the United States and the Soviet Union, having relations with both, but an alliance with neither. They had sought to maneuver both powers to provide them with a maximum opportunity to defeat Iraq in the war and overthrow Saddam Hussein. The nine-point plan represented a failure of the American part of their strategy.

---

[77] "Charles Allen interview," John G. Tower et al., *Report of the President's Special Review Board: February 26, 1987* (Washington, D.C.: GPO, 1987), B-169.
[78] Ibid. Draper, *Very Thin Line*, 446, says of Casey here that he was "either playacting, or already so weakened by illness that he was incapable of facing "a disaster of major proportions.'"
[79] "Mainz Transcript, October 29, 1986," *Iran-Contra Affair*, Appendix A, volume 1, 1647.

Iran had spent some ten months attempting to bring about a change in United States policy from neutrality (of sorts) to full support of Iran against Iraq, with all of its attendant weapons benefits. They had held out the prospect of parleying arms for hostages into reestablishment of full diplomatic relations, although they wanted no alliance. They had changed interlocutors, offering direct contact with Rafsanjani, to increase their credibility, even as they grudgingly acknowledged only limited influence with the hostages' captors.

Having failed to draw the United States into full support against Iraq forced a change in Iranian calculations. Iran had sought full-scale weapons support, but no political alliance. Reagan had declined this bargain, shifting to a simple and limited exchange of weapons for the remaining hostages. The 9-point plan reflected that position.

The Iranians, of course, could not deliver the hostages without satisfying Mugniyeh's demands that the United States assist in obtaining the freedom of the Dawa 17. In the 9-point plan, Hakim had offered a "plan" to mediate between Iran and Kuwait over these prisoners, but not a commitment to intervene in internal Kuwaiti politics. To accept this plan would mean that the best that could be hoped for was limited U.S. weapons support for Iran, and then only if the hostages were released.

On the other hand, there was the Soviet factor in the equation. They had offered to normalize relations and on October 9, Iran had declared that it was "ready to consolidate its good neighborly relations with the USSR."[80] Russian intelligence had obviously been following the negotiations with the Americans closely and timed their offer accordingly.

The Soviet agreement to "consolidate" relations implied a Soviet willingness to reduce support for Saddam again, as they had done in February. No doubt, the Soviets pointed out that although Saddam continued air attacks, he was reinforcing his defenses by constructing strengthened barriers, minefields, and dug-in tanks, rather than

---

[80] "Middle East and South Asia Review," FBIS-South Asia, October 10, 1986, 1.

preparing his forces for offensive operations.[81] There can also be little doubt that Soviet restraint of Saddam would be contingent upon Tehran stepping away from Washington.

Thus, with full U.S. support for Iran not possible, the choice before the Iranian leaders appeared to be at best limited U.S. support for Iran against full Soviet support for Saddam, unless consolidation of relations with Moscow would be accompanied by reduced support for Saddam. One bright spot was the large increase in arms from China, spare U.S. parts from Greece, and arms from Soviet client, Czechoslovakia, which offered some hope that Iran could satisfactorily prosecute the war.[82]

As the Iranian leadership struggled over these options, Rafsanjani advocated making another attempt to draw the United States in, to which Ayatollah Montazeri violently objected. Montazeri, the designated successor to Khomeini, opposed the deal with the Great Satan and so directed his top lieutenant, Mehdi Hashemi to distribute "five million" leaflets throughout Tehran to expose Rafsanjani's secret negotiations with the United States. Presumably advocating the Soviet option, publicizing the negotiations was an attempt to prevent the continuation of efforts to draw the United States into support of Iran.[83] The timely arrival of information confirming McFarlane's trip to Tehran added fuel to the struggle.[84]

But Khomeini himself censured Montazeri, authorized the arrest of Hashemi and some two hundred of his men, and ordered an investigation of his "underground operations."[85] The fact that

---

[81] Anthony Cordesman, The Iran-Iraq War and Western Security, 1984-1987 (London: Jane's, 1987), 111.
[82] Ibid, 109.
[83] *Iran-Contra Affair*, 259.
[84] Segev, *Iranian Triangle*, 283-86. The editor of *Al Shiraa* was Hassan Sabra, who was also a supporter of Montazeri. Segev discusses Sabra's role in attempting to confirm McFarlane's trip to Tehran in October.
[85] Cordesman, *Iran-Iraq War and Western Security*, 123. See also "Clandestine Radio Reports 'Verbal Clash,'" *FBIS-South Asia*, October 22, 1986, I-1; "Khomeyni Answers Reyshahri on Arrest of Hashemi," *FBIS-South Asia*, October 28, 1986, I-1.

Montazeri continued to be referred to as the "appointed next leader" indicated that their differences had been over policy and was not the beginning of a succession crisis, as some Americans believed.[86]

In short, Khomeini overruled the objections of Montazeri, and authorized another meeting with the Americans, but sent only Ali Samii and kept Rafsanjani's man, Bahramani, in Tehran. This was no doubt punishment for his earlier failed negotiation of the 9-point plan. Thus, on October 19, the Iranians confirmed their acceptance of the 9-point plan and agreed to another meeting in Frankfurt to discuss its implementation. Their intent, however, was to change its terms.

On October 21, North and Secord flew to Geneva to conclude a complicated arrangement with Nir.[87] The U.S. had agreed to sell 500 *TOWs* to Iran as part of the 9-point plan. Earlier, in May, the U.S. had finally replaced the missiles Israel had sent to Iran in August 1985. The Israelis had rejected them as outmoded, but kept them in storage. The deal with Nir was that Israel would send these outmoded models to Iran and receive new models from the U.S.[88]

Part of their discussion involved Gorbanifar, as Nir recounted the Iranian's payment demands. Secord was struck by North's passive, even phlegmatic reaction, not realizing that North had heard all this two weeks before from Casey. Secord thought of North that "maybe he was just tired." The two Americans also informed Nir that they were on their way to a meeting with Bahramani, but, as the Iranians had objected to an Israeli presence, he would not be invited.[89] Thus, part of the reason for the missile switch was to keep the Israelis on board.

---

[86] "AFP Told Montazeri 'Still' Khomeyni Successor," *FBIS-South Asia,* October 28, 1986, I-1. On the succession interpretation, see "Teicher Prof Note to Poindexter," November 4, 1986, *Tower Report,* B-171-72.

[87] *Tower Report,* B-171, says that North's calendar showed him departing for Frankfurt on October 26, but, in fact, as noted above, North and his team departed for Europe five days earlier, soon after hearing from the Iranians.

[88] Segev, *Iranian Triangle,* 309.

[89] Richard Secord and Jay Wurts, Honored and Betrayed: Irangate, Covert Affairs, and the Secret War in Laos (New York: Wiley, 1992), 303-04.

On October 24, North and Secord flew to Frankfurt, joining Hakim, who had preceded them. They were to meet Bahramani and Samii at the Steigenburger Hotel. The first inkling that all was not well came when Hakim told them that Bahramani would not be coming. It immediately became obvious when they met that Samii, the "monster," had been sent to take a hard line. The Iranian began the meeting by telling them that he could only obtain the freedom of one hostage for the 500 *TOWs*. He had "tried hard for a second 'box,' but could only guarantee one."[90]

This news upset North, who felt "the Iranians already seemed to be welching on the deal." (In fact, according to the 9-point plan, the Iranians had promised to obtain the release of "one definitely and the second with all effective possible effort.")[91] Next, Samii claimed "with a straight face" that the "U.S. had promised to intercede with the Kuwaitis" regarding the Dawa 17. Secord immediately said that this was "a step backward and a bald-faced lie."[92] He was correct, the 9-point plan specified only that "Albert [Hakim] will provide the plan" for their release and it was understood that Washington would "mediate," not "intercede."[93]

Exasperated, North and Secord "demanded that the Relative [Bahramani] fly up for the meeting, or they could forget about the TOW delivery." Samii countered with the argument that to call Bahramani now would be "an insult" to him. But North said that as Bahramani had been "presented as the representative of Speaker Rafsanjani," he insisted that he be present. "After numerous phone calls [to Tehran], the Relative agreed the next day to join us."[94]

---

[90] Ibid, 305.
[91] *Iran-Contra Affair*, 257.
[92] Ibid.
[93] *Iran-Contra Affair*, 257.
[94] Secord, *Honored and Betrayed*, 305, notes "Ollie considered going back to Washington," but "after discussions with Poindexter, he agreed to wait while Cave flew over to join us." Reagan's instructions, conveyed through Poindexter, were to focus on the 9-point plan, get the hostages out, and press for more later.

Cave arrived on the morning of October 26, joining North, Secord, and Hakim. At noon, they "picked up the Relative [Bahramani] at the Frankfurt airport and drove directly to Mainz about thirty minutes away." They went to Mainz ostensibly because no rooms were available in Frankfurt due to the International Book Fair then going on. Whether this was true or not, the fact was the CIA had bugged their rooms at the Mainz Hilton.[95]

Reviewing the 9-point plan, Bahramani confirmed that "only one release was feasible" in the next few days before the election. After lengthy discussion about the irrelevance of the coming election and the importance of obtaining the release of at least one more hostage, North closed the meeting with a threat to terminate their negotiations.

> Unless we could get the nine-point plan in motion to our mutual benefit without these acrimonious after-the-fact lapses of faith, it would be best for both sides to table the program—at least until more meaningful talks could be held between our two governments.[96]

North's threat, relayed immediately back to Tehran, seemed to have an effect. When they resumed talks the next morning, October 27, Bahramani and Samii both became much more forthcoming. Bahramani revealed they were trying to locate hostages Reed and Cicippio, but could not. He also revealed that the reason behind the attempt to obtain U.S. intercession with Kuwait was because the 9-point plan "required ambassadorial-level communication" between Iran and Kuwait that they did not have. "Eventually," however, Bahramani "agreed that the Kuwait plan was acceptable as written."[97]

North also offered a major concession, reducing the price for the *TOW* missiles. Where, earlier, the unit price had been $13,000, North lowered it to $7,200, making the total for 500 $3.6 million. The Iranians seemed grateful for this concession and offered to

---

[95] Ibid, 306.
[96] Ibid, 307.
[97] Ibid.

demonstrate their bona fides. After the meeting, Hakim accompanied Bahramani and Samii to the Frankfurt branch of Credit Suisse to confirm deposit of the $3.6 million to the Lake Resources account. When it was confirmed, they offered to deposit an additional $40 million (!) to demonstrate their "good faith." On Secord's advice Hakim wisely declined this offer because "it might be construed as committing the U.S. government," which, of course, was its purpose.[98] The deposit immediately triggered the delivery of the 500 *TOWs* from Israel the next day, October 28, and set the stage for the climactic meeting between the two sides.

Meeting in Mainz, October 29

From the U.S. point of view the meeting of the 29th was intended to reach agreements on implementing the 9-point plan. For the Iranians, however, it was designed to make another attempt to range the U.S. firmly on the side of Iran as a major weapons supplier. Bahramani began the meeting divulging the news that there was "dissension in Iran over the initiative"[99] and recounted the story of the leaflets spread around Tehran by "Montazeri's loyalists."[100] He reported that Montazeri's chief lieutenant, Mehdi Hashemi, had been arrested and the situation 'brought ...under control," but the crisis had "almost prevented" the two of them from coming to the meeting.[101]

This was both an adroit attempt to explain away the fact of Bahramani's own initial absence and turn it to advantage. He thought that the revelations "would hasten the exposure of the entire affair," and that, therefore, they should "expedite" the 9-point plan.[102] North agreed. He "immediately sent a KL-43 message to Admiral Poindexter telling him the news and recommending that we press on to do everything possible to get out more hostages before the Iran initiative

---

[98] Ibid, 309.
[99] *Iran-Contra Affair*, 259.
[100] Segev, *Iranian Triangle*, 310.
[101] Draper, *Very Thin Line*, 452.
[102] Segev, Iranian Triangle, *310.*

met the same end as Project Democracy. In his reply, the Admiral okayed what would be our final transaction."[103]

North's "message to Admiral Poindexter" was somewhat disingenuous. He was in constant contact with Poindexter and presumably was being briefed on current developments in Tehran essential to his mission. There can be little doubt, therefore, that North was fully apprised of the "dissension" in Iran before Bahramani recounted it to him because news of Montazeri's opposition was all over the Iranian press, which American intelligence assiduously monitored.[104]

Talk of dissension in Tehran led naturally to the state of play in Washington. Bahramani asked who supported the initiative besides the president and Poindexter? North replied that in addition to the two of them, the Vice-President, Casey, and Regan supported the initiative, while Shultz and Weinberger opposed. "After that," he said, "nobody else counts....Nobody in our Congress knows about it. And we're not going to tell them until we get all the hostages out."[105]

In return, Bahramani revealed that there were three groups in Iran, which he described as a "shareholding company," participating in this "venture." There was Rafsanjani's group, a right-wing group, whose leader was not named, but was probably either Ayatollah Khamenei's, or Ayatollah Farsi's group, and Montazeri's. Montazeri, however, "had lost ground...and been forced to withdraw from public activity."[106] Although Montazeri's objection had been public and therefore known to the Americans, the fact that Rafsanjani had included all three groups in the opening to the United States had stunned them.

Bahramani's revelation meant that Reagan had not been supporting a moderate faction against hard-liners after all, but dealing with what

---

[103] North, *Under Fire*, 299.
[104] See footnotes 85 and 86 above.
[105] "Mainz Transcript, October 29, 1986," *Iran-Contra Affair*, Appendix A, volume 1, 1592.
[106] Ibid, 1573-4. In another place, 1588-90, Montazeri was said to have "closed himself in."

had been, up until then, a united leadership. The entire effort of shifting from Gorbanifar to a second channel had been a charade, cleverly managed by the Iranians to give the Americans the impression that they were moving closer to developing a political relationship.

The unity of the Iranian leadership was further reinforced when, in naming the Iranian members to the proposed joint Iranian-American commission, Bahramani named none other than Kangarlu, who was Montazeri's man, and Najafabadi, the Majlis member who had participated in the McFarlane talks in Tehran.[107] Bahramani and Samii were apparently the other two.[108] The inclusion of Kangarlu meant that Gorbanifar was also part of the scheme.

Much of the discussion revolved around arms and hostages. Going beyond the 9-point plan, Bahramani asked, "in Rafsanjani's name," that the U.S. send technicians to repair the inoperative *Phoenix* missiles in their inventory. He also wanted helicopters, which were embargoed, and reconnaissance cameras for their Phantom jets.[109] Finally, he raised again the question of the funds that had been frozen years earlier.

North recognized that in asking for the *Phoenix* assistance "they are making a change—step six is the hawk," referring to point six of the 9-point plan. He then countered by demanding that they obtain the release of all three of the hostages, not just two.[110] North said, "we have known for over a year that you need technical help, and we have offered to send it." North affirmed that he was prepared to stick by the proposal he had given the Iranians in May: "all the hostages [out] All terrorism stops." [111] But nothing could go forward until the hostages were freed. If they were freed, then everything was possible. Their

---

[107] Segev, *Iranian Triangle*, 310.
[108] Draper, *Very Thin Line*, 657, n.20.
[109] "Mainz Transcript, October 29, 1986," 1604-5 and Segev, *Iranian Triangle*, 310.
[110] "Mainz Transcript," 1604-5.
[111] Ibid, 1607-08.

meeting ended with Bahramani's promise that Jacobson would be released in a few days, and perhaps Sutherland.[112]

Afterward, the Americans discussed among themselves the prospects of actually freeing the hostages. North thought that "the only thing that was necessary [was] for the Imam to make very clear to people" his wishes. Hakim thought that they "do not want to use Khomeini...they don't want to use the big gun." Secord thought they could simply "send an order to the revolutionary guard to get them," but thought they didn't know where they were. North and Cave disagreed, arguing that they know "exactly where they are."[113]

There were several conclusions that emerged from this meeting. Despite all the hints and even outright admissions the Iranian interlocutors had given, especially Bahramani, the Americans still persisted in the erroneous belief that Khomeini's influence would govern Mugniyeh's decisions. Even though it was clear that the Americans knew Mugniyeh held the hostages, they believed that Khomeini's will prevailed.

The revelation that the Iranian leadership had been manipulating the Reagan team, not the other way around, raised even more fundamental questions. It was impossible to avoid the conclusion that the hostages were simply being dangled as bait for weapons and that the prospects for a full-blown political rapprochement were nil. Before any of these points could sink in, however, the president's initiative came crashing down, the result of the new world order faction's time bomb planted months earlier.

---

[112] If Iranian intelligence were monitoring U.S. publications, an item in *Newsweek*, October 20, 1986 would certainly have removed doubts about the U.S. understanding of the hostage situation. The news item declared that Imad Mugniyeh was holding Jacobson, Anderson, and Sutherland. *Islamic Jihad* "had snatched their victims to trade for seventeen confreres in terror jailed in Kuwait. But intelligence sources believe they might settle for springing just three Lebanese Shiites among them, who have been sentenced to death."

[113] "Mainz Transcript," 1618.

Chapter 12
The Struggle for Power

The irony of President Reagan's Iran initiative was that his policy was failing even as it was being exposed by the new world order faction. Exposure of the initiative led immediately to a sustained effort by Secretary Shultz to seize control of foreign policy under the guise of a demand to end what he charged was an arms-for-hostages scheme.

Reagan's response was first to attempt to sustain the initiative. When it became clear that the Iranians had rejected rapprochement, he attempted to end the initiative but retain control of policy. Finally, Shultz revealed the entrapment of the president in the November 1985 *Hawk* shipment and its subsequent cover-up. The entrapment combined with the promise of additional revelations through a congressional investigation, with its threat of a Watergate-style outcome—that is, the possibility of impeachment—led Reagan to give up the struggle for power with Shultz and focus on salvaging his presidency.

Exposure of the Iran Initiative

At the end of the Mainz meeting, Bahramani had assured North that he could arrange for two of the remaining three hostages, Jacobson and Sutherland, to be released. Samii had sought to extract 500 more *TOWs* as the price for a second hostage, which didn't go over well with Secord and the matter was dropped.[1] Nevertheless,

---

[1] Report of the Congressional Committees Investigating the Iran-Contra Affair (Washington, D.C.: GPO, 1987), 261. [cited hereafter as Iran-Contra Affair.]

assuming that two hostages would be released, North made preparations to pick them up. Seeking to disguise Washington's role, he arranged for Terry Waite, a well-known British humanitarian and Anglican Church envoy, to travel to Beirut to receive them. Waite arrived in Beirut on October 31, with the story that he was expecting the imminent release of two hostages.[2]

At 7:00 A.M. on Sunday morning, November 2, David Jacobson was dropped off near the site of the old American embassy compound in west Beirut. According to Jacobson, Terry Anderson was also supposed to have been released later that day. He had been in contact with Anderson, as both men were being held in the same building, but in different cells. The third hostage, Sutherland was being held in a different place.[3] In a statement announcing Jacobson's release, *Islamic Jihad*, that is, Imad Mugniyeh, urged the U.S. government to proceed with unspecified "current approaches that could lead, if continued, to a solution of the hostage issue," a veiled reference to the Dawa prisoners in Kuwait mentioned in the nine-point agreement.[4]

Everything seemed to be going according to plan, but two hours after Jacobson was released, at 9:00 A.M., the newspaper *Al Shiraa* "hit the streets" with its weekend edition. In it was an article describing the ongoing Byzantine policy struggle in Tehran, including a jumbled account of McFarlane's trip to Tehran tacked on at the end.[5] The article apparently spooked Imad Mugniyeh, if not also Rafsanjani, and Anderson's release was canceled.[6]

---

[2] Bernard Gwertzman, "U.S. Looks for Sign in Captors' Move," *New York Times*, November 4, 1986, 11, and Jane Mayer and Doyle McManus, *Landslide: The Unmaking of the President* (Boston: Houghton Mifflin, 1988), 290.
[3] Deborah H. Strober and Gerald S. Strober, *The Reagan Presidency: An Oral History of the Era* (Washington: Brassey's, 2003*)*, 472.
[4] Ihsan A. Hijazi, "Hostage's Release is Linked to Shift in Iranian Policy," *New York Times*, November 4, 1986, 1.
[5] Mayer and McManus, *Landslide*, 293.
[6] Strober and Strober, *The Reagan Presidency*, 472. Most sources state that the newspaper appeared the following day, November 3, but the *New York Times* articles cited above establish the date as November 2.

Hoping that the second hostage's release was being delayed, not canceled, President Reagan decided to refuse comment to reporters' increasingly insistent questions about the *Al Shiraa* article, saying that it had no foundation.[7] Not so, Shultz. On his way to Vienna for a meeting with Shevardnadze, he cabled Poindexter from the plane with contrary advice to "get everything out in the open, and fast."[8] Seeing an opportunity to put an end to the president's initiative, Shultz continued: "we could make clear that this was a special, one-time operation based on humanitarian grounds…[but] that our policies toward terrorism and the Iran-Iraq war stand."[9]

The president disregarded Shultz's advice and decided to wait. Asked on the campaign trail in Las Vegas about his efforts to secure the release of the hostages, Reagan simply said that the government was working through channels that he couldn't "discuss."[10] Poindexter, in a reply to Shultz, said that the vice president, Weinberger, and Casey had all agreed with the president to decline comment for the time being, but Shultz refused "to go along." In remarks to his staff, he was already saying the president was stonewalling, which to him meant, "it was somewhat like Watergate."[11]

To say that Shultz was panicking, or jumping to conclusions at this early date would be a misinterpretation. The exposure of the initiative was his opportunity to make yet another attempt to shut down the initiative and take control of policy. Shultz's exchange with Poindexter marked the beginning of a fierce policy struggle between the president and the new world order faction.

The president immediately instructed Poindexter to gather together the relevant facts "to determine how the policy initiative had been

---

[7] Mayer and McManus, *Landslide*, 295-96.
[8] George Shultz, *Turmoil and Triumph* (New York: Macmillan, 1993), 786.
[9] *Iran-Contra Affair*, 293. Shultz omitted this portion of his message to Poindexter from his memoir.
[10] Gwertzman, "U.S. Looks for Sign in Captors' Move."
[11] Shultz, *Turmoil and Triumph*, 787.

conducted, conceived, approved, and so forth."[12] The problem was there was no record, no paper trail detailing the origins of the initiative. Recall, as part of the new world order faction's entrapment scheme, McFarlane had authorized Israeli action in the president's name and had made no record of his actions.

Unable to document the origins of the initiative, Poindexter had no choice but to ask the former national security adviser for his "help," and he readily acceded. In his PROF note reply to Poindexter, on November 7, McFarlane complained that he had "heard" Regan was "indicating to one and all that the whole Iran business had been my idea" and wanted to set out "just what the truth is." It was only years later, in his memoir, that McFarlane divulged the source of his information. It had come from none other than Brent Scowcroft, who called to tell him that "Regan is hanging you out to dry." Scowcroft's call should properly be understood as a signal for McFarlane to go into action.[13] Scowcroft would be one of the leaders of the new world order faction, who would be part of the later "investigation" of the president's policies.

If Regan had been attempting to pin "the whole Iran business" on McFarlane at this time it was not evident in press reports, as Scowcroft claimed. Quite the contrary. A *Los Angeles Times* report of November 6 cited Regan on the hostage issue, but he refused to discuss "how we negotiated." Nor was there any hint of recrimination or casting of blame, just an expressed concern to protect the hostages.[14] However, Mayer and McManus say that Regan, speaking on background to reporters from weekly newsmagazines, like *Newsweek* and *Time*, as a "senior administration official," said that the Iran initiative was "all McFarlane's idea."

---

[12] "McFarlane Testimony," February 21, 1987, in John G. Tower et al., *Report of the President's Special Review Board: February 26, 1987* (Washington, D.C.: GPO, 1987), D-3.
[13] Robert C. McFarlane, *Special Trust* (New York: Cadell & Davies, 1994), 91.
[14] Doyle McManus, "U.S. Offer to Iran Seen as Subtle Policy Shift," *Los Angeles Times*, November 6, 1986, 13. Mayer and McManus, *Landslide*, 296.

As the scandal unfolded, the charges against the president would hinge entirely upon the changing, self-serving, muddled, contradictory, and unprovable claims of McFarlane, crucially assisted by Shultz's open opposition, combined with massive, almost daily, well-informed leaks to the press, asserting that President Reagan had been engaged in an illegal, arms-for-hostages scheme.

In his PROF note to Poindexter, McFarlane said that the "Israelis approached us in June 1985" and the president "approved" of "engaging in a dialogue," with "no mention at all of any arms exchange." Then, "we heard nothing until August when the Israelis introduced the requirement for TOWs. I told Kimche no." The Israelis "went ahead on their own, but then asked that we replace the TOWs and after checking with the president, we agreed." Benjamin Weir was released "as a consequence of their action."

In this carefully hedged statement, McFarlane truthfully said the president had approved *only* of a "dialogue" with the Iranians, not an "arms exchange." Nor did he claim that the president had authorized the Israeli shipment of arms, but said the Israelis had shipped arms "on their own." Finally, there was no charge of arms for hostages, as McFarlane assigned responsibility for the initiative to the Israelis.

However, McFarlane omitted the crucial facts that it had been he, not the president, who had given the Israelis the go ahead to ship arms and "agreed" to replace the *TOWs* the Israelis had shipped. Indeed, much of the new world order entrapment scheme had occurred while the president was recuperating at his ranch in Santa Barbara.[15] McFarlane also omitted any mention of the November *Hawk* fiasco, and concluded with a discussion of his trip to London in December, turning off the initiative, and resigning from government.[16] This memo would constitute but the first of several versions of the initiative by McFarlane that either ignored or carefully obfuscated his own role.

---

[15] See Chapter 5.
[16] "McFarlane PROF note to Poindexter," November 7, 1986, *Tower Report*, D-4. See also *Iran Contra Affair*, 299.

McFarlane's first story contained some truth, but omitted crucial facts. However, in the absence of any written record, there was no one in the U.S. government who could contradict him except the president himself, and he said nothing for the moment. Neither Poindexter, nor North, nor Casey, nor Weinberger, had been involved in the summer of 1985, as McFarlane played his cards close to his vest. His liaison to the Israelis had been Michael Ledeen, a private citizen. McFarlane had made an "explicit arrangement" with Ledeen that "we would not put anything on paper."[17] But, he, too, acted on the assumption that McFarlane had been carrying out the orders of the president.

The Iranians Say No to Rapprochement

Meanwhile, a burst of commentary from Iranian leaders not only fed the press frenzy surrounding the president, but it also signaled that the president's initiative had failed. On November 4, at a rally marking the seventh anniversary of the seizure of the American embassy, Rafsanjani and Prime Minister Moussavi spoke before a large crowd. Acknowledging the McFarlane trip, Rafsanjani said, "the Americans' immediate aim was to secure Iranian mediation in Lebanon, though their distant goal was to create amicable relations with Iran." Although "we have left the door open...Iranian action on the hostages is conditional on the United States proving that it is not engaging in 'senseless hostility' against Iran." However, he said, Iran's friends in Lebanon "do not owe us anything" and "have not pledged themselves to follow our orders."[18]

If Rafsanjani suggested that the door was still open, if only a crack, Moussavi immediately declared it was closed shut. He stressed that there was "no possibility at all of holding talks with the United States" outside of the framework of existing negotiations taking place at The Hague. He claimed that the reason for president Reagan's denials of

---

[17] Michael Ledeen, *Perilous Statecraft: An Insider's Account of the Iran Contra Affair* (New York: Scribner, 1988), 255, "took notes at the meetings I attended at McFarlane's instructions, but once I had briefed him, I destroyed the notes."
[18] "Middle East and South Asia Review," *FBIS-Daily Report*, November 5, 1986, i.

the McFarlane mission were because "such news could create disgrace inside America."[19] Indeed, as far as Iran was concerned, "any talks" with this "clandestine delegation would be interpreted as unofficial." To make his position clear, he declared, actual "negotiations with the U.S. in the light of its crimes against the Islamic Revolution will never take place."[20]

The thrust of Iranian leaders' remarks was difficult to gauge because, immediately after the rally, Bahramani called North to arrange another meeting in Geneva on the November 8.[21] The president decided to stay his course, at least through the meeting, even though the questions and criticisms from the press about trading arms for hostages were reaching a crescendo. Indeed, a cascade of well-informed press stories began to appear based on official but unnamed sources.[22]

Under this growing cloud, North, Secord, Hakim, and Cave headed off to Geneva for what they thought would be a meeting with Bahramani and Samii, their usual interlocutors. But, upon arriving, they learned that only Samii and Bahramani's aide, but not Bahramani himself, were there. According to Samii, Bahramani was "lying low because the *Al-Shiraa* piece had raised his profile a little too high." Although the absence of Bahramani was a bad sign, Samii assured the Americans that both Bahramani and Rafsanjani "were anxious to

---

[19] Ibid.
[20] "Public Disclosure of the McFarlane Trip-Musavi Announcement in Tehran," *FBIS-Middle East and South Asia*, November 5, 1986, 13-14.
[21] *Iran-Contra Affair*, 261.
[22] William Drodziak and Walter Pincus, "Iran Says McFarlane Carried Out Secret Mission to Tehran," *Washington Post*, November 5, 1986, 1; John Walcott and Youssef Ibrahim, "U.S. Suggests It Would Allow Weapons For Iran in Return for Hostages' Release," *Wall Street Journal*, November 5, 1986, 3; Walter Pincus, "Secret Talks With Iran Described," *Washington Post*, November 6, 1986, 1; Michael Dobbs, "Tehran Visit May Hurt U.S.-Iraqi Ties," *Washington Post*, November 6, 1986, 38; Walter Pincus, "Shultz Protested Iran Deal," *Washington Post*, November 6, 1986, 1.

continue with the plan although we should expect to hear some anti-American propagandizing to appease the opposition."[23]

If the American team was being kept up to date on current developments in Tehran, as one would expect, this was a transparent attempt by Samii to deny what had been Rafsanjani's public repudiation of the "plan" just the day before. At Friday Prayers on November 7, Rafsanjani carefully acknowledged that he had lost the policy struggle over whether or not to establish relations with the United States.

As the loser in the policy struggle, he was required to repudiate his own policy. He now claimed that McFarlane had come without "permission" and denied any purchase of arms from Israel, our "main enemy." Indeed, "as long as the United States backs Israel, we will consider the United States as the arch Satan. We will never be friendly with a country that financially supports Israel..."

Then, he said that Khomeini, the grand imam, had "commanded that as long as the United States is not chastised, we will not establish relations with it. This declaration by the imam of the Islamic nation has clarified our foreign policy course. Grand Ayatollah Montazeri also elucidated this issue in his recent speech." Finally, he concluded, "we have no responsibility whatsoever" for the U.S. hostages in Lebanon. Indeed, in view of all the crimes the U.S. has committed there, "what could the wronged people of Lebanon do if not take hostages?"[24]

For North, if not for his companions, the meeting in Geneva was a last-gasp attempt to get Anderson and Sutherland out, not to continue with the initiative, which was dead. In fact, neither the establishment of political relations, nor the subject of arms sales came up. The two sides

---

[23] Richard Secord and Jay Wurts, *Honored and Betrayed: Irangate, Covert Affairs, and the Secret War in Laos* (New York: Wiley, 1992), 320. Oliver North and William Novak, *Under Fire: An American Story* (New York: Harper Collins, 1991), 306, claims that the "Nephew" was present in Geneva, but, while North may have had a conversation with him, it could only have been over the phone.

[24] "Majlis Speaker: 'No Responsibility' for Hostages," *FBIS-Middle East-South Asia*, November 7, 1986, I1.

first traded charges about the *Al Shiraa* article. Samii wanted the Americans to know that it had not been their doing and claimed that the newspaper was "under Syrian control." This, he said, "had led some in Tehran to conclude that the U.S. might have had a hand in the expose`."

Cave replied that the U.S. had "considerable information which clearly indicates that Hizbollah is involved with the newspaper... [and that] Mèhdi Hashemi may have used it as a means of channeling his leak."[25] Cave certainly knew that Mehdi Hashemi was already in jail and that Samii's suspicions were correct. The Iranians had sent a "high level" delegation to Damascus to look into the matter of Syrian involvement and evidently had been satisfied that Assad had played no role. Thus, their suspicion of an American "hand."[26]

North said how "keenly disappointed" the Americans were "about getting only Jacobson out." Samii "made it clear that the freeing of the Dawa prisoners was a prerequisite to the release of the 'other two hostages.'" He conceded that even if only "some" prisoners were released "something" might be possible. North said that "we had done all that was humanly possible by talking directly to the Kuwaitis" and recommended that the Iranians send a delegation to Kuwait, promising that it would be "warmly received."[27] Samii replied that there had to be a deal before any senior Iranian officials would go to Kuwait.[28]

Samii also went to some lengths to cut ties to Gorbanifar, claiming that the Iranians now "suspected" him of being an Israeli agent. This was a clear signal that he was out of favor in Tehran. But, in his next breath, he wanted the Americans to "appease" him to forestall any "trouble." Interestingly, the next day, when North and his team met with Nir, who had also come to Geneva, the Israeli disclosed that Gorbanifar was spreading the word that "the United States was spending Iranian money in Nicaragua." The double irony here was that

---

[25] "George Cave Briefing of HPSCI Staffers," *Iran-Contra Affair*, Appendex A, volume 1, 1762.
[26] "Teicher PROF note to Poindexter," November 4, 1986, *Tower Report*, B-171-2.
[27] *Iran-Contra Affair*, 262.
[28] Theodore Draper, *A Very Thin Line: The Iran-Contra Affairs* (New York: Hill and Wang, 1991), 460.

North informed Nir that the Lake Resources account had been closed because "some of the Iranian funds had become "mixed" with funds for Nicaragua."[29]

They had reached the end of the line. Both sides were shutting down the operation. As North concluded: "the Iran initiative was finally over."[30] But, if he thought that the initiative would fade quietly into the background he was in for a rude shock. When he returned to Washington the next day, he found the administration embroiled in a full-blown crisis.

The Battle Lines Are Drawn

In view of the pummeling the administration was receiving in the press and on the Sunday talk shows, the president called a meeting of the NSPG group on Monday morning, November 10. He decided that it was now necessary to put out a public defense of his policy and hoped to present a united administration to the public. He was under no illusions about Shultz, who, he knew, opposed his policy. An additional purpose of the meeting, it seems, was to learn how much the secretary knew and what kind of attack to expect from him.

Shultz saw the burgeoning crisis as the moment "to get policy on Iran and on antiterrorism back on track, into my hands and away from the NSC staff."[31] It would be, he said, a "battle royal." To do it, he would need the support of key members of the NSPG. He believed he could count on Weinberger, who had opposed the policy, and sought to persuade the vice president and later Regan to support him, against the president.

In a telephone conversation with Nick Brady, Bush's close friend and adviser, on Saturday, Shultz warned, "the vice president could get drawn into a web of lies. If he blows his integrity, he's finished. He should be very careful how he plays the 'loyal lieutenant' role now."

---

[29] *Iran-Contra Affair*, 262.
[30] North, *Under Fire*, 306.
[31] Shultz, *Turmoil and Triumph*, 808.

On Sunday, Shultz visited Bush at his home and "reminded him that he had been present at a meeting where arms for Iran and hostage releases had been proposed and that he had made no objection despite the objection of both Cap and me."[32] This was a signal that Bush should support Shultz in the coming arguments, at the risk of his political future.

Meeting in the Situation Room, Monday morning, were the president, Bush, Schultz, Casey, Weinberger, Meese, Regan, Poindexter, and Alton Keel, Poindexter's deputy. Reagan opened the meeting, stating that what we were doing regarding the Iran initiative was "right, and legal, and justifiable." We were trying to "turn around the strategic situation in the Persian Gulf, to move Iran to a constructive role, to help the Iranians with their problem with the Soviets. And, of course…we wanted the hostages back."[33] In this regard, he said, "we have not dealt directly with terrorists, no bargaining, no ransom."[34]

Poindexter next gave a history of the initiative, which, was based on McFarlane's memo, North's inputs, and his own analysis. It was filled with errors, half-truths, and mis-statements because both North and McFarlane were determined to protect themselves and thus gave contradictory information and Poindexter could not sort out truth from fiction. In fact, Poindexter's history was so blatantly wrong as to guarantee a negative response from Shultz. Indeed, as the discussion proceeded, it was plain to all around the table that the argument was between Shultz and the president, in which Meese attempted to support the president.

Poindexter stated that the origins of the initiative came earlier the previous year when North "stumbled onto an Israeli warehouse in Portugal." The Israelis claimed they were selling arms to Iran to get Jews out of the country and shipped five hundred missiles to Iran in August and September 1985 "without the knowledge of the United

---

[32] Ibid, 808-9.
[33] Ibid, 812.
[34] Draper, *Very Thin Line*, 464.

States. We were told after the fact."[35] Poindexter omitted any reference to the November *Hawk* shipment, just as McFarlane had.

In January, the president had signed a finding authorizing the initiative and instructing Casey to defer notification to the Congress. This led, Poindexter said, to the Gorbanifar-Kangarlu channel, which culminated in McFarlane's trip to Tehran. This channel never "achieved anything," and was closed. Subsequently, a second channel was opened with Rafsanjani's "nephew," which was much more productive. The United States sold a thousand *TOWs* and some *Hawk* missile battery parts; and three hostages were released.[36]

Poindexter concluded by claiming that "we have achieved…solid contact with Rafsanjani," a middle of the road politician opposed to Khomeini, who had the support of the Revolutionary Guards. The radical elements were for "war, terrorism, revolution.… They were the ones who were linked to Hezbollah in Lebanon and who were responsible for the last three hostage takings [Reed, Cicippio, and Tracy]." Montazeri, Khomeini's heir apparent, was "an independent player." We have convinced them that they can't win the war, that the hostages have to be released, and that the Soviets are a threat. The political situation, in short, "was fluid and susceptible to influence in a way that would be positive for us."[37]

Poindexter's rendition of the initiative's history was so obviously skewed that it bore little relationship to reality, especially the tale about the discovery of the Israeli warehouse in Portugal, one of North's concoctions, and the long and tangled relationship with Gorbanifar. Ironically, the Israelis had a warehouse in Portugal, but its discovery had not marked the start of the initiative. But, it was his analysis of the Iranian leadership dynamic and the assertion of a "solid contact" with Rafsanjani that jarred. He knew that the initiative had failed, and that Rafsanjani had just three days before publicly

---

[35] Mayer and McManus, *Landslide*, 297.
[36] Shultz, *Turmoil and Triumph*, 812.
[37] Ibid, 813.

repudiated it, but to admit that rejection would also acknowledge the failure of the president's policy.

Shultz predictably "exploded" at what he said was a "ludicrous" tale riddled with "preposterous assertions." Reacting to the revelation of the January 17 finding, he claimed, "this is the first I ever heard of such a finding."[38] In fact, the president and Shultz had had a "long discussion" of the initiative at lunch on the same day that he had signed the finding, although he had not shown him the actual document.[39] Shultz, therefore, had never known of the crucial, legal basis for proceeding with the initiative, which was the Economy Act and not the Arms Export and Control Act. His explosion related to his realization that Reagan had outmaneuvered him.

Shultz would claim falsely that he had known little to nothing of what had happened in 1986 to avoid even a taint of complicity in the initiative. Nevertheless, as Walsh documents in great detail, Shultz and his aides were fully knowledgeable about the president's policy, followed it closely from the outset, and carefully prepared a false story for the secretary after the crisis erupted.[40]

Poindexter's revelation of the January 17 finding meant that the president's policy had been entirely legal from that point. Shultz could and would criticize the advisability of the policy, but not its legality. He was left with McFarlane's entrapment schemes of 1985. There were few grounds on which to attack the president about the initial Israeli shipments of *TOWs* because it was essentially his word against McFarlane's. Shultz's only leverage was the November *Hawk* shipment, in which the CIA had become entangled, and that would be his main line of attack against the president.

---

[38] Shultz, *Turmoil and Triumph*, 812-13.
[39] Lawrence E. Walsh, *Final Report of the Independent Counsel for Iran-Contra Matters* (Washington, D.C.: United States Court of Appeals for the District of Columbia Circuit, August 4, 1993), 338. "On January 17, 1986 there was another meeting at the White House to discuss the initiative. [Nick] Platt noted Shultz's report of that meeting as follows: "long discussion of Polecat [North] at lunch. [Shultz]...want it to be recorded as: A, unwise, B, illegal."
[40] Ibid, 325-374.

Shultz charged that the president was paying ransom for the hostages, that it was "an arms for hostages deal." Reagan said, "it's not linked" and Meese interjected to say that "we didn't sell; Israel sold."[41] The president was literally correct, but essentially disingenuous. The January 17, 1986 finding had authorized the sale of weapons to an authorized cut-out, who then re-sold them to Iran; the Iranians then attempted to exercise their influence over the hostage-taker, Imad Mugniyeh, in Lebanon. The linkage was indirect, but it was clear enough. It appeared to be a distinction without a difference.

Israel's role was to facilitate meetings with the Iranians, provide warehouse space for weapons, and to transport them as needed. Shultz charged that "conspiring with the Israelis…gave Israel a clear field, and they would then supply Iran with equipment that really mattered." Meese sought to distinguish between "trading directly with those who held the hostages and doing it through Iran," but Shultz warned against saying "something that's technically correct but not exactly representative of what we've done." In his view, the Iranians and the Israelis were "playing us for suckers."[42]

The president said he would "appreciate people saying you support policy" and Meese suggested the release of a public statement. Shultz, however, balked, saying, "I support you, Mr. President, but I am concerned about policy." Casey then "produced a draft statement to be released to the press," but signing such a statement was something Shultz "was not prepared to do." The tension in the room was palpable, as everyone, even Weinberger, who Shultz thought would unreservedly support him, wanted to rally around the president. Shultz left the meeting feeling that he was now "the most unpopular man in town."[43]

The meeting ended without agreement, as Shultz hurried off to a previously scheduled flight to Guatemala for an OAS meeting. While

---

[41] Shultz, *Turmoil and Triumph*, 813 and Draper, *Very Thin Line*, 465.
[42] Shultz, *Turmoil and Triumph*, 814 and Draper, *Very Thin Line*, 466.
[43] Draper, *Very Thin Line*, 468 and Shultz, *Turmoil and Triumph*, 814. See Frank Morring, "Weinberger Defends Iran Arms Shipments, *Washington Times*, November 14, 1986, 9 and Molly Moore, "Weinberger Backs Policy Toward Iran," *Washington Post*, November 20, 1986, 24.

in flight, Poindexter contacted the secretary with a press release regarding the American hostages in Lebanon whose main thrust was that "there was unanimous support for the President's decisions." The national security adviser said that the vice president, Weinberger, Casey, and Meese "had already cleared it."[44]

Again, Shultz balked, declaring that "I did not support this operation and I would not join in lying about it." It was "a lie.... It's Watergate all over again," he complained to his aides. He argued with Poindexter, demanding that the key sentence be revised to say simply "there was unanimous support for the President," omitting any reference to "decisions." Even with this change, Shultz "was uncomfortable."[45]

Democrats Attack; Reagan Defends

While Shultz was bolting on Iran policy, the newly elected Congress, with both houses under Democrat control, planned investigations to determine "whether the National Security Council has been used to circumvent Congress, the Pentagon and the State Department in arranging for arms to be shipped to Iran in exchange for American hostages." The inquiries were expected "to go beyond the Iranian operation to the role of the NSC in supplying arms to the rebels in Nicaragua." In short, congressional Democrats were already connecting the president's Iran and Contra policies two weeks before the so-called diversion would be acknowledged. The House planned to hold hearings as early as December, with Senate hearings delayed until January when Democrats would assume control.[46]

Of course, aside from the merits of the case, which had generated a congressional uproar, investigations to determine whether the NSC

---

[44] Shultz, *Turmoil and Triumph*, 814. Draper, *Very Thin Line*, 469, says Poindexter "obtained the approval of Reagan, Weinberger, Meese, and Casey," omitting the vice president, which, if true, meant that Shultz's warning to him had had an impact.
[45] Shultz, *Turmoil and Triumph*, 814-15.
[46] Walter Pincus, "Hill Probes of NSC Planned," *Washington Post*, November 10, 1986, 1.

was being used to circumvent Congress were a transparent and time-honored means whereby an opposition-controlled Congress could attack a President. To Reagan, it meant that he had to get out front, brief Congress and attempt to counter by obtaining the support of the people. He assembled his NSPG principals in the Situation Room on November 12 to brief key members of Congress: Senate leaders Robert Dole (R-KS) and Robert Byrd (D-WV); and House leaders Jim Wright (D-TX) and Dick Cheney (R-WY).

Reagan opened the meeting by defending his policy, affirming that no laws were broken, that there was no trade of arms for hostages, and that no officials were bypassed. The president reportedly argued "we would be at fault if Khomeini died and we had not made any preparations for contacts with a future regime.... The arms were necessary for that." However, an unnamed "official" who attended the meeting "conceded that the supply of arms was 'intertwined' with the release of the hostages."[47]

Poindexter also gave a briefing, which focused on the policy after the January finding, intimating that the Israeli shipments of 1985 had occurred without authorization, and that the United States delivered only 1000 *TOWs* and 240 *Hawk* spare parts, a relatively small outlay for a potentially significant outcome.[48] He did acknowledge, however, that the White House may have "made a miscalculation on who it could trust in Iran." [49]

Congressional leaders, especially the Democrats, reacted with great skepticism. Senator Byrd declared: "Iran is a terrorist state. You are selling arms. You want others *not* to sell arms. It's selling arms for hostages...and it's a bad mistake."[50] Representative Wright issued a statement after the meeting, stating that the discussions had been

---

[47] Bernard Weinraub, "Reagan Confirms Iran Got Arms Aid; Calls Deals Vital," *New York Times*, November 13, 1986, 1.
[48] *Iran-Contra Affair*, 295-96. The actual number of TOWs was later corrected to be 2,008.
[49] Walter Pincus and David Hoffman, "White House Briefs Hill on Iran Contacts," *Washington Post*, November 11, 1986, 1.
[50] Shultz, *Turmoil and Triumph*, 818.

"frank and candid," and that he had "expressed certain convictions regarding the direction of our foreign affairs and how to improve future relations between the executive and legislative branches."[51] Sen. Dole thought the entire operation "a little inept," and Sen. Barry Goldwater (R-AZ) charged, "laws had been broken."[52]

Immediately afterward, as word leaked that the United States had sold arms for hostages, Shultz sought out Regan. He wanted him "to help me get Ronald Reagan out of the line of fire and turn this mess over to me to clean it up." He wanted the president to include a statement in his major speech the next day, that he would publicly transfer "Iran policy and terrorist policy back in my hands."[53] But Reagan was not ready to relinquish control, or to give up on his policy.

The next evening, November 13, the president addressed the nation. The Iran initiative was in the national interest, he maintained. He sought to reestablish relations with Tehran, bring an honorable end to the Iran-Iraq war, eliminate state-sponsored terrorism, and effect the safe return of all hostages. The United States, he said, had not "swapped" arms for hostages. "I authorized the transfer of small amounts of defensive weapons and spare parts…to send a signal that the United States was prepared to replace the animosity between us with a new relationship." At the same time, we insisted as a condition of progress, that Tehran "oppose all forms of international terrorism" and "the most significant step which Iran could take, we indicated, would be to use its influence in Lebanon to secure the release of all hostages held there."[54]

Despite making what appeared to be a defensible, if not compelling case, an *L.A. Times* poll taken afterwards showed conclusively that the American people did not believe the president

---

[51] Weinraub, "Reagan Confirms Iran Got Arms…"
[52] Joseph Harsch, "The Iran Operation—…a Little Inept," *Christian Science Monitor*, November 18, 1986, 21.
[53] Shultz, *Turmoil and Triumph*, 818.
[54] Ronald Reagan, "Address to the Nation on the Iran Arms Controversy," November 13, 1986. See also Walter Pincus, "Reagan Told Deal Key to Iran's Help," *Washington Post*, November 14, 1986, 1.

was telling the truth. Only 14 percent believed Reagan's statement that he did not trade arms for hostages. Asked whether they thought that the United States had upheld its policy of not negotiating with terrorists, 44 percent believed it was only "technically true," while 29 percent believed it "essentially false." Only 20 percent of those polled believed that the U.S. government was in "full compliance with federal law." Forty-six percent believed that the statement was "essentially true," 24 percent believed it was "essentially false."[55]

Shultz went to see the president the next day saying that he intended to resign, but was willing to stay on for the next few weeks "to get him through the crisis." Reagan did not want him to resign, but the two men "argued" over Iran inconclusively, as the president insisted that his policy was correct. The secretary also sought out Regan again, importuning him to attempt to persuade the president to "transfer the President's policy…to me." Regan "seemed to agree," he recalled, and urged that Shultz go on one of the Sunday talk shows. Shultz agreed.[56]

British Prime Minister Margaret Thatcher met with President Reagan at Camp David on Saturday, November 15. Shultz hoped to be able to find time to discuss with the president what he would say on television the next day, "with the aim of getting control of the policy shifted away from Poindexter and back to State." As there was no opportunity for a private discussion, Shultz handed to Regan the memo he had crafted authorizing the transfer of power to State. Looking at it, Regan sided with the president, saying: "we are not in a position to do what you're asking for."[57]

The next day, on *Face The Nation*, Shultz threw down the "gauntlet," declaring his total opposition to the president's policy. "It is clearly wrong to trade arms for hostages," he said, "because it encourages taking more." Will there be any more arms shipments, he was asked? "Under the

---

[55] "Poll Shows Americans Doubt Reagan on Iran," *Washington Post*, November 18, 1986, 14.
[56] Shultz, *Turmoil and Triumph*, 819-20.
[57] Ibid, 821.

circumstances of Iran's war with Iraq, its pursuit of terrorism, its association with those holding our hostages, I would certainly say, as far as I'm concerned, no." Asked whether he had "authority to speak for the administration?," Shultz responded, "no."[58]

Reagan Engages, Loses, and Switches

Not only had the president's Iran initiative failed, his defense of the Iran initiative had failed.[59] The many holes in the story had generated a profound skepticism. He had defended his decision as a matter of "national interest," claimed "progress continues to be made," and asked the American people for their support.[60] The response was overwhelmingly negative: from the political establishment, with Shultz's open rebellion; from Democrat-controlled Congress, which was in an uproar; from the Republican leadership itself, which would not back him; from the media, which spewed an outpouring of critical articles laying bare minute details of arms shipments; and from public opinion, which demonstrated that the president's prize asset, his credibility, had been seriously impaired. He was condemned without trial for secretly trading arms for hostages, ignoring Congress, and violating his own policy.

So, Reagan decided to do what he had done before, in 1983 after the KAL-007 crisis. He would relinquish policy control to Shultz temporarily, but retain ultimate decision-making authority over strategy. In the meantime, the president would defend his policy against Shultz's charge that he had ransomed arms for hostages, which

---

[58] Ibid.

[59] Perhaps the final nail in the president's Iran initiative was news on November 15 that Bahramani had fled Iran for Toronto, Canada, with an "investigator" hard on his heels. See Scott Armstrong et al., *The Chronology: The Documented Day-by-Day Account of the Secret Military Assistance to Iran and the Contras* (New York: Warner Books, 1987), 558.

[60] Ronald Reagan, "Address to the Nation on the Iran Arms Controversy," November 13, 1986.

necessitated a convincing history of events, and prepare to defend himself against the attack on the presidency that was clearly building.

His immediate public reaction was to assert that he and Shultz were united. The day after Shultz's appearance on *Face The Nation*, the White House issued a statement declaring that the secretary "did speak for the administration," that "the President has no plans to send further arms to Iran," and that both were in "complete accord on this."[61] The president was asked at a picture-taking ceremony whether he would fire Shultz. "I'm not firing anyone," he replied.

At separate briefings, White House and State Department spokesmen sparred over who controlled what, differing "in their description of administration decision-making processes." White House spokesman Larry Speakes declared "the president makes the decisions," while State Department spokesman Charles Redman said "this building, the State Department, is the focal point of foreign policy. That includes Iran, as well as all other areas of the world."[62]

Regarding the incipient challenge to the presidency, Reagan sought advice from former President Nixon and instructed Pat Buchanan, a White House speechwriter who had worked for him, to contact the ex-president. Nixon advised Reagan to admit that he had made a mistake, get the truth out, and avoid even the appearance of a cover-up.[63] Reagan agreed that it was vital to get the truth out and avoid a cover-up, but rejected the idea of admitting a mistake. Reagan believed that his policy of reestablishing relations with Iran was the right one and would adhere to it firmly.

Nixon's advice was not as valuable as his example. The lesson Reagan took from Nixon was that to fight the new world order establishment the way Nixon had would lead to the same outcome, the threat of impeachment and loss of the presidency. Reagan decided that it was more important to retain the presidency than it was to contend

---

[61] Shultz, *Turmoil and Triumph*, 823.
[62] Lou Cannon and Walter Pincus, "Reagan Has 'No Plans' To Ship Iran More Arms, But Order Still in Effect," *Washington Post*, November 18, 1986, 1.
[63] Mayer and McManus, *Landslide*, 307.

over a policy that had already failed. His plan would be to distance himself from the implementation of policy and place the blame on his aides for its improper execution.

Meanwhile, pursuant to Poindexter's direction, North prepared a sanitized "maximum chronology" of the arms shipments, based in part on McFarlane's memo of November 7, which dealt with the Israeli arms shipments of 1985, conversations with other government personnel, and his own records of the events. A chronology of events would establish the basic "party line" officials could rely on in testimony to Congress and in remarks to the public. It would contain the essential information on which the president's upcoming press conference would be based.

Only McFarlane had known of the genesis of the 1985 Israeli arms sales. North and Poindexter had become involved only in November with the *Hawk* fiasco. Thus, North's November 17 chronology accurately described the three arms shipments of 1986, but followed McFarlane's memo for the events of 1985. The U.S. Government was "not aware" of the Israeli *TOW* deliveries of August-September until afterward and was "silent" on the questions of "knowledge and approval" of the November *Hawk* shipment.[64] North and McFarlane both had an interest in avoiding any discussion of the November shipment.

When the crisis broke, Meese had assigned his aide Charles Cooper the task of determining the legality of the arms deals and he had had no difficulty determining that the policy authorized by the January 17 finding was legal.[65] When he looked at North's November 17 chronology, however, and saw that Israel had shipped weapons in 1985, he realized that this information was a potential time bomb. The shipments violated the Arms Export Control Act (AECA) and there had been no congressional notification.

---

[64] *Iran Contra* Affair, 299. Mayer and McManus, *Landslide*, 308, say that this chronology stated that the "Israel had delivered the HAWK missiles over the objections of the United States."
[65] See *Iran-Contra Affair*, 380-81, for a discussion of the legality of presidential findings.

Cooper called Meese and Paul Thompson, Poindexter's counsel. Poindexter then called McFarlane in to review North's chronology and directed Thompson to call a meeting of the government's national security lawyers. The next day, November 18, Cooper, Thompson, Peter Wallison of the White House, Dave Doherty of CIA, Lawrence Garrett of DOD, and Abe Sofaer of State gathered in Wallison's office. The meeting was designed for Cooper and Thompson to brief the others, to test whether or not their story would pass muster.

Sofaer, State's counsel, thought Cooper's justification of the 1986 arms sales, based on the January 17 finding, was acceptable, but "it was unclear...whether [his] legal theory could be applied to the September 1985 shipment or to other pre-1986 shipments." Referring to North's chronology, Cooper stated that the "United States had no knowledge of the [1985] transaction until after the sale had occurred."[66] Cooper, too, made no mention of the November *Hawk* shipment.

Sofaer "asked them what they had and whether we could be given copies," but Thompson "refused to let us see it or to provide any additional information." We had "no need to know," he said, shocking those "who had been excluded." Sofaer thought it "ridiculous" that the very people "supposed to help their clients satisfy legal obligations" were being denied the information needed to do so. Sofaer became convinced that "Poindexter was blocking access to information that could undermine the story he was attempting to develop."[67]

Later that same day, Poindexter briefed Sofaer and Armacost, but still not Wallison, providing more information than had Thompson, but "still not all of the facts." He "claimed that the United States had not sanctioned the September 1985 shipment of TOWs," but he, too, "did not mention the shipment of HAWKs..." Sofaer and Armacost

---

[66] Abraham Sofaer, "Iran-Contra: Ethical Conduct and Public Policy," *Houston Law Review* (December 2003), 1090-91. Peter J. Wallison, *Ronald Reagan: The Power of Conviction and the Success of His Presidency* (Boulder: Westview, 2003), 188-89, claimed that the purpose of the meeting was to "share our knowledge," but omits the fact that Cooper and Thompson were briefing from the NSC chronology.
[67] Sofaer, "Iran-Contra..." 1091.

left the meeting "certain that Poindexter was making things up as he went along."⁶⁸

They were only partly correct. Poindexter and North were scrambling to string together the basic facts of the initiative and did not want to release it until they had done so. Their chronology obviously could not be comprehensive, but they hoped that it would be sufficiently accurate to be plausible and defensible. Potentially, it seemed, Reagan could be legally vulnerable in terms of the Arms Export Control Act for the 1985 Israeli *TOW* and *Hawk* shipments, but the November *Hawk* deal presented the more serious problem of the CIA's entanglement. Both, recall, had been the result of the new world order's entrapment scheme.

On the *TOW* shipments, in his earlier memo to Poindexter, McFarlane had accurately related that the president had not authorized the Israeli shipment of arms, (even though, in fact, McFarlane had given the Israelis to believe that the president had authorized their action). Thus, the administration's position consistently would be that the president had not authorized the August-September shipments.

On the *Hawk* affair, McFarlane again acted without presidential authorization and the Israelis had, for their own protection, entangled the CIA peripherally in the delivery to insure U.S. government commitment in what the Israelis considered to be a joint venture. McFarlane had informed the president of Israel's action in November just before it commenced, but in no sense was approval requested, or given. In both cases, as McFarlane knew, the Arms Export Control Act required congressional notification in advance.⁶⁹

There were three findings in question, which provided presidential authorization for policy, the January 17, 1986 finding, the December 5, 1985 finding, and also the mistakenly signed finding of January 6, 1986. Poindexter argued that the January 17

---

⁶⁸ Ibid, 1092.

⁶⁹ A new section had been added to the AECA on August 27, 1986, prohibiting the export of arms to countries the Secretary of State determined were supporters of international terrorism, but it did not apply in the case of the January 17, 1986 finding, which was based on a different law, the Economy Act.

finding, which formally authorized the initiative, superseded the previous two.[70] The relevant laws governing the initiative in 1986 were the Economy Act and the Foreign Assistance Act, not the AECA. Congressional reporting requirements were less stringent for these and the president had specifically instructed Casey to defer notification to Congress until a later time.[71]

More serious was the December 5 finding that sought retroactively to ratify the CIA's involvement and expressly described an arms-for-hostages trade. The finding was almost literally the only direct evidence of what seemed to be the president's authorization of Israel's November *Hawk* shipment, and that had come after the fact. Thus, it could be construed as a cover-up. There was only one signed copy of this finding, which was in Poindexter's possession. The existence of the December finding appeared to explain why neither North nor Poindexter wanted to mention the November *Hawk* deal.

When McFarlane arrived at North's office on the evening of November 18, he changed North's chronology and the president's opening statement for his news conference the next day. In the process, he exonerated himself from any responsibility for the November 1985 *Hawk* shipment, but cleverly left the president open to a charge of a cover-up. North's chronology, as it had evolved to this point, simply stated that the November *Hawk* shipment was "not an authorized exception to [U.S.] policy."

McFarlane deleted that sentence and inserted the following in its place: "Later in the fall, other transfers of equipment were made between Israel and Iran although some of the items were returned to Israel."[72] McFarlane had pinned the operation on Israel, removed all

---

[70] He was incorrect. Findings "remain valid until formally cancelled." See NSDD-159, in Simpson, *National Security Directives," 494*.

[71] Bob Woodward, "Reagan Ordered Casey to Keep Iran Mission From Congress," *Washington* Post, November 15, 1986, 1. "The president issued [a] written order to Casey in an attempt to protect his intelligence chief from the anticipated wrath of Congress." See also, *Iran Arms Sales: DOD's Transfer of Arms to the Central Intelligence Agency*, GAO Report, no. 132738, March 1987.

[72] *Iran-Contra Affair*, 300.

references to any U.S. involvement, or even that a shipment of arms had occurred, and, according to Mayer and McManus, he inserted into the chronology that he, himself, "had actually objected to the sale."[73]

North confirmed that McFarlane "totally altered the facts about the [*Hawk*] delivery and our role in facilitating it, and made it appear that we didn't even know about it at the time." North had his own reasons for going along with McFarlane's decision not "to reveal our connection with that 1985 shipment." It not only could have led to disclosure of the December 5 finding, which "would have been enormously embarrassing for the administration,"[74] but also could have led to revelation of his own involvement in its formulation. Of course, in the fall of 1985 North could not have anticipated what would lie ahead for the initiative a year later.

Shultz Marshals His Forces

Shultz realized that the crisis was fast approaching a critical point and mobilized his forces for action. Aside from confronting the president directly, with support from his State Department team he sent legal counsel Sofaer into action with the charge that the president had lied about the November *Hawk* fiasco. Charging the president with an illegal action, however, also was a decision to sacrifice his ally, McFarlane, who would also be exposed as lying about the *Hawk* shipment. Shultz's attack splintered the upper ranks of the administration as everyone took cover. As will be discussed in the next chapter, as soon as McFarlane learned that Shultz had sacrificed him, he began to claim that the president had authorized "everything" the Israelis did. Reagan, on the other hand, would move to protect his position by sacrificing his top aides.

---

[73] Mayer and McManus, *Landslide,* 310-11, seeing a multiple cover-up, say "McFarlane wanted to obscure the circumstances under which he approved the first Israeli shipment in August 1985, which was almost certainly illegal under the Arms Export Control Act" and to deny his role in the November *Hawk* deal.
[74] North, *Under Fire,* 313.

Shultz saw the president alone in the early afternoon of November 19 before his press conference that evening, trying again to persuade him to relinquish control of Iran policy. After asserting, "terrible mistakes had been made," he "read to the president a statement that I wanted him to make on television declaring that there would be no more arms sales and that our Iran policy would be managed by the secretary of state." Reagan refused to turn over control to Shultz, insisting that the "operation was a good one and argued, furthermore, that Iran had "tempered its support for terrorism." Shultz strongly disagreed, insisting that even if it were true it was a "terrible deal to make."[75]

Shultz maintained that "terrorism is an international problem and we must treat it that way," but did not elaborate. Instead, he showed Reagan a report by his aide Jerry Bremer, which said "Lebanese groups associated with Iran" had taken the three recent hostages, Reed, Cicippio, and Tracy. (Bremer's argument was misleading and simplistic, but Shultz's main concern was its political utility, not the truth. The hostage takers were Lebanese, all right, and all may have had ties to Iran, but some, at least, also had ties to Qadaffi and the Russians, which he did not note.)[76]

Reagan did not know the details, and responded, "this is news to me." Shultz immediately said, "you are not fully informed. You must not continue to say we made no deals for hostages. You have been deceived and lied to. I plead with you...*don't* say that Iran has let up on terrorism." Reagan again responded, "you're telling me things I don't know." Shultz replied, "if I'm telling you something you don't know—I don't know much—then something is terribly wrong here!"[77]

---

[75] Shultz, *Turmoil and Triumph*, 828.
[76] The so-called Revolutionary Justice Organization, a Libyan-controlled group that also did work for other clients, had taken all three. Indeed, Kangarlu had evidently sanctioned the taking of Cicippio. See "North PROF note to Poindexter," October 10, 1986, *Tower Report*, B-167 and Samuel Segev, *The Iranian Triangle: The Untold Story of Israel's Role in the Iran-Contra Affair* (New York: Free Press, 1988), 305-6.
[77] Shultz, *Turmoil and Triumph*, 828.

Either wittingly or unwittingly this exchange between Reagan and Shultz would provide the president with his exit strategy. His defense would be that he had been "not fully informed" and "deceived and lied to" by his subordinates. At the time, however, Shultz had no inkling that Reagan was on the verge of a major decision. Returning to his office he thought he had failed to make an impression. "The president's staff was continuing to deceive him," he thought, but "he was allowing himself to be deceived."

Receiving the White House text of what the president would say at his press conference, Shultz became alarmed, fearing that the president would continue to run Iran policy out of the NSC. So he called Regan, seeking his help once again. He "went over...the same points I had made to the president": the structure of the deals was clearly arms for hostages; Iran was still involved in terrorism; it was "disastrous" to intermingle intelligence and operations; running operations out of the White House was "idiocy," depriving the president of any insulation. Shultz felt that Regan "was increasingly awake to the fact that he, too, had been misled."[78]

During his press conference that evening, Reagan threw several curves, hoping to placate Shultz, while justifying his policy. In his opening statement, which was not the one McFarlane had prepared for him,[79] the president reiterated his purposes: to improve relations with Tehran, negotiate an end to the Iran-Iraq war, end terrorism, and effect release of the hostages.

Finessing Shultz's objections, the president said, "these policy objectives were never in dispute." The differences were in "how best to proceed." Several top advisers, he said, opposed making a limited exception of our arms embargo "as a signal of our serious intent." Others felt that "no progress could be made without this sale."

---

[78] Ibid, 829. Shultz's charge that running operations out of the White House was "idiocy," was simply gamesmanship. Every president in the modern era has directed foreign policy, or policies, from the Oval Office.

[79] McFarlane, *Special Trust*, 98, "he didn't use the opening statement I had prepared."

Weighing their views, and the risks as well as the rewards, the president declared, "I decided to proceed."[80]

Shultz had demanded that the president announce that he would end the initiative and hand over control of Iran policy to the State Department. Instead, the president said:

> to eliminate the widespread but mistaken perception that we have been exchanging arms for hostages, I have directed that no further sales of arms of any kind be sent to Iran. I have further directed that all information relating to our initiative be provided to the appropriate members of Congress.[81]

Reagan had terminated arms sales, as Shultz demanded, but retained control of the policy reins. In a tense exchange with reporters involving forty-one questions, the president maintained that the policy was not a "mistake," but a "high-risk gamble" that the circumstances warranted. He said, "we still have those contacts. We still have made some ground," with the recovery of three hostages. "What we did was right, and we're going to continue on this path." His answer referred to continuing efforts to recover the remaining hostages, but Shultz chose to interpret his answer as meaning the continuation of arms for hostages, ignoring the opening statement in which the president had said he had ended them.

Four of the questions directly asked whether the United States had "condoned shipments by Israel." The president, not wanting to identify Israel by name, but continuing to maintain that he had not authorized any third country arms shipments, replied each time that "we did not condone and do not condone the shipment of arms from other countries." Twice reporters said erroneously that chief of staff Regan had acknowledged Israel's arms shipments to Iran and the president disputed their claim.[82]

---

[80] Ronald Reagan, "The President's News Conference," November 19, 1986.
[81] Ibid.
[82] Immediately after the press conference the White House issued a clarification in the president's name acknowledging that "a third country [was] involved in our

As Regan saw it, the president had "carried off a difficult news conference better than his enemies wished to concede," although Shultz and his aides thought the president's performance disastrous.[83] Weinberger publicly backed the president, defending the initiative as "well justified," and backing away from any association with Shultz's criticisms. "It is certainly understandable that the president would want to do what he could to try to change [Iran's] policies....Now if that doesn't succeed, why then, obviously, we'll not pursue it."[84]

The article on Weinberger was stuffed in the back pages of the *Washington Post*, but it was an interview with McFarlane, that made front-page headlines. The former national security adviser, associating himself with Shultz, claimed in an interview "the administration made a 'mistake' in providing arms to Iran as part of an arrangement that included release of U.S. hostages."[85] Senior White House officials immediately pronounced themselves "flabbergasted" at McFarlane's comments.[86]

Don Regan, siding with the president and against Shultz, lashed out at McFarlane for his remarks. In a report leaked from a senior staff meeting, Regan declared, "let's not forget whose idea this was. It was Bud's [McFarlane's] idea. When you give lousy advice, you get lousy results." Other leaks noted, "second-guessing and increasingly bitter

---

secret project with Iran," but still not naming Israel, and said that "all of the shipments...I have authorized or condoned taken in total could be placed aboard a single cargo aircraft." See Mayer and McManus, *Landslide*, 314.

[83] Don Regan, *For the Record*, (New York: Harcourt, Brace, Jovanovich, 1988), 36. Shultz, *Turmoil and Triumph*, 830. Lou Cannon, "Reagan Defends Iran Arms Deal, Says It Freed 3 Hostages," *Washington Post*, November 20, 1986, 1.

[84] Molly Moore, "Weinberger Backs Policy Toward Iran," *Washington Post*, November 20, 1986, 24.

[85] Lou Cannon, "McFarlane Calls Sending Arms to Iran a 'Mistake,'" *Washington Post*, November 20, 1986, 1.

[86] Bernard Weinraub, "White House 'Flabbergasted' at McFarlane's Comments That Iran Deal Was Mistake," *New York Times*, November 21, 1986, 6.

criticism...[had] swept the White House.... Everybody is running from this thing."[87]

Meanwhile, as soon as the press conference had ended, Shultz called the president and claimed that he had made "a great many factual errors," which he wanted to point out to him. Reagan agreed to see him the next morning, leading Shultz to believe that he "now had a shot at turning this fiasco around." Shultz's plan was to force Poindexter out and take his place. "I would be willing," Shultz said, "to turn State over to my deputy, John Whitehead, and become acting NSC adviser for a month. I would clean house and then turn the job over to whoever would be permanently appointed."[88]

When Shultz arrived at the White House, the president would not see him so he spoke to Regan, instead. The secretary went through all of the president's mistakes and "put this idea" of taking control of the NSC to Regan. The chief of staff told him that the president had told Bush and Poindexter of the charge that he had been factually misled. Reagan, he said, wanted to "think it over at the ranch" over the weekend and convene a meeting of the NSPG on Monday "to go over what everybody knows and get it all together."[89]

At this, Shultz flew into a rage, exclaiming "that's a formula for catastrophe!...We have to make decisions. Here they are. Make them! The longer you wait, the worse it gets. It's not a matter of getting our lines straight! Think of the future!" Regan was "uncharacteristically subdued" and made no response. The president was not available. Shultz insisted on seeing him and said he would call Regan that afternoon and "push him on this again."[90]

Returning to his office, Shultz decided to apply greater pressure on the White House and use his trump card. He would bring in legal adviser Sofaer as his unwitting attack dog. As Sofaer recounted it, Shultz "decided to give me and Armacost access to some of the notes

---

[87] David Hoffman, "Reagan Aides Cast Blame For Dealings With Iran," *Washington Times*, November 21, 1986, 1.
[88] Shultz, *Turmoil and Triumph*, 831.
[89] Ibid.
[90] Ibid.

that Charlie Hill had kept of meetings and calls from the time Shultz became Secretary of State." One of Hill's notes was of McFarlane's call to Shultz in Geneva in November 1985 during which he "told Shultz that a shipment of HAWKs was being made to Iran that month by Israel with U.S. approval for the purpose of securing the release of hostages."[91]

Sofaer jumped or was led to conclude, "this single note established beyond any doubt that the White House knew of and had approved that shipment."[92] Sofaer assumed incorrectly, but not unreasonably based on what he was being told, that what McFarlane knew, the president knew, and thus took Hill's use of the term "with U.S. approval" to mean Reagan had approved the *Hawk* shipment as part of an arms-for-hostages deal, when he had not.

As it happened, that Thursday morning of November 20 Poindexter's office was a scene of hectic activity, as aides prepared statements for both the national security adviser and Casey, who were scheduled to testify before the House and Senate Intelligence Committees the next morning. Schultz had just received an early draft of Casey's testimony and handed it to Sofaer just "after [he] had obtained the readout from Hill." Sofaer "immediately noticed" the statement that no one "at the CIA" had known that the November shipment had been an arms shipment. He then concluded "McFarlane's statement to Shultz did not establish that the CIA also knew that the shipment was arms, not oil-drilling equipment, but it made the truthfulness of the draft testimony statement highly unlikely."[93]

Mike Armacost jumped in to say that the CIA "had used its own airline, Southern Air Transport, to handle the work." (Armacost was

---

[91] Sofaer, "Iran-Contra..." 1094. Shultz, *Turmoil and Triumph*, 831, turns it around, claiming that "Abe Sofaer asked me to authorize him to tell White House counsel Wallison and Attorney General Ed Meese of the evidence that we had that administration officials knew of arms shipments that had been made before the January 17, 1986, finding."
[92] Sofaer, "Iran-Contra...." 1094.
[93] Ibid.

incorrect. St. Lucia airlines was used, but saying it had been Southern Air Transport allowed him to make a connection with the Contras.)[94] He then surmised, "the testimony was false and possibly reflected some sort of conspiracy involving Central America as well. We agreed to demand that the CIA make the necessary changes in Casey's testimony."[95]

Shultz and his aides were carefully building the case for arguing there was a conspiracy involving both Iran and the Contras. Carefully primed, Sofaer immediately placed calls to Meese and Wallison "to report the information I had learned from Hill's note....that the U.S. government undoubtedly was aware that the November 1985 shipment was of HAWK missiles and that Casey's testimony was probably false in claiming that the CIA had no knowledge of that fact." Meese was not there, but called back later to reassure Sofaer that he "knew of certain facts that explained all these matters," but Sofaer "refused to accept that response as adequate reassurance."[96]

In his call to Wallison, Sofaer claimed that the president's lawyer did not know about the *Hawk* shipment and implied that he was being deceived by "the people around him at the White House."[97] Wallison, however, said that he had a "vague recollection of having been told by Poindexter" earlier of the *Hawk* shipment. While he was on the phone, Cooper and Thompson had come into his office having finished working on the testimony for Poindexter and Casey. Sofaer claims that when Wallison asked if they knew about the shipment they "admitted that they knew about it but had not told him," but Wallison denies this charge, too, saying that when he asked if they had been aware of it, "they said they were not."[98]

By the time Sofaer had called about Casey's testimony, the draft had undergone several iterations, particularly about the November Israeli

---

[94] See Bob Woodward, *Veil: The Secret Wars of the CIA, 1981-1987* (New York: Simon and Schuster, 1987), 420-21
[95] Sofaer, "Iran-Contra...." 1095.
[96] Ibid.
[97] Ibid, 1096.
[98] Wallison, *Ronald Reagan*, 194.

arms shipment. North, seeking to protect the NSC and himself, had insisted that Casey's testimony be broadened from "we in CIA" to "no one in the US Government" knew that the agency's proprietary airline had hauled missiles to Iran until mid-January of the following year.[99]

All in the meeting, including Poindexter, Casey, Meese, Gates, Thompson, Cooper and North knew that this was untrue, but agreed to it. Meese penciled in the change, which conveniently placed their knowledge of the event *after* the January 17 finding, legalizing it.[100] After Sofaer's blast, Casey's testimony was changed again eliminating all reference to the shipment, which satisfied Sofaer. It wasn't the whole truth, he said, but "at least there wasn't a lie out there."[101]

Shultz's revelation of Hill's note through Sofaer documenting McFarlane's call to him about the November *Hawk* shipment was the straw that broke the camel's back. He had raised the ante, not only charging Reagan with an illegal act, but also with a cover-up. McFarlane had entangled the CIA in the *Hawk* shipment, but Reagan had attempted to cover it up with a clearly illegal, after-the-fact finding, the so-called December 5 finding. Worst of all, the finding justified a purely arms-for-hostages policy, which the president had consistently denied authorizing. The new world order entrapment had succeeded.[102]

That afternoon of November 20, Shultz arrived at the White House family quarters armed for a battle with the president. Reagan claims he had agreed to the meeting because Shultz had issued an "ultimatum," threatening to quit unless the president fired Poindexter.[103] Reagan

---

[99] James McCullough, "Personal Reflections on Bill Casey's Last Month at CIA," *Studies in Intelligence*, vol. 39, no. 5 (1996), and Draper, *Very Thin Line*, 488.

[100] "Meese testimony," *Iran-Contra Affair*, 100-9, 218-19.

[101] Mayer and McManus, *Landslide*, 321.

[102] But at the cost of sacrificing McFarlane, which did not sit well with Shultz's aide, Charles Hill. Hill was upset because Sofaer's disclosure could "be read as GPS [Shultz] fingering McF [McFarlane] on something that could get him prison." See "Hill note," November 24, 1986, Walsh, *Final Report*, 353n.225.

[103] Ronald Reagan, *An American Life* (New York: Simon and Schuster, 1990), 529.

also may have wanted to hear directly from Shultz about the November *Hawk* shipment.

Shultz had hoped Nancy would be there, but she stayed away; Regan was the only other person present. In an hour-long "tirade," Shultz went over prepared talking points denouncing every aspect of the president's policy. In a "hot and heavy" argument Shultz declared that Iran still supported terrorism and was the "main banker, patron, arms supplier, and adviser" of Hezbollah; the Iranians we had dealt with were "unscrupulous and untrustworthy"; we had traded arms for hostages; there was serious questions about the president's "right to defer for so long reporting to Congress."[104] When he raised the subject of McFarlane's November 1985 call to him of the *Hawk* shipment, Reagan disarmingly said that he "knew about that," but "that wasn't arms-for-hostages."[105] (No hostages had been released as a result of that shipment.)

Shultz's approach had been to say that he "agreed with the president's objective but parted company with the way it had been carried out." Placing the blame squarely on the national security adviser, he said that he had been "a victim of Poindexter's misinformation."[106] Shultz demanded that Reagan fire Poindexter on the spot, but the president demurred. "He still wanted to have a meeting on Monday at which everyone could exchange information." Reagan had heard him out without rancor and Shultz seemed surprised that he "didn't seem to resent my efforts, but I didn't shake him one bit."[107]

Shultz didn't realize it, but he was like a bull charging through an open door into the china shop. The president had already decided on a carefully choreographed preemptive maneuver to extricate himself from any danger to his presidency. Reagan knew that Shultz had one more bomb to throw. The secretary had attended the May 16 NSPG meeting at which the president had exclaimed, "Can't Ollie find

---

[104] Draper, *Very Thin Line*, 484.
[105] Shultz, *Turmoil and Triumph*, 832.
[106] Draper, *Very Thin Line*, 485.
[107] Shultz, *Turmoil and Triumph*, 833.

funds" for the Contras, so he knew of the president's direct involvement in the search for funds.[108]

Shultz had raised the issue of the use of Iran surplus funds for the Contras among his aides. As Armacost had put it to Sofaer earlier that very day, they thought there was "some sort of conspiracy involving Central America [and Iran]."[109] Recall, congressional leaders in both houses had planned probes of both the Iran and Contra policies, already suggesting that connection.[110] Rumors were also flying around the administration of the use of Iran funds to support the Contras. Gorbanifar had made the same charge and so had Furmark. If Shultz charged the president with illegal actions in regard to both Iran and the Contras, it would put him squarely on the road to impeachment.

Reagan and his close aides concluded that the game was up. The president had lost the struggle for power and it was time to insulate himself from all complicity, especially with regard to the November *Hawk* affair. It was important to move as quickly as possible for time was now a factor. With a Democrat-controlled Congress set to convene and begin investigations, it was imperative to take preemptive action to establish the president's innocence immediately.

---

[108] See Chapter 10.
[109] Sofaer, "Iran-Contra...." 1095.
[110] Walter Pincus, "Hill Probes of NSC Planned," *Washington Post*, November 10, 1986, 1.

Chapter 13
The Defeat and Survival of Ronald Reagan

President Reagan had lost the struggle for power to his Secretary of State. Worse, the prospect of the exposure of his cover up of the CIA's involvement in the November 1985 *Hawk* shipment threatened a major scandal. The issue was no longer Iran policy, which had in any case failed, but his own position, which had to be protected at all costs. So, he reluctantly relinquished control of policy to Shultz, employing a variation on a tactic he had used twice earlier in his presidency when a policy conflict had reached a tipping point. Each time the issue was control over the NSC and each time the president triggered an incident to disguise what had happened.

In two previous instances involving a change of control at the NSC, Richard Allen in 1981 and William Clark in 1983, the president employed a minor, domestic incident to divert attention away from a change at NSC.[1] In 1981, he had authorized a Justice Department investigation into Allen's alleged mismanagement of a $1,000 gratuity he had accepted on behalf of Nancy Reagan for an interview the first lady had given to a Japanese magazine. Allen had taken the money, placed it in his office safe, and forgotten about it.

Although the investigation uncovered no wrongdoing, the president used the incident to justify moving Allen out of his NSC post and replacing him with Judge Clark. Politically, the shift gave the

---

[1] See Richard C. Thornton, *The Reagan Revolution, I: The Politics of U.S. Foreign Policy* (Victoria: Trafford, 2003), 995-102, for Allen's removal; and *The Reagan Revolution, III: Defeating the Soviet Challenge* (Victoria: Trafford, 2009), 359 and 399, for Clark's.

president greater control over foreign policy, as the shift in personnel also marked a change in the structure of the policy-making process. Allen, as part of the president's compact with the new world order establishment, had had no policy role during his tenure, while Clark would play a major role in managing the president's foreign policy against the policy preferences of Secretary of State Haig and his successor Shultz.

A similar incident surrounded Judge Clark's removal from his NSC post in October 1983. As a result of the KAL 007 crisis Shultz had demanded Clark's removal and the president had acquiesced, but took the opportunity of the resignation of his Secretary of Interior, James Watt, to disguise this political defeat by shifting Clark from NSC to Interior. Although the maneuver kept Clark in the cabinet for another year, the NSC post went to Shultz's ally, Robert McFarlane. From that position, as recounted in this volume, the new world order faction had engineered the entrapment of the president that had led to the current crisis.

Reagan's Action Plan

The struggle with Shultz over Iran policy was the most serious crisis of Reagan's presidency, but his response was the same in principle as in the Allen and Clark instances. The difference was that this time the president had not merely suffered a setback, but had lost power. Therefore, stakes were higher, and so the incident disguising the defeat was larger. To cover his defeat, the president would "discover" that his aides had diverted funds from Iran arms sales to the Contras without his knowledge. Taking command, he would dismiss those deemed responsible, then initiate measures to investigate and make public all of the information about it, including full disclosure to the Congress ensuring that there would be no possibility of a cover-up.[2]

---

[2] Lou Cannon, *Reagan*, (New York: Putnam, 1982), 132-38, relates a lesson well learned from his California governorship. Reagan's staff had discovered a homosexual ring operating in the governor's office. Reagan forced those identified to resign, but tried to keep the mess quiet. The cover-up failed, however, and the resultant scandal

In reality, the president decided to drape a political scandal over his policy failure and political defeat, the so-called "Iran-Contra diversion." He would claim that he was "uninformed," place the blame on his aides, and turn over policy control to the secretary.[3] Poindexter and North were prepared to shoulder the burden of blame for their chief, and would do so, but were not apprised of the true nature and extent of their sacrifice, which would involve criminal not merely political liability and stretch out over several years after the president had left office.

Connecting the Contra program to the Iran initiative was also Reagan's subtle threat to the new world order establishment because it could implicate Vice President Bush, who was a strong supporter of the Contra program. If Bush were drawn into the scandal it would compromise his own prospects as Reagan's successor. The message was that if Reagan went down, Bush would go down with him and the new world order establishment would lose control of the presidency.

Attorney General Meese, Reagan's long-time fixer from the days of his California governorship, acting, he said, as the president's "legal adviser," not as Attorney General, would manage the exit strategy.[4] But, it must be emphasized, as this account demonstrates, the president was not a passive player in the drama; he was deeply involved in his own defense strategy and decided if not directed the policy, which Meese executed.

The process actually commenced with Casey's testimony before the Intelligence Committees on Friday morning, November 21, 1986. During his remarks, Casey three times volunteered that North had been responsible for "problems at the NSC." He had been "active

---

had a negative effect on his presidential candidacy. The lesson was that it was eminently preferable to divert attention away from a crisis than to cover it up.

[3] Stephen Engelberg, "Iran Defense For Reagan," *New York Times*, January 8, 1987, 1. "Senior White House aides have apparently decided it was better to suggest that Mr. Reagan was unaware of or misinformed about key decisions than to allow continued speculation about his involvement."

[4] "Meese testimony," Report of the Congressional Committees Investigating the Iran-Contra Affair (Washington, D.C.: GPO, 1987), 100-9, 224. [Cited hereafter as Iran-Contra Affair.]

operationally to help the Nicaraguan resistance" and "active in the private provision of weapons to the contras." [5] Casey had "kept away from the details because [he] was barred from doing anything...[but, he] knew that others were doing it."[6] Casey's remarks foreshadowed the decision to place the blame on North.

While Casey was giving his testimony, Meese called Poindexter to arrange a meeting with the president, Regan and himself for later that morning. Poindexter immediately called North to tell him that an investigation was beginning and that Meese would be sending over his aides to look at documents, clearly a "heads up" call. North reassured his boss not to worry, that "it's all taken care of," obviously meaning that he had *already* disposed of all incriminating documents.[7]

At that moment, North was more worried about something else. It was Michael Ledeen, the one man besides McFarlane who knew the details about the events of 1985. Ledeen "wanted to speak publicly" about his role and North wanted to make sure he knew what to say, especially about the *Hawk* shipment.[8] North jumped into a taxi and sped off to Ledeen's home in Bethesda, Maryland, arriving at 11:00 A.M.

In what was a most unusual, indeed, startling coincidence, when North arrived at Ledeen's home, he found McFarlane already there. McFarlane wanted Ledeen to deny that he had "gone to Israel originally to carry out a specific mission for him at his request." Ledeen thought that McFarlane was trying to "protect" him, while in fact he was attempting to protect himself. North was concerned with "not what happened but what are you [Ledeen] going to say happened." Ledeen reassured both men that his "role" had been

---

[5] Oliver North and William Novak, *Under Fire: An American Story* (New York: Harper Collins, 1991), 325.

[6] Jane Mayer and Doyle McManus, *Landslide: The Unmaking of the President* (Boston: Houghton Mifflin, 1988), 323.

[7] Ibid, 325, say "Poindexter's warning to North touched off a frenzied weekend of destroying documents and warning confederates...sometimes only steps ahead of Meese's investigators," but North had been shredding documents for weeks.

[8] "Michael Ledeen deposition," *Iran-Contra Affair*, Appendix B, volume 15, 1472-73.

"nothing more than being a person who listened at meetings and reported what I heard."⁹

North declined to get into the *Hawk* issue in depth in McFarlane's presence, but arranging for Ledeen to come to his office later that afternoon, accepted a lift from McFarlane back to Washington. North then returned to his office where he, his aide Robert Earl and secretary Fawn Hall proceeded to shred or otherwise dispose of every remaining document, PROF note and KL-43 message that could conceivably be incriminating.

When Ledeen arrived that afternoon North asked him: "what would you say if you are asked about a shipment of HAWK missiles in November 1985?" Ledeen responded: "I would tell the truth which was that I was aware of it, that I knew that it had happened, but that I was not aware or could not recall who had made the decision to do it or when that decision had been made." North answered: "fine."¹⁰

Earlier that morning at 11:30, Meese had gone over to the White House for his meeting with the president, Poindexter, and Regan. His purpose was ostensibly to obtain the president's "approval" to interview those involved, review documents, "and pull together a coherent account."¹¹ Meese's true purpose, however, as Walsh concludes, was to build "a case of deniability for his client-in-fact, President Reagan."¹² Draper also argues that his purpose was to insure that the president could not be implicated in any illegal act, particularly in regard to the November *Hawk* shipment.¹³ Reagan told

---

⁹ Lawrence E. Walsh, *Final Report of the Independent Counsel for Iran-Contra Matters* (Washington, D.C.: United States Court of Appeals for the District of Columbia Circuit, August 4, 1993), 98-99. See the exchange between Ledeen and McFarlane: Michael Ledeen, "How the Iran Initiative Went Wrong," *Wall Street Journal*, August 10, 1987, 26; Robert McFarlane, "Retreat, Then Rewrite," Ibid, August 14, 1987, 15; and Michael Ledeen, "Reread, Then Reconsider," Ibid, August 21, 1987, 15.
¹⁰ "Michael Ledeen Grand Jury testimony," Ibid, 99, fn 175.
¹¹ Ibid.
¹² Walsh, *Final Report*, 525.
¹³ Theodore Draper, *A Very Thin Line: The Iran-Contra Affairs* (New York: Hill and Wang, 1991), 499. See also, *Iran-Contra Affair*, 644-47, for the skeptical

Meese to wrap things up over the weekend and be prepared to report back on Monday, November 24, to an NSPG meeting.

Meese returned to the Justice Department to select trusted aides to assist him in reviewing documents and accompany him in interviews with key individuals. Meese picked Charles Cooper, his own counsel, who had been working on the problem since the crisis had broken, along with two of his deputies, William Bradford Reynolds and John Richardson. All three were loyal political appointees and competent lawyers, but with no investigative experience. The focus of their inquiry was supposed to be the November 1985 *Hawk* shipment, but would turn out to be something very different.

Meese's men drew up a list of witnesses to be interviewed. They were: Bush, McFarlane, Shultz, Weinberger, North, Sporkin, McMahon, Thompson, Allen, the CIA's counsel and "operations officers." Curiously, there were no plans to interview the president, Poindexter, or Casey, although they would be "contacted" for assistance.[14] Nor was Secord or Hakim or anyone else identified as persons of interest. In fact, Meese would only "interview" McFarlane, Shultz, Sporkin, and North in his effort to establish an alibi for the president.

Meanwhile, Poindexter, too, had been busy shredding and deleting documents and memos about the initiative. In fact, Poindexter had been far more "productive" by himself than North had been with his entire team. According to Walsh, Poindexter had deleted 5,012 messages from his computer to North's 736.[15] More important, that afternoon Poindexter calmly tore up the one piece of hard evidence that documented the president's after-the-fact authorization for the *Hawk*, arms-for-hostages deal, the only signed copy of the December 5 finding.[16]

---

observations of Congressmen Peter Rodino (D-NJ), Dante Fascell (D-FL), Jack Brooks (D-TX), and Louis Stokes (D-OH) regarding Meese's investigation.

[14] *Iran-Contra Affair*, 306.
[15] Walsh, *Final Report*, 124.
[16] Ibid, 142, "Paul Thompson deposition," *Iran-Contra Affair*, Appendix B, volume 26, 1067, and Draper, *Very Thin Line*, 500. Mayer and McManus, *Landslide*, 329, say that Poindexter "simply" considered the document a "C.Y.A." finding to protect the CIA, and tore it up.

The signed finding was a double-edged sword. While it seemed to show that the president had attempted to authorize an arms-for-hostages deal, it actually proved that he had not authorized the November *Hawk* shipment. If he had there would have been no need to sign an after-the-fact finding to justify it. Unfortunately, the president decided that the risks attending to the arms-for-hostages charge were greater than the benefit of using the finding to demonstrate that he had not authorized the November shipment, and so it was destroyed.

Poindexter, a computer expert, surely understood that there were backups in the computer system that could not be destroyed and copies of other documents distributed throughout government offices, so his and North's deletion and shredding operations were only delaying tactics to buy time. A more devious interpretation would be that they anticipated that investigators subsequently would view their efforts as attempts to destroy evidence. (Indeed, Poindexter would be indicted on one charge of destroying evidence.)

Twice that afternoon North went over to the White House to see Poindexter, at 1:30 and 2:25.[17] The first time was with his "spiral notebook," which detailed his involvement in the November shipment. North read out his note of November 26, 1985, which said that Poindexter had told him that Reagan had "directed the operation to proceed." When North expressed his intention to destroy the notebook, Poindexter "did not object."[18] (As discussed in Chapter 6, Poindexter had merely passed on to North what McFarlane had told him.)

The second time North saw Poindexter, Meese was with him. According to North's aide, Robert Earl, when North came back from that meeting, he told him that "It's time for North to be the scapegoat, Ollie has been designated the scapegoat." North reportedly asked Meese if he could have twenty-four or forty-eight hours to finish cleaning up the document trail, but Meese replied, "he did not know

---

[17] *Iran-Contra Affair*, 306.
[18] *Ibid*, 307.

whether he could have that much time."[19] (Both Meese and North later denied Earl's account, but there was no reason for Earl to have prevaricated.[20])

Meese's 'Investigation'

While Poindexter and North were tending to their records tasks, Meese put his plan into action. He declined to bring in the criminal division of the Justice Department because, he said, it was a political not a criminal problem, which left him in control. He also declined to seal the offices of the NSC, which gave North and Poindexter continued access to NSC files. North's office would not be sealed until November 25. Meese began his weekend "interviews" that afternoon of the 21st.

First on his list was McFarlane, who came to his office in the Justice Department at 3:30 P.M. Cooper, the only other person present, took notes. Meese asked McFarlane for his views "without distortion," and the former national security adviser generally went over the interpretation he had written in the November 7 memo to Poindexter and the November 18 rewrite of North's chronology, but, abjuring Meese's admonition, further distanced himself from responsibility.[21]

The Israelis, McFarlane said, through David Kimche had suggested arms sales in July 1985. Reagan had not authorized arms sales, but was interested in a political opening. McFarlane emphasized that "no one in [the] U.S. government...had contact with Israel" on the August-September *TOW* shipments. In this version, McFarlane sought to airbrush himself entirely out of the picture. The Israelis were the initiators and McFarlane simply a passive recipient of information. He

---

[19] "Robert Earl testimony," *Iran-Contra Affair*, Appendix B, volume 9, 624-26. See also Mayer and McManus, *Landslide*, 327.
[20] "Meese testimony," Ibid, 100-9, 335-6 and "North testimony," 100-7, 144.
[21] "Charles Cooper deposition," *Iran-Contra Affair*, Appendix B, volume 7, 142.

had "learned of the 1985 shipment of *TOW*s from Ledeen," his *non-governmental* go-between with the Israelis.[22]

When he got to the November *Hawk* shipment, he diverged even further from his earlier position. He now claimed that in November 1985 "he learned that Israel had shipped oil equipment," remembering "no mention...of arms." It was not until the following May, when he was preparing to go to Tehran, that he "learned" that the Israeli shipment had been *Hawk* missiles. At this, Meese surprised him with the revelation that Shultz had contemporaneous notes that said while in Geneva McFarlane had told him that the Israelis were shipping *Hawk* missiles in a planned arms-for-hostages swap.[23]

McFarlane, stunned at the realization that Shultz was sacrificing him in his battle with Reagan and flustered at being caught in a flagrant lie, mumbled that he "doesn't remember a chat with [George Shultz], but probably had one."[24] In his typical fashion, McFarlane responded elliptically to Meese's charge that he had contemporaneous proof of McFarlane's knowledge of the *Hawk* shipment, by admitting only that he had "probably" had a "chat" with Shultz. Of course, the issue was not whether he had had a "chat" with Shultz, but what he had said.

When the interview had ended and Cooper had left the room, McFarlane asked Meese if he could talk to him for a moment. Thinking fast, he said he wanted the attorney general to know that the "president was 'four square behind' the arms sales from the beginning." According to McFarlane, "Meese expressed relief at this because the president's approval in advance of sales would constitute a finding." In Meese's view, the president's "legal position [was] far better the earlier he made the decision."[25] But, he said, there must be no suggestion of a cover-up.

---

[22] Ibid. Walsh, *Final Report*, 100; Robert C. McFarlane, *Special Trust* (New York: Cadell & Davies, 1994), 99; Mayer and McManus, *Landslide*, 329.
[23] *Iran-Contra Affair*, 308.
[24] "Cooper deposition," 142.
[25] Walsh, *Final Report*, 100.

Discussing McFarlane's performance afterward, both Meese and Cooper thought that he had been flustered and "not entirely forthcoming."[26] Indeed, from this point onward, McFarlane would change his story further to claim that the president had authorized Israeli arms sales from the beginning, indeed, asserting that he had done so from the first briefing at the hospital. He would make this assertion even though he could provide no evidence to support it. Meese would also back this notion for its legal value to the president, not because it was the truth.[27] Then, when the story would not hold up, Meese would deny that the president knew anything.

Precisely because there was no evidence for his claim, McFarlane fell back on his notion of a "mental finding," which he had first sold to North during the *Hawk* shipment a year earlier. In a panic, as soon as he left the Justice Department, McFarlane attempted to cover his tracks. His first call was to North, which he made from a telephone booth on the street. According to North's note of the call, McFarlane recounted his interview with Meese and said "RR said he [would] support 'mental finding,'" the exact phrase he had used in his call to North a year earlier.[28]

---

[26] "Cooper deposition," 142.

[27] Edwin Meese, *With Reagan: The Inside Story*, (Washington, D.C.; Regnery, 1992), 266-67, claimed that the Hughes-Ryan Amendment did not require a *written* finding and that "approval was given orally by the president," based on McFarlane's say so. But this is sheer sophistry, as only the most literal reading would admit of this interpretation. Hughes-Ryan required that the president provide a finding to the appropriate committees of Congress. Even if the president made an oral finding, he would have to deliver it to appropriate committees of Congress, not to his national security adviser, which would involve a written document. See Hughes-Ryan Amendment to the Foreign Assistance Act, Pub. L. 87–195, pt. III, §662, as added Pub. L. 93–559, § 32, Dec. 30, 1974, 88 Stat. 1804, codified at 22 U.S.C. 2422 (repealed in 1991). But Meese also overlooked NSDD 159, of January 18, 1985, which explicitly required a written finding for all covert operations. Meese's memoir was published in 1992 before NSDD 159 was declassified, but he knew of its existence. The directive specifically included the Attorney General in all NSPG meetings dealing with covert operations. See Christopher Simpson, *National Security Directives of the Reagan and Bush Administrations* (Boulder: Westview, 1995), 493-95.

[28] "North notebook entry," November 21, 1986, in Walsh, *Final Report*, 100 n.187.

Twisting Meese's words, McFarlane told North that Meese "was relieved to learn" the president had approved the Iran initiative, which subsequently justified their actions. Of course, Meese had said nothing of the kind. He had said Reagan's legal position *would* be better the earlier he approved of the initiative–a conditional that McFarlane turned into a "fact." (Meese later testified that he never used, or would have used, the phrase, "mental finding," which, of course, had no legitimacy except in McFarlane's imagination.)[29]

McFarlane's next step was to call Shultz at the State Department "to try to obtain a copy of the Charles Hill note."[30] On the advice of Sofaer not to speak to anyone "likely to be under investigation," Shultz refused to take his call. McFarlane then called Sofaer, asking "to see the Hill note." Sofaer refused to let him see it, but "read the note to him." Sofaer did this for two reasons. He "wanted him to know that the effort to cook the facts about the November shipment was untenable and should be abandoned" and also to give him "information that could lead him to avoid committing perjury."[31]

That night an increasingly worried McFarlane sent a PROF note to Poindexter in which he doubled down on the "mental finding" notion. Referring to the November *Hawk* shipment as his "only blind spot," he said that "the matter…can be covered if the President made a 'mental finding' before the transfer took place." Then, he said, "on that score we ought to be ok because he was all for letting the Israelis do anything they wanted at the very first briefing in the hospital."[32] McFarlane seemed to believe that if he repeated his falsehood enough times to enough people it would become true. Actually, McFarlane was caught in a double lie: regarding the *Hawk* shipment and about Reagan's briefing at the hospital and his only way out was to claim that Reagan had authorized everything from the beginning.

---

[29] "Meese testimony," *Iran-Contra Affair*, 100-9, 231.
[30] Walsh, *Final Report*, 101.
[31] Sofaer, "Iran-Contra: Ethical Conduct and Public Policy," 1099. In "Abraham Sofaer deposition," *Iran-Contra Affair*, Appendix B, volume 26, 288-89, Sofaer appears to suggest that the call to him came first.
[32] Walsh, *Final Report*, 101.

The president, meanwhile, was playing his part. While North and Poindexter were working late destroying documents and McFarlane was attempting to puzzle out a plausible defense for himself, Reagan was attending a post-election, Capitol Hill dinner for Senate Republicans. Unfortunately, there were more losers than winners—seven had lost and three retired- making the proceedings less than festive.[33] Indeed, in a major defeat, the Republicans had lost control of the Senate, which they had controlled since 1980.

Meese, however, was busy. He spoke with Shultz to arrange an interview for the next morning, and called Poindexter, Weinberger and Casey to alert them to the investigation. The content of their conversations is unknown. He also arranged for one of his attorneys, John McGinnis, to go over to the CIA that night to review intelligence reports relating to Iran arms sales. Briefing Meese early the next morning, McGinnis confirmed that the U.S. government had been involved in the November *Hawk* shipment and determined that "excess profits" had accrued from the arms sales.[34]

McGinnis' information was intriguing but vague. CIA entanglement in the *Hawk* shipment was clear enough, based on an incomplete but sufficiently conclusive message trail, but the only way he could have determined that "excess profits" existed was by examining the bank account of Lake Resources, Secord and Hakim's vehicle for managing Iran arms sales. The CIA had an account at Compagnie de Services Fiduciaires (CSF) in Geneva where the Lake Resources account also was. Did the agency have access to Secord's account, as McGinnis implied? At that time, CSF was reportedly being "operated by former CIA officials," so that possibility cannot be discounted.[35]

According to Richardson, however, McGinnis' "excess profits" determination had been based on "rumors at CIA [that Iran arms sales]

---

[33] Mayer and McManus, *Landslide*, 331.
[34] *Iran-Contra Affair*, 309.
[35] Scott Armstrong et al., The Chronology: The Documented Day-by-Day Account of the Secret Military Assistance to Iran and the Contras (New York: Warner Books, 1987), 598-99.

money was funneled through Southern Air Transport" to the Contras, not facts. Undermining this "rumor" was his discovery that "the CIA did not use Southern Air Transport" for the November *Hawk* shipment, although it had been used later.[36] A different proprietary, St. Lucia Airlines, had been used in November. McGinnis' findings occurred before discovery of North's diversion memo the next day, but it is obvious that the existence of "excess profits" was a necessary precondition to any charge of a diversion of funds.

The next morning, November 22, at 8:00, Meese and Cooper met with Shultz and Hill in the secretary's office at the State Department. Meese focused on the November *Hawk* shipment stating that he wanted to "get the facts.... and no cover-up." Shultz recounted his statement to the president two days before of "Bud's phone call to me on November 19, 1985, in Geneva" and Reagan's reply that he "knew all about that, but that wasn't arms for hostages." Shultz maintained, "no one looking at the record would believe that."[37]

Meese's concern was to insulate Reagan from any knowledge of the *Hawk* shipment. So, referring to Hill's note of the McFarlane conversation, Meese said, "the president had no notes and had trouble remembering meetings." Signaling the line he intended to take, he said, "certain things could be a violation of the law," but "the president didn't know about the HAWKS in November 1985. If it happened and the president didn't report to Congress, it's a violation." Hill "thought

---

[36] "John Richardson deposition," *Iran-Contra Affair*, Appendix B, volume 23, 312-15. See Michael Tackett, "Air Carrier In Thick of Iran Tangle," *Chicago Tribune*, December 21, 1986, 1, notes that SAT flew one mission from Kelly AFB to Tel Aviv in May 1986.

[37] George Shultz, *Turmoil and Triumph* (New York: Macmillan, 1993), 835. According to Cooper's notes, Shultz said that McFarlane had come to his hotel, not made a phone call. See Draper, *Very Thin Line*, 503. In Shultz's testimony before Congress, he said "McFarlane had told him on November 18, 1985, in Geneva, that four hostages would be released..." The correct date was the 19th, not the 18th, and the number of hostages was five not four. See John G. Tower et al., *Report of the President's Special Review Board: February 26, 1987* (Washington, D.C.: GPO, 1987), B-31. See also chapter 5 above.

Meese was trying to get Shultz to back off of his claim that the President had admitted knowing about the HAWK shipment."[38]

Meese wanted specifically to know whether there was "any contact that I knew of between Bud and the president on this topic then?" Shultz replied "not to my knowledge, though I don't know." That, apparently, was all Meese needed to assert definitively, standing over Shultz in what Hill interpreted as an intimidating "back on your heels" manner, "the president had not known of the [HAWK] shipment that might be illegal, and that the shipments he did know of were not illegal."[39]

Shultz thought that this was a weak position, saying "I would not want to be the president arguing it in public." Then, he offered up the very argument Meese and Reagan had decided to use in the president's defense, when he said, "another angle worries me. This could get mixed in with help for the freedom fighters in Nicaragua. One thing may be overlapping with another. There may be a connection." Meese "did not reply to this suggestion."[40]

Shultz claimed that Mike Armacost was the inspiration for his assertion of an Iran-Contra "connection," based on his view "that a contractor in the Iran arms deliveries, Southern Air Transport, had also been used in support of the Contras." He speculated "they may have shifted funds between the two trades."[41]

Behind their speculation lay a Justice Department investigation of Southern Air Transport, which had begun after the Hasenfus shoot down in early October. The department had begun to conduct "field interviews" of SAT crewmembers. Poindexter, responding to North's concerns that these interviews would interfere with ongoing hostage rescue operations, called Meese, who requested a postponement of the

---

[38] Walsh, *Final Report*, 539, 544, citing Hill's note.
[39] Ibid. and Shultz, *Turmoil and Triumph*, 836.
[40] Ibid. Indeed, Meese would later deny that Shultz had made such a connection, but Hill's notes corroborated Shultz's account. See *Iran-Contra Affair*, 309.
[41] Shultz, *Turmoil and Triumph*, 836.

investigation. The Justice Department put off further interviews for over three weeks, although their investigation continued.[42]

Meese had remained silent about Shultz's suggestion of an Iran-Contra connection because it was a bombshell. If Shultz leaked that news to the press before Reagan could make it public himself, the disclosure would immediately sound the tocsin of a Watergate-style cover up. It meant that there was no time to lose. It was imperative for Reagan to make that revelation before Shultz did, in order to retain the initiative and not be forced onto the defensive.

Meese had planned on sending some of his men to review NSC files, but now it was urgent to get them over to North's office as soon as possible. Thus, immediately following his interview with Shultz, at ten-thirty Meese told Cooper to call Thompson to tell him that two of his men, William Bradford Reynolds and John Richardson, were heading to North's office right away. They arrived at the Old Executive Office Building a little after 11:00 A.M.

"Discovery" of the Diversion Memorandum

In the entire history of the Iran-Contra Affair, the so-called "chance" discovery of North's memorandum proposing the use of Iran arms sales surplus funds for the Contras, stands out as what Reagan called a "smoking gun."[43] On the face of it, however, given the immense significance of the memo, its discovery fit Meese's plan to protect the president far too perfectly for it to have been a chance occurrence.[44]

---

[42] Ronald Ostrow, "Said It Could Blow Lid Off Arms Deal: North Warning to FBI on Probe of Airline Alleged," *Los Angeles Times*, January 14, 1987, 1, and Walsh, *Final Report*, 551-52.

[43] Ronald Reagan, *An American Life* (New York: Simon and Schuster, 1990), 530.

[44] As Draper, *Very Thin Line*, 507, notes: "It was…pure chance that enabled Reynolds to hit on the one paragraph that North had been most determined to conceal. One wonders what might have happened if North had successfully destroyed the telltale document and had obliged the two lawyers to come back without their revelation."

In short, when Meese sent Reynolds and Richardson to North's office he was confident of what they would find. North and his colleagues, including Poindexter, had for weeks, since the Hasenfus shoot down, been carefully pruning their files of potentially damaging information. North had confidently told Poindexter just the day before that he had "taken care of" everything in his files. It therefore seems highly unlikely that North would have overlooked an obviously incriminating memo.

The high probability is that the memo was planted in North's files. The question is: by whom? There are two persons who had means, motive, and opportunity: Reynolds and Poindexter. Reynolds, Meese's long-time confidant, who "discovered" the memo, could have brought it with him when he went to North's office and inserted it into North's files during an unobserved moment. There were several stretches of time during which he and Richardson were alone at their table and the only other person present, Col. Earl, was in an adjacent room.

More likely, however, it was Poindexter, who planted the memo. He was committed to taking responsibility for the diversion. He had full access to NSC offices and had a copy of North's memo. (North had sent five memos to Poindexter discussing use of residuals.[45]) The national security adviser could have pulled a copy from his files and simply walked over to the EOB and inserted it into North's files.

On Saturday morning, when Reynolds and Richardson arrived at the EOB, NSC Counsel Paul Thompson let them into the building and showed them to North's office. Earl was the only one in the office at that time and he had laid out on a table numerous accordion-style file folders. Richardson thought they were there to look into the 1985 events, to determine whether the U.S. government had "authorized or acquiesced in" the Israeli arms shipments.[46] After looking at the material laid out on the desk, Reynolds "suggested it would be easier if he just took all this [the files] over to Justice," but Richardson advised

---

[45] "William Bradford Reynolds deposition," *Iran-Contra Affair*, B, volume 22, 1128.
[46] "John Richardson deposition," *Iran-Contra Affair*, B, volume 25, 260-61.

against it, saying they could be "open to attack if we take custody out of the NSC..."[47]

"Sometime during the first hour of their review" of the files, the congressional report notes, Reynolds suddenly "found an item that seemed out of place." Standing out among the files contained in the reddish-brown accordion folders was a "white folder stamped with a red White House label."[48] According to Reynolds, Earl "was not in the room" when he discovered the memo.[49] Indeed, Thompson said that "no one at the NSC" saw Reynolds and Richardson find the memo, or even knew that it had been found.[50]

Inside the folder was a longer version of a memo Reynolds had come across earlier, but this one included a paragraph discussing how "residual funds" from arms sales to Iran would be used. It stated "$12 million will be used to purchase critically needed supplies for the Nicaraguan Democratic Resistance Forces." These funds would "bridge the period between now and when congressionally approved lethal assistance...can be delivered."[51]

The two men, even though realizing the importance of what they had found, decided nonchalantly to place the document with other documents they had selected for copying later in the day. Then, around 1:45 P.M. they broke for lunch and walked over to the Old Ebbitt Grill to join the attorney general and Cooper. As they were leaving North arrived. They exchanged pleasantries and asked if there were any additional files for the 1985 period. North said he would check his files.

Meanwhile, Meese and Cooper had been interviewing Judge Sporkin and also been surprised by what they had learned. Sporkin told them about his drafting of the December 5 finding, when he

---

[47] Ibid, 282.
[48] *Iran-Contra Affair*, 310. Mayer and McManus, *Landslide*, 333, described it as a "white manila folder with the letter W.H. in red." "Reynolds deposition," *op cit*, 1132, said the memo "was in a discrete manila folder that was readily identifiable."
[49] Ibid, 1129.
[50] "Paul Thompson deposition," Ibid, Appendix B, volume 26, 924.
[51] Draper, *Very Thin Line*, 505. See also chapter 9 above.

learned about the CIA's role in the November *Hawk* shipment.[52] He knew that arms were involved, not oil drilling equipment, and that the purpose of the finding was to justify an after-the-fact CIA role in an arms-for-hostages transaction. Whether Meese already knew that Poindexter had destroyed the December 5 finding, or not, learning of the December 5 finding made it all the more imperative to act promptly to deflect attention from the entire affair with the "diversion."[53]

At lunch in the Old Ebbitt Grill, the four men discussed their discoveries. Reynolds disclosed the contents of North's memo, but noted that there was no indication that any money transfer had actually occurred. It was, Reynolds said, an "aspiration," not a fact.[54] Meese said it would be necessary to query North directly about it. In this analysis, Meese now had his evidence; what was necessary was to obtain North's admission that he had written the memo, but also to insure that it had never reached the president.

While Meese and his team were having lunch at the Old Ebbitt Grill, Casey, Poindexter and North were meeting in Poindexter's office in the White House. Afterward, Casey called Meese and arranged for him to visit him that evening at his home. At the same time, Meese called North and arranged for him to be interviewed the next afternoon at the Justice Department.

That evening, Meese went alone to Casey's home. He later claimed that Casey told him about the visit from Furmark over six weeks earlier. Reportedly, this involved the threat by Gorbanifar and the Canadian financiers to go public with the charge that money had been diverted to the Contras.[55] Meese denied that he discussed the discovery of North's diversion memo, which seems highly improbable, given the

---

[52] *Iran-Contra Affair*, 309.
[53] "William Bradford Reynolds deposition," 1141. Reynolds, at least, learned for the first time that there had been such a finding, which was, he said, "a new revelation for him."
[54] Ibid, 1143.
[55] *Iran-Contra Affair*, 311 and "Meese testimony," Ibid, 100-9, 236-38.

fact that the reason Casey called him was to discuss that very subject, even if in a different context.

At the very least, Meese would most certainly have taken the opportunity to alert Casey to the imminent break in the crisis. Meese took no notes of their discussion, nor did Casey; but immediately after Meese left, Casey composed and sent a letter to the president urging him to fire Shultz. It read, in part:

> The public pouting of George Shultz and the failure of the State Department to support what we did [in Iran] inflated the uproar on this matter. If we all stand together and speak out I believe we can put this behind us quickly. Mr. President, you need a new pitcher.[56]

On Sunday, November 23, before going to his interview at the Justice Department, North went to see McFarlane at his office in downtown Washington. The main topic of their conversation was the diversion. Unless North were already informed, and was attempting to prepare the ground for his defense, he had uncannily homed in on the issue which was about to explode in his face.[57] Yet, when it happened, not three hours later, he seemed oddly unprepared.

North arrived at the attorney general's office at 2:15 Sunday afternoon. With Meese were Cooper, Reynolds, and Richardson. Meese wanted North to go through the early history of the initiative, admonishing him to tell it straight to avoid any implication of a cover-up. But North had his own idea. Clearly assuming that he was to be the fall guy, North spun Meese a tale that put the Israelis at the center of the arms deals, the president interested solely in getting the hostages out, and the NSC and CIA as uninvolved in anything more than peripheral roles.

After about an hour discussing the 1985 events, in which North "dissembled" about the *Hawk* missiles and the retroactive finding of

---

[56] Mayer and McManus, *Landslide*, 336.
[57] *Iran-Contra Affair*, 312.

December 5,[58] Meese pulled out the nine-page, unsigned "diversion memo" and asked North if he had prepared it. North said yes. Looking at it he thought that it was "precisely the kind of document I had shredded. Or so I thought." North asked, "where did this come from?" But Meese merely replied, "that's not important." North asked if there had been a "cover memo," which he knew would indicate where the memo had been routed and who had received it. Reynolds answered that there had been no cover memo.[59]

As the memo was unsigned and had no cover letter it meant that there was no proof that it had ever reached Poindexter, let alone the president. Meese then pointed to the paragraph describing the diversion. When North saw it, he was startled and "visibly surprised." Meese asked if the transaction proposed in the memo had occurred and North answered that it had not. Meese then probed further: "did anything like this ever take place," and North answered, "yes."[60]

Meese asked whether the president had authorized the diversion and North said, "he didn't think so." At least, it had never been discussed at any meeting in his presence. Was there any government involvement, he was asked? North replied: "our involvement was none....The CIA, NSC, none." Only three people knew, he said: himself, Poindexter, and McFarlane. The diversion was the Israelis' idea. Wanting to be "helpful," they offered to share some of the profits from the arms sales with the Contras.[61]

When Meese asked him how the diversion worked, North told another completely false story, omitting Secord and Lake Resources entirely, and asserting that the Israelis, specifically Amiram Nir, decided how much money would go to the Contras and deposited funds directly into accounts set up by Adolfo Calero in Switzerland. North's only role had been to advise Calero to set up the accounts and

---

[58] Walsh, *Final Report*, 540-41.
[59] North, *Under Fire*, 327-28.
[60] Ibid. See also Draper, *Very Thin Line*, 511-18, for a discussion of the interview, based on comparison of the accounts of North, Cooper, Reynolds, and Richardson.
[61] "John Richardson notes," *Iran-Contra Affair*, 100-9, 1413-15.

give the account numbers to the Israelis.[62] The truth was that North could not say, as Secord notes, "that Contra-related payouts from Iranian profits ever *had* taken place....Only Secord, Hakim, and Zucker [the Swiss banker who handled the Lake Resources account] had definitive knowledge in this area."[63]

Despite North's efforts at what he undoubtedly believed would be helpful prevarication, Meese got what he needed. North had told a false story that exonerated the president, the NSC, and the CIA, while taking the blame on himself. He admitted writing the diversion memo, yet assured Meese that it had not reached the president. The attorney general thus had in hand the main ingredients for the president's defense, which he could spring at any time.

Last Chance

But Reagan wasn't ready to accept defeat just yet. He decided to make one last attempt to obtain Shultz's agreement before throwing in the towel. This would come at the NSPG meeting, Monday afternoon, November 24. The plan was to present Shultz with a united front in support of the president in hopes that he would back down from his challenge. To prepare for it, the president had stories threatening Shultz's removal placed in the *Washington Post* and *Wall Street Journal* that morning divulging news of an imminent "shake up" in the administration. Shultz himself thought, "everything in [these stories] was likely to be a message dropped into the hands of reporters in the hope of influencing decisions and events."[64]

The *Wall Street Journal* article had Meese and former national security adviser William Clark "quietly...looking for candidates to replace" Regan, Shultz, and Poindexter. Former Transportation Secretary Drew Lewis, retiring Senator Paul Laxalt (R-NV), and Clark "have been rumored as possible choices." Forecasting the exact

---

[62] *Iran-Contra Affair*, 312-13 and Draper, *Very Thin Line*, 515-16.
[63] Richard Secord and Jay Wurts, Honored and Betrayed: Irangate, Covert Affairs, and the Secret War in Laos (New York: Wiley, 1992), 331.
[64] Shultz, *Turmoil and Triumph*, 837.

outcome, the story went on to say that, as Reagan had "long been reluctant to fire people," Regan and Shultz might stay, while Poindexter and North would go. Nancy Reagan was reportedly "furious" that "former advisers first backed the arms sales and now are trying to blame others." The reference was to "McFarlane, who originally initiated the Iran policy," and suggested that the axe would fall on him, too.[65]

The *Washington Post* piece had California "friends of Ronald Reagan," the name of the influential group that had supported the president at the outset of his political career, urging the president to replace Shultz, Regan, and Poindexter with Weinberger, Lewis, and Jeane Kirkpatrick, former delegate to the UN. Here, too, Nancy Reagan was cited as being "particularly upset" with the president's advisers, again meaning McFarlane, who were "more interested in protecting their own hindsight than in protecting the president."[66]

The *Wall Street Journal* also carried an op-ed by Poindexter justifying the president's Iran policy and its continuation, but admitting "a pro-U.S. leadership that invites us back into Iran is not in the cards." It was nevertheless important to pursue a policy that seeks "an Iran that lives at peace with its neighbors" and that "no longer supports terror as an instrument of policy." The United States accepted the Iranian revolution and sought a nation at peace and "a force for stability in the region."[67]

The news stories set the stage for the NSPG meeting that afternoon, but it was Shultz's deputy, John Whitehead's testimony before the House Foreign Affairs Committee that morning that

---

[65] Ellen Hume and Jane Mayer, "Reagan Faces Political Crisis in Choosing Whether to Oust Top Aides in Iran Flap," *Wall Street Journal*, November 24, 1986, 64.

[66] David Hoffman and Lou Cannon, "White House Shake-Up Sought," *Washington Post*, November 24, 1986, 1. Weinberger wrote in his diary, November 21, 1986, that he would replace Shultz and that William Clark would return to replace Poindexter. See Walter Pincus and George Lardner, "Shultz Sought Nancy Reagan as Iran-Contra Ally," *Washington Post*, February 20, 1993, 1.

[67] John Poindexter, "The Prudent Option in Iran," *Wall Street Journal*, November 24, 1986, 30.

ratcheted up the level of tension. Whitehead, testifying in place of Shultz, openly defended his chief, "denounced arms for hostages, said Iran supported terrorism, and pointed out the impossibility of coping with operations run clandestinely by the NSC staff." His testimony, regarded as a declaration of "open warfare on the White House basement," sent shock waves around Washington, igniting talk of another Watergate crisis.[68]

Meanwhile, Meese spent that morning touching base with all of the members of the NSPG, except Shultz. He also spoke with McFarlane to determine whether he did in fact know about the diversion, as North said, and whether he had told anyone else about it. McFarlane's answers were that North had told him about it in passing after the Tehran trip, but he had not talked to anyone else about it. No notes were taken at any of these meetings and Meese consistently could not recall that anything of substance had been discussed.[69]

Meese went to the White House later that morning, at eleven o'clock, to speak to Regan. The president's chief of staff had been largely uninvolved in the initiative, but Meese needed him to take the lead from this point and also, later, to take some of the blame.[70] As Regan recalled, Meese said that "he had to see the president at once: his investigation had discovered...'things the president did not know' including a possible diversion of funds from the Iran arms sale."[71]

Regan was horrified, but misunderstood what Meese was saying. He thought, "Meese meant money had been siphoned directly from the U.S. Treasury," which truly would have been a disaster.[72] In any case, Regan immediately ushered Meese in to see the president, who was riffling through his three-by-five cards preparing for his meeting with South African Zulu nation chief, Mangosuthu Buthulezi.

---

[68] Shultz, *Turmoil and Triumph*, 837.
[69] *Iran-Contra Affair*, 314.
[70] The *Tower Report*, IV-11, would conclude that Regan "must bear *primary responsibility* [!] for the chaos that descended upon the White House" when the crisis broke. (emphasis supplied)
[71] Regan, *For the Record*, 37.
[72] Mayer and McManus, *Landslide*, 341.

Oddly, despite telling Regan that he "had to see the president at once" about a "possible diversion," when he entered the Oval Office, he did not tell the president about the diversion. He said simply that he "wanted to forewarn him that something was very wrong in regard to the arms transaction." What he had found was "a terrible mess." Meese said he still had "a few things to button up" before giving a full report, but it was "going to be bad news." So they agreed to meet after the NSPG meeting that afternoon.[73]

The NSPG meeting was the president's last attempt to obtain Shultz's support. They were all there: the president, Bush, Meese, Shultz, Casey, Regan, Weinberger, Poindexter, and also Cave. Shultz thought the purpose of the meeting was to hear Meese "present the results of his quick probe."[74] In fact, it was to put out the president's line on the November *Hawk* shipment to see if Shultz would buy it. The diversion was not discussed. (It was only five years later, in 1991, when Walsh discovered Regan's and Weinberger's mutually reinforcing notes, that it became possible to present an accurate portrayal of what happened at this meeting.)[75]

Poindexter, Shultz recounts, ran the meeting and reviewed the Iran initiative, as if nothing had happened. Cave gave the CIA's assessment on Iran, and then was excused from the meeting. Casey described the government's improved intelligence on Iran and Weinberger discussed the Iran-Iraq conflict, but "did not take [Shultz's] side of the argument with the vigor he had in such sessions long ago." Poindexter informed the group "we would proceed without changing the project or the policy." When Shultz strongly objected, Poindexter "ignored what [he] said."[76]

---

[73] Don Regan, *For the Record*, (New York: Harcourt, Brace, Jovanovich, 1988), 38. Meese claimed that he told the president the whole story of the discovery of the North memorandum, as well as North's and McFarlane's "confirmation" of the diversion. See *Iran-Contra Affair*, 314.

[74] Shultz, *Turmoil and Triumph*, 838.

[75] Walsh, *Final Report*, 542-43. Draper, *Very Thin Line*, 525, calls it a "peculiarly uninformative" meeting; Mayer and McManus, *Landslide*, 342, describe a "stilted discussion;" *Iran-Contra Affair*, 315, mentions Meese's notes, but not what he said.

[76] Shultz, *Turmoil and Triumph*, 838, and Walsh, *Final Report*, 542.

At this point, Regan raised the November *Hawk* issue and whether we objected to the Israeli shipment?[77] Poindexter responded first, saying "from July '85 to Dec. 7 McFarlane handled this all alone—no documentation." Meese then took the floor to discuss at length the position that the president would take, placing all the blame on McFarlane.

McFarlane, he said, had told Shultz about the delivery and possible hostage release, and noted that Shultz "didn't approve." The president was "only told maybe hostages out in short order." He gave "no specific OK for HAWKs." McFarlane told Shultz that the hostages were to come out first before arms were sent, but "that did not take place." Meese noted that it could be a violation of the law if arms were shipped without a finding, but "the president did not know."[78]

Although all knew that Meese was incorrect as to what the president knew, they all supported the president, except Shultz. The secretary declared that he "knew something of what [McFarlane] did." It seemed to him that "once again, ...they were rearranging the record."[79] As Shultz had suspected, they were trying to "lay all this off on Bud [McFarlane]. That won't be enough." Hill thought that the "White House was carrying out 'thru Meese' a 'carefully thought out strategy' to insulate the President and 'blame it on Bud [McFarlane].'"[80]

The president, Shultz said, was "in a steamy, angry mood clearly directed at me." He insisted, "we were right in what we were doing. Pounding the table, he said: "we are right...We had to take the opportunity! And we were successful! History will never forgive us if we don't do this!" To Shultz, the president was sending an

---

[77] Lawrence E. Walsh, *Firewall: The Iran-Contra Conspiracy and Cover-Up* (New York: Norton & Co., 1997), 364. Although Regan later denied it, Meese had evidently prompted him to raise the issue before the meeting.
[78] "Regan note," November 24, 1986, in Walsh, *Final Report*, 512-13.
[79] Shultz, *Turmoil and Triumph*, 838.
[80] "Charles Hill note," November 24, 1986, in Walsh, *Final Report*, 543.

"unmistakable message: understand me, and get off my back.... He was angry in a way I had never seen before."[81]

But Shultz would not be intimidated. In an unprecedented act, he got up from the table—and walked out! Shultz claimed that he "had to leave while the meeting was still going on for a previously scheduled appointment with South African Zulu Chief Buthelezi," but the plain fact is that he had figuratively dismissed the president.[82] The meeting ended a few minutes later. Shultz's answer to the implied question of whether or not he would accept the interpretation put forward by Meese and support the president and his policy was an emphatic NO.

Reagan Surrenders Policy Control

Had Shultz caved in the president could have weathered the storm, placed the blame for the Iran fiasco on conveniently retired McFarlane, and retained control of policy. But Shultz's walkout and refusal to agree meant that the struggle would continue and grow. The illegal aspects of the November *Hawk* deal would deal a severe blow to the president's credibility. Worse, if Shultz and the new world order faction leaked the diversion, it could easily have led to charges of a cover-up. Reagan, Meese and their closest confidants decided that the president's position had to be saved above all other considerations. And they had to act quickly.

Immediately after the NSPG meeting, Meese met with Poindexter for five minutes, ostensibly to find out what he knew about the diversion, but in reality to signal that it was time for him to play his role and take responsibility. Poindexter dutifully admitted that he knew "what was going on, but that he had not inquired further." He had justified his inaction on the grounds that "he wanted the president and his staff to retain deniability." He also "knew that when the diversion became public, he would have to resign."[83]

---

[81] Shultz, *Turmoil and Triumph*, 838.
[82] Ibid.
[83] "John Poindexter testimony," *Iran-Contra Affair*, 100:8, 119-20.

Meese then joined Regan and the president for a brief meeting of sixteen minutes as Meese laid out for Regan's benefit what he knew about the diversion. According to Regan, Meese said that Iran had paid $30 million for arms and the CIA received $12 million. "Where the other $18 million had gone and what had been done with it, nobody seemed to know." Meese said, "North had admitted ...that he had diverted some of these funds to the Nicaraguan contras," but there were questions about the location of the rest.[84]

The purpose of the meeting was to have a third party, Regan, verify that the president had no knowledge of the diversion and the chief of staff reacted perfectly. The president, he said, received Meese's report with "deep distress" and "he blanched when he heard Meese's words." Regan was convinced. "This guy I know was an actor, and he was nominated at one time for an Academy Award, but I would give him an Academy Award if he knew anything about [the diversion] when you watched his reaction to express complete surprise at this news."[85] Of course, the president was a good actor and he played his part well here, (but he had never been nominated for an Academy Award).

Reagan asked "did any Americans get their hands on that money" and Meese told him North's lie that "no U.S. person" had handled the money, which had gone from Iranian to Israeli to Swiss bank accounts and then to the Contras. The question of Poindexter's fate came up and it was agreed that he would have to go, but North, oddly, was not mentioned.

Regan offered two suggestions. First, congressional leaders must be told forthwith, which should be followed by a press conference "to make sure the White House could announce the problem before it leaked." Second, the president should appoint a bipartisan commission "to establish the facts, and make recommendations." There was also talk of an independent counsel, but Reagan, agreeing with this plan, emphasized that he wanted a commission, not an independent counsel,

---

[84] Regan, *For the Record*, 38.
[85] "Donald Regan testimony," *Iran-Contra Affair*, 100:10, 29-30.

which would take too long. The president decided to "wait overnight and make a decision in the morning."[86]

The policy battle was finally over and Reagan had given up. The president would hand over policy control to Shultz and concentrate on preserving his position. Poindexter was tasked with conveying the news. A little over an hour after the NSPG meeting, he called Shultz's office and talked to Whitehead. The national security adviser's demeanor was "entirely different now."

> He wanted to assure Whitehead that the uproar over his testimony was no problem. Poindexter would tell the president it was okay. He said he hoped State would 'get involved' with Iran policy. 'State can take the lead if it wants to,' Poindexter said. In fact, he went on, 'I want to get out of it. I haven't been able to do anything else for weeks.'[87]

Shultz professed to be "stunned" at this news, hurriedly telling Whitehead to call Poindexter back to "firm up the details of how State would take charge of Iran policy and this operation." The secretary said, "we just crossed the Great Divide...Something dramatic must have happened. What, I did not know. I could not believe that Poindexter had simply had a change of heart or was putting this issue aside in order to attend to other matters. I was mystified but elated at this dramatic shift from the White House."[88]

That evening, while Shultz and the new world order faction were rejoicing over their victory, Meese and Regan were busy contacting their colleagues to tell them that the president would be making the results of the attorney general's investigation public the next day. Regan stopped by Casey's house on the way home to tell him of the plan. Casey objected strenuously, saying that it would probably mean

---

[86] Mayer and McManus, *Landslide*, 343.
[87] Shultz, *Turmoil and Triumph*, 839.
[88] Ibid.

the end of both the Iran and Contra programs. But Regan was adamant. "It's the only thing we can do."[89]

Poindexter and North commiserated with each other, realizing that the game was up, but not fully aware of what lay in store for them. Exchanging PROF notes, Poindexter told him about his offer to resign and said that Meese was "one of the few beside the President that I can trust." He thought that if "we don't leave," perhaps North could be assigned as Casey's assistant. North said that he was "prepared to depart at the time you and the President decide it to be in the best interests of the Presidency and the country."[90] Clearly, neither man had an inkling they were about to become scapegoats for the president.

The next morning, November 25, Meese asked Thompson "to do a search one more time of the presidential records to ascertain that the president had not seen or signed any memorandum dealing with Iran during the time period 1 April to the end of May, '86." Thompson tasked staff member Brenda Reger to do the search, which turned up negative.[91] Meese was now ready to announce the diversion and turn the Iran policy flap into the Iran-Contra scandal.[92]

Springing the Diversion

After briefing the NSPG and congressional leaders about the diversion and the dismissals of Poindexter and North, the president and Meese went to the White House briefing room. Reagan said that "after becoming concerned" about the inability of the national security staff to provide a "complete factual record with respect to the implementation of my policy toward Iran, I directed the attorney general to undertake a review of this matter over the weekend and report to me on Monday." Meese's report "led me to conclude that I

---

[89] Mayer and McManus, *Landslide*, 344.
[90] Draper, *Very Thin Line*, 534-35.
[91] "Paul Thompson deposition," *Iran-Contra Affair*, Appendix B, volume 26, 1076.
[92] Don Oberdorfer and Walter Pincus, "Iran-Contra Connection Tipped the Scale: Meese's White House Revelation Turned a Flap Into a Scandal," *Washington Post*, November 30, 1986, 1.

was not fully informed on the nature of one of the activities undertaken in connection with this initiative."[93]

The president announced that the Department of Justice would be undertaking an investigation and that he would appoint a special review board to evaluate the "role and procedures" of the NSC staff in the conduct of foreign and national security policy. He said that he would share their findings with the Congress and American people. He then announced that Poindexter, "although not directly involved," had "asked to be relieved," and that North "has been relieved," but did not explain why. Then, as he attempted to turn the meeting over to Meese, reporters shouted several times asking whether Shultz was also going to be let go, but Reagan ignored the questions, and left the room.

Meese then took over, saying that "all the information is not yet in," but he did want to "make available immediately what we know at the present time." He then proceeded to surprise everyone. Instead of laying the blame on McFarlane, as virtually everyone expected, especially Shultz, he placed the blame on North and Israel and introduced an entirely new issue, the diversion of Iran arms sale funds to the Contras. Virtually everything he said skirted to the edge of truth, or went over the line into clever obfuscation, but it all was designed to divert blame from the president and show that he was in charge of his administration.

The attorney general then laid out the story of the diversion, based in large part on his interview with North. "In the course of the arms transfers" to Iran, he said, "certain monies which were received in the transaction between representatives of Israel and representatives of Iran were taken and made available to the forces in Central America...." [94] He continued: "a certain amount of money was negotiated by representatives outside the United States with Iran for arms. This amount of money was then transferred to... representatives of Israel. They, in turn, transferred to the CIA, which was the agent for the United States government under a finding...signed by the president

---

[93] "Reagan: 'I Was Not Fully Informed,'" *Washington Post*, November 26, 1986, A6.
[94] Ibid, A8-9, "Transcript of Attorney General Meese's News Conference."

in January 1986. And, incidentally, all of these transactions…took place between January 1986 and the present time."

The Israelis paid the CIA "the exact amount… that was owed…for the weapons" and the CIA then repaid the Department of Defense. "All government property was accounted for and statements of that have been verified by us up to the present time…. the difference between the money owed to the United States…and the money received from…Iran was then deposited in bank accounts which were under the control of representatives of the forces in Central America."

The general reaction, in the briefing room and across the nation, was shock and surprise at what was a bolt out of the blue. Then, the question and answer session began. Reporters asked over a hundred probing questions, a sampling of which is included below, in italics. Meese's answers to all but a handful regarding the diversion were either "we don't know yet, or we're still looking into it." Increasingly, the tone was one of general skepticism, verging on disbelief, in the tale they were being told, which appeared to have no relevance to the Iran story.

How much money was involved? "We don't know the exact amount, yet. Our estimate is that it is somewhere between $10 million and $30 million." *How did you find out?* "In the course of a thorough review of a number of intercepts, and other materials…the hint of a possibility that there was some monies being made available for some other purpose came to our attention." *Did the president know?* "The president knew nothing about it until I reported it to him."

Were you looking for this when you began, or was this just something that turned up in the course of the investigation? "It turned up in the course of the investigation." Reflecting McFarlane's view, one reporter asked: *We have been told that the president was operating from the beginning of this operation in June or July of 1985 on legal opinions—not written, but oral—from you. Are you sorry that you gave that advice?* "The only legal opinion that was involved had to do with the routine concurrence with the finding of January 1986."

Who knew that money was being transferred to the Contras? "The only person in the United States Government that knew precisely about this, the only person, was Lt. Col. North. Adm. Poindexter did know that something of this nature was occurring, but he did not look into it further." *What about Casey?* "CIA Director Casey, Secretary of State Shultz, Secretary of Defense Weinberger, myself, the other members of the NSC—none of us knew." Everyone was innocent, Meese claimed. The only culprit was North. McFarlane was not mentioned.

Is it correct to say that we have heard "nothing new" from you about the central questions that have been asked for the past three or four weeks about the propriety of shipments to...Iran? Meese answered in the affirmative: "we have heard nothing new that hasn't been testified to essentially on the Hill." The discovery of the diversion "does not drive to any of those other questions." *Was what North did a crime? Will he be prosecuted?* "We are presently looking to the legal aspects of it as to whether there's any criminality involved." *Is it time to appoint a special prosecutor?* "No. If we find that there is any criminality...then that would be the time to request an independent counsel."

What were the diverted funds used for? "I don't know. I don't know that anyone does." *How did you discover it?* "There were some references to this in one particular document that we found." *Did these transfers go through one man—Col. North? Were there no other people involved?* "No transfers of money went through anyone. Bank accounts were established...by representatives of the forces in Central America. And this information was provided to representatives of...Israel...and then these funds were put into the accounts....No American person actually handled any of the funds that went to the forces in Central America."

Have you done anything about the spectacle of top members of this administration fighting one another like cats and dogs over policy, damaging the president's credibility? "I think...this would involve commenting on other members of the administration, which I won't do....I think anyone who is a member of the president's...cabinet has an obligation either to support the policy decisions of the president or to get out." *Where does that leave the Secretary of State?* "I'm not talking about any particular person. Conclusions are your business, not mine."

At what point did the president know about all this? "The president was informed generally that there had been an Israeli shipment of weapons to Iran sometime during the late summer, early fall of 1985, and then he later learned in February of 1986 details about another shipment that had taken place in November of '85." *If he didn't know, then why did he call Shimon Peres to thank him right after Benjamin Weir was released?* Surprised by the question, Meese stumbled through an answer: "Well, he thanked—he called—I don't know, because that's something I have not discussed with the president...but I think there was no question that the Israelis had been helpful in terms of their contacts with other people in regard to Weir."

Did the president authorize the September 1985 Israeli shipment to Iran? "Well, nobody—to my knowledge....To my knowledge, nobody authorized that particular shipment specifically." *The Israelis did it on their own?* "That's my understanding, yes." *The Israelis claim they never did anything without the full knowledge, understanding and consent of the U.S. Government.* "My understanding is that in terms of that particular shipment...it was done at their—on their own motion.... [but] after the fact, at least, it was condoned by the United States government."

What's to prevent an increasingly cynical public from thinking that you went looking for a scapegoat and you came up with this whopper, [which] doesn't have a lot to do with the original controversy? Meese's answer to this penetrating question was quite revealing, even through the mangled syntax. "The president felt that in the interests of getting the full story out, that he should make the statement that he did today and that I should appear before you and answer questions— which I think you will agree is doing everything we can do to be sure that there is no hint that anything is trying to be concealed."

How high did this go? Are we being asked to believe that a lieutenant colonel took this initiative and had these funds transferred, and that only Adm. Poindexter knew about it? How high did it go? Again, attempting to insulate the president, Meese answered: "To the best of our knowledge —and we have checked this rather extensively —it did not go any higher than that."

What did Col. North actually tell you? Why did he do it, and where was the money deposited? Meese did not answer directly, but what he said, perhaps inadvertently, went well beyond North to the president, saying: "it was done during a time...that provisions had been made by congress to permit the United States to seek funding...from third countries." As to where the money was deposited, "the bank accounts were in Switzerland."

Are you suggesting that Congress authorized what Col. North did in seeking funds for the contras from third countries? Meese hastily corrected himself and changed the subject, saying: "Congress never specifically authorized what Col. North did. The question that has to be looked at, as a legal matter, is whether he committed any violation of law at the time he did that."

Was the $30 million owed to the U.S. Government? "No, it was not owed to the U.S. Government. All the money that was owed to the United States Government was paid to the United States Government." *Will you seek to recover the money that went to the Contras?* "We have no control over that money. It was never U.S. funds, it was never the property of United States officials, so we have no control over that whatsoever." *If it wasn't U.S. Government funds, whose money was it?* Meese's answer: "I think it would probably be the party that had sold the weapons to the Iranians."

Who set the price for the weapons? Was it North, or the Israelis? "My understanding is that all of that took place in negotiations between people...representing Israel and people representing Iran....This was not done in the presence of, or with the participation of any American persons, to the best of my knowledge." *Was it North's idea to bid up the price the Iranians were paying?* "I don't know.... It's a matter that is still up for investigation."

How can so much of this go on and the president not know about it? "Because somebody didn't tell him, that's why....No one in the chain of command was informed." The last question was about Eugene Hasenfus. *Was his fateful mission in any way funded by any of these diverted funds?* Meese's answer: "I have no knowledge and I doubt if we'll ever find out since we have no information about how those funds were used once they were ultimately received."

"Survival" of the President

Meese had quite deliberately left the impression that it had been North who diverted Iran surplus funds to the Contras and reporters jumped to that conclusion, but that is not what he had actually said. He said that North was the only person "that knew precisely about" the diversion, not that he had actually done it. Furthermore, he said, "no American person handled any of the funds." It had been "representatives of Israel" who put the money into Contra bank accounts.[95]

"People...representing Israel and people representing Iran" had determined prices. No American persons participated in that either. Meese had no idea what the diverted funds had been used for, and didn't think "anyone" did. The money was not U.S. money; it belonged to the "party that had sold the weapons," whom he never identified. But his main point reiterated several times was that the president had been uninformed and that it had all happened without his knowledge because nobody told him. Once Meese informed him, he took action to correct the problem. It was imperative, he concluded, to rally around the president, to stand "shoulder to shoulder with him" in this time of crisis.

The "diversion" was a brilliant stratagem clumsily implemented, but it served its purpose of diverting attention away from the failed Iran policy and the president's political defeat. It changed the trajectory of inquiry from Iran to Contra, from policy failure to an apparent illegal transaction. Three investigations would focus on Reagan's policy toward Iran, the Contras, and their interconnections. The Tower Report and the Congressional Investigation were published in February and November 1987, while the Independent Counsel report would not be completed until five years after Reagan left office. Although unearthing valuable details, none of them even remotely

---

[95] Both the Israelis and Contra leaders immediately objected to Meese's thesis. See Glen Frankel, "Israel Denies Funding Contras," *Washington Post*, November 26, 1986, A1 and Julia Preston, "Contra Leaders Deny Receiving Funds," *Ibid, A10.*

addressed the central dynamic that conflicted the Reagan presidency from its outset–the continuous factional struggle for control over American foreign policy between the president and the new world order faction.

The president emerged bloodied and weakened by the cumulative impact of the investigations, but the argument Meese laid out at his news conference that the president was uninformed and the victim of mismanagement by his aides held. No evidence was ever produced showing that Reagan knew about or authorized a diversion of funds. Indeed, Brent Scowcroft, one of the Tower board's principals, admitted: "we were unable to develop any clear independent evidence—either in terms of money in bank accounts with the Contras or in terms of flows of equipment—that the diversion had in fact taken place."[96]

The closest Reagan would come to acknowledging that his policy had been a mistake was in his speech to the nation on March 4, 1987 when, after reviewing the Tower Report, he said "what began as a strategic opening to Iran deteriorated, in its implementation, into trading arms for hostages."[97] The speech was not only an admission of policy failure, but it also masked what appeared to be his last feeble attempt to regain power.

In late January, on the 22nd, as the president was preparing for his appearance before the Tower Board on the 26th, he disclosed to Bush, Regan, Abshire, and Wallison, who were briefing him, that notes he had made on the briefing materials had come "from his diary." They were surprised because, up until that moment, no one had known that the president had a diary.[98]

---

[96] Mary Belcher, "Tower Says Arms Proceeds Vanished 'into a black hole,'" *Washington Times*, March 2, 1987, 1. See also Gaylord Shaw and James Gerstenzang, "Weinberger Skeptical Profits Were Diverted," *Los Angeles Times*, January 7, 1987, 11.

[97] Ronald Reagan, "Address to the Nation on the Iran Arms and Contra Aid Controversy, March 4, 1987. *Presidential Speeches.*

[98] Peter J. Wallison, *Ronald Reagan: The Power of Conviction and the Success of His Presidency* (Boulder: Westview, 2003), 249.

Before the Tower Board four days later, the existence of the president's diary did not come up, but Reagan surprised everyone, including his briefers, when he declared that, although he was "still digging," he thought that he had approved the first Israeli arms shipment "in advance." He also said that, "the Israelis had shipped the HAWKs without our permission." Wallison was dumbfounded; the president's testimony was mutually contradictory and "muddled the record," as far as he knew it.

Attempting to determine how the president had come to these positions, which had contradicted what he had said to them privately, Wallison realized that he had included copies of North's chronology of November 19 and McFarlane's testimony of December 11, but not apparently Regan's testimony of January 7, in the president's briefing materials, which contained these respective arguments. This explained for Wallison how the president thought he had approved the first Israeli shipment in advance and could say that the Israelis shipped the *Hawks* in November without his permission.[99]

When the president's testimony leaked, it was assumed that he was siding with McFarlane against Regan in the dispute over whether he had authorized the Israeli shipments in advance or not.[100] However, the president had in fact adopted the legal strategy developed by Meese that the earlier the president had approved of the Israeli shipments the better for the president, because all subsequent actions would be covered by what would have amounted to an oral finding.

News of the existence of the president's diary, or notes as they decided to call them, appeared in the *Washington Post* on February 1, provoking intense interest in what information the notes might hold. The clear implication was that they held the key to whether or not Reagan had authorized Israeli arms sales in advance. After discussions between Wallison and staff of the Tower Board to arrange for a second

---

[99] Ibid, 252-53. Walsh, *Final Report*, 521, omits the fact that Wallison included McFarlane's testimony in Reagan's briefing materials.
[100] John G. Tower, *Consequences: A Personal and Political Memoir* (New York: Little, Brown & Co., 1991), 283-84.

appearance, the president announced that he would turn over "relevant excerpts" from his notes to investigators.[101] In a statement he said he would "furnish copies of the relevant notes" to the Tower Board.[102]

McFarlane was scheduled to testify to the Tower Board on February 10 and the president on the 11th. As news of the president's notes trickled out the pressure on McFarlane mounted. He had to assume that the notes would show that the president had not authorized arms sales in advance and would thus expose the former national security adviser as having acted in contravention to the president's wishes. The implications for the new world order faction were equally grave, for it would give Reagan the leverage he needed to reclaim power.

There can be little doubt that either Tower or Scowcoft, close friends of McFarlane's, informed him of what the notes contained. McFarlane was faced with a major quandary. It was vital for him to avoid testifying first at the risk of being exposed as a liar a day later. The way out he chose was to take an overdose of Valium. McFarlane claimed that he had attempted suicide "for the wrong [he] believed [he] had done [his] country." The Iran-Contra scandal, he believed, was "all [his] fault." He had "disgraced [his] country."[103] That may be true. He may well have been guilt-stricken, but his action was also consistent with the need to avoid the president's public repudiation.

Although it is a common method to attempt suicide by taking an overdose of drugs, medical experts say that even taking "extremely large quantities" of Valium "is unlikely to cause death." McFarlane reportedly took between 30 and 40 tablets. "Experts said individuals had survived many times that amount."[104] McFarlane took what would be a drug overdose on the night of February 9, and was rushed to the

---

[101] Steven Roberts," Reagan Would Turn Over 'Excerpts' From Notes," *New York Times*, February 3, 1987, 14.
[102] Wallison, *Ronald Reagan*, 258.
[103] McFarlane, *Special Trust*, 3, 6, 8.
[104] Harold Schmeck, "Valium, Often a Suicide Step, Seldom Works," *New York Times*, February 11, 1987.

hospital the next morning "two hours before he was scheduled to testify before the Tower Commission."[105]

President Reagan appeared before the Tower Commission the next day and reversed his testimony. He now declared that he had *not* approved the Israeli arms shipments in advance, but there was no mention that the president had come to that conclusion based on a review of his notes. Wallison said that the president had actually read from a memorandum that he had prepared for him to use as a reference.[106]

The next day's press account, quoting an official who was in a position to know, reported that "they've got something," but subsequent accounts said he had reached the conclusion that he had not authorized the Israeli shipment in advance after "he and Regan talked at length about the issue following the first interview with the panel."[107] The impression left was that the president had been persuaded by Regan, not his own notes.

On February 19, Tower and Scowcroft met with McFarlane in the hospital for his interview. He admitted that in writing the November 18 memorandum he had laid out how the president could deny authorizing the Israelis shipment in advance, but continued to insist that he had given his "private approval" in advance.[108] This new position seemed to explain the president's own contradictory accounts and it was at this point that the president decided to end his struggle with the new world order faction.

The next day, Friday February 20, Reagan sent a note to the Tower Board "clarifying" his position. It read:

---

[105] Susan Okie and Chris Spolar, "McFarlane Suffers Drug Overdose," *Washington Post*, February 10, 1987, 1.
[106] Wallison, *Ronald Reagan*, 265-66 and Walsh, *Final Report*, 521.
[107] Steve Roberts, "Tower Panel Data Said to Link N.S.C., Illicit Contra Aid," *New York Times*, February 12, 1987, 1 and "President Changed Statement on 1985 Iran Arms Approval," *Washington Post*, February 19, 1987, A1.
[108] *The Chronology*, 642.

> I'm afraid that I let myself be influenced by others' recollections, not my own....*I have no personal notes or records to help my recollection on the matter.* The only honest answer is that try as I might I cannot recall anything whatsoever about whether I approved an Israeli sale in advance, or whether I approved replenishment of Israeli stocks around August of 1985. My answer therefore—and the simple truth is, 'I don't remember—period.'[109]

In short, the president now *denied* that he had any "personal notes" to help his recollection, a statement that flew in the face of the facts, but which removed the role of the notes from the issue. If Reagan had hoped to use them to establish the truth about his decision he had failed.

Although the battle was over, it was nevertheless necessary for the new world order faction to make sure the notes, or any other evidence, would never appear at any future time to endanger their political victory. Their decision was to gain control of the paper flow to and from the president, which meant it was necessary to force out Regan and his counsel Wallison and replace them with their own men.

Both Nancy Reagan and George Bush now played key roles in the drama that unfolded, both demanding that Regan resign immediately.[110] For months, Nancy's contact with him had been solely by telephone, pressing him to leave. The president had staunchly defended his chief of staff all through the Iran-Contra crisis. Now, following resolution of the notes issue, the president had agreed to expedite Regan's departure and the chief of staff had agreed to depart after the Tower Board's report had been published. On February 23, however, Vice-President Bush called him into his office and suggested that he speak to the president immediately "about your situation."[111]

---

[109] Mayer and McManus, *Landslide*, 378. (emphasis supplied)
[110] Walter Pincus and George Lardner, "Schultz Sought Nancy Reagan as Iran-Contra Ally," *Washington Post*, February 20, 1993, 1. Nancy Reagan had been furious with Shultz, at first, for not supporting the president, but later came around to support him.
[111] Regan, *For the Record*, 96-97.

Regan went to the president and asked directly when he should resign and the president replied that "now" would be a good time. Flabbergasted, Regan exploded, demanding "better treatment than that." The president, taken aback, then asked when he thought he should leave. Regan thought the following Monday, March 2 would be appropriate, which would be after the publication of the Tower Board's report.

He would not last that long. Three days later, on February 26, the Tower Board briefed the president an hour before releasing its report. The report contained a harsh criticism of Regan, who had counted on the board to exonerate him of any wrongdoing.[112] Within hours of the report's release, Nancy Reagan had solicited the recommendations of influential "friends of Reagan," including Mike Deaver, Paul Laxalt, Republican party chairman Frank Fahrenkopf, and pollster Richard Wirthlin. They all agreed that former Senator Howard Baker should immediately replace Regan.[113]

The next morning Baker was shown in to the president's private quarters and offered the job, which he accepted on the spot. However, the president did not want to announce the appointment until the following Monday, when it had been agreed Regan would leave. The first lady refused to wait and leaked word of Baker's appointment. When reporters called her office to confirm the rumors, her press secretary said that Mrs. Reagan wished Regan "good luck," and "welcomed Howard Baker."[114]

Regan was shocked. He had known nothing of the back door dealings and appointment of Baker and could not understand the urgency about his departure. But as reports began appearing on the news wire confirming the appointment of Baker, he immediately

---

[112] David Hoffman and Dan Morgan, "Tower Panel Details Administration Breakdown, Blames Reagan, Top Aides for Failed Policies," *Washington Post*, February 27, 1987, 1
[113] Mayer and McManus, *Landslide*, 383.
[114] Ibid, 384.

resigned. His twenty-two-word letter, dated February 27, 1987, read:[115]

> Dear. Mr. President:
>
> I hereby resign as Chief of Staff to the President of the United States.
>
> Respectfully yours,
>
> Donald R. Regan.

Baker immediately assumed the job of Chief of Staff and brought along with him his long-time aide A. B. Culvahouse, as legal counsel replacing Wallison. Culvahouse now re-negotiated the rules regarding the president's notes. Instead of providing "copies of relevant notes" to congressional investigators, as agreed by Wallison, Culvahouse himself "copied verbatim" the president's notes.[116] According to Senators Daniel Inouye (D-HI) and Warren Rudman, (R-NH) chairmen of the Senate Select Committee, Culvahouse "personally reviewed all of the president's handwritten diaries...and represented to us that he had copied all relevant entries."[117]

According to public agreement, "the excerpts would be typewritten, shown to Reagan for his approval and then shown to senior members of the House and Senate committees or designated staff aides."[118] This was an extraordinary and flawed procedure. What should have been done, of course, was to provide photocopies of the relevant portions of the president's handwritten notes alongside the

---

[115] Regan, *For the Record*, 370-72.
[116] Lou Cannon, *President Reagan: Role of a Lifetime* (New York: Simon & Shuster, 1991), 616.
[117] *Iran-Contra Affair*, 637.
[118] David Espo, "Congressional Investigators to Get Reagan Iran-Contra Notes," *Associated Press*, April 8, 1987.

typewritten transcription. Instead, the typewritten excerpts were accepted as a matter of "faith."[119]

While the approach taken may have been politically expedient and satisfied Nancy Reagan, who objected to the release of any notes at all, the procedure introduced the obvious possibility of human error, if not outright tampering. In short, all of the president's typewritten "notes" must be considered to have been "tainted" for purposes of authenticity until verified against the original handwritten material. The notes, as "copied," played no further role in the Iran-Contra Affair. The president had lost his battle with the new world order faction. His speech of March 4, 1987 was his statement of surrender.

---

[119] Despite the president's promise of full cooperation, Culvahouse would staunchly refuse congressional committee requests for additional information from the White House. See *Iran-Contra Affair*, 639-40.

Conclusion

The Iran-Contra scandal was a pivotal moment in U.S. history. Beyond the domestic political impact of the transfer of power from President Ronald Reagan to Secretary of State George Shultz, the scandal disguised a fundamental and long-lasting change in national security strategy. Shultz repudiated President Reagan's Victory program, even while claiming to be carrying it out. In fact, none of Reagan's fundamental objectives—reducing strategic weapons and negotiating a transition to strategic defense, strengthening the containment of the Soviet Union, building a strategic relationship with China, reestablishing relations with Iran, containing terrorism, and bringing democracy to Nicaragua and other Soviet client regimes—were accomplished.

Instead, Shultz moved to bring about an accommodation with the Soviet Union based on the new world order faction's strategy of détente and mutual assured destruction. He abandoned the shift to strategic defense, allowed relations with China to atrophy, terminated the policy of pursuing the normalization of relations with Iran, ineffectually pressed the struggle against international terrorism, and negotiated "solutions" with Soviet client regimes that left them all in power. The hostages would remain in captivity (Terry Anderson and Thomas Sutherland were not released until 1991).

In fact, not a single U.S.-supported anti-Soviet resistance movement came to power—not in Nicaragua, Angola, Cambodia, Mozambique, Ethiopia, and not in Afghanistan. Reagan deployed the *Stinger* anti-aircraft missile to Afghanistan in the fall of 1986 to great effect, but with Shultz in control afterward, even after the Soviets withdrew in defeat, a Soviet client regime remained in power. Throughout, Shultz and his allies proclaimed that he and Reagan were in total agreement and that he was merely carrying out the president's wishes, but no one who followed American politics was fooled.

Shultz's decision to terminate the Iran Initiative had predictable consequences. Contrary to his view that "Iran needed the United States....We didn't need to chase after the Iranians," a quite different outcome occurred.[1] With no effective source of support or weapons to counter Soviet-armed Iraq, Iran would suffer military defeat and move to an accommodation with Moscow, resulting in a de facto alliance that continues to the present. Indeed, the Russians adroitly parleyed withdrawal from Afghanistan into alliance with Iran.

The relationship with China, which Reagan had so carefully nurtured, atrophied once Shultz took power. A strong U.S.-China relationship was contrary to the détente relationship Shultz and the new world order faction sought with the Soviet Union and was allowed to stagnate. The Tiananmen crisis in mid-1989 witnessed the removal of pro-American Chinese leaders and marked China's shift away from the United States toward closer ties to the Soviet Union. It would not be until the collapse of the Soviet Union in 1991—which dramatically altered the global strategic situation—that U.S.-China relations improved again.

Consistent with the new world order strategy of dismantling the containment structure, both West Germany and Japan edged to the middle between American and Soviet power, benefitting from both. In the two years Shultz controlled American foreign policy the Western Alliance, which President Reagan had labored so strenuously to rebuild, had loosened measurably. In part, this was due to what appeared to be Shultz's lone accomplishment—the INF Treaty to eliminate intermediate-range weapons.[2]

What appeared to be a successful demonstration of the fruits of detente, in fact, simply returned the missile balance to what it had been before the deployment of the Pershing II in the fall of 1983, restoring

---

[1] George Shultz, *Turmoil and Triumph* (New York: Macmillan, 1993), 841.
[2] Angelo Codevilla and L. Francis Bouchey, "Bringing Out The Worst in European Politics," *Strategic Review*, (Winter 1988): 14-23

Soviet leverage. Structurally, the outcome was closer to what Soviet leader Yuri Andropov had proposed than to what Reagan proposed, to the consternation of allies and friends around the Eurasian landmass.[3]

The U.S. withdrew the Pershing II missiles from West Germany, removing a major advantage in both strategic and intermediate-range weapons. While the Soviets removed most of the SS-20s, they hid others, perhaps as many as they had destroyed. They also replaced the SS-20 with weapons of similar if not superior capacity and of shorter and longer ranges not prohibited by the treaty.

The treaty prohibited weapons with ranges between 500 and 3500 kilometers. Just before the treaty was signed, however, the Soviets secretly rushed 73 SS-23 shorter-range missiles, which were explicitly prohibited by the treaty, into Eastern Europe to East Germany, Czechoslovakia, and Bulgaria.[4] When they were discovered in 1990 the State Department conducted a compliance review. The remarkable conclusion was that "Soviet control over the SS-23 missiles did not constitute actual possession of them.... The missiles were the property of the three East European states. The presence of the missiles, therefore, was *not* a violation of the INF Treaty ban on all Soviet shorter-range missiles."[5]

The Russians also deployed the SS-25, which was classified as an ICBM, with a maximum range of 10,000km, and thus outside the scope of the INF Treaty. However, the SS-25 could also strike targets down to a range of 2,000km, well within the prohibited range. By the end of 1988 the Soviets had deployed over 200 SS-25s, many at former SS-20 sites. The United States made no similar compensatory moves, nor voiced any complaint.

---

[3] For Andropov's proposal, see Richard C. Thornton, *The Reagan Revolution, III: Defeating the Soviet Challenge* (Victoria: Trafford, 2009), chapter 4.
[4] Kenneth Timmerman, "Russia's Hidden Nuclear Missiles," *World Net Daily*, June 5, 2000 and "Why is Moscow Cheating on the INF Treaty and is Washington Minimizing the Implications?" *Center For Security Policy*, March 14, 1990.
[5] "Case Study: SS-23 Missiles in Eastern Europe," *Department of State*, October 1, 2005 (emphasis added).

Under Secretary Shultz's stewardship, as the price of détente, the United States insured that the Soviet Union's three main objectives, as argued in this study, were fulfilled. Moscow's strategic deterrent remained intact; there would be no treaty to reduce strategic weapons, or shift to the strategic defensive. The Soviets reestablished nuclear weapons domination over the Eurasian landmass, with the withdrawal of the Pershing II missile from West Germany; and the Soviets drew Iran into their orbit, with the termination of the Iran initiative. This last would encourage a strong Soviet and later Russian drive to gain leverage over Middle East Oil.[6] Thus, not only would Iran be lost, but also American leverage over Middle Eastern oil would be sharply attenuated.

The Iran-Contra affair was also pivotal in a deeper sense, marking the end of a quarter-century-long struggle within the American political establishment, spanning Republican and Democrat administrations, over the transcendent issue of American strategy. On the question of whether to continue the strategy of anti-Soviet Containment, known in the Reagan administration as the Victory strategy, or to change to a strategy of détente and accommodation with Moscow, the decision was to terminate the former and embrace the latter. The United States has pursued an accommodationist course ever since.

The deeply troubling aspect, however, was that the question of American strategy was not decided by America's elected leaders, but by an unelected political elite, many of whom were appointed to high office in several administrations, but none of whom was elected by the American people. Shultz claimed that as an appointed cabinet officer he was accountable, but by accountable he meant that he could be called to testify before Congress.[7] This form of "accountability" should not be confused with electoral accountability. According to the

---

[6] See the author's "The U.S.-Russian Struggle for World Oil, 1979-2010," in Alain Beltran, ed., *Le Pétrole et la Guerre*, (Brussels: Peter Lang, 2012), 299-312.
[7] Shultz, *Turmoil and Triumph*, 919.

U.S. Constitution, only the president *decides* strategy and policy, not appointed officials.

Both Presidents Nixon and Reagan pursued strategies that defeated Soviet strategy, putting the United States in position to exploit victory and create beneficial outcomes for the West and possibly for the Soviet Union, too, through the regime change that invariably accompanies strategic defeat. But, at the moment of success in both cases the new world order faction of the political establishment shrank from victory and, instead, demanded negotiated settlements. Opposing their elected leaders, the new world order faction employed the stratagem of entrapment to achieve political power and, once gaining power, reversed strategy to seek accommodation with Moscow.

In Nixon's case, with his entanglement in Watergate, Henry Kissinger reversed the president's strategy and took the nation onto the path of détente and accommodation with Moscow with disastrous results, including America's first defeat in Vietnam.[8] Despite the failure of detente, Jimmy Carter campaigned on and when elected continued with the détente strategy with further negative outcomes, including and especially the collapse of the U.S. relationship with Iran. Even though he belatedly realized the folly of détente, Carter's inability to defend American interests cast him as one of the worst presidents in American history.[9] Indeed, during these years, the Soviet Union accumulated enormous military power and wielded it to great effect in an effort to alter the global balance of power according to Moscow's design.

The election of Ronald Reagan brought with it a change in American strategy. Reagan jettisoned détente, in favor of a more vigorous Containment strategy. He accepted the idea of a negotiated settlement with Moscow, but one negotiated from strength, which meant victory in the cold war. Victory required establishing the

---

[8] Richard C. Thornton, *The Nixon –Kissinger Years: The Reshaping of American Foreign Policy* (St. Paul: Paragon House, 2001, 2nd Ed.), chapter 4.
[9] Richard C. Thornton, *The Carter Years: Toward A New Global Order* (New York: Paragon House, 1991).

superiority of the United States and the West in every dimension-political, military, economic, and cultural. I have presented much of that record in the four volumes of this study.

NSDD-75 laid out the objectives of Reagan's strategy as a long-term action plan. America's fundamental objective was an advantageous change in the global balance of power, which involved the gradual elimination of offensive ballistic missiles and a shift to a new order based on the primacy of missile defense, including space-based defense. Although the president had signed NSDD-75, it had not gone uncontested by Shultz and the new world order faction, which opposed it.[10]

In his second term and no longer beholden to the political establishment, the president sought to press forward with his Victory strategy. The new world order faction, desperate to reverse the president's strategy, entangled him in a presumably illegal policy toward Iran, contrived to expose it, triggering a major crisis over policy. In the struggle for power that ensued, the president's strategy was deemed a failure. Facing the same fate as Richard Nixon, Reagan chose to surrender power over confrontation with the new world order faction and super imposed a bigger scandal to obscure his political defeat.

It was an unnecessary choice, borne of the timidity of his advisers, especially his wife, who was seduced by the idea of ending the Cold War and her husband's political legacy as a peacemaker.[11] The political establishment could not afford to put the country through a second constitutional crisis to impeach a second Republican president in a dozen years. The risk to the American democratic system was too great.

In fact, as this account demonstrates, impeachment was not a likely possibility. Attorney General Edwin Meese cited it afterward to justify the actions he had taken, but not all the Democrats' men and all their

---

[10] Richard C. Thornton, *The Reagan Revolution, III: Defeating the Soviet Challenge* (Victoria: Trafford, 2009), 207-09.
[11] Nancy Reagan and William Novak, *My Turn: The Memoirs of Nancy Reagan* (New York: Random House, 1989), 336-37; and Thomas C. Reed, *At The Abyss: An Insider's History of the Cold War*, (New York: Ballantine, 2004), 258-75.

horses could impeach Ronald Reagan.[12] Indeed, once he had gained power, Shultz and the new world order faction *needed* Reagan to remain in office, but as a figurehead, to confer legitimacy on them as well as to demonstrate the essential stability and viability of the American political system.

The new world order faction, for example, controlled the President's Review Board. John Tower, Brent Scowcroft, and Edward Muskie were all part of the political establishment, and were not Reagan's men. Shultz named several State Department aides to research and write the *Tower Report*, which endorsed McFarlane's views over the president's.[13] Yet, none of the three investigations into *Iran-Contra* blamed the president for anything other than poor management skills. All blame was heaped upon his men. Neither did any of the investigations even remotely touch on the factional struggle over U.S. strategy that suffused his presidency from the beginning.

Nevertheless, Reagan agreed to a second Faustian bargain. The first, recall, was in 1980 when he agreed to include representatives of the new world order faction in his government in return for their support in the election.[14] Now, he agreed to relinquish control over foreign policy in return for continuation in office to serve out his term and a positive legacy afterward. If the first bargain was a political necessity, the second was a terrible blunder, which only confounded his followers, and also degraded his legacy.[15]

Worst of all, Reagan's failure to clarify the fundamental issues in dispute permitted the new world order faction to blur the fact that a

---

[12] Peter Wallison, "Iran-Contra: The Butlers Did It," *Washington Post*, January 31, 1994, A21, concurs. "Neither the American people nor a Democratic Congress would have seriously contemplated the impeachment of this or any other president simply because he did not recognize that arms shipments to Iran were not legal unless certain ambiguous technical requirements were met."

[13] See "Q&A: Gorbanifar calls McFarlane a 'fool,' North a 'genius,'" *Washington Times*, March 23, 1987, 9B, for an incisive critique of the Tower Report

[14] Richard C. Thornton, *The Reagan Revolution, I: The Politics of U.S. Foreign Policy* (Victoria: Trafford, 2003), chapter 1.

[15] Lynn Nofziger, "A Reaganite's Lament," *Washington Post*, August 4, 1991, C-7.

great strategic choice had been made. The United States, from late in 1986, embarked on a course of détente and accommodation with Moscow that continues to the present day. Who would argue that the country has been better off for it?

In the Orwellian world of Washington-speak, Reagan's defeat was hailed as a victory; the repudiation of his strategy its continuation; and Moscow's continued assault against the West through proxies and support of international terrorism, the blossoming of détente and the end of the Cold War. Failing even to identify the Russians as state supporters of international terrorism was perhaps the most grievous fault, which gave them a blank check in their long-term 'death by a thousand cuts' strategy against the United States and the West. In the immortal words of Pogo: "We have met the enemy and he is us."

Biblio

Martin Anderson and Annelise Graebner Anderson, *Reagan's Secret War* (New York: Crown, 2009),

Scott Armstrong et al., *The Chronology: The Documented Day-by-Day Account of the Secret Military Assistance to Iran and the Contras* (New York: Warner Books, 1987)

Milt Bearden and James Risen, *Main Enemy: The Inside Story of the CIA's Final Showdown with the KGB* (New York: Random House, 2003)

Alain Beltran, ed., *Le Pétrole et la Guerre*, (Brussels: Peter Lang, 2012), 299-312.

Ari Ben-Menashe, *Profits of War* (New York: Sheridan Square Press, 1992)

Ronen Bergman, *The Secret War With Iran* (New York: Free Press, 2007)

Yossef Bodansky, *Target America: Terrorism in the U.S. Today*, (New York: S.P.I. Books, 1993

Michael Bohn, *The Achille Lauro Hijacking: Lessons in the Politics and Prejudice of Terrorism* (Dulles: Potomac Books, 2004).

Daniel Bolger, *Americans At War, 1975-1986* (San Francisco: Presidio, 1988)

Douglas Brinkley, ed., *The Reagan Diaries*, (New York: Harper Collins, 2007)

Lou Cannon, *Reagan*, (New York: Putnam, 1982)

Lou Cannon, *President Reagan: Role of a Lifetime* (New York: Simon & Shuster, 1991)

Duane R. Clarridge, *A Spy For All Seasons: My Life in the CIA* (New York: Scribner, 1997)

Joseph Churba, ed., *Focus On Libya: February 1984 to June 1989* (Washington, D.C.: Pemcon publishers, 1989)

Steve Coll, *Ghost Wars* (New York: Penguin, 2004)

Anthony Cordesman, *The Iran-Iraq War and Western Security, 1984-1987* (London: Jane's, 1987)

Anthony H. Cordesman and Abraham R. Wagner, *The Lessons of Modern War*, Vol. II (Boulder: Westview, 1990)

George Crile, *Charlie Wilson's War*, (New York: Grove Press, 2003)

Chester Crocker, *High Noon in Southern Africa* (New York: Norton, 1992),

Admiral William J. Crowe, *The Line of Fire*, (New York: Simon & Shuster, 1993)

J.E. Davies, *Constructive Engagement? (Oxford: James Curry, 2007*

Michael K. Deaver, *Behind the Scenes*, (New York: William Morrow, 1987),

Theodore Draper, *A Very Thin Line: The Iran-Contra Affairs* (New York: Hill and Wang, 1991)

Pete Early, *Confessions of a Spy: The Real Story of Aldrich Ames* (New York: Putnam, 1997)

Michael Fredericks, *The Octopus Eagle* (Tallahassee: Loiry Publishing, 1987)

Robert Gates, *From the Shadows: The Ultimate Insider's Story of Five Presidents and How They Won the Cold War* (New York: Simon & Schuster, 1996)

Donald Goddard with Lester Coleman, *Trail of the Octopus* (New York: Signet, 1994)

Roy Gutman, *Banana Diplomacy* (New York: Simon & Shuster, 1988)

The Jonathan Pollard Affair, National Security Archive, The George Washington University, 2013

Robert Kagan, *Twilight Struggle*: American Power and Nicaragua, 1977-1990 (New York: Free Press, 1992)

David Kimche, *The Last Option: After Nasser, Arafat & Saddam Hussein* (London: Weidenfeld and Nicolson, 1991)

Peter Kornbluh and Malcom Byrne, *The Iran-Contra Scandal: The Declassified History* (New York: New Press, 1993)

Vladimir Kuzichkin, *Inside the KGB*, (New York: Ballantine, 1990)

Michael Ledeen, *Perilous Statecraft: An Insider's Account of the Iran Contra Affair* (New York: Scribner, 1988)

Libya's Qadaffi: The Challenge to U.S. and Western Interests (Washington: Central Intelligence Agency, 1985)

Kirsten Lundberg, *Politics of a Covert Action: The US, the Mujahideen, and the Stinger Missile*, (Boston: Harvard, 1999)

David C. Martin and John Walcott, *Best Laid Plans: The Inside Story of America's War Against Terrorism* (New York: Touchstone, 1988)

Jack Matlock, *Reagan and Gorbachev* (New York: Random House, 2004)

Jane Mayer and Doyle McManus, *Landslide: The Unmaking of the President* (Boston: Houghton Mifflin, 1988)

Robert C. McFarlane, *Special Trust* (New York: Cadell & Davies, 1994)

Edwin Meese, *With Reagan: The Inside Story*, (Washington, D.C.; Regnery, 1992)

Herb Meyer, ed., *Scouting the Future: The Public Speeches of William J. Casey,* (Washington, D.C.: Regnery, 1989)

J.A. Mizzi, *Massacre in Malta: The Hijack of Egyptair MS 648* (Valletta: Techonografia, 1989).

Paul Nitze et al., *From Hiroshima to Glasnost* (New York: G. Weidenfeld, 1989)

Oliver North and William Novak, *Under Fire: An American Story* (New York: Harper Collins, 1991)

Edgar O'Ballance, *The Gulf War* (London; Washington: Brassey's Defence Publishers, 1988)

Don Oberdorfer, *The Turn: From the Cold War to a New Era: The United States and the Soviet Union, 1983-1990* (New York: Poseidon Press, 1991)

John W. Parker, *Kremlin in Transition/ Vol. II, Gorbachev, 1985 to 1989* (Boston: Unwin Hyman, 1991),

John W. Parker, *Persian Dreams: Moscow and Tehran Since the Fall of the Shah* (Washington: Potomac Books, 2009)

Trita Parsi, *Treacherous Alliance: The Secret Dealings of Israel, Iran, and the U.S.* (New Haven: Yale, 2007)

Stephen Pelletiere, Douglas Johnson, and Leif Rosenberger, *Iraqi Power and U.S. Security in the Middle East* (Carlisle: U.S. Army War College, 1990)

Itamar Rabinovitch and Haim Shaked, eds, *Middle East Contemporary Survey, 1986*, vol. 10 (Syracuse: Syracuse University Press, 1986)

Farhang Rajaee, ed., *The Iran-Iraq War: The Politics of Aggression* (Gainesville: University of Florida Press, 1993)

Dan Raviv and Yossi Melman, *Every Spy a Prince* (New York: Houghton Mifflin, 1990)

Nancy Reagan and William Novak, *My Turn: The Memoirs of Nancy Reagan* (New York: Random House, 1989)

Ronald Reagan, *An American Life* (New York: Simon and Schuster, 1990)

Thomas C. Reed, *At The Abyss: An Insider's History of the Cold War*, (New York: Ballantine, 2004)

Don Regan, *For the Record*, (New York: Harcourt, Brace, Jovanovich, 1988)

Report of the Congressional Committees Investigating the Iran-Contra Affair (Washington, D.C.: GPO, 1987)

Peter Rodman, *More Precious Than Peace: The Cold War and the Struggle for the Third World* (New York: Scribner's, 1994)

Henry Rowen and Charles Wolfe, *The Impoverished Superpower: Perestroika and the Soviet Military Burden* (San Francisco: ICS Press, 1990)

Edward L. Rowny, *It Takes One To Tango* (Washington: Brassey's, 1992)

Peter Schweitzer, *Victory: The Reagan Administration's Secret Strategy That Hastened the Collapse of the Soviet Union* (New York: Atlantic Monthly Press, 1994)

James M. Scott, *Deciding to Intervene* (Durham: Duke University Press, 1996)

Richard Secord and Jay Wurts, *Honored and Betrayed: Irangate, Covert Affairs, and the Secret War in Laos* (New York: Wiley, 1992)

Samuel Segev, *The Iranian Triangle: The Untold Story of Israel's Role in the Iran-Contra Affair* (New York: Free Press, 1988)

Haim Shemesh, *Soviet-Iraqi Relations, 1968-1988: In the Shadow of the Iraq-Iran Conflict* (Boulder: Lynne Rienner, 1992

George Shultz, *Turmoil and Triumph* (New York: Macmillan, 1993)

Christopher Simpson, *National Security Directives of the Reagan and Bush Administrations* (Boulder: Westview, 1995)

John Singlaub, *Hazardous Duty* (New York: Summit, 1991)

Gerard Smith, *Doubletalk: The Story of SALT I* (New York: Doubleday, 1980)

Joseph Stanik, *El Dorado Canyon: Reagan's Undeclared War with Qadaffi*, (Annapolis: Naval Institute Press, 2003), 95-97.

Deborah H. Strober and Gerald S. Strober, *The Reagan Presidency: An Oral History of the Era* (Washington: Brassey's, 2003*)*

Amir Taheri, Nest of Spies: America's Journey to Disaster in Iran (New York: Pantheon, 1988)

Strobe Talbott, *The Master of the Game* (New York: Knopf, 1988)

Howard Teicher and Gayle Radley Teicher, *Twin Pillars to Desert Storm* (New York: William Morrow, 1993)

John Testrake, *Triumph Over Terror, On Flight 847* (Eastbourne: Kingsway Publications, 1988),

Thomas, *Gideon's Spies: The Secret History of the Mossad*, (New York: Thomas Dunn, 2009)

Richard C. Thornton, *China: A Political History, 1917-1980* (Boulder: Westview Press, 1982)

Richard C. Thornton, *The Nixon –Kissinger Years: The Reshaping of American Foreign Policy* (St. Paul: Paragon House, 2001, 2nd Ed.)

Richard C. Thornton, *The Carter Years: Toward A New Global Order* (New York: Paragon House, 1991).

Richard C. Thornton, *The Reagan Revolution, I: The Politics of U.S. Foreign Policy* (Victoria: Trafford, 2003)

Richard C. Thornton, *The Reagan Revolution, II: Rebuilding the Western Alliance* (Victoria: Trafford, 2005),

Richard C. Thornton, *The Reagan Revolution, III: Defeating the Soviet Challenge* (Victoria: Trafford, 2009)

Robert Timberg, *The Nightingale's Song* (New York: Touchstone, 1995)

Kenneth Timmerman, *The Death Lobby: How the West Armed Iraq* (New York: Houghton-Mifflin, 1991)

John G. Tower et al., *Report of the President's Special Review Board: February 26, 1987* (Washington, D.C.: GPO, 1987)

John G. Tower, *Consequences: A Personal and Political Memoir* (New York: Little, Brown & Co., 1991)

Robert Venkus, *Raid on Qadaffi* (New York: St. Martin's, 1993)

Peter J. Wallison, *Ronald Reagan: The Power of Conviction and the Success of His Presidency* (Boulder: Westview, 2003)

Lawrence E. Walsh, *Final Report of the Independent Counsel for Iran-Contra Matters* (Washington, D.C.: United States Court of Appeals for the District of Columbia Circuit, August 4, 1993)

Lawrence E. Walsh, *Firewall: The Iran-Contra Conspiracy and Cover-Up* (New York: Norton & Co., 1997)

Caspar W. Weinberger, *Fighting for Peace: Seven Critical Years in the Pentagon* (New York: Warner Books, 1990)

David C. Wills, The *First War on Terrorism: Counter-Terrorism Policy During the Reagan Administration* (Lanham: Rowman & Littlefield, 2003)

Jay Winik, *On the Brink*, (New York: Simon & Schuster, 1996)

Bob Woodward, *Veil: The Secret Wars of the CIA, 1981-1987* (New York: Simon and Schuster, 1987)

Daniel Yergin, *The Prize*, (New York: Free Press, 1992)

Mohammad Yousaf and Mark Adkin, *The Bear Trap* (London: Leo Cooper, 1992)

The Reykjavik File, National Security Archive, The George Washington University.

Iran-Contra Collection, National Security Archive, The George Washington University

Index

27th Party Congress, USSR, 271, 276, 352

A-7 Corsair, 304

Abdel-Rahman, 303

ABM Treaty, 14, 17, 18, 165, 166, 167, 168, 184, 354, 355, 356, 357, 394, 395, 397, 399, 403, 405, 407, 408, 409, 410

ABM Treaty, Article IV, 395

Abshire, David, 502

Achille Lauro, 160, 163, 177, 222, 248, 519

Aegis, 297, 298

Afghanistan, U.S. support for resistance, 33

Agreed Statement 'D', 166

Air Branch Chief, 211, 212

Akhromeyev, Sergei, 401

Al Faw battle, 277

Al Haim prison, 246, 250

Alboher, Yehuda, 199

Allen, Charles, 149, 157, 160, 211, 262, 292, 416, 418, 421

Allen, Richard, 467

Al-Rashid, Gen. Abdul, 278

Al-Shiraa, 437

Amal, 48, 78, 82, 84, 85, 91, 93, 96, 108, 109, 113, 115, 232

Anderson, Terry, 66, 151, 172, 432, 511

Andreotti, Giulio, 303

Andropov, Yuri, 513

Angola, U.S. support for resistance, 33

Arafat, Yasir, 160

Arbatov, Georgi, 403

Armacost, Michael, 118, 119, 159

Arms Export Control Act, 44, 240, 253, 261, 264, 368, 451, 453, 455

Asmar, Tony, 377, 378

Assad, Hafez, 91, 104, 109, 115

Atlit prison, 83, 88, 94, 100, 104, 112

Atwa, Ali, 81, 84, 87, 97

Azziz, Tariq, 274

Badredienne, Mustafa, 49, 86, 116

Bahramani, Ali, 376

Bahramani, in Washington, 381

Baker, Howard, 507

Baker, James, 1

Baldridge, Malcolm, 53

Bandar Abbas, 64, 185, 286, 287, 320

Bartholomew, Reggie, 101, 151

Begin, Menachem, 47

Benjadid, Chadli, 83

Ben-yosef, Avram, 188

Berri, Nabih, 91, 93, 96, 104, 105, 113

Bessmyrtnekh, Alexander, 401

Boland Amendments, 309, 350

Bonici, Mifsud, 222

Bonnici, Carmelo, 109

Bremer, Jerry, 456

Brezhnev, Leonid, 28, 164, 180, 270, 277

Buchanan, Patrick, 450

Buckley, William, 49, 51, 54, 151, 159, 160, 162

Burghardt, Raymond, 330

Bush, George H.W., 130, 506

Buthulezi, Mangosuthu, 489

Byrd, Sen. Robert, 446

Caanan, Gen. Ghazi, 111

Calero, Adolfo, 311, 486

Cambodia, U.S. support for resistance, 33

Cannistraro, Vince, 193, 194

Carlson, Kurt, 83

Caron, 297

Carter, and détente, xi

Carter, James E., xi, 33, 515

Casey, William, xvii

Cave, George, 292, 324, 327, 335, 338, 344, 358, 360, 362, 363, 439

Central Intelligence Agency, 45, 79, 217, 247, 454, 521

Central Intelligence Agency (CIA), 45, 79, 217, 247, 454, 521

Cheney, Cong. Dick, 446

Chernayev, Rudolph, 371

Chernenko, Konstantin, xix, 18

Chernobyl, 353

Chin, Larry Wu-tai, 201

China, xi, xii, 41, 43, 71, 134, 271, 292, 293, 333, 392, 399, 423, 511, 512, 524

China, in Reagan's strategy, 392

Chirac, Jacques, 302

Ciccippio, Joseph, 380

Clark, William, 3, 467, 487, 488

Clarke, George, 263

Clarridge, Duane, 194, 205, 520

Clift, Eleanor, 176

Coleman, Lester, 377, 378, 521

Compagnie de Services Fiduciaire (CSF), 285

Congressional Investigation, 431, 501

Contadora, 29, 314

Containment, ix, x, xi, xii, xiv, xviii, 8, 9, 23, 29, 41, 43, 44, 51, 273, 350, 511, 512, 514, 515

Cooper, Charles, 451, 472, 474

Coral Sea, 259, 297

Cordovez, Diego, 275

Counterterrorism Task Force, 148, 149

Cranston, Sen. Alan, 419

Crawford, Jay, 371

Craxi, Bettino, 68

Creagan, James, 195

Cruise Missile, xiii, 271

Cruz, Arturo, 311

Cuba, 19, 52, 114

Culvahouse, A. B., 508

Daniloff, Nicholas, 370

Dawa 17, 49, 116, 152, 177, 341, 344, 385, 387, 388, 422, 425

Deaver, Michael, 1, 507

December 5, 1985 finding, 453

DefEx, 186, 195

Delta Force, 86, 89, 223

Deng Xiaoping, 332

Derickson, Uli, 81, 82

Diversion, 481, 495

Djerejian, Edward, 176, 330

Doherty, David, 419

Dole, Sen. Robert, 446

Douglas, Leigh, 323

Doust, Rafiq, 122

Druze, 78, 92, 101, 232

Durrenberger, Sen. David, 314

Economy Act, 44, 45, 253, 254, 255, 260, 261, 264, 266, 267, 281, 369, 443, 453, 454

EF-111 Raven, 304

Egyptair flight 648, 221

Eitan, Rafi, 58, 201

El Dorado Canyon, 247, 248, 249, 256, 259, 297, 298, 299, 300, 303, 304, 524

Enger, Valdik, 371

Ethiopia, U.S. support for resistance, 33

Executive Order 12543, 256

F-111 Ardvark Qadaffi, Hana, 304

FA-18 Hornet, 304

Fadlallah, Sheik, 86

Fahd, King, 18, 20, 22, 23, 26, 43, 60, 62, 63, 123, 240, 311, 330

Fahrenkopf, Frank, 507

Fairbanks, Richard, 45

Fielding, Fred, 5, 217

Fiers, Alan, 330

Ford, Gerald, xi

Foreign Assistance Act, 44, 45, 204, 261, 454, 476

Fortier, Donald, 68, 71, 252, 265

Fuller, Graham, 70, 71

Furmark, Roy, 62, 63, 136, 383, 415, 419, 420

Gabriel, Gen. Charles, 145

Gaffney, Henry, 192

Garnel, Jose, 195

Garrett, Lawrence, 452

Gates, Robert, xvii, 40, 416, 520

Gazit, Schlomo, 63, 69

Geneva meeting, 181

Genscher, Hans-Dietrich, 302

George, Claire, 292

Goldwater, Sen. Barry, 447

Gonzalez, Felipe, 302

Gorbachev, and Afghanistan, 35

Gorbachev, and arms control, 270

Gorbachev, and Iran, 156

Gorbachev, defense spending, 40

Gorbachev, Mikhail, and Soviet strategy, xvi, xix, 18, 28, 35, 39, 77, 113, 180, 271

Gorbanifar, Manuchur, 55, 56, 60, 110, 119

Grenada, xiii, 30

Gromyko, Andrei, 11, 274

Haig, Alexander, 8, 229, 377

Hakim, Albert, 287

Hamadi, Mohamad, 81

Hamilton, Cong. Lee, 314

HARM missile, 298

Harpoon, 161, 294, 298

Hasenfus, Eugene, 386, 391, 500

Hashemi, Cyrus, 62, 118, 325

Hashemi, Manuchur, 54

Hashemi, Mehdi, 423, 427, 439

Hawk Missile, 170, 173, 187, 192, 203, 212, 214, 215, 475, 485

Hawk shipment, November 1985, 431, 454, 467, 472

Hezbollah /Hizbollah, 48, 66, 78, 82, 85, 86, 92, 93, 96, 97, 100, 101, 104, 105, 110, 111, 115, 123, 149, 152, 153, 170, 232, 236, 239, 242, 286, 323, 324, 439, 442, 464

Hill, Charles, 53, 118, 177, 192, 463, 477, 491

Hill, Peter, 90, 100

Howard, Edward, 201

Howiza marshes, 277

Hughes-Ryan Amendment, 193, 476

Hussein, Saddam, 21, 40, 43, 59, 125, 156, 274, 278, 293, 382, 421, 521

Hussein, Saddam, visit to Moscow, 293

Ibrahim, Abu, 299

ICBM, ix, 397, 513

Ikle, Fred, 182

INF negotiations, 13

Inouye, Sen. Daniel, 508

Iran, and grey market sales, 46

Iran, and hostages, 389

Iran-Contra 'Diversion', 469

Iran-Iraq war, 21, 39, 121, 231, 274, 377, 382, 433, 447, 457

Iraq, 24, 25, 39, 40, 58, 60, 272, 277, 349, 422, 449, 512

Iraq, in Soviet strategy, 47

Islamic Jihad, 48, 85, 105, 108, 113, 123, 160, 162, 176, 232, 233, 379, 430, 432

Israel, vii, 22, 31, 46, 47, 56, 57, 58, 59, 62, 63, 64, 65, 68, 70, 71, 72, 73, 74, 78, 82, 83, 84, 88, 90, 91, 92, 94, 95, 97, 98, 100, 101, 104, 107, 109, 110, 111, 112, 117, 122, 123, 124, 126, 127, 128, 129, 130, 131, 132, 133, 134, 135, 136, 138, 142, 143, 148, 151, 155, 157, 160, 161, 172, 173, 174, 177, 178, 179, 180, 185, 186, 187, 188, 189, 190, 192, 199, 200, 201, 202, 203, 209, 219, 229, 230, 231, 233, 238, 239, 241, 244, 246, 250, 253, 255, 259, 260, 261, 263, 264, 265, 266, 267, 281, 282, 283, 287, 299, 310, 320, 321, 329, 334, 341, 376, 379, 381, 384, 388, 416, 424, 427, 438, 444, 451, 453, 454, 456, 458, 459, 461, 470, 474, 475, 496, 498, 500, 501, 522, 523

Israel, arms sales to Iran, 39

Israeli Historical Chronology, 135, 144, 225, 226, 238

Izz al Din, Hasan, 81

Jacobson, David, 66, 151, 172, 432

Jalloud, Abdel Salam, 106

Jamison, W. George, 45

January 17, 1986 Finding, 444, 453

Jenco, Lawrence, 66, 151, 363

Joubert, Christian, 48

Juchniewicz, Edward, 209

Jumblat, Walid, 92

KAL-007 Crisis, 449

Kangarlu, Moshen, 63, 118, 119, 122, 135, 144, 289

Karami, Rashid, 112

Karoubi, Mehdi, 55

Kassebaum, Sen. Nancy, 316

Keel, Alton, 441

Kelso, Adm. Frank, 296

Kennedy, Sen. Edward, 377

Kerr, Malcolm, 48

KGB, terrorist plots, 300

Khamenei, Ali, 124

Khashoggi, Adnan, 24, 56, 60, 62, 118, 123, 284, 328, 415

Khomeini, Ayatollah, 43, 47, 52, 53, 55, 58, 59, 65, 71, 74, 75, 122, 124, 125, 267, 283, 327, 341, 381, 423, 424, 430, 438, 442, 446

Kilburn, Peter, 49, 151, 172, 323

Kimche, David, 57, 59, 125, 128, 163, 170, 177, 209, 229, 474, 521

Kirkpatrick, Jeane, 3, 488

Kissinger, and new world order faction, xi

Kissinger, Henry, xi, xii, 157, 292, 418, 515

Koch, Noel, 149, 247, 259

Kohl, Helmut, 413

Korea, xi, 29, 52, 59, 114

Kornienko, Georgi, 276

Kostosgeorges, Agamemnon, 89

Krasnoyarsk radar station, 17, 167

Kuzichkin, Vladimir, 44, 45, 521

La Belle Discotheque, 299

Labor Alignment, 57

Lake Resources, 190, 209, 285, 311, 312, 318, 320, 329, 330, 331, 383, 417, 427, 440, 478, 486

Lakenheath Air Base, 301

Larijani, Ali, 364

Laxalt, Sen. Paul, 487

Leahy, Sen. Patrick, 419

Ledeen, Michael, 56, 67, 110, 127, 143, 161, 221, 436, 470, 471, 521

Levin, Jeremy, 48

Lew, Drew, 487

Lewis, Samuel, 57

Libya, 8, 25, 39, 52, 79, 80, 90, 106, 109, 114, 116, 126, 247, 248, 250, 255, 256, 257, 258, 259, 297, 298, 299, 300, 302, 303, 304, 305, 322, 323, 324, 352, 520, 521

Libya, air strike, 323

Libya, in Soviet strategy, 39

Likud, 58

Line of death, 259, 297

Linhard, Robert, 401, 409

Mahdavi-Kani, Reza, 50

Mainz, meeting, 427

Majnoon oil complex, 277

Makowka, Edward, 216, 219

Mansur, Mary Elias, 299

Maresca, Phillip, 81

Maronites, 78

Matlock, Jack, 15, 16, 183, 351, 369, 401, 521

McFarlane, and 'mental finding', 477

McFarlane, Robert, 2, 6, 65, 66, 96, 240, 378, 468, 471

McGinnis, John, 478

McMahon, John, 36, 53, 55, 139, 178, 216, 217, 308

Meese, Edwin, 1, 210, 217, 252, 476, 516, 521

Meron, Mindy, 230

Meyer, Herbert, 19, 103, 522

Mi-24 Hind, 31, 308, 313

Miller, Richard, 201

Mitterand, Francois, 302

Montazeri, Ayatollah, 382, 423, 438

Moreau, Vice-Adm. John, 149

Morrison, Samuel, 201

Mossad, 58, 63, 200, 524

Moussavi, Mir Hossein, 122

Moynihan, Sen. Daniel, 419

Mozambique, U.S. support for resistance, 33

Mubarak, Hosni, 224

Mugniyeh, Imad, 48, 85, 91, 105, 115, 116, 123, 152, 232, 235, 247, 248, 324, 332, 430, 432, 444

Mujahideen, 23, 33, 34, 35, 37, 53, 308, 521

Murphy, Richard, 25, 55, 118, 119

Muskie, Sen. Edward, 517

Mutual Assured Destruction, xiv, xviii, 7, 12, 42, 43, 349, 351, 392, 393, 511

Najafabadi, Ali, 339

Najavi, Ali, 337

Najibullah, 275

Naliotes, Costas, 89

National Security Act, 44

National Security Planning Group (NSPG), 2

Netanyahu, Benjamin, 107

Nevada submarine, 353

New World Order faction, x, xi, xii, xviii, xix, 4, 5, 6, 8, 9, 10, 39, 41, 42, 43, 61, 66, 67, 77, 116, 117, 120, 127, 129, 146, 153, 155, 163, 174, 201, 215, 216, 217,

218, 229, 235, 243, 261, 271, 273, 291, 292, 307, 308, 309, 332, 333, 346, 348, 349, 350, 351, 358, 363, 364, 366, 375, 377, 378, 381, 412, 430, 431, 433, 434, 468, 492, 494, 502, 504, 505, 506, 509, 511, 512, 515, 516, 517

Newlin, Michael, 83

Nidal, Abu, 221, 247, 248, 249, 258, 299

Nimrodi, Yakov, 56, 59

Nir, Amiram, 58, 137, 175, 177, 246, 334, 486

Nitze, Paul, 3, 13, 167, 353, 354, 395, 401, 402, 522

Nixon, relinquishes control, xi

Nixon, Richard M., x, xii, 516

North, Oliver, 148, 157, 187, 205, 310, 378, 386, 417, 438, 470, 522

NSC-68, xiii

NSDD-138, 52, 247

NSDD-159, 5, 6, 61, 193, 204, 454, 476

NSDD-173, 181

NSDD-179, 248

NSDD-205, 257

NSDD-75, January 17, 1983, xiii, 7

Oakley, Robert, 55, 118, 149, 196

Ogarkov, Nikolai, xix

Oil, price decline, xv

OPEC, and prices, xv, 24

Operation Cappuccino, 142

Operation Cosmos, 64

Operation Espresso, 174, 230

Operation Recovery, 267

Operation Rose, 248

Operation Staunch, 45, 47, 51, 53, 59, 70, 71

Operation Tulip, 248

Orlov, Yuri, 375

Padfield, Philip, 323

Palestine Liberation Organization (PLO), 31, 78, 92, 106, 160, 247

Papandreou, Andreous, 89

Pelton, Ronald, 201

Peres, Shimon, 57, 68, 230, 499

Perle, Richard, 4, 16, 182, 401, 409

Pershing II Missile, 399, 513, 514

Persian Gulf, xii, xvi, 10, 43, 185, 441

Phoenix, 161, 170, 172, 176, 177, 230, 242, 289, 294, 429

Platt, Nicholas, 158, 177

Pogo, 518

Poindexter, John, 7, 68, 149, 159, 218, 237, 238, 351, 367, 488, 492

Pollard, Anne Henderson, 200

Pollard, Jonathan, 199

Poseidon submarine, 353

Powell, Colin, 145, 150

Prairie Fire, 297, 298

Price, Charles, 325

Qadaffi, 48, 77, 80, 90, 91, 104, 105, 106, 109, 115, 116, 123, 153, 222, 224, 247, 248, 249, 252, 255, 256, 257, 258, 259, 270, 296, 297, 298, 299, 300, 301, 302, 303, 304, 305, 307, 323, 352, 456, 521, 524, 525

Qadaffi, and terrorism, 247

Rabin, Yitzhak, 57

Rafsanjani, Hashemi, 49

Rafsanjani, Mahmoud, 364, 365, 376

Reagan Doctrine, 6, 7, 18, 19, 22, 28, 42, 43, 61, 307, 315

Reagan, and diary, 228

Reagan, and Iran-Contra, xii

Reagan, and opposition to S.U., 30

Reagan, and struggle with new world order faction, xii

Reagan, and test ban, 405

Reagan, and U.S. strategy, 41, 517

Reagan, defeats Soviet strategy, xii, 39, 180, 349

Reagan, July 25 letter, 358

Reagan, land zero option, xiv, 271, 352, 399

Reagan, Nancy, 130, 131, 144, 467, 488, 506, 507, 509, 516, 523

Reagan, rejects détente, xii

Reagan, Ronald W., vii, xii, xiii, 20, 21, 28, 36, 115, 126, 146, 165, 168, 351, 411, 447, 449, 452, 458, 462, 463, 467, 481, 488, 502, 504, 505, 511, 515, 517, 523, 525

Redeye missile, 309

Redman, Charles, 450

Reed, Frank, 379

Regan, Donald, 1, 220, 241, 493

Reger, Brenda, 495

Regier, Frank, 48

Relative, the, 279, 361, 362, 364, 377, 425, 426

Rentschler, James, 109

Reykjavik, 10, 270, 356, 369, 375, 389, 391, 392, 393, 396, 397, 398, 402, 403, 404, 405, 406, 409, 410, 411, 412, 413, 526

Reynolds, William Bradford, 472, 481, 482, 484

Rezai, Moshen, 122

Rezaq, Omar, 221, 223

Richardson, John, 472, 479, 481, 482, 486

Ridgway, Rosalind, 401

Robelo, Alfonso, 311

Robinson, Davis R., 44

Rockefeller, Nelson, and new world order faction, xi

Rockeye, 298

Rodman, Peter, 272, 280, 308, 523

Rome airport massacre, 248

Rowland, Roland 'Tiny', 325

Rowny, Edward, 3, 4, 401, 523

Rudman, Sen. Warren, 508

Sabra, Hassan, 378, 423

SAM-5 missile, 298, 352

Samii, Ali, 384, 424

Sandinistas, 30, 31, 32, 313, 314, 315, 386

Saratoga, 259, 297

Saud, Al-Faisal, 61

Saudi Arabia, xii, 7, 8, 18, 20, 21, 24, 25, 26, 27, 56, 123, 240, 310, 311, 313

Savimbi, Jonas, 23

Schwimmer, Adolf, 56

Scott, 297

Scowcroft, Brent, 434, 502, 517

Scranage, Sharon, 201

Second channel, 359, 362, 363, 366, 376, 377, 378, 380, 384, 415, 417, 429, 442

Secord, Richard, 31, 186, 190, 194, 214, 242, 266, 284, 310, 312, 382, 424, 438, 487, 523

Shackley, Theodore, 54

Shaheen, John, 119

Shakespeare, Frank, 195

Shamir, Yitzhak, 47, 57, 95, 201, 379

Shamkhani, Ali, 144

Shevardnadze, Eduard, 163, 371

Shiites, 61, 78, 82, 100, 101, 106, 108, 430

Shultz, and Daniloff, 371

Shultz, and détente, xiii

Shultz, and new world order faction, xviii

Shultz, George P., xii, xix, 3, 6, 29, 36, 45, 88, 118, 167, 241, 280, 313, 355, 396, 433, 475, 479, 485, 511, 512, 524

Shultz, opposes naming Moscow, xvii

Shultz, reverses Reagan's policy, xiii

Shultz, SDI as bargaining chip, xviii

Sidewinder, 161, 170, 172

Smith, William French, 44, 253

Sofaer, Abraham, 166, 167, 452, 477

Sokolov, Oleg, 373

Soprofina, 186

Southern Air Transport, 461, 479, 480

Soviet Union, ix, xi, xii, xiii, xv, xvi, xvii, xviii, xx, 5, 6, 7, 8, 9, 10, 13, 15, 17, 18, 20, 23, 24, 25, 27, 28, 29, 30, 34, 39, 40, 42, 49, 51, 60, 67, 71, 75, 77, 78, 79, 80, 103, 114, 115, 122, 124, 164, 166, 168, 169, 183, 200, 269, 270, 271, 272, 273, 275, 276, 305, 307, 324, 332, 339, 349, 350, 352, 353, 354, 358, 367, 375, 392, 393, 394, 395, 400, 403, 405, 406, 407, 412, 414, 421, 511, 512, 514, 515, 522, 523

Soviet Union, and Middle East terror network, 39

Soviet Union, and support for international terrorism, xvii

Soviet Union, economic decline, xviii

Soviet Union, espionage, 369

Soviet Union, policy toward Iraq, 52

Speakes, Larry, 97, 98, 107, 450

Special National Intelligence Estimate (SNIE), 52

Spetznaz, 35, 308

Sporkin, Stanley, 216
SR-71 Blackbird, 304
SS-18 missile, 356
SS-20 Missile, 271, 354, 399, 403, 406, 513
SS-23 Missile, 513
SS-25 Missile, 272, 513
St. Lucia Airlines, 462, 479
START talks, 13
Stethem, Robert, 82
Stinger missile, 36, 308, 309, 350, 521
Strategic Defense Initiative, xii, xiii, xviii, 7, 14, 43, 271, 412
Sutherland, George, 66
Suzuki, Zenko, 332
Tabatabai, Sadegh, 361
Task Force 60, 296
Tehran, trip, 489
Teicher, Howard, 66, 71, 202, 296, 302, 334, 337, 340, 342, 343, 344, 345, 347, 524
Terrorist Incident Working Group (TIWG), 148
Testrake, John, 80, 81, 524
Thatcher, Margaret, 26, 448

The Enterprise, 281, 287, 318, 319
Thompson, Paul, 237, 238, 452, 472, 482, 483, 495
Ticonderoga, 297, 298
TOW Missile, 64, 119, 129, 138, 142, 144, 150, 171, 250, 259, 266, 282, 378, 426
TOW missile, price of, 150
Tracy, Edward, 380
Trident submarine, 353
Trouras, Athanassios, 90
Tudeh Party, 44
TWA-840, 299
TWA-847, 222
Twetten, Thomas, 283
U.S., and counter terrorism policy, 87
Vance, Cyrus, xii
Velyati, Akbar, 240, 276
Vessey, John, 5, 92, 139
Victory strategy, 514, 516
Vienna airport massacre, 248
Vietnam, xi, 19, 515
Waheed, Libyan patrol boat, 297
Waite, Terry, 432

Walker, John, 201
Wallison, Peter, 419, 452, 517
Walters, Vernon, 3, 55, 302
Weinberger, Casper, xviii, 2
Weinberger, opposes use of U.S. military power, xviii
Weir, Benjamin, 49, 148, 151, 158, 435, 499
Whitehead, John, 118, 159, 460, 488
Whitworth, Jerry, 201
Wirthlin, Richard, 507
Wright, Cong. James, 446
Yamal pipeline, xv
Zakharov, Gennady, 369
Zia ul-Haq, 33
Zimmerman, Christian, 81
Zucker, Willard, 285